Time Out

London
2012

timeout.com/london

D0928689

Time Out Guides Ltd
Universal House
251 Tottenham Court Road
London W1T 7AB
United Kingdom
Tel: +44 (0)20 7813 3000
Fax: +44 (0)20 7813 6001
Email: guides@timeout.com
www.timeout.com

Published by Time Out Guides Ltd, a w̲
Time Out and the Time Out logo are trademarks of Time Out Group Ltd.

This edition first published in Great Britain in 2012 by Ebury Publishing
A Random House Group Company
20 Vauxhall Bridge Road, London SW1V 2SA

Random House Australia Pty Ltd 20 Alfred Street, Milsons Point, Sydney, New South Wales 2061, Australia

Random House New Zealand Ltd 18 Poland Road, Glenfield, Auckland 10, New Zealand

Random House South Africa (Pty) Ltd Isle of Houghton, Corner Boundary Road & Carse O'Gowrie,
Houghton 2198, South Africa

Random House UK Limited Reg. No. 954009

Distributed in the US and Latin America by Publishers Group West (1-510-809-3700)

For further distribution details, see www.timeout.com.

ISBN: 978-1-84670-287-7

A CIP catalogue record for this book is available from the British Library.

Printed and bound in Great Britain by Butler Tanner & Dennis, Frome, Somerset.

The Random House Group Limited supports The Forest Stewardship Council (FSC®), the leading international forest
certification organisation. Our books carrying the FSC label are printed on FSC® certified paper. FSC is the only
forest certification scheme endorsed by the leading environmental organisations, including Greenpeace. Our paper
procurement policy can be found at www.randomhouse.co.uk/environment

Time Out carbon-offsets its flights with Trees for Cities (www.treesforcities.org).

While every effort has been made by the author(s) and the publisher to ensure that the information contained in this
guide is accurate and up to date as at the date of publication, they accept no responsibility or liability in contract,
tort, negligence, breach of statutory duty or otherwise for any inconvenience, loss, damage, costs or expenses of
any nature whatsoever incurred or suffered by anyone as a result of any advice or information contained in this
guide (except to the extent that such liability may not be excluded or limited as a matter of law). Before travelling, it
is advisable to check all information locally, including without limitation, information on transport, accommodation,
shopping and eating out. Anyone using this guide is entirely responsible for their own health, well-being and
belongings and care should always be exercised while travelling.

MIX
Paper from
responsible sources
FSC
www.fsc.org   **FSC® C023561**

Contents

Introduction

The date is 6 July 2005; the place Trafalgar Square. At precisely 12.49pm, the face of International Olympic Committee President Jacques Rogge beams out across the square from a giant screen, live from Singapore. The thousands of expectant Londoners who have turned up to witness history in the making hold their breath. 'The Games of the XXX Olympiad in 2012 are awarded to the city of...', Rogge pauses, '...London.' The square erupts with delight.

Seven years later, on Friday 27 July 2012, Trafalgar Square's Countdown Clock will reach zero, another screen will broadcast the Opening Ceremony of the London 2012 Olympic Games, and another crowd will go ape. At time of writing, the new Olympic Park in east London looked sure to be completed well in advance of the starter's gun. Some 5,000 employees, 70,000 volunteers, 9,800 officials, 21,000 members of the media and 8,000 Torchbearers will be swinging into action – not forgetting 15,000 or so athletes. With competitors for whom the epithet 'world-class' is no hyperbole facing off in headline sports such as Athletics, Cycling and Aquatics, we expect endeavour, drama and excellence.

London will rise to the challenge. Its parks, monuments and stadiums will provide a memorable setting for many of the sports. Cultural institutions here and nationwide will lay on a spread of landmark events for the London 2012 Festival. Many venue openings, arts projects, blockbuster exhibitions and insfrastructure improvements have been timed to complete in 2012, so come 27 July the city will be in peak form (though the influx of millions of ticketholders will test its capacity). It's Diamond Jubilee year, too (marking 60 years of the reign of Queen Elizabeth II), so citizens will be in celebratory mood. If you're visiting for the Games, you can expect a feast of sporting action, a dynamic metropolis and a party atmosphere. And if you're not, you can take in the iconic sights, free museums, bubbling restaurant scene, east-side art innovations and real-ale renaissance and just enjoy the world's greatest city. Generally New York and Paris compete fiercely for this crown, but in 2012 London scores the perfect ten.

Ruth Jarvis, Editor

London in Brief

IN CONTEXT

Recession, terrorism, war, rioting – they've all had their impact on London. But this is a city that's survived 2,000 years of turbulence. From adapting old buildings to modern needs to regenerating entire areas – not least the new Olympic Park – the capital is meeting its challenges with renewed creativity, as we show in these features.
▶ For more, see pp14-40.

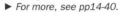

LONDON 2012

Whether you're a ticketholder or a TV viewer, this dedicated section tells you all you need to know about the London 2012 Games, from planning a visit to getting around. It lists every venue in the South-east, and provides full maps and event schedules.
▶ For more, see pp43-71.

SIGHTS

Some of London's attractions write their own headlines: the British Museum, Buckingham Palace or the riverside Tates. But within these pages, you'll also find everything from ancient palaces to shiny new developments, quirky museums to expansive parks.
▶ For more, see pp76-186.

CONSUME

The London 2012 Games have provoked a frenzy of hotel openings – most notably the restored St Pancras Renaissance. With a restaurant scene that has won some serious respect (and stars), a bevy of new boutiques and some innovative pubs and bars, London no longer lags behind in the spending stakes.
▶ For more, see pp188-280.

ARTS & ENTERTAINMENT

London's nightlife is famously lively. When you throw in the finest theatrical tradition in the world, some great symphony orchestras and a whole slew of heavyweight events timed to coincide with the Games, you have a cultural scene as vibrant as anywhere in the world.
▶ For more, see pp282-350.

ESCAPES & EXCURSIONS

When trying to get round the innumerable attractions of London has started to feel too much like hard work, take a break. Breezy Brighton is an easy train ride from the city and nothing but cheery seaside fun; other escapes covered here range from austere Dungeness to the discreet joys of Cambridge and Canterbury.
▶ For more, see pp352-362.

London in 24 Hours

During Games time

London will be a fantasically exciting place to visit at Games time. This central London itinerary can be followed on foot – but do check for road closures before you set out.

9AM Take breakfast at your hotel or one of London's funky new coffee shops (*see p250* **Hot Coffee**) and plan your day, using *Time Out* magazine, website or app to check on the latest events and exhibitions, and www.london2012.com for any Games-related bulletins.

10.30AM Get a taste of traditional London: watch the **Changing of the Guard** at Buckingham Palace (the classic) or Horse Guards Parade (less crowded, but offering a better view of the action; *for both, see p290* **Standing on Ceremony**); and proceed to **St James's Park** for great London views and, if you're lucky, to catch a brass band.

NOON Head for a **Live Site** (*see p64*), where giant screens will relay Games action. There are two in central London. Walk up the Mall to the one in Trafalgar Square, or along Constitution Hill to the Hyde Park location. Pick up a picnic lunch from one of the chain cafés on the way, or, if you'd like a longer walk and fancier food, divert to **Fortnum & Mason** (*see p256*) on Piccadilly, which is en route to either destination.

Several London 2012 Games events are being staged on the streets of central London, including the Marathon and the cycling element of the Triathlon. If you are lucky enough to be in town on these days, save the Live Sites for the evening and join the roadside crowds cheering on the competitors as they pass the city's iconic sights.

2.30PM Depending on energy levels, either immerse yourself in Olympic history at the **Royal Opera House**'s free 'The Olympic Journey: The Story of the Games' exhibition (*see p112*), or take a stroll along the ever-dynamic South Bank. You will see several Cultural Olympiad artworks. Look out for 'A Room for London' (*see p84*) rising out of the roof of the **Queen Elizabeth Hall**, and pop into **Tate Modern** (*see p82*) to contemplate Tino Sehgal's Turbine Hall commission. You could also take a short river trip to **Tate Britain** (*see p138*) for great views of the Houses of Parliament and a 21st-centry afternoon tea. Oh, and some art...

6PM Take dinner early to avoid the crowds. Book in advance and see if you can find a pre-theatre deal (we recommend the **Arbutus** group; *see p232*).

8PM Treat yourself to one of the world-class performances in the London 2012 Festival; a restored Hitchcock film at the **BFI Southbank** (*see p308*), for example, or a Shakespeare play at the **World Shakespeare Festival** (*see p345*). (Book in advance for both.) Alternatively, just enjoy the night-time atmosphere: rent a Transport for London bicycle and explore the more residential neighbourhoods of central London, such as Mayfair, Soho, Fitzrovia, Bloomsbury, Marylebone and Clerkenwell, where there are plenty of traditional pubs to discover. Watch the sporting action on TV or take your drinks outside and enjoy the street life.

At other times

9AM Breakfast is a good time to experience the best of British. Try the Wolseley (*see p228*) for a grand-café sense of occasion, or St John Hotel (*see p198*) for hearty born-again British cooking.

11AM Take a guided tour of the Olympic Park area (*see p55; before the Games only*). You won't have access to the site, but you'll be able to see many of the key features from the perimeter. Finish with lunch at Forman's Restaurant (*see p235*) for London-cured salmon and a to-die-for view of the Olympic Stadium.

2PM Several central London must-sees clamour for an afternoon of your time: the South Bank, the top-rank major museums and Hyde Park, with its new art attractions, among them. But since this is east London's year, we suggest instead a visit to Greenwich. Here you can take a look at another Games site: **Greenwich Park**, which stages the Equestrian events. Near to the river is a clutch of historic maritime institutions: Greenwich was the naval powerbase for the monarchy from the 1300s onward and is now a UNESCO World Heritage Site. To find out more, and celebrate the Queen's Diamond Jubilee, visit 'Royal River: Power, Pageantry and the Thames' at the **National Maritime Museum** (*see p173*; from April 27).

5.30PM Greenwich was a key player in London's real-ale renaissance, thanks to the Meantime Brewery, so grab a pre-dinner pint at the **Old Brewery** (*see p172*).

6.30PM Return to town on a Thames Clipper boat (*see p366*), for unforgettable views.

7.30PM Tapas-style dish-sharing is the current dining vogue. Try it at **Morito** (*see p219*), **Caravan** (*p218*), **Dehesa** (*p223*), **Bocca di Lupo** (*p223*) or **Brawn** (*p234*).

10PM Explore London's alternative nighlife scene, a pop-up paradise of dress-up speakeasies, blitz parties, vintage balls and other irregular entertainments. *See p305* **All Dressed Up**.

VISITING DURING LONDON 2012

Over ten million tickets have been issued for the London 2012 Olympic and Paralympic Games, and the city will be unprecedentedly crowded, particularly from 25 July to 12 August. We strongly recommend that you reserve as much as possible well ahead. Book major cultural events and attractions as soon as tickets become available – sign up for Twitter feeds and newsletters. Restaurants, too, should be reserved in advance.

At press time, some places had yet to decide whether they would be open during the Games, notably theatres and venues near the route of public-view events. In addition, restaurants and bars may close for private functions. Always call before you visit – websites may be out of date.

Key websites to scan are london 2012.com (official Games info), www.tfl. gov.uk (transport), visitlondon.com (tourist info), http://festival.london2012.com and www.timeout.com (events).

London in Profile

THE SOUTH BANK & BANKSIDE

Running along the Thames from the London Eye to Gabriel's Wharf, the **South Bank** is the centre of the nation's arts scene. Directly east is **Bankside**, which has risen to prominence thanks to Tate Modern and Borough Market.
▶ *For more, see pp76-85.*

THE CITY

Reminders of London's long, ramshackle and occasionally great history jostle with latter-day citadels of high finance in the City, the fascinating 'square mile' (it's actually slightly larger) that essentially was London for centuries.
▶ *For more, see pp86-101.*

HOLBORN & CLERKENWELL

Just west of the City lie two different, distinct locales. Quietly historic **Clerkenwell** boasts some of London's best bars and restaurants. Adjacent **Holborn**, meanwhile, is the city's legal quarter, and sits on the fringes of the West End.
▶ *For more, see pp102-104.*

BLOOMSBURY & KING'S CROSS

North-west of Holborn, literary **Bloomsbury** draws millions to the British Museum. North of Bloomsbury is fast-improving **King's Cross**, while to the west the restaurant-packed area of **Fitzrovia** concerns itself mainly with its media-industry locals.
▶ *For more, see pp105-110.*

COVENT GARDEN & THE STRAND

Covent Garden, just south of Bloomsbury, is a real visitor magnet; tourists adore its open-plan piazza and cheerful street entertainers. Between here and the Thames lies the traffic-choked, theatre-lined **Strand**.
▶ *For more, see pp111-115.*

SOHO & LEICESTER SQUARE

The hub of the West End, **Soho** is London's most notorious district. These days, it's far more civilised than its naughty reputation suggests, but is still fun to wander in. Just south sit bustling **Chinatown** and touristy **Leicester Square**.
▶ *For more, see pp116-120.*

OXFORD STREET & MARYLEBONE

London's shoppers get to choose from countless different shopping areas, but chain-heavy **Oxford Street** is where much of the money is spent. Oxford Street separates Soho and Mayfair from Fitzrovia and **Marylebone**, an agreeably villagey district dotted with boutiques and restaurants.
▶ *For more, see pp121-125.*

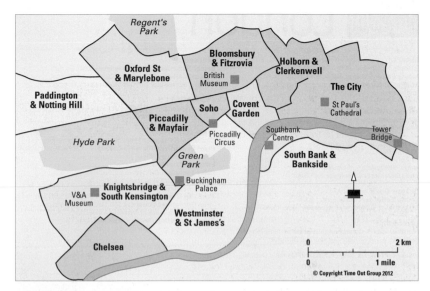

© Copyright Time Out Group 2012

PADDINGTON & NOTTING HILL

Millions have been spent improving north-westerly **Paddington** in recent years, but the area still lacks focus. It's better to head west to the market, bars and boutiques of **Notting Hill**.

▶ *For more, see pp126-127.*

PICCADILLY CIRCUS & MAYFAIR

The neon beguiles small-town tourists, but **Piccadilly Circus** is little more than a charmless traffic junction nowadays. Instead of lingering there, stroll west into **Mayfair**, home to London's most upmarket shops and prestigious hotels.

▶ *For more, see pp128-132.*

WESTMINSTER & ST JAMES'S

With the northern edge of Trafalgar Square pedestrianised, the centre of London is a pleasant place to be. Just south is historic **Westminster**, the home of government; go south-west and you'll reach immaculate, aristocratic **St James's**.

▶ *For more, see pp133-142.*

CHELSEA

Chelsea starts in earnest at Sloane Square, before stretching west and ebbing outwards off the shop-lined King's Road. It's southern border is the Thames.

▶ *For more, see pp143-145.*

KNIGHTSBRIDGE & SOUTH KENSINGTON

Knightsbridge draws devotees with a welter of high-class, high-priced shops. Adjoining **South Kensington** is where the throngs pile into London's three palatial Victorian museums.

▶ *For more, see pp146-150.*

Time Out London

Editorial

Editor Ruth Jarvis
Deputy Editor Edoardo Albert, Simon Coppock
Listings Editors William Crow, Jamie Warburton
Proofreader Tamsin Shelton
Indexer Holly Pick

Editorial Director Ruth Jarvis
Editorial Manager Holly Pick
Management Accountants Margaret Wright, Clare Turner

Design

Art Director Scott Moore
Art Editor Pinelope Kourmouzoglou
Senior Designer Kei Ishimaru
Group Commercial Designer Jodi Sher

Picture Desk

Picture Editor Jael Marschner
Picture Desk Assistant/Researcher Ben Rowe

Advertising

New Business & Commercial Director Mark Phillips
Magazine & UK Guides Commercial Director
  St John Betteridge
Account Managers Jessica Baldwin, Michelle Daburn,
  Ben Holt

Marketing

Senior Publishing Brand Manager Luthfa Begum
Guides Marketing Manager Colette Whitehouse
Group Commercial Art Director Anthony Huggins

Production

Group Production Manager Brendan McKeown
Production Controller Katie Mulhern-Bhudia

Time Out Group

Chairman & Founder Tony Elliott
Chief Executive Officer David King
Chief Operating Officer Aksel Van der Wal
Editor-in-Chief Tim Arthur
Chief Technical Officer Remo Gettini
Group Financial Director Paul Rakkar
Group General Manager/Director Nichola Coulthard
Time Out Communications Ltd MD David Pepper
Time Out International Ltd MD Cathy Runciman
Cultural Development Director Mark Elliott
Group Marketing Director Andrew Booth

Contributors

Introduction Ruth Jarvis. **History** Simon Coppock (*Time Machine* Museum of London curators; *Thanks for the Memories* Ruth Jarvis). **London Today** Peter Watts. **Architecture** Simon Coppock (*Spotter's Guides* Simon Coppock, Peter Watts; *Olympic Park Art* Ossian Ward). **London 2012** Simon Coppock, Peter Watts, Ruth Jarvis (*Torch Song; Beside the Seaside; Whatever Next?* Simon Coppock). **Sights** Simon Coppock, Charlie Godfrey-Faussett, Peter Watts (*Animal Passion, Thou Shalt Not Steal* Ruth Jarvis; *Profile: London Eye* Ronnie Haydon; *Snapshots* Simon Coppock, Sally Harrild; *Profile: Museum of London, Walk: Book Stops* Patrick Welch; *Walk: The Sidestreet Shuffle* Helen Walasek; *Artistic Revival* Nuala Calvi). **Hotels** Simon Coppock (*The Grand Tour* Ruth Jarvis; *Have Bike, Will Travel* Charli Plant). **Restaurants & Cafés** contributors to *Time Out London's Best Restaurants*. **Pubs & Bars** contributors to *Time Out London's Best Bars* (*The Gin Craze* Simon Coppock). **Shops & Services** Anna Norman. **Calendar** Jamie Warburton, William Crow, Loren Harway (*Please, Sir, Can We Have Some More?* Charli Plant; *Happy and Glorious* Loren Harway). **Children** Emma Perry. **Comedy** Ben Williams, Patrick Welch (*Our Own Edinburgh?* Edoardo Albert). **Dance** Lyndsey Winship. **Film** Dave Calhoun, John Watson. **Gay & Lesbian** Patrick Welch. **Music** Eddy Lawrence, Simon Coppock, Chris Parkin. **Nightlife** Kate Hutchinson. **Sport & Fitness** Rob Greig, Ruth Jarvis, Simon Coppock, Patrick Welch. **Theatre** Caroline McGinn, Nuala Calvi. **Escapes & Excursions** Holly Pick, Anna Norman & contributors to *Time Out Great Days Out*. **Directory** William Crow, Jamie Warburton.

Thanks to Caroline Drayton, Jennie Fancett, Pete Fiennes, Will Fulford-Jones, Tim Goodfellow, Sarah Guy, Jackie McDevitt, Sandra Reynolds, Royden Stock, Paul Sullivan and all Guides staff past and present.

Maps john@jsgraphics.co.uk

Cover photography © branchlake/Alamy
Back cover photography Abigail Lelliott, Jitka Hynkova, Britta Jaschinski, LOCOG

Photography by pages 3, 6 Shutterstock; 4, 48, 56, 57, 59, 61, 62, 64, 120, 289 LOCOG; 5 (top left), 7, 39 (bottom), 41, 49, 63 ODA; 5 (top right), 38 ArcelorMittal; 5 (middle left), 28, 92, 165, 167, 187, 224, 236, 239, 240, 241, 245, 254, 277, 328, 337, 343, 351 Rob Greig; 5 (middle right), 9 (right), 13, 103, 112, 139, 150, 157, 158, 177, 246, 251, 263, 315, 326, 334 Jonathan Perugia; 5 (bottom left) Elena Rostunova; 5 (bottom right), 342 Sean Ebsworth Barnes; 8, 115, 127, 168 (bottom), 232, 235, 262, 255 Scott Wishart; 8 (top left) Kaspars Grinvalds; 8 (middle left) David Poultney; 8 (middle right) Rogan MacDonald; 8 (bottom left), 96, 119, 253 (bottom), 256, 257, 309 Alys Tomlinson; 8 (bottom right), 258 Olivia Rutherford; 9 (top left) 282, 294, 312 Heloise Bergman; 9 (middle left) Rob Wilson/Shutterstock.com; 9 (bottom left) www.simonleigh.com; 14 London Transport Museum; 15, 16, 18, 22, 23108 © Trustees of the British Museum; 17 Corbis; 20, 33, 109, 118, 123, 137, 148, 156, 160, 182, 209 (bottom right), 252, 253 (top), 304, 307 Ben Rowe; 32 Elena Elisseeva; 36, 122, 130, 147, 159, 168 (top) 188, 189, 199, 205, 206, 233, 313, 316, 319, 323 Michelle Grant; 39 (top) Courtesy of David Kohn Architects and Fiona Banner; 43, 44, 45 copyright of and reproduced with the consent of the International Olympic Committee; 53 © Matthew Andrews; 65, 67 (right) Getty Images; 67 (left), 79 (left) Rob Wilson / Shutterstock.com; 70, 363 © ODA 2008; 73, 295 Mandeville TM © LOCOG 2009-10 and Wenlock TM © LOCOG 2009-10; 75 Peter Nadolski; 77, 301 Belinda Lawley; 79 (right) Richard Bowden; 80, 81, 144, 153, 175, 185, 193, 196, 215, 249, 268, 270, 273, 275, 361 Britta Jaschinski; 82, 104 Tove K. Breitstein; 85, 131, 140, 181, 292, 298 Andrew Brackenbury; 87, 223, 225, 229 Michael Franke; 89 Neil Lang; 90, 94, 95 (bottom), 218 Ed Marshall; 99 S.Borisov/Shutterstock.com; 100 Rene Ramos; 129 nito / Shutterstock.com; 134 Transport for London 2005; 138 (top) Andrei Nekrassov; 138 (bottom) Luciano Mortula; 141 Sverlova Mariya / Shutterstock.com; 151 Marzena Zoladz; 152 Abi Lelliott; 154 Jael Marschner; 161 David Fearn; 170 Nerida Howard; 172, 296 Nick Ballon; 173 Kate Beatty; 178 Rachael Russell; 186, 230 Tricia de Courcy Ling; 201 Ashley Morrison; 202 Niall Clutton; 217, 230 (bottom left), 248, 259, 261, 279 Ming Tang-Evans; 271, 293 Christina Theisen; 272, 276 Gemma Day; 281 Mark Oxley; 284 National Portrait Gallery London; 287, 288, 340 Elisabeth Blanchet; 290 Sue Robinson/ Shutterstock.com; 291 Sean Nel; 303 Tom Nelson; 329 Peter Kindersley; 335 Neil Balderson/Shutterstock.com; 346 Alastair Muir; 347 Manuel Harlan/RSC; 348 Lee Woodgate; 352 Adrian Zenz; 354 Simon Gurney; 356 Rachelle Burnside; 359 © 2011 Warner Bros. Ent. Harry Potter Publishing Rights © J.K.R.
The following images were supplied by the featured establishments/artists: pages 40, 46, 60, 95 (top), 117, 162, 190, 194, 195, 209, 213, 260, 283, 305, 310, 311, 325, 330, 345, 355

About the Guide

LONDON 2012 OLYMPIC AND PARALYMPIC GAMES

Time Out Guides is proud to be the official book publisher of travel and tourism guides for the London 2012 Olympic and Paralympic Games. This guide contains full information for visitors to the Games, along with Games-related features, all identified with **Pink headings**.

However, it is also a fully comprehensive guidebook for all visitors to London, no matter when they are in town. Those visiting outside Games time should bear in mind that events in the Cultural Olympiad are not by any means confined to Games time; indeed many of the standouts take place earlier in the year.

GETTING AROUND

The back of the book contains street maps of London, as well as overview maps of the city and its surroundings. The maps start on page 392; on them are marked the locations of hotels (❶), restaurants and cafés (❶), and pubs and bars (❶). The majority of businesses listed in this guide are located in the areas we've mapped; the grid-square references in the listings refer to these maps.

THE ESSENTIALS

For practical information, including visas, disabled access, emergency numbers, lost property, useful websites and local transport, please see the Directory. It begins on page 364.

THE LISTINGS

Addresses, phone numbers, websites, transport information, hours and prices were all checked and correct at press time. However, business owners may alter their arrangements at any time – particularly during the London 2012 Games.

The very best venues in the city, the must-sees and must-dos in every category, have been marked with a red star (★). In the Sights chapters, we've also marked venues with free admission with a FREE symbol.

PHONE NUMBERS

The area code for London is 020, but within the city, dialling from a landline, you only need the eight-digit number as listed. The UK country code is 44; calling from abroad, add 20 for London (dropping the initial zero) and the eight-digit number as listed in the guide. For more on phones, *see pp375-376*.

Time Out Guides

Founded in 1968, Time Out has grown from humble beginnings into the leading resource for anyone wanting to know what's happening around the world. The company remains proudly independent, still owned by Tony Elliott over four decades after he launched *Time Out London*. Alongside our influential weeklies in London, New York, Chicago and Dubai, we publish more than 20 magazines in cities as varied as Beijing and Beirut. Our websites, apps, blogs and tweets keep you connected to the best events, entertainment and eating out wordwide – check www.timeout.com to join the global conversation.

This book is one of over 50 Time Out City Guides now joined by the pocket-size Shortlist series. Written by local experts and packed with original photography, our books also retain their independence. No business has been featured because it has advertised, and all restaurants are visited and reviewed anonymously.

ABOUT THE EDITOR

Long-time east London resident **Ruth Jarvis** is Editorial Director of Time Out Guides and an expert on travel and tourism worldwide. She was a member of the development team for Time Out's London 2012 publishing programme.

In Context

Tower of London. *See p101.*

History

Plague, fire and disaster – enjoy 2,000 years of London.

TEXT: SIMON COPPOCK

Over the 2,000 years since London was born, a small trading station by a broad and marshy river, the city has faced plagues and invasions, fires and wars, religious turbulence and financial turmoil. Its history is a sequence of wars, natural disasters and acts of terrorism, borne by Londoners with their characteristic upbeat pessimism and gloomily forthright moaning until the moment arrives when the frenzy of commerce can begin again. Once-beloved leaders are cruelly dismissed, then their departure lamented. Booms beget depressions beget booms. More than anything, this city's past is a tale of resilience, of locals grinning while bearing their burdens of disaster.

In the City, Wren churches – built from the ruins of the Great Fire – have walls still blackened by the German incendiary bombs dropped during the Blitz, and shrapnel scars around Cleopatra's Needle beside the Thames remain from a World War I biplane raid. A fragment of glass, deeply embedded in a wall at the Old Bailey, tells of an IRA terrorist attack back in 1973, while 52 austere steel columns in Hyde Park commemorate those killed by suicide bombers in the summer of 2005.

Evidence of strife is everywhere in this city and the true Londoner will cheerfully insist there's more and worse to come. Just don't bet against them handling their portion of strife with aplomb.

LATIN LESSONS

The city's origins are hardly grand. Celtic tribes lived in scattered communities along the banks of the Thames before the Romans arrived in Britain, but there's no evidence of a settlement on the site of the future metropolis before the invasion of the Emperor Claudius in AD 43. During the Roman conquest, they forded the Thames at its shallowest point (probably near today's London Bridge) and, later, built a timber bridge there. A settlement developed on the north side of this crossing.

Over the next two centuries, the Romans built roads, towns and forts in the area. Progress was halted in AD 61 when Boudicca, the widow of an East Anglian chieftain, rebelled against the imperial forces who had seized her land, flogged her and raped her daughters. She led the Iceni in a revolt, destroying the Roman colony at Colchester before marching on London. The Romans were massacred and their settlement razed.

After order was restored, the town was rebuilt; around AD 200, a two-mile, 18-foot wall was put up around it. Chunks of the wall survive today; the early names of the original gates – Ludgate, Newgate, Bishopsgate and Aldgate – are preserved on the map of the modern city, with the street known as London Wall tracing part of its original course. But through to the fourth century, racked by invasions and internal strife, the Roman Empire was clearly in decline (*see below* **Time Machine**). In 410, the last troops were withdrawn, and London became a ghost town.

INTO THE DARK

During the fifth and sixth centuries, history gives way to legend. The Saxons crossed the North Sea; apparently avoiding the ruins of London, they built farmsteads and trading posts outside the city walls. Pope Gregory sent Augustine to convert the English to Christianity in 596; Mellitus, one of his missionaries, was appointed the first Bishop of London, founding a cathedral dedicated to St Paul inside the old city walls in 604.

From this period, the history of London is one of expansion. Writing in 731, the Venerable Bede described 'Lundenwic' as 'the mart of many nations resorting to it by land and sea'. Yet the city faced a new danger during the ninth century: the Vikings. The city was ransacked in 841 and again in 851, when Danish raiders returned with 350 ships. It was not until 886 that King Alfred of Wessex, Alfred the Great, regained the city, re-establishing London as a major trading centre.

Throughout the tenth century the city prospered. Churches were built, parishes established and markets set up. However, the 11th century brought more harassment

IN CONTEXT

Time Machine AD 290s

By Jenny Hall, Roman curator at the Museum of London.

Who's in control? Carausius declares Home Rule for Britain in AD 293 and makes London his base; Constantius Chlorus, junior emperor of the Roman Empire, is charged with returning Britain to Roman control. **Average wage** Unskilled labourer, 25 to 50 silver denarii a day. **Life expectancy** 26 to 45. **Key concerns** How long could this unofficial empire last? What would happen to Londoners who sided with Carausius and Allectus if the Roman Empire won back Britain? **Local legislation** Coins are minted in London for the first time after a period of rampant inflation.

Flash point Allectus assassinates Carausius, giving Constantius the opportunity to make a two-pronged attack from the sea and save London from Allectus's rebel army in AD 296. Constantius's son was Constantine.

from the Vikings, and the English were forced to accept a Danish king, Cnut (Canute, 1016-35), during whose reign London replaced Winchester as the capital of England.

After a brief spell under Danish rule, the country reverted to English control in 1042 under Edward the Confessor, who devoted himself to building England's grandest church two miles west of the City on an island in the river marshes at Thorney: 'the West Minster' (Westminster Abbey; *see p137*). Just a week after the consecration, he died. London now had two hubs: Westminster, centre of the royal court, government and law; and the City of London, centre of commerce.

On Edward's death, foreigners took over. Duke William of Normandy was crowned king on Christmas Day 1066, having defeated Edward's brother-in-law Harold at the Battle of Hastings. The pragmatic Norman resolved to win over the City merchants by negotiation rather than force, and in 1067 granted the burgesses and the Bishop of London a charter – still available to researchers in the London Metropolitan Archives – that acknowledged their rights and independence in return for taxes. He also ordered strongholds to be built at the city wall 'against the fickleness of the vast and fierce population', including the White Tower (the tallest building in the Tower of London; *see p101*) and the now-lost Baynard's Castle that stood at Blackfriars.

PARLIAMENT AND RIGHTS

In 1295, the Model Parliament, held at Westminster Hall by Edward I and attended by barons, clergy and representatives of knights and burgesses, agreed the principles of English government. The first step towards establishing personal rights and political liberty, not to mention curbing the power of the king, had already been taken in 1215 with the signing of the Magna Carta by King John (*see below* **Time Machine**). Then, in the 14th century, subsequent assemblies gave rise to the House of Lords and the House of Commons. During the 12th and 13th centuries, the king and his court travelled the kingdom, but the Palace of Westminster was now the permanent seat of law and government; noblemen and bishops began to build palatial houses along the Strand from the City to Westminster, with gardens stretching down to the river.

Relations between the monarch and the City were never easy. Londoners guarded their privileges, and resisted attempts by kings to squeeze money out of them to finance wars and construction projects. Subsequent kings were forced to turn to Jewish and Lombard moneylenders, but the City merchants were intolerant of foreigners too.

The self-regulation privileges granted to the City merchants under Norman kings were extended by the monarchs who followed – in return for finance. In 1191, the City of London was recognised by Richard I as a self-governing community; six years later, it won control of the Thames. King John had in 1215 confirmed the city's right 'to elect every year a mayor', a position of authority with power over the sheriff and the Bishop of London. A month later, the mayor joined the rebel barons in signing the Magna Carta.

IN CONTEXT

Time Machine 1210s

By Jackie Keily, medieval curator at the Museum of London.

Who's in control? Nominally, King John.
Average wage Unskilled labourer, 2d a day; skilled craftsman, 3d to 5d a day.
Key concerns Fire, fighting, Frenchmen.
Local legislation After a Southwark fire in 1212, straw roofs are banned.
Flash point In 1215, the inhabitants of London side with the barons against

King John; and in 1216, they support Prince Louis of France when he arrives in the city. Never crowned king, Louis is defeated at the Battle of Lincoln in 1217.

Over the next two centuries, the power and influence of the trade and craft guilds (later known as the City Livery Companies) increased as dealings with Europe grew. The City's markets drew produce from miles around: livestock at Smithfield, fish at Billingsgate, poultry at Leadenhall. The street markets ('cheaps') around Westcheap (now Cheapside) and Eastcheap were crammed with a variety of goods. The population within the city walls grew from about 18,000 in 1100 to well over 50,000 in the 1340s.

WAKE UP AND SMELL THE ISSUE

Lack of hygiene became a serious problem. Water was provided in cisterns, but the supply, more or less direct from the Thames, was limited and polluted. The street of Houndsditch was so named because Londoners threw their dead animals into the furrow there; in the streets around Smithfield (the Shambles), butchers dumped entrails into the gutters. These conditions helped foster the greatest catastrophe of the Middle Ages: the Black Death of 1348 and 1349, which killed about 30 per cent of England's population. The plague came to London from Europe, carried by rats on ships, and was to recur in London several times during the next three centuries.

Disease left the harvest short-handed, causing unrest among the peasants whose labour was in such demand. Then a poll tax of a shilling a head was imposed. It was all too much: the Peasants' Revolt began in 1381. Thousands marched on London, led by Jack Straw from Essex and Wat Tyler from Kent; the Archbishop of Canterbury was murdered and hundreds of prisoners were set free. After meeting the Essexmen near Mile End, the 14-year-old Richard II rode out to the rioters at Smithfield and spoke with Tyler. During their discussion, Tyler was fatally stabbed by the Lord Mayor; the revolt collapsed and the ringleaders were hanged. But no more poll taxes were imposed.

IN CONTEXT

Gin Lane by William Hogarth.
See p21.

Time Machine 1480s

By Jackie Keily, medieval curator at the Museum of London.

Who's in control? Complicated! Four kings in three years: Edward IV and his son, Edward V, both die in 1483 and are succeeded by Edward IV's brother Richard III, who is defeated and killed at Bosworth Field in 1485 by Henry Tudor, the future Henry VII.
Average wage Unskilled labourer, 4d a day.
Unusual imports In 1480-81, Portuguese ships bring 300,000 oranges; a single Venetian galley brings a mixed cargo including coral beads, pepper, sponges, ginger, satin, silk, Corinth raisins and two apes.

Key concerns Avoiding major unrest.
Local legislation In 1484, statutes are passed to stop the importation of certain foreign manufactured goods, so as to protect local jobs.
Flash point In June 1483, London supports Richard III as king instead of the 12-year-old Edward V, who is in prison. The young prince never leaves the Tower (*see p101*) – he and his brother, Richard of Shrewsbury, are later known as the 'Princes in the Tower'.

ROSES, WIVES AND THE ROYAL DOCKS

Its growth spurred by the discovery of America and the opening of ocean routes to Africa and the Orient, London became one of Europe's largest cities under the Tudors (1485-1603). The first Tudor monarch, Henry VII, had ended the Wars of the Roses by might, defeating Richard III at the Battle of Bosworth, and policy, marrying Elizabeth of York, a daughter of his rivals (*see above* **Time Machine**). By the time his son took the throne, the Tudor dynasty was firmly established. But progress under Henry VIII was not without its hiccups. His first marriage to Catherine of Aragon failed to produce an heir, so in 1527 he determined the union should be annulled. When the Pope refused to co-operate, Henry defied the Catholic Church, demanding to be recognised as Supreme Head of the Church in England and ordering the execution of anyone who opposed the plan (including Sir Thomas More, his otherwise loyal chancellor). The subsequent dissolution of the monasteries transformed the face of the medieval city.

When not transforming the politico-religious landscape, Henry found time to develop a professional navy, founding the Royal Dockyards at Woolwich in 1512. He also established palaces at Hampton Court (*see p180*) and Whitehall, and built a residence at St James's Palace. Much of the land he annexed for hunting became today's Royal Parks, among them Greenwich Park, Hyde Park and Regent's Park.

RENAISSANCE MEANS REBIRTH

Elizabeth I's reign (1558-1603) saw the founding of the Royal Exchange in 1566, which enabled London to emerge as Europe's commercial hub. Merchant venturers and the first joint-stock companies established new trading enterprises, as pioneering seafarers Francis Drake, Walter Raleigh and Richard Hawkins sailed to the New World. As trade grew, so did London: it was home to some 200,000 people in 1600, many living in dirty, overcrowded conditions. The most complete picture of Tudor London is given in John Stow's *Survey of London* (1598), a fascinating first-hand account by a diligent Londoner whose monument stands in the church of St Andrew Undershaft.

These were the glory days of English drama. The Rose (1587) and the Globe (1599, now recreated; *see p82*) were erected at Bankside, providing homes for the works of popular playwrights Christopher Marlowe and William Shakespeare. Deemed officially

'For all its devastation, the Great Fire of 1666 at least allowed planners the chance to rebuild London as a modern city.'

'a naughty place' by royal proclamation, 16th-century Bankside was a vibrant mix of entertainment and 'sport' (bear-baiting, cock-fighting), drinking and whoring – and all within easy reach of the City, which had outlawed theatres in 1575.

In 1605, two years after the Tudor dynasty ended with Elizabeth's death, her Stuart successor, James I, escaped assassination on 5 November, when Guy Fawkes was found underneath the Palace of Westminster. Commemorated with fireworks each year as Bonfire Night, the Gunpowder Plot was hatched in protest at the failure to improve conditions for the persecuted Catholics, but only resulted in an intensification of anti-papist sentiment. James I is more positively remembered for hiring Inigo Jones to design court masques (musical dramas) and London's first influential examples of the classical Renaissance architectural style: the Queen's House (1616; *see p173*), the Banqueting House (1619; *see p136*) and St Paul's Covent Garden (1631; *see p112*).

ROYALISTS AND ROUNDHEADS

Charles I succeeded his father in 1625, but gradually fell out of favour with the City of London and an increasingly independent-minded Parliament over taxation. The country slid into civil war (1642-49), the supporters of Parliament (the Roundheads, led by Puritan Oliver Cromwell) opposing the supporters of the King (the Royalists).

Both sides knew that control of the country's major city and port was vital for victory, and London's sympathies were with the Parliamentarians. In 1642, 24,000 citizens assembled at Turnham Green to face Charles's army, but the King withdrew. The move proved fatal: Charles never threatened the capital again, and was eventually found guilty of treason. Taken to the Banqueting House in Whitehall on 30 January 1649, he declared himself a 'martyr of the people' and was beheaded. A commemorative wreath is still laid at the site of the execution on the last Sunday in January each year.

For the next decade, the country was ruled as a Commonwealth by Cromwell. But his son Richard's subsequent rule was brief: due to the Puritans closing theatres and banning Christmas (a Catholic superstition), the Restoration of the exiled Charles II in 1660 was greeted with great rejoicing. The Stuart king had Cromwell exhumed from Westminster Abbey, and his body was hung in chains at Tyburn (near modern-day Marble Arch). His severed head was displayed on a pole outside the abbey until 1685.

PLAGUE, FIRE AND REVOLUTION

The year 1665 saw the most serious outbreak of bubonic plague since the Black Death, killing nearly 100,000. Then, on 2 September 1666, a second disaster struck. The fire that spread from a carelessly tended oven in Thomas Farriner's baking shop on Pudding Lane raged for three days and consumed four-fifths of the City.

The Great Fire at least allowed planners the chance to rebuild London as a modern city. Many blueprints were considered, but Londoners were so impatient to get on with business that the City was reconstructed largely on its medieval street plan (albeit in brick and stone rather than wood). The prolific Sir Christopher Wren oversaw work on 51 of the 54 rebuilt churches. Among them was his masterpiece: the new St Paul's (*see p90*), completed in 1710 and effectively the world's first Protestant cathedral.

In the wake of the Great Fire, many well-to-do City dwellers moved to new residential developments west of the old quarters, an area subsequently known as the West End. In the City, the Royal Exchange was rebuilt, but merchants increasingly used the new

IN CONTEXT

coffeehouses to exchange news. With the expansion of the joint-stock companies and the chance to invest capital, the City emerged as a centre not of manufacturing but of finance. Even at this early stage, economic instability was common: the 1720 financial disaster known as the South Sea Bubble ruined even Sir Isaac Newton.

Anti-Catholic feeling still ran high. The accession in 1685 of Catholic James II aroused such fears of a return to papistry that a Dutch Protestant, William of Orange, was invited to take the throne with his wife, Mary Stuart (James's daughter). James fled to France in 1688 in what became known (by its beneficiaries) as the 'Glorious Revolution'. It was during William's reign that the Bank of England was founded, initially to finance the King's religious wars with France.

IN CONTEXT

Thanks for the Memories

London's newest blue plaques, celebrating famous residents.

Charles Rolls (1877-1910)
The building was the West End headquarters of Rolls-Royce; the man put together the famous partnership behind the company. His interest in speed led to his premature death, in a plane crash.
14-15 Conduit Street, W1S 2XJ.

Graham Greene (1904-1991)
The home of the great 20th-century novelist from 1935 to 1940; he wrote Brighton Rock here.
14 Clapham Common North Side, SW4.

Marie Stopes (1880-1958)
The future sex education and birth control pioneer spent her girlhood here.
28 Cintra Park, SE19 2LH.

John Lennon (1940-1980)
Yoko Ono unveiled the plaque at this ground floor and basement flat, the first home she shared with Lennon. He was working on 'The White Album' at the time (the second half of 1968).
34 Montagu Square, W1H 2LH.

Richard D'Oyly Carte (1844-1901)
The family home of the man behind the comic operas of Gilbert and Sullivan and the founder of the Savoy hotel (where he employed Messrs Ritz and Escoffier).
2 Dartmouth Park Road, NW5.

John Rae (1813-1893)
The Arctic explorer and discoverer of the missing link in the vital Northwest Passage shipping route spent the last 24 years of his life here.
4 Lower Addison Gardens, W14.

Sir Basil Spence (1907-1976)
The home and office of the prolific modern architect, best known for his ground-breaking design for Coventry Cathedral.
1 Canonbury Place, N1.

Sir Malcolm Campbell (1885-1948) and Donald Campbell (1921-1967)
Father and son between them set ten land and 11 water speed records; but dad failed to cover the few yards from a neighbour's house to see his son born. Their home is now a school.
Canbury, Kingston Hill, Kingston Upon Thames, Surrey KT2 7LN.

Sir William Ramsay (1852-1916)
The chemist and Nobel-honoured discoverer of five of the noble gases ived here from 1887 to 1902.
12 Arundel Gardens, W11.

David Gestetner (1854-1939)
This imposing villa was the home for 41 years to Gestetner, a Hungarian Jewish immigrant whose clever office copying technology changed the way business was done.
125 Highbury New Park, N5.

ENGLISH HERITAGE
JOHN
LENNON
1940~1980
Musician
and Songwriter
lived here in
1968

CREATION OF THE PRIME MINISTER

In 1714, the throne passed to George, the Hanover-born great-grandson of James I. The German-speaking king (he never learned English) became the first of four long-reigning Georges in the Hanoverian line.

During George I's reign (1714-27), and for several years after, Sir Robert Walpole's Whig party monopolised Parliament. Their opponents, the Tories, supported the Stuarts and had opposed the exclusion of the Catholic James II. On the king's behalf, Walpole chaired a group of ministers (the forerunner of today's Cabinet), becoming, in effect, Britain's first prime minister. Walpole was presented with 10 Downing Street (built by Sir George Downing) as a residence; it remains the official prime ministerial home.

During the 18th century, London grew with astonishing speed. New squares and terraced streets spread across Soho, Bloomsbury, Mayfair and Marylebone, as wealthy landowners and speculative developers cashed in on the new demand for leasehold properties. South London also became more accessible with the opening of the first new bridges for centuries: Westminster Bridge (opened 1750) and Blackfriars Bridge (completed 1769) joined London Bridge, previously the only Thames crossing.

GIN-SOAKED POOR, NASTY RICH

In London's older districts, people were living in terrible squalor. Some of the most notorious slums were located around Fleet Street and St Giles's (north of Covent Garden), only a short distance from fashionable residences. To make matters worse, gin ('mother's ruin') was readily available at low prices; many poor Londoners drank excessive amounts in an attempt to escape the horrors of daily life. The well-off seemed complacent, amusing themselves at the popular Ranelagh and Vauxhall Pleasure Gardens or with trips to mock the patients at the Bedlam lunatic asylum. Public executions at Tyburn were popular events in the social calendar; it's said that 200,000 people gathered to see the execution (after he had escaped from prison four times) of the folk-hero thief Jack Sheppard in 1724.

The outrageous imbalance in the distribution of wealth encouraged crime, and there were daring daytime robberies in the West End. Reformers were few, though there were exceptions. Henry Fielding, author of the picaresque novel *Tom Jones*, was also an enlightened magistrate at Bow Street Court. In 1751, he and his blind half-brother John set up a volunteer force of 'thief-takers' to back up the often ineffective efforts of the parish constables and watchmen who were, until then, the city's only law-keepers. This crime-busting group of proto-cops, known as the Bow Street Runners, were the earliest incarnation of today's Metropolitan Police (established in 1829).

Meanwhile, five major new hospitals were founded by private philanthropists. St Thomas's and St Bartholomew's were long-established monastic institutions for the care of the sick, but Westminster (1720), Guy's (1725), St George's (1734), London (1740) and the Middlesex (1745) went on to become world-famous teaching hospitals. Thomas Coram's Foundling Hospital (*see p108*) was another remarkable achievement.

INDUSTRY AND CAPITAL GROWTH

It wasn't just the indigenous population of London that was on the rise. Country folk, whose common land had been replaced by sheep enclosures, were faced with a choice between starvation wages or unemployment, and so drifted into the towns. Just outside the old city walls, the East End drew many poor immigrant labourers to build the docks towards the end of the 18th century. London's total population had grown to one million by 1801, the largest of any city in Europe. By 1837, when Queen Victoria came to the throne (*see p22* **Time Machine**), five more bridges and the capital's first passenger railway (from Greenwich to London Bridge) gave hints of huge expansion.

As well as being the administrative and financial capital of the British Empire, London was its chief port and the world's largest manufacturing centre. On one hand, it had splendid buildings, fine shops, theatres and museums; on the other, it was a

IN CONTEXT

Time Machine 1830s

By Alex Werner, head of history at the Museum of London.

Who's in control? In 1837, 18-year-old Queen Victoria arrives on the throne. Prime Minister Lord Melbourne holds together a divided cabinet and mentors the young Queen, who turns a blind eye to past indiscretions (and his wife's affair with Lord Byron). **Population** About two million. **Average wage** Tailor, 5s a day; about half of the total female labour force are servants.

Key concerns Stopping cholera: many die in epidemics during the 1830s.

Local legislation The London to Birmingham Railway opens in 1837, but the line is not yet ready; early riders can only get as far as Hemel Hempstead.

city of poverty, pollution and disease. Residential areas were polarised into districts of fine terraces maintained by squads of servants and overcrowded, insanitary slums.

The growth of the metropolis in the century before Victoria came to the throne had been spectacular, but during her reign (1837-1901), thousands more acres were covered with roads, houses and railway lines. If you visit a street within five miles of central London, its houses will be mostly Victorian. By the end of the 19th century, the city's population had swelled to more than six million, an incredible growth of five million in just 100 years.

Despite social problems of the Victorian era, memorably depicted in the writings of Charles Dickens, steps were being taken to improve conditions for the majority of Londoners by the turn of the century. The Metropolitan Board of Works installed an efficient sewerage system, street lighting and better roads. The worst slums were replaced by low-cost building schemes funded by philanthropists such as the American George Peabody, whose Peabody Donation Fund continues to provide subsidised housing to the working classes. The London County Council (created in 1888) also helped to house the poor.

The Victorian expansion would not have been possible without an efficient public transport network with which to speed workers into and out of the city from the new suburbs. The horse-drawn bus appeared on London's streets in 1829, but it was the opening of the first passenger railway seven years later that heralded the commuters of the future. The first underground line, which ran between Paddington and Farringdon Road, opened in 1863 and proved an instant success, attracting 30,000 travellers on the first day. The world's first electric track in a deep tunnel – the 'tube' – opened in 1890 between the City and Stockwell, later becoming part of the Northern line.

THE CRYSTAL PALACE

If any single event symbolised this period of industry, science, discovery and invention, it was the Great Exhibition of 1851. Prince Albert, the Queen's Consort, helped organise the triumphant showcase, for which the Crystal Palace, a vast building of iron and glass, was erected in Hyde Park. It looked like a giant greenhouse; hardly surprising as it was designed not by a professional architect but by the Duke of Devonshire's gardener, Joseph Paxton. Condemned by art critic John Ruskin as the model of dehumanisation in design, the Palace came to be presented as the prototype of modern architecture. During the five months it was open, the Exhibition drew six million visitors. The profits were used by the Prince Consort to establish a permanent centre for the study of the applied arts and sciences; the enterprise survives today in the South Kensington museums of natural history, science, and decorative and applied arts (*see pp147-149*), and in three colleges (of art, music and science). After the Exhibition, the Palace was moved to Sydenham and used as an exhibition centre until it burned down in 1936.

ZEPPELINS ATTACK FROM THE SKIES

London entered the 20th century as the capital of the largest empire in history. Its wealth and power were there for all to see in grandstanding monuments such as Tower Bridge (*see p101*) and the Midland Grand Hotel at St Pancras Station (*see p192*), both of which married the retro stylings of High Gothic with modern iron and steel technology. During the brief reign of Edward VII (1901-10), London regained some of the gaiety and glamour it had lacked in the later years of Victoria's reign. Parisian chic came to London with the opening of the Ritz (*see p204*); Regent Street's Café Royal hit the heights as a meeting place for artists and writers; gentlemen's clubs proliferated; and 'luxury catering for the little man' was provided at the new Lyons Corner Houses (the Coventry Street branch held 4,500 people).

Road transport, too, was revolutionised. By 1911, horse-drawn buses were abandoned, replaced by motor cars, which put-putted around the city's streets, and the motor bus, introduced in 1904. Disruption came in the form of devastating air raids during World War I (1914-18). Around 650 people lost their lives in Zeppelin raids, but the greater impact was psychological – the mighty city had experienced helplessness.

CHANGE, CRISIS AND SHEER ENTERTAINMENT

Political change happened quickly after the war. At Buckingham Palace (*see p140*), the suffragettes had fiercely pressed the case for women's rights before hostilities began (*see below* **Time Machine**) and David Lloyd George's government averted revolution in 1918-19 by promising 'homes for heroes' (the returning soldiers). It didn't deliver, and in 1924 the Labour Party, led by Ramsay MacDonald, formed its first government.

A live-for-today attitude prevailed in the Roaring '20s among the young upper classes, who flitted from parties in Mayfair to dances at the Ritz. But this meant little to the mass of Londoners, who were suffering in the post-war slump. Civil disturbances, brought on by the high cost of living and rising unemployment, resulted in the nationwide

IN CONTEXT

Time Machine 1910s

By Jenny Hall, curator of social history at the Museum of London.

Who's in control? In 1910, the London County Council assumes greater responsibility for governing London, particularly in areas such as education, health and housing.

Life expectancy Men, 52; women, 55.

Average wage 31s 6d.

Prices The maximum retail price of a 4lb loaf in 1912 is 6d.

Key concerns The death of a whole generation of young men during World War I: about 60,000 Londoners will die in the trenches.

Local legislation In 1918, the Representation of the People Act gives eight million women over 30 the right to vote in parliamentary elections for the first time, and also enfranchises all adult males over the age of 21 who are resident householders.

Flash point In May 1914, police stop suffragettes entering Buckingham Palace (*see p140*) in a bid to present a 'Votes for Women' petition to the King; 66 women are arrested, among them Emmeline Pankhurst.

Let the games begin

Wenlock and Mandeville, the official
London 2012 mascots in stores now.
london2012.com/shop

Paralympic Games

General Strike of 1926, when the working classes downed tools en masse in support of striking miners. Prime Minister Baldwin encouraged volunteers to take over the public services, and the streets teemed with army-escorted food convoys, aristocrats running soup kitchens and students driving buses. After nine days of chaos, the strike was finally called off.

The economic situation only worsened in the early 1930s following the New York Stock Exchange crash of 1929. By 1931, more than three million Britons were jobless. During these years, the London County Council (LCC) began to have a greater impact on the city, clearing slums and building new houses, creating parks and taking control of public services. All the while, London's population increased, peaking at nearly 8.7 million in 1939. To accommodate the influx, the suburbs expanded, particularly to the north-west with the extension of the Metropolitan line to an area that became known as 'Metroland'. Identical gabled houses sprang up in their thousands.

At least Londoners were able to entertain themselves with film and radio. Not long after London's first radio broadcast was beamed from the roof of Marconi House in the Strand in 1922, families were gathering around huge Bakelite wireless sets to hear the BBC (the British Broadcasting Company; from 1927 the British Broadcasting Corporation). TV broadcasts started on 26 August 1936, when the first telecast went out from Alexandra Palace, but few Londoners could afford televisions until the 1950s.

BLITZKRIEG

Abroad, events had taken on a frightening impetus. Neville Chamberlain's policy of appeasement towards Hitler's Germany collapsed when the Germans invaded Poland. Britain duly declared war on 3 September 1939. The government implemented precautionary measures against air raids, including the evacuation of 600,000 children and pregnant mothers, but the expected bombing raids didn't happen during the autumn and winter of 1939-40 (the so-called 'Phoney War'). Then, in September 1940, hundreds of German bombers dumped explosives on east London and the docks, destroying entire streets and killing or injuring more than 2,000 in what was merely an opening salvo. The Blitz had begun. Raids on London continued for 57 consecutive nights, then intermittently for a further six months. Londoners reacted with stoicism, famously asserting 'business as usual'. After a final raid on 10 May 1941, the Nazis had left a third of the City and the East End in ruins.

From 1942 onwards, the tide began to turn, but Londoners had a new terror to face: the V1 or 'doodlebug'. Dozens of these deadly, explosive-packed, pilotless planes descended on the city in 1944, causing widespread destruction. Later in the year, the more powerful V2 rocket was launched. The last fell on 27 March 1945 in Orpington, Kent, around six weeks before Victory in Europe (VE Day) was declared on 8 May 1945.

'NEVER HAD IT SO GOOD'

World War II left Britain almost as shattered as Germany. Soon after VE Day, a general election was held and Winston Churchill was defeated by the Labour Party under Clement Attlee. The new government established the National Health Service in 1948, and began a massive nationalisation programme that included public transport, electricity, gas, postal and telephone services. For most people, however, life remained regimented and austere. In war-ravaged London, local authorities struggled with a critical shortage of housing. Prefabricated bungalows provided a temporary solution for some (60 years later, six prefabs on the Excalibur estate in Catford, south-east London, were given protection as buildings of historic interest), but the huge new high-rise housing estates that the planners devised proved unpopular with their residents.

There were bright spots. London hosted the Olympic Games in 1948; three years later came the Festival of Britain, resulting in the first full redevelopment of the riverside site into the South Bank (now Southbank) Centre. As the 1950s progressed, life and prosperity returned, leading Prime Minister Harold Macmillan in 1957 to

IN CONTEXT

proclaim that 'most of our people have never had it so good'. However, Londoners were leaving. The population dropped by half a million in the late 1950s, causing a labour shortage that prompted huge recruitment drives in Britain's former colonies. London Transport and the National Health Service were both particularly active in encouraging West Indians to emigrate to Britain. Unfortunately, as the Notting Hill race riots of 1958 illustrated, the welcome these new immigrants received was rarely friendly. Still, there were several areas of tolerance: Soho, for instance, which became famous for its mix of cultures and the café and club life they brought with them.

THE SWINGING '60S
By the mid 1960s, London had started to swing. The innovative fashions of Mary Quant and others broke the stranglehold Paris had on couture: boutiques blossomed along the King's Road, while Biba set the pace in Kensington. Carnaby Street became a byword for hipness as the city basked in its new-found reputation as music and fashion capital of the world – made official, it seemed, when *Time* magazine devoted its front cover to 'swinging London' in 1966. The year of student unrest in Europe, 1968, saw the first issue of *Time Out* hit the streets in August; it was a fold-up sheet, sold for 5d. The decade ended with the Rolling Stones playing a free gig in Hyde Park that drew around 500,000 people.

Then the bubble burst. Many Londoners remember the 1970s as a decade of economic strife, the decade in which the IRA began its bombing campaign on mainland Britain. After the Conservatives won the general election in 1979, Margaret Thatcher instituted an economic policy that cut public services and widened the gap between rich and poor. Riots in Brixton (1981) and Tottenham (1985) were linked to unemployment and heavy-handed policing, keenly felt in London's black communities. The Greater London Council (GLC), led by Ken Livingstone, mounted vigorous opposition to the government with a series of populist measures, but it was abolished in 1986. The replacement of Margaret Thatcher by John Major in October 1990 signalled a short-lived upsurge of hope among Londoners.

THINGS CAN ONLY GET BETTER?
In May 1997, the British electorate ousted the Tories and gave Tony Blair's Labour Party the first of three election victories. Blair left London with two significant legacies.

First, the government commissioned the Millennium Dome, whose turn-of-the-century celebrations it hoped would be a 21st-century rival to the Great Exhibition of 1851. Instead, the Dome ate £1 billion and became a national joke. However, even as Labour's fortunes declined, the Dome's saw an upturn. In its guise as the O2 Arena (*see p321*), it has hosted concerts by the likes of Prince and Lady Gaga; as the North Greenwich Arena (*see p61*), it will be a key venue in the London 2012 Olympic and Paralympic Games. Second, following a referendum, Labour instituted the Greater London Assembly (GLA) and London mayoralty. Thus 2000 saw Ken Livingstone return to power as London's first directly elected mayor. He was re-elected in 2004, a thumbs-up for policies that included a traffic congestion charge. Summer 2005 brought elation, as London won the bid to host the 2012 Games, and devastation, as bombs on tube trains and a bus killed 52 people and injured 700.

Aided by support from the suburbs that Livingstone had neglected, thatch-haired Tory Boris Johnson became mayor in 2008 with a healthy majority. Publicity-friendly early policies, such as the introduction of a bike rental scheme, have more recently taken a back seat to the sober realities of working with the new national government, a Conservative–Liberal Democrat coalition – whose policies and spending cuts don't always favour city life – and ensuring a smooth run-up to the Games. The disturbing riots of August 2011 (*see pp28-31*), whose flashpoint was again in Tottenham, have made this a task to be taken seriously. Electors will judge his success, with Johnson due to face old adversary Livingstone once more in the mayoral elections of May 2012.

Key Events

London in brief.

43 The Romans invade; the settlement of Londinium is founded.
61 Boudicca burns Londinium; the city is rebuilt and made provincial capital.
200 A city wall is built.
410 Roman troops evacuate Britain.
c600 Saxon London is built to the west.
841 The Norse raid for the first time.
c871 The Danes occupy London.
886 Alfred the Great takes London.
1042 Edward the Confessor builds a palace and 'West Minster' upstream.
1066 William I is crowned in Westminster Abbey.
1078 The Tower of London is begun.
1123 St Bart's Hospital is founded.
1197 Henry Fitzalwin is the first mayor.
1215 The mayor signs the Magna Carta.
1240 First Parliament at Westminster.
1290 Jews are expelled from London.
1348 The Black Death arrives.
1381 The Peasants' Revolt.
1397 Richard Whittington is Lord Mayor.
1476 William Caxton sets up the first printing press at Westminster.
1534 Henry VIII cuts Britain off from the Catholic Church.
1555 Martyrs burned at Smithfield.
1565 Sir Thomas Gresham proposes the Royal Exchange.
1572 First known map of London.
1599 The Globe Theatre opens.
1605 Guy Fawkes's plot to blow up James I fails.
1642 The start of the Civil War.
1649 Charles I is executed; Cromwell establishes Commonwealth.
1664 Beginning of the Great Plague.
1666 The Great Fire.
1675 Building starts on the new St Paul's Cathedral.
1694 The Bank of England is set up.
1766 The city wall is demolished.
1773 The Stock Exchange is founded.
1824 The National Gallery is founded.
1836 The first passenger railway opens; Charles Dickens publishes *The Pickwick Papers*, his first novel.

1843 Trafalgar Square is laid out.
1851 The Great Exhibition takes place.
1858 The Great Stink: pollution in the Thames reaches hideous levels.
1863 The Metropolitan line opens as the world's first underground railway.
1866 London's last major cholera outbreak; the Sanitation Act is passed.
1868 The last public execution is held at Newgate prison (now the Old Bailey).
1884 Greenwich Mean Time is established as a global standard.
1888 Jack the Ripper prowls the East End; London County Council is created.
1890 The Housing Act enables the LCC to clear the slums; the first electric underground railway opens.
1897 Motorised buses are introduced.
1908 London hosts the Olympic Games for the first time.
1915 Zeppelins begin three years of bombing raids on London.
1940 The Blitz begins.
1948 London again hosts the Olympic Games; forerunner of the Paralympics, the Stoke Mandeville Games are organised in Buckinghamshire by neurologist Sir Ludwig Guttman.
1951 The Festival of Britain is held.
1952 The last 'pea-souper' smog.
1953 Queen Elizabeth II is crowned.
1981 Riots in Brixton.
1982 The last London docks close.
1986 The GLC is abolished.
1992 One Canada Square tower opens on Canary Wharf.
2000 Ken Livingstone becomes London's first directly elected mayor; Tate Modern and the London Eye open.
2005 The city wins its bid to host the 2012 Games; suicide bombers kill 52 on public transport.
2008 Boris Johnson becomes mayor.
2010 Hung parliament leads to new Conservative–Lib Dem coalition.
2011 Riots and looting around the city.
2012 London 2012 Olympic Games and Paralympic Games take place.

IN CONTEXT

London Today

Counting down to the London 2012 Games.

TEXT: PETER WATTS

London's capacity to recover within weeks from seemingly bone-crunching blows can still surprise even veteran Londoners. It happened during the Blitz, it happened after the 7 July 2005 bombings and it happened within hours of London being convulsed by a series of vicious riots last August. These mass looting sprees had left the city in a state of seemingly irreparable shellshock, but the very next day Londoners took to the streets by the hundreds to clean up the damage for themselves. It was impossible not to take heart at the speed and motivation of these self-organised, community-motivated 'riot clean-up' crews who gathered behind raised brooms in a show of strength that seemed to take holidaying politicians almost as much by surprise as the riots themselves.

Peter Watts is a freelance journalist who writes for Prospect *and the* New Statesman *and blogs at http:// greatwenlondon. wordpress.com.*

London remains a magnet for oligarchs, sheikhs and Chinese and Indian billionaires, who live in the same city but a different world to most Londoners.

HARD TIMES

But underneath these moments of unity, a hard truth remains – London, for all its charms, is a tough city to live in and it isn't getting any easier. House prices, already the steepest in the country and beyond the means of most first-time buyers, continue to rise, but now rents are going up as well, squeezing many people out of newly gentrified areas. For parents, state schools are incredibly variable in quality and living on the wrong side of the street can be devastating for a child's educational development. Transport, while the envy of other capital cities across the world, is eye-wateringly expensive, with inflation-busting rises arriving every year. Add the general social problems caused by the lingering recession – employment is high and social services are being reduced in most boroughs – and you have a fairly uncomfortable stew. The riots may not have been political in focus, but they did represent a wider dissatisfaction at the unfairness of life in London. London's increasing inequality remains a focus of the *Evening Standard*, London's only daily newspaper, which continues to examine the extremes of poverty that are present in most London boroughs.

Living alongside the 'squeezed middle' and 'feral underclass', as current political parlance divides society, are the super-rich. London remains a magnet for oligarchs, sheikhs and Chinese and Indian billionaires, who live in the same city but a different world to most Londoners. London's super-prime housing market – for estate agents that is anything over £15 million – remains remarkably robust in these straitened times, with London's most expensive housing development, the Candy Brothers' huge building at One Hyde Park, doing brisk business through 2011 despite some properties being priced as high as £136 million. It seems nobody has yet managed to build a penthouse that is so expensive a buyer can't be found for it.

A CUT ABOVE THE REST

The next must-have homes to hit the market will be the dozen or so apartments at the top of the Shard, Europe's tallest building, which has rapidly risen over London Bridge Station throughout the past year and is now almost ready for occupancy. This 1,017-foot skyscraper designed by Italian architect Renzo Piano is a mixed-use development of offices, housing and a hotel, and is expected to transform Bermondsey almost as much as the Olympic Park will change Stratford. Thousands of jobs will be created and the flood of money into the area is predicted to expand London's South Bank district as far east as Bermondsey Street, making it an economic powerhouse to rival the West End, City and Canary Wharf. One beneficiary will be the long-beleaguered London Bridge Station itself, which is now scheduled to receive a refurbishment to rival that of St Pancras, whose renaissance was confirmed last year with the reopening after 75 years of the former Midland Grand Hotel as the extraordinary St Pancras Renaissance.

One of the first new arrivals to the new 'London Bridge Quarter', as the developers have named it, is the cavernous White Cube, Jay Jopling's contemporary art gallery, which already has outposts in Hoxton and Piccadilly and opened at the end of 2011 in an old warehouse on Bermondsey Street. Bermondsey Street already has more than its fair share of independent boutiques and trendy bars, but White Cube is its best-known inhabitant and will certainly draw similar enterprises to the area.

IN CONTEXT

From a White Cube to white elephants. One of the unforeseen consequences of the London 2012 Olympic and Paralympic Games appears to be a belated desire for designers and planners to come up with the 'new London Eye', a headline-grabbing tourist-nabbing initiative that will be heralded as iconic and distinctive while also raking in the cash. One such scheme is the planned Thames River Park, a series of pontoons on the north bank that will provide tourists with an alternative means of getting between St Paul's and the Tower of London during the Games. The floating walkway will support eight glass pod-like pavilions that will contain museums, concert halls, cinemas, swimming pools and eco-parks. It's an intriguing concept, a sort of floating Festival of Britain, but local residents are not impressed, and nor are some of the local heritage attractions such as Shakespeare's Globe, which claim views of the Thames will be damaged. Although the structure is said to be temporary, campaigners are unconvinced, pointing out the same thing was said when the London Eye went up.

SKY RIDE

Even more controversial has been Boris Johnson's scheme for a cable car over the Thames between North Greenwich and the Isle of Dogs, which is hoped to be open for the London 2012 Games. The estimated cost for this odd creation is said to be around £60 million, £36 million of which will come from the sponsors Emirates and the rest from Transport for London – the public company that runs London's transport network. Some Londoners are furious with the deal: the line will appear on tube maps in company colours as the Emirates Air Line and the two stations linked by the cable car will be called Emirates Greenwich Peninsula and Greenwich Royal Docks, even though a significant portion of the funding will come from the public purse. Commuters, already stung by some of the highest fares in Europe, are not happy at being asked to fund a scheme that is being built almost entirely for tourists – it links the O2 and the ExCeL exhibition centre. The cable car will certainly offer great views, but it is not being built in a particularly useful place (it's not quite next to the O2 or ExCeL) and it's not exactly what London is crying out for.

In this sense, it's rather typical of Mayor Johnson's initiatives, which often seem to be generated more for publicity than to alleviate the frequently aggravating lives of Londoners. You can see the attraction, however, as it was one such proposal that helped get Johnson elected in the first place, when he promised to replace the unpopular articulated single-deck 'bendy buses' with a new version of London's condemned but iconic Routemaster. It sounded good and won votes, but the new Routemaster has proved to be rather expensive and not particularly helpful given that bendy buses are the quickest, if not the most comfortable, way for commuters to navigate London's busiest bus routes. Worse still was Johnson's proposal to build a new airport in the Thames Estuary, an idea that had been exposed as a planning impossibility as far back as the 1970s. As with the cable car and Routemaster, it was hard to shake off the suspicion that Johnson was more interested in self-publicising gimmicks than actually solving London's transport problems.

And it's obviously no coincidence that the cable car, Thames River Park and Routemaster were all scheduled to be ready for 2012 – along with much else. The 2012 Games have certainly helped to focus the mind of London, and summer 2012 is the date given for a multitude of new arrivals: the Shard's completion, the opening of the first stage of the Tate Modern extension, major exhibitions on Pablo Picasso and David Hockney, a much-delayed £15.5 million refurbishment of Leicester Square, the reopening of the *Cutty Sark* in Greenwich and the redevelopment of Piccadilly Circus. With public and private funding as scarce as it's ever been thanks to the global and European financial crises, being able to promise delivery in time for the Games has helped push through a lot of projects that may otherwise have fallen by the wayside. Which begs the question: what will Londoners have to look forward to when the Olympic Games party has left town?

IN CONTEXT

Architecture

A wonderful jumble of architectural highlights.

TEXT: SIMON COPPOCK

For the first decade of this century, it seemed every central London street was obliged by some arcane law to engage a cluster of cranes. Then the recession made loans expensive, property returns unpredictable and investors wary. Suddenly, the city's mania for redevelopment seemed to be over.

After the shock, some reality. News of projects – notably any tall building – hits the press when planning permission is sought, but the buildings might take three years from site-clearance to topping out. So several monster blocks that outraged columnists are only now approaching completion. Renzo Piano's 1,016-foot Shard is one of them, its concrete core a major London landmark months ahead of completion.

For all the annual top ten lists of loathed new buildings, the best modern architecture is taken to the city's heart. Some is swiftly loved (the Gherkin a classic example), other buildings become favourites over time: Centre Point, the BT Tower, the Barbican and the National Theatre are once-hated structures that increasingly find themselves dearly loved.

None of this is new. In the 17th century, the authorities objected to Sir Christopher Wren's magnificent St Paul's Cathedral because it looked far too Roman Catholic for their Anglican sensibilities. In late 2010, other sensibilities were offended by Jean Nouvel's 'groundscraper' One New Change, a block of shops and offices right opposite the cathedral.

In fact, this city's defining characteristic is its aesthetically unhappy mix of buildings. As it always has been, London is a mess of historic bits and modern bobs, giving the city's built landscape its unique capacity to surprise and delight.

THE NEW CITY

Modern London sprang into being after the Great Fire of 1666. The Fire destroyed four-fifths of the City of London, burning 13,200 houses and 89 churches. The devastation was commemorated by Sir Christopher Wren's 202-foot **Monument** (*see p99*), recently renovated, but many of the finest buildings in the City still stand as testament to the talents of Wren, the architect of the great remodelling, and his successors.

London was a densely populated place built largely of wood, and fire control was primitive. It was only after the three-day inferno that the authorities insisted on a few basic regulations. Brick and stone became the construction materials of choice, and key streets were widened to act as firebreaks. Despite grand, classical proposals from several architects, Wren among them, London reshaped itself around its old street pattern, with buildings that survived the Fire standing as monuments to earlier ages. Chief of these was the Norman **Tower of London** (*see p101*), begun soon after William's 1066 conquest and extended over the next 300 years; the Navy saved the Tower from the flames by blowing up surrounding houses before the inferno could reach it.

Another longstanding building, **Westminster Abbey** (*see p137*) was begun in 1245 when the site lay far outside London's walls; it was completed in 1745 by Nicholas Hawksmoor's west towers. The abbey is the most French of England's Gothic churches, but the chapel begun by Henry VII is pure Tudor. Centuries later, Washington Irving gushed: 'Stone seems, by the winning labour of the chisel, to have been robbed of its weight and density, suspended aloft, as if by magic.'

IN CONTEXT

Spotter's Guide to Tudor Windows

An ancient architectural style made new friends in the 19th century.

Reputedly built so he could keep tabs on his monks praying without having to leave his quarters, Prior Bolton's oriel window at **St Bartholomew-the-Great** (*see p88*) is a classic example of the characteristic Renaissance design. The bay window bears the Prior's rebus (an arrow from a crossbow piercing a wine barrel; bolt + tun = bolton), and shows a parabolic arch (a flatter curve than the more steeply curving Gothic arch) with a plain trefoil design at the top of the upper panes. The form found popularity with Victorian architects, as they sought a style sufficiently British to support their imperial aims; this is why oriel windows are so common in London's institutional buildings.

IN CONTEXT

A LATE FLOWERING

The European Renaissance came late to Britain, making its London debut with Inigo Jones's 1622 **Banqueting House** (*see p136*). The sumptuously decorated ceiling, added in 1635 by Rubens, celebrated the Stuart monarchy's Divine Right to rule, although 14 years later King Charles I provided a greater spectacle as he was led from the room and beheaded on a stage outside. Tourists also have Jones to thank for **St Paul's Covent Garden** (*see p112*) and the immaculate **Queen's House** (*see p173*), but they're not his only legacies. He mastered the art of piazzas (such as the one at Covent Garden), porticos and pilasters, changing British architecture forever. His work influenced the careers of succeeding generations of architects and introduced a habit of venerating the past that it would take 300 years to kick.

Nothing cheers a builder like a natural disaster, and one can only guess at the relish with which Wren and co began rebuilding after the Fire. They brandished classicism like a new broom: the pointed arches of English Gothic were duly rounded off, Corinthian columns made an appearance and church spires became as complex, frothy and multi-layered as a wedding cake.

Wren blazed the trail with his daring plans for **St Paul's Cathedral** (*see p90*), spending an enormous (for the time) £500 on the oak model of his proposal. But the scheme, incorporating a Catholic dome rather than a Protestant steeple, was too Roman for the establishment and the design was rejected. Wren quickly produced a redesign and gained planning permission by incorporating a spire, only to set about a series of mischievous U-turns to give us the building, domed and heavily suggestive of an ancient temple, that's survived to this day.

Wren's baton was picked up by Nicholas Hawksmoor and James Gibbs, who benefited from a 1711 decree that 50 extra churches should be built (*see below* **Spotter's Guide**). Gibbs became busy around Trafalgar Square with the steepled Roman temple of **St Martin-in-the-Fields** (*see p135*), as well as the Baroque **St Mary-le-Strand** and the tower of **St Clement Danes** (for both, *see p114*). His work was well received, but the more experimental Hawksmoor had a rougher ride. For one thing, not everyone admired his stylistic innovations; for another, even fewer approved of his financial planning, or lack of it: **St George's Bloomsbury** (*see p109*) cost three times its £10,000 budget and took 15 years to build.

Spotter's Guide to Baroque Spires

How Hawksmoor reinvented the English church.

Under the Fifty New Churches Act of 1711, which used a coal tax to fund the building of 'churches of stone... with Towers and Steeples', Nicholas Hawksmoor designed, in whole or part, eight new places of worship. Like Wren, Hawksmoor loved the classical temple, a style at odds with the Act's Anglican insistence on spires. **St George-in-the-East**, **St Anne Limehouse** and **St Mary Woolnoth** (*see p96*) are all unorthodox resolutions of this contradiction, but the 'spire' of **St George's Bloomsbury** (*see p109*) is the barmiest. Apeing the Mausoleum of Halicarnassus,

Hawksmoor created a peculiar stepped pyramid design, plopped a giant statue of George I in a toga on top and then added unicorns and lions.

Hawksmoor's ruinous overspends (St Anne's was so costly no money was left for the rector's salary) was one reason why just a dozen of the proposed 50 churches were built. Still, the four corner towers of Thomas Archer's **St John's, Smith Square** (*see p318*) and the spire 'portholes' of **St Martin-in-the-Fields** (*see p135*) today provide further delightful evidence of Baroque invention.

One of a large family of Scottish architects, Robert Adam found himself at the forefront of a movement that came to see Italian Baroque as a corruption of the real thing, with architectural exuberance dropped in favour of a simpler interpretation of ancient forms. The best surviving work of Adam and his brothers James, John and William can be found in London's great suburban houses **Osterley Park**, **Syon House** (*see p185*) and **Kenwood House** (*see p155*), but the project for which they're most famous no longer stands: the cripplingly expensive Adelphi housing estate off the Strand. Most of the complex was pulled down in the 1930s and replaced by an office block, and only a small part of the original development survives; it's now the **Royal Society of Arts** (8 John Adam Street, Covent Garden, WC2N 6F7)

SOANE AND NASH

Just as the first residents were moving into the Adelphi, a young unknown called John Soane was embarking on a domestic commission in Ireland. It was never completed, but Soane eventually returned to London and went on to build the **Bank of England** (*see p93*) and **Dulwich Picture Gallery** (*see p169*). The Bank was demolished between the wars, leaving only the perimeter walls and depriving us of Soane's masterpiece, though his gracious Stock Office has been reconstructed in the museum. A further glimpse of what those bankers might have enjoyed can be gleaned from his house, the quirky **Sir John Soane's Museum** (*see p103*), an exquisite architectural experiment.

A near-contemporary of Soane's, John Nash was a less talented architect, but his contributions – among them the inner courtyard of **Buckingham Palace** (*see p140*), the **Theatre Royal Haymarket** (Haymarket, SW1Y 4HT) and **Regent Street** (W1) – have proved comparable to those of Wren. Regent Street began as a proposal to link the West End to the planned park further north, as well as a device to separate the toffs of Mayfair from the riff-raff of Soho; in Nash's own words, a 'complete separation between the Streets occupied by the Nobility and Gentry, and the narrow Streets and meaner houses occupied by mechanics and the trading part of the community'.

By the 1830s, the classical form of building had been established in England for some 200 years, but this didn't prevent a handful of upstarts from pressing for change. In 1834, the **Houses of Parliament** (*see p136*) burned down, leading to the construction of Sir Charles Barry's Gothic masterpiece. Barry sought out Augustus Welby Northmore Pugin. Working alongside Barry, if not always in agreement with him (of Barry's symmetrical layout, he famously remarked, 'All Grecian, sir. Tudor details on a classic body'), Pugin created a Victorian fantasy that would later be condemned as the Disneyfication of history.

GETTING GOTHIC

This was the beginning of the Gothic Revival, a move to replace what was considered foreign and pagan with something that was native and Christian. Architects would often decide that buildings weren't Gothic enough; as with the **Guildhall**'s 15th-century Great Hall (*see p97*), which gained its corner turrets and central spire only in 1862. The argument between Classicists and Goths erupted in 1857, when the government hired Sir George Gilbert Scott, a leading light of the Gothic movement, to design a new home for the Foreign Office. Scott's design incensed anti-Goth Lord Palmerston, then prime minister, whose diktats prevailed. But Scott exacted his revenge by building an office in which everyone hated working, and by going on to construct Gothic edifices all over town, among them the **Albert Memorial** (*see p147*) and the impressive frontage of what is now **St Pancras International** train station (*see p110*), which returned to its original function as a hotel in early 2011 (*see p192*).

St Pancras was completed in 1873, after the Midland Railway commissioned Scott to build a London terminus that would dwarf that of its rivals next door at King's Cross. Using the project as an opportunity to show his mastery of the Gothic form, Scott built an asymmetrical castle that obliterated views of the train shed behind, itself an engineering marvel completed earlier by William Barlow. Other charming and imposing neo-Gothic buildings around the city include the **Royal Courts of Justice** (*see p87*), the **Natural History Museum** (*see p147*) and **Tower Bridge** (*see p101*). Under the influence of the Arts and Crafts movement, medievalism morphed into such mock Tudor buildings as the wonderful half-timbered **Liberty** department store (*see p258*).

BEING MODERN

World War I and the coming of modernism led to a spirit of renewal and a starker aesthetic. **Freemasons' Hall** (*see p113*) and the BBC's **Broadcasting House** (*see p122*) are good examples of the pared-down style of the 1920s and '30s, but perhaps the finest example of between-the-wars modernism can be found at **London Zoo** (*see p125*). Built by Russian émigré Bertold Lubetkin and the Tecton group, the spiral ramps of the Penguin Pool were a showcase for the possibilities of concrete. The material was also put to good use on the London Underground, enabling the quick, cheap building of cavernous spaces with sleek lines and curves. There was nothing quick or cheap about the art deco **Daily Express** building (*see below* **Spotter's Guide**).

The bombs of World War II left large areas of London ruined, providing another opportunity for builders to cash in. Lamentably, the city was little improved by the

Spotter's Guide to Art Deco

London wasn't short of curves in the Roaring '20s.

Dating from the mid 1920s, the art deco architectural style favoured streamlined geometrical simplicity, in keeping with the Jazz Age's wide-eyed belief in a bright and beautiful future. From tube stations to cinemas, London has some prime examples of the style, but one of the best art deco buildings is the old **Daily Express Building** (121-128 Fleet Street, the City). Built in 1931, it's an early example of 'curtain wall' construction, its radical black vitrolite and glass façade (by Sir Owen Williams) hung on an internal frame, and demonstrates the modernist belief that form should reflect function. Public access is restricted to very occasional tours (sometimes during Open-City events; *see p288*), but stick your head around the door to glimpse the Robert Atkinson interior of plaster reliefs, with an oval staircase and lots of silver and gilt. The *Architects' Journal* called it a 'defining monument of 1930s London'.

rebuild; in many cases, it was left worse off. The destruction left the capital with a dire housing shortage, so architects were given a chance to demonstrate the grim efficiency with which they could house large numbers of families in tower blocks.

There were post-war successes, however, including the **Royal Festival Hall** (*see p78*) on the South Bank. The sole survivor of the 1951 Festival of Britain, the RFH was built to celebrate the end of the war and the centenary of the Great Exhibition, held in 1851 and responsible for the foundation in South Kensington of the Natural History Museum, the Science Museum and the V&A. Next door to the RFH, the **Hayward** gallery (*see p80*) is an exemplar of the 1960s vogue for Brutalist architecture, a style more thoroughly explored at the **Barbican** (*see p316*), loved by many but never fully rehabilitated from the vilification it received in the years after it opened in 1982.

HERE COME THE STARCHITECTS

The 1970s and '80s offered up a pair of alternatives to concrete: postmodernism and high-tech. The former is represented by César Pelli's blandly monumental **One Canada Square** (*see p163*) in Docklands, an oversized obelisk that's perhaps the archetypal expression of late '80s architecture. Richard Rogers's high-tech **Lloyd's of London** building (*see p98*) is much more widely admired. A clever combination of commercial and industrial aesthetics that adds up to one of the most significant British buildings since the war, it was mocked on completion in 1986, but outclasses newer projects.

Apart from Rogers, the city's most visible contemporary architect has been Norman Foster, whose **City Hall** and **30 St Mary Axe** (aka 'the Gherkin'; *see p40* **Spotter's Guide**) have caught up with Big Ben and black taxis as movie shorthand for 'Welcome to London!'. His prolific practice set new standards in sports design with the soaring arch of the new **Wembley Stadium** (*see p336*); the exercise in complexity that is the £100 million Great Court at the **British Museum** (*see p106*) did the same for London's cultural gem. The Great Court is the largest covered square in Europe, but every one of its 3,300 triangular glass panels is unique.

Much new architecture is to be found cunningly inserted into old buildings. Herzog & de Meuron's fabulous transformation of a Bankside power station into **Tate Modern** (*see p82*) is perhaps the most famous example – the firm aims to repeat its success with an ambitious new extension. Now due to be completed in 2013, it will look something like a pyramid folded out of origami. Equally ground-breaking was Future Systems' NatWest Media Centre at **Lord's Cricket Ground** (*see p337*). Built from aluminium in a boatyard and perched high above the pitch, it's one of London's most daring constructions to date, especially given the traditional setting. More recently, the arty new **Town Hall Hotel & Apartments** (*see p211*) redeveloped an Edwardian town hall in Bethnal Green by adding a new top floor under a laser-cut metal 'veil', but keeping intact as many characterful aspects of the exterior and interior as possible, right down to brass fire-hose reels and lift numbers.

LOCAL COLOUR AND OPEN ARTS

Architecture hasn't all been about headline projects and eye-troubling commercial developments. Will Alsop's multicoloured **Peckham Library** (122 Peckham Hill Street, SE15 5JR) has helped redefine community architecture, as did David Adjaye's later **Idea Stores** (www.ideastore.co.uk) in Poplar (1 Vesey Path, East India Dock Road, E14 6BT) and Whitechapel (321 Whitechapel Road, E1 1BU); the crisp aesthetic of these buildings is a world away from the traditional Victorian library. Adjaye's inspiration in shop design is even more explicit in the **Rivington Place** gallery (Rivington Place, Shoreditch, EC2A 3BA), with the main entrance tucked to the side so that passers-by are drawn into the main gallery by a display window – just like that of a department store. The subtle Robbrecht en Daem expansion of **Whitechapel Gallery** (*see p160*) into the stylistically very different former library next door reversed the process, giving a new democratic openness to a pair of landmark Victorian buildings.

IN CONTEXT

London 2012 Art

Ossian Ward picks eight of the biggest new public works for London 2012.

Anish Kapoor.

Anish Kapoor

If an Olympic-size swimming pool sounds big, try an Olympic Park sculpture for size. Anish Kapoor's *ArcelorMittal Orbit* for the Olympic Park will dwarf Big Ben at 115 metres. It's essentially a pair of viewing platforms on a steel tower, but a tower that plays with its great height and strength in a series of twists and rolls.

Martin Creed

Martin Creed may have jumped the gun with his *Work No 850 (Runners)*, in which athletes sprinted down the Tate's Duveen Galleries – indeed Seb Coe launched the Cultural Olympiad by taking part in the 2008 piece. But the Glaswegian minimalist has big plans for 2012, based on a performance staged in Italy in 2000, entitled *All of the Bells in a City or Town Rung as Quickly and as Loudly as Possible for Three Minutes (Work No 245)*. Creed's 'Big

Ring' for London will herald the start and finish of the Olympic Games with a similar clapper-call across the city.

Monica Bonvicini

Best known for provocative public works in neon, steel and glass (like her see-through, one-way mirror loo), Monica Bonvicini has come up with a nine-metre high sculpture, *Run*, to be sited in the Olympic Park. Her references include the Velvet Underground song 'Run Run Run' and 'Running Dry' by Neil Young, so the work might be more melancholic imperative than cheerful suggestion.

Rachel Whiteread

Strange to say, there's no permanent work in London by local luminary Whiteread. The perfect blank canvas has been here all along: the frontage of the Whitechapel Gallery has remained undecorated since it was built in 1901, the designers installing electric lights

IN CONTEXT

(unlike most museums at the time), but running out of money for the façade.

Fiona Banner

Those looking for accommodation next summer could do worse than spend a night in a boat. Fiona Banner and architect David Kohn have teamed up with Artangel and Living Architecture to create *A Room for London*, a steamboat run aground on the roof of the Southbank Centre, where paying guests will be treated to a flag-raising ceremony as well as spectacular views.

Tino Sehgal

Tate Modern's annual Turbine Hall commission is usually a licence to scale up your artistic practice, but Tino Sehgal's human approach means there will likely be nothing bigger than you on display. His performing actors, dancers and gallery invigilators converse or cajole visitors, forcing you into the picture.

Olafur Eliasson

After dazzling Londoners with his artificial sun, Olafur Eliasson returns for a project with the Serpentine Gallery, which is launching a new space in Kensington Gardens for 2012.

World in London

The Photographers' Gallery has comissioned portraits of 204 Londoners hailing from each of

Fiona Banner.

the nations participating in the Olympic Games (including St Kitts) for *The World in London*. The first portrait, taken by Andres Serrano, was of Alexander McQueen, representing Team GB, and the entire series will be splashed across prominent hoardings and buildings all over the city and online as well.

IN CONTEXT

Monica Bonvicini.

PLANNING THE FUTURE

The Open-City London festival (*see p288*) does a terrific job of getting locals engaged with their built environment, but for an overview of what the city might look like in a few years' time, get off the tube at Goodge Street and visit **New London Architecture** (26 Store Street, WC1E 7BT, 7636 4044, www.newlondonarchitecture.org). The centre's centrepiece is a 39-foot-long scale model of London.

In the north, the transformation of King's Cross is continuing apace. St Pancras International Station, **Kings Place** (*see p319* **Profile**) and the University of the Arts London – which began autumn term 2011 here in a redeveloped Victorian granary – are just the vanguard of the 67-acre brownfield redevelopment known as King's Cross Central. As well as the arts and education, 20 new streets are being built to service 1,900 new homes in a part of London that has its very own new postcode: N1C.

Even more impressive – and also with its own postcode, E20, the same as the fictional Walford borough in TV soap *EastEnders* – is the **Olympic Park** (*see p52*). The new stadiums in this formerly disregarded corner of east London are impressive, but the changes being wrought around the Park and other Games venues are every bit as fascinating: the huge cluster of buildings planned south of the **O2 Arena** (at Games time, the North Greenwich Arena, *see p61*); the new 'town centre' at Stratford, on the eastern flank of the Olympic Park; and the ambitious £30 million Siemens sustainability centre on the Royal Docks, due for completion in 2012, possibly along with a cable car link across the river to the O2. Planners have been pointing to this bit of London, start of the Thames Gateway, as the city's future for many years now – are the 2012 Games finally leading it into existence?

Spotter's Guide to City Skyscrapers

The City shoots for the skies.

When some wag dubbed Lord Foster's 40-storey Swiss Re Tower, now **30 St Mary Axe**, 'the Erotic Gherkin' in 2004, it wasn't with fondness. Yet the name became such a badge of honour that the planners now routinely give each skyscraper a nickname: the Walkie-Talkie, Helter-Skelter and, overlooking the City from London Bridge, Babel-size Shard. **Lloyd's of London**, finished to Foster's rival architect Lord Rogers's design in 1986, has never had a nickname nor been as loved as the Gherkin, despite its innovative inside-out design. Perhaps Rogers' 48-storey **122 Leadenhall Street** ('the Cheese Grater'), now under way again right opposite, will win him some affection. But our money's on the City's current tallest building. At 110 Bishopsgate, **Heron Tower** stands a proud 755 feet (including radio mast) and 46 storeys tall. It is by no means as beautiful as Lloyd's or the Gherkin, but – like the equally plain **Tower 42** (*see p98*), just over the junction – has the advantage of regular public access: the designers thoughtfully included the Japanese-Brazilian Sushisamba bar-restaurant on Levels 38-40, reached by exterior glass lifts. It is due to open in early 2012.

Heron Tower.

London 2012

Olympic Stadium. *See p53*.

Stef Reid,
Runner

On the scoreboard:
THE IMPORTANT THING
THE OLYMPIC GAMES IS N
WINNING BUT TAKING PAR
THE ESSENTIAL THING
LIFE IS NOT CONQUERING
BUT FIGHTING WELL.
BARON de COUBE

Olympic City

London has proper Games pedigree.

Peter Watts is a freelance journalist who writes for Prospect *and the* New Statesman, *and blogs about London at* greatwenlondon. wordpress.com.

On 27 July, London will become the first city to host the modern Olympic Games for a third time. Yes, the Games originated in Athens in 776 BC, were revived there in 1896 and returned in 2004, but the London Games of 1908 and 1948 were pivotal in establishing the character and some cherished traditions of the modern Olympic Movement.

Nor is the United Kingdom's role confined to those two years. Key to the revival of the Games was the work of Dr William Penny Brookes, a Victorian educationist and believer in physical exercise as a means for moral improvement. He began staging a sporting competition inspired by the ancient Olympic Games in the tiny Shropshire hamlet of Much Wenlock from the 1850s. In 1890, this annual event was attended by Baron Pierre de Coubertin, who was inspired to organise the first modern Games.

The Paralympic Games also have their origins in this country: at Stoke Mandeville Hospital in Buckinghamshire the first wheelchair games were organised in 1948 by Sir Ludwig Guttmann, a doctor who worked with World War II veterans suffering from spinal injuries.

Women's Archery at the **1908 Games**.

VOLCANIC INTERRUPTION

It isn't just the faded black-and-white photos of the 1908 Olympic Games that make it seem they were from a distant era. There was the inclusion of keenly contested events that from this distance seem rather quaint: Bicycle Polo (recently enjoying something of an international revival), Tug-of-War, the Standing Long Jump. There was the sheer dominance of the hosts, who won 99 more medals than the second-placed United States. But the most amazing thing is that the 1908 Games happened at all.

The Games had originally been allocated to Rome but, when Vesuvius erupted in 1906, the Italian government felt it couldn't afford the cost. So London stepped in to save the day, hastily building an athletics stadium at White City, which was being redeveloped for the Franco-British Exhibition. It was an impressive arena, able to hold 70,000 spectators and with a swimming pool in the centre. Other venues included the All England Club at Wimbledon for Tennis (a role it will reprise for London 2012; *see p62*), Hurlingham for Polo and Queen's Club for Real Tennis.

There was a great deal about the 1908 Games that was novel. For the first time, athletes competed not as individuals, but in national teams (the first ever national flag parade inaugurated these Games). Many regulations were still being worked out, from the length of running shorts to the rules for the 400m. Indeed, disagreement about whether a runner had to stay in lane in the 400m led to all three US competitors boycotting a re-run of the four-man final. British athlete Wyndham Halswelle thus won the only walkover in Olympic history. A make-it-happen attitude pervaded the Games: British middleweight Johnny Douglas won gold in the Boxing on a split decision decided by his father, who happened to be the referee, and the American Tug-of-War team was defeated by a team of Liverpudlian policemen.

The event that defined the 1908 Games was the Marathon. This was to begin at Windsor Castle, and King Edward VII and Queen Alexandra wanted it to end at the stadium. Problem. The accepted Marathon distance was 25 miles – that's the distance between Athens and Marathon, after all – but Windsor Castle was 26 miles from White City. So the length of the race was increased to accommodate the Royal Couple, plus an extra 385 yards so it could finish directly beneath the Royal Box. This became the established distance from 1924, but it was a mile too far for several competitors in the un-British summer heat of 1908. The race leader, Italian baker Dorando Pietri, collapsed inches from the end. He was helped over the finishing line by supporters –

LONDON 2012

and promptly disqualified. (As a consolation prize, Queen Alexandra gave Pietri a silver cup.) The race favourite, an Onondaga Indian from Canada called Tom Longboat, lasted just 19 miles, perhaps due to the champagne runners routinely supped.

THE AUSTERITY GAMES

If there is something charming about the can-do brio of competitors in 1908, the 1948 Olympic Games were played out against a much graver backdrop. Their predecessor had been the infamous Berlin Games of 1936, while the 1940 event would have been held, at the height of World War II, in Tokyo. After the war, it was felt Europe needed something to celebrate and London duly volunteered as host. Intended to be called the Reconciliation Games, the '48 Olympics became, in British folklore, the Austerity Games.

In Britain, rationing was even worse after 1945 than it had been during the war. To help out, all participants were asked to bring food: the United States team flew in white flour daily and ate steak, and it's said the French brought champagne. British athletes were given 'double rations', 5,467 calories a day – the same as dockers and miners, almost twice as much as ordinary Londoners. The city was desperately short of housing after years of bombing and there was no money to build an Olympic Village, so male athletes lived in RAF camps in Richmond and Uxbridge, while the women stayed at Southlands College in West Drayton. A volunteer programme was for the first time established to help run the Games, and Wembley (*see p336*), the principal venue, was hastily converted into an athletics stadium. Other surviving venues include Earls Court (which London 2012 revisits, *see p58*) and the Herne Hill Velodrome (*see p339*).

The Opening Ceremony on 29 July was seen as a landmark occasion for the post-war world – many had believed there would never be another Games after '36 – and 2,500 pigeons were released as a symbol of its significance. Technological advances were also being made: the ceremony was broadcast live by the BBC (these were the first televised Games) and the result of the 100m final was the first determined by photo-finish (the equipment was in place, but unused, in '32 and '36).

The 1948 Games uncovered several heroes. One was Károly Takács, a Hungarian, who won gold in the Rapid-Fire Pistol event. Takacs' favoured right hand had been shattered by a grenade in the war, so he trained himself to shoot with his left. Another success was Bob Mathias, an American who

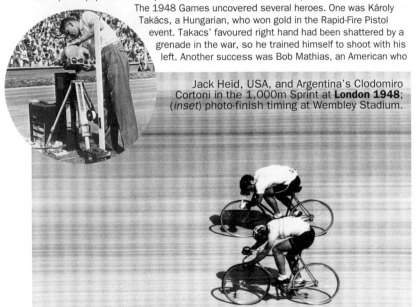

Jack Heid, USA, and Argentina's Clodomiro Cortoni in the 1,000m Sprint at **London 1948**; (*inset*) photo-finish timing at Wembley Stadium.

LONDON 2012

LONDON 2012

Herne Hill Velodrome. *See p45.*

won the Decathlon four months after taking up the sport. At 17, he became the youngest man to win an Olympic Athletics event. British weightlifter Jim Haldaway was more than a mere sporting hero: he weighed just four and a half stones when he was liberated from a Japanese prisoner-of-war camp, but won a bronze in the lightweight class.

The undoubted king and queen of the 1948 Games were Emil Zatopek and Fanny Blankers-Koen. Zatopek was a Czech long-distance runner, one of the best of all time, and he first made an impact at London 1948, winning the 10,000m in only his second ever race at the distance. His achievements four years later were even more impressive – golds at the 5,000m, 10,000m and Marathon.

Blankers-Koen was Dutch and probably the first great female athlete. Nicknamed the 'Flying Housewife', she won four gold medals (in the 100m, 200m, 400m and 4x100m relay) despite being (gasp) 30, (wince) married and (gulp) a mother of two. Another female success story was France's Micheline Ostermeyer, who won the Shot Put and Discus. Her day job: a concert pianist.

Birth of the Paralympic Games

How a global movement grew from one doctor's vision.

While the 1948 Games were happening in London, a small event took place in nearby Buckinghamshire that would later become the Paralympic Games. The 1948 International Wheelchair Games were organised at Stoke Mandeville Hospital for 16 ex-soldiers by Dr Ludwig Guttmann. Guttmann was responsible for a special unit treating those who had suffered spinal injuries in World War II.

A German-Jewish neurologist who fled the Nazis in the 1930s, Guttmann used sport as part of his rehabilitation programme. 'Paraplegia is not the end of the way,' he said. 'It is the beginning of a new life.' He encouraged the ex-servicemen to participate in sports including darts, billiards, skittles, polo and basketball. 'We're so bloody busy in this place, we haven't got time to be ill,' a patient is said to have remarked.

The Games began on 29 July, the same day as the London Olympic Games. The Stoke Mandeville Games were then held every year in the last week of July. Word spread quickly: the arrival in 1952 of Dutch athletes made it an international competition, and by 1960 it was no longer reserved for war veterans, with Guttmann taking 400 athletes in wheelchairs to compete alongside the Olympic Games in Rome.

From this, the new competition took its name – 'Paralympics' is an abbreviated form of 'Parallel Olympics' – and the Paralympic Games have followed every Olympic Games since. In 2012, 162 countries and 4,200 athletes are expected to take part in 20 sports.

Athletes are of mixed disabilities and events are split into different classes, depending on the capabilities of the competitors. For instance, Archery is open to amputees, those with cerebral palsy and wheelchair-users, and has three classes, two for standing athletes and one for wheelchair-users. There are also sports unique to the Paralympic Games, such as Boccia – pronounced 'botcha', it is a game like boules that was specifically designed to be played by those with cerebral palsy.

The Games returned to Stoke Mandeville in 1984 in a dual event shared with New York. The British section was at Stoke Mandeville Stadium, the national centre for disability sport where such home Paralympians as Baroness Tanni Grey-Thompson, multi-gold medallist, have trained. The street on which the stadium is located is called Guttmann Road, in tribute to the pioneering doctor who made the Paralympic Games possible.

LONDON 2012

Venues

What's where for the London 2012 Games.

An extraordinary transformation has been made to the mostly derelict, former industrial land between Stratford International Station and the River Lea. In just a few years, a cluster of remarkable stadiums have sprung up, impressive in scale and design – and all of them on target for completion well before you read this.

Unless you're lucky enough to get a place on a guided tour of the site, there's no access to the **Olympic Park** (*see p52*) until the London 2012 Olympic and Paralympic Games are under way, but its riverside location makes for a fascinating day out on foot or by bicycle.

You can, of course, already visit the several historic venues that are also to be used in the 2012 Games. **Horse Guards Parade** (*see p59*), **Hyde Park** (*see p61*), **Greenwich Park** (*see p59*), **Wimbledon** (*see p63*), **Lord's Cricket Ground** (*see p61*) and **Wembley Stadium** (*see p62*) are among them.

THE BASICS

The London 2012 Games are divided into concentric circles: at its heart, the Olympic Park; next the London venues; and then a number of venues outside London.

The **Olympic Park** (*see pp52-58*) is quite staggering – as an architectural, environmental and logistical achievement, for sure, but also in its sheer scale as you walk or cycle beside it. More than half the bridges were complete by summer 2010, and planting in the parklands was well under way – the 'golden meadow', carefully planted to flower in July and August 2012, first bloomed in summer 2010, then right on cue again in summer 2011.

In this chapter, we list the sporting venues and the events they will host in 2012, but there are many other significant structures in the Park. The most eye-catching is alongside the Olympic Stadium: Anish Kapoor's lofty, spiralling, red **Orbit** (*see p52* **Inside Track**). The innovative, eco-friendly **Energy Centre**

> 🏃 Pictograms in this colour represent events in the **Olympic Games**.
> 🏃 Pictograms in this colour represent events in the **Paralympic Games**.

will be operational from the end of 2010, while the 'brown roof' of the **Main Press Centre** is being made out of wood and seeds recycled from the developing parkland habitat around it. In **Stratford City**, to the west of the Olympic Park, the vast Westfield shopping mall (*see p259*) opened to huge crowds in 2011, while the apartment blocks that will house some 17,000 athletes and officials during the Games have taken shape in the Olympic & Paralympic Village. It is a rare boon for competitors that they'll be staying within walking distance of the major competition venues for London 2012. Everything will be connected to central London by the new Javelin® shuttle service, promising journey times of just seven minutes to St Pancras International come the Games.

Beyond the Olympic Park, the **London venues** (*see pp58-62*) bring events for the 2012 Games into the parts of the city that most postcard-collectors will recognise: **Horse Guards Parade** (*see p59*) and **The Mall** (*see p61*) are just down the road from Buckingham Palace, while **Hyde Park** is alongside the posh shops, hotels and embassies of Mayfair (*see pp129-131*). Visitors interested in getting a flavour of London 2012 venues prior to the events themselves are able to explore all of these – given good weather, a day spent

Velodrome. *See p55.*

watching a cricket match at **Lord's Cricket Ground**, for example, is a holiday highlight for many sports fans.

The Olympic Park has transformed a vast, once-decrepit area of east London, but the riverbank venues to the south of the park (*see pp58-62*) may prove to have a subtler long-term influence on how Londoners understand their city. Locals generally conceive of London as divided by the River Thames into south and north, but infrastructure improvements, linking south bank venues such as **Greenwich Park** (*see p59*) and the **North Greenwich Arena** (*see p61*) to **ExCeL** (*see p58*) on the north bank, may encourage them to consider the Thames as less of an absolute barrier – especially when Mayor Boris Johnson's eye-catching cable car across the river (*see p59* **Inside Track**) is completed. Whatever your level of interest in the Games, the UNESCO World Heritage Site of Maritime Greenwich (*see pp17-174*) is likely to be included on your list of must-sees.

The 2012 Games will visit four further historic London venues – **Wembley Stadium** (*see p62*) and **Wimbledon** (*see p63*), respectively the heart of English football and the centre of world tennis, **Wembley Arena** (*see p62*), and regal **Hampton Court Palace** (*see p59*) – as well as a number of improved or purpose-built sites **outside London** (*see pp62-64*).

Our chapter **Visit** (*see pp69-71*) provides succint practical details and advice on tickets, basic orientation, transport, health & safety advice and accommodation. For indicative **venue maps** of the Olympic Park, *see pp50-51*, and of the Greater London venues, *see p47*. For details on general transport around London, *see pp365-368* **Getting Around**.

INSIDE TRACK SEE FOR FREE

Several London 2012 events offer great roadside viewing. The Cycling Road Race events take place on 28-29 July; the route runs from The Mall via Hampton Court Palace to Box Hill before looping back. Time Trials are at Hampton Court Palace on 1 Aug. The cycling element of the Triathlon (women's, 4 Aug; men's, 7 Aug), a 40km course passing several iconic sights, can also be viewed by all. Road-based Athletics events, in and around town, are the Marathon (women's, 5 Aug; men's, 12 Aug) and Race Walk (men's 20km, 4 Aug; men's 50km and women's 20km, 11 Aug). For the Paralympic Games, road-side viewing is possible for the Cycling Road Race around Brands Hatch (6-8 Sept) and the Marathon (9 Sept).

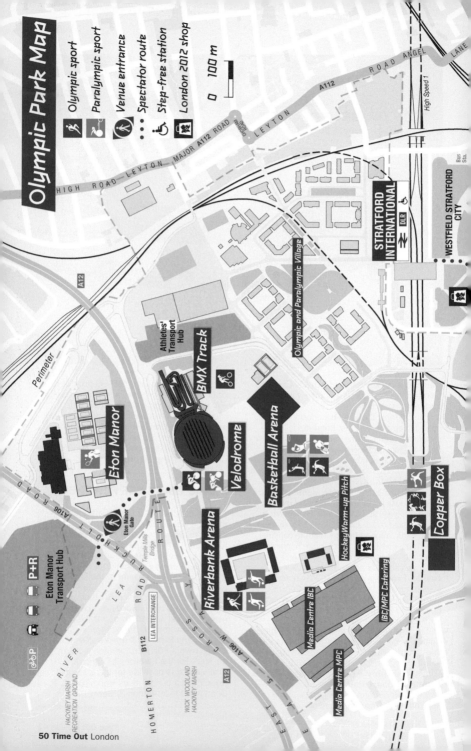

Olympic Park Map

Olympic sport
Paralympic sport
Venue entrance
Spectator route
Step-free station
London 2012 shop

0 100 m

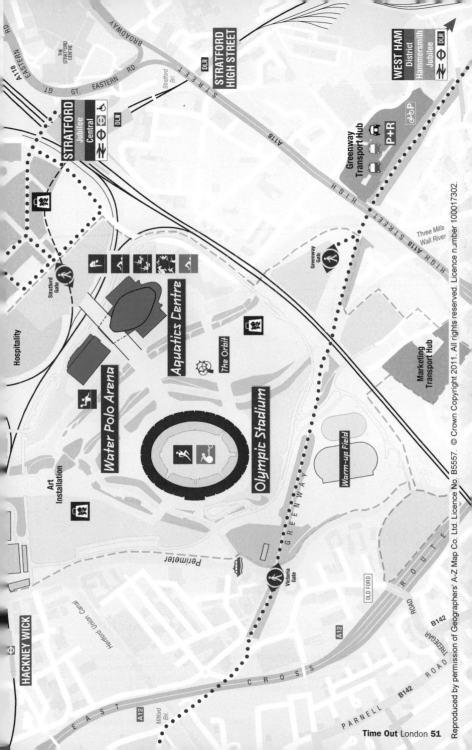

STRATFORD HIGH STREET

WEST HAM
District
Hammersmith
Jubilee

A118 EASTERN RD.

THE STRATFORD CENTRE

BROADWAY

GT. EASTERN RD.

STRATFORD
Jubilee
Central

Stratford Bri.

STRATFORD HIGH STREET

A118

HIGH STREET A118

Greenway Transport Hub

P+R

Three Mills Wall River

Stratford Gate

Greenway Gate

Hospitality

Aquatics Centre

The Orbit

Marketing Transport Hub

Water Polo Arena

Olympic Stadium

Art Installation

Warm-up Field

Perimeter

GREENWAY

Victoria Gate

OLD FORD

ROUTE

HACKNEY WICK

Hertford Union Canal

Mitford Bri.

A12

A12

OLD FORD ROAD

TREDEGAR ROAD

B142

B142

EAST CROSS ROUTE

PARNELL ROAD

Jessica Ennis,
Heptathlete

Join Jessica to help offset the Carbon Footprint of London 2012.

Register at bptargetneutral.com and we will offset the carbon emissions from your travel to the Games. Join us in an attempt to set a world record for offsetting carbon emissions from spectator journeys to a single event. It's easy to register and free of charge.

bp targetneutral

London 2012. Fuelling the Future.

The Olympic Park's Kingsgate footbridge, with waterfall art by Peter Lewis.

OLYMPIC PARK

Stratford or West Ham tube/DLR/rail,
or Stratford International DLR/rail.
Maps p50 & p54.

The centre of the Games is the combination of permanent stadiums and temporary venues that make up the **Olympic Park** in east London, as listed below. The Park will be landscaped with both natural and artistic features, including new bridges over the channels of the River Lea, around which it is built, and is set to provide a fitting visual backdrop for a feast of sport.

If you are visiting before the Games, a guided tour (*see p57* **Inside Track**) or self-guided walk or cycle around the perimeter is the best way to see the Olympic Park. The raised Greenway foot- and cyclepath offers a good perspective, with the **View Tube** (*see p166*) supplying fine vistas and café food. (Note that the View Tube and part of the Greenway will be inside the perimeter fence during the Games and so accessible only to ticket-holders.)

The London 2012 shop within the John Lewis store at Westfield Stratford City (*see p259*) offers good Olympic Stadium views.

Olympic Stadium

On Stadium 'island', in the south section of the Park, alongside the Aquatics Centre and Water Polo Arena.
The focal venue in the Olympic Park – host to the Opening and Closing Ceremonies, as well as both the Olympic and the Paralympic Athletics – looks like a kind of giant mechanical lotus flower, especially when you see its 14 stanchions of floodlights, open like 60m-long petals, reflected in the junction of the Lea Navigation and Hertford Union Canal. It sits on an island between three rivers, crossed by a total of five bridges. When the stadium is complete, its top layer will be covered by material stretched over a cable-net roof to provide perfect conditions for the competitors and shelter for two-thirds of the 80,000 spectators in the stands.

Within the Stadium, there are 700 rooms (medical facilities, changing rooms, toilets) and a 60m warm-up track, but most of the normal stadium functions have been moved outside: refreshments, merchandising and information desks are to be stationed around the perimeter, giving the Park a festival feel.

This – and the use of temporary stands above the permanent seats – has allowed the weight of materials to be kept low, reducing the carbon footprint created by their manufacture and transport.
🏃 *Athletics*
🏃 *Paralympic Athletics*

Aquatics Centre & Water Polo Arena

In the south-east of the Park, between the Olympic Stadium and Westfield Stratford City.
Another of the Olympic Park's iconic buildings, the Aquatics Centre will be the first building many spectators see – it's on the approach from Stratford Regional station, with visitors crossing a vast bridge that conceals the training pool, a river and a railway line. The Aquatics Centre was designed by Iraqi-born starchitect Zaha Hadid in typically uncompromising style. Its talking point is the huge, wave-shaped roof – steel and glass on the outside, treated timber within – that is flanked by 42m-high temporary stands on either side. Inside, there are a 50m competition pool, 25m competition diving pool and a 50m warm-up pool. The first of 180,000 pool tiles was laid by world record-holding swimmer Mark Foster in autumn 2010; the venue as a whole has used more than 800,000 ceramic tiles.

Located opposite the Aquatics Centre, the Water Polo Arena is one of several temporary structures in the Olympic Park. *Photo p62.*
🤿 *Aquatics – Diving*
🏊 *Aquatics – Swimming*
🏊 *Aquatics – Synchronised Swimming*
🤽 *Aquatics – Water Polo*
🏊 *Modern Pentathlon – swimming*
🏊 *Paralympic Swimming*

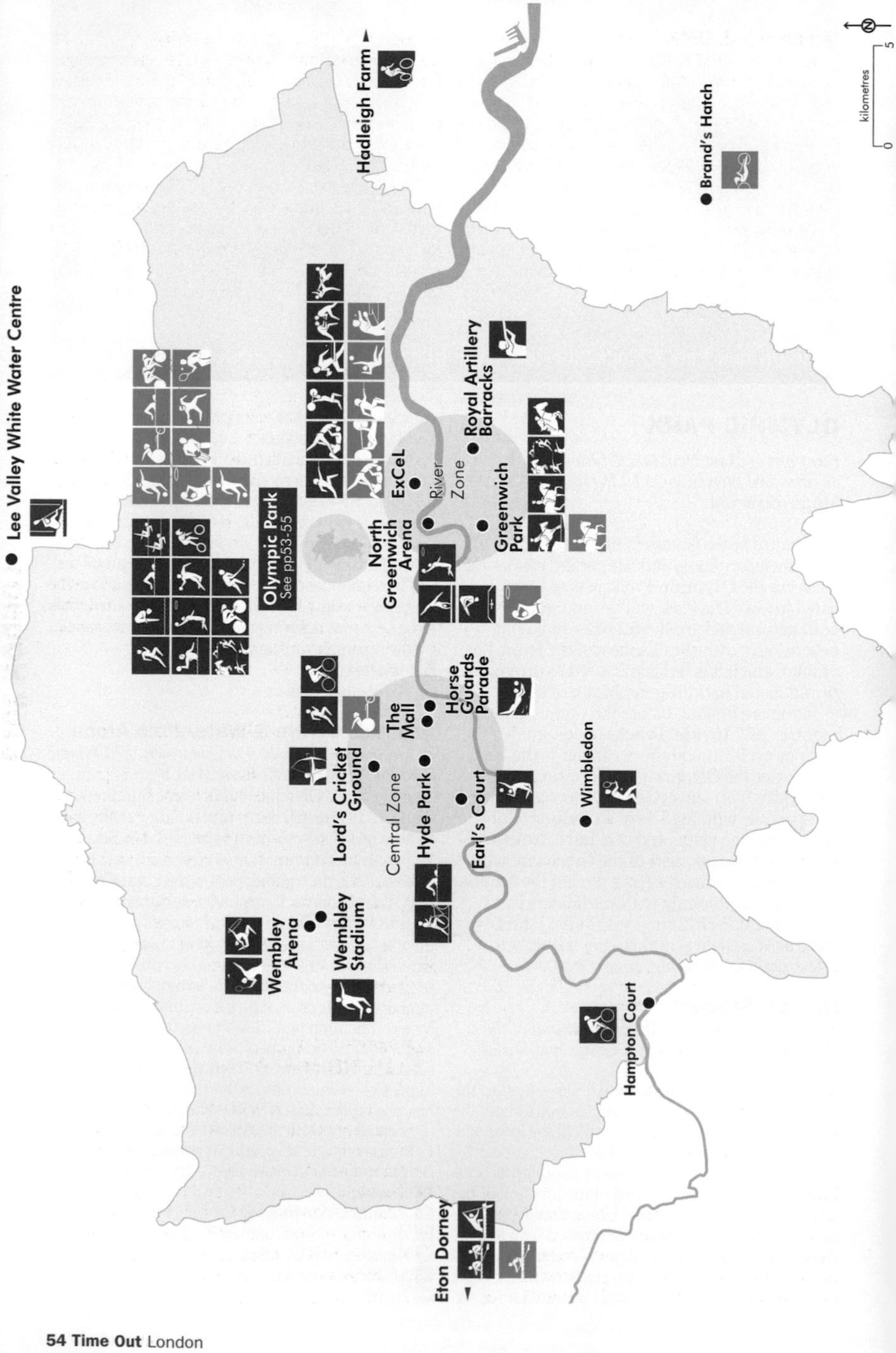

Lee Valley White Water Centre

Hadleigh Farm

Brand's Hatch

Olympic Park
See pp53-55

Royal Artillery
Barracks

ExCeL

River
Zone

North
Greenwich
Arena

Greenwich
Park

Horse
Guards
Parade

The Mall

Lord's Cricket
Ground

Central Zone

Hyde Park

Wimbledon

Earl's Court

Wembley
Arena

Wembley
Stadium

Hampton Court

Eton Dorney

N

kilometres
0   5

Velodrome & BMX Track

At the northern end of the North-East Concourse,
between the Basketball Arena and Eton Manor.
Until the Olympic Park opens to ticket-holders, the
Velodrome will remain the least accessible of the three
key venues to curious onlookers: the Stadium (*see*
p52) and Aquatics Centre (*see left*) can be admired
from the riverbank, but the Velodrome is set back
from the river beside a major arterial road. It's a
shame, because this venue, shaped like a Pringle crisp,
is a stunner. Sir Chris Hoy – with three gold medals,
a major part of the UK's cycling triumph at Beijing
2008 – helped to select the winning design team for
the Velodrome. Inside, the slope of the track and the
best temperature have been carefully worked out to
produce the optimal conditions for fast rides. The
track is made of sustainable Siberian pine wood and
the whole structure built from lightweight materials
(including another cable-net roof) to keep transport
and manufacture emissions low. Great pains have
been taken to use daylight, rather than artificial
lighting, and natural ventilation. The Velodrome
even catches rainwater for recycling. Unimpressed
by the engineering? Aesthetes will get great views
of east London via a glass wall between upper and
lower seating. All in all, it was no surprise the venue
was shortlisted for a major architecture award from
RIBA in 2011. **Photo** *p49*.

The BMX Track, right next door, has temporary
seating. After the Games, the track is to be relocated
to form part of the VeloPark.

🚴 *Cycling – BMX*
🚴 *Cycling – Track*
🚴 *Paralympic Cycling – Track*

Basketball Arena

In the north-east of the Park, between the
Velodrome and the Olympic & Paralympic Village.
It is the Olympic Park's third-largest venue, and will
be one of the busiest parts of the Olympic Park, with
events occurring daily throughout the Games, but
The Basketball Arena is, in fact, only a temporary
structure. Looking deeper, it's one of the largest
impermanent structures to be built for any Games.
Erected in only three months, it is covered with a
stretched material that will be used for light projections during London 2012, in a style perhaps reminiscent of the Beijing 2008 Water Cube.

🏀 *Basketball (preliminary rounds; women's*
quarter-finals)
🤾 *Handball (men's quarter-finals; men's &*
women's semi-finals, finals)
♿ *Wheelchair Basketball*
♿ *Wheelchair Rugby*

Copper Box

On the west side of the Park, between the Olympic
Stadium and The Riverside Arena.
The Copper Box is a sleek, blocky modernist structure, but its appearance is designed to change over
time: the exterior is adorned with around 3,000sq m

of copper cladding that is intended to age and
weather. Green initiatives include 88 pipes through
the roof to let in natural light and reduce the need
for artificial lighting, and rainwater pipes for recycling water. The sportsmen and -women might be
more excited about the sprung wood floor in the
competition area.

After the Games, a combination of permanent and
retractable seating will enable the venue to be converted into a flexible indoor sports centre.

🤾 *Handball (preliminary rounds; women's*
quarter-finals)
🤺 *Modern Pentathlon – fencing*
🥅 *Goalball*

Eton Manor

In the most northerly section of the Olympic Park.
Perhaps the lowest profile of the Park's new, permanent constructions, this venue is on the site of the early
20th-century Eton Manor Sports Club, which had
fallen into disuse by 2001. For the Games themselves,
it will have three 50m training pools for Swimming
and smaller pools for the other Aquatics disciplines,
as well as a show court set aside for the Wheelchair
Tennis. Memorials to sportsmen from the original
club who died in World War I and II, moved off-site
during construction, have been returned now work is
complete – and will remain here after the Games,
when Eton Manor becomes a sports centre with facilities for tennis, hockey and five-a-side football.

♿ *Wheelchair Tennis*

Riverbank Arena

At the north end of the North-West Concourse,
west of the Velodrome.
The Riverbank Arena will have two Hockey pitches:
the main one is for competition, while the smaller is
principally intended for warming up. For the first
time, the playing surfaces will be bright blue in contrast to yellow (rather than white) balls, an innovation for London 2012 that will improve visibility for
players and spectators alike. It is hoped that, after
the Games, both pitches will be moved north to be
added to the facilities at Eton Manor (*see p57*).

🏑 *Hockey*
⚽ ⚽ *Paralympic 5-a-side & 7-a-side Football*

INSIDE TRACK
TALKING THE WALK

In the run-up to the Games, you won't be
able to get into the Olympic Park, but you
can spot the key venues in the course of a
pleasant guided walk on the Greenway,
including the View Tube, and the banks of
the Lea Navigation. Walks run daily: for
more information, call 7936 2568 or visit
www.toursof2012sites.com. Guides are
knowledgeable and enthusiastic.

Torch Song

Passing on the flame.

The key symbolic precursor to the London 2012 Games will be the arrival of the Olympic Torch at Land's End, in the far west of the United Kingdom, on 18 May. The Torch Relay doesn't arrive in London until 21 July, where it completes a 70-day, 8,000-mile journey that encompasses the whole country. The last of the long chain of Torchbearers – athletes and ordinary members of the sport-loving British public, half of whom will be under 25 – will enter the Olympic Stadium on 27 July, at the climax of the Opening Ceremony.

The Opening Ceremony itself promises to be an elaborate affair, overseen by Oscar-winning film director Danny Boyle and Tony Award winner Stephen Daldry. The details are top secret, but Boyle is said to be keen to start at sunset, using the darkness to create spectacular lighting effects. Certain traditions are always observed at an Olympic Opening Ceremony, however. The key ones are the Parade of Athletes (led by Greece, and with the Host Country, Team GB, entering the Stadium last), the raising of the Olympic Flag, and the finally the lighting of the Olympic Cauldron.

The Closing Ceremony on 12 August 2012 is in the capable hands of Kim Gavin, who was the choreographer behind Take That's immensely successful Circus tour. Among the ceremonials laid out in the Olympic Charter are the march of the Flagbearers for each national team, now gathered as a single group of athletes rather than divided up into their rival teams; the raising of the three national flags – of Greece, the Host Country (UK) and the next Host Country (Brazil) – and the extinguishing of the Olympic Cauldron.

The Paralympic Games then has its own Torch Relay, which starts on 24 August, when flames will be lit in London, Belfast, Edinburgh and Cardiff, the capitals of the four nations of the United Kingdom. These four flames will be brought together at Stoke Mandeville, in Buckinghamshire, the inspirational origin of the Paralympic Games (*see p47* **Birth of the Paralympic Games**). There, the Paralympic Flame begins a 24-hour Torch Relay, arriving in the Olympic Stadium on 29 August. Details of the Paralympic Opening and Closing Ceremonies are as closely guarded a secret as their Olympic Games counterparts – and they promise to be every bit as spectacular. The former is being run by Bradley Hemmings (Artistic Director of the alfresco Greenwich+Docklands Festival) and Jenny Sealey (artistic director of Graeae, a major disabled-led theatre company), the latter – on 9 September – again by Kim Gavin. When the Paralympic Flame goes out, the London 2012 Games are officially over.

LONDON 2012

Lord Coe showcases the first prototype of the London 2012 Olympic Torch.

Hyde Park. *See p59.*

LONDON VENUES

A mixture of locations that are famous as sights, such as **Horse Guards Parade** and **The Mall**, **Hyde Park**, or for their sporting heritage – **Lord's Cricket Ground**, **Earls Court** – take the 2012 Games right into the heart of tourist London.

A further selection of venues is scattered north and south across the River Thames, bringing the city together. These are **Greenwich Park** (*see p59*), **North Greenwich Arena** (*see p61*) and **The Royal Artillery Barracks** (*see p61*) on the southern side, and **ExCeL** (*see p58*) among the docklands to the north.

Providing a counterweight to the east London focus of the 2012 Games are iconic sporting venues in the city's north-west (**Wembley**) and west (**Wimbledon**), and the spectacular **Hampton Court Palace** in the south-west.

Earls Court
Warwick Road, SW5 9TA. Earl's Court tube. **Travel time** allow 1hr from central London, 2hrs from the Olympic Park. **Map** p54.
Usually associated with trade shows and concerts (this is where Pink Floyd built *The Wall*), the concrete Exhibition Centre has a strong Olympic past: it hosted the Boxing, Gymnastics, Weightlifting and Wrestling for the 1948 Games. Built in 1937, the building has a certain retro flair: its architect also designed 1920s movie palaces.
Volleyball

ExCeL
1 Western Gateway, Royal Victoria Dock, E16 1XL. Arrive: Custom House or West Silvertown DLR; depart: Prince Regent or Pontoon Dock DLR.

Travel time allow 2hrs from central London, at least 1hr from the Olympic Park. **Map** p54.
Located between Canary Wharf and London City Airport, this convention centre (*see p163*) is right on Royal Victoria Dock. For the London 2012 Games, ExCeL's 45,000sq m and two halls will be divided into five arenas accommodating 13 sports – it is to host the largest number of events of any venue outside the Olympic Park.
Boxing
Fencing
Judo
Table Tennis
Taekwondo
Weightlifting
Wrestling
Boccia
Paralympic Judo
Paralympic Powerlifting
Paralympic Table Tennis
Volleyball – Sitting
Wheelchair Fencing

Greenwich Park
Greenwich Park, Greenwich, SE10 8XJ. Greenwich DLR/rail, Maze Hill or Blackheath rail. **Travel time** allow 2hrs from central London, 2hrs from the Olympic Park. **Map** p54.
Greenwich Park was, appropriately enough, a former royal hunting ground. For London 2012's Equestrian events, an arena will be set behind the National Maritime Museum and the wonderfully grand colonnades of the Old Royal Naval Hospital. *Photo p64.*
Equestrian – Dressage
Equestrian – Eventing
Equestrian – Jumping
Modern Pentathlon – riding
Paralympic Equestrian

IT'S TIME TO FLY THE FLAG.
AND THE T-SHIRT, THE APRON,
THE CUDDLY TOY...

OFFICIAL MERCHANDISE NOW AVAILABLE
AT ALL LONDON 2012 SHOPS.

WWW.LONDON2012.COM/SHOP

TEAM GB

ParalympicsGB

Hadleigh Farm. *See p64.*

Hampton Court Palace

Hampton Court rail, or riverboat to Hampton Court Pier. **Travel time** check the London 2012 website for up-to-date information. **Map** p54.
Hampton Court Palace (*see p180*) is the grand former home of both Henry VIII and Elizabeth I, but the men's and women's Road Cycling Time Trials are open to the hoi polloi – both are free to spectators. The riders will pedal a circuit beginning and ending at the Palace, and in Bradley Wiggins there's likely to be a London hero to cheer along in the contest.
🚴 *Cycling – Road (Time Trial)*

Horse Guards Parade

Horse Guards Road, SW1A 2BJ. Charing Cross, Victoria or Waterloo tube/rail, or Embankment, Piccadilly Circus or Green Park tube. **Travel time** allow 1hr from the Olympic Park. **Map** p54
Best known for the Changing of the Guard and Trooping the Colour ceremonies (*see p290* **Standing on Ceremony**), and likely to have already seen heavy use during the Queen's Golden Jubilee on 2-5 June 2012, this large parade ground is open along its eastern side to lovely, sleepy St James's Park (*see p140*). For London 2012, it will bring crowds to temporary stands to watch the Beach Volleyball – which might bring a smile to the lips of even the legendarily deadpan Horse Guards.
🏐 *Volleyball – Beach*

Hyde Park

Hyde Park, W2 2UH. Green Park, Bond Street, Knightsbridge, Hyde Park Corner or Marble Arch tube, or Victoria or Paddington tube/rail. **Travel time** allow 2hrs from the Olympic Park. **Map** p54.
Hyde Park will provide a scenic backdrop for London 2012. Triathletes will swim 1,500m in the beautiful

Serpentine boating lake, run 10,000m around the lake in four equal laps, and then cycle 40,000m over seven laps of the park, along a route taking in Constitution Hill and Buckingham Palace. The Marathon Swimmers will do six 1,670m laps of the Serpentine. A temporary grandstand will have a clear view of the finish lines. *Photo p57.*
🏊 *Aquatics – Swimming (Marathon Swimming)*
🏃 *Triathlon*

Lord's Cricket Ground

St John's Wood Road, NW8 8QN. St John's Wood tube. **Travel time** allow at least 1hr from the Olympic Park. **Map** p54.
Established in 1814, Lord's is the home of cricket (*see p337*). But, since much of the world remains immune to the charms of our summer sport, the 2012 Games will use this splendid setting to showcase a sport of even longer pedigree: Archery. Spectators will get to enjoy the juxtaposition of the regal Victorian pavilion and the strikingly modern media centre. Two world records have already been broken here, despite blustery conditions, during the London Archery Classic, a test event held in autumn 2011.
🎯 *Archery*

The Mall

Between Buckingham Palace (see p140) & Trafalgar Square (see p133). Green Park, Piccadilly Circus or St James's Park tube, or Charing Cross, Victoria or Waterloo tube/rail. **Travel time** allow 1hr from the Olympic Park. **Map** p54.
Once a fenced-off pitch for the 17th-century sporting predecessor to polo known as *paille-maille*, this long straight road was a promenade for more than 150 years, and has been a ceremonial route

LONDON 2012

Beside the Seaside

How to make the most of your visit to Weymouth and Portland.

Long before Weymouth and Portland were chosen as the venue for the Olympic and Paralympic Sailing, the area was already a popular tourist destination.

King George III (1760-1820) popularised sea bathing in Weymouth (his statue surveys the holiday throng) and the tradition continues, courtesy of a fine sandy beach and jolly seaside Esplanade. If the weather's inclement, you can check out the Weymouth Sea-Life Park and Marine Sanctuary (www.visitsealife.com) in Lodmoor Country Park.

On the Isle of Portland, just to the south of Weymouth, there are two 'raised beaches' (rock platforms that once touched the shore) and Church Ope Cove, a secluded spot below the ruins of Rufus Castle, supposedly built by the famously red-bearded Norman king, William Rufus, who met a mysterious end at the wrong end of a hunting arrow in the New Forest.

Formerly a naval base, Portland is a limestone outcrop best known for its quarries, which produce the famous stone that is used in many grand London buildings. From breezy Portland Bill, the rocky southern promontory, the 300-year-old lighthouse museum (www.trinityhouse.co.uk) provides a perch for watching the racing.

While you're there, nip into the pleasingly old-fashioned Pulpit Inn (01305 821237), which serves fresh seafood and even offers B&B, or the Lobster Pot café (01305 820242), with its veranda.

For more secluded beaches, head west along Lyme Bay. The sea can be reached from any of a series of villages, with West Bexington perhaps the prettiest. West Bay, with its dramatic cliffs, shingle beach and fishing trips from the harbour is very atmospheric. Further west, on the way to Lyme Regis, Seatown has a wonderful little sandy beach in the shadow of Golden Cap, the highest point on the south coast of England. The beach is overlooked by the convivial Anchor Inn (www.theanchorinn seatown.co.uk), popular with fossil hunters.

Those fossil hunters are here for the 'Jurassic Coast', a UN-designated World Heritage Site that dates back some 185 million years. At the southern end of its 95-mile stretch, Chesil Beach was brought to wider attention by the 2007 Ian McEwan novel. A massive rampart of flint and chert pebbles – technically a very rare type of 'tombolo' (barrier spit) – it is a place of extraordinary, melancholy beauty.
For more details, see the tourist website www.visitweymouth.co.uk.

Weymouth.

Oscar Pistorius at the Olympic Stadium. *See p52.*

since the early 1900s. Expect the Cycling to be especially well attended – no one was surprised to see British hope Mark Cavendish (the 'Manx Missile') win the test event on this course, shortly before heading to Copenhagen to win the World Championship. Key viewing areas will be ticketed, but spectators will be welcome to line the rest of the route for free.

Athletics – Marathon
Athletics – Race Walk
Cycling – Road (Road Race)
Paralympic Athletics – Marathon

North Greenwich Arena
Millennium Way, North Greenwich, SE10 OPH. North Greenwich tube or Charlton rail then shuttle bus. **Travel time** allow 1hr from central London, 1hr from the Olympic Park. **Map** p54.
Derided as an exorbitant New Labour vanity project when it opened in 2000, Lord Rogers' striking Millennium Dome has made a major comeback (*see p321* **O2 Arena**). As the North Greenwich Arena, it will play a major role in London 2012. A proposed cable-car link with ExCeL across the Thames may be completed in time for the Games.

Basketball (men's quarter-finals; men's & women's semi-finals, finals)
Gymnastics – Artistic
Gymnastics – Trampoline
Wheelchair Basketball

The Royal Artillery Barracks
Greenwich, SE18 4BH. Woolwich Arsenal DLR/rail. **Travel time** allow 2hrs from central London, 2hrs from the Olympic Park. **Map** p54.

Built in 1776, The Royal Artillery Barracks has the country's longest Georgian façade. To convert the area for Shooting and Paralympic Archery, a 62ft-high safety screen is due to be erected shortly after we go to press, along with the three outdoor ranges (for Trap and Skeet). The additional three indoor ranges (for Pistol and Rifle shooting) have already been completed, using 1,200 tonnes of plywood and steel. Grandstands have been built for each range, and the enclosures surrounded by a white PVC skin, enlivened with brightly coloured spots.

INSIDE TRACK
GETTING DRESSED

In the run-up to the Games, the city will be 'dressed' with Games symbols and London 2012 colours – there are plans to provide £50,000 grants to the city's boroughs so they can decorate their streets and public spaces appropriately. St Pancras International Station (*see p110*), home to one of the dedicated London 2012 Shops (*see p275*) and a key transport hub for the Games (the Javelin® will run to the Olympic Park from here), was decked out with Olympic rings in spring 2011; plans are afoot to do the same to a range of London icons – new and old – as we approach the Games, with both Tower Bridge (*see p101*) and the Shard (*see p83*) rumoured to be contenders.

Aquatics Centre. *See p53.*

Shooting
Paralympic Archery
Paralympic Shooting

Wembley Arena

Arena Square, Engineers Way, Wembley, Middx HA9 0DH. Wembley Park tube, Wembley Central tube/rail, or Wembley Stadium rail. **Travel time** allow 2hrs from central London, 2hrs from the Olympic Park. **Map** p54.

Most Londoners know Wembley Arena as a music venue (*see p322*), but it was built, in 1934, to host the Empire Games (the forerunner of the Commonwealth Games). It also has good Olympic credentials, having been the location for the Swimming in the 1948 Games.

Badminton
Gymnastics – Rhythmic

Wembley Stadium

Stadium Way, Wembley, Middx HA9 0WS. Wembley Park tube, Wembley Central tube/rail, or Wembley Stadium rail. **Travel time** allow 2hrs from central London, 2hrs from the Olympic Park. **Map** p54.

Lord Foster's reworked Wembley Stadium will be an impressively grand setting for the finals of the London 2012 Football. With a 90,000-seat capacity, it is Europe's second-largest stadium, and its 317m arch became an instant landmark when the new stadium opened back in 2007.

Football

Wimbledon

All England Lawn Tennis Club, Church Road, Wimbledon, SW19 5AE. Wimbledon or Southfields tube then shuttle bus. **Travel time** allow 2hrs from central London, 2hrs from the Olympic Park. **Map** p54.

There could only be one setting for the London 2012 Tennis: the world's only world-class grass-court venue, home of the game's most prestigious Grand Slam tournament (*see p335*). The revamped Centre Court seats 13,800 spectators.

Tennis

OUTSIDE LONDON

The following venues range from those on the fringes of London – **Hadleigh Farm**, **Eton Dorney Rowing Centre**, **Lee Valley White Water Centre**, **Brands Hatch** – to the south coast, a hundred miles away (**Weymouth & Portland**). The Olympic Football preliminary rounds will take place in Scotland (**Hampden Park**, Glasgow) and Wales (the **Millennium Stadium**, Cardiff), as well as the north of England (**Old Trafford**, Manchester; **St James' Park**, Newcastle) and the Midlands (**City of Coventry Stadium**).

Brands Hatch

Fawkham, Longfield, Kent DA3 8NG (01474 872331, www.motorsportvision.co.uk). Swanley rail then shuttle bus. **Travel time** approx 1hr from London Victoria. **Map** p54.

This famous motor-racing circuit began life as a dirt-track for motorbikes but went on to host a dozen British Grand Prix races from 1964 to 1986. For the Paralympic Road Cycling, around half the circuit will take place on the circuit itself; the rest heads out into the Kentish countryside.

Paralympic Cycling – Road (Road Race)
Paralympic Cycling – Road (Time Trial)

Whatever Next?

How the 2012 Games are creating a whole new area of London.

'It will be very different to any park that anyone's seen before.' John Hopkins, Project Sponsor for Parklands and Public Realm for the Olympic Delivery Authority (ODA), is justifiably proud of the largest urban river and wetland planting in the UK – some 300,000 plants and 2,000 British trees, among them ash, birch, hazel and London plane. He is describing the extraordinarily complex work that has been going on in the Olympic Parklands, work that was almost entirely unnoticed until the wild flowers of the 'golden meadow' bloomed into the headlines back in July 2010. The meadow is right on schedule to come to life again for the opening of the Olympic Games.

Through the northern section of the Olympic Park (*see p52*), there's a single river, which Hopkins says was almost lost under 'factories, warehouses and dereliction – a huge Victorian tip site', the leftovers from a hundred years of the Industrial Revolution. There the ODA has created 45 hectares of intricate marshland. Flood modelled to cope with 'a 100-year storm' (a water-level rise of 4m), this new habitat protects 4,000 buildings from extreme weather – by returning the area to an earlier natural state. 'It's really ironic: we ran flood models and the only places that didn't flood were the marshes.'

In the southern part of the Olympic Park, the major sporting venues were set on islands between the Waterworks River, City Mill River and the River Lea. Here problems were as much structural as environmental, with vast bridges having to be built over railtracks and rivers, and ground made accessible to every active user.

After the Games, this whole area will open to the public as the Queen Elizabeth Olympic Park. The permanent facilities – the Olympic Stadium, the Aquatics Centre, the Velodrome, Eton Manor, The Copper Box – will take on new roles, the Orbit is expected to become a tourist attraction, and improvements to the transport infrastructure will benefit the entire local community. The Olympic and Paralympic Village will be joined from 2014 by further new buildings, perhaps 8,000 new homes in five new districts: Chobham Manor, East Wick, Sweetwater, Marshgate Wharf, Pudding Mill Lane. The Olympic Park Legacy Company (OPLC), which will oversee the transition from sporting venue to public space, talks of 'traditional family neighbourhoods of terraced and mews houses, set within tree-lined avenues' – 40% of the Chobham Manor new-builds are projected to have gardens. No doubt these new homes will be quickly snapped up.

LONDON 2012

Greenwich Park. *See p57.*

Eton Dorney
Dorney Lake, off Court Lane, Dorney, Windsor, Berks SL4 6QP. Maidenhead, Slough or Windsor & Eton Riverside rail then shuttle bus. **Travel time** allow at least 2hrs from central London, and at least 3hrs from the Olympic Park.
Map p54.

INSIDE TRACK LIVE SITES

Live Nation Music UK, producers of Live 8 and the Wireless Festival, will run four 'Festival Live Sites' in London during the 2012 Games. These join Park Live East and West within the Olympic Park to bring the thrills of Olympic and Paralympic competition to **Hyde Park** (*see p61*), **Victoria Park** (*see p164*), **Trafalgar Square** (*see p133*) and **Potter's Field**, next door to City Hall (*see p84*). Along with sporting action on big screens, there'll be free music and other entertainments. Further screens will be placed in Walthamstow Town Square and General Gordon Place in Woolwich. As Royal Parks chief executive, Mark Camley, noted: 'the atmosphere at the Live Site[s] promises to be electric'.

The London 2012 Games should liven things up at Eton College, posh alma mater of Prime Minister David Cameron and London Mayor Boris Johnson. The school owns the lake, set in 400 acres of park, where the Rowing and Canoe Sprint will be held. The lake has already hosted the 2006 Rowing World Championships, but further improvements to the eight-lane, 2,200m course and the warm-up lanes were completed in summer 2010, along with a new cut-through and two bridges.
Canoe Sprint
Rowing
Paralympic Rowing

Hadleigh Farm
Castle Lane, Benfleet, Essex SS7 2AP. Leigh-on-Sea rail then shuttle bus. **Travel time** allow at least 2hrs from central London, at least 3hrs from the Olympic Park. **Map** p54.
Hadleigh Farm is a lovely mix of woodland, pasture, hay meadow and marsh, with views of the Thames Estuary and even a ruined 13th-century castle. The hilly terrain will be perfect for the Mountain Bike competition. *Photo p59.*
Cycling – Mountain Bike

Lee Valley White Water Centre
Station Road, Waltham Cross, Herts EN9 1AB. Cheshunt rail. **Travel time** allow 2hrs from central London, 2hrs from the Olympic Park.
Map p54.
The brand-new White Water Centre is at the far northern end of Lee Valley Regional Park. The first new London 2012 venue to open to the public, in spring 2011, it has two white-water courses. The 300m competition course and 160m training course are both fed from a starting lake filled with 25,000 cubic metres of water – enough to fill 5,000 Olympic-sized swimming pools. The lake pumps 15 cubic metres of water per second down the course, with parts of the course reaching 7mph. For an account of Time Out's preview of riding the waves, *see p340* **Ride the Rapids**.
Canoe Slalom

Weymouth & Portland
Weymouth & Portland National Sailing Academy, Osprey Road, Portland, Dorset DT5 1SA. Park-and-ride, the 2012 Games coach or local bus services. **Travel time** check the London 2012 website for details.
Improvements to the Weymouth & Portland National Sailing Academy were ready for competition by 2008 – making this the first London 2012 venue of any type to be finished. The new slipway, moorings and other facilities have already been used for several international events. *See also p60* **Beside the Seaside**.
Sailing
Paralympic Sailing

Faster, higher, stronger.

TEXT: SIMON COPPOCK

Sporting Glory

Citius, Altius, Fortius. The ambitions expressed by the Olympic motto are simple, but the quest to be faster, higher and stronger is always an intoxicating spectacle. The great joy of any sporting competition is that no one can predict what will happen – favourites will fail and rank outsiders snatch gold medals; there will be controversy and heartbreak alongside the world records and floods of joyful podium tears. Even so, the indications are that the 2012 Games will be exceptional.

London 2012 is, of course, the 'Olympic and Paralympic Games'. Competition in the Paralympic Games will be every bit as intense as in its Olympic counterpart, with plenty of home-grown stars to keep the atmosphere buoyant. In fact, there is the distinct possibility of Paralympic Games hopefuls also taking part in the Olympic Games: several have already met the Olympic qualifying standards. Never did the Paralympic Movement motto – 'Spirit in motion' – seem more appropriate.

In this chapter, we stick our neck out and give our tips for London 2012's big stars and key dates. But expect the unexpected and – wherever you might be at Games time, however you plan to get involved – we hope you enjoy the greatest multi-sport event on earth. In the words of Baron Pierre de Coubertin, the founder of the modern Olympic Games: 'The most important thing in the Olympic Games is not to win but to take part, just as the most important thing in life is not the triumph but the struggle.'

LONDON 2012

GLOBAL GAMES

During the 2012 Olympic Games, two contests are likely to stand out. The 100m final is one of the centrepieces of any Games, but the prospect of seeing the hugely talented and charming Usain Bolt take on Asafa Powell, Tyson Gay and a host of young pretenders is fervently anticipated. It could be the most exciting 100m final since Atlanta 1996, when the defending gold medallist, the reigning world champion and the man with the year's fastest time all raced head to head. Worryingly for his rivals, Bolt has said he will attempt to equal Carl Lewis's four gold medals at Los Angeles 1984 – adding the 4 x 400m Relay to the 100m, 200m and 4 x 100m Relay.

The other mouthwatering prospect is a potential Swimming duel between the USA's Michael Phelps, the eight-times gold medallist of Beijing 2008, and Australian Ian Thorpe, a five-times career Olympic gold medallist who is returning from five years in retirement (though had yet to qualify for the Games at press time). They could compete in the 100m Freestyle, 200m Freestyle and 200m Individual Medley. Interestingly, Phelps and Thorpe both play down the importance of a head-to-head contest, pointing instead to the challenge in the 200m Freestyle and Individual Medley from American Ryan Lochte; and on 2011 World Championships form, 200m gold-winning Australian James Magnussen will be right in among the medals for the 100m Freestyle.

The headline event for the Paralympic Games is also likely to be the 100m, with Oscar Pistorius – the South African double amputee, famous as 'the Blade Runner' – facing Jerome Singleton, the USA athlete who took silver to Pistorius's 100m (T44) gold at Beijing 2008, and beat Pistorius at the IPC World Athletics 100m in New Zealand in 2011. The final is on 6 September. Watch out, too, for Irishman Jason Smyth, who matched Pistorius in taking both 100m and 200m golds at Beijing 2008, but in the T13 (visually impaired) rather than T44 category; the T13 final is on 1 September. Like Pistorius, Smyth may well qualify for the Olympic Games as well as the Paralympic Games.

BACKING THE BRITS

There are a number of potential red-letter days for the home crowd. Jessica Ennis's bid to add Olympic gold to her 2009 World Championship and 2010 European Championship golds in the Heptathlon will hopefully come to a climax on 4 August. The following day, Paula Radcliffe will attempt to make one of the comebacks of all time and beat her Olympic Games hex to take gold in the Marathon. Holder of the world record at the distance since 2003, Radcliffe has struggled with injury (as well as giving birth to a second child), but a reasonably successful race in Berlin in autumn 2011 has her many fans hoping again. There should be a mighty battle between charismatic local hero Phillips Idowu (from Hackney, one of the Host Boroughs) and Frenchman Teddy Tamgho in the Triple Jump, and Mo Farah could well be among the medals in the 5000m final and 10,000m. Although born in Somalia and now training in Oregon, we still claim him as a Londoner: he spent a decade running for the Newham and Essex Beagles – based in another Host Borough, Newham.

In the pool, names to watch will probably include Rebecca Adlington, who is due to contest the 400m and 800m Freestyle swimming events, and Fran Halsall, who took gold in the 100m Individual Medley at the Fina World Cup in late 2011, as well as silver in the 100m Butterfly and bronze in the 50m Freestyle. Gemma Spofforth holds the world record for the 100m Backstroke, but has recently been troubled by illness and injury.

Given how fashionable bicycles now are in London – and Team GB's dramatic success at Beijing 2008 – events in the Velodrome might yet generate the keenest interest. In the Track Cycling, watch out for Victoria Pendleton, Geraint Thomas and Sir Chris Hoy. There are high hopes that sprinter Mark Cavendish – the 'Manx Missile' – will overcome Beijing disappointment to win gold in the Cycling Road Race. The signs are promising: Cavendish won the test event on the 2012 course in summer

2011, in between becoming the first Briton to win the sprinters' coveted *maillot vert* in the Tour de France and taking the World Championships. Cav's female counterpart, Nicole Cooke, looks to defend her Road Race gold from Beijing 2008 on 29 July, while Londoner Bradley Wiggins is likely to be a major contender in the Cycling Time Trial.

Among home Paralympians, support will be strong for wheelchair athlete David Weir (*see below* **Leading Londoners**) and swimmer Ellie Simmonds, both double gold winners at Beijing 2008. Weir – described in the *Telegraph* as 'Britain's Goliath' – plans to defend his T54 golds for the 800m and 1500m, as well as seeking to better his 2008 bronze in the 5000m; but the Marathon, in which he should face key rivals Marcel Hug from Switzerland and Australian Kurt Fearnley, may prove the most compelling contest. The mind games have already begun, with Fearnley suggesting the tight turns on the London 2012 course will give Weir an advantage. Simmonds,

Leading Londoners

DAVID WEIR
PARALYMPIC ATHLETE
What will be unique about a London 2012 Paralympic Games?
The weather! I also think it will be a special Paralympics because it's coming back home to where it was invented. I think the atmosphere will be electric!
Do you have any mental tricks?
When I was at the World Championships in 2010 [he won three gold medals], I won the first race. Just before, I'd had a toasted cheese-and-ham sandwich with brown sauce in it. Because that had worked for me, I had it every day.
What's your favourite London spot?
Probably the Ministry of Sound. Once I'm there, I love it. I'd love to DJ there when I retire from sport.

David Weir.

LONDON 2012

Zoe Smith.

ZOE SMITH
OLYMPIC WEIGHTLIFTER
What will be unique about a London 2012 Olympic Games?
I've grown up in Greenwich, which is a Host Borough, so to have the Olympics here is amazing.
Do you have any mental tricks?
Other than listening to 'All the Small Things' before I lift, I don't have much of a routine. A lot of lifters – me included – are just in the zone when we get to the platform, so we're on autopilot, really.
What's your favourite London spot?
Probably Camden Town.

meanwhile, is hoping to defend the golds she won as a 13-year-old in the S6 100m Freestyle, in which she may well race her nemesis, Dutchwoman Mirjam de Koning-Pepper, and S6 400m Freestyle. Simmonds was the second youngest British Paralympic medal-winner and the youngest MBE.

EXCITING ALTERNATIVES

The Paralympic Games combine sports with Olympic Games counterparts (Cycling, Athletics, Judo and so on) with unique sports such as Boccia ('botcha'), a game similar to pétanque or bowls – Nigel Murray, winner of Britain's first gold for Boccia at Sydney 2000, hopes to retire after London 2012 with another one. For visually impaired athletes, both Goalball and 5-a-side Football are played with a ball with a sound-making device inside and spectators keeping silent; in the latter, Briton Dave Clarke, still starring in his sport at the age of 40, aims to go one better than his World and European Championship silvers. At the opposite end of the noise spectrum is the intensely physical Wheelchair Rugby, originally called 'murderball' due to the ferocity of the clashes between competitors. Steve Brown, the Wheelchair Rugby player who led the London parade to celebrate British successes at Beijing 2008, told Time Out that preparing his chair, gloves and kit before a game is 'like putting your armour on before battle'.

Terrific stories seem to surround the Paralympic Games. Bob Matthews, for instance, is looking to compete in his eighth Paralympic Games at London 2012. The Briton is an MBE and has 13 medals – among them eight golds for Paralympic Athletics. Approaching 50 years old, Matthews hopes to compete in Paralympic Cycling in 2012, but having emigrated would now race for New Zealand rather than Britain. British patriots will be relieved that Paralympian Sarah Storey is still resident in this country. She won medals for Swimming at Barcelona 1992, Atlanta 1996, Sydney 2000 and Athens 2004, then took two golds in Cycling at Beijing 2008, and is currently in contention to join the Olympic Pursuit team for London 2012.

In the Olympic Games, there might be a rare opportunity to see siblings contest the same event – world champion Alistair Brownlee and his brother Jonathan share medal aspirations in the Triathlon – and an even rarer opportunity to see some British tennis success, should Andy Murray make it to the Singles Tennis final. And, for the first time since the men competed at Rome 1960, there will be British players contesting the Football, with a Home Nations team aspiring to reach the men's final on 11 August; the women's team hope to reach theirs on 9 August.

There are high hopes in Diving (Tom Daley) and Sailing (Ben Ainslie in the Finn, Iain Percy and Andrew Simpson in the Star and Paul Goodison in the Laser), and the men's and women's Hockey should be pretty exciting, with the purpose-built bright blue pitch playing true and very quick. Men's hockey star Richard Alexander is characteristically forthright: 'People think [hockey is] a bit of a girls' sport. But if you speak to any rugby players who come to watch us, they say they wouldn't go out on the pitch. The ball flies at 100 miles an hour, and it's dangerous.'

British competitors also look strong in the Boxing. Bantam Weight Luke Campbell, Super Heavy Weight Anthony Joshua and Fly Weight Andrew Selby are all in with a good chance of a medal, having reached the finals of the World Amateur Boxing Championship in Baku in late 2011. Female Boxing is new for London 2012 – and the British delegation has strong contenders: Nicola Adams at Fly Weight, Natasha Jones at Light Weight and Savannah Marshall at Middle Weight could be among the medals after showing well in the European Women's Championship in the Netherlands. Those in the mood for the pugilistic arts should also check out the Taekwondo: Aaron Cook and Sarah Stevenson are both hot prospects.

● *For a day-by-day schedule of the Olympic events, see p72; for Paralympic events, see p73; and for Live Sites see p64* **Inside Track**.

Visit

TICKETS

During the **initial application phase** for tickets for the London 2012 Olympic Games in spring 2011, more than 20m applications were made for 6.6m Olympic tickets. A similar phase for the Paralympic Games in September saw 1.14m Paralympic tickets applied for before the deadline. Headline sports and events such as the Opening and Closing Ceremonies, Track Cycling, Swimming and Athletics finals were immediately heavily oversubscribed; **remaining tickets** will have been on sale – first come, first served – since late winter 2011, with any that haven't yet been snapped up available to be bought from box offices during the Games. There will be a fresh window of opportunity to grab tickets in early 2012, when the **official resale site** for London 2012 Olympic and Paralympic tickets opens. For the latest ticketing information and news, register at **www. tickets.london2012.com**.

It is likely that, by the time you read this, there will be Olympic Games tickets left only for team sports in large venues with lots of sessions (the earlier rounds of the men's and women's Football, for example); late availability for the Paralympic Games is harder to predict, but it is pretty clear the headline sessions will also be sold out – Archery, Athletics, Track Cycling, Football, Judo, Rowing, Shooting, Swimming, Table Tennis, Wheelchair Basketball and Wheelchair Rugby were all oversubscribed in the initial Paralympic ballot.

There are also several unticketed (apart from seats in the stands at the start/finish), roadside spectating opportunities during the Olympic Games: in Cycling, the Road Race and Road Time Trial; and in Athletics, the Race Walk and Marathon (the Paralympic Marathon can also be watched from the roadside). The cycling section of the Triathlon affords another such opportunity. *See also p64* **Inside Track**.

Beware of bogus websites. Only the official website (www.london2012com), National Olympic Committees, National Paralympic Committees and Authorised Ticket Resellers (Thomas Cook, Prestige Ticketing and Jet Set Sports) can sell or resell London 2012 tickets.

ORIENTATION

The venues for the 2012 Games can be thought of in three concentric rings: east London's Olympic Park venues (map pp50-51); London venues spread across the city (map p54) and venues outside London. They are all listed on pp52-64, with closest transport links – some normal transport arrangements will be changed in the run-up to the Games, so check precise details when you plan your journeys.

On days when you are heading to a London 2012 sports event or ceremony, plan your travel using www.london2012.com/travel and the spectator journey planner at www.london2012.com/journey.

For travel in and around London on other days, visit www.tfl.gov.uk.

AT THE GAMES

● Do keep your tickets and photo ID with you at all times.
● Do arrive in plenty of time for the start of your session. The London 2012 website provides recommended arrival times.
● There are no on-site refunds – instead, apply for a refund using the forms available at www.tickets. london2012.com. Refunds are only made to the purchaser of the ticket, not the ticket-holder.
● Only one soft-sided bag per person is allowed into venues, and this must be no larger than is specified on the London 2012 website for the specific venue. No suitcases or luggage are allowed inside venues, and there will be nowhere to store them. There will just be limited space to store prams, buggies and wheelchairs.
● LOCOG will publish a comprehensive list of items you are not permitted to take into venues. As a rule of thumb, leave at your hotel anything you would not be permitted to take on a plane.
● Spectators are expected to behave in a way that is respectful to athletes, other spectators and London 2012 staff. If you misbehave, you may be removed from the venue.

GETTING TO THE GAMES

In summer 2012, events starting with the Queen's Diamond Jubilee (2-5 June) and continuing through both the Olympic Games and the Paralympic Games will add up to what Transport for London has described as 'around 100 continuous days of extraordinary operation', peaking on 3 Aug with some 750,000 spectators moving between different venues. This extra volume will have an impact not only on Games spectators, but on all journeys around the capital, whatever their purpose.

For day-by-day advice, *see p71* **Travel Calendar**.

Planning

Throughout this period, it is essential to plan your journey well in advance and leave a generous margin of error. For route-planning and details of how to use London's transport system, *see pp365-368* **Getting Around**; and for a map of the London underground, *see pp414-415*.

● Unless you're heading to or leaving a Games session, avoid travelling at peak times each day, especially on weekdays.
● Allow plenty of time to travel to, from and between venues, because

LONDON 2012

Stratford Station.

LONDON 2012

London's transport system will be significantly busier than usual. Remember to allow extra time to get through the transport system, and substantial time for queuing and walking within large venues. TfL are predicting waits for the tube of up to an hour at certain peak times.

● National rail across the country will be very busy during the Games. We strongly recommend pre-booking rail tickets. The earlier you buy, the lower the price, generally speaking.

● Some of the co-Host City venues are a significant distance from London and from each other. The furthest – Hampden Park Stadium in Glasgow – is more than 400 miles north of London, with a train journey of around four and a half hours from London Euston and Glasgow.

● There is no public parking at venues, so do not drive unless you have booked a Blue Badge space or park-and-ride. To travel to and from venues use public transport, walk or cycle – cycle parking areas are already planned to the north, east and south-west of the Olympic Park.

● Spectators with a ticket for a Games event in London or at certain venues outside London will receive a one-day 'Games Travelcard' for the day of that event with their event ticket. The Games Travelcard will entitle you to travel in zones 1 to 9 in London and by National Rail between London and recommended stations for certain venues outside London (Brands Hatch, Eton Dorney, Hadleigh Farm, Hampton Court Palace and Lee Valley White Water Centre). The Games

Travelcard covers travel on London Underground, London Overground, DLR, bus, tram and some mainline rail services, but not the Heathrow, Stansted or Gatwick Express trains or taxis. Ticket holders will also be entitled to a one-third discount on river services.

● London 2012 ticket holders have been able to book travel from around Great Britain to venues since summer 2011 on several additional, Games-specific travel services. These include National Rail (for journeys from any National Rail station in the country to London and the co-Host Cities), dedicated park-and-ride for venues, specially organised coach services (to the Olympic Park, Greenwich Park, ExCeL and Weymouth & Portland) and even Blue Badge parking.

Games-time travel

In London, operational hours for public transport will be extended. The Underground, Overground, DLR and some mainline rail services will run until around 1.30am; starting times will be normal, except for Sunday mornings when trains will begin earlier. There will also be more trains running through the Games: the Underground will run a peak service in the late evenings to mop up spectators leaving the venues after the final session each day, the DLR will run peak services all day, and the frequency of National Rail services will be increased. The Javelin® fast train will operate a shuttle service between St Pancras International, Stratford International and Ebbsfleet.

Many buses will operate 24 hours a day, but with different services from normal – the Oympic and Paralympic Route Network (ORN/PRN) will be in operation from a few days before the Opening Ceremony, reorganising London's roads to ensure the athletes and VIPs get to the Games venues on time. Confirmed details of the ORN/PRN should be available by the time you read this guide.

During the Games, the operation of certain important London stations will change. Details of entry- or exit-only stations and one-way arrangements within stations will be confirmed in spring 2012, but Stratford, West Ham, Earl's Court, St Pancras, London Bridge and Waterloo are likely to be among those affected. London Bridge and Bank stations may well be very busy, and should be avoided if possible – Charing Cross and Cannon Street stations make useful alternatives to London Bridge for National Rail travellers, while extra DLR trains will be running from Tower Gateway to ease the pressure on Bank. Pudding Mill Lane DLR station will be closed to the public throughout the Games (it is within the perimeter of the Olympic Park).

Visit www.london2012. com/travel for information and travel tools and tips that will make planning your travel easier.

It's possible that London's already congested roads will creak badly during the Games. Use your common sense when travelling by bus or bicycle, avoid the major centres and try not to drive anywhere – particularly as some roads will be designated as Games

Lanes for athletes, officials, the media and emergency services only.

HEALTH & SAFETY

For health information and advice visit **NHS Choices** at www.nhs.uk/2012 or call **NHS Direct** on 0845 4647. For health emergencies, *see p370*. Also bear the following advice in mind:

● If you're on any medication, bring an adequate supply and take it as prescribed.

● You will be spending lots of time outside, so regularly apply sunscreen (at least SPF15, with a four- or five-star rating).

● Drink plenty of water, especially when the sun is out or when drinking alcohol. Drink alcohol responsibly.

● Don't bring or take illegal drugs.

There will be police within and outside of the Olympic Park.

● Walk as much as you can – it's the best way to enjoy the sights.

ACCOMMODATION

People have, understandably, been worried about being able to find accommodation for the 2012 Games. There's no need to be concerned. More than 200 new hotels have opened in London over the last five years; many more are due before the Games, including several hotels near the Olympic Park – you're unlikely to find anywhere closer to it than the three hotels being built in Westfield Stratford City (*see p204* **Inside Track**). By 2012, there will be over 123,000 rooms in London. For our favourite places to stay, across town and to suit all

pockets, *see pp188-214* **Hotels**. Book ahead if you can, but bear in mind that rooms that have been block-booked far in advance by corporate interests and VIPs are likely to be released early in 2012 – so there's no need to despair if you haven't already arranged accommodation.

Homestays will be a popular option for visitors wanting a taste of lived-in London and for residents looking to make money. London & Partners (www.visitlondon.com/ accommodation) has a useful list of agencies, listed under 'London Homestay Accommodation'.

If you are staying in central London, we advise that you plan your journey carefully and allow plenty of time for travelling around the city. For information on London transport, *see p365*.

TRAVEL CALENDAR

27 JULY In addition to extended services on National Rail, the Tube and DLR will run to 2.30am on the night of the **Olympic Games Opening Ceremony**. Those not attending the Olympic Park or London's Live Sites (*see p64*) are advised to get home as early as they can.

28-29 JULY There will be major disruption on the roads in central and south-west London for the **Cycling Road Race**, with roads closed and buses routes changed from Sat morning to Sun afternoon.

30 JULY The start of **Equestrian events** in Greenwich Park and a busy day at ExCeL mean Canning Town, London Bridge and Waterloo East stations should be avoided. If you're travelling to Greenwich, allow plenty of time and use the alternative rail route from Victoria, Cannon Street and Charing Cross to Blackheath and Greenwich, then walk. Allow lots of extra time.

3 AUG This Friday has been earmarked as the busiest for transport of the Games. Avoid any unnecessary travel, especially through St Pancras International – mainland rail arrivals to London are better arranged through Liverpool Street station.

4-5 AUG Olympic Games road events have been planned to fall on the weekends to minimise disruption. Expect major alterations to bus routes and consequently busier Tube and rail journeys all weekend. The women's **Marathon** on 5 Aug will see major road closures from 9am to noon – avoid west London and the City if you're not planning to watch the race.

6-10 AUG The **second week** of the Games is, in general, expected to be busier for transport than the first. Plan your movements carefully, whether you're seeing the sights or watching the sport,

and allow plenty of extra time for journeys. Walk where you can.

11-12 AUG This is likely to be a difficult weekend for the DLR, due to the **Modern Pentathlon** in Greenwich Park and the Olympic Park. On 12 Aug, unless you're planning to cheer the athletes for the men's **Marathon** avoid west London and the City between 9am and noon.

13-28 AUG Between the Olympic and Paralympic Games, transport should return to normal. The ORN and PRN road alterations will not be in operation. On 13 Aug, however, avoid Paddington station and Heathrow airport if you can – many Olympic dignitaries, VIPs and workers will be leaving. Other London airports are likely to be busy too.

29 AUG-9 SEPT With venues clustered in east London, throughout the **Paralympic Games** expect the DLR, Central and Jubilee lines to be busy – Liverpool Street, Fenchurch Street and West Ham stations will remain the essential to Olympic Park transport links, and City and Docklands services (especially to Stratford, Canary Wharf and ExCeL) are likely to be packed during the morning and evening rush hours. Although there are fewer spectators for the Paralympic Games than the Olympic Games, the school holidays will be over, increasing the pressure on public transport, and last services on National Rail will be best avoided.

The Tube will be running a weekday service on Sundays (that is, finishing later), with extra evening Stratford trains and Jubilee line services to the North Greenwich Arena, and National Rail will maintain an Olympic level of service; the Javelin®, however, will return to its normal timetable, but with additional shuttle services between Ebbsfleet, St Pancras International and Stratford International.

LONDON 2012

London 2012 Olympic Games Schedule

		JULY							AUGUST											
SPORT	VENUE	W 25	Th 26	F 27	Sa 28	Su 29	M 30	Tu 31	W 1	Th 2	F 3	Sa 4	Su 5	M 6	Tu 7	W 8	Th 9	F 10	Sa 11	Su 12
Opening Ceremony	Olympic Stadium p53			•																
Closing Ceremony	Olympic Stadium p53																			•
Archery	Lord's Cricket Ground p59			•	•	•	•	•	•	•	•									
Athletics	Olympic Stadium p53										•	•	•	•	•	•	•	•	•	
Athletics – Marathon	The Mall p59												•							•
Athletics – Race Walk	The Mall p59											•							•	
Badminton	Wembley Arena p62				•	•	•	•	•	•	•	•	•							
Basketball	Basketball Arena p55				•	•	•	•	•	•	•	•	•	•	•					
	North Greenwich Arena p61															•	•	•	•	•
Beach Volleyball	Horse Guards Parade p59				•	•	•	•	•	•	•	•	•	•	•	•	•			
Boxing	ExCeL p57				•	•	•	•	•	•	•	•	•	•	•	•	•	•	•	•
Canoe Slalom	Lee Valley White Water Centre p64					•	•	•	•	•										
Canoe Sprint	Eton Dorney p64													•	•	•	•	•	•	
Cycling – BMX	BMX Track p55															•	•			
Cycling – Mountain Bike	Hadleigh Farm p64																		•	•
Cycling – Road	The Mall p59				•	•														
	Hampton Court Palace p59								•											
Cycling – Track	Velodrome p55									•	•	•	•	•	•					
Diving	Aquatics Centre p53					•	•	•	•		•	•	•	•	•	•	•	•	•	
Equestrian – Dressage	Greenwich Park p57									•	•		•		•					
Equestrian – Eventing	Greenwich Park p57				•	•	•	•												
Equestrian – Jumping	Greenwich Park p57											•		•	•		•			
Fencing	ExCeL p57				•	•	•	•	•	•	•	•								
Football	City of Coventry Stadium, Coventry	•	•		•	•			•	•					•					
	Hampden Park, Glasgow	•	•		•				•	•										
	Millennium Stadium, Cardiff	•	•		•				•		•				•					
	Old Trafford, Manchester		•			•	•			•	•				•					
	St James' Park, Newcastle		•			•	•			•	•									
	Wembley Stadium p62					•	•		•					•	•		•		•	
Gymnastics – Artistic	North Greenwich Arena p61				•	•	•	•	•	•				•	•	•				
Gymnastics – Rhythmic	Wembley Arena p62																•	•	•	•
Gymnastics – Trampoline	North Greenwich Arena p61									•	•									
Handball	Copper Box p55				•	•	•	•	•	•	•	•	•	•	•					
	Basketball Arena p55															•	•	•	•	•
Hockey	Riverbank Arena p55					•	•	•	•	•	•	•	•	•	•	•	•	•	•	
Judo	ExCeL p57				•	•	•	•	•	•	•									
Modern Pentathlon	Copper Box p55, Aquatics Centre p53 & Greenwich Park p57																		•	•
Rowing	Eton Dorney p64				•	•	•	•	•	•	•	•								
Sailing	Weymouth & Portland p64					•	•	•	•	•	•	•	•	•	•	•	•	•	•	
Shooting	The Royal Artillery Barracks p61				•	•	•	•	•	•	•	•	•							
Swimming	Aquatics Centre p53				•	•	•	•	•	•	•	•								
Swimming – Marathon	Hyde Park p59																•	•		
Synchronised Swimming	Aquatics Centre p53													•	•	•		•	•	
Table Tennis	ExCeL p57				•	•	•	•	•	•	•	•	•	•	•	•				
Taekwondo	ExCeL p57															•	•	•	•	
Tennis	Wimbledon p62				•	•	•	•	•	•	•	•	•							
Triathlon	Hyde Park p59											•			•					
Volleyball	Earls Court p55				•	•	•	•	•	•	•	•	•	•	•	•	•	•	•	•
Water Polo	Water Polo Arena p53					•	•	•	•	•	•	•	•	•	•	•	•	•	•	•
Weightlifting	ExCeL p57				•	•	•	•	•		•	•	•	•						
Wrestling – Freestyle	ExCeL p57															•	•	•	•	•
Wrestling – Greco-Roman	ExCeL p57												•	•	•					

NOTES For session-by-session details, see www.london2012.com.

London 2012 Paralympic Games Schedule

SPORT	VENUE	AUGUST			SEPTEMBER								
		W 29	Th 30	F 31	Sa 1	Su 2	M 3	Tu 4	W 5	Th 6	F 7	Sa 8	Su 9
Opening Ceremony	Olympic Stadium p53	•											
Closing Ceremony	Olympic Stadium p53												•
Archery	The Royal Artillery Barracks p61		•	•	•	•	•	•	•				
Athletics	Olympic Stadium p53			•	•	•	•	•	•	•	•	•	
Athletics – Marathon	The Mall p59												•
Boccia	ExCeL p57						•	•	•	•	•	•	
Cycling – Road	Brands Hatch p62								•	•	•	•	
Cycling – Track	Velodrome p55		•	•	•	•							
Equestrian	Greenwich Park p57		•	•	•	•	•	•					
Football 5-a-side	Riverbank Arena p55					•		•		•		•	
Football 7-a-side	Riverbank Arena p55					•		•		•		•	•
Goalball	Copper Box p55		•	•	•	•	•	•	•	•	•		
Judo	ExCeL p57		•	•	•								
Powerlifting	ExCeL p57		•	•	•	•	•	•	•				
Rowing	Eton Dorney p64			•	•	•							
Sailing	Weymouth & Portland p64				•	•	•	•	•	•			
Shooting	The Royal Artillery Barracks p61		•	•	•	•	•	•	•	•			
Swimming	Aquatics Centre p53		•	•	•	•	•	•	•	•	•	•	
Table Tennis	ExCeL p57		•	•	•	•	•		•	•	•	•	
Volleyball (Sitting)	ExCeL p57		•	•	•	•	•	•	•	•	•	•	
Wheelchair Basketball	North Greenwich Arena p61		•	•	•	•	•	•	•	•	•	•	
	Basketball Arena p55		•	•	•	•	•						
Wheelchair Fencing	ExCeL p57							•	•	•	•	•	
Wheelchair Rugby	Basketball Arena p55								•	•	•	•	•
Wheelchair Tennis	Eton Manor p55				•	•	•	•	•	•	•	•	
ExCeL day pass			•	•	•	•	•	•	•	•	•	•	
Olympic Park day pass			•	•	•	•	•	•	•	•	•	•	

NOTES *For session-by-session details, see www.london2012.com.*

Sights

Houses of Parliament. *See p136.*

The South Bank & Bankside

Capital views and cultural clout.

An estimated 14 million people come this way each year, and it's easy to see why. Between the **London Eye** and **Tower Bridge**, the south bank of the Thames offers a two-mile procession of diverting, largely state-funded arts and entertainment venues and events, while also affording breezy, traffic-free views of the succession of landmarks (Big Ben, St Paul's, the Tower of London) on the other side of the water.

The area's modern-day life began in 1951 with the Festival of Britain, staged in a bid to boost morale in the wake of World War II. The **Royal Festival Hall** stands testament to the inclusive spirit of the project; it was later expanded into the Southbank Centre, alongside **BFI Southbank** and the concrete ziggurat of the **National Theatre**. However, it wasn't until the new millennium that the riverside really took off, with the arrival of the **London Eye**, **Tate Modern**, the **Millennium Bridge** and the expansion of **Borough Market**. Ever since, the area has been top of most tourists' itineraries and pulses with life, all the more so since several Cultural Olympiad events are taking place here. They include the 'Room for London' installation, which resembles a steamboat run aground on the roof of the Southbank Centre.

Map p399 & pp402-403	**Restaurants & cafés** pp216-217
Hotels p189	**Pubs & bars** p241

THE SOUTH BANK

Lambeth Bridge to Hungerford Bridge

Embankment or Westminster tube, or Waterloo tube/rail.

Thanks to the sharp turn the Thames makes around Waterloo, **Lambeth Bridge** lands you east of the river, not south, opposite the Tudor gatehouse of **Lambeth Palace**. Since the 12th century, it's been the official residence of the Archbishops of Canterbury. The palace is not normally open to the public, except on holidays. The church next door, St Mary at Lambeth, is now the **Garden Museum** (*see p77*).

The benches along the river here are great for viewing the Houses of Parliament opposite, before things get crowded after **Westminster Bridge**, where London's major riverside tourist zone begins. Next to the bridge is **County Hall**, once the seat of London government, now home to the **Sea Life London Aquarium**. The massive wheel of the **London Eye** (*see p77*) rotates slowly in front of you.

Florence Nightingale Museum

St Thomas's Hospital, 2 Lambeth Palace Road, SE1 7EW (7620 0374, www.florence-nightingale. co.uk). Westminster tube or Waterloo tube/rail. **Open** 10am-5pm daily. **Admission** £5.80; £4.80 reductions; £16 family; free under-5s. **Credit** AmEx, MC, V. **Map** p399 M9.

Festival fo Britain at the Southbank Centre.

The nursing skills and campaigning zeal that made Nightingale a Victorian legend are honoured here. Reopened after refurbishment for the centenary of her death in 2010, the museum is a chronological tour through a remarkable life under three key themes: family life, the Crimean War, health reformer. Among the period mementoes – clothing, furniture, books, letters and portraits – are Nightingale's lantern and stuffed pet owl, Athena.

Garden Museum
Lambeth Palace Road, SE1 7LB (7401 8865, www.gardenmuseum.org.uk). Lambeth North tube or Waterloo tube/rail. **Open** 10.30am-5pm Mon-Fri; 10.30am-4pm Sat; closed 1st Mon of mth. **Admission** £6; £3-£5 reductions; free under-16s. **Credit** AmEx, MC, V. **Map** p399 L10.
The world's first horticulture museum (formerly the Museum of Garden History) fits neatly into the old church of St Mary's. A 'belvedere' gallery (built from eco-friendly Eurban wood sheeting) contains the permanent collection of artworks, antique gardening tools and horticultural memorabilia, while the ground floor is used for interesting temporary exhibitions. In the small back garden, the replica of a 17th-century knot garden was created in honour of John Tradescant, intrepid plant hunter and gardener to Charles I; Tradescant is buried here. A stone sarcophagus contains the remains of William Bligh, the captain of the mutinous HMS *Bounty*.

★ London Eye
Jubilee Gardens, SE1 7PB (0870 500 0600, www.londoneye.com). Westminster tube or

Waterloo tube/rail. **Open** *Sept-Mar* 10am-8.30pm daily. *Apr-June* 10am-9pm daily. *July, Aug* 10am-9.30pm daily. **Admission** £18.60; £9.54-£15 reductions; free under-4s. **Credit** AmEx, MC, V. **Map** p399 M8.
See p79 **Profile**.

London Film Museum
County Hall, Riverside Building, SE1 7PB (7202 7040, www.londonfilmmuseum.com). Westminster tube or Waterloo tube/rail. **Open** 10am-5pm Mon-Fri; 10am-6pm Sat, Sun. **Admission** £13.50; £9.50-£11.50 reductions; free under-5s. **Credit** MC, V. **Map** p399 M8.
Dedicated to British film since the 1950s (the brief is for films that were *made* in Britain, which allows

---

INSIDE TRACK STREET VIEW

Unseen Tours' walks are led by homeless guides, who bring their own stories and perspectives to well-known landmarks and quirkier nooks and crannies around Mayfair, Covent Garden, Brick Lane, Shoreditch and London Bridge. Run by Sock Mob, a volunteer network that provides socks, food and a friendly ear to London's homeless, the tours have drawn a steady stream of locals, tourists and school groups since they started in 2010. Check www.sockmobevents.org.uk to see when the next tour is taking place.

unexpected blockbusters such as *Star Wars* and the Indiana Jones movies to be sneaked in alongside the more obvious *Kind Hearts and Coronets* and *Brief Encounter*), the London Film Museum is at the heart of the former home of London's metropolitan government, County Hall. The interactive displays tell the stories of great studios such as Pinewood and Ealing, discussing David Lean and other major directors, and detail different types of movie that have come from these islands. The box-like offices lining the corridors contain sets and props – among thousands of original artefacts, you can see the Rank gong. 'Charlie Chaplin: The Great Londoner' explores the Tramp's life, while 'Ray Harryhausen: Myths & Legends' (to June 2012) looks at his pioneering stop-motion techniques.

Sea Life London Aquarium

County Hall, Riverside Building, Westminster Bridge Road, SE1 7PB (0871 663 1678, tours 7967 8007, www.sealife.co.uk). Westminster tube or Waterloo tube/rail. **Open** *July, Aug* 10am-8pm daily. *Sept-June* 10am-6pm Mon-Thur, Sun; 10am-7pm Fri, Sat. **Admission** £19.02; £14.04 reductions; £60 family; free under-3s. **Credit** MC, V. **Map** p399 M8.

This is one of Europe's largest aquariums and a huge hit with kids. The inhabitants are grouped by geographical origin, beginning with the Atlantic, where blacktail bream swim alongside the Thames Embankment. The 'Rainforests of the World' exhibit has introduced poison arrow frogs, crocodiles and piranha. The Ray Lagoon is still popular, though touching the friendly flatfish is no longer allowed (it's bad for their health). Starfish, crabs and anemones can be handled in special open rock pools instead, and the clown fish still draw crowds. There's a mesmerising Seahorse Temple, a tank full of turtles and, new in 2011, enchanting Gentoo penguins. The centrepieces, though, are the two massive Pacific and Indian Ocean tanks, with menacing sharks quietly circling fallen Easter Island statues and dinosaur bones. *Photo p77.*

FREE Topolski Century

150-152 Hungerford Arches, behind the Royal Festival Hall, SE1 8XU (7928 5433, www.topolskicentury.org.uk). Waterloo tube/rail. **Open** 11am-7pm Mon-Sat; noon-6pm Sun. **Admission** free. **Map** p399 M8.

Underneath the arches near Waterloo, this extensive mural depicts an extraordinary procession of 20th-century events and faces, from Bob Dylan to Winston Churchill via Chairman Mao and Malcolm X. It's the work of Feliks Topolski, a Polish-born artist who travelled the world from 1933 until his death in 1989, popping up at just about every major event from the liberation of Bergen-Belsen to the coronation of Queen Elizabeth II. Refurbished, the space has lost some of its bombed-out atmosphere, but it's much better annotated and easier to decipher.

Hungerford Bridge to Blackfriars Bridge

Embankment or Temple tube, Blackfriars rail or Waterloo tube/rail.

When the **Southbank Centre** (*see p318*) was built in the 1950s, the big concrete boxes that together contain the Royal Festival Hall (RFH), the Queen Elizabeth Hall (QEH) and the Purcell Room were hailed as a daring statement of modern architecture. Along with the Royal National Theatre and the Hayward, they comprise one of the largest and most popular arts centres in the world.

The centrepiece is Sir Leslie Martin's **Royal Festival Hall** (1951), given a £75 million overhaul in 2007. The main auditorium has had its acoustics enhanced and seating refurbished; the upper floors include an improved Poetry Library, and event rooms in which readings are delivered against the backdrop of the Eye and, on the far side of the river, Big Ben. Behind the hall on Belvedere Road, **Festival Square** now hosts off-beat but crowd-pulling events, markets and exhibitions, and there are busy cafés and chain restaurants all around.

Next door, just across from the building housing the QEH and the Purcell Room, the **Hayward** (*see p80*) is a landmark of Brutalist architecture. *Waterloo Sunset*, the gallery's elliptical glass pavilion, was designed in collaboration with light artist Dan Graham. Tucked under Waterloo Bridge is **BFI Southbank** (*see p308*); the UK's premier arthouse cinema, it's run by the British Film Institute. At the front is a second-hand book market – fun, but not brilliant for real finds. Due to its relative height and location just where the Thames bends from north–south to east–west, **Waterloo Bridge** provides some of the finest views of London, especially at dusk. It was designed by Sir Giles Gilbert Scott, the man behind Tate Modern (*see p82*), in 1942.

East of the bridge is Denys Lasdun's terraced **National Theatre** (*see p344*), another Brutalist concrete structure, and one that still divides opinion like few other London buildings. There are popular free performances outside in the summer and free chamber music within during winter. Shaded by trees dotted with blue LEDs, the river path leads past a rare sandy patch of riverbed, busy with sculptors in warm weather, to **Gabriel's Wharf**, a collection of small independent shops that range from stylish to kitsch.

Next door, the deco tower of **Oxo Tower Wharf** was designed to circumvent advertising regulations for the stock-cube company that used to own the building. Saved by local action group Coin Street Community Builders, it

Profile London Eye

It took less than a decade for the Eye to become an icon of modern London.

At the hub of the South Bank's millennial makeover rolls the **London Eye** (for listings, *see p77*), here only since 2000 but already up there with Tower Bridge and the Houses of Parliament as the capital's most postcard-friendly tourist asset. Assuming you choose a clear day, a 30-minute circuit on the Eye affords predictably great views of the city. Take a few snaps from the comfort of your pod and your sightseeing's done.

The London Eye was the vision of husband-and-wife architect team Julia Barfield and David Marks, who entered a 1992 competition to design a structure for the millennium. The Marks' giant wheel idea came second in the contest; the winning entry is conspicuous by its absence. The Eye was planned as a temporary structure but its removal now seems unthinkable. Indeed, the wheel's popularity is such that owner Merlin Entertainments has seen fit to future-proof its investment with a three-year renovation ready for 2012.

By then, each of the wheel's 32 pods (there's one for every London borough) will have been in turn unpinned from its cantilevered moorings. The first ten-ton pod was detached in 2009, placed on to a pontoon and floated down the Thames on the tide to Tilbury Docks, from where it was loaded on to a truck and escorted by road to a Worcester workshop. So the wheel can keep its balance, a dummy capsule is put in place of the one that is missing. The renovation has been a knotty problem for Merlin; a spokesman tells us that more than 20 companies have been involved.

So what can we expect from the shiny new Eye pods? They will be, said a press spokesman, more high-tech with improved climate control. Some will be given screens, so business folk can hire them for high-level presentations. So while it's not exactly a case of Pimp my Eye (the attraction won't look any different), we're promised a snappier, happier ride.

Oxo Tower.

now provides affordable housing, interesting designer shops and galleries, and restaurants (including a rooftop restaurant and bistro with more wonderful views). Behind, **Bernie Spain Gardens** is great for a break from the crowds.

Shortly after the **Oxo Tower**, the path along the south bank path is blocked by current redevelopment to Blackfriars Station – by 2012, it is to have become a single station spanning both sides of the river. Until then, you'll have to divert inland to ugly Southwark Street if you're continuing to Bankside.

Hayward

Southbank Centre, Belvedere Road, SE1 8XX, (0844 875 0073, www.southbankcentre.co.uk). Embankment tube or Waterloo tube/rail. **Open** 10am-6pm Mon-Wed, Sat, Sun; 10am-8pm Thur, Fri. **Admission** varies; check website for details. **Credit** AmEx, MC, V. **Map** p399 M8.
This versatile gallery is continuing with its excellent programme of exhibitions, many of them loaned from around the world. It's carved out a particular niche for itself with participatory installations – Antony Gormley's fog-filled chamber for 'Blind Light', the rooftop rowing boat for group show 'Psycho Buildings' – but there's always plenty of variety on display. Visitors can hang out in the industrial-look café downstairs (it's a bar at night), aptly called Concrete, before visiting free contemporary exhibitions at the inspired Hayward Project Space; take the stairs to the first floor from the glass foyer extension.

Highlights for 2012 include David Shrigley (1 Feb-13 May) and Jeremy Deller (22 Feb-13 May).

Around Waterloo

Waterloo tube/rail.

Surprisingly, perhaps, there's plenty of interest around the stone-meets-glass rail terminus of London Waterloo. The most obvious attraction is the massive **BFI IMAX** (*see p308*), located in the middle of a roundabout at the southern end of Waterloo Bridge. The £20-million cinema makes imaginative use of a desolate space that, in the 1990s, was notorious for its 'Cardboard City' population of homeless residents.

South, on the corner of Waterloo Road and the Cut, is the restored Victorian façade of the **Old Vic** theatre (*see p344*), now overseen by Kevin Spacey. Further down the Cut is the renovated home of the **Young Vic** (*see p350*), a hotbed of theatrical talent with a stylish balcony bar. Both bring a touch of West End glamour across the river. To the north of the Cut, off Cornwall Road, are a number of atmospheric terraces made up of mid 19th-century artisans' houses.

BANKSIDE

Borough or Southwark tube, or London Bridge tube/rail.
In Shakespeare's day, the area known as Bankside was the centre of bawdy Southwark, neatly located just beyond the jurisdiction of the City fathers. As well as playhouses such as the Globe and the Rose, there were the famous 'stewes' (brothels) presided over by the Bishops

of Winchester, who made a tidy income from the fines they levied on the area's 'Winchester Geese' (or, in common parlance, prostitutes). There's less drinking, carousing and mischief-making here these days, but the area's cultural heritage remains alive thanks to the reconstructed **Shakespeare's Globe** (*see p82*) and, pretty much next door to it, **Tate Modern** (*see p82*), a former power station that's now a gallery.

Spanning the river in front of the Tate, the **Millennium Bridge** opened in 2000, when it became the first new Thames crossing in London since Tower Bridge (1894). Its early days were fraught with troubles; after just two days, the bridge was closed because of a pronounced wobble, and didn't reopen until 2002. Its troubles long behind it, the bridge is an extremely elegant structure; a 'ribbon of steel' in the words of its conceptualists, architect Lord Foster and sculptor Anthony Caro. Cross it and you're at the foot of the stairs leading up to St Paul's Cathedral (*see p90*).

Continuing past the Globe and Southwark Bridge, you'll reach the **Anchor Bankside** pub (34 Park Street, 7407 1577). Built in 1775 on the site of an even older inn, the Anchor has, at various points, been a brothel, a chapel and a ship's chandlers. The outside terrace, across the pathway, offers fine river views – a fact lost on no one each summer, when it's invariably crammed with people.

All that's left of the Palace of Winchester, home of successive bishops, is the ruined rose window of the Great Hall on Clink Street. It stands next to the site of the bishops' former Clink prison, where thieves, prostitutes and debtors all served their sentences; it's now the **Clink Prison Museum** (1 Clink Street, SE1 9DG, 7403 0900, www.clink.co.uk). Around the corner is the entrance to the wine showcase **Vinopolis** (*see p83*). At the other end of Clink Street, St Mary Overie's dock contains a terrific full-scale replica of Sir Francis Drake's ship, the **Golden Hinde** (*see below*).

FREE Bankside Gallery

48 Hopton Street, SE1 9JH (7928 7521, www.banksidegallery.com). Southwark or London Bridge tube/rail. **Open** 11am-6pm daily. **Admission** free; donations appreciated. **Credit** MC, V. **Map** p402 O7.

In the shadow of Tate Modern, this tiny gallery is the home of the Royal Watercolour Society and the Royal Society of Painter-Printmakers. The gallery runs a frequently changing programme of delightful print and watercolour exhibitions throughout the year; many of the works on show are for sale. Both societies hold frequent events here, including talks and demonstrations.

Golden Hinde

Pickfords Wharf, Clink Street, SE1 9DG (7403 0123, www.goldenhinde.com). London Bridge tube/rail. **Open** 10am-5.30pm daily. **Admission** £6; £4.50 reductions; £18 family; free under-4s. **Credit** AmEx, MC, V. **Map** p402 P8.

This meticulous replica of Sir Francis Drake's 16th-century flagship is thoroughly seaworthy: the ship has even reprised the privateer's circumnavigatory

SIGHTS

Royal Festival Hall. *See p78.*

SIGHTS

voyage. 'Living History Experiences' (some overnight) allow participants to dress in period clothes, eat Tudor fare and learn the skills of the Elizabethan seafarer; book well in advance. On weekends, it swarms with children dressed up as pirates for birthday dos.

★ Shakespeare's Globe

21 New Globe Walk, SE1 9DT (7401 9919, www.shakespeares-globe.org). Southwark tube or London Bridge tube/rail. **Open** *Exhibition* 10am-5pm daily. *Globe Theatre tours* Oct-Apr 10am-5pm daily. May-Sept 9.30am-12.30pm Mon-Sat; 9.30-11.30am Sun. *Rose Theatre tours* May-Sept 1-5pm Mon-Sat; noon-5pm Sun. *Tours* every 30mins. **Admission** £12.50; £8-£11 reductions; £35 family; free under-5s. **Credit** AmEx, MC, V. **Map** p402 O7.

The original Globe Theatre, where many of William Shakespeare's plays were first staged and which he co-owned, burned to the ground in 1613 during a performance of *Henry VIII.* Nearly 400 years later, it was rebuilt not far from its original site, using construction methods and materials as close to the originals as possible, and is now open to the public for tours throughout the year (allow 90 minutes for the visit). During matinées, the tours go to the site of the Rose (21 New Globe Walk, SE1 9DT, 7261 9565, www.rose theatre.org.uk), built by Philip Henslowe in 1587 as the first theatre on Bankside; red lights show the position of the original theatre. Funds are being sought to continue excavations and preserve the site.

Under the adventurous artistic directorship of Dominic Dromgoole, the Globe is also a fully operational theatre. From 23 April, conventionally regarded as the bard's birthday, into early October, Shakespeare's plays and the odd new drama are performed. For more on the theatre, *see p346.*

★ FREE Tate Modern

Bankside, SE1 9TG (7887 8888, www. tate.org.uk). Southwark tube or London Bridge tube/rail. **Open** 10am-6pm Mon-Thur, Sun; 10am-10pm Fri, Sat. *Tours* 11am, noon, 2pm, 3pm daily. **Admission** free. *Temporary exhibitions* vary. **Credit** AmEx, MC, V. **Map** p402 O7.

Thanks to its industrial architecture, this powerhouse of modern art is awe-inspiring even before you enter. Built after World War II as Bankside Power Station, it was designed by Sir Giles Gilbert Scott, architect of Battersea Power Station (*see p176*). The power station shut in 1981; nearly 20 years later, it opened as an art museum, and has enjoyed spectacular popularity ever since. The gallery attracts five million visitors a year to a building intended for half that number; work on the ambitious, £215m TM2 extension began in 2010. The vast new origami structure, designed by Herzog & de Meuron (who were behind the original conversion), isn't due for completion until after 2012, but works won't interrupt normal service in the main galleries.

Old Operating Theatre, Museum & Herb Garret. *See p84.*

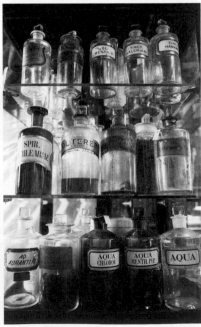

The original cavernous turbine hall is used to jaw-dropping effect as the home of large-scale, temporary installations. Beyond, the permanent collection draws from the Tate's collections of modern art (international works from 1900) and features heavy hitters such as Matisse, Rothko and Beuys. There are vertiginous views down inside the building from outside the galleries, which group artworks according to movement (Surrealism, Minimalism, Post-war abstraction) rather than theme. The year's highlights are likely to be a major Damien Hirst retrospective (4 April-9 September; see below **Inside Track**) and Tino Sehgal's Turbine Hall commission, unveiled on 17 July. Both are highlights of the Cultural Olympiad.

The tanks that once housed oil to power the generators are being converted into performance and event-based art spaces. From 6 July to 25 November events held here are part of the Cultural Olympiad.

▶ *The polka-dotted Tate-to-Tate boat zooms to Tate Britain (see p138) every 40 minutes, with a stop-off at the London Eye (see p77). Tickets are available at both Tates, on board, online or by phone (7887 8888; £5, £1.65-£3.75 reductions).*

Vinopolis

1 Bank End, SE1 9BU (7940 8300, www.vinopolis.co.uk). London Bridge tube/rail. **Open** 2-10pm Thur, Fri; noon-10pm Sat; noon-6pm Sun. **Admission** £22.50-£40. **Credit** AmEx, MC, V. **Map** p402 P8.

Glossy Vinopolis is more of an introduction to wine-tasting than a resource for cognoscenti, but you do need to have some prior interest to get a kick out of it. Participants are introduced to systematic wine tasting and then given a wine glass. Exhibits are set out by country, with opportunities to taste wine or champagne from different regions. Gin crashes the party courtesy of a Bombay Sapphire cocktail, and you can also sample Caribbean rum, whisky and beer.

BOROUGH

Borough or Southwark tube, or London Bridge tube/rail.

At Clink Street, the route cuts inland, skirting the edge of the district of Borough. The landmark here is the Anglican **Southwark Cathedral** (*see p84*), formerly St Saviour's and before that the monastic church of St Mary Overie. Shakespeare's brother Edmund was buried in the graveyard; there's a monument to the playwright inside.

Just south of the cathedral you'll find the roof of **Borough Market**, a buoy food market dating from the 13th century. It's wholesale only for most of the week, but hosts London's foodiest public food market (*see p272*) on Thursdays, Fridays and Saturdays (when it gets very crowded). It's surrounded by good places to eat and drink. Not far away, the quaint

George (77 Borough High Street, 7407 2056) is London's last surviving galleried coaching inn.

Around London Bridge Station, tourist attractions clamour for attention. One of the grisliest, with its body parts and surgical implements, is the **Old Operating Theatre, Museum & Herb Garret** (*see p84*), but it's the less scary **London Dungeon** (*see p84*) that draws the biggest queues. Underneath the arches almost opposite the Dungeon is a rival gore-fest: the **London Bridge Experience** (*see below*). Competing with the blood-curdling shrieks from the Dungeon's entrance are the dulcet tones of Vera Lynn, broadcast from **Winston Churchill's Britain at War Experience** (*see p84*). And towering over them all is the vast, 1,017-foot **Shard** development at London Bridge station.

London Bridge Experience

2-4 Tooley Street, SE1 2SY (0844 847 2287, www.thelondonbridgeexperience.com). London Bridge tube/rail. **Open** 10am-5pm Mon-Fri; 10am-6pm Sat, Sun. **Admission** £23; £17-£21 reductions; £74 family; free under-6s. **Credit** MC, V. **Map** p403 Q8.

This costumed whistle-stop tour comprises a family-friendly lesson on the history of London Bridge, as well as a scary walk through the haunted foundations of the bridge for over-11s only and a less scary visit under ground for under-11s. Upstairs, it's all smoke-filled fun as actors ham it up in front of wobbly sets and a bewildered, rapidly bonding audience. A Viking warrior urges us to heave hawsers to pull the bridge down; a chamber of gore is hosted by the chap in charge of putting chopped-off heads on poles. Below, pestilential corridors are peopled by crazed zombies, animatronic torture victims and a butcher wielding a chainsaw. The calmness of Peter Jackson's London Bridge artefacts comes as a real relief.

INSIDE TRACK
FIRST FOR HIRST

Damien Hirst's best-known works pretty well defined the 1990s generation that became known as the Young British Artists, so it's surprising that the forthcoming retrospective of his career at Tate Modern (for listings, *see p82*) will be the first on this scale to be held in Britain. Running from 5 April to 9 September 2012, it's part of the London 2012 Festival. The exhibition draws work from across his 25-year career, including, yes, *The Physical Impossibility of Death in the Mind of Someone Living* – Hirst's notorious shark art, with the fish preserved as if it is swimming through a vitrine of formaldehyde.

SIGHTS

SIGHTS

London Dungeon

28-34 Tooley Street, SE1 2SZ (0871 423 2240, www.thedungeons.com). London Bridge tube/rail. **Open** times vary; check website for details. **Admission** £23.52; £17.52-£21.54 reductions. **Credit** AmEx, MC, V. **Map** p403 Q8.

Enter the Victorian railway arches of London Bridge for this jokey and rather expensive celebration of torture, death and disease. Visitors are led through a dry-ice fog past gravestones and hideously rotting corpses to experience nasty symptoms from the Great Plague exhibition: an actor-led medley of corpses, boils, projectile vomiting, worm-filled skulls and scuttling rats. The death-dealing exploits of Bloody Mary are explored alongside those of Sweeney Todd and the Ripper. Extremis: Drop Ride to Doom re-enacts an execution – with you as victim. Vengeance is based on the séances that were once held at 50 Berkeley Square.

★ Old Operating Theatre, Museum & Herb Garret

9A St Thomas's Street, SE1 9RY (7188 2679, www.thegarret.org.uk). London Bridge tube/rail. **Open** 10.30am-5pm daily. **Admission** £5.90; £3.40-£4.90 reductions; £13.80 family; free under-6s. **No credit cards**. **Map** p403 Q8.

The tower that houses this reminder of the surgical practices of the past used to be part of the chapel of St Thomas's Hospital. Before moving there, operations took place in the wards. Visitors enter via a vertiginous spiral staircase to inspect a pre-anaesthetic operating theatre dating from 1822, with tiered viewing seats for students. The operating tools look more like torture implements. *Photo p82.*

INSIDE TRACK
PENTHOUSE DREAMS

If you've ever enjoyed a night at the Southbank Centre so much you didn't want to go home, A Room for London will be your idea of heaven. Part of the London 2012 Cultural Olympiad, this unique artistic and architectural collaboration places a boat-shaped, timber-built room on the roof of the Southbank Centre's Queen Elizabeth Hall, offering guests and invited artists a place of refuge and reflection, high above the riverfront throng. The designers hope occupants will keep a 'logbook' of their experiences; during each stay, a flag will be raised to indicate the boat has been boarded. Members of the public will be able to spend a single night in A Room for London between January and December 2012; booking opens in September 2011 (www.living-architecture.co.uk).

FREE Southwark Cathedral

London Bridge, SE1 9DA (7367 6700, www.southwark.anglican.org). London Bridge tube/rail. **Open** 9am-5pm daily (closing times vary on religious holidays). *Services* 8am, 8.15am, 12.30pm, 12.45pm, 5.30pm Mon-Fri; 9am, 9.15am, 4pm Sat; 8.45am, 9am, 11am, 3pm, 6.30pm Sun. *Choral Evensong* 5.30pm Mon, Thur (girls); 5.30pm Tue (boys & men); 5.30pm Fri (men only). **Admission** free; suggested donation £4. **Credit** MC, V. **Map** p402 P8.

The oldest bits of this building date back more than 800 years. The retro-choir was the setting for several Protestant martyr trials during the reign of Mary Tudor. The courtyard is one of the area's prettiest places for a rest, especially during the summer. Inside, there are memorials to Shakespeare, John Harvard (benefactor of the American university) and Sam Wanamaker (the force behind the reconstruction of the Globe); Chaucer features in the stained glass. There are displays throughout the cathedral explaining its history.

Winston Churchill's Britain at War Experience

64-66 Tooley Street, SE1 2TF (7403 3171, www.britainatwar.co.uk). London Bridge tube/rail. **Open** *Apr-Oct* 10am-5pm daily. *Nov-Mar* 10am-4.30pm daily. **Admission** £12.95; £5.50-£6.50 reductions; £29 family; free under-5s. **Credit** AmEx, MC, V. **Map** p403 Q8.

This old-fashioned exhibition recalls the privations endured by the British during World War II. Visitors descend from street level in an ancient lift to a reconstructed tube station shelter. The experience continues with displays about London during the Blitz, including bombs, rare documents, photos and reconstructed shopfronts. The displays on rationing, food production and Land Girls are fascinating, and the set-piece walk-through bombsite is quite disturbing.

LONDON BRIDGE TO TOWER BRIDGE

Bermondsey tube/London Bridge tube/rail.

Across the street from the Dungeon is **Hay's Galleria**. Once an enclosed dock, it's now dominated by a peculiar kinetic sculpture called *The Navigators*. Exiting on the riverside, you can walk east past the great grey hulk of **HMS Belfast** (*see right*) to Tower Bridge.

Beyond the battleship you pass the pristine, but rather soulless environs of **City Hall**, home of London's current government. There's a pleasant outside 'amphitheatre' called the Scoop, used for lunch breaks and outdoor events.

South of here, many of the historic houses on Bermondsey Street now host hip design studios or funky shops. This is also where you'll find the **Fashion & Textile Museum** (*see right*).

HMS Belfast.

At the street's furthest end, the redevelopment of Bermondsey Square created an arthouse cinema and the Bermondsey Square Hotel, but old-timers linger on. There's the eel and pie shop M Manze and a Friday antiques market (6am-2pm) – great for browsing, but get there early for the real bargains.

Back on the riverfront, a board announces when **Tower Bridge** is next due to be raised, which happens several hundred times a year. The bridge is one of the lowest to span the Thames, hence its twin lifting sections or bascules. The original steam-driven machinery can still be seen at the **Tower Bridge Exhibition** (*see p101*), which also offers the visitor fantastic views from the top. Further east, the former warehouses of **Butler's Wharf** are now mainly given over to expensive riverside dining; one of them currently houses the **Design Museum** (*see below*).

Design Museum

Shad Thames, SE1 2YD (7403 6933, www. designmuseum.org). Tower Hill tube or London Bridge tube/rail. **Open** 10am-5.45pm daily. **Admission** £11; £7-£10 reductions; free under-12s. **Credit** AmEx, MC, V. **Map** p403 S9.
Exhibitions in this former banana warehouse focus on modern and contemporary design. The temporary shows run from major installations to design artefacts, from architects' travel photographs to retrospectives of key theorists of the built environment. The Blueprint Café has a balcony overlooking the Thames, and you can buy designer books and items relating to the current show in the museum shop. In 2011,

Terence Conran made a major donation that will enable the museum to move to new premises in the former Commonwealth Institute by 2014.

Fashion & Textile Museum

83 Bermondsey Street, SE1 3XF (7407 8664, www.ftmlondon.org). London Bridge tube/rail. **Open** 11am-6pm Tue-Sat. **Admission** £7; £4 reductions; free under-12s. **Credit** MC, V. **Map** p403 Q9.
As flamboyant as its founder, fashion designer Zandra Rhodes, this pink and orange museum holds 3,000 of Rhodes's garments, some on permanent display, and her archive of paper designs, sketchbooks, silk screens and show videos. Temporary shows explore the work of particular trend-setters or themes such as the development of underwear. A quirky shop sells ware by new designers.

HMS Belfast

Morgan's Lane, Tooley Street, SE1 2JH (7940 6300, www.iwm.org.uk). London Bridge tube/rail. **Open** *Mar-Oct* 10am-6pm daily. *Nov-Feb* 10am-5pm daily. **Admission** £13.50; £6.75-£10.80 reductions; free under-16s (must be accompanied by an adult). **Credit** MC, V. **Map** p403 R8.
This 11,500-ton 'Edinburgh' class large light cruiser is the last surviving big gun World War II warship in Europe. A floating branch of the Imperial War Museum, it makes an unlikely playground for children, who tear around its complex of gun turrets, bridge, decks and engine room. The *Belfast* was built in 1938, ran convoys to Russia, supported the Normandy Landings and helped UN forces in Korea before being decommissioned in 1965.

The City

Where London began – and where much of its wealth is made.

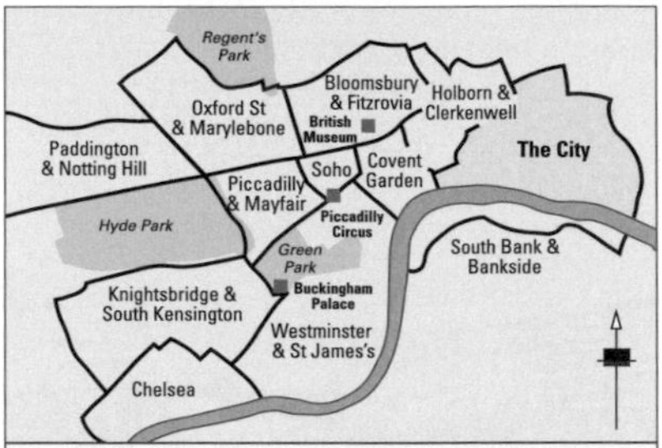

The City's current fame merely as the financial heart of London does no justice to its 2,000 years of history. This was where the Romans founded the city they called Londinium, building a bridge to the west of today's **London Bridge**. Here were a forum-basilica, an amphitheatre, public baths and, eventually, the surrounding defensive wall that still more or less defines the area we call the Square Mile (actually an area of 1.21 square miles).

Although the City has just over 9,000 residents, 330,000 people arrive each weekday to work as bankers, brokers, lawyers and traders, taking over 85 million square feet of office space. Tourists come, too, to see **St Paul's Cathedral** and the **Tower of London**, but there's much else besides. No area of London offers quite so much to see in so small a space. Roman ruins? Medieval remains? Iconic 21st-century offices? You've come to the right place.

Map pp400-403	**Hotels** pp189-191
Pubs & bars p242	**Restaurants & cafés** pp217-218

INTRODUCING THE CITY

London has long been divided in two, with Westminster the centre of politics and the City the capital of commerce. Many of the City's administrative affairs are still run on a feudal basis under the auspices of the City of London, Britain's richest local authority. The wealth of the area has always been hard to comprehend; this is, after all, an area that was able to bounce back after losing half its population to the Black Death and half its buildings first to the Great Fire and, later, to the Blitz.

To understand the City properly, visit on a weekday when the great economic machine is running at full tilt and the commuter is king. At weekends, many of the streets fall eerily quiet, though others are animated by streetmarkets, particularly on Sunday mornings.

FREE City of London Information Centre

St Paul's Churchyard, EC4M 8BX (7332 1456, www.cityoflondon.gov.uk). St Paul's tube. **Open** 9.30am-5.30pm Mon-Sat; 10am-4pm Sun. **Credit** (shop) MC, V. **Map** p402 O6.

Run by the City of London, this spiky-roofed modern tourist office is just opposite St Paul's, at the top of the stairs that lead up from the Millennium Bridge. As well as information and brochures on sights, events, walks and talks, it offers tours with well-trained specialist guides.

TEMPLE & THE INNS OF COURT

Temple tube.

At its western end, the Strand (*see p113*) becomes Fleet Street (*see p88*) at **Temple Bar**, the City's ancient western boundary and once the site of Wren's great gateway (now relocated to Paternoster Square beside St

---

INSIDE TRACK LONDON PASS

The London Pass (www.londonpass.com) gives pre-paid access and queue-jumping privileges at more than 50 sights and attractions. It's worth looking at if you are planning some intensive sightseeing.

Paul's; *see p90*). A newer, narrower, but still impressive griffin-topped monument marks the original spot. The area has long been linked to the law, and here, on the edge of Holborn, stands the splendid neo-Gothic **Royal Courts of Justice** (*see below*). On the other side of the road, stretching almost to the Thames, are the several courtyards that make up **Middle Temple** (7427 4800, www.middletemple.org.uk) and **Inner Temple** (7797 8250, www.innertemple.org.uk), two of the Inns of Court that provided training and lodging for London's medieval lawyers. Anybody may visit the grounds, but access to the grand, collegiate buildings is reserved for lawyers and barristers. Tours of Inner Temple cost £10 per person (minimum ten people; book on 7797 8241).

The site was formerly the headquarters of the Knights Templar, an order of warrior monks founded in the 12th century to protect pilgrims travelling to the Holy Land. The Templars built the original **Temple Church** (*see below*) in 1185, but they fell foul of Catholic orthodoxy during the Crusades and the order was disbanded for heresy. Dan Brown used the Temple Church as a setting for his bestselling conspiracy novel *The Da Vinci Code* (2003). Robin Griffith-Jones, the master of Temple Church, has produced a robust response to his claims at www.beliefnet.com/templechurch.

FREE Royal Courts of Justice

Strand, WC2A 2LL (7947 6000, tours 7947 7684, www.hmcourts-service.gov.uk). Temple tube. **Open** 9am-4.30pm Mon-Fri. **Admission** free. *Tours* £10. **Credit** MC, V. **Map** p397 M6.
Two of the highest civil courts in the land sit in these imposing buildings: the High Court and the Appeals Court, justice at its most bewigged and ermine-robed. Visitors are welcome to observe the process of law in any of the 88 courtrooms, but very little happens in August and September. There are also two-hour tours on the first and third Tuesday of the month (11am or 2pm; pre-book on 7947 7684 or rcj-tours@talktalk.net). Cameras and children under 14 are not allowed on the premises.

FREE Temple Church

Fleet Street, EC4Y 7HL (7353 8559, www.templechurch.com). Chancery Lane or Temple tube. **Open** 2-4pm Tue-Fri; phone or check website for details. *Services* 1.15pm Thur; 8.30am, 11.15am Sun. **Admission** free. **Map** p402 N6.
Inspired by Jerusalem's Church of the Holy Sepulchre, the Temple Church was the chapel of the Knights Templar. The rounded apse contains the worn grave-stones of several Crusader knights, but the church was refurbished by Wren and the Victorians, and was damaged in the Blitz. Not that it puts off the wild speculations of *Da Vinci Code* fans. There are organ recitals most Wednesdays (phone for details).

Temple Church.

SIGHTS

SIGHTS

INSIDE TRACK
PRIVATE PROPERTY

If you'd like to see inside the City's most interesting buildings but are keen to avoid the queues at September's **Open-City London** weekend (*see p288*), try the **City of London Festival** (*see p317* **Festivals**). There are special tours at Mansion House, Bank and St Paul's Cathedral.

FLEET STREET

Temple tube or Blackfriars rail.

Without Fleet Street, the daily newspaper might never have been invented. Named after the vanished River Fleet, Fleet Street was a major artery for the delivery of goods into the City, including the first printing press, which was installed behind **St Bride's Church** (*see right*) in 1500 by William Caxton's assistant, Wynkyn de Worde, who also set up a bookstall in the churchyard of St Paul's. London's first daily newspaper, the *Daily Courant*, rolled off the presses in 1702; in 1712, Fleet Street saw the first of innumerable libel cases when the *Courant* leaked the details of a private parliamentary debate.

By the end of World War II, half a dozen offices were churning out scoops and scandals between the Strand and Farringdon Road. Most of the newspapers moved away after Rupert Murdoch won his war with the print unions in the 1980s; the last of the news agencies, Reuters, finally followed suit in 2005. Until recently, the only periodical published on Fleet Street was a comic, the much-loved *Beano*. However, in 2009, left-wing weekly the *New Statesman* moved into offices around the corner from Fleet Street on Carmelite Street. Interesting relics from the media days remain: the Portland-stone **Reuters building** (no.85), the Egyptian-influenced **Daily Telegraph building** (no.135) and the sleek, black **Daily Express building** (nos.121-128), designed by Owen Williams in the 1930s and arguably the only art deco building of note in London. Tucked away on an alley behind St Bride's Church is the **St Bride Foundation Institute**, its library (7353 4660, www.st bride.org; open noon-5.30pm Tue, Thur; noon-9pm Wed) dedicated to printing and typography. The library mounts temporary exhibitions showing off its collections, which include rare works by Eric Gill and maquettes for Kinnear and Calvert's distinctive road signs.

At the top of Fleet Street itself is the church of **St Dunstan-in-the-West** (7405 1929,

www.stdunstaninthewest.org; free tours 11am-3pm Tue), where the poet John Donne was rector in the 17th century. The church was rebuilt in the 1830s, but the eye-catching clock dates to 1671. The clock's chimes are beaten by clockwork giants who are said to represent Gog and Magog, tutelary spirits of the City. Next door, no.186 is the house where Sweeney Todd, the 'demon barber of Fleet Street', reputedly murdered his customers before selling their bodies to a local pie shop. The legend, sadly, is a porky pie: Todd was invented by the editors of a Victorian penny dreadful in 1846 and propelled to fame rather later by a stage play.

Fleet Street was always known for its pubs; half the newspaper editorials in London were composed over liquid lunches, but there were also more literary imbibers. If you walk down Fleet Street, you'll see **Ye Olde Cheshire Cheese** (no.145, 7353 6170), a favourite of Dickens and Yeats. In its heyday, it hosted the bibulous literary salons of Dr Samuel Johnson, who lived nearby at 17 Gough Square (*see below* **Dr Johnson's House**). It also had a famous drinking parrot, the death of which prompted hundreds of newspaper obituaries. At no.66, the **Tipperary** (7583 6470) is the oldest Irish pub outside Ireland: it sold the first pint of Guinness on the British mainland in the 1700s.

Dr Johnson's House

17 Gough Square, off Fleet Street, EC4A 3DE (7353 3745, www.drjohnsonshouse.org). Chancery Lane tube or Blackfriars tube/rail. **Open** *May-Sept* 11am-5.30pm Mon-Sat. *Oct-Apr* 11am-5pm Mon-Sat. *Tours* by arrangement, groups of 10 or more only. **Admission** £4.50; £1.50-£3.50 reductions; £10 family; free under-5s. *Tours* free. **No credit cards. Map** p402 N6.
Famed as the author of one of the first – as well as the most significant and unquestionably the wittiest – dictionaries of the English language, Dr Samuel Johnson (1709-84) also wrote poems, a novel and one of the earliest travelogues, an acerbic account of a tour of the Western Isles with his biographer James Boswell. You can tour the stately Georgian townhouse off Fleet Street where Johnson came up with his inspired definitions – 'to make dictionaries is dull work,' was his definition of the word 'dull'. The house has been open to the public since 1911.
▶ *A neat statue of Johnson's cat Hodge sits contentedly in the square outside.*

FREE St Bride's Church

Fleet Street, EC4Y 8AU (7427 0133, www.st brides.com). Temple tube. **Open** 8am-6pm Mon-Fri; 11am-3pm Sat; 10am-6.30pm Sun. Times vary Mon-Sat, so phone ahead to check. *Services* 8.30am Mon, Tue, Thur, Fri; 8.30am, 1.15pm Wed; 11am, 5.30pm Sun. **Admission** free. **No credit cards. Map** p402 N6.

Hidden down an alley south of Fleet Street, St Bride's is known as the journalists' church: in the north aisle, a shrine is dedicated to hacks killed in action. Down in the crypt a surprisingly interesting little museum displays fragments of the churches that have existed on this site since the sixth century.

▶ *The Wren-designed spire is said to have inspired the traditional tiered wedding cake.*

ST PAUL'S & AROUND

St Paul's tube.

The towering dome of **St Paul's Cathedral** (*see p90*) is, excluding the Big Ben clocktower, probably the definitive symbol of traditional London. It was also an architectural two fingers to the Great Fire and, later, to the Nazi bombers that pounded the city in 1940 and 1941. Immediately north of the cathedral itself is the redeveloped **Paternoster Square**, a modern plaza incorporating a sundial that only rarely tells the time. The name harks to the days when priests from St Paul's walked the streets chanting the Lord's Prayer (*Pater noster* is Latin for 'Our Father', the first words of that prayer).

Also of interest is Wren's statue-covered **Temple Bar**. It once stood at the intersection of Fleet Street and the Strand (*see p113*), marking the boundary between the City of London and neighbouring Westminster; during the Middle Ages, the monarch was only allowed to pass through the Temple Bar into the City with the approval of the Lord Mayor of London. The archway was dismantled as part of a Victorian road-widening programme in 1878 and became a garden ornament for a country estate in Hertfordshire, before being installed in its current location, as the gateway between St Paul's and Paternoster Square, in 2004. The gold-topped pillar in the centre of the square looks as if it commemorates something important, but's just an air vent for the Underground. Victorians would admire such spirited decoration of the mundane.

South of St Paul's, a cascade of steps runs down to the **Millennium Bridge**, which spans the river to Tate Modern (*see p82*) and now offers the main gateway to the City for tourists. The stairs take you close to the 17th-century **College of Arms** (*see p90*), the official seat of British heraldry.

East of the cathedral, the huge **One New Change** shopping mall and office development (www.onenewchange.com) opened in late 2010. Designed by French starchitect Jean Nouvel, its most interesting aspects are a gash that gives views straight through the building to St Paul's and, for a fine roof-level panorama, the sixth-floor public terrace and bar-restaurant. Meekly hidden among the alleys behind it, you'll find narrow Bow Lane. At one end sits **St Mary-le-Bow** (7248 5139, www.stmarylebow.co.uk; open 7.30am-6pm Mon-Wed; 7.30am-6.30pm Thur;

Millennium Bridge.

7am-4pm Fri), built by Wren between 1671 and 1680. The church bell's peals once defined anyone born within earshot as a true Cockney. At the other end of Bow Lane is **St Mary Aldermary** (7248 9902, www.stmary aldermary.co.uk; open 11am-3pm Mon-Fri). With a pin-straight spire designed by Wren's office, this was the only Gothic church by him to survive World War II. Inside, there's a fabulous moulded plaster ceiling and original wooden sword rest (London parishioners carried arms until the late 19th century). Roman coins are sold here to fund renovation work.

There are more Wren creations south of St Paul's. On Garlick Hill, named for the medieval garlic market, is **St James Garlickhythe** (7236 1719, www.stjamesgarlickhythe.org.uk; open 10.30am-4pm Thur). The official church of London's vintners and joiners, it was built by Wren in 1682. Hidden in the tower are the naturally mummified remains of a young man, nicknamed Jimmy Garlick, discovered in the vaults in 1855. The church was hit by bombs in both World Wars, and partly ruined by a falling crane in 1991, but the interior has been convincingly restored. Off Victoria Street, **St Nicholas Cole Abbey** was the first church rebuilt after the Great Fire.

Built on the site of the infamous Newgate prison to the north-west of the cathedral is the **Old Bailey** (*see below*). A remnant of the prison's east wall can be seen in Amen Corner.

FREE College of Arms

130 Queen Victoria Street, EC4V 4BT (7248 2762, www.college-of-arms.gov.uk). St Paul's tube or Blackfriars tube/rail. **Open** 10am-4pm Mon-Fri. *Tours* by arrangement. **Admission** free. **No credit cards. Map** p402 O7.

Originally created to identify competing knights at medieval jousting tournaments, coats of arms soon became an integral part of family identity for the landed gentry of Britain. Scriveners still work here to create beautiful heraldic certificates. Only the Earl Marshal's Court is open to the general public, but visitors can book for evening tours (Mon-Fri) around the historic interior, led by a herald who will usually be able to show you documents from the archive.

FREE Old Bailey
(Central Criminal Court)

Corner of Newgate Street & Old Bailey, EC4M 7EH (7248 3277, www.cityoflondon.gov.uk). St Paul's tube. **Open** *Public gallery* 9.45am-12.45pm, 2-4.30pm Mon-Fri. **Admission** free. No under-14s; 14-16s only if accompanied by adults. **No credit cards. Map** p402 O6.

A gilded statue of blind (meaning impartial) justice stands atop London's most famous criminal court. The current building was completed in 1907; the site itself has hosted some of the most famous trials in

St Paul's Cathedral.

British history, including that of Oscar Wilde. Anyone is welcome to attend a trial, but bags, cameras, dictaphones, mobile phones and food are banned (and no storage facilities are provided).

▶ *A blocked-up door in St Sepulchre Without is the visible remains of a priest tunnel into the court; the Newgate Execution Bell is also there.*

★ St Paul's Cathedral

Ludgate Hill, EC4M 8AD (7236 4128, www.st pauls.co.uk). St Paul's tube. **Open** 8.30am-4pm Mon-Sat. *Galleries, crypt & ambulatory* 9.30am-4.15pm Mon-Sat. Special events may cause closure; check before visiting. *Tours of cathedral & crypt* 10.45am, 11.15am, 1.30pm, 2pm Mon-Sat. *Services* 7.30am, 8am, 12.30pm, 5pm Mon-Sat; 8am, 10.15am, 11.30am, 3.15pm, 6pm Sun. **Admission** *Cathedral, crypt & gallery* (incl tour) £14.50; £5.50-£13.50 reductions; £34.50 family; free under-6s. **Credit** AmEx, MC, V. **Map** p402 O6.

The first cathedral to St Paul was built on this site in 604, but fell to Viking marauders. Its Norman replacement, a magnificent Gothic structure with a 490ft spire (taller than any London building until the 1960s), burned in the Great Fire. The current church was commissioned in 1673 from Sir Christopher Wren as the centrepiece of London's resurgence from the ashes. Modern buildings now encroach on the cathedral from all sides, but the passing of three centuries has done nothing to diminish the appeal of London's most famous cathedral.

Start with the exterior. Over the last decade, a £40m restoration project has painstakingly removed most of the Victorian grime from the walls and the extravagant main façade looks as brilliant today as it must have when the last stone was placed in 1708. On the south side of the cathedral, an austere park has been laid out, tracing the outline of the medieval chapter house whose remains lie 4ft under it.

The vast open spaces of the interior contain memorials to national heroes such as Wellington and Lawrence of Arabia. The statue of John Donne, metaphysical poet and former Dean of St Paul's, is often overlooked, but it's the only monument to have been saved from Old St Paul's. There are also more modern works, including a Henry Moore sculpture and temporary Arts Project displays of major contemporary art. The Whispering Gallery, inside the dome, is reached by 259 steps from the main hall; the acoustics here are so good that a whisper can be bounced clearly to the other side of the dome. Steps continue up to first the Stone Gallery (119 tighter, steeper steps), with its high external balustrades, then outside to the Golden Gallery (152 steps), with its giddying views.

Before leaving St Paul's, head down to the maze-like crypt (through a door whose frame is decorated with skull and crossbones), which contains a shop and café and memorials to such dignitaries as Alexander Fleming, William Blake and Admiral Lord Nelson, whose grand tomb (purloined from Wolsey by Henry VIII but never used by him) is right beneath the centre of the dome. To one side is the small, plain tombstone of Christopher Wren himself, inscribed by his son with the epitaph, 'Reader, if you seek a monument, look around you'; at their request, Millais and Turner were buried near him.

As well as tours of the main cathedral and self-guided audio tours (which are free), you can join special tours of the Triforium, visiting the library and Wren's 'Great Model', at 11.30am and 2pm on Monday and Tuesday and at 2pm on Friday (pre-book on 7246 8357, £19.50 incl admission).

▶ *The crypt now also houses Oculus – a 270° film that tells the cathedral's history and flies you up the dome, past the Whispering Gallery, to look out over the City from the Golden Gallery.*

NORTH TO SMITHFIELD

Barbican or St Paul's tube.

North of St Paul's Cathedral on Foster Lane is **St Vedast-alias-Foster** (7606 3998; open 8am-5.30pm Mon-Fri; 11am-4pm Sat), another finely proportioned Wren church, restored after World War II using spare trim from other churches in the area. Off nearby Aldersgate Street, peaceful **Postman's Park** contains the Watts Memorial to Heroic Sacrifice: a wall of ceramic plaques, each of which commemorates a heroic but doomed act of bravery. Most date

to Victorian times – pantomime artiste Sarah Smith, for example, who received 'terrible injuries when attempting in her inflammable dress to extinguish the flames which had engulfed her companion (1863)' – but the first new plaque for 70 years was added in 2009. It was dedicated to 30-year-old Leigh Pitt, who died in 2007 while saving a child from drowning in Thamesmead.

Further west on Little Britain (named after the Duke of Brittany) is **St Bartholomew-the-Great** (*see p92*), founded along with **St Bartholomew's Hospital** in the 12th century. Popularly known as St Bart's, the hospital treated air-raid casualties throughout World War II; shrapnel damage from German bombs is still visible on the exterior walls. Scottish nationalists now come here to lay flowers at the monument to William Wallace, executed in front of the church on the orders of Edward I in 1305. Just beyond St Bart's is the handsome ironwork of Smithfield Market (*see p104*).

FREE Museum of St Bartholomew's Hospital

St Bartholomew's Hospital, North Wing, West Smithfield, EC1A 7BE (3465 5798, www.barts andthelondon.nhs.uk/museums). Barbican tube or Farringdon tube/rail. **Open** 10am-4pm Tue-Fri. **Admission** free; donations welcome. **No credit cards. Map** p400 O5.

Be glad you're living in the 21st century. Many of the displays in this small museum inside St Bart's

SIGHTS

Thou Shalt Not Steal

Doctor on the loose.

Dr Peter Turner, a 17th-century doctor at St Bartholomew's hospital, might have hoped to be remembered, but not for a caper of looting and art fraud 400 years after his death. His statue stood in the medieval St Olave church (*see p98*) near the Tower of London, where it watched quietly over the grave of Samuel Pepys, who lived round the corner. So far, so peaceful; but in 1941 the church sustained bomb damage, and the statue was looted. It was missing for nearly 70 years before its appearance on an auctioneer's bill provoked suspicion. Detective work by the Art Loss Register tracked it back through several changes of ownership to an antiques dealer who some serious form. The statue was expected to take up its rightful place by Christmas 2011. Fittingly, Turner's expression is one of slight surprise.

Hospital relate to the days before anaesthetics, when surgery and carpentry were kindred occupations. Every Friday at 2pm, visitors can take a guided tour of the museum (£5; for information, call 7837 0546) that takes in the Hogarth paintings in the Great Hall, the little church of St Bartholomew-the-Less, neighbouring St Bartholomew-the-Great and Smithfield.

St Bartholomew-the-Great

West Smithfield, EC1A 9DS (7606 5171, www. greatstbarts.com). Barbican tube or Farringdon tube/rail. **Open** 8.30am-5pm Mon-Fri (until 4pm Nov-Feb); 10.30am-4pm Sat; 8.30am-8pm Sun. **Services** 12.30pm Tue; 8.30pm Thur; 9am, 11am, 6.30pm Sun. **Admission** £4; £3 reductions; £10 family; free under-7s. **Credit** AmEx, MC, V. **Map** p400 O5.

This atmospheric medieval church was built over the remains of the 12th-century priory hospital of St Bartholomew, founded by Prior Rahere, a former courtier of Henry I. The church was chopped about during Henry VIII's reign and the interior is now firmly Elizabethan, although it also contains donated works of modern art. You may recognise the main hall from *Shakespeare in Love* or *Four Weddings and a Funeral*.

▶ *If you need refreshment, the church has a bar-café in the 15th-century cloister, serving coffee, monastery beers and home-made weekday lunches.*

NORTH OF LONDON WALL

Barbican tube or Moorgate tube/rail.

From St Bart's, the road known as London Wall runs east to Bishopsgate, following the approximate route of the old Roman walls. Tower blocks have sprung up here like daisies, but the odd lump of weathered stonework can still be seen poking up between the office blocks, marking the path of the old City wall. You can patrol the remaining stretches of the wall, with panels (some barely legible) pointing out highlights on a route of two miles. The walk starts near

---

Happy Birthday, Barbican

The concrete arts palace turns 40.

Under its saw-toothed, concrete towers, the Barbican (Silk Street, EC2Y 8DS, 7638 8891, www.barbican.org.uk) is Europe's largest multiarts centre. Its angular, Brutalist architecture has attracted plenty of opprobrium since it opened in 1982 – but up close, the Barbican is a much more friendly place. The austerie architecture is softened by water features – a rectangular lake with fountains, and several square duck ponds – and there's a steamy Conservatory (open noon-4pm Sundays and bank holidays) that's full of tropical plants, exotic fish and twittering birds.

Learn to love the Barbican by taking one of the regular, 90-minute architectural tours of the complex (www.barbican.org.uk/education) – which will also help you navigate its famously confusing layout. Of course, the main reason to visit is the impressive arts programme. Highlights for the Barbican's birthday year include a Bauhaus exhibition and several projects for the London 2012 Festival (Cate Blanchett in *Gross und Klein*, Philip Glass's *Einstein on the Beach*, a season of Pina Bausch's contemporary dance and a collaboration between African singer Rokia Traoré and novelist Toni Morrison among them). Even better, there are free foyer events themed to complement the performances in the main halls.

the brilliant **Museum of London** (*see p95* **Profile**) and runs to the Tower of London.

The area north of London Wall was reduced to rubble by German bombs in World War II. In 1958, the City of London and London County Council clubbed together to buy the land for the construction of 'a genuine residential neighbourhood, with schools, shops, open spaces and amenities'. What Londoners got was the **Barbican**, a vast concrete estate of 2,000 flats that feels a bit like a university campus after the students have gone home. Casual visitors may get the eerie feeling they have been miniaturised and transported into a giant architect's model, but design enthusiasts will recognise the Barbican as a prime example of 1970s Brutalism, softened a little by time and rectangular ponds of friendly resident ducks.

The main attraction here is the Barbican arts complex, with its library, cinema, theatre and concert hall – each reviewed in the appropriate chapters – plus an art gallery (*see below*) and the **Barbican Conservatory** (open noon-5pm Sun), a huge greenhouse full of exotic plants. Sadly, pedestrian access wasn't high on the architects' list of priorities: the Barbican is a maze of blank passages and dead-end walkways. Marooned amid the towers is the only pre-war building in the vicinity: the restored 16th-century church of **St Giles Cripplegate** (7638 1997, www.stgilescripplegate.com; open 11am-4pm Mon-Fri), where Oliver Cromwell was married and John Milton buried.

North-east of the Barbican on City Road are **John Wesley's House** (*see below*) and **Bunhill Fields**, the nonconformist cemetery where William Blake, the preacher John Bunyan and novelist Daniel Defoe are buried.

Barbican Art Gallery

Barbican Centre, Silk Street, EC2Y 8DS (7638 8891, www.barbican.org.uk). Barbican tube or Moorgate tube/rail. **Open** 11am-8pm Mon, Fri-Sun; 11am-6pm Tue, Wed; 11am-10pm Thur. **Admission** varies; check website for details. **Credit** AmEx, MC, V. **Map** p400 P5.

The art gallery at the Barbican Centre on the third floor isn't quite as 'out there' as it would like you to think, but the exhibitions on design, architecture and pop culture are usually pretty diverting, as are their often attention-grabbing titles.

▶ *On the ground floor, the Curve is a long, thin gallery (yes, it's curved) that commissions free large-scale installations. They're often superb.*

FREE John Wesley's House & the Museum of Methodism

Wesley's Chapel, 49 City Road, EC1Y 1AU (7253 2262, www.wesleyschapel.org.uk). Moorgate or Old Street tube/rail. **Open** 10am-4pm Mon-Sat; after the service until 1.45pm Sun. *Tours* arrangements

on arrival; groups of 10 or more phone ahead. **Admission** free; donations welcome. **Credit** AmEx, MC, V. **Map** p401 Q4.

John Wesley (1703-91), the founder of Methodism, was a man of legendary self-discipline. You can see the minister's nightcap, preaching gown and personal experimental electric-shock machine on a tour of his austere home on City Road. The adjacent chapel has a small museum on the history of Methodism and fine memorials of dour, sideburn-sporting preachers. Downstairs (to the right) are some of the finest public toilets in London, built in 1899 with original fittings by Sir Thomas Crapper.

★ FREE Museum of London

150 London Wall, EC2Y 5HN (7001 9844, www.museumoflondon.org.uk). Barbican or St Paul's tube. **Open** 10am-6pm daily. **Admission** free; suggested donation £3. **Credit** MC, V. **Map** p400 P5. *See p95* **Profile**.

BANK & AROUND

Mansion House tube or Bank tube/DLR.

Above Bank station, seven streets come together to mark the symbolic heart of the Square Mile, ringed by some of the most important buildings in the City. Constructed from steely Portland stone, the Bank of England, the Royal Exchange and Mansion House form a stirring monument to the power of money: most decisions about the British economy are still made within this small precinct. Few places in London have quite the same sense of pomp and circumstance.

Easily the most dramatic building is the **Bank of England**, founded in 1694 to fund William III's war against the French. It's a fortress, with no accessible windows and just one public entrance (leading to the **Bank of England Museum**; *see p97*). The outer walls were designed in 1788 by Sir John Soane, whose own museum can be seen in Holborn (*see p103* **Sir John Soane's Museum**). Millions have been stolen from its depots elsewhere in London, but the bank itself has never been robbed. Today, it's responsible for printing the nation's banknotes and setting the base interest rate. On the south side of the junction is the Lord Mayor

SIGHTS

Clockmakers' Museum. See p97.

of London's official residence, **Mansion House** (7626 2500, www.cityoflondon.gov.uk, group visits by written application to Diary Office, Mansion House, Walbrook, EC4N 8BH, or by phone), an imposing neoclassical building constructed by George Dance in 1753. It's the only private residence in the country to have its own court and prison cells for unruly guests. Just behind Mansion House is the superbly elegant church of **St Stephen Walbrook** (7626 9000, www.ststephenwalbrook.net; open 10am-4pm Mon-Fri), built by Wren in 1672. Its gleaming domed, coffered ceiling was borrowed from Wren's original design for St Paul's; other features include an incongruous modernist altar, sculpted by Sir Henry Moore and cruelly dubbed 'the camembert'. The Samaritans were founded here in the 1950s.

To the east of Mansion House is the **Royal Exchange**. It's the Parthenon-like former home of the London Stock Exchange, founded back in 1565 to facilitate the newly invented trade in stocks and shares with Antwerp. In 1972, the exchange shifted to offices on Threadneedle Street, thence to Paternoster Square in 2004; today, the Royal Exchange houses a posh champagne bar and some expensive fashion and gift shops. Flanking the Royal Exchange are statues of James Henry Greathead, who invented the machine that cut the tunnels for the London Underground, and Paul Reuter, who founded the Reuters news agency here in 1851.

The period grandeur is undermined by the monstrosity on the west side of the square, **No.1 Poultry**. The name fits: it's a turkey. A short walk down Queen Victoria Street will lead you to the eroded foundations of the **Temple of Mithras**, built by Roman soldiers in AD 240-50. Beliefs from the cult of Mithras were incorporated into Christianity when Rome abandoned paganism in the fourth century, but what remains of the site is rather unimpressive. Further south, on Cannon Street, you can see the **London Stone**. Depending who you talk to, it marks the Roman's measuring point for distances across Britain, it's a druidic altar or it's just a lump of rock. Whichever way, it's a small thing, easily missed and preserved behind a grille in the wall. Nearby Cannon Street station is being refurbished beneath a new eight-storey office, Cannon Place, due for completion this year.

Nearby on College Hill is the late Wren church of **St Michael Paternoster Royal** (7248 5202; open 9am-5pm Mon-Fri), the final resting place of Richard 'Dick' Whittington. Later transformed into a rags-to-riches pantomime hero, the real Dick Whittington was a wealthy merchant who was elected Lord Mayor of London four times between 1397 and 1420. The role of Dick Whittington's cat is less

Profile Museum of London

The story of London's past, gloriously told.

When a museum opening is attended not just by Mayor Boris Johnson, who sometimes seems happy to open anything at all if he's asked nicely enough, but by Sir Michael Caine (born in Rotherhithe) and Barbara Windsor, MBE (Shoreditch), you know it's somewhere special. And the **Museum of London** (*see p93*) is certainly that.

A five-year, £20 million refurbishment came to completion in 2010 with the unveiling of a thrilling lower-ground-floor gallery that covers the city from 1666 to the present day. The new space features everything from an unexploded World War II bomb, suspended in a room where the understated and very moving testimony of ordinary Blitz survivors is screened, to clothes by the late Alexander McQueen.

The museum's biggest obstacle has always been its location: the entrance is two floors above street level, hidden behind a grim wall. To solve this, a new space was created on the ground floor, allowing one key exhibit – the Lord Mayor's gold coach – to be seen from the outside. The architects Wilkinson Eyre also managed to increase gallery space by a quarter,

enabling the museum to focus on the city's relationship with the rest of the world and how it was changed by trade, war and empire. There are displays and brilliant interactives on poverty (they've reconstructed an actual debtor's cell, complete with graffiti), finance, shopping and 20th-century fashion, including a recreated Georgian pleasure garden, with mannequins that sport Philip Treacy masks and hats. Some displays are grand flourishes – the suspended installation that chatters London-related web trivia in the Sackler Hall, a printing press gushing changing newsheets – but others ingeniously solve problems: games to engage the kids, glass cases in the floors to maximise display space.

Upstairs, the chronological displays begin with 'London Before London', where artefacts include flint axes from 300,000 BC, found near Piccadilly, and the bones of an aurochs. 'Roman London' includes an impressive reconstructed dining room complete with mosaic floor. Windows overlook a sizeable fragment of the City wall, whose Roman foundations have clearly been built upon many times over the centuries. Sound effects and audio-visual displays illustrate the medieval, Elizabethan and Jacobean city, with particular focus on the plague and the Great Fire.

TWO TO SEE
The Museum of London has issued two excellent free apps, Streetmuseum and Streetmuseum Londinium. They offer images and information about historic sites near your current location.

SIGHTS

Guildhall.

clear – many now believe that 'cat' was actually slang for a ship – but an excavation to find Whittington's tomb in 1949 did uncover a mummified medieval moggy. The happy pair are shown in the stained-glass windows.

Returning to Bank, stroll north along Prince's Street, beside the Bank of England's blind wall. Look right along Lothbury to find **St Margaret Lothbury** (7726 4878, www. stml.org.uk; open 7am-5.15pm Mon-Fri). The grand screen dividing the choir from the nave was designed by Wren himself; other works here by his favourite woodcarver, Grinling Gibbons, were recovered from various churches damaged in World War II. Lothbury also features a beautiful neo-Venetian building, now apartments, built by 19th-century architect Augustus Pugin, who worked with Charles Barry on the Houses of Parliament.

South-east of Bank on Lombard Street is Hawksmoor's striking, twin-spired church of **St Mary Woolnoth** (7626 9701; open 9.30am-4.30pm Mon-Fri), squeezed in between what were 17th-century banking houses. Only their gilded signboards now remain, a hanging heritage artfully maintained by the City's planners. The gilded grasshopper at 68 Lombard Street is the heraldic emblem of Sir Thomas Gresham, who founded the Royal Exchange and **Gresham College**.

Further east on Lombard Street is Wren's **St Edmund the King** (7621 1391, www.

spiritualitycentre.org; open 10am-6pm Mon-Fri), which now houses a centre for modern spirituality. Other significant churches in the area include Wren's handsome red-brick **St Mary Abchurch**, off Abchurch Lane, and **St Clement**, on Clement's Lane, immortalised in the nursery rhyme 'Oranges and Lemons'. Over on Cornhill are two more Wren churches: **St Peter-upon-Cornhill**, mentioned by Dickens in *Our Mutual Friend*, and **St Michael Cornhill**, which contains a bizarre statue of a pelican feeding its young with pieces of its own body – a medieval symbol for the Eucharist, it was sculpted by someone who had plainly never seen a pelican.

North-west of the Bank of England is the **Guildhall**, the City of London headquarters. 'Guildhall' can either describe the original banqueting hall or the cluster of buildings around it, of which the **Guildhall Art Gallery**, the **Clockmakers' Museum & Library** (for all three, *see p98*) and the church of **St Lawrence Jewry** (7600 9478, www.stlawrencejewry.org.uk; open 8am-5pm Mon-Fri), opposite the hall, are also open to the public. St Lawrence is another restored Wren, with an impressive gilt ceiling. Within, you can hear the renowned Klais organ at lunchtime organ recitals (usually from 1pm Tue).

Glance north along Wood Street to see the isolated tower of **St Alban**, built by Wren in 1685 but ruined in World War II and now an eccentric private home. At the end of the street is **St Anne & St Agnes** (7606 4986; open 10.30am-5pm Mon-Fri, Sun), laid out in the form of a Greek cross. Recitals take place here on weekday lunchtimes.

FREE Bank of England Museum

Entrance on Bartholomew Lane, EC2R 8AH (7601 5545, www.bankofengland.co.uk/museum). Bank tube/DLR. **Open** 10am-5pm Mon-Fri. **Admission** free. **No credit cards.** **Map** p403 Q6.
Housed inside the former Stock Offices of the Bank of England, this engaging and surprisingly lively museum explores the history of the national bank. As well as ancient coins and original artwork for British banknotes, the museum offers a rare chance to lift nearly 30lbs of gold bar (you reach into a secure box, closely monitored by CCTV). One exhibit looks at the life of Kenneth Grahame, author of *The Wind in the Willows* and a long-term employee of the bank. Child-friendly temporary exhibitions take place in the museum lobby.

FREE Clockmakers' Museum & Guildhall Library

Aldermanbury, EC2V 7HH (Guildhall Library 7332 1868, www.clockmakers.org). St Paul's tube or Bank tube/DLR. **Open** 9.30am-4.45pm Mon-Sat. **Admission** free. **No credit cards.** **Map** p402 P6.
Hundreds of clocks and watches are displayed in this single-room museum, from the egg-sized Elizabethan pocket watches to marine chronometers via a 'fuse for a nuclear device'. Highlights include Marine Chronometer H5, built by John Harrison (1693-1776) to solve the problem of longitude, and the plain Smith's Imperial wristwatch worn by Sir Edmund Hillary on the first (Rolex-sponsored) ascent of Everest. Just down the corridor, the library has books, manuscripts and prints relating to the history of London – original historic works can be requested for browsing (bring ID), but much of the archive has been moved to the London Metropolitan Archives. *Photo p94.*

FREE Guildhall

Gresham Street, EC2P 2EJ (7606 3030, www. guildhall.cityoflondon.gov.uk). St Paul's tube or Bank tube/DLR. **Open** *May-Sept* 10am-5pm daily.

INSIDE TRACK
THE WRITE STUFF

In the shadow of the Gherkin, **St Andrew Undershaft** has a statue of John Stow, who wrote London's first guidebook, the *Survey of London* in 1598. In a ceremony every 5 April, the Lord Mayor places a new quill in the statue's hand; the old quill is given to the child deemed to have written the best essay on London.

Oct-Apr 10am-5pm Mon-Sat. Closes for functions; phone ahead. **Admission** free. **No credit cards.** **Map** p402 P6.
The City of London and its progenitors have been holding grand ceremonial dinners in this hall for eight centuries. Memorials to national heroes line the walls, shields of the 100 livery companies grace the ceiling, and every Lord Mayor since 1189 gets a namecheck on the windows. Many famous trials have taken place here, including the treason trial of 16-year-old Lady Jane Grey, 'the nine days' queen', in 1553. Above the entrance to the Guildhall are statues of Gog and Magog. Born of the union of demons and exiled Roman princesses, these two mythical giants are said to protect the City of London. The current statues replaced 18th-century forebears that were destroyed during the Blitz.

★ Guildhall Art Gallery

Guildhall Yard, off Gresham Street, EC2P 2EJ (7332 3700, www.guildhall-art-gallery.org.uk). St Paul's tube or Bank tube/DLR. **Open** 10am-5pm Mon-Sat; noon-4pm Sun. **Admission** free. *Temporary exhibitions* £5; £3 reductions; free under-16s. **Credit** MC, V. **Map** p402 P6.
The City of London's gallery contains numerous dull or unimpressive portraits of royalty and long-gone mayors, but also some wonderful surprises, including a brilliant Constable, some superbly camp Pre-Raphaelite works (Clytemnestra looks mighty riled) and a number of absorbing paintings of London, from moving depictions of war and melancholy working streets to the likes of the grandiloquent (and never-enacted) George Dance plan for a new London Bridge. The collection's centrepiece is the massive *Siege of Gibraltar* by John Copley, which spans two entire storeys of the purpose-built gallery. A sub-basement contains the scant remains of London's 6,000-seater Roman amphitheatre, built around AD 70; *Tron*-like figures and crowd sound effects give a quaint inkling of scale.

MONUMENT & THE TOWER OF LONDON

Aldgate or Monument tube, Liverpool Street tube/rail, Tower Hill tube or Tower Gateway DLR.

From Bank, King William Street runs south-east towards London Bridge, passing the small square containing the **Monument** (*see p99*). South on Lower Thames Street is the moody-looking church of **St Magnus the Martyr** (*see p100*); nearby are several relics from the days when this area was a busy port, including the old Customs House and **Billingsgate Market**, London's main fish market until 1982 (when it was relocated to east London).
North of the Monument along Gracechurch Street is the atmospheric **Leadenhall Market**,

SIGHTS

SIGHTS

INSIDE TRACK
LONDON RIVER PARK

The London 2012 Games will bring a host of daring temporary initiatives to the city – not least the London River Park. This 39-foot wide, half-mile-long river pontoon is expected to sit below Blackfriars Bridge, providing a continuous walkway north of the river to rival the South Bank promenade. Along it, eight pavilions devoted to culture, sport and other aspects of city life are planned.

Even without the River Park, Blackfriars Bridge is worth a look. It not only has splendid red-and-white painted Victorian ironwork, but offers a great vantage point on London's first cross-river train station, due to complete in time for the Games. The new Blackfriars station has incorporated environmentally friendly features into its design. It makes use of pillars left over from an 1864 rail bridge, and its roof is home to the capital's largest array of photovoltaic solar panels, which will supply half of its energy.

constructed in 1881 by Horace Jones (who also built the market at Smithfield; *see p104*). The vaulted roof was restored to its original Victorian finery in 1991 and City workers come here in droves to lunch at the pubs, cafés and restaurants, including the historic Lamb Tavern. Fantasy fans may recognise the market as Diagon Alley in *Harry Potter & the Philosopher's Stone*.

Behind the market is Lord Rogers's high-tech **Lloyd's of London** building, constructed in 1986, with all its ducts, vents, stairwells and lift shafts on the outside, like an oil rig dumped in the heart of the City. The original Lloyd's Register of Shipping, decorated with evocative bas-reliefs of sea monsters and nautical scenes, is on Fenchurch Street. South on Eastcheap (derived from the Old English 'ceap' meaning 'barter') is Wren's **St Margaret Pattens**, with an original 17th-century interior.

Several of the City's tallest buildings are nearby. To the north, the ugly and rather dated **Tower 42** (25 Old Broad Street) was the tallest building in Britain until the construction of 1 Canada Square in Docklands in 1990. And topped out at 755 feet (including a radio mast), **Heron Tower** (110 Bishopsgate, www. herontower.com) became the City's tallest building at the end of 2009. Its 46 storeys are to include a restaurant and bar (due to open in early 2012), a bit under 600 feet up. Also on

Bishopsgate, behind Tower 42, is **Gibson Hall**, ostentatious former offices of the National Provincial Bank of England.

A block south, St Mary Axe is an insignificant street named after a vanished church that is said to have contained an axe used by Attila the Hun to behead English virgins. It is now known for Lord Foster's **30 St Mary Axe**, arguably London's finest modern building. The building is known as 'the Gherkin' (and, occasionally, more suggestive nicknames) for reasons that are obvious. On curved stone benches either side of 30 St Mary Axe are inscribed the 20 lines of Scottish poet Ian Hamilton Finlay's 'Arcadian Dream Garden', a curious counterpart to Lord Foster's popular building. Nearby are two more medieval churches that survived the Great Fire: **St Helen's Bishopsgate** (*see p100*) and **St Andrew Undershaft** (*see p97* **Inside Track**).

The north end of St Mary Axe intersects with two interesting streets. The more northerly, Houndsditch, is where Londoners threw dead dogs and other rubbish in medieval times – the ditch ran outside the London Wall (*see p92*), dividing the City from the East End. The southerly one is Bevis Marks, home to the superbly preserved **Bevis Marks Synagogue** (7626 1274; open 10.30am-2pm Mon, Wed, Thur; 10.30am-1pm Tue, Fri; 10.30am-12.30pm Sun), founded in 1701 by Sephardic Jews fleeing the Spanish Inquisition. Services are still held in Portuguese as well as Hebrew. On neighbouring Heneage Lane is the classy kosher **Bevis Marks Restaurant** (no.4, 7283 2220, www.bevismarkstherestaurant.com).

South along Bevis Marks are **St Botolph's-without-Aldgate** (*see p100*) and the tiny stone church of **St Katharine Cree** (7283 5733; open 9.30am-4pm Mon-Fri) on Leadenhall Street, one of only eight churches to survive the Great Fire. Inside is a memorial to Sir Nicholas Throckmorton, Queen Elizabeth I's ambassador to France, who was imprisoned for treason on numerous occasions, despite – or perhaps because of – his friendship with the temperamental queen. Just north of St Katharine is Mitre Square, site of the fourth Jack the Ripper murder.

Further south, towards the Tower of London, streets and alleys have evocative names: Crutched Friars, Savage Gardens, Pepys Street and the like. The famous diarist lived in nearby Seething Lane and observed the Great Fire of London from **All Hallows by the Tower** (*see p99*). Pepys is buried in the church of **St Olave** (*see p91* **Thou Shalt Not Steal**) on Hart Street, nicknamed 'St Ghastly Grim' by Dickens for the skulls at the entrance.

Marking the eastern edge of the City, the **Tower of London** (*see p101*) was the palace of the medieval kings and queens of England. Home to the Crown Jewels and the Royal Armoury, it's one of Britain's best-loved tourist attractions and, accordingly, is mobbed by visitors seven days a week. Overlooking the Tower from the north, beside the tube station, **Trinity Square Gardens** are a humbling memorial to the tens of thousands of merchant seamen killed in the two World Wars, and across the road is a small square in which London's druids celebrate each spring equinox with an elaborate ceremony. Just beyond is one of the City's finest Edwardian buildings: the former **Port of London HQ** at 10 Trinity Square, with a huge neoclassical façade and gigantic statues symbolising Commerce, Navigation, Export, Produce and Father Thames. It's now being turned into a superluxury hotel. Next door is **Trinity House**, the home of the General Lighthouse Authority, founded by Henry VIII for the upkeep of shipping beacons along the river.

At the south-east corner of the Tower is **Tower Bridge** (*see p101*), built in 1894 and still London's most distinctive bridge. Used as a navigation aid by German bombers, it escaped the firestorm of the Blitz. East across Bridge Approach is **St Katharine Docks**, the first London docks to be formally closed. The restaurants around the marina, slightly hidden behind modern office blocks, offer more dignified dining than those around the Tower.

FREE All Hallows by the Tower

Byward Street, EC3R 5BJ (7481 2928, www. ahbtt.org.uk). Tower Hill tube or Tower Gateway DLR. **Open** 9am-5pm Mon-Fri; 10am-4pm Sat, Sun. *Tours* phone for details; donation requested. *Services* 6pm Wed; 11am Sun. **Admission** free; donations appreciated. **No credit cards.** **Map** p403 R7.

Often described as London's oldest church, All Hallows is built on the foundations of a seventh-century Saxon church. Much of what survives today was reconstructed after World War II, but several Saxon details can be seen in the main hall, where the Knights Templar were tried by Edward II in 1314. The undercroft contains a museum with Roman and Saxon relics and a Crusader altar. William Penn, the founder of Pennsylvania, was baptised here in 1644.

★ Monument

Monument Street, EC3R 8AH (7626 2717, www.themonument.info). Monument tube. **Open** 9.30am-5pm daily. **Admission** £3; £1.50-£2 reductions; free under-5s. **No credit cards.** **Map** p403 Q7.

One of 17th-century London's most important landmarks, the Monument reopened in 2009 after an 18-month refurbishment – the column's magnificent Portland stone was cleaned and repaired, and the golden orb at the top restored with more than 30,000 leaves of gold. The Monument was designed by Sir Christopher Wren and his (often overlooked) associate Robert Hooke as a memorial to the Great Fire. The world's tallest free-standing stone column, it

SIGHTS

Tower Bridge. *See p101.*

Tower of London

measures 202ft from the ground to the tip of its golden flames, exactly the distance east to Farriner's bakery in Pudding Lane, where the fire is supposed to have begun on 2 September 1666. New lighting has been installed, and the cumbersome old iron bars of the viewing platform replaced with a new, lightweight mesh cage – you still have to walk the 311 steps up the internal spiral staircase to enjoy the sights, though. At least everyone who makes it to the top gets a certificate. A stone and glass pavilion at the bottom has been specially designed to reflect the gleaming orb and gilded flames from its roof.

FREE St Botolph's-without-Aldgate
Aldgate High Street, EC3N 1AB (7283 1670, www.stbotolphs.org.uk). Aldgate tube. **Open** 10am-2pm Mon, Wed; 10am-3pm Tue, Thur, Fri; 10am-12.30pm Sun. *Eucharist* 1.05pm Tue, Thur; 10.30am Sun. **Admission** free; donations appreciated. **No credit cards. Map** p403 R6.
The oldest of three churches of St Botolph in the City, this handsome monument was built at the gates of Roman London as a homage to the patron saint of travellers. The building was reconstructed by George Dance in 1744 and a beautiful ornamental ceiling was added in the 19th century by John Francis Bentley, who also created Westminster Cathedral.

FREE St Ethelburga Centre for Reconciliation & Peace
78 Bishopsgate, EC2N 4AG (7496 1610, www.stethelburgas.org). Bank tube/DLR or Liverpool Street tube/rail. **Open** 11am-3pm Fri. **Admission** free; donations appreciated. **No credit cards. Map** p403 R6.
Built around 1390, the tiny church of St Ethelburga was reduced to rubble by an IRA bomb in 1993 and

rebuilt as a centre for peace and reconciliation. Behind the chapel is a Bedouin tent where events are held to promote dialogue between the faiths (phone or check the website for details), an increasingly heated issue in modern Britain. Lunchtime meditation classes are held here on Thursdays.

FREE St Helen's Bishopsgate
Great St Helen's, off Bishopsgate, EC3A 6AT (7283 2231, www.st-helens.org.uk). Liverpool Street tube/rail or Bank tube/DLR. **Open** 9.30am-12.30pm Mon-Fri, afternoons by appointment only. *Services* 10.30am, 4pm, 6pm Sun. *Lunchtime meetings* 1-2pm Tue, Thur. **Admission** free. **No credit cards. Map** p403 R6.
Founded in 1210, St Helen's Bishopsgate is actually two churches knocked into one, which explains its unusual shape. The church survived the Great Fire and the Blitz, but was partly wrecked by IRA bombs in 1992 and 1993. The hugely impressive 16th- and 17th-century memorials inside include the grave of Thomas Gresham, founder of the Royal Exchange (*see p95*).

FREE St Magnus the Martyr
Lower Thames Street, EC3R 6DN (7626 4481, www.stmagnusmartyr.org.uk). Monument tube. **Open** 10am-4pm Tue-Fri; 10am-1pm Sun. *Mass* 12.30pm Tue, Thur, Fri; 11am Sun. **Admission** free; donations appreciated. **No credit cards. Map** p403 Q7.
Downhill from the Monument, this looming Wren church marked the entrance to the original London Bridge. A cute scale model of the old bridge is displayed inside the church, along with a statue of axe-wielding St Magnus, the 12th-century Earl of Orkney. The church is mentioned at one of the cli-

maxes of TS Eliot's *The Waste Land*: 'Where the walls/Of Magnus Martyr hold/Inexplicable splendour of Ionian white and gold.'

► *St Mary Woolnoth (see p96) is another star of* The Waste Land*: keeping 'the hours/With a dead sound on the final stroke of nine'.*

Tower Bridge Exhibition

Tower Bridge, SE1 2UP (7403 3761, www.tower bridge.org.uk). Tower Hill tube or Tower Gateway DLR. **Open** *Apr-Sept* 10am-6.30pm daily. *Oct-Mar* 9.30am-6pm daily. **Admission** £8; £3.40-£5.60 reductions; £12.50-£18 family; free under-5s. **Credit** AmEx, MC, V. **Map** p403 R8.

Opened in 1894, this is the 'London Bridge' that wasn't sold to America. Originally powered by steam, the drawbridge is now opened by electric rams when big ships need to venture upstream (check when the bridge is next due to be raised on the bridge's website or follow the feed on Twitter). The bridge is looking particularly resplendent after a three-year restoration, completed in 2011. An entertaining exhibition on its history is displayed in the old steamrooms and the west walkway, which provides a superb crow's-nest view along the Thames. *Photo p99.*

★ Tower of London

Tower Hill, EC3N 4AB (0844 482 7777, www. hrp.org.uk). Tower Hill tube or Tower Gateway DLR. **Open** *Mar-Oct* 10am-5.30pm Mon, Sun; 9am-5.30pm Tue-Sat. *Nov-Feb* 10am-4.30pm Mon, Sun; 9am-4.30pm Tue-Sat. **Admission** £18; £9.50-£15.50; £50 family; free under-5s. **Credit** AmEx, MC, V. **Map** p403 R8.

If you haven't been to the Tower of London before, go now. Despite the exhausting crowds and long climbs up inaccessible stairways, this is one of Britain's finest historical attractions. Who would not be fascinated by a close-up look at the crown of Queen Victoria or the armour (and prodigious codpiece) of King Henry VIII? The buildings of the Tower span 900 years of history and the bastions and battlements house a series of interactive displays on the lives of British monarchs, and the often excruciatingly painful deaths of traitors. There's easily enough to do here to fill a whole day, and it's worth joining one of the highly recommended and entertaining free tours led by the Yeoman Warders (or Beefeaters).

Make the Crown Jewels your first stop, and as early in the day as you possibly can: if you wait until you've pottered around a few other things the queues are usually immense. Beyond satisfyingly solid vault doors, you get to glide along a set of travelators (each branded with the Queen's official 'EIIR' badge) past such treasures of state as the Monarch's Sceptre, mounted with the Cullinan I diamond, and the Imperial State Crown, which is worn by the Queen each year for the opening of Parliament.

The other big draw to the tower is the Royal Armoury in the central White Tower, with its swords, armour, poleaxes, halberds, morning stars (spiky maces) and other gruesome tools for separating human beings from their body parts. Kids are entertained by swordsmanship games, coin-minting activities and a child-sized longbow. The garderobes (medieval toilets) also seem to appeal.

Back outside, Tower Green – where executions of prisoners of noble birth were carried out, continuing until 1941 – is marked by a poem and a stiff glass pillow, sculpted by poet and artist Brian Catling. Overlooking the green, Beauchamp Tower, dating to 1280, has an upper floor full of intriguing graffiti by the prisoners that were held here (including Anne Boleyn, Rudolf Hess and the Krays).

Towards the entrance, the 13th-century Bloody Tower is another must-see that gets overwhelmed by numbers later in the day. The ground floor is a reconstruction of Sir Walter Raleigh's study, the upper floor details the fate of the Princes in the Tower. In the riverside wall is the unexpectedly beautiful Medieval Palace, with its reconstructed bedroom and throne room, and spectacularly complex stained glass in the private chapel. The whole palace is deliciously cool if you've been struggling round on a hot summer's day.

► *For the new exhibition Strange Beasts, see below* **Animal Passion**.

Animal Passion

The Tower's menagerie.

What animal is most associated with the Tower of London (*see left*)? If you think it's the raven, then you should take yourself to the new Royal Beasts exhibition for a royal re-education. The monarch kept an extravagant collection of animals at the Tower for over 600 years (until the early 19th-century), to use as high-status gifts and for the gawking amusement of the royal household and its guests. The exhibition traces their sad story, from the first inhabitants – lions and elephants from Europe and North Africa – to exotic captives from the New World, as it opened up. It shows you, though wall panels and the latest electronic technology, how the animals lived, what they smelled like and what happened when they escaped. You'll learn about the polar bear that fished in the Thames and the leopard that stole umbrellas, along with the history of the Brick Tower, newly opened to the public, in which the exhibition is situated. There aren't any actual animals, of course, but the Tower grounds contain dynamic life-size sculptures of some of the Tower's royal beasts.

SIGHTS

Holborn & Clerkenwell

Vestiges of the medieval past abound alongside present-day pleasures.

Along Fleet Street and Holborn, the West End dives into the City of London and heads for St Paul's Cathedral. The newspapers that once called **Fleet Street** home have long since jumped ship for Docklands and Kensington, but some of their grand old offices remain, flanked by the collegiate quiet of the barristers' ancient **Inns of Court**.

Meanwhile, across Farringdon Road, the boom years have transmogrified **Clerkenwell** from an earnest and shabby suburb of Grub Street into a playground for afterwork City boys, bambi-eyed clubbers and design-led media businesses. And in a typically startling juxtaposition, the butchers of **Smithfield Market** still ply their bleeding trade right in the thick of the party.

Map p397 & p400	Hotels pp191-192
Pubs & bars pp242-243	Restaurants & cafés p218-219

HOLBORN

Holborn tube.

A sharp left turn out of Holborn tube and then another left again leads into the unexpectedly lovely **Lincoln's Inn Fields**. Surely London's largest square (indeed, it's more of a park), it's blessed with gnarled oaks casting dappled shade over a tired bandstand. On the south side of the square, the neoclassical façade of the Royal College of Surgeons hides the **Hunterian Museum**; facing it from the north is the magical **Sir John Soane's Museum** (for both, *see p103*).

East of the square lies **Lincoln's Inn** (7405 1393, www.lincolnsinn.org.uk), one of the city's four Inns of Court. Its grounds are open to the public, ogling an odd mix of Gothic, Tudor and Palladian buildings. On nearby Portsmouth Street lies the **Old Curiosity Shop** (nos.13-14, WC2A 2ES, 7405 9891, www.curiosityuk.com; *photo p104*), its timbers apparently known to Charles Dickens, but now selling Daita Kimura's decidedly modern shoes. Nearby, Gray's Inn

Road runs north beside the second Inn of Court. The sculpted gardens at **Gray's Inn** (7458 7800, www.graysinn.org.uk), dating to 1606, are open on weekdays, noon-2.30pm.

Opened in 1876 on Chancery Lane as a series of strongrooms in which the upper classes could secure their valuables, the **London Silver Vaults** (7242 3844, www.thesilvervaults.com) are now a hive of dealers buying, selling and repairing silverware. There are also glittering window displays on **Hatton Gardens**, the jewellery and diamond centre of London. It's a short walk but a million miles from the Cockney fruit stalls and sock merchants of the market on **Leather Lane** (10am-2.30pm Mon-Fri).

Further on is **Ely Place**, its postcode absent from the street sign as a result of it technically falling under the jurisdiction of Cambridgeshire. The church garden of ancient **St Etheldreda** (*see p103*) produced strawberries so delicious that they made the pages of Shakespeare's *Richard III*; a celebratory Strawberrie Fayre is still held on the street each June. The 16th-century **Ye Old Mitre** (1 Ely Court, EC1N 6SJ, 7405 4751) remains an atmospheric pub.

FREE Hunterian Museum

*Royal College of Surgeons, 35-43 Lincoln's Inn
Fields, WC2A 3PE (7869 6560, www.rcseng.
ac.uk/museums). Holborn tube.* **Open** 10am-5pm
Tue-Sat. **Admission** free. **No credit cards.**
Map p397 M6.

The collection of medical specimens once held by
John Hunter (1728-93), physician to King George III,
can be viewed in this museum. The sparkling glass
cabinets of the main room offset the goriness of the
exhibits, which include Charles Babbage's brain and
Winston Churchill's dentures, as well as shelf after
shelf of diligently classified pickled body parts. The
upper floor holds a brutal account of surgical techniques. Notably interesting kids' activities have
included demonstrations by a 'barber surgeon'.

FREE St Etheldreda

*14 Ely Place, EC1N 6RY (7405 1061, www.
stetheldreda.com). Chancery Lane tube.* **Open**
8am-5pm Mon-Sat; 8am-12.30pm Sun. **Admission**
free; donations appreciated. **No credit cards.**
Map p400 N5.

Dedicated to the saintly seventh-century Queen of
Northumbria, this is Britain's oldest Catholic church
and London's only surviving example of 13th-cen-
tury Gothic architecture; it was saved from the Great
Fire by a change in the wind. The crypt is darkly
atmospheric, untouched by traffic noise, and the
stained glass (actually from the 1960s) is stunning.

Lincoln's Inn Fields.

★ FREE Sir John Soane's Museum

*13 Lincoln's Inn Fields, WC2A 3BP (7405 2107,
www.soane.org). Holborn tube.* **Open** 10am-5pm
Tue-Sat; 10am-5pm, 6-9pm 1st Tue of mth.
Tours 11am Sat. **Admission** free; donations
appreciated. *Tours* £5; free reductions. **Credit**
(shop) MC, V. **Map** p397 M5.

When he wasn't designing notable buildings, among
them the original Bank of England, Sir John Soane
(1753-1837) obsessively collected art, furniture and
architectural ornamentation. In the 19th century, he
turned his house into a museum to which, he said,
'amateurs and students' should have access. The
result is this perfectly amazing place.

Much of the museum's appeal derives from the
domestic setting. The modest rooms were modified
by Soane with ingenious devices to channel and
direct daylight, and to expand space, including walls
that open out like cabinets to display some of his
many paintings (Canaletto, Turner, Hogarth). The
Breakfast Room has a beautiful domed ceiling, inset
with convex mirrors. The extraordinary Monument
Court contains a sarcophagus of alabaster, so fine
that it's almost translucent, that was carved for the
pharaoh Seti I (1291-78 BC) and discovered in his
tomb in Egypt's Valley of the Kings. There are also
numerous examples of Soane's eccentricity, not least
the cell for his imaginary monk 'Padre Giovanni'.

The museum has launched an appeal that will
open Soane's top-floor 'private apartments', recreated from contemporary watercolours, with Phase I
due to be completed by 2012.

CLERKENWELL & FARRINGDON

Farringdon tube/rail.

Few places encapsulate London's capacity for
reinvention quite like Clerkenwell, an erstwhile
religious centre that takes its name from the
parish clerks who once performed Biblical
mystery plays on its streets. The most lasting
holy legacy is that of the 11th-century knights
of the **Order of St John**; the remains of their

SIGHTS

Old Curiosity Shop. *See p102.*

priory can still be seen at St John's Gate, a crenellated gatehouse that dates from 1504 and is home to the **Museum & Library of the Order of St John** (*see right*).

By the 17th century, this was a fashionable locale, but the Industrial Revolution soon buried it under warehouses and factories. Printing houses were established, and the district gained a reputation as a safe haven for radicals, from 16th-century Lollards to 19th-century Chartists. In 1903, Lenin is believed to have met Stalin for a drink in what is now the **Crown Tavern** (43 Clerkenwell Green, 7253 4973), one year after moving the publication of *Iskra* to neighbouring 37A (now the **Marx Memorial Library**; 7253 1485, www.marx-memorial-library.org).

Industrial dereliction and decay were the theme until property development in the 1980s and '90s turned Clerkenwell into a desirable area. The process was aided by a slew of artfully distressed gastropubs (following the lead of the **Eagle**; *see p219*), and the food stalls, fashion boutiques, restaurants and bars along the colourful strip of **Exmouth Market**.

INSIDE TRACK
TOP DECK TREAT

Part of the Cultural Olympiad, the Bus Tops project (http://bus-tops.com) will be positioning 33 digital art installations – one for each of the 32 London boroughs, plus the City of London – on the roofs of bus shelters across the city by January 2012. They'll continue to brighten commuters' journeys until the end of the Paralympic Games, on 9 September.

FREE Islington Museum

245 St John Street, Finsbury, EC1V 4NB (7527 3235, www.islington.gov.uk). Angel tube. **Open** 10am-5pm Mon, Tue, Thur-Sat. **Admission** free. **No credit cards. Map** p400 O3.

The Islington Museum covers local history and the political and ethical credentials of the borough, exemplified by local residents such as reformist preacher John Wesley, playwright Joe Orton and eminent feminist Mary Wollstonecraft.

FREE Museum of the Order of St John

St John's Gate, St John's Lane, Clerkenwell, EC1M 4DA (7324 4005, www.sja.org.uk/museum). Farringdon tube/rail. **Open** 10am-5pm Mon-Sat. *Tours* 11am, 2.30pm Tue, Fri, Sat. **Admission** free. *Tours* free. Suggested donation £5; £4 reductions. **Credit** MC, V. **Map** p400 O4.

This museum celebrates the Order of St John. Now best known for its ambulance service, the Order's roots lie in the Christian medical practices developed during the Crusades of the 11th to 13th centuries. Artefacts related to the Order of Hospitaller Knights, from Jerusalem, Malta and the Ottoman Empire, are displayed; there's a separate collection relating to the evolution of the modern ambulance service. A major refurbishment has reorganised the galleries in the Tudor gatehouse and, across St John's Square, opened the Priory Church, its garden and its 12th-century crypt to the public for the first time. A 'pavement museum' helps visitors visualise the contours of the lost medieval priory.

SMITHFIELD

Farringdon tube/rail.

Smithfield Market provides a colourful, not to say visceral, link to an age when the quality of British beef was a symbol of national virility and good humour. Meat has been traded here for a millennium or more; the current market, designed by Horace Jones, opened in 1868, though it's since been altered (in part out of necessity, thanks to World War II bombs). Meat trucks start arriving around 11pm; early risers will find traders setting up stalls at first light.

The meat traders are joined at night these days by revellers settling in for dinner at vast **Smiths of Smithfield** (67-77 Charterhouse Street, EC1M 6HJ, 7251 7950, www.smithsof smithfield.co.uk) or nearby **St John** (*see p219*), tucking into a glass or two at **Vinoteca** (*see p243*) or taking to the dancefloor at superclub **Fabric** (*see p331*). For a little peace and quiet, stroll by the **Charterhouse**. This Carthusian monastery, founded in 1370, is now Anglican almshouses that retain the original 14th-century chapel and a 17th-century library. It's right beside the **Malmaison** (*see p191*).

SIGHTS

Bloomsbury & King's Cross

Culture – global, intellectual and literary bohemian – is celebrated here.

London's neighbourhoods north of Oxford Street are full of bookishness and bohemianism. **Bloomsbury** is best known as the home of the **British Museum** (*see p106*), but the presence of University College London (UCL) also helps lend the area a youthful, if studious, tone. The unofficial heart of the area is the redeveloped **Brunswick Centre** and the buzzing network of surrounding streets.

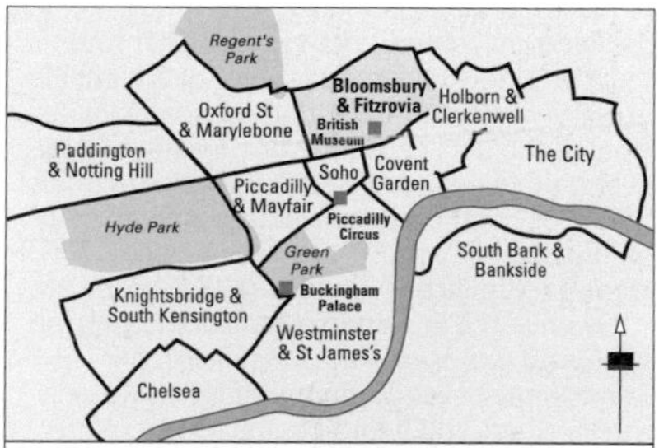

Next door to the west, **Fitzrovia** is a favourite source of stories for London nostalgists, but those days of postwar spivs and never-knowingly-sober poets have almost vanished beneath a tide of new media offices. Centred on Charlotte Street, they at least keep the pubs lively and the restaurants high-quality.

To the north of Bloomsbury, the legendarily seedy **King's Cross** may be going the way of raffish Fitzrovia. The arrival of the **British Library** (*see p109*) and the rebirth of **St Pancras Station** (*see p110*) as an international rail hub are leading the redevelopment of a former blackspot into a destination and des res.

| Map pp396-397 & p416 | Restaurants & cafés pp219-220 |
| Hotels pp192-195 | Pubs & bars p243 |

SIGHTS

BLOOMSBURY

Euston Square, Holborn, Russell Square or Tottenham Court Road tube.

Bloomsbury's florid name is, prosaically, taken from 'Blemondisberi' – the manor ('bury') of William Blemond, who acquired the area in the 13th century. It remained rural until the 1660s, when the fourth Earl of Southampton built Bloomsbury Square around his house. The Southamptons intermarried with the Russells, the Dukes of Bedford; together, they developed the area as one of London's first planned suburbs.

Over the next two centuries, the group built a series of grand squares. **Bedford Square** (1775-80) is London's only complete Georgian square (regrettably, its garden is closed to the public); huge **Russell Square** has been restored as a public park with a popular café.

To the east, the cantilevered postwar **Brunswick Centre** is full of shops, flats, restaurants and a cinema. The nearby streets, particularly **Marchmont Street**, are some of the most characterful in the West End.

Bloomsbury's charm is the sum of its parts, best experienced on a meander through its bookshops (many on **Great Russell Street**) and pubs. The blue plaques are a *Who's Who* of literary modernists (*see p107* **Walk**), with a few interlopers from more distant history: Edgar Allan Poe (83 Southampton Row), Anthony Trollope (6 Store Street) and, of course, Dickens (48 Doughty Street; *see p108* **Charles Dickens Museum**).

On Bloomsbury's western border, Malet Street, Gordon Street and Gower Street are dominated by the **University of London**. The most notable building is Gower Street's University College, founded in 1826. Inside is

Time Out London **105**

INSIDE TRACK
ALL THE WORLD'S A STAGE

From 19 July to 25 November, the British Museum is hosting Shakespeare: Staging the World, as part of the London 2012 Festival's Shakespeare celebrations (see also p345). The exhibition sets the great playwright in the context of his age and explores his universal appeal.

the 'autoicon' of utilitarian philosopher and founder of the university Jeremy Bentham: his preserved cadaver, fully clothed, sits in a glass-fronted cabinet. The university's main library is housed in towering **Senate House** on Malet Street, one of the city's most imposing examples of monumental art deco. It was the model for Orwell's Ministry of Truth in *1984*.

South of the university sprawls the **British Museum** (*see below*), the must-see of all London must-sees. Running off Great Russell Street, where you'll find the museum's main entrance, are three attractive parallel streets (Coptic, Museum and Bury) and, nearby, the **Cartoon Museum** (*see right*); also close by, Bloomsbury Way is home to Hawksmoor's restored **St George's Bloomsbury** (*see p109*). Across from here, **Sicilian Avenue** is a fancy-pants, Italianate, pedestrian precinct of colonnaded shops.

North-east of the British Museum, **Lamb's Conduit Street** is a convivial neighbourhood lined with interesting shops. At the top of the street is **Coram's Fields** (*see p297*), a delightful children's park on the grounds of the former Thomas Coram's Foundling Hospital. Coram's legacy is commemorated in the beautiful **Foundling Museum** (*see p108*).

★ FREE British Museum

Great Russell Street, WC1B 3DG (7323 8299, www.britishmuseum.org). Russell Square or Tottenham Court Road tube. **Open** *Galleries* 10am-5.30pm Mon-Wed, Sat, Sun; 10am-8.30pm Thur, Fri. *Great Court* 9am-6pm Mon-Wed, Sun; 9am-11pm Thur-Sat. *Multimedia guides* 10am-4.30pm Mon-Wed, Sat, Sun; 10am-7.30pm Thur, Fri. *Eye Opener tours* (40mins) phone for details. **Admission** free; donations appreciated. *Temporary exhibitions* prices vary. *Multimedia guides* £4.50; £3-£4 reductions. *Eye Opener tours* free. **Credit** (shop) AmEx, DC, MC, V. **Map** p397 K5.
Officially the country's most popular tourist attraction, the British Museum opened to the public in 1759 in Montagu House, which then occupied this site. The current building is a neoclassical marvel built in 1847 by Robert Smirke, one of the pioneers

of the Greek Revival style. The most high profile addition since then was Lord Foster's popular if rather murky glass-roofed Great Court, open since 2000 and now claimed to be 'the largest covered public square in Europe'. This £100m landmark surrounds the domed Reading Room (used by the British Library until its move to King's Cross; *see p109*), where Marx, Lenin, Dickens, Darwin, Hardy and Yeats once worked.

Star exhibits include ancient Egyptian artefacts – the Rosetta Stone on the ground floor (with a barely noticed, perfect replica in the King's Library), mummies upstairs – and Greek antiquities, including the marble friezes from the Parthenon known as the Elgin Marbles. The Celts gallery upstairs has Lindow Man, killed in 300 BC and so well preserved in peat you can see his beard, while the Wellcome Gallery of Ethnography holds an Easter Island statue and regalia collected during Captain Cook's travels. The King's Library provides a calming home to a permanent exhibition that is entitled 'Enlightenment: Discovering the World in the 18th Century', a 5,000-piece collection devoted to the extraordinary formative period of the museum. The remit covers archaeology, science and the natural world; the objects displayed range from Indonesian puppets to a beautiful orrery.

You won't be able to see everything in one day, so buy a souvenir guide and pick out the showstoppers, or plan several visits. Highlights tours focus on specific aspects of the huge collection; Eye Opener tours offer specific introductions to world cultures. There are also regular blockbuster exhibitions, for which it may be necessary to book. In 2012, these include 'Hajj: Journey to the Heart of Islam' (26 January to 15 April) and 'Shakespeare: Staging the World' (*see above* **Inside Track**).
► *The historic Museum Tavern (49 Great Russell Street, 7242 8987), by the front gate, is no mere tourist trap. It has a fine range of ales.*

Cartoon Museum

35 Little Russell Street, WC1A 2HH (7580 8155, www.cartoonmuseum.org). Tottenham Court Road tube. **Open** 10.30am-5.30pm Tue-Sat; noon-5.30pm Sun. **Admission** £5.50; free-£4 reductions. **Credit** (shop) MC, V. **Map** p416 Y1.
The best of British cartoon art is displayed on the ground floor of this former dairy. The displays start in the early 18th century, when high-society types back from the Grand Tour introduced the Italian practice of *caricatura* to polite company. From Hogarth, it moves through Britain's cartooning 'golden age' (1770-1830) to examples of wartime cartoons, ending up with modern satirists such as Gerald Scarfe and the wonderfully loopy Ralph Steadman. Upstairs is a celebration of UK comic art, with original 1921 *Rupert the Bear* artwork by Mary Tourtel, Frank Hampson's Dan Dare, Leo Baxendale's Bash Street Kids and a painted *Asterix* cover by that well-known Briton, Albert Uderzo.

Walk Book Stops

A stroll round Bloomsbury's fine array of modern literary luminaries.

One of Britain's most important publishing houses, **Faber & Faber** was founded in 1929 on the north-west corner of Russell Square (no.24), where this walk begins. The poet TS Eliot was appointed literary advisor, and pored over the work of authors and poets such as Ted Hughes and Sylvia Plath. Eliot romanced his secretary Valerie Fletcher for eight years at the **Russell Hotel** (nos.1-8), marrying her in 1957 to the astonishment of his fellow staff.

Head south along Southampton Row and turn left down Cosmo Place until you reach Queen Square. No.3 served as Faber's home from 1971 to 2008. And on the right is **St George-the-Martyr** (www.stgeorges bloomsbury.org.uk), where Plath and Hughes married on 16 June 1956.

No.44 **Mecklenburgh Street** was home to Hilda Doolittle, an imagist poet. Doolittle's husband was the writer Richard Aldington; his mistress, Dorothy Yorke, lived in another part of the house. Yorke was friends with DH Lawrence, who came here in 1917 to write *Women in Love*.

Head through the alleyway that skirts around the Coram Trust, then weave your way through to **Woburn Walk**. From 1895 to 1919, no.5 (marked by a square metal plaque) was home to WB Yeats, who later became one of Faber's 11 Nobel laureates.

Down the road, Virginia Woolf lived for a time at 52 Tavistock Square (now the **Tavistock Hotel**). Woolf published Eliot's *Poems* in 1919. Close by, Woolf and her assorted Bloomsbury Group cohorts (the likes of EM Forster, Lytton Strachey and Duncan Grant) would discuss literature, art, politics and, above all, each other at **50 Gordon Square**; many were Faber authors.

Go past **Senate House**, then left behind the **British Museum** (*see p102*). From here, cross the corner of Russell Square to **28 Bedford Place**; Eliot briefly lived in this 'cheap boarding house' in 1914.

Turn right on to Great Russell Street and stop outside nos.74-77: **Bloomsbury House**, the current home of Faber & Faber. Congratulations: you've just completed 80 years of literary history in an hour.

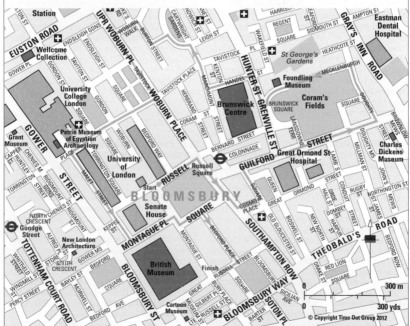

Snapshot Iron Age London

Where to see how London lived.

Even before the Romans transformed a cluster of settlements into the walled city of Londinium, there was civilisation on the site that is now London. The Iron Age treasures displayed in the Britain and Europe room of the **British Museum** (*see p106*) testify to the flamboyance and complexity of life here prior to the invasion of AD 43. The Battersea Shield – unearthed from the Thames at Battersea Bridge in 1857, but dating back as far as 350 BC – is more pretty than protective. Too short and flimsy to have been used in battle, it was more likely to have been thrown or placed in the river as a showy sacrifice for someone of high status. Its intricate design is a clear indication of the sophistication of the tribal craftsmen.

SIGHTS

Charles Dickens Museum

48 Doughty Street, WC1N 2LX (7405 2127, www.dickensmuseum.com). Chancery Lane or Russell Square tube. **Open** 10am-5pm daily. *Tours* by arrangement. **Admission** £6; £3-£5 reductions; free under-11s. **Credit** AmEx, DC, MC, V. **Map** p397 M4.

London is scattered with plaques marking addresses where Dickens lived, but this is the only building still standing. He lived here from 1837 to 1840, writing *Nicholas Nickleby* and *Oliver Twist* while in residence. Ring the doorbell to gain access to four floors of Dickensiana, collected over the years from various former residences. Some rooms are arranged as they might have been when he lived here; others deal with different aspects of his life, from struggling hack to famous performer.

Foundling Museum

40 Brunswick Square, WC1N 1AZ (7841 3600, www.foundlingmuseum.org.uk). Russell Square tube. **Open** 10am-5pm Tue-Sat; 11am-5pm Sun. **Admission** £7.50; £5 reductions; free under-16s. **Credit** MC, V. **Map** p397 L4.

The Foundling Museum recalls the social history of the Foundling Hospital, set up in 1739 by shipwright and sailor Thomas Coram. Returning to England from America in 1720, Coram was appalled by the number of abandoned children he saw. Securing royal patronage, he persuaded Hogarth and Handel to become governors; it was Hogarth who made the building Britain's first public art gallery; works by artists as notable as Gainsborough and Reynolds are on display. The most heart-rending display is a tiny case of mementoes that were all mothers could leave the children they abandoned here.

★ FREE Grant Museum

Rockefeller Building, 21 University Street, WC1E 6JJ (3108 2052, www.ucl.ac.uk/museums/zoology). Goodge Street tube. **Open** 1-5pm Mon-Fri. **Admission** free. **No credit cards. Map** p397 K4.

Now re-housed in a former Edwardian library in the University College complex, the Grant Museum retains the air of an avid Victorian collector's house. Its 67,000 specimens include the remains of many rare and extinct creatures, including skeletons of the dodo and the zebra-like quagga, which was hunted out of existence in the 1880s. Visitors are engaged in dialogue about the distant evolutionary past via the most modern means available, including iPads and smartphones.

► *If the grisliness of body parts in jars appeals, check out the Hunterian as well; see p103.*

FREE Petrie Museum of Egyptian Archaeology

University College London, Malet Place, WC1E 6BT (7679 2884, www.petrie.ucl.ac.uk). Goodge Street or Warren Street tube. **Open** 1-5pm Tue-Sat. **Admission** free; donations appreciated. **No credit cards. Map** p397 K4.

Set up in 1892 by eccentric traveller and diarist Amelia Edwards, the refurbished (and now much easier to find) museum is named after Flinders Petrie, tireless excavator of ancient Egypt. Where the British Museum's Egyptology collection is strong on the big stuff, the Petrie is dim case after dim case of minutiae: pottery shards, grooming accessories, beads. Highlights include artefacts from the heretic pharaoh Akhenaten's capital Tell el Amarna. Wind-up torches illuminate gloomy corners and computers offer 3D views of select objects.

FREE St George's Bloomsbury
Bloomsbury Way, WC1A 2HR (7242 1979,
www.stgeorgesbloomsbury.org.uk). Holborn or
Tottenham Court Road tube. **Open** times vary;
phone for details. *Services* 1.10pm Wed, Fri;
10.30am Sun. **Admission** free. **No credit cards.**
Map p397 L5.
Consecrated in 1730, St George's is a grand and disturbing Nicholas Hawksmoor church, with an offset, stepped spire which was inspired by Pliny the Elder's account of the Mausoleum at Halicarnassus. Highlights of its recent renovation include the mahogany reredos and the sculptures of lions and unicorns clawing at the base of the steeple. The hours are erratic, but on Sundays, the church always remains open for visitors after the regular service. Check online for details of concerts.

★ FREE Wellcome Collection
183 Euston Road, NW1 2BE (7611 2222,
www.wellcomecollection.org). Euston Square
tube or Euston tube/rail. **Open** 10am-6pm Tue,
Wed, Fri, Sat; 10am-10pm Thur; 11am-6pm Sun.
Library 10am-6pm Mon-Wed, Fri; 10am-8pm
Thur; 10am-4pm Sat. **Admission** free. **Credit**
MC, V. **Map** p397 K4.
Sir Henry Wellcome, a pioneering 19th-century pharmacist, amassed a vast and idiosyncratic collection of implements and curios relating to the medical trade, now displayed here. In addition to these fascinating and often grisly items – ivory carvings of pregnant women, used guillotine blades, Napoleon's toothbrush – there are several serious works of modern art, most on display in a smaller room to one side of the main chamber of curiosities. The temporary exhibitions are wonderfully interesting and come with all manner of associated events, from lectures and walks to gigs and experimental food.

KING'S CROSS & ST PANCRAS

King's Cross tube/rail.

North-east of Bloomsbury, King's Cross is becoming a major European transport hub, thanks to a £500-million makeover of the area. The renovated and restored **St Pancras International** (*see p110*) was the key arrival, but neighbouring King's Cross station will itself be getting an expanded station concourse and, in front of the original 1851 façade, a new public square. The gaping badlands to the north are being transformed into a mixed-use nucleus called **King's Cross Central**, with the University of the Arts London due to take up residence in a converted granary building by 2012. Other elements of the development are taking shape, and it is worth a stroll to see the new roads and public areas on a site so large it has its own new postcode (N1C). There are already several places to explore: the **London**

Canal Museum (*see right*), north of King's Cross Station by the **Kings Place** arts complex (*see p319* **Profile**); and charming **St Pancras Old Church** (*see p110*).

★ FREE British Library
96 Euston Road, NW1 2DB (7412 7332,
www.bl.uk). Euston or King's Cross tube/rail.
Open 9.30am-6pm Mon, Wed-Fri; 9.30am-8pm Tue; 9.30am-5pm Sat; 11am-5pm Sun.
Admission free; donations appreciated.
Credit (shop) AmEx, MC, V. **Map** p397 K3.
'One of the ugliest buildings in the world,' opined a Parliamentary committee on the opening of the new British Library in 1997. But don't judge a book by its cover: the interior is a model of cool, spacious functionality, the collection is unmatched (150 million items and counting), and the reading rooms (open only to cardholders) are so popular that regular users are now complaining that they can't find a seat. The focal point of the building is the King's Library, a six-storey glass-walled tower housing George III's collection, but the library's main treasures are displayed in the John Ritblat Gallery: Magna Carta, the Lindisfarne Gospels, original Beatles lyrics. There is also a great programme of temporary exhibitions and associated events.

London Canal Museum
12-13 New Wharf Road, off Wharfdale Road,
N1 9RT (7713 0836, www.canalmuseum.org.uk).
King's Cross tube/rail. **Open** 10am-4.30pm Tue-Sun; 10am-7.30pm 1st Thur of mth. **Admission**
£4; £2-£3 reductions; free under-5s. **Credit**
AmEx, MC, V. **Map** p397 M2.
Housed in a former 19th-century ice warehouse, the little London Canal Museum has a barge cabin to sit in and models of boats, but the displays (photos and videos about ice-importer Carlo Gatti) on the history of the ice trade are perhaps the most interesting. The

SIGHTS

Brunswick Centre. *See p105.*

SIGHTS

installation of new, low-energy lighting should help make the most of the collections. The canalside walk from here to Camden Town is pleasant.
▶ *The museum arranges various canal boat trips. In summer, don't miss the dank exploration of the Islington Tunnel.*

FREE St Pancras International

Pancras Road, N1C 4QP (7843 7688, www.stpancras.com). King's Cross tube/rail. **Open** 24hrs daily. **Admission** free. **No credit cards.** **Map** p397 L3.

William Barlow's gorgeous Victorian glass and iron train shed welcomes high-speed Eurostar trains from Paris. The redeveloped station has become somewhere to linger, but for all the public art, 'the longest champagne bar in Europe', the high-end boutiques, the gastropubs, the restaurants and the farmers' market, St Pancras is really worth a diversion because of the beauty of the original structure.
▶ *Stop for a sip at the Booking Hall café-bar at the newly restored St Pancras Renaissance Hotel to admire classic Victorian station architecture.*

FREE St Pancras Old Church & St Pancras Gardens

St Pancras Road, NW1 1UL (7387 4193). Mornington Crescent tube or King's Cross tube/rail. **Open** *Gardens* 7am-dusk daily. *Services* times vary; check website for details. **Admission** free. **No credit cards.** **Map** p397 K2.

St Pancras Old Church has been ruined and rebuilt many times. The current structure is handsome, but it's the churchyard that delights. Among those buried here are writer William Godwin and his wife, Mary Wollstonecraft; over their grave, their daughter Mary Godwin (author of *Frankenstein*) declared her love for poet Percy Bysshe Shelley. Also here is the last resting place of Sir John Soane, one of only two Grade I-listed tombs (the other is Karl Marx's, in Highgate Cemetery; *see p155*). Designed for his wife, the tomb's dome influenced Gilbert Scott's design for the red British phone box.

FITZROVIA

Goodge Street or Tottenham Court Road tube.

Squeezed in between Tottenham Court Road, Oxford Street, Great Portland Street and Euston Road, Fitzrovia isn't as famous as Bloomsbury, but its history is just as rich. The origins of the name are hazy: some believe it comes from **Fitzroy Square**, named after Henry Fitzroy (son of Charles II); others insist it's due to the famous **Fitzroy Tavern** (16 Charlotte Street, 7580 3714), focal venue for London bohemia of the 1930s and '40s and a favourite with the likes of Dylan Thomas and George Orwell. Fitzrovia also had its share of artists: James McNeill Whistler lived at 8 Fitzroy Square, later taken over by British Impressionist Walter Sickert, while Roger Fry's Omega Workshops, blurring the distinction between fine and decorative arts, had its studio at no.33. However, this raffish image is largely a thing of the past, and the area is better known as a high-powered media hub.

The district's icon is the **BT Tower**, completed in 1964 as the Post Office Tower. Its revolving restaurant and observation deck featured in any film that wanted to prove how much London was swinging (*Bedazzled* is just one example). The restaurant is now reserved for corporate functions, but **Charlotte Street** and neighbouring byways have plenty of good options for earthbound food and drink.

FREE All Saints

7 Margaret Street, W1W 8JG (7636 1788, www.allsaintsmargaretstreet.org.uk). Oxford Circus tube. **Open** 7am-7pm daily. *Services* 7.30am, 8am, 1.10pm, 6pm, 6.30pm Mon-Fri; 7.30am, 8am, 6pm, 6.30pm Sat; 8am, 10.20am, 11am, 5.15pm, 6pm Sun. **Admission** free. **No credit cards.** **Map** p416 U1.

Respite from the tumult of Oxford Street, this 1850s church was designed by William Butterfield, one of the great Gothic Revivalists. The church looks as if it has been lowered into its tiny site, so tight is the fit; its lofty spire is the second-highest in London. Behind the polychromatic brick façade, the lavish interior is one of the capital's finest ecclesiastical triumphs, with luxurious marble, flamboyant tile work and glittering stones built into its pillars. A three-year cleaning and restoration project to return it to Butterfield's original conception was completed in late 2011.

Pollock's Toy Museum

1 Scala Street, W1T 2HL (7636 3452, www.pollockstoymuseum.com). Goodge Street tube. **Open** 10am-5pm Mon-Sat. **Admission** £5; £2.50-£4 reductions; free under-3s. **Credit** AmEx, MC, V. **Map** p396 J5.

Pollock's is named after Benjamin Pollock, the last of the Victorian toy theatre printers. By turns beguiling and creepy, it's a nostalgia-fest of old board games, tin trains, porcelain dolls and Robertson's gollies. It's fascinating for adults but less so for children; describing a pile of painted woodblocks stuffed in a cardboard box as a 'Build a skyscraper' kit may make them feel lucky to be going home to their Wii.

INSIDE TRACK HAWK EYES

If a distant movement from above catches your eye in St Pancras International Station, you might just have spotted Comet or Electra, the two Harris hawks employed, along with their handler, to ensure the great shed stays pigeon-free.

Covent Garden & the Strand

An eminently strollable area of markets, boutiques and theatres.

From the capital's wholesale fruit and veg market, decades-since relocated to Vauxhall, to the Royal Opera House, still regal overlord of the market's north-east corner, **Covent Garden** has always been an index of the extremes of London life. At which end of the slippery scale you think it sits will depend on your tolerance for crowds. The masses descend daily on the restored 19th-century market and its cobbled 'piazza' to peruse the la-di-da shops and gawp at the street entertainment. Yet even the most crowd-averse Londoner finds plenty that's irresistible: the **London Transport Museum** (*see p112*); the **Royal Opera House** (*see p112*), eager nowadays to draw in all kinds of visitor; and, down towards the river on the grubbily historic **Strand**, the **Courtauld Gallery** just off the vast courtyard of **Somerset House** (for both, *see p114*).

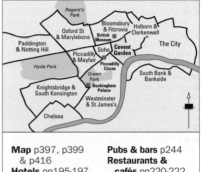

Map p397, p399 & p416
Hotels pp195-197

Pubs & bars p244
Restaurants & cafés pp220-222

COVENT GARDEN

Covent Garden or Leicester Square tube.

Covent Garden was once the property of the medieval Abbey ('convent') of Westminster. When Henry VIII dissolved the monasteries, it passed to John Russell, first Earl of Bedford, in 1552; his family still owns land hereabouts. During the 16th and 17th centuries, they developed the area: the fourth Earl employed Inigo Jones to create the Italianate open square that remains the area's centrepiece.

A market was first documented here in 1640 and grew into London's pre-eminent fruit and vegetable wholesaler, employing over 1,000 porters; its success led to the opening of coffee-houses, theatres, gambling dens and brothels. A flower market was added (where the London Transport Museum now stands).

In the second half of the 20th century, it became obvious that the congested streets of central London were unsuitable for such market traffic and the decision was taken to move the traders out. In 1974, with the market gone, the threat of property development loomed for the empty stalls and offices. It was only through demonstrations that the area was saved. It's now a pleasant place for a stroll, especially if you catch it early on a fine morning before the crowds descend.

Covent Garden Piazza

Centred on Covent Garden Piazza, the area now offers a combination of gentrified shops, restaurants and cafés, supplemented by street artists and busking musicians in the lower courtyard. The majority of the entertainment takes place under the portico of **St Paul's Covent Garden** (*see p112*).

Tourists favour the 180-year-old **covered market** (7836 9136, www.coventgarden londonuk.com), which combines upmarket chain stores with a collection of small, sometimes quirky but often rather twee

SIGHTS

independent shops. Its handsome architecture is best viewed from the Amphitheatre Café Bar's terrace loggia at the **Royal Opera House**. The whole area is currently undergoing a major revamp (*see p115* **Market Makeover**).

Change is barely evident elsewhere. The **Apple Market**, in the North Hall, still has arts and crafts stalls from Tuesday to Sunday, and antiques on Monday. Across the road, the tackier **Jubilee Market** deals mostly in novelty T-shirts and other tat.

★ London Transport Museum

Covent Garden Piazza, WC2E 7BB (7379 6344, www.ltmuseum.co.uk). Covent Garden tube. **Open** 10am-6pm Mon-Thur, Sat, Sun; 11am-6pm Fri. **Admission** £13.50; £10 reductions; free under-16s. **Credit** AmEx, MC, V. **Map** p416 Z3.

The London Transport Museum traces the city's transport history from the horse age to the present day. It does so in an engaging and inspiring fashion, with a focus on social history and design, illustrated by a superb array of preserved buses, trams and trains, and backed up by some brilliant temporary exhibitions. The collections are in broadly chronological order, beginning with the Victorian gallery, where a replica of Shillibeer's first horse-drawn bus service in 1829 takes pride of place. Another gallery is dedicated to the museum's truly impressive collection of poster art. Under the leadership of Frank Pick, in the early 20th century London Transport developed one of the most coherent brand identities in the world. The new museum also raises some interesting and important questions about the future of public transport in the city, with a display on ideas that are 'coming soon'.

Royal Opera House

Bow Street, WC2E 9DD (7304 4000, www.roh.org.uk). Covent Garden tube. **Open** 10am-3.30pm Mon-Sat. **Admission** free. *Stage tours* £10.50; £7-£9.50 reductions. **Credit** AmEx, DC, MC, V. **Map** p416 Y3.

**INSIDE TRACK
THE OLYMPIC JOURNEY**

Between 27 July and 12 August 2012, to co-incide with the London 2012 Olympic Games, the Royal Opera House (*see above*; www.roh.org.uk/theolympicjourney) is hosting 'The Olympic Journey: The Story of the Games'. This free exhibition draws on archive film, audio and artefacts from the Olympic Museum in Lausanne, and includes an example of a medal from every Games since Athens 1896, as well as all the Olympic Torches since the tradition began at Berlin 1936, among its highlights.

Neal's Yard.

The Royal Opera House was founded in 1732 by John Rich on the profits of his production of John Gay's *Beggar's Opera*; the current building, constructed roughly 150 years ago but extensively remodelled since, is the third on the site. Visitors can explore the massive eight-floor building as part of an organised tour, including the main auditorium, the costume workshops and sometimes even a rehearsal. Certain parts of the building are also open to the general public, including the glass-roofed Paul Hamlyn Hall, the Crush Bar (so named because in Victorian times the only thing served during intermissions was orange and lemon crush) and the Amphitheatre Café Bar.

▶ *For the ROH as a music venue, see p320.*

FREE St Paul's Covent Garden

Bedford Street, WC2E 9ED (7836 5221, www.actorschurch.org). Covent Garden or Leicester Square tube. **Open** 8.30am-5pm Mon-Fri; 9am-1pm Sat. Times vary Sat; phone for details. *Services* 1.10pm Tue, Wed; 6pm Thur; 11am Sun. *Choral Evensong* 4pm 2nd Sun of mth. **Admission** free; donations appreciated. **No credit cards. Map** p416 Y3.

Known as the Actors' Church for its long association with Covent Garden's theatres, this pleasingly spare building was designed by Inigo Jones in 1631. A lovely limewood wreath by the 17th-century master carver Grinling Gibbons hangs inside the front door as a reminder that he and his wife are interred in the crypt. For the many thespians commemorated on its walls, *see left* **Plaques, Decay**.

Elsewhere in Covent Garden

Outside Covent Garden Piazza, the area offers a mixed bag of entertainment, eateries and shops. Nearest the markets, most of the more unusual shops have been superseded by a homogeneous mass of cafés, while big fashion chains – and the new **St Martin's Courtyard** mall (www.stmartinscourtyard.co.uk) – have all but domesticated Long Acre. There are more interesting stores north of here on Neal Street and Monmouth Street; Earlham Street is also home to the **Donmar Warehouse** (see p349), a former banana-ripening depot that's now an intimate and groundbreaking theatre. On tiny Shorts Gardens next door is the **Neal's Yard Dairy** (see p274), purveyor of exceptional UK cheeses; down a passageway one door along is **Neal's Yard** itself, known for its co-operative cafés, herbalists and head shops.

South of Long Acre and east of the Piazza, historical depravity is called to account at the former **Bow Street Magistrates Court**. Once home to the Bow Street Runners, the precursors of the Metropolitan Police, this was also where Oscar Wilde entered his plea when arrested for 'indecent acts' in 1895. It's currently being converted into a hotel. To the south, Wellington and Catherine streets mix restaurants and theatres, including the grand **Theatre Royal**. Other diversions in and around Covent Garden include the museum at **Freemasons' Hall** (7831 9811, www.freemasonry.london.museum; call for details of tours), the eye-catchingly bombastic white stone building where Long Acre becomes Great Queen Street; and, at opposite ends both of St Martin's Lane and the cultural spectrum, lap-dancing club **Stringfellows** (16-19 Upper St Martin's Lane, 7240 5534, www.stringfellows.co.uk) and the **Coliseum** (see p318), home of the English National Opera.

THE STRAND & EMBANKMENT

Embankment tube or Charing Cross tube/rail.

Until as recently as the 1860s, the Strand ran beside the Thames; indeed, it was originally the river's bridlepath. In the 14th century, it was lined with grand residences with gardens that ran down to the water. It wasn't until the 1870s that the Thames was pushed back with the creation of the Embankment and its adjacent gardens. By the time George Newnes's famed *Strand* magazine was introducing its readership to Sherlock Holmes (1891), the street boasted the Cecil Hotel (long since demolished), **Simpson's**, **King's College** and **Somerset House** (see p114). Prime Minister Benjamin Disraeli described it as 'perhaps the finest street in Europe'. Nobody would make such a claim today – there are too many overbearing office blocks and underwhelming restaurants – but there's still plenty to interest visitors.

In 1292, the body of Eleanor of Castile, consort to King Edward I, completed its

funerary procession from Lincoln in the small hamlet of Charing, at the western end of what is now the Strand. The occasion was marked by the erection of the last of 12 elaborate crosses. A replica of the Eleanor Cross (originally set just south of nearby Trafalgar Square; see p133) was placed in 1865 on the forecourt of **Charing Cross Station**; it remains there today, looking like the spire of a sunken cathedral. It emerged from under tarpaulins in summer 2010 after major refurbishments. Across the road, behind **St Martin-in-the-Fields** (see p135), is Maggie Hambling's weird memorial to a more recent queen, *A Conversation with Oscar Wilde*.

The Embankment itself can be reached down Villiers Street. Pass through the tube station to the point at which boat tours with on-board entertainment depart. Just to the east stands **Cleopatra's Needle**, an obelisk presented to the British nation by the viceroy of Egypt, Mohammed Ali, in 1820 but not set in place by the river for a further 59 years. The obelisk was originally erected around 1500 BC by the pharaoh Tuthmosis III at a site near modern-day Cairo, before being moved to Alexandria, Cleopatra's capital, in 10 BC. By this time, however, the great queen was 20 years dead.

Back on the Strand, the majestic **Savoy** hotel (see p197) has just reached the end of a tortuously long and thorough refurbishment. The hotel first opened in 1889, financed by profits from Richard D'Oyly Carte's productions of Gilbert and Sullivan's light operas at the neighbouring **Savoy Theatre** (see p347 **Legally Blonde**). The theatre, which pre-dates the hotel by eight years, was the first to use electric lights.

SIGHTS

INSIDE TRACK
CHANGING TITIAN

The National Gallery (*see p112*) and the Royal Opera House (*see p134*) are pooling their considerable artistic resources for the London 2012 Festival to create a new work called *Metamorphosis: Titian 2012* (14-20 July). Seven choreographers will collaborate to produce three new works, inspired by three of Titian's paintings on display in the National – the dramatic *Diana & Actaeon*, *The Death of Actaeon* and *Diana & Callisto*. It will also be shown on the BP Summer Big Screens (details via the ROH), for free.

Benjamin Franklin House
36 Craven Street, the Strand, WC2N 5NF (7925 1405, www.benjaminfranklinhouse.org). Charing Cross tube/rail. **Open** noon-5pm Wed-Sun. *Tours* noon, 1pm, 2pm, 3.15pm, 4.15pm Wed-Sun. **Admission** £7; £5 reductions; free under-16s. **Credit** AmEx, MC, V. **Map** p416 Y5.

This is the house where Franklin – scientist, diplomat, philosopher, inventor and Founding Father of the US – lived between 1757 and 1775. It isn't a museum in the conventional sense, but can be explored on 'experiences' lasting a short but intense 45 minutes (noon, 1pm, 2pm, 3.15pm and 4.15pm Wed-Sun; booking advised). The tours are led by an actress playing Franklin's landlady's daughter Polly Stevenson, using projections and sound to conjure up the world and times in which Franklin lived. From noon on Mondays, the house offers more straightforward, 20-minute tours given by house interns (£3.50).

THE ALDWYCH
Temple tube.

At the eastern end of the Strand is the Aldwych. This grand crescent dates only from 1905, but the name 'ald wic' (old settlement or market) has its origins in the 14th century. To the south is **Somerset House**; even if you're not interested in the galleries, it's worth visiting the regal fountain courtyard. Almost in front of it is **St Mary-le-Strand** (7836 3126, open 11am-4pm Tue-Sat, 10am-3pm Sun), James Gibbs's first public building, completed in 1717. On Strand Lane, reached via Surrey Street, is the so-called **'Roman' bath** where Dickens took the waters – you have to peer through a dusty window.

On a traffic island just east of the Aldwych is **St Clement Danes** (7242 2380). It's believed that a church was first built here by the Danish in the ninth century, but the current building is mainly Wren's handiwork. It's the principal church of the RAF. Just beyond the church are the Royal Courts of Justice (*see p87*) and the original site of Temple Bar (*see p89*).

★ Courtauld Gallery
The Strand, WC2R 1LA (7848 2526, www.courtauld.ac.uk/gallery). Temple tube or Charing Cross tube/rail. **Open** 10am-6pm daily. *Tours* phone for details. **Admission** £6; £4.50 reductions. Free 10am-2pm Mon; students & under-18s daily. **Credit** MC, V. **Map** p399 M7.

Located for the last two decades in the north wing of Somerset House (*see below*), the Courtauld has one of Britain's greatest collections of paintings, and contains several works of world importance. Although there are some outstanding early works (Cranach's wonderful *Adam & Eve*, for one), the collection's strongest suit is in Impressionist and Post-Impressionist paintings. Popular masterpieces include Manet's astonishing *A Bar at the Folies-Bergère*, alongside plenty of superb Monets and Cézannes, important Gauguins (such as *Nevermore*), and some Van Goghs and Seurats. On the top floor, there's a selection of gorgeous Fauvist works, a lovely room of Kandinskys and plenty more besides.

Hidden downstairs, the sweet little gallery café is frequently forgotten, but it feels delightfully separate from the rest of Somerset House. Note that bulky backpacks must be carried, not worn, through the collection; there are coin-operated lockers downstairs.

FREE Somerset House & the Embankment Galleries
The Strand, WC2R 1LA (7845 4600, www.somersethouse.org.uk). Temple tube or Charing Cross tube/rail. **Open** 10am-6pm (last entry 5.15pm) daily. *Tours* phone for details. **Admission** *Courtyard & terrace* free. *Embankment Galleries* prices vary; check website for details. *Tours* phone for details. **Credit** MC, V. **Map** p399 M7.

The original Somerset House was a Tudor palace commissioned by the Duke of Somerset. In 1775, it was demolished to make way for the first purpose-built office block in the world. Architect Sir William Chambers spent the last 20 years of his life working on the neoclassical edifice overlooking the Thames, built to accommodate learned societies such as the Royal Academy and government departments.

The taxmen are still here, but the rest of the building is open to the public. Attractions include the Courtauld (*see above*), the handsome fountain court, and a terraced café and a classy restaurant. The Embankment Galleries explore connections between art, architecture and design in temporary exhibitions, and at Christmas usually host an adventurous market; downstairs, a ceremonial Thames barge and information boards explain the place's history, to the accompaniment of Handel's *Water Music*. In summer, children never tire of running through the choreographed fountains while parents watch from café tables; in winter, a popular ice rink is erected.

Market Makeover

Covent Garden is undergoing a transformation.

While all eyes have been focused on the new Westfield Stratford City, another shopping district has quietly been undergoing a nip and tuck. By 2012, central London's Covent Garden will be completely altered, from a slightly rough-edged cobbled square to a plumped-up, youthful shopping district.

Since 2006, property investor Capco has consumed great chunks of prime real estate in Covent Garden, scooping up property on the Piazza, King Street, James Street, Long Acre and beyond – £780 million of it, to be exact. And it's Capco's marketing and communications director, Bev Churchill, who is charged with re-editing the neighbourhood. One-time marketing director of Selfridges, she knows a thing or two about retail. And she certainly thinks big. A slew of shops have been replaced by high street heavyweights and luxury brands. Fred Perry, Whistles, L'Artisan Parfumier, Kurt Geiger, Rugby Ralph Lauren and Burberry Brit have all appeared; last year, the world's largest Apple store set up shop and, until recently, a giant inflatable Jeff Koons bunny hung in the Market Building.

Perhaps most tellingly, the West Cornwall Pasty Co has become a Ladurée café, where waistcoat-wearing staff dispense dainty orange-blossom macaroons where steak and Stilton pastries were once shovelled out.

'We've seen so many changes in the last couple of years,' says Jane Shepherdson, CEO of Whistles. 'We've started to see a serious fashion customer come back to the area.' Food brands popular with the style set have also been lured back. Russell Norman's Da Polpo opened in May *(see p 225)* and the Icecreamists' shock-concept ice-cream *(see p221)* sits in the Market Building, where travelling burger kitchen Meateasy will have a permanent site.

But what of Covent Garden's bawdy personality? To Bev, it's all about plonking niche, indie shops, bars and restaurants up against luxury retailers and contemporary art, and also about uncovering what's already there. The Rugby store, a late-1600s townhouse with library-like rooms and grand façade, is a case in point. 'Covent Garden has great bone structure,' explains Bev. 'It just needed a little facelift.'

SIGHTS

Soho & Leicester Square

Soho has a character all of its own – Leicester Square wants one.

For more than two centuries, poseurs, spivs, tarts, whores, toffs, drunks and divas have gathered in **Soho** to ply their trades. Many of the area's music, film and advertising businesses have moved on, but the gay scene still thrives, and contributes to a non-stop party atmosphere.

Hemmed in by Oxford Street to the north, Charing Cross Road to the east, Shaftesbury Avenue to the south and Regent Street to the west, Soho is packed with a huge range of restaurants, shops, clubs and bars, sharing the streets with a sizeable residential community. There are a few more chains than there used to be, but independent businesses (and an independent frame of mind) still dominate.

Just to the south, beyond London's tiny but thriving **Chinatown**, **Leicester Square** – mainly known for its cinemas – is many a drunken exhibitionist's favourite late-night stamping ground, though classier activities are reappearing.

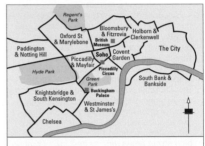

| **Map** p416 | **Hotels** pp197-198 |
| **Pubs & bars** pp245-247 | **Restaurants & cafés** pp222-226 |

SOHO SQUARE

Tottenham Court Road tube.

Forming the area's northern gateway, **Soho Square** was laid out in 1681. It was initially called King's Square; a weather-beaten statue of Charles II stands just north of the centre. On warmer days, the grassy spaces are filled with courting couples as snacking workers occupy its benches; one of these benches is dedicated to singer Kirsty MacColl, in honour of her song named after the square. The denominations of the two churches on the square testify to the area's long-standing European credentials: as well as the French Protestant church, you'll find St Patrick's, one of the first Catholic churches built in England after the Reformation.

Two classic Soho streets run south from the square. **Greek Street**, its name a nod to a church that once stood here, is lined with restaurants and bars, among them 50-year-old Hungarian eaterie the **Gay Hussar** (no.2, 7437 0973) and the nearby **Pillars of Hercules** pub (no.7, 7437 1179), where the literati once enjoyed long liquid lunches. Just by the Pillars, an arch leads to Manette Street and the Charing Cross Road, where you'll find **Foyles** (*see p261*). Back on Greek Street, no.49 was once Les Cousins, a folk venue (note the heldover mosaic featuring a musical note); Casanova lived briefly at no.46.

Parallel to Greek Street is **Frith Street**, once home to Mozart (1764-65, no.20) and painter John Constable (1810-11, no.49). Humanist essayist William Hazlitt died in 1830 at no.6, now a discreet hotel named in his memory (*see p198* **Hazlitt's**). Further down the street are **Ronnie Scott's** (*see p327*), Britain's best-known jazz club, and, across from Ronnie's, the similarly mythologised **Bar Italia** (no.22, 7437 4520). A large portrait of Rocky Marciano dominates Italia's narrow, chrome bar, but it's the place's 24-hour opening that makes it likely you'll have to fight for a seat.

SIGHTS

This area has been suffering from major disruption caused by works on the Crossrail link. It's tedious and unsightly, but you can usually find your way around it down one of the area's characteristic back streets or alleys.

OLD COMPTON STREET & AROUND

Leicester Square or Tottenham Court Road tube.

Linking Charing Cross Road to Wardour Street and crossed by Greek, Frith and Dean streets, **Old Compton Street** is London's gay catwalk. Tight T-shirts congregate around **Balans** (*see p310*), **Compton's** (nos.51-53) and the **Admiral Duncan** (no.54). However, the street has an interesting history that dates back long before rainbow flags were hung above its doors. Now the **Boulevard Bar & Dining Room**, 59 Old Compton Street was formerly the 2i's Coffee Bar, the skiffle venue where stars and svengalis mingled in the late 1950s and early '60s

Visit Old Compton Street in the morning for a sense of the mostly vanished immigrant Soho of old. Cheeses and cooked meats from **Camisa** (no.61, 7437 7610) and roasting beans from the **Algerian Coffee Stores** (*see p271*) scent the air, as **Pâtisserie Valerie** (no.44, 7437 3466, www.patisserie-valerie.co.uk) does a brisk trade in croissants and cakes. Its traditional French rival is the older **Maison Bertaux** (*see p223*), an atmospheric holdover from the 19th century that sits near the southern end of Greek Street.

Maison Bertaux is far from the only point of interest on the roads south of Old Compton Street. At the corner of Greek and Romilly streets sits the **Coach & Horses** (no.29, 7437 5920), where irascible Soho flâneur Jeffrey Bernard held court for decades. It's almost opposite the members' club **Soho House** (no.40, 7734 5188), where a current crop of wannabes hopes to channel the same vibe. Two streets along, Dean Street holds the **French House** (*see p246*); formerly the York Minster pub, it was de Gaulle's London

---

A Better Leicester Square?

Central London's least appealing space begins to pull its socks up.

SIGHTS

Locals have for many years scorned the fast food, expensive cinemas and tacky pavement artists of **Leicester Square**. Apart from the **tkts** booth, selling cut-price, same-day theatre tickets, and Leicester Place's unlikely neighbours the **Prince Charles** cinema (*see p308*) and the French Catholic church of **Notre Dame de France** (no.5, 7437 9363, www.ndfchurch.org), with its Jean Cocteau murals, there was no reason to venture here. The green patch in the centre might be bearable on a sunny day, but woe betide anyone caught in the jostle of drunken suburban idiots and lost tourists at night.

When Westminster Council announced plans for an £18m redevelopment in 2008, there were serious doubts the fortunes of the square could be turned round. The idea of a new layout for the square's centre (improved lighting, modish 'ribbon' seating doubtless designed to prevent drunks and the homeless getting a good kip) conjured visions of another clean, characterless, commerce-friendly space. Certainly the pitch is high-end: the Grade II-listed, Frank Matcham-designed **Hippodrome** (*see p120*) on the north-east corner is to reopen as a casino, and there are two new swish hotels: boutique **W Leicester Square** (*see p197*) from Starwood and the **St John Hotel** (*see

p198*), an outpost of the nose-to-tail eating restaurant chain. But not all memories of the square's cheerfully tacky phase will be erased: the glockenspiel clock that used to command the attention of crowds outside the Swiss Centre every hour has returned, redesigned (27 bells, mechanical mountain farmers) but still chiming out the time on behalf of Switzerland Tourism.

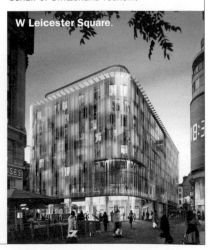

W Leicester Square.

Old Compton Street. *See p117.*

base for French resistance in World War II and in later years became a favourite of painters Francis Bacon and Lucian Freud. Upstairs is **Polpetto** (*see p246*), one of a clutch of related Italian wine-bar restaurants to have taken the area by storm last year. Nearby speakeasy-style **Spuntino** (*see p225*) is another fêted newcomer.

North of Old Compton Street on Dean Street sits the **Groucho Club** (no.45), a members-only media hangout that was founded in the mid 1980s and named in honour of the familiar Groucho Marx quote about not wanting to join any club that would have him as a member. A few doors along, **Quo Vadis** (nos.26-29) has a costly grill room and an upstairs bar for members; Karl Marx, who lived in the garret at no.28 from 1850 to 1856, would probably not have approved. To the north is the **Soho Theatre** (*see p350*), which programmes comedy shows and new plays.

WARDOUR STREET & AROUND

Leicester Square or Tottenham Court Road tube.

Parallel to Dean Street, **Wardour Street** provides offices for film and TV production companies, but is also known for its rock history. What's now upscale tapas joint **Meza** (no.100) was, for nearly three decades, the Marquee, where Led Zeppelin played their

INSIDE TRACK SO LONG, SOHO

With so much of Soho lost except to history, it's pleasing to see someone is trying to keep track of the ephemera: **www.themuseumofsoho.org.uk** has the stories of the Colony Room, Windmill Girls, the Pierpoint Monument and all sorts of interesting odds and ends.

first London gig and Hendrix appeared four times. The latter's favourite Soho haunt was the nearby **Ship** pub (no.116), still with a sprinkling of music-themed knick-knacks. There's more music history at Trident Studios on nearby **St Anne's Court**: Lou Reed recorded *Transformer* here, and David Bowie cut both *Hunky Dory* and *The Rise and Fall of Ziggy Stardust* on the site.

Back when he was still known as David Jones, Bowie played a gig at the Jack of Clubs on Brewer Street, now **Madame JoJo's** (*see p331*). But this corner of Soho is most famous not for music but for its position at the heart of Soho's dwindling but still notorious sex trade. The **Raymond Revuebar** opened on the neon alleyway of Walker's Court in 1958, swiftly becoming London's most famous strip club. It closed in 2004, but numerous smaller, seedier establishments continue to tout for business close by on Brewer Street and Tisbury Court.

North of here, **Berwick Street** is a lovely mix of old-school London raffishness and new-Soho style. The former comes courtesy of the amiable food market (support it: more custom needed), and the egalitarian, old-fashioned and unceasingly popular **Blue Posts** pub (no.22, 7437 5008), where builders, post-production editors, restaurateurs and market traders gabble and glug as one beneath a portrait of Berwick Street-born star of stage and radio Jessie Matthews (1907-81). It's quite a contrast with the **Endurance** (no.90, 7437 2944), the street's gastropub and **Flat White** (no.17, 7734 0370), a shabby-chic coffee bar.

WEST SOHO

Piccadilly Circus tube.

West of Berwick Street, Soho has been branded 'West Soho' in a misplaced bid to give some kind of upmarket identity to its shops. **Brewer**

SIGHTS

Street does have some interesting places; among them is the **Vintage Magazine Store** (nos.39-43, 7439 8525), offering everything from retro robots to pre-war issues of *Vogue*. Star restaurant **Hix** (*see p219* **Hix Oyster & Chop House**) is also here. On Great Windmill Street is the **Windmill Theatre** (nos.17-19), which gained fame in the 1930s and '40s for its 'revuedeville' shows with erotic 'tableaux' – naked girls who remained stationary in order to stay within the law. The place is now a lap-dancing joint. North of Brewer Street is **Golden Square**. Developed in the 1670s, it became the political and ambassadorial district of the late 17th and early 18th centuries, and remains home to some of the area's grandest buildings (many now bases for media firms).

Just north of Golden Square is **Carnaby Street**, which became a fashion mecca shortly after John Stephen opened His Clothes here in 1956; Stephen, who went on to own more than a dozen fashion shops on the street, is now commemorated with a plaque at the corner with Beak Street. After thriving during the Swinging Sixties, Carnaby Street became a rather seamy commercialised backwater. However, along with nearby **Newburgh Street** and **Kingly Court** (*see p263*), it's undergone a revival, with the tourist traps and chain stores joined by a wealth of independent stores.

Close to Oxford Street, the **Photographers' Gallery** (16-18 Ramillies Street, 0845 262 1618, www.photonet.org.uk), London's largest devoted to the medium, reopens in early 2012.

CHINATOWN & LEICESTER SQUARE

Leicester Square tube.

Shaftesbury Avenue is the very heart of Theatreland. The Victorians built seven grand theatres here, six of which still stand. The most impressive is the gorgeous **Palace Theatre** on Cambridge Circus, which opened in 1891 as the Royal English Opera House; when grand opera flopped, the theatre reopened as a music hall two years later. Appropriately, it's most famous for the musicals it has staged: *The Sound of Music* (1961) and *Jesus Christ Superstar* (1972) had their London premières here, and *Les Misérables* racked up 7,602 performances between 1985 and 2004. The current resident is *Singin' in the Rain*.

Just opposite the Palace Theatre, what's now the Med Kitchen occupies premises that were once home to Marks & Co, the shop that was made famous by Helene Hanff's *84 Charing Cross Road*. A few (and, sadly, getting fewer) second-hand bookshops line **Charing Cross Road** to the south, heading towards Leicester Square, where **Cecil Court** (*see p262*) is a better bet for bibliophiles, despite some closures. West of Charing Cross Road and south of Shaftesbury Avenue, and officially just outside Soho, is the city's **Chinatown**.

The Chinese are relative latecomers to this part of town. London's original Chinatown was set around Limehouse in east London, but hysteria about Chinese opium dens and criminality led to 'slum clearances' in 1934 (interestingly, the surrounding slums were deemed to be in less urgent need of clearance). It wasn't until the 1950s that the Chinese put down roots here, attracted by the cheap rents along Gerrard and Lisle streets.

The ersatz oriental gates, stone lions and pagoda-topped phone boxes around Gerrard Street suggest a Chinese theme park, but this

Chinatown.

SIGHTS

remains a close-knit residential and working enclave, a genuine focal point for the Chinese community in London. The area is crammed with restaurants, Asian grocery stores, some great bakeries and a host of small shops selling iced-grass jelly, speciality teas and cheap air tickets to Beijing.

South of Chinatown, **Leicester Square** was one of London's most exclusive addresses in the 17th century; in the 18th, it became home to the royal court of Prince George (later George II). Satirical painter William Hogarth had a studio here (1733-64), as did 18th-century artist Sir Joshua Reynolds; both are commemorated by busts in the small gardens that lie at the heart of the square, although it's the statue of a tottering Charlie Chaplin that gets all the attention. There's no particular reason for Chaplin to be here, other than the fact that Leicester Square is considered the home of

British film thanks to its numerous cinemas. The monolithic **Odeon Leicester Square** (*see p307*) once boasted the UK's largest screen, and probably still has the UK's highest ticket prices. Like the neighbouring **Empire**, it's regularly used for movie premières.

The **Hippodrome**, on the corner of Cranbourn Street and Charing Cross Road beside the tube station, is an impressive red-brick edifice designed by the prolific theatre architect Frank Matcham. It became famous as the 'Talk of the Town' cabaret venue in the 1960s, featuring the likes of Shirley Bassey and Judy Garland. It is currently being refurbished to reopen as a casino, due to open in 2012. This, and the arrival of two new hotels on the north-western corner of the square, are encouragement for the council in its attempts to revivify a square most locals cordially loathe (*see p117* **A Better Leicester Square?**).

Sebastian Coe's London

What the Olympian loves about the city.

Sebastian Coe.

I've been a lifelong Chelsea Football Club supporter, so for years the Shed End of Stamford Bridge has been my home on match days. Recent seasons have seen some great successes – though I try to tell my children that despite this, winning the double is not a regular occurrence. I was there for the 27 years between winning FA Cups.

Throughout my athletics career, hill training was an integral part of conditioning, and I spent many hours running up and down Richmond Hill, working on my speed, strength and fitness. Despite the exertions, it was the view that made it that little bit more bearable. Many artists and writers have been inspired by

its beauty; it appears in a Sir Walter Scott novel, and has a mention in a Wordsworth sonnet. Whether I'm at a flat-out pace at 6am or with the family for a Sunday stroll, the views are breathtaking.

I have many fond memories of days spent watching Test matches at Lord's Cricket Ground. Lovingly referred to as the 'home of cricket', Lord's is steeped in history. You don't even need the excuse of a match to draw you there; the MCC Museum, the oldest sports museum in the world, contains an absolutely amazing collection of cricket memorabilia. What makes the venue even more special for 2012 is that we will be using it as a backdrop for the Olympic Games Archery competition.

SIGHTS

Oxford Street & Marylebone

The main(stream) shopping drag, and its more interesting environs.

Oxford Street is working hard to stay top of London's shopping destinations. A revamped roundabout at **Marble Arch** (*see p122*), wider pavements, innovative pedestrian crossings and an all-new 'eastern gateway' development should, come the London 2012 Games, make sunset on 'London's High Street' memorable for more of the right reasons. Until then, crowd-phobic locals will continue to favour the luxury cafés and boutiques of **Marylebone** and the flowering green acres of **Regent's Park** (*see p124*).

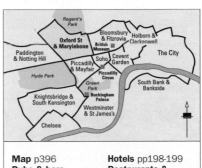

Map p396	**Hotels** pp198-199
Pubs & bars p247	**Restaurants & cafés** p226

SIGHTS

OXFORD STREET

Bond Street, Marble Arch, Oxford Circus or Tottenham Court Road tube.

Official estimates put the annual footfall at somewhere near 200 million people per year, but few Londoners love **Oxford Street**. A shopping district since the 19th century, it's unmanageably busy on weekends and in the run-up to Christmas. Even outside these times, it's never pretty, lined with over-familiar chain stores and choked with bus traffic. The New West End Company (www.newwestend.com) has been charged with changing all that, and Oxford Circus, Marble Arch and Regent Street are feeling the benefits.

The street gets smarter as you walk from east to west. The eastern end around Tottenham Court Road station is under major redevelopment for Crossrail, but has anyway lacked destination shops for years. The string of big department stores – **John Lewis** (nos.278-306, 7629 7711), **Debenhams** (nos.334-348, 0844 561 6161) and **Selfridges** (no.400; *see p258*) – are west of chaotic **Oxford Circus**, where there are more Crossrail works at Bond Street station. Apart from the art deco splendour of Selfridges, architectural interest along Oxford Street is

largely limited to Oxford Circus's four identical convex corners, constructed between 1913 and 1928. The crowds and rush of traffic hamper investigations, a problem the council attempted to address a couple of years ago by widening pavements, removing street clutter and creating Tokyo Shibuya-style diagonal crossings – which, much to the surprise of London's habitual jaywalkers, work well.

Oxford Street gained notoriety as the route by which condemned men were conveyed from Newgate Prison to the old Tyburn gallows, stopping only for a last pint at the **Angel** (61-62 St Giles High Street, 7240 2876). Thousands gathered to watch the countless executions that

---

INSIDE TRACK
SCRAMBLED EGGS

A young Paul McCartney woke up one morning in 1965 at **57 Wimpole Street**, the house of then-girlfriend Jane Asher's parents. He dashed to the piano to transcribe a tune that had been playing in his dreams: only the lyrics didn't quite work. Until, that is, he decided to change 'Scrambled Eggs' into 'Yesterday'.

Marble Arch.

than one. Prominent among the carvings is a statue of Shakespeare's Prospero and Ariel, his spirit of the air – or, in this case, the airwaves. The statue caused controversy when it was unveiled due to the flattering size of the airy sprite's manhood; artist Eric Gill was recalled and asked to make it more modest. Major renovations are due to be completed in 2012/13. Over the road is the **Langham Hotel**, which opened in 1865 as Britain's first grand hotel and has been home at various points to Mark Twain, Napoleon III and Oscar Wilde.

North, Langham Place turns into **Portland Place**, designed by Robert and James Adam as the glory of 18th-century London. Its Georgian terraced houses are now mostly occupied by embassies and swanky offices. At no.66 is the **Royal Institute of British Architects** (RIBA). Parallel to Portland Place are **Harley Street**, famous for its high-cost dentists and doctors, and **Wimpole Street**, erstwhile home to the poet Elizabeth Barrett Browning (no.50) and Sir Arthur Conan Doyle (2 Upper Wimpole Street).

MARYLEBONE

Baker Street, Bond Street, Marble Arch, Oxford Circus or Regent's Park tube.

North of Oxford Street, the fashionable district known to its boosters as 'Marylebone Village' has become a magnet for moneyed Londoners. Many visitors to the area head directly for the waxworks of **Madame Tussauds** (*see p124*); there's also a small and oft-overlooked museum at the neighbouring **Royal Academy of Music** (7873 7300, www.ram.ac.uk). However, the area's beating heart is **Marylebone High Street**, teeming with interesting shops.

St Marylebone Church stands in its fourth incarnation at the northern end of the street. The name of the neighbourhood is a contraction of the church's earlier name, St Mary by the Bourne; the 'bourne' in question, Tyburn stream, still filters into the Thames near Pimlico, but its entire length is now covered. The church's lovely garden hosts designer clothing and artisan food stalls at the **Cabbages & Frocks** market on Saturdays (www.cabbagesandfrocks.co.uk).

More lovely boutiques can be found on winding **Marylebone Lane**, along with the **Golden Eagle** (no.59, 7935 3228), which hosts regular singalongs around its piano. There's fine food here, too, with smart, often upmarket eateries snuggling alongside delicatessens such as **La Fromagerie** (2-6 Moxon Street, 7935 0341, www.lafromagerie.co.uk) and century-old lunchroom **Paul Rothe & Son** (35 Marylebone Lane, 7935 6783). **Marylebone**

SIGHTS

were held at Tyburn over six centuries; held in 1783, the final execution to be carried out here is marked by an X on a traffic island at the junction of the Edgware and Bayswater roads.

Close by, at the western end of Oxford Street, stands **Marble Arch**, with its Carrara marble cladding and sculptures celebrating Nelson and Wellington. It was designed by John Nash in 1827 as the entrance to a rebuilt Buckingham Palace, but the arch was moved here in 1851, after – it is said – a fuming Queen Victoria found it to be too narrow for her coach. Now given a £2-million revamp, it's been joined by renovated water fountains and gardens that contain an ongoing series of public sculpture commissions. The current incumbent is Nic Fiddian-Green's giant *Horse at Water*, a vast horse's head poised on its lips amid the lawns.

North of Oxford Circus

Great Portland Street, Oxford Circus or Regent's Park tube.

North of Oxford Circus runs **Langham Place**, notable for the Bath stone façade of John Nash's **All Souls Church** (Langham Place, 2 All Souls Place, 7580 3522, www.allsouls.org). Its bold combination of a Gothic spire and classical rotunda wasn't popular: in 1824, a year after it opened, the church was condemned in the House of Commons as 'deplorable and horrible'.

Opposite the church you'll find the BBC's **Broadcasting House**, an oddly asymmetrical art deco building that's shipshape in more ways

Farmers' Market takes place in the Cramer Street car park every Sunday.

Further south, the soaring neo-Gothic interior of the 19th-century **St James's Roman Catholic Church** (22 George Street) is lit dramatically by stained-glass windows; Vivien Leigh (née Hartley) married barrister Herbert Leigh Hunt here in 1932. Other cultural diversions include the **Wallace Collection** (*see below*) and the **Wigmore Hall** (*see p318*).

Madame Tussauds

Marylebone Road, NW1 5LR (0870 400 3000, www.madametussauds.com/london). Baker Street tube. **Open** times vary; check website for details. **Admission** £28.80; £24.60 reductions; £99 family; free under-4s. **Credit** MC, V. **Map** p396 G4.

Streams of humanity jostle excitedly here for the chance to take pictures of each other planting a smacker on the waxen visage of fame and fortune. Madame Tussaud brought her show to London in 1802, 32 years after it was founded in Paris, and it's been expanding ever since, on these very premises since 1884. There are some 300 figures in the collection now, under various themes: 'A-list Party' (Brad, Keira, Kate Moss, Will Smith), 'Première Night' (Monroe, Chaplin, Arnie as the Terminator), 'Sports Zone' (Tendulkar, Rooney, Muhammad Ali), 'By Royal Appointment' and so on. If you're not already overheating, your palms will be sweating by the time you descend to the Chamber of Horrors in 'Scream', where only teens claim to enjoy the floor drops and scary special effects. Much more pleasant is the kitsch 'Spirit of London' ride, whisking you through 400 years of London life in a taxi pod. New arrivals include Justin Bieber, Captain Jack Sparrow and World Champion heptathlete Jessica Ennis.

Tussauds also hosts Marvel Super Heroes 4D. Interactives and waxworks of Iron Man, Spiderman and an 18ft Hulk provide further photo opportunities, but the highlight is the nine-minute film in '4D'

INSIDE TRACK
CITY OF SCULPTURE

You can't help but notice the large and colourful figures near Marble Arch, at once jolly and sinister. These are Mauro Perucchetti's *Jelly Baby Family*, one of a series of sculptures installed by Westminster Council to present the city at its best for London 2012. Others of note around town are *Room in Rome* by Franz West, on The Mall; *Hand of God* by Lorenzo Quinn, on Park Lane; *Yuri Gagarin* by Pavel Medvedev, Spring Gardens; *The Search for Enlightenment* by Simon Gudgeon, in Riverwalk Gardens and some naturalistic (albeit nude) Bruce Denny figures enjoying a rest in Soho Square.

(as well as 3D projections, there are 'real' effects such as a shaking floor and smoke in the auditorium) in the dome that used to house the planetarium. For 2012, the Sports Zone will have an Olympic theme. ▶ *Get here before 10am to avoid the enormous queues, and book online in advance to make the steep admission price more palatable.*

★ FREE Wallace Collection

Hertford House, Manchester Square, W1U 3BN (7935 0687, www.wallacecollection.org). Bond Street tube. **Open** 10am-5pm daily. **Admission** free. **Credit** (shop) MC, V. **Map** p396 G5.

Built in 1776, this handsome house contains an exceptional collection of 18th-century French furniture, painting and objets d'art, as well as an amazing array of medieval armour and weaponry. It all belonged to Sir Richard Wallace, who, as the illegitimate offspring of the fourth Marquess of Hertford, inherited in 1870 the treasures his father had amassed in the last 30 years of his life. Room after grand room contains

SIGHTS

ZSL London Zoo. *See p125.*

Louis XIV and XV furnishings and Sèvres porcelain; the galleries are hung with paintings by Titian, Gainsborough, Velázquez, Fragonard and Reynolds; Franz Hals's *Laughing Cavalier* (neither laughing nor a cavalier) is one of the best known, along with Fragonard's *The Swing*. Since summer 2010, refurbished West Galleries have displayed the museum's 19th-century and Venetian works, including paintings by Canaletto, and the collections of miniatures and gold boxes have been on show in the Boudoir Cabinet; new East Galleries should be complete by early 2012 and will be dedicated to Dutch paintings.

▶ *The museum restaurant is beautifully set in a glass-roofed courtyard and a good choice for a shopping-day lunch.*

REGENT'S PARK

Baker Street or Regent's Park tube.

Regent's Park (open 5am-dusk daily) is one of London's most delightful open spaces. Originally a hunting ground for Henry VIII, it remained a royals-only retreat long after it was

Walk The Sidestreet Shuffle

Avoid Oxford Street's clogged pavements with a trail through the back streets.

This hour-long walk follows the hinterlands of Oxford Street, which offer not only useful routes parallel to the main drag but a back-street take on retail and London life.

Rathbone Place marks the lower reaches of Fitzrovia, where the worlds of media and design collide with the rag trade. The fun begins at Hobgoblin (no.24, 7323 9040), a folk music store where musicians test-drive zithers, banjos and ukuleles. Close by on Percy Street, **Contemporary Applied Arts** (*see p274*) sells outstanding British crafts, from jewellery to furniture.

Keep north up restaurant-lined Charlotte Street, buzzing with media types, then turn left beside the suave **Charlotte Street Hotel** (*see p192*) through Percy Passage. Cross the dog-leg of Rathbone Street, and head on via Dickensian Newman Passage to emerge in Newman Street. Pause for a snap of the **BT Tower**, then go left and right

on to Eastcastle Street. Detour up Margaret Street to **All Saints** church (*see p110*).

Back on Eastcastle Street sits cutting-edge gallery **Stuart Shave/Modern Art** (nos.23-25). Over the road, **Fever** (no.52, 7636 6326) mixes cute retro-inspired clothing and accessories with vintage, while the **Getty Images Gallery** (no.46, 7291 5380) holds great photography exhibitions. Market Place opens ahead, a mellow collection of sidewalk cafés yards from the frenzy of Oxford Street. Stop for refreshment and then head across Oxford Street down Argyll Street, aiming for the half-timbered **Liberty** building (*see p258*).

Next, cross Regent Street towards Conduit Street, where a visit to **Vivienne Westwood**'s flamboyant flagship store (no.44, 7439 1109, www.vivienne westwood.com) provides a taste of punky London couture. Continue to New Bond

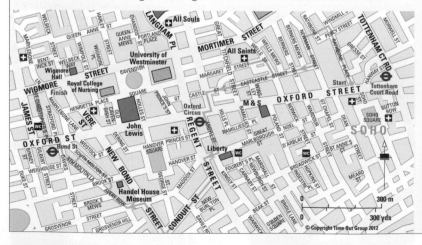

formally designed by John Nash in 1811; only in 1845 did it open to the public as a spectacular shared space. Attractions run from the animal noises and odours of **ZSL London Zoo** (*see below*) to the enchanting **Open Air Theatre** (*see p344*); rowing boat hire, beautiful rose gardens, ice-cream stands and the **Garden Café** (7935 5729, www.companyofcooks.com) complete the postcard-pretty picture.

West of Regent's Park rises the golden dome of the **London Central Mosque** (www.iccuk.org), while the northern end

---

Street into Grosvenor Street, then right up Avery Row. This is the land of Victorian London's great aristocratic estates, where narrow service alleys brought tradesmen to the rear entrances of the grand residences. The alleys still offer services to the gentry, but they're now exclusive little boutiques and restaurants that are hidden from the dazed tourists wandering nearby. On Avery Row, check out the **Paul Smith Sale Shop** (*see p267*).

Adjoining Lancashire Court is home to restaurants and the **Handel House Museum** (*see p130*), which faces Brook Street and, close by, Italian design legend **Alessi** (no.22, 7518 9091). Move on to pedestrianised South Molton Street and its strong mix of chain stores, cafés and independents, among them glittery **Butler & Wilson** (no.20, 7409 2955). Take the passage to the left of fashion queen **Browns** (*see p265*) and pop out by the imposing terracotta structure of **Grays Antique Market** (*see p278*).

Cross Oxford Street again, battling your way to the freestanding clock signposting the narrow entrance to St Christopher's Place. This warren of little streets houses a traffic-free complex of cafés and shops, including Finnish designer **Marimekko** (nos.16-17, 7486 6454). There's also a fountain and a flower-decked Victorian WC.

Need a rest? Head north to Wigmore Street for one last stop at **Robert Clergerie Shoes** (no.67, 7935 3601), before heading a couple of doors down to **Comptoir Libanais** (no.65, 7935 1110, www.lecomptoir.co.uk). This colourful and inviting Lebanese eaterie is the perfect place to mull over your purchases with a rosewater macaroon and a mint tea.

---

of **Baker Street** is unsurprisingly heavy on nods of respect to the world's favourite freelance detective. At the **Sherlock Holmes Museum** (no.221B, 7935 8866, www.sherlock-holmes.co.uk), Holmes stories arc earnestly re-enacted using mannequins, but serious fans may find more of interest among the books and photos of the **Sherlock Holmes Collection** at Marylebone Library (7641 1206, by appointment only); or, for that matter, at Arthur Conan Doyle's former home on Upper Wimpole Street and the Langham Hotel (for both, *see p122*), which plays a role in a number of the Holmes stories.

The Beatles painted 94 Baker Street with a psychedelic mural before opening it in December 1967 as the Apple Boutique, a clothing store run on such whimsical hippie principles that it had to close within six months due to financial losses. Fab Four pilgrims head to the **London Beatles Store** (no.231, 7935 4464, www.beatlesstorelondon.co.uk), where the ground-floor shop offers a predictable array of Beatles-branded accessories alongside genuine collectables. Next door, **Elvisly Yours** (7486 2005) caters to the blue-suede-shoed fraternity.

★ ZSL London Zoo

Regent's Park, NW1 4RY (7722 3333, www.zsl.org/london-zoo). Baker Street or Camden Town tube then bus 274, C2. **Open** times vary; check website for details. **Admission** £18.60; £14.50-£17.10 reductions; free under-3s. **Credit** AmEx, MC, V. **Map** p396 G2.

London Zoo has been open in one form or another since 1826. Spread over 36 acres and containing more than 600 species, it cares for many of the endangered variety – part of the entry price (pretty steep at nearly £20, in peak season and including the voluntary donation) goes towards the ZSL's projects around the world. The emphasis is on upbeat education. Regular events include 'animals in action' and keeper talks; explanations are simple, short and lively. Exhibits are entertaining: look out, in particular, for the re-creation of a kitchen overrun with large cockroaches. The relaunched 'Rainforest Life' biodome and the 'Meet the Monkeys' attractions allow visitors to walk through enclosures that recreate the natural habitat of, respectively, tree anteaters and sloths, and black-capped Bolivian squirrel monkeys, while personal encounters of the avian kind can be had in the Victorian Blackburn Pavilion. 'Gorilla Kingdom' is another highlight, and the reptile house delights and horrifies in equal measure. Bring a picnic basket and you could easily spend the entire day here. The newest attraction is Penguin Beach, where the birds have plenty of room to frolic in and out of the water and the public can watch them swim through underwater windows. *Photo p123.*

▶ *Excellent for children, the petting zoo in Battersea Park is much cheaper; see p295.*

SIGHTS

Paddington & Notting Hill

Mecca for London's Middle Easterners.

Sprawled beneath the Westway flyover, with its railway terminus and branch of the Grand Union Canal, **Paddington** is where central London meets the west of England. It's not an attractive area, but it holds appeal thanks to the Arab influence around the Edgware Road and the goodies hidden away in Alfie's Antique Market. There's nothing hidden away about **Notting Hill**, where **Portobello Market** is surrounded by some of the most desirable addresses in west London, one of which houses the inimitable **Museum of Brands, Packaging & Advertising**.

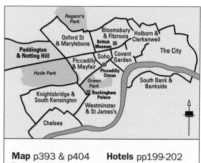

Map p393 & p404	**Hotels** pp199-202
Pubs & bars p247	**Restaurants & cafés** p231-232

EDGWARE ROAD & PADDINGTON

Edgware Road, Lancaster Gate or Marble Arch tube, or Paddington tube/rail.

Part of the Romans' Watling Street from Dover to Wales, **Edgware Road** rules a definite north–south line marking where the West End stops and central west London begins. It's now the heart of the city's Middle East end: if you want to pick up your copy of *Al Hayat*, cash a cheque at the Bank of Kuwait or catch Egyptian football, head here. North of the Marylebone Road, **Church Street** is home to the wondrous **Alfie's Antique Market** (*see p278*).

INSIDE TRACK MARKET FINDS

Portobello Green Market has the area's best vintage fashion stalls. Look out for the excellent second-hand boot and shoe stall and brilliant vintage handbag stall (usually outside Falafel King), along with vintage clothing stall Sage Femme, often outside the Antique Clothing Shop.

The fact that the name Paddington has been immortalised by a certain small, ursine Peruvian émigré is appropriate, given that the area has long been home to refugees and immigrants. It was a country village until an arm of the Grand Union Canal arrived in 1801, linking London to the Midlands, followed in the 1830s by the railway. **Paddington Station**, with its fine triple roof of iron and glass, was built in 1851 to the specifications of the great engineer Isambard Kingdom Brunel.

Paddington's proximity to central London eventually drew in developers. To the east of the station, gleaming **Paddington Central** now provides a million square feet of office space, canalside apartments and restaurants. In St Mary's Hospital, the old-fashioned **Alexander Fleming Laboratory Museum** gives a sense of what the district used to be like.

Alexander Fleming Laboratory Museum
St Mary's Hospital, Praed Street, W2 1NY (7886 6528, www.imperial.nhs.uk/aboutus/museumsand archives/index.htm). Paddington tube/rail. **Open** 10am-1pm Mon-Thur. *By appointment* 2-5pm Mon-Thur; 10am-5pm Fri. **Admission** £4; £2 reductions; free under-5s. **No credit cards.** **Map** p393 D5.

Notting Hill location for film *Alfie*.

Buzz in at the entrance on your left as you enter the hospital and head up the stairs to find this tiny, dusty, instrument-cluttered lab. Enthusiastic guides conjure up the professor who, in 1928, noticed that mould contamination had destroyed some staphylococcus bacteria on a set-aside culture plate: he had discovered penicillin. The keen entrepreneurs across the street immediately began to advertise their pub's healthful properties, claiming the miracle fungus had blown into the lab from them. The video room has a documentary on Fleming's life and discovery.

NOTTING HILL

Notting Hill Gate, Ladbroke Grove or Westbourne Park tube.

Head north up Queensway from Kensington Gardens and turn west along **Westbourne Grove**. The road starts humble but gets posher the further west you go; cross Chepstow Road and you're in upmarket **Notting Hill**. A host of fashionable restaurants and bars exploit the lingering street cred of the fast-disappearing black and working-class communities; posh shops are a better reflection of the area's current character. **Notting Hill Gate** isn't a pretty street, but the leafy avenues to the south are; so is **Pembridge Road**, to the north, leading to the boutique-filled streets of Westbourne Grove and Ledbury Road, and to **Portobello Road** and its renowned market (*see p261*).

Halfway down, **Blenheim Crescent** boasts a couple of independent booksellers, but the **Travel Bookshop** (nos.13-15), the store on which Hugh Grant's bookshop was based in the movie *Notting Hill*, has now closed down. Under the Westway, that elevated section of the M40 motorway linking London with Oxford, is the small but busy **Portobello Green Market** (*see left* **Inside Track**).

North of the Westway, Portobello's vitality fizzles out. It sparks back to life at **Golborne Road**, the heartland of London's North African community. Here, too, is a fine Portuguese café-deli, the **Lisboa Pâtisserie** (no.57, 8968 5242). At the north-eastern end of the road stands **Trellick Tower**, an architecturally significant, like-it-or-loathe-it piece of Ernö Goldfinger modernism. At its western end, Golborne Road connects with Ladbroke Grove, which can be followed north to spooky **Kensal Green Cemetery**.

FREE Kensal Green Cemetery

Harrow Road, Kensal Green, W10 4RA (8969 0152, www.kensalgreen.co.uk). Kensal Green tube. **Open** *Apr-Sept* 9am-6pm Mon-Sat; 10am-6pm Sun. *Oct-Mar* 9am-5pm Mon-Sat; 10am-5pm Sun. **Tours** *Mar-Oct* 2pm Sun. *Nov-Feb* 2pm 1st & 3rd Sun of mth. **Admission** free. *Tours* £5 (£4 reductions) donation. **No credit cards.**
Behind a neoclassical gate is a green oasis of the dead. It's the resting place of both the Duke of Sussex, sixth son of George III, and his sister, Princess Sophia; also buried here are Wilkie Collins, Anthony Trollope and William Makepeace Thackeray.

Museum of Brands, Packaging & Advertising

Colville Mews, Lonsdale Road, W11 2AR (7908 0880, www.museumofbrands.com). Notting Hill Gate tube. **Open** 10am-6pm Tue-Sat; 11am-5pm Sun. **Admission** £6.50; £2.25-£4 reductions; £15 family; free under-7s. **Credit** MC, V. **Map** p404 Y4.
Robert Opie began collecting the things others throw away when he was 16. His collection now includes anything from milk bottles to vacuum cleaners and cereal packets. The emphasis is on the last century of British consumerism, design and domestic life, but there are older items, such as an ancient Egyptian doll.

Piccadilly Circus & Mayfair

Beyond the neon frenzy of Piccadilly lies the deep calm of old money.

Top dog since the 1930s, when it was a playground for London's aristocracy, **Mayfair** oozes wealth. The area is now the haunt of hedge funders, who defy the lingering recession as they flash cash in restaurants and hotel bars. There are vestiges of old Mayfair: the tailors of Savile Row, marginally destuffed; the galleries of Cork Street; the bijou shopping rookery of Shepherd Market. To the south-east, the neon-lit frenzy of **Piccadilly Circus** remains the one part of town that every Londoner does their best to avoid.

Map p396, p398 & p416	**Pubs & bars** p247
Hotels pp202-204	**Restaurants & cafés** pp226-228

PICCADILLY CIRCUS & REGENT STREET

Oxford Circus or Piccadilly Circus tube.

Frantic **Piccadilly Circus** is an uneasy mix of the tawdry and the grand, a mix with little to do with the vision of its architect. John Nash's 1820s design for the intersection of Regent Street and Piccadilly, two of the West End's most elegant streets, was a harmonious circle of curved frontages. But 60 years later, Shaftesbury Avenue muscled in, creating the

lopsided and usually pandemonious traffic junction still in place today. This should have all changed by the end of 2011 when a £14-million revamp is due to complete. Almost a mile of ugly, pedestrian-funnelling and cyclist-shredding railings are to be ripped out by the same design consultants who successfully remodelled Oxford Circus.

Alfred Gilbert's memorial fountain in honour of child-labour abolitionist Earl Shaftesbury was erected in 1893. It's properly known as the **Shaftesbury Memorial**, with the statue on top intended to show the Angel of Christian Charity, but critics and public alike recognised the likeness of **Eros** and their judgement has stuck. The illuminated advertising panels around the intersection appeared late in the 19th century and have been present ever since: a Coca-Cola ad has been here since 1955, making it the world's longest-running advertisement. Running Sky News broadcasts indicate the likely media-saturated future for the illuminations.

Opposite the memorial, the **Trocadero Centre** (www.londontrocadero.com) has seen several ventures come and go, driven out by high rents and low footfall in a prime but tired location, although **Ripley's Believe It or Not!** (*see p129*) seems already to be well established. Plans for a massive revamp

SIGHTS

of the site, including a huge new hotel, had drifted off the radar as we went to press.

Connecting Piccadilly Circus to Oxford Circus to the north and Pall Mall to the south, the broad curve of **Regent Street** was designed by Nash in the early 1800s with the aims of improving access to Regent's Park and bumping up property values in Haymarket and Pall Mall. Much of Nash's architecture was destroyed in the early 20th century, but the grandeur of the street remains impressive. Among the highlights are the mammoth children's emporium **Hamleys** (nos.188-196, 0871 704 1977, www.hamleys.com), landmark department store **Liberty** (*see p258*) and, perhaps the first of a new Regent Street pedigree, **Anthropologie** (*see p266*).

Ripley's Believe It or Not!

1 Piccadilly Circus, W1J 0DA (3238 0022, www. ripleyslondon.com). Piccadilly Circus tube. **Open** 10am-midnight daily (last entry 10.30pm). **Admission** £25.95; £19.95-£23.95 reductions; £81.95 family; free under-4s. **Credit** MC, V. **Map** p416 W4.
This 'odditorium' follows a formula more or less unchanged since Robert Ripley opened his first display at the Chicago World Fair in 1933: an assortment of 800 curiosities is displayed, ranging from the world's smallest road-safe car to da Vinci's *Last Supper* painted on a grain of rice – via the company's signature shrunken heads.

MAYFAIR

Bond Street or Green Park tube.

The gaiety suggested by the name of Mayfair, derived from a long-gone spring celebration, isn't matched by its latter-day atmosphere today. Even on Mayfair's busy shopping streets, you may feel out of place without the reassuring heft of a platinum card. Nonetheless, there are many pleasures to enjoy if you fancy a stroll, not least the concentration of blue-chip commercial art galleries.

The Grosvenor and Berkeley families bought the rolling green fields that would become Mayfair in the middle of the 17th century. In the 1700s, they developed the pastures into a posh new neighbourhood, focused on a series of landmark squares. The most famous of these, **Grosvenor Square** (1725-31), is dominated by the supremely inelegant US Embassy, its only decorative touches a fierce eagle and a mass of post-9/11 protective barricades. Out front, pride of place is taken by a statue of President Dwight Eisenhower, who stayed in nearby **Claridge's** (*see p202*) when in London; Roosevelt is in the park nearby. Plans are in place to move the embassy to the much less salubrious (but apparently more secure) environs of Vauxhall – in 2017.

Brook Street has impressive musical credentials: GF Handel lived and died at no.25, and Jimi Hendrix roomed briefly next door at no.23, adjacent buildings that have been combined into the **Handel House Museum** (*see p130*). For most visitors, however, this part of town is all about shopping. Connecting Brook Street with Oxford Street to the north, **South Molton Street** is home to the fabulous boutique-emporium **Browns** (*see p265*) and the excellent **Grays Antique Market** (*see p278*), while **New Bond Street** is an A-Z of top-end, mainstream fashion houses.

Beyond New Bond Street, **Hanover Square** is another of the area's big squares, now a busy traffic chicane. Just to the south is **St George's Church**, built in the 1720s and once everyone's

SIGHTS

Piccadilly Circus.

favourite place to be seen and to get married. Handel, who married nobody, attended services here. South of St George's, salubrious **Conduit Street** is where fashion shocker Vivienne Westwood (no.44) faces staid Rigby & Peller (no.22A), corsetière to the Queen.

Running south off Conduit Street is the most famous Mayfair shopping street of all, **Savile Row**. Gieves & Hawkes (no.1) is a must-visit for anyone interested in the history of British menswear; at no.15, the estimable Henry Poole & Co has cut suits for clients including Napoleon III, Charles Dickens and 'Buffalo' Bill Cody. No.3 was the home of the Beatles' Apple Records and their rooftop farewell concert.

Two streets west, **Cork Street** is known as the heart of the West End art scene; more than half a dozen galleries are strung along its few hundred feet of shopfront. A couple of streets over is Albemarle Street, where you'll find the handsomely rejuvenated **Royal Institution**, home to the **Faraday Museum** (*see p131*).

★ Handel House Museum

25 Brook Street (entrance in Lancashire Court), W1K 4HB (7399 1953, www.handelhouse.org). Bond Street tube. **Open** 10am-6pm Tue, Wed, Fri, Sat; 10am-8pm Thur; noon-6pm Sun. **Admission** £6; £2-£5 reductions; free under-5s. **Credit** MC, V. **Map** p396 H6.

Handel moved to Britain from his native Germany aged 25 and settled in this house 12 years later, remaining here until his death in 1759. The house has been beautifully restored with original and recreated furnishings, paintings and a welter of the composer's scores (in the same room as photos of Jimi Hendrix, who lived in the attic, now used as the museum office). The programme of events includes Thursday recitals.

Death and Dignity

London remembers those killed in terrorist attacks.

Few Londoners will ever forget the terrorist attacks of 7 July 2005, when 52 people were killed by suicide bombers. The city has a calm, surprisingly unrhetorical memorial to the tube and bus passengers who died. In the south-east corner of Hyde Park between the Lovers' Walk and busy Park Lane, the £1m monument consists of 52 ten-foot-tall, square steel columns, one for each of the fatalities. Each is marked with the date, time and location of that person's death; they're arranged in four groups, according to which of the four explosions killed the person in question. Designed by architects Carmody Groarke in close consultation with the victims' families, with Antony Gormley as an independent adviser, the monument is an austerely beautiful, quietly modern and human-scale tribute.

Elsewhere, London has a memorial to the 202 victims of the 2002 Bali bombings (just by the Churchill War Rooms, *see p136*), as well as a memorial garden for the victims of 9/11 (Grosvenor Square, near the US Embassy). Interestingly, and despite widespread commemoration events for the 70th anniversary of the beginning of the Blitz (57 consecutive nights of German bombing which began on 7 September 1940), there is still no unified memorial to the perhaps 20,000 London civilians killed across the capital.

★ FREE **Royal Institution**
& Faraday Museum
21 Albemarle Street, W1S 4BS (7409 2992,
www.rigb.org). Green Park tube. **Open** 9am-9pm
Mon-Fri. Closes for events; phone ahead.
Admission free. *Multimedia tours* £3.
Credit MC, V. **Map** p416 U4.
The Royal Institution was founded in 1799 for
'diffusing the knowledge… and application of science to the common purposes of life'; from behind
its neoclassical façade, it's been at the forefront of
London's scientific achievements ever since. In 2008,
Sir Terry Farrell completed a £22m rebuild, inside
and out, with the brief of improving accessibility and
finding ways to lure people inside. The result is a
more open frontage, a restaurant, a bar and a café.

The Michael Faraday Laboratory, a complete
replica of Faraday's former workspace, is in the
basement, alongside a working laboratory in which
RI scientists can be observed researching their current projects. Some 1,000 of the RI's 7,000-odd scientific objects are on display, including the world's first
electric transformer, a prototype Davy lamp and,
from 1858, a print of the first transatlantic telegraph
signal. The RI also holds a terrific rolling programme of talks and demonstrations in its lecture
theatre, most famously at Christmas.

Handel House Museum.

Shepherd Market

Just west of Albemarle Street, **44 Berkeley
Square** is one of the original houses in this
grand square. Built in the 1740s, it was
described by architectural historian Nikolaus
Pevsner as 'the finest terrace house of London'.
Curzon Street, which runs off the south-west
corner of Berkeley Square, was home to MI5,
Britain's secret service, from 1945 until the '90s.
It's also the northern boundary of **Shepherd
Market**, named after a food market set up here
by architect Edward Shepherd in the early 18th
century and now a curious little enclave in the
heart of this exclusive area.

From 1686, this was where the raucous May
Fair was held, until it was shut down in the late
18th century due to 'drunkenness, fornication,
gaming and lewdness'. You'll still manage the
drunkenness easily enough at a couple of good
pubs (such as **Ye Grapes**, at 16 Shepherd
Market). The cobbler on adjoining White Horse
Street ('Don't throw away old shoes, they can be
restored!') and the ironmongers on Shepherd
Street keep things from becoming too genteel.

PICCADILLY & GREEN PARK

Green Park, Hyde Park Corner or Piccadilly
Circus tube.
Piccadilly's name is derived from the 'picadil',
a type of suit collar that was in vogue during
the 18th century. The first of the area's main

buildings was built by tailor Robert Baker and,
indicating the source of his wealth, nicknamed
'Piccadilly Hall'. A stroll through the handful
of Regency shopping arcades confirms that the
rag trade is still flourishing mere minutes away
from Savile Row and Jermyn Street. At the
renovated **Burlington Arcade** (*see p259*), the
oldest and most famous of these arcades, top-
hatted security staff known as 'beadles' ensure
there's no singing, whistling or hurrying in the
arcade: such uncouth behaviour is prohibited
by archaic bylaws. Formerly Burlington House
(1665), the **Royal Academy of Arts** (*see p132*)
is next door to the arcade's entrance. It hosts
several lavish, crowd-pleasing exhibitions each
year and has a pleasant courtyard café.

On Piccadilly are further representatives
of high-end retail. **Fortnum & Mason** (*see
p256*), London's most prestigious food store,
was founded in 1707 by a former footman to
Queen Anne. Look for the fine clock: a 1964
articulated effort, it features 18th-century
effigies of Mr Fortnum and Mr Mason, who
bow to each other on the hour. The plain church

SIGHTS

INSIDE TRACK DEEP WATER

The water feature in the basement of
Grays Antique Market (*see p278*) is
formed from the Tyburn Brook. One of
London's buried rivers, it runs underground
from Hampstead to Westminster.

SIGHTS

at no.197 is **St James's Piccadilly** (*see right*), where William Blake was baptised.

To the west along Piccadilly, smartly uniformed doormen mark the **Wolseley** (*see p228*), a former car showroom that is now a fine (if tiresomely frequently lauded) restaurant, and the expensive, exclusive **Ritz** (*see p204*). The dull, flat, green expanse just beyond the Ritz is **Green Park**. Work your way along Piccadilly, following the northern edge of Green Park past the queue outside the Hard Rock Café (where the Vault's displays of memorabilia are free to visit and open every day) to the Duke of Wellington's old home, **Apsley House**, opposite **Wellington Arch** (for both, *see below*). This is hectic **Hyde Park Corner**; Buckingham Palace (*see p140*) is just a short walk south-east, while Hyde Park (*see p149*) and the upper-crust enclave of Belgravia (*see p146*) are to the west.

Apsley House

149 Piccadilly, W1J 7NT (7499 5676, www. english-heritage.org.uk). Hyde Park Corner tube. **Open** *Nov-Mar* 11am-4pm Sat, Sun. *Apr-Oct* 11am-5pm Wed-Sun. *Tours* by arrangement. **Admission** £6.30; £3.80-£5.70 reductions; free under-5s. *Tours* phone in advance. *Joint ticket with Wellington Arch* £7.90; £4.70-£7.10 reductions; £20.50 family. **Credit** MC, V. **Map** p398 G8.
Called No.1 London because it was the first London building encountered on the road to the city from the village of Kensington, Apsley House was built by Robert Adam in the 1770s. The Duke of Wellington kept it as his London home for 35 years. Although his descendants still live here, several rooms are open to the public, providing a superb feel for the man and his era. Admire the extravagant porcelain dinnerware and plates or ask for a demonstration of the crafty mirrors in the scarlet and gilt picture gallery, where a fine Velázquez and a Correggio hang near Goya's portrait of the Iron Duke after he defeated the French in 1812. This was a last-minute edit: X-rays have revealed that Wellington's head was painted over that of Joseph Bonaparte, Napoleon's brother.
► *Come here for the atmospheric twilight tours in winter to appreciate the dazzling floor- and ceiling-mounted chandeliers.*

FREE Royal Academy of Arts

Burlington House, W1J 0BD (7300 8000, www. royalacademy.org.uk). Green Park or Piccadilly Circus tube. **Open** 10am-6pm Mon-Thur, Sat, Sun; 10am-10pm Fri. **Admission** free. *Exhibitions* vary. **Credit** AmEx, MC, V. **Map** p416 U4.
Britain's first art school was founded in 1768 and moved to the extravagantly Palladian Burlington House a century later, but it's now best known not for education but exhibitions. Ticketed blockbusters are generally held in the Sackler Wing or the main galleries; shows in the John Madejski Fine Rooms are drawn from the RA's holdings, which range from Constable to Hockney, and are free. The Academy's biggest event is the Summer Exhibition, which for more than two centuries has drawn from works entered by the public.

FREE St James's Piccadilly

197 Piccadilly, W1J 9LL (7734 4511, www. st-james-piccadilly.org). Piccadilly Circus tube. **Open** 8am-6.30pm daily. *Evening events* times vary. **Admission** free. **Credit** (concerts only) AmEx, DC, MC, V. **Map** p416 V4.
Consecrated in 1684, St James's is the only church Sir Christopher Wren built on an entirely new site. A calming building with few architectural airs or graces, it was almost destroyed in World War II, but painstakingly reconstructed. Grinling Gibbons's delicate limewood garlanding around the sanctuary survived and is one of the few real frills. Beneath a new tiled roof, the church stages regular classical concerts, provides a home for the William Blake Society and hosts markets in the churchyard: food on Monday, antiques on Tuesday, and arts and crafts from Wednesday to Saturday. There's also a handy café in the basement with plenty of tables.

Wellington Arch

Hyde Park Corner, W1J 7JZ (7930 2726, www. english-heritage.org.uk). Hyde Park Corner tube. **Open** *Apr-Oct* 10am-5pm Wed-Sun. *Nov-Mar* 10am-4pm Sat, Sun. **Admission** £3.90; £2.30-£3.50 reductions; free under-5s. *Joint ticket with Apsley House* £7.90; £4.70-£7.10 reductions; £20.50 family. **Credit** AmEx, MC, V. **Map** p398 G8.
Built in the late 1820s to mark Britain's triumph over Napoleonic France, Decimus Burton's Wellington Arch was initially topped by an out-of-proportion equestrian statue of Wellington. However, since 1912 Captain Adrian Jones's 38-ton bronze *Peace Descending on the Quadriga of War* has finished it with a flourish. It has three floors of displays, covering the history of the arch and the Blue Plaques scheme, and great views in winter from the balcony. Note that the Wellington Arch will be closed for renovation until 31 May 2012.
► *Hyde Park Corner contains one of London's finest war memorials: Charles Sargeant Jagger's moving tribute to the Royal Artillery.*

Westminster & St James's

For members' clubs and members of Parliament.

England is ruled from **Westminster**. The monarchy has been in residence here since the 11th century, when Edward the Confessor moved west from the City, and the government of the day also calls it home. It's a key destination for visitors as well, with the most significant area designated a UNESCO World Heritage Site back in 1987.

For such an important part of London, it's surprisingly spacious. **St James's Park** is one of London's finest parks, **Trafalgar Square** (overlooked by the **National Gallery**) is a tourist hotspot, and the **Mall** offers a properly broad and regal route to Buckingham Palace.

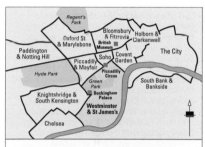

Map pp398-399 & p416	**Restaurants & cafés** p228
Hotels pp204-206	**Pubs & bars** p247

SIGHTS

TRAFALGAR SQUARE

Leicester Square tube or Charing Cross tube/rail.

Laid out in the 1820s by John Nash, Trafalgar Square is the heart of modern London. Tourists come in their thousands to pose for photographs in front of **Nelson's Column**. It was erected in 1840 to honour Vice Admiral Horatio Nelson, who died at the point of victory at the Battle of Trafalgar in 1805. The statue atop the 150-foot Corinthian column is foreshortened to appear in perfect proportion from the ground. The granite fountains were added in 1845; Sir Edwin Landseer's bronze lions joined them in 1867.

Once surrounded on all sides by busy roads, the square was improved markedly by pedestrianisation in 2003 of the North Terrace, right in front of the **National Gallery**. A ban on feeding pigeons was another positive step. The square feels more like public space now, and is a focus for performance and celebration.

Around the perimeter are three plinths bearing statues of George IV and two Victorian military heroes, Henry Havelock and Sir Charles James Napier. The **fourth plinth** is used to display temporary, contemporary art. For 2012, sculptor Yinka Shonibare's large-scale model of HMS *Victory* in a glass bottle will be replaced by Elmgreen and Dragset's *Powerless Structures, Fig.101*, a bronze cast of a boy on a rocking horse playing on the militarism of the other statues. Nearby, a 21ft Omega digital clock counts down the time to the London 2012 Olympic and Paralympic Games.

Other points of interest around the square include an equestrian statue of Charles I, dating from the 1630s, with a plaque behind it that marks the original site of Edward I's Eleanor Cross, the official centre of London. (A recently renovated Victorian replica of the cross stands outside Charing Cross Station; *see p113.*) At the square's north-east corner is the refurbished **St Martin-in-the-Fields** (*see p135*).

INSIDE TRACK BIRD WATCH

Discover what's ruffling the feathers of a typical London pigeon – like the feeding ban at Trafalgar Square – at the Pigeon Blog: http://pigeonblog.wordpress.com.

Get There Greener

Hop on or hail a more eco-friendly form of transport.

The Routemaster, London's original, hop-on, hop-off bus, was finally sent to the great garage in the sky in 2005 by then-mayor Ken Livingstone. Noting the buses perennial popularity, his successor, Boris Johnson, promised to bring a new generation of Routemasters to London's streets. A design was unveiled in spring 2010 (www.london.gov.uk/priorities/transport/new-bus-london) – not looking much like the old Routemasters, it must be said, but at least you'll be able to hop on and off the back. Transport for London promises the new buses will be '15 per cent more fuel efficient than existing hybrid buses, 40 per cent more efficient than conventional diesel double decks and much quieter on the streets'; innovations include a battery that is recharged using energy generated by braking. The first five prototypes will be in operation by spring 2012.

Until then, experience the joy of the old on two 'heritage routes'. Refurbished buses from the 1960-64 Routemaster fleet run on routes 9 (from Aldwych via the Strand, Trafalgar Square and Piccadilly Circus to the Royal Albert Hall) and 15 (from Trafalgar Square to Tower Hill, with glimpses of the Strand, Fleet Street and St Paul's Cathedral); head to stops B or S in the south-west corner of Trafalgar Square. Buses run every 15 minutes from 9.30am;

fares match ordinary buses, but you must buy a ticket before boarding (*see p366*).

It's not just buses that are getting greener; taxis are too. The following firms use hybrid electric and petrol engine cars, and also carbon-offset their emissions. The luxurious fleet of grey Toyota Prius cabs at Climate Cars (7350 5960, www.climatecars.com) come complete with newspapers and free mineral water, while Ecoigo (0800 032 6446, www.ecoigo.com) runs a 24-hour service that promises to offset considerably more carbon than its fleet omits, through the World Land Trust. Green Tomato Cars (8568 0022, www.greentomatocars.com), meanwhile, are branded with the trademark tomato, offering competitive prices and a dependable service.

★ **FREE** **National Gallery**

Trafalgar Square, WC2N 5DN (7747 2885, www.nationalgallery.org.uk). Leicester Square tube or Charing Cross tube/rail. **Open** 10am-6pm Mon-Thur, Sat, Sun; 10am-9pm Fri. *Tours* 11.30am, 2.30pm daily. **Admission** free. *Special exhibitions* vary. **Credit** (shop) MC, V. **Map** p416 X5.

Founded in 1824 to display 36 paintings, the National Gallery is now one of the world's great repositories for art. There are masterpieces from virtually every European school of art, from austere 13th-century religious paintings to the sensual delights of Caravaggio and Van Gogh.

Furthest to the left of the main entrance, the modern Sainsbury Wing extension contains the gallery's earliest works: Italian paintings by masters such as Giotto and Piero della Francesca, as well as the *Wilton Diptych*, the finest medieval English picture in the collection, showing Richard II with the Virgin and Child. The basement of the Sainsbury Wing is the setting for important temporary exhibitions.

In the West Wing (left of the main entrance) are Italian Renaissance masterpieces by Correggio, Titian and Raphael. Straight ahead on entry, in the North Wing, are 17th-century Dutch, Flemish, Italian and Spanish Old Masters, including works such as Rembrandt's *A Woman Bathing in a Stream* and Caravaggio's *Supper at Emmaus*. Velázquez's *Rokeby Venus* is one of the artist's most famous paintings, a reclining nude asking herself – and us – 'How do we look?' Also in this wing are works by the great landscape artists Claude and Poussin. Turner insisted that his *Dido Building Carthage* and *Sun Rising through Vapour* should hang alongside two Claudes here that particularly inspired him.

In the East Wing (to the right of the main entrance, and most easily reached via the new street-level entrance on Trafalgar Square) are some of the gallery's most popular paintings: works by the French Impressionists and Post-Impressionists, including Monet's *Water-Lilies*, one of Van Gogh's *Sunflowers* and Seurat's *Bathers at Asnières*. Don't miss Renoir's astonishingly lovely *Les Parapluies*. You shouldn't plan to see everything in one visit, but free guided tours, audio guides and the superb Art Start computer (which allows you to tailor and map your own itinerary of must-sees) help you make the best of your time. The highlight for 2012 is 'Metamorphosis: Titian 2012' (11 July-23 Sept; *see p114* **Inside Track**). *Photo p137.*

★ FREE National Portrait Gallery

St Martin's Place, WC2H 0HE (7306 0055, www.npg.org.uk). Leicester Square tube or Charing Cross tube/rail. **Open** 10am-6pm Mon-Wed, Sat, Sun; 10am-9pm Thur, Fri. **Admission** free. *Special exhibitions* vary. **Credit** AmEx, MC, V. **Map** p416 X4.

Portraits don't have to be stuffy. The excellent National Portrait Gallery has everything from oil paintings of stiff-backed royals to photographs of soccer stars and gloriously unflattering political caricatures. The portraits of musicians, scientists, artists, philanthropists and celebrities are arranged in chronological order from the top to the bottom of the building, with the oldest at the top.

At the top of the escalator up from the main foyer, on the second floor, are the earliest works, portraits of Tudor and Stuart royals and notables, including Holbein's 'cartoon' of Henry VIII and the 'Ditchley Portrait' of his daughter, Elizabeth I, her pearly slippers placed firmly on a colourful map of England. On the same floor, the 18th-century collection features Georgian writers and artists, with one room devoted to the influential Kit-Cat Club of bewigged Whig (leftish) intellectuals, Congreve and Dryden among them. More famous names include Wren and Swift. The second floor also shows Regency greats, military men such as Wellington and Nelson, plus Byron, Wordsworth and other Romantics. The first floor is devoted to the Victorians (Dickens, Brunel, Darwin) and to 20th-century luminaries, such as TS Eliot and Ian McKellen.

Key exhibitions in 2012 are 'Lucien Freud Portraits' (9 Feb-27 May; *see right* **Inside Track**) and 'The Queen: Art & Image' (17 May-21 Oct). ▶ *'The Road to 2012' photographic project, which has been beautifully documenting people preparing for London 2012, reaches its finale this summer.*

FREE St Martin-in-the-Fields

Trafalgar Square, WC2N 4JJ (7766 1100, www.smitf.org). Leicester Square tube or Charing Cross tube/rail. **Open** 8am-6pm Mon-Fri; 9am-6pm Sat; 8am-7.30pm Sun. *Services* 8am, 1.15pm, 6pm Mon, Tue, Thur, Fri; 8am, 1pm, 5pm, 6.15pm Wed; 8am, 10am, 5pm, 6.30pm Sun. *Brass Rubbing Centre* 10am-6pm Mon-Wed; 10am-8pm Thur-Sat; 11.30am-5pm Sun. **Admission** free. *Brass rubbing* £4.50. **Credit** MC, V. **Map** p416 X4. There's been a church 'in the fields' between Westminster and the City since the 13th century, but the current one was built in 1726 by James Gibbs,

using a fusion of neoclassical and Baroque styles. The parish church for Buckingham Palace (note the royal box to the left of the gallery), St Martin's recently benefited from a £36m Lottery-funded refurbishment. The bright interior has been fully restored, with Victorian furbelows removed and the addition of a brilliant altar window that shows the Cross, stylised as if rippling on water. The crypt, its fine café and the London Brass Rubbing Centre have all been modernised.

▶ *For lunchtime and evening concerts, see p318.*

WHITEHALL TO PARLIAMENT SQUARE

Westminster tube or Charing Cross tube/rail.

The offices of the British government are lined along **Whitehall**, itself named after Henry VIII's magnificent palace, which burned to the ground in 1698. Walking south from Trafalgar Square, you pass the old **Admiralty Offices** and **War Office**, the **Ministry of Defence**, the **Foreign Office** and the **Treasury**, as well as the **Banqueting House** (*see p136*), one of the few buildings to survive the blaze. Also here is **Horse Guards**, headquarters of the Household Cavalry, the elite army unit that protects the Queen. The parade ground is to do rather different service during London 2012, as the venue for Beach Volleyball (*see p59*).

Either side of **Downing Street** – home to the prime minister (no.10) and chancellor (no.11), but closed to the public after IRA attacks in the 1980s – are significant war memorials. The millions who died in the service of the nation in World Wars I and II are commemorated by Sir Edwin Lutyens's dignified **Cenotaph**, focal point of Remembrance Day (*see p291*), while a

INSIDE TRACK
LUCIAN FREUD

A portrait by the late Lucian Freud matures and grows much as it was painted. Not only did the reclusive artist spend many hours transferring each sitter's personality and likeness to canvas, he built up the surfaces of his pictures until they took on a life of their own, erupting into nodules and pustules like fungi or real faces. The exhibition at the **National Portrait Gallery** (*see left*) brings together Freud's friends, lovers and other 'people in my life', while also exploring his stylistic development from his early surrealist works to the portraiture that would mark him as Britain's greatest postwar figurative artist.

SIGHTS

separate memorial to the women of World War II, by sculptor John Mills, recalls the seven million women who contributed to the war effort. Just past the Cenotaph and hidden beneath government offices at the St James's Park end of King Charles Street, the claustrophobic **Churchill War Rooms** (*see right*) are where Britain's wartime PM planned his campaigns and delivered his fiery speeches.

The broad sweep of Whitehall is an apt introduction to the monuments of **Parliament Square**. Laid out in 1868, this tiny green space is flanked by the extravagant **Houses of Parliament** (*see right*), the neo-Gothic Middlesex Guildhall and the twin, square spires of **Westminster Abbey** (*see p137*). Like a pre-pedestrianised Trafalgar Square, Parliament Square can seem little more than a glorified traffic island, despite all the statues of British politicians (Disraeli, Churchill) and foreign dignitaries (Lincoln, Mandela), but its symbolic value has been brought back into focus in recent years as a site for political protests.

Parliament itself simply dazzles. An outrageous neo-Gothic fantasy, the seat of the British government is still formally known as the Palace of Westminster, though the only remaining parts of the medieval palace are **Westminster Hall** and the **Jewel Tower** (*see p137*). At the north end of the palace is the clocktower housing the huge 'Big Ben' bell that gives the tower the name by which it's popularly known; more than seven feet tall, the bell weighs over 13 tons.

Banqueting House

Whitehall, SW1A 2ER (0844 482 7777, www.hrp.org.uk). Westminster tube or Charing Cross tube/rail. **Open** 10am-5pm Mon-Sat. **Admission** £5; £4 reductions; free under-16s. **Credit** MC, V. **Map** p399 L8.

This handsome Italianate mansion, which was designed by Inigo Jones and constructed in 1620, was the first true Renaissance building in London. The sole surviving part of the Tudor and Stuart kings' Whitehall Palace, the Banqueting House features a lavish painted ceiling by Rubens, glorifying James I, 'the wisest fool in Christendom' (*see also p139* **Snapshot**). Regrettably, James's successor, Charles I, did not rule so wisely. After losing the English Civil War to Cromwell's Roundheads, he was executed in front of Banqueting House in 1649 (the event is marked every 31 Jan). Lunchtime concerts are held on the first Monday of every month except August. Call before you visit: the mansion is sometimes closed for corporate functions.

Churchill War Rooms

Clive Steps, King Charles Street, SW1A 2AQ (7930 6961, www.iwm.org.uk). St James's Park or Westminster tube. **Open** 9.30am-6pm daily. **Admission** £15.95; £8-£12.80 reductions; free under-16s. **Credit** MC, V. **Map** p399 K9.

Out of harm's way beneath Whitehall, this cramped and spartan bunker was where Winston Churchill planned the Allied victory in World War II. Open to the public since 1984, the rooms powerfully bring to life the reality of a nation at war. The cabinet rooms were sealed on 16 August 1945, keeping the complex in a state of suspended animation: every pin stuck into the vast charts was placed there in the final days of the conflict. The humble quarters occupied by Churchill and his deputies give a tangible sense of wartime hardship, an effect reinforced by the wailing sirens and wartime speeches on the audio guide (free with admission).

FREE Houses of Parliament

Parliament Square, SW1A 0AA (Commons information 7219 4272, Lords information 7219 3107, www.parliament.uk). Westminster tube. **Open** (when in session) *House of Commons Visitors' Gallery* 2.30-10.30pm Mon, Tue; 11.30am-7.30pm Wed; 10.30am-6.30pm Thur; 9.30am-3pm Fri. *House of Lords Visitors' Gallery* 2.30-10.30pm Mon, Tue; 3-10pm Wed; 11am-7.30pm Thur; 10am Fri. *Tours* 9.15am-4.30pm Sat & summer recess; check website for details. **Admission** *Visitors' Gallery* free. *Tours* £15; £6-£10 reductions; £37 family; free under-5s. **Credit** MC, V. **Map** p399 L9.

After strict security checks at St Stephen's Gate (the only public access to Parliament), visitors are welcome to observe the debates at the House of Lords and House of Commons. The experience is usually soporific, but an exception is Prime Minister's Question Time at noon on Wednesday, when the incumbent PM fields a barrage of hostile questions from the opposition (and occasionally some of their own rebellious backbenchers) and soft questions from loyal backbenchers eager to present the government in a good light. Tickets must be arranged in advance through your embassy or MP, who can also arrange tours. The best time to visit Parliament is during the summer recess, when the main ceremonial rooms, including Westminster Hall and both Houses, are thrown open to the general public as part

---

INSIDE TRACK
LONDON BY GASLIGHT

Although most of London's street lights now use electric bulbs, there are still hundreds of gas-powered lamps dotted around the capital. You'll find them at the Tower of London, outside Buckingham Palace, and along the Mall and Pall Mall, among other locations. Casting a softer glow than their modern-day counterparts, they're in operation from dusk until dawn.

National Gallery. *See p134.*

of an organised tour (book in advance online). The first parliamentary session was held in St Stephen's Chapel in 1275, but Westminster only became the permanent seat of Parliament in 1532, when Henry VIII moved to a new des-res in Whitehall. Designed by Charles Barry, the Palace of Westminster is now a wonderful mish-mash of styles, dominated by Gothic buttresses, towers and arches. It looks much older than it is: the Parliament buildings were created in 1860 to replace the original Houses of Parliament, destroyed by fire in 1834. The compound contains 1,000 rooms, 11 courtyards, eight bars and six restaurants, plus a small cafeteria for visitors. Of the original palace, only the Jewel Tower (*see below*) and the ancient Westminster Hall remain.

Jewel Tower
Abingdon Street, SW1P 3JY (7222 2219, www. english-heritage.org.uk). Westminster tube. **Open** Apr-Oct 10am-5pm daily. *Nov-Mar* 10am-4pm Sat, Sun. **Admission** £3.20; £1.90-£2.90 reductions; free under-5s. **Credit** AmEx, MC, V. **Map** p399 L9.
This easy-to-overlook little stone tower opposite Parliament was built in 1365 to house Edward III's treasure. It is, with Westminster Hall, all that remains of the medieval Palace of Westminster. It contains a small exhibition on Parliament's history.
► *Nowadays, the Crown Jewels are on display in the Tower of London; see p101.*

FREE St Margaret's Church
Parliament Square, SW1P 3PA (7654 4840, www.westminster-abbey.org). St James's Park or Westminster tube. **Open** 9.30am-3.30pm Mon-Fri; 9.30am-1.30pm Sat; 2-4.30pm Sun (times vary due to services). *Services* 11am Sun. **Admission** free. **No credit cards. Map** p399 L9.

Tucked in under the grandeur of Westminster Abbey, this little church was founded in the 12th century; since 1614, it's served as the official church of the House of Commons. The interior features some of the most impressive pre-Reformation stained glass in London. The east window (1509) commemorates the marriage of Henry VIII and Catherine of Aragon; others celebrate Britain's first printer, William Caxton (buried here in 1491), explorer Sir Walter Raleigh (executed in Old Palace Yard in 1618), and writer John Milton (1608-74), who married his second wife here in 1656.

Westminster Abbey
20 Dean's Yard, SW1P 3PA (information 7222 5152, tours 7654 4834, www.westminster-abbey.org). St James's Park or Westminster tube. **Open** 9.30am-4.30pm Mon, Tue, Thur, Fri; 9.30am-7pm Wed; 9.30am-2.30pm Sat. *Abbey Museum, Chapter House & College Gardens* 10am-4pm daily. *Tours* phone for details. **Admission** £16; £6-£13 reductions; £32 family; free under-10s with adult. *Tours* £3. **Credit** AmEx, MC, V. **Map** p399 K9.
The cultural, historic and religious significance of Westminster Abbey is impossible to overstate, but also hard to remember as you're shepherded around, forced to elbow fellow tourists out of the way to read a plaque or see a tomb. The best plan is to get here as early in the day as you can. Edward the Confessor commissioned a church to St Peter on the site of a seventh-century version, but it was only consecrated on 28 December 1065, eight days before he died. William the Conqueror subsequently had himself crowned here on Christmas Day 1066 and, with just two exceptions, every English coronation since has taken place in the abbey.

Trafalgar Square.
See p133.

Many royal, military and cultural notables are interred here. The most haunting memorial is the Grave of the Unknown Warrior, in the nave. Elaborate resting places in side chapels are taken up by the tombs of Elizabeth I and Mary Queen of Scots. In Innocents Corner lie the remains of two lads believed to be Edward V and his brother Richard (their bodies were found at the Tower of London), as well as two of James I's children. Poets' Corner is the final resting place of Chaucer, the first to be buried here. Few of the other writers who have stones here are buried in the abbey, but the remains of Dryden, Johnson, Browning and Tennyson are all present. Henry James, TS Eliot and Dylan Thomas have dedications – on the floor, fittingly for Thomas.

In the vaulted area under the former monks' dormitory, one of the abbey's oldest parts, the Abbey Museum celebrated its centenary in 2008. You'll find effigies and waxworks of British monarchs, among them Edward II and Henry VII, wearing the robes they donned in life. The Choir School is the only school in Britain exclusively for the education of boy choristers from eight to 13. Its Christmas services are truly magnificent. The 900-year-old College Garden is one of the oldest cultivated gardens in Britain and a useful place to escape the crowds.

An ongoing refurbishment revealed the restored Cosmati Pavement to the public in spring 2010, and new visitor facilities, and a new gallery and refectory should be completed during 2012. *Photo p140*.

MILLBANK

Pimlico or Westminster tube.

Running south from Parliament along the river, Millbank leads eventually to **Tate Britain** (*see below*), built on the site of an extraordinary pentagonal prison that held criminals destined for transportation to Botany Bay. If you're walking south from the Palace of Westminster, look out on the left for **Victoria Tower Gardens**, which contain a statue of suffragette leader Emmeline Pankhurst and the rather colourful Buxton Drinking Fountain, which commemorates the emancipation of slaves. There's also a version of Rodin's sombre *Burghers of Calais*.

On the other side of the road, Dean Stanley Street leads to Smith Square, home to the architecturally striking **St John's Smith Square** (*see p318*), built as a church in grand Baroque style and now a popular venue for classical music. **Lord North Street**, the elegant row of Georgian terraces running north from the square, has long been a favourite address of politicians; note, too, the directions on the wall for wartime bomb shelters.

Across the river from Millbank is **Vauxhall Cross**, the oddly conspicuous HQ of the Secret Intelligence Service (SIS), commonly referred to by its old name MI6. In case any enemies of the state were unaware of its location, the cream and green block appeared as itself in the 1999 James Bond film *The World is Not Enough*.

★ **FREE Tate Britain**
Millbank, SW1P 4RG (7887 8888, www.tate.org.uk). Pimlico tube. **Open** 10am-6pm daily; 10am-10pm 1st Fri of mth. *Tours* 11am, noon, 2pm, 3pm Mon-Fri; noon, 3pm Sat, Sun. **Admission** free. *Special exhibitions* vary. **Credit** MC, V. **Map** p399 K11.
Tate Modern (*see p82*) gets the attention, but the original Tate Gallery, founded by sugar magnate Sir Henry Tate, has a broader brief. Housed in a stately building on the riverside, Tate Britain is second only to the National Gallery (*see p134*) when it comes to British art. The historical collection includes work by Hogarth, Gainsborough, Reynolds, Constable (who gets three rooms) and Turner (in the superb Clore Gallery). Many contemporary works were shifted to the other Tate when it opened in 2000, but Stanley Spencer, Lucian Freud and Francis Bacon are well represented here, and Art Now installations showcase up-and-coming British artists. Temporary exhibitions include headline-hungry blockbusters

and the controversy-courting Turner Prize exhibition (Oct-Jan). The gallery has a good restaurant and a well-stocked gift shop.

Major exhbitions for 2012 include: 'Picasso and Modern British Art' (15 Feb-15 July) and 'Another London' (27 July-16 Sept), classic photographs of the city to coincide with the London 2012 Games.

▶ *The handy Tate-to-Tate boat (see p83) zips along the river to Tate Modern every 40mins.*

VICTORIA

Pimlico tube or Victoria tube/rail.

As you might expect from London's main backpacker hangout, Victoria is colourful and chaotic. Victoria rail station is a major hub for trains to southern seaside resorts and ferry terminals, while the nearby coach station is served by buses from all over Europe. Catering to new arrivals, Belgrave Road provides an almost unbroken line of cheap and often shabby B&Bs, hotels and hostels, most set in fading townhouses. The theatres dotted around Victoria form a western outpost of the West End's Theatreland, with a similar programme of star-vehicle dramas and musicals.

Not to be confused with Westminster Abbey (*see p137*), **Westminster Cathedral** is the headquarters of the Roman Catholic church in England. South and east of Victoria Station are the Georgian terraces of **Pimlico** and **Belgravia**. Antiques stores and restaurants line Pimlico Road; the intriguing independent shops of Tachbrook Street are worth a look.

North of Victoria Street towards Parliament Square is **Christchurch Gardens**, burial site of Thomas ('Colonel') Blood, who stole the Crown Jewels in 1671. He was apprehended making his getaway but, amazingly, managed to talk his way into a full pardon. Also in the area are **New Scotland Yard**, with its famous revolving sign, and the art deco headquarters of **London Underground** at 55 Broadway. Public outrage about Jacob Epstein's graphic nudes on the façade almost led to the resignation of the managing director in 1929.

FREE Westminster Cathedral

42 Francis Street, SW1P 1QW (7798 9055, www.westminstercathedral.org.uk). Victoria tube/rail. **Open** 7am-6pm Mon-Fri; 8am-6.30pm Sat; 8am-7pm Sun. *Exhibition* 10am-5pm Mon-Fri; 10am-6pm Sat, Sun. *Bell tower* 9.30am-4.30pm daily. *Services* 7am, 8am, 10.30am, 12.30pm, 1.05pm, 5.30pm Mon-Fri; 8am, 9am, 10.30am, 12.30pm, 6pm Sat; 8am, 9am, 10.30am, noon, 5.30pm, 7pm Sun. **Admission** free; donations appreciated. *Exhibition* £5; free-£2.50 reductions; £11 family. *Bell tower & exhibition* £8; free-£4 reductions; £17.50 family. **Credit** MC, V. **Map** p398 J10.

With its domes, arches and soaring tower, the most important Catholic church in England looks surprisingly Byzantine. There's a reason: architect John Francis Bentley, who built it between 1895 and 1903, was heavily influenced by Hagia Sophia in Istanbul. Compared to the candy-cane exterior, the interior is surprisingly restrained (in fact, it's unfinished), but there are still some impressive marble columns and mosaics. Eric Gill's sculptures of the Stations of the Cross (1914-18) were dismissed as 'Babylonian' when they were first installed, but worshippers have come to love them. A new permanent exhibition, 'Treasures of the Cathedral', opened in the upper gallery in 2010 to celebrate the centenary of the cathedral's consecration. It displays an impressive

Snapshot
Stuart London

Where to see how London lived.

Peter Paul Rubens' painted ceiling in the **Banqueting House** (*see p136*) is as fine a piece of Stuart propaganda as you could wish to see, its chubby cherubs commissioned by Charles I to celebrate his father James I's rule under bombastic titles: 'The Union of the Crowns', 'The Apotheosis of James I', 'The Peaceful Reign of James I'. Inigo Jones, the building's architect, also built the **Queen's House** (*see p173*) and **St Paul's Covent Garden** (*see p112*).

SIGHTS

Westminster Abbey. *See p137.*

SIGHTS

Arts & Crafts coronet, a Tudor chalice, holy relics and Bentley's amazing architectural model of his cathedral, complete with tiny hawks. A lift runs to the top of the 273ft bell tower, for great views.

AROUND ST JAMES'S PARK

St James's Park tube.

Handsome **St James's Park** was founded as a deer park for the royal occupants of St James's Palace, and remodelled by John Nash on the orders of George IV. The central lake is home to various species of wildfowl; pelicans have been kept here since the 17th century, when the Russian ambassador donated several of the bag-jawed birds to Charles II. The pelicans are fed at 3pm daily, though they supplement their diet at other times of the day with the occasional pigeon. Lots of humans picnic here, too, notably around the bandstand during the summer weekend concerts. The bridge over the lake offers good views of Buckingham Palace.

Along the north side of the park, the Mall connects Buckingham Palace with **Trafalgar Square** (*see p133*). It looks like a classic processional route, but the Mall was actually laid out as a pitch for Charles II to play 'pallemaille' (an early version of croquet imported from France) after the pitch at Pall Mall became too crowded. On the south side of the park, Wellington Barracks contains the

Guards Museum (*see p141*) to the east, Horse Guards contains the **Household Cavalry Museum** (*see p141*).

Along the north side of the Mall, **Carlton House Terrace** was the last project completed by John Nash before his death in 1835. Part of the terrace now houses the **ICA** (*see p141*). Just behind is the **Duke of York column**, commemorating Prince Frederick, Duke of York, who led the British Army against the French. He's the nursery rhyme's 'Grand old Duke of York', who marched his 10,000 men neither up nor down Cassel hill in Flanders.

Buckingham Palace & Royal Mews

The Mall, SW1A 1AA (Palace 7766 7300, Royal Mews 7766 7302, Queen's Gallery 7766 7301, www.royalcollection.org.uk). Green Park tube or Victoria tube/rail. **Open** times vary; check website for details. **Admission** prices vary; check website for details. **Credit** AmEx, MC, V. **Map** p398 H9.
Although nearby St James's Palace (*see p142*) remains the official seat of the British court, every monarch since Victoria has used Buckingham Palace as their primary home. Originally known as Buckingham House, the present home of the British royals was constructed as a private house for the Duke of Buckingham in 1703, but George III liked it so much he purchased it for his German bride Charlotte in 1761. George IV decided to occupy the mansion himself after taking the throne in 1820 and John Nash was hired to convert it into a palace

befitting a king. Construction was beset with problems, and Nash – whose expensive plans had always been disliked by Parliament – was dismissed in 1830. When Victoria came to the throne in 1837, the building was barely habitable. The job of finishing the palace fell to the reliable but unimaginative Edward Blore ('Blore the Bore'). The neoclassical frontage now in place was the work of Aston Webb in 1913.

As the home of the Queen, the palace is usually closed to visitors, but you can view the interior for a brief period each year while the Windsors are away on their holidays; you'll be able to see the State Rooms, still used to entertain dignitaries and guests of state, and part of the garden. There's even a café – paper cups, sadly, but coloured a pretty blue-green and clearly marked with the palace crest for souvenir-hunters. At any time of year, you can visit the Queen's Gallery to see her personal collection of treasures, including paintings by Rubens and Rembrandt, Sèvres porcelain and the Diamond Diadem crown. Further along Buckingham Palace Road, the Royal Mews is a grand garage for the royal fleet of Rolls-Royces and home to the splendid royal carriages and the horses, individually named by the Queen, that pull them.

Guards Museum

Wellington Barracks, Birdcage Walk, SW1E 6HQ (7414 3428, www.theguardsmuseum.com). St James's Park tube. **Open** 10am-4pm daily. **Admission** £4; £2 reductions; free under-16s. **Credit** (shop) AmEx, MC, V. **Map** p398 J9.
Just down the road from Horse Guards, this small museum tells the 350-year story of the Foot Guards, using flamboyant uniforms, period paintings, medals and intriguing memorabilia, such as the stuffed body of Jacob the Goose, the Guard's Victorian mascot, who was regrettably run over by a van in barracks. Appropriately, the shop is well stocked with toy soldiers of the British regiments.
▶ *The Guards assemble on the parade ground here before the Changing of the Guard; see p290* **Standing on Ceremony**.

Household Cavalry Museum

Horse Guards, Whitehall, SW1A 2AX (7930 3070, www.householdcavalrymuseum.co.uk). Westminster tube or Charing Cross tube/rail. **Open** *Apr-Oct* 10am-6pm daily. *Nov-Mar* 10am-5pm daily. **Admission** £6; £4 reductions; £15 family ticket; free under-5s. **Credit** MC, V. **Map** p399 K8.
Household Cavalry is a fairly workaday name for the military peacocks who make up the Queen's official guard. They get to tell their stories through video diaries at this small but entertaining museum, which also offers the chance to see medals, uniforms and shiny cuirasses (breastplates) up close. You'll also get a peek – and sniff – of the magnificent horses that parade just outside every day: the stables are separated from the main museum by no more than a screen of glass. Interactive displays on the horses have recently been added. Note: the museum will be closed 18 June-1 Oct for the London 2012 Games.
▶ *The parade ground outside the Household Cavalry Museum will host the Beach Volleyball for the London 2012 Games.*

FREE ICA (Institute of Contemporary Arts)

The Mall, SW1Y 5AH (information 7930 0493, tickets 7930 3647, www.ica.org.uk). Piccadilly

Buckingham Palace.

SIGHTS

SIGHTS

Circus tube or Charing Cross tube/rail. **Open**
Galleries (during exhibitions) noon-7pm Wed,
Fri-Sun; noon-9pm Thur. **Admission** free.
Credit AmEx, MC, V. **Map** p399 K8.
Founded in 1947 by a collective of poets, artists and
critics, the ICA has recently found itself somewhat
adrift. The institute moved to the Mall in 1968 and
set itself up as a venue for arthouse cinema, performance art, philosophical debates, exhibitions, art-
themed club nights and anything else that might
challenge convention – but 'convention' is much
harder to challenge now, when everyone's doing it.
New director Gregor Muir has some interesting
ideas, including a redesigned interior and Friday
lunchtime talks from topline contemporary artists.

ST JAMES'S

Green Park or Piccadilly Circus tube.

One of London's most refined residential areas,
St James's was laid out in the 1660s for royal
and aristocratic families, some of whom still live
here. It's a rewarding district, a sedate bustle of
intriguing mews and grand squares. Bordered
by Piccadilly, Haymarket, the Mall and Green
Park, the district is centred on **St James's
Square**. Just south of the square, **Pall Mall** is
lined with exclusive, members-only gentlemen's
clubs (in the old-fashioned sense of the word).
Polished nameplates reveal such prestigious
establishments as the **Institute of Directors**
(no.116) and the **Reform Club** (nos.104-105),
site of Phileas Fogg's famous bet in *Around
the World in Eighty Days*. Around the corner
on St James's Street, the **Carlton Club** (no.69)
is the official club of the Conservative Party;
Lady Thatcher remains the only woman to be
granted full membership. Nearby on King Street
is **Christie's** (7839 9060, www.christies.com),
the world's oldest fine art auctioneers.

At the south end of St James's Street, **St
James's Palace** was built for Henry VIII in
the 1530s. Extensively remodelled over the
centuries, the red-brick palace is still the official
address of the Royal Court, even though every

monarch since 1837 has lived at Buckingham
Palace. From here, Mary Tudor surrendered
Calais and Elizabeth I led the campaign
against the Spanish Armada; this is also
where Charles I was confined before his 1649
execution. The palace is home to the Princess
Royal (the title given to the monarch's eldest
daughter, currently Princess Anne); it's closed
to the public, but you can attend Sunday
services at its historic **Chapel Royal** (1st Sun
of mth, Oct-Easter Sunday; 8.30am, 11.15am).

Adjacent to St James's Palace is **Clarence
House** (*see below*), former residence of the
Queen Mother; a few streets north, delightful
Spencer House (*see below*) is the ancestral
home of the family of the late Princess Diana.
Across Marlborough Road lies the pocket-sized
Queen's Chapel, designed by Inigo Jones
in the 1620s for Charles I's Catholic Queen
Henrietta Maria, at a time when Catholic places
of worship were officially banned. The Queen's
Chapel can only be visited for Sunday services
(Easter-July; 8.30am, 11.15am).

Clarence House

*The Mall, SW1A 1AA (7766 7303, www.
royalcollection.org.uk). Green Park tube.* **Open**
Aug-early Sept 10am-4pm Mon-Fri; 10am-5.30pm
Sat, Sun. **Admission** £8.50; £4.50 reductions; free
under-5s. *Tours* pre-booked tickets only. **Credit**
AmEx, MC, V. **Map** p398 J8.
Currently the official residence of Prince Charles and
the Duchess of Cornwall, this austere royal mansion
was built between 1825 and 1827 for Prince William
Henry, Duke of Clarence, who stayed on in the house
after his coronation as King William IV. Designed
by John Nash, the house has been much altered by
its many inhabitants, among them the late Queen
Mother. Five receiving rooms and the Queen
Mother's British art collection usually open to the
public in summer, but for advance bookings only.

Spencer House

*27 St James's Place, SW1A 1NR (7499 8620,
www.spencerhouse.co.uk). Green Park tube.* **Open**
Feb-July, Sept-Dec 10.30am-5.45pm Sun. Last tour
4.45pm. *Gardens* phone or see website for details.
Admission £9; £7 reductions. Under-10s not
allowed. **Credit** MC, V. **Map** p398 J8.
One of the last surviving private residences in St
James's, this handsome mansion was designed for
John Spencer by John Vardy, but was completed in
1766 by Hellenophile architect James Stuart, which
explains the mock Greek flourishes. Lady
Georgiana, the 18th-century socialite and beauty,
and subject of bodice-ripping film *The Duchess*, lived
here, but the Spencers left generations before their
most famous scion, Diana, married into the Windsor
family. The palatial building has painstakingly
restored interiors, now mainly used for corporate
entertaining, and a wonderful garden.

Chelsea

Blue bloods, red coats and an exquisite green space.

Chelsea is where London's wealthy classes play in cultural and geographical isolation. Originally a fishing hamlet, the area was a 'village of palaces' by the 16th century, home to the likes of Henry VIII's ill-fated advisor Sir Thomas More. Artists and poets (Whistler, Carlyle, Wilde) followed from the 1880s, before the fashionistas arrived with the opening of Mary Quant's Bazaar in 1955. Soon after, Chelsea had a raffish reputation and was at the forefront of successive youth culture revolutions. Those days are long gone. Now there are smart shops and street after sleepy street of immaculate terraced housing, but cultural pleasures are few, making the arrival of the **Saatchi Gallery** (*see p144*) especially welcome.

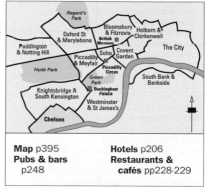

Map p395	**Hotels** p206
Pubs & bars p248	**Restaurants & cafés** pp228-229

SLOANE SQUARE & THE KING'S ROAD

Sloane Square tube then various buses.

Synonymous with the Swinging Sixties and immortalised by punk, the dissipated phase of the King's Road is now a matter for historians as the street teems with pricey fashion houses and air-conditioned poodle parlours. Yet on a sunny day, it does make a vivid stroll. For one thing, you don't have to take yourself as seriously as the locals. And for another, the area is figuratively rich with historical associations and literally so, with the expensive red-brick houses that slumber down leafy mews and charming, cobbled sidestreets.

At the top (east end) of the King's Road is **Sloane Square**. It's named after Sir Hans Sloane, who provided the land for the Chelsea Physic Garden (*see p145*), invented milk chocolate in the early 18th century and was instrumental in the founding of the British Museum (which was set up to hold his collections when he died). In the middle of the square sits a fountain erected in 1953, a gift to the borough from the Royal Academy of Arts (*see p132*). The shaded benches in the middle of the square provide a lovely counterpoint to the looming façades of Tiffany & Co and the enormous Peter Jones department store, in a 1930s building with excellent views from its top-floor café. A certain edginess is lent to proceedings by the **Royal Court Theatre** (*see p344*), which shocked the nation with its 1956 première of John Osborne's *Look Back in Anger*.

To escape the bustle and fumes, head to the **Duke of York Square**, a pedestrianised enclave of boutiques and restaurants that's presided over by a statue of Sir Hans. In the summer, the cooling fountains attract hordes of children, their parents sitting to watch from the outdoor areas of the cafés or taking advantage of the Saturday food market. The square is also home to the mercilessly modern art of the **Saatchi Gallery** (*see p144*), housed in former military barracks. Around the corner on Chelsea Bridge Road sit more disused army lodgings; the proposed redevelopment of **Chelsea Barracks** became a controversial topic a couple of years back, thanks to the intervention of Prince Charles.

The once-adventurous shops on the King's Road are now a mix of trendier-than-thou fashion houses and high-street chains, but there are still a few gems around if you're prepared to look off the beaten path: **Shop at Bluebird** (*see p266*) and London's second branch of **Anthropologie** (*see p266*) suggest future directions. Wander Cale Street for some pleasing boutiques, or head for the **Chelsea Farmers' Market** on adjoining Sydney Street to find a clutter of artfully distressed rustic sheds housing restaurants and shops selling everything from cigars to garden products. Sydney Street leads to **St Luke's Church**, where Charles Dickens married Catherine Hogarth in 1836.

Towards the western end of the King's Road is **Bluebird**, a dramatic art deco former motor garage housing a café, a restaurant and the hip shop mentioned above. A little further up the road, the **World's End** store (no.430) occupies what was once Vivienne Westwood's notorious leather- and fetishwear boutique Sex; a green-haired Johnny Rotten auditioned for the Sex Pistols here in 1975 by singing along to an Alice Cooper record on the shop's jukebox.

FREE Saatchi Gallery
Duke of York's HQ, off the King's Road, SW3 4SQ (7811 3070, www.saatchi-gallery.co.uk). Sloane Square tube. **Open** 10am-6pm daily. **Admission** free. **Credit** (shop) AmEx, MC, V. **Map** p395 F11.
Charles Saatchi's gallery offers 50,000sq ft of space for temporary exhibitions. Given his fame as a promoter in the 1990s of what became known as the Young British Artists – Damien Hirst, Tracey Emin, Gavin Turk, Sarah Lucas et al – it will surprise many

that the opening exhibition a few years back was devoted to new Chinese art. More recent shows have continued with the international feel.

CHEYNE WALK & CHELSEA EMBANKMENT
Sloane Square tube then various buses.

Chelsea's riverside has long been noted for its nurseries and gardens. The borough's horticultural curiosity is still alive, lending a village air that befits a place of retirement for the former British soldiers living in the **Royal Hospital Chelsea** (*see p145*). In summer, the Chelsea Pensioners, as they're known, regularly don red coats and tricorn hats when venturing beyond the gates. The Royal Hospital's lovely gardens host the **Chelsea Flower Show** (*see p285*) in May each year. Next door is the **National Army Museum** (*see p145*).

West from the river end of Royal Hospital Road is **Cheyne Walk**, less peaceful than it once was due to Embankment traffic. Its river-view benches remain good spots for a sit-down, but the tranquillity of **Chelsea Physic Garden** (*see p145*) is the real treat.

Further west on Cheyne Walk, the park benches of **Chelsea Embankment Gardens** face Albert Bridge, where signs still order troops to 'Break step when marching over this

Chelsea Physic Garden.

bridge'. In the small gardens, you'll find a statue of the great historian Thomas Carlyle – the 'sage of Chelsea', whose home is preserved (*see below* **Carlyle's House**). Nearby, a gold-faced statue of Sir Thomas More looks out over the river from the garden of **Chelsea Old Church** (*see below*), where he once sang in the choir and may well be (partially) buried. Follow Old Church Street north and you'll find the **Chelsea Arts Club** (no.143), founded in 1871 by Whistler.

North of the western extremity of Cheyne Walk are **Brompton Cemetery** (*see p183*) and the home ground of Chelsea FC, **Stamford Bridge** (*see p337*). Football fans might be interested in the **Chelsea Centenary Museum** (www.chelseafc.com, 10.30am-4.30pm daily, £10, £8-£9 reductions), which contains perhaps the only photograph of Raquel Welch wearing football kit to be found in any museum in England.

Carlyle's House
24 Cheyne Row, SW3 5HL (7352 7087, www.nationaltrust.org.uk). Sloane Square tube or bus 11, 19, 22, 49, 170, 211, 319. **Open** *Mar-Oct* 11am-5pm Wed-Sun. **Admission** £5.10; £2.60 children; £12.80 family. **No credit cards.** **Map** p395 E12.

Thomas Carlyle and his wife Jane moved to this four-storey, Queen Anne house in 1834. The house was inaugurated as a museum in 1896, 15 years after Carlyle's death, offering an intriguing snapshot of Victorian life. The writer's quest for quiet (details of his valiant attempts to soundproof the attic) strikes a chord today: he was plagued by the sound of revelry from Cremorne Pleasure Gardens.

FREE Chelsea Old Church
Old Church Street, SW3 5DQ (7795 1019, www.chelseaoldchurch.org.uk). Sloane Square tube or bus 11, 19, 22, 49, 319. **Open** 2-4pm Tue-Thur; 1.30-5pm Sun. *Services* 8am, 10am, 11am, 12.15pm Sun. *Evensong* 6pm Sun. **Admission** free; donations appreciated. **No credit cards. Map** p395 E12.

Legend has it that the Thomas More Chapel, which remains on the south side, contains More's headless body buried somewhere under the walls (his head, after being spiked on London Bridge, was 'rescued' and buried in a family vault in St Dunstan's church, Canterbury). There's a striking statue of More outside the church. Guides are on hand on Sundays.

★ Chelsea Physic Garden
66 Royal Hospital Road, SW3 4HS (7352 5646, www.chelseaphysicgarden.co.uk). Sloane Square tube or bus 11, 19, 22. **Open** *Apr-Oct* noon-5pm Tue-Fri; noon-6pm Sun. *Tours* times vary; phone to check. **Admission** £8; £5 reductions; free under-5s. *Tours* free. **Credit** MC, V. **Map** p395 F12.

The capacious grounds of this gorgeous botanic garden are filled with healing herbs and vegetables, rare trees and dye plants. The garden was founded in 1673 by Sir Hans Sloane with the purpose of cultivating and studying plants for medical purposes. The first plant specimens were brought to England and planted here in 1676, with the famous Cedars of Lebanon (the first to be grown in England) arriving a little later. The garden opened to the public in 1893.
► *Sloane's specimens began the botany collection of the Natural History Museum; see p147.*

FREE National Army Museum
Royal Hospital Road, SW3 4HT (7730 0717, www.national-army-museum.ac.uk). Sloane Square tube or bus 11, 137, 170. **Open** 10am-5.30pm daily. **Admission** free. **Credit** (shop) AmEx, MC, V. **Map** p395 F12.

More entertaining than its modern exterior suggests, this museum dedicated to the history of the British Army kicks off with 'Redcoats', a gallery that starts at Agincourt in 1415 and ends with the American War of Independence. Upstairs, 'The Road to Waterloo' marches through 20 years of struggle against the French, featuring 70,000 model soldiers. Men of a certain age will welcome the exhibition of art from *Commando* comics with cries of 'Take that, Fritz' and 'Die Englander, schweinhund', while Major Michael 'Bronco' Lane, conqueror of Everest, has donated his frostbitten fingertips.

FREE Royal Hospital Chelsea
Royal Hospital Road, SW3 4SR (7881 5200, www.chelsea-pensioners.org.uk). Sloane Square tube or bus 11, 19, 22, 137, 170. **Open** *Apr-Sept* 10am-noon, 2-4pm Mon-Sat; 2-4pm Sun. *Oct-Mar* 10am-noon, 2-4pm Mon-Sat. **Admission** free. **Credit** MC, V. **Map** p395 F12.

Roughly 350 Chelsea Pensioners (retired soldiers) live at the Royal Hospital, founded in 1682 by Charles II and designed by Sir Christopher Wren (with adjustments by Robert Adam and Sir John Soane). Retired soldiers are still eligible to apply for a final posting here if they're over 65 and in receipt of an Army or War Disability Pension for Army Service. The pensioners have their own club room, bowling green and gardens, and get tickets to Chelsea FC home games. The museum, open at the same times as the Hospital, has more about their lives.

INSIDE TRACK ESPIONAGE

Chelsea has long been a popular haunt for spies, real and fictional. KGB agent Kim Philby held meetings at the Markham Arms at 138 King's Road, now a branch of the Santander bank, and both James Bond and George Smiley were given homes in the area by their respective creators.

SIGHTS

Knightsbridge & South Kensington

Shop 'til you pop into a museum.

A certain type of Londoner goes to **Knightsbridge** to spend, spend, spend. Or, at least, to hang around people who are spend, spend, spending. Many of the key designer labels have major shops in the area, which gets plenty of foot traffic thanks to its world-famous department stores and high-end restaurants. Nearby, **South Kensington**'s footprint is cultural rather than commercial: you'll find three of the world's greatest museums, some extraordinary colleges, a concert hall and a cutting-edge contemporary art gallery.

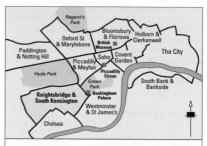

| Map pp392-393 & p395 | Restaurants & cafés pp229-231 |
| Hotels pp207-208 | Pubs & bars p248 |

KNIGHTSBRIDGE

Knightsbridge tube.

Knightsbridge in the 11th century was a village celebrated for its taverns, highwaymen and the legend that two knights once fought to the death on the bridge spanning the Westbourne River (later dammed to form Hyde Park's Serpentine lake). In modern Knightsbridge, urban princesses would be too busy unsheathing the credit card to notice such a farrago. Voguish **Harvey Nichols** (*see p257*) holds court at the top of **Sloane Street**, which leads down to Sloane Square. Expensive brands – Gucci, Prada, Chanel – dominate. East of Sloane Street is **Belgravia**, characterised by a cluster of embassies around **Belgrave**

Square. Hidden behind the stucco-clad parades fronting the square are numerous mews, worth exploring for the pubs they conceal, notably the **Nag's Head** (53 Kinnerton Street, 7235 1135).

For many tourists, Knightsbridge means one thing: **Harrods** (*see p257*). From its tan bricks and olive green awning to its green-coated doormen, it's an instantly recognisable retail legend. Further along is the imposing **Brompton Oratory** (*see below*).

FREE Brompton Oratory

Thurloe Place, Brompton Road, SW7 2RP (7808 0900, www.bromptonoratory.com). South Kensington tube. **Open** 6.30am-8pm daily. **Admission** free; donations appreciated. **No credit cards. Map** p395 E10.

The second-biggest Catholic church in the country (after Westminster Cathedral; *see p139*) is formally the Church of the Immaculate Heart of Mary, but almost universally known as the Brompton Oratory. Completed in 1884, it feels older, partly because of the Baroque Italianate style but also because much of the decoration pre-dates the structure: Mazzuoli's 17th-century apostle statues, for example, are from Siena cathedral. The 11am Solemn Mass sung in Latin on Sundays is enchanting, as are Vespers, at 3.30pm; the website has details. During the Cold War, KGB agents used the church as a dead-letter box.

SIGHTS

▶ *A new chapel, in honour of the recently beatified Cardinal Newman, is now complete.*

SOUTH KENSINGTON

Gloucester Road or South Kensington tube.

As far as cultural and academic institutions are concerned, this is the land of plenty. It was Prince Albert who oversaw the inception of its world-class museums, colleges and concert hall, using the profits of the 1851 Great Exhibition; the area was nicknamed 'Albertopolis' in his honour. You'll find the **Natural History Museum** (*see right*), the **Science Museum** (*see p149*) and the **Victoria & Albert Museum** (*see p149*), **Imperial College**, the **Royal College of Art** and the **Royal College of Music** (Prince Consort Road, 7589 3643; call for details of the musical instrument museum), which forms a unity with the **Royal Albert Hall** (*see p317*), open since 1871 and variously used for boxing, motor shows, marathons, table tennis tournaments, fascist rallies and rock concerts. Opposite is the **Albert Memorial** (*see below*).

FREE Albert Memorial
Kensington Gardens (7936 2568). South Kensington tube. **Tours** *Mar-Dec* 2pm, 3pm 1st Sun of mth. **Admission** *Tours* £6; £5 reductions. **No credit cards. Map** p393 D8.
'I would rather not be made the prominent feature of such a monument,' was Prince Albert's reported response when the subject of his commemoration arose. Hard, then, to imagine what he would have made of this extraordinary thing, unveiled 15 years after his death. Created by Sir George Gilbert Scott, it centres around a gilded Albert holding a catalogue of the 1851 Great Exhibition, guarded on four corners by the continents of Africa, America, Asia and

Europe. The pillars are crowned with bronze statues of the sciences, and the frieze at the base depicts major artists, architects and musicians. It's one of London's most dramatic monuments.

★ FREE Natural History Museum
Cromwell Road, SW7 5BD (7942 5000, www.nhm.ac.uk). South Kensington tube. **Open** 10am-5.50pm daily. **Admission** free; charges apply for special exhibitions. *Tours* free. **Credit** MC, V. **Map** p395 D10.
Both a research institution and a fabulous museum, the NHM opened in Alfred Waterhouse's purpose-built, Romanesque palazzo on the Cromwell Road in 1881. Now joined by the splendid Darwin Centre extension, the original building still looks quite magnificent. The pale blue and terracotta façade just about prepares you for the natural wonders within.

Taking up the full length of the vast entrance hall is the cast of a Diplodocus skeleton. A left turn leads into the west wing or Blue Zone, where long queues form to see animatronic dinosaurs – the endlessly popular T Rex is back after hip surgery in 2010. A display on biology features an illuminated, man-sized model of a foetus in the womb along with graphic diagrams of how it might have got there.

A right turn from the central hall leads past the 'Creepy Crawlies' exhibition to the Green Zone. Stars include a cross-section through a Giant Sequoia tree and an amazing array of stuffed birds, including the chance to compare the egg of a hummingbird, smaller than a little finger nail, with that of an elephant bird (now extinct), almost football-sized. Beyond is the Red Zone. 'Earth's Treasury' is a mine of information on a variety of precious metals, gems and crystals; 'From the Beginning' is a brave attempt to give the expanse of geological time a human perspective. Outside, the delightful Wildlife Garden (Apr-Oct only) showcases a range of British lowland habitats, including a 'Bee Tree', a hollow tree trunk that opens to reveal a busy hive.

SIGHTS

Hyde Park. *See p149.*

Profile Science Museum

One of London's greatest museums takes on the world's greatest challenge.

SIGHTS

Only marginally less popular with kids than its natural historical neighbour, the **Science Museum** (for listings, *see p149*) is a celebration of the wonders of technology in the service of our daily lives. On the ground floor, the shop – selling wacky toys – is part of the 'Energy Hall', which introduces the museum's collections with impressive 18th-century steam engines. In 'Exploring Space', rocket science and the lunar landings are illustrated by dramatically lit mock-ups and models, before the museum gears up for its core collection in 'Making the Modern World'. Introduced by Puffing Billy, the world's oldest steam locomotive (built in 1815), the gallery also contains Stephenson's Rocket. Also here are the Apollo 10 command module, classic cars and an absorbing collection of everyday technological marvels from 1750 right up to the present.

In the main body of the museum, the second floor holds displays on computing, marine engineering and mathematics; the third floor is dedicated to flight, among other things, including the hands-on Launchpad gallery, which has levers, pulleys, explosions and all manner of experiments for children (and their associated grown-ups). On the fifth floor, you'll find an old-fashioned but intriguing display on the science and art of medicine.

Beyond 'Making the Modern World', bathed in an eerie blue light, the three floors of the Wellcome Wing are where the museum makes sure it stays on the cutting edge of science. On the ground floor, 'Antenna' is a web-savvy look at breaking science stories, displaying video interviews and Q&As with real research scientists alongside the weird new objects they've been working on. Upstairs, the enjoyable and troubling 'Who Am I?' gallery was relaunched in summer 2010. The dozen silver pods that surround brightly lit cases of objects have engaging interactive displays – from a cartoon of ethical dilemmas that introduces you to your dorsolateral prefrontal cortex to a chance to find out what gender your brain is. Compelling objects include a jellyfish that's 'technically immortal', the statistically average British man (he's called Jose, by the way) and a pound of human fat, displayed alongside a gastric band. There's also contemporary art, including installations and Stephen Wiltshire's amazingly detailed drawing, from memory, of the Houses of Parliament.

THREE TO SEE
There's more brilliant science at the **Wellcome Collection** (*see p109*), the **Royal Institution & Faraday Museum** (*see p131*) and the **Royal Observatory** (*see p173*).

Many of the museum's 22 million insect and plant specimens are housed in the new Darwin Centre, where they take up nearly 17 miles of shelving. With its new eight-storey Cocoon, this is also home to the museum's research scientists, who can be watched at work. But a great deal of this amazing institution is hidden from public view, given over to labs and specialised storage.

The major exhibition for 2012 (to 2 September) is 'Scott's Last Expedition', looking at the explorer's Terra Nova odyssey, including specimens collected by the team and a full-size replica of base camp.

★ FREE **Science Museum**
Exhibition Road, SW7 2DD (switchboard 7942 4000, information 0870 870 4868, www.sciencemuseum.org.uk). South Kensington tube. **Open** 10am-6pm daily. **Admission** free; charges apply for special exhibitions. **Credit** MC, V. **Map** p395 D9.
Major exhibitions for 2012 include 'Hidden Heroes – the Genius of Everyday Things', looking at some of the foundation stones of modern life, including the zip and the tea bag, and 'Oramics to Electronica: Revealing Histories of Electronic Music'.
See p148 **Profile.**

★ FREE **Victoria & Albert Museum**
Cromwell Road, SW7 2RL (7942 2000, www.vam.ac.uk). South Kensington tube. **Open** 10am-5.45pm Mon-Thur, Sat, Sun; 10am-10pm Fri. *Tours hourly, 10.30am-3.30pm daily.* **Admission** free; charges for special exhibitions. **Credit** MC, V. **Map** p395 E10.
The V&A is one of the world's most magnificent museums, its foundation stone laid on this site by Queen Victoria in her last official public engagement in 1899. It is a superb showcase for applied arts from around the world, appreciably calmer than its tear-away cousins on the other side of Exhibition Road. Some 150 grand galleries on seven floors contain countless pieces of furniture, ceramics, sculpture, paintings, posters, jewellery, metalwork, glass, textiles and dress, spanning several centuries. Items are grouped by theme, origin or age, but any attempt to comprehend the whole collection in a single visit is doomed. For advice, tap the patient staff, who field a formidable combination of leaflets, floorplans, general knowledge and polite concern.

Highlights include the seven Raphael Cartoons painted in 1515 as tapestry designs for the Sistine Chapel; the finest collection of Italian Renaissance sculpture outside Italy; the Ardabil carpet, the world's oldest and arguably most splendid floor covering, in the Jameel Gallery of Islamic Art; and the Luck of Edenhall, a 13th-century glass beaker from Syria. The Fashion galleries run from 18th-century court dress right up to contemporary chiffon numbers; the Architecture gallery has videos, models, plans and descriptions of various styles; and the famous Photography collection holds over 500,000 images.

The V&A's ongoing FuturePlan transformation has been a revelation. The completely refurbished Medieval & Renaissance Galleries are stunning, but there are many other eye-catching new or redisplayed exhibits: the Gilbert Collection of silver, gold and gemmed ornaments has arrived from Somerset House (*see p114*); the Ceramics Galleries have been renovated and supplemented with an eye-catching bridge; there's lovely Buddhist sculpture in the Robert HN Ho Family Foundation Galleries; and the new Theatre & Performance Galleries take over where Covent Garden's defunct Theatre Museum left off. The restored mosaic floors and beautiful stained glass of the 14th- to 17th-century sculpture rooms, just off the central John Madejski Garden, enhance the already striking statuary.

Two major 2012 exhibitions are 'British Design 1948-2012' and, as part of the Cultural Olympiad, 'Heatherwick Studio: Designing the Extraordinary' (31 May-30 Sept).

HYDE PARK & KENSINGTON GARDENS
Hyde Park Corner, Knightsbridge, Lancaster Gate or Queensway tube.

At one and a half miles long and about a mile wide, **Hyde Park** (7298 2000, www.royalparks. gov.uk) is one of the largest of London's Royal Parks. The land was appropriated in 1536 from the monks of Westminster Abbey by Henry VIII for hunting deer. Although opened to the public in the early 1600s, the parks were favoured only by the upper echelons of society.

At the end of the 17th century, William III, averse to the dank air of Whitehall Palace, relocated to **Kensington Palace** (*see p150*). A corner of Hyde Park was sectioned off to make grounds for the palace and closed to the public, until King George II opened it on Sundays to those wearing formal dress. Nowadays, **Kensington Gardens** is delineated from Hyde Park only by the line of the Serpentine and the

SIGHTS

Long Water. Beside the Long Water is a bronze statue of **Peter Pan**, erected in 1912: it was in Kensington Gardens beside the Round Pond eight years earlier that playwright JM Barrie met Jack Llewelyn Davies, the boy who was the inspiration for Peter. The **Diana, Princess of Wales Memorial Playground** (*see p297*) is a kids' favourite, as is Kathryn Gustafson's ring-shaped **Princess Diana Memorial Fountain**. Near the fountain, Simon Gudgeon's giant bird *Isis* was in 2009 the first sculpture added to the park for half a century. There are changing exhibitions of contemporary art at the **Serpentine Gallery** (*see right*).

The **Serpentine** itself is London's oldest boating lake. Home to ducks, coots, swans, tufty-headed grebes and, every summer, gently perspiring dads rowing their children about, the Serpentine will be a great setting for the Triathlon and Marathon Swimming during the 2012 Games (*see p59*). The lake is at the bottom of **Hyde Park**, which isn't especially beautiful, but is of historic interest. The legalisation of public assembly in the park led

to the establishment of **Speakers' Corner** in 1872 (close to Marble Arch tube), where political and religious ranters – sane and otherwise – still have the floor. Marx, Lenin, Orwell and the Pankhursts all spoke here.

The park perimeter is popular with skaters, as well as with bike- and horse-riders. If you're exploring on foot and the vast expanses defeat you, look out for the **Liberty Drives** (May-Oct). Driven by volunteers, these electric buggies, each with space for a wheelchair, pick up groups of sightseers and ferry them around; there's no fare, but offer a donation if you can.

Kensington Palace
Kensington Gardens, W8 4PX (information 0844 482 7777, reservations 0844 482 7799, www.hrp.org.uk). High Street Kensington or Queensway tube. **Open** *Mar-Oct* 10am-6pm daily. *Nov-Feb* 10am-5pm daily. **Admission** £12.50; £6.25-£11 reductions; £34 family; free under-5s. **Credit** AmEx, MC, V. **Map** p392 B8.

Sir Christopher Wren extended this Jacobean mansion to palatial proportions on the instructions of William III. After extensive renovations aimed at restoring lost vistas of the building, the palace will reopen in March 2012. The first of a planned four new exhibitions to open will be 'Victoria: Love, Duty and Loss'. The future monarch was born and spent much of her childhood at Kensington Palace, and she was there when the Archbishop of Canterbury and Lord Chamberlain conveyed to her the news that William IV was dead and she was now queen.

★ FREE Serpentine Gallery
Kensington Gardens, nr Albert Memorial, W2 3XA (7402 6075, www.serpentinegallery.org). Lancaster Gate or South Kensington tube. **Open** 10am-6pm daily. **Admission** free; donations appreciated. **Credit** (shop) AmEx, MC, V. **Map** p393 D8.

The secluded location south-west of the Long Water and Serpentine makes this small and airy former tea house an attractive destination for lovers of contemporary art. The rolling two-monthly programme of exhibitions features up-to-the-minute artists. Every spring, a renowned architect, who's never before built in the UK, is commissioned to build a new pavilion. It then opens to the public, running a programme of cultural events from June to September.

2012 is a big year for the Serpentine. First, the Serpentine Sackler Gallery, devoted to emerging art in all forms, is set to open across the Serpentine in an 1815 building whose Palladian styling belies its original function as a gunpowder store. Zaha Hadid is supervising the transformation.

In addition, Olafur Eliasson is teaming up with the Serpentine to create a new space in Kensington Gardens. Swiss duo Fischli & Weiss will also create a new piece for the park, installing two giant rocks in a state of precarious balance.

Snapshot
Victorian London

Where to see how London lived.

The legacy of Queen Victoria's reign is everywhere in London, even in buildings that preceded the Victorians: the likes of **St Paul's Cathedral** (*see p90*) and the **Houses of Parliament** (*see p136*) received 19th-century alterations to make them look more 'historic' and less plain. St Paul's, for example, gained amazing giltwork and mosaics. But South Kensington's three palatial museums and the **Albert Memorial** (*see p147*) must be the finest testaments to the self-confidence and ingenuity of the Victorians, with the coloured brickwork and extravagant detailing of the **Natural History Museum** (*see p147*) almost as arresting as the exhibits within.

Natural History Museum.

North London

Life at the top.

The list of famous residents gives an idea of the scope of north London: from Amy Winehouse to Karl Marx and John Keats, a huge variety of people have been drawn to its mix of pretty, sleepy retreats and buzzing, creative party zones. First stop for most is **Camden Town**, with its markets, indie pubs and alternative vibe, but there's fun to be found in the squares of **Islington** and among the grown-up bohemians of **Stoke Newington** and fashionable **Dalston**. To the north, **Hampstead** and **Highgate** offer genteel village life.

Map p404	**Hotels** p210
Pubs & bars p250	**Restaurants & cafés** pp232-234

CAMDEN

Camden Town or Chalk Farm tube.

Despite the pressures of gentrification, Camden refuses to leave behind its grungy history as the cradle of British rock music. Against a backdrop of social deprivation in Thatcher's Britain, venues such as the Electric Ballroom and Dingwalls provided a platform for musical rebels. By the 1990s, the Creation label was based in nearby Primrose Hill (*see p153*), unleashing My Bloody Valentine and the Jesus & Mary Chain on the world, before making it big with Oasis. The Gallaghers were often seen trading insults with Blur at the **Good Mixer** (30 Inverness Street, 7916 7929). The music still plays at Camden icon the **Roundhouse** (*see p321*) and at **Koko** (*see p321*).

Before the Victorian expansion of London, Camden was a watering stop on the highway to Hampstead (*see p154*), with two notorious taverns – the Mother Black Cap and Mother Red Cap (now the **World's End** pub, opposite the tube) – frequented by highwaymen and brigands. After the gaps were filled in with terraced houses, the borough became a magnet for Irish and Greek railway workers, many of them working in the engine turning-house that is now the Roundhouse. The squalor of the area had a powerful negative influence on the young Charles Dickens, who lived briefly on Bayham Street; a blue plaque commemorates his stay. From the 1960s, things started to pick up for

Camden, helped by an influx of students, lured by low rents and the growing arts scene that nurtured punk, then indie, then Britpop – and now any number of short-lived indie-electro and alt-folk hybrids.

Much of Camden still has a rough quality – dealers and junkies loiter around Camden Town tube station – but the hardcore rebellion of the rock 'n' roll years has been replaced by a more laid-back carnival vibe, as goths, indie kids, emos and the last punks vie for attention. Tourists travel here in their thousands for the sprawling mayhem of **Camden Market** (*see p152*), which stretches north from the tube along boutique-lined Camden High Street and Chalk Farm Road. A dozen different countercultures depend on the market for thigh-length Frankenstein boots, studded collars and leather jackets emblazoned with the mispunctuated mantra 'Punks not Dead'.

There are unmistakeable signs of a move upmarket: the summer 2010 opening of **Shaka Zulu** (Stables Market, Chalk Farm Road, 3376 9911, www.shaka-zulu.com), a hugely over-the-top Zulu-themed bar-restaurant, right beneath **Gilgamesh** (7428 4922, www.gilgameshbar.com), a hugely over-the-top Sumerian-themed bar-restaurant, may point to the future. Drop in to **Proud** (*see p332*) if you want to reset your cultural compass.

Cutting through the market is **Regent's Canal**, which opened in 1820 to provide a link between east and west London for horse-drawn narrowboats loaded with coal. Today, the canal is used by the jolly tour-boats of the London Waterbus Company (7482 2550, www.london waterbus.com) and Walker's Quay (7485 4433, www.walkersquay.com), which run between Camden Lock and **Little Venice** in summer and on winter weekends. Locals use the canal towpath as a convenient walking route west to Regent's Park and **ZSL London Zoo** (*see p125*), or east to Islington (*see p156*).

Camden's one avowed 'sight' is west of Camden Town – the excellent **Jewish Museum** (*see right*) – but it's still a good bit of town for gigs. As well as Koko and the Roundhouse, there are plenty of pub stages where this year's hopefuls try to get spotted: try the **Barfly** (*see p322*), **Underworld** (*see p324*) and the **Dublin Castle** (94 Parkway, 7485 1773), where Madness and, later, Blur were launched. The **Jazz Café** (*see p324*) and the **Blues Kitchen** (*see p323*) offer a different vibe.

Camden Market

Camden Lock *Camden Lock Place, off Chalk Farm Road, NW1 8AF (7485 7963, www.camdenlockmarket.com).* **Open** 10am-6pm Mon-Thur, Sun; 10am-6.30pm Fri, Sat. Note: there are fewer stalls Mon-Fri.
Camden Lock Village *east of Chalk Farm Road, NW1 (www.camdenlock.net).* **Open** 10am-6pm daily.
Camden Market *Camden High Street, at Buck Street, NW1 (www.camdenmarkets.org).* **Open** 10am-5.30pm Thur-Sun.
Inverness Street Market *Inverness Street, NW1 (www.camdenlock.net).* **Open** 8.30am-5pm daily.
Stables Market *off Chalk Farm Road, opposite Hartland Road, NW1 8AH (7485 5511, www. stablesmarket.com).* **Open** 10.30am-6pm Mon-Fri (reduced stalls); 10am-6pm Sat, Sun.
All *Camden Town or Chalk Farm tube.* **Map** p404 Y2.
Camden Market actually refers to the microcosm of markets that make up the northern Camden Town area. The Camden Market, née Buck Street Market, is the place for neon sunglasses and pseudo-witty slogan garments. Almost next door, and perennially threatened by proposed tube station expansions, is

Camden.

the listed building the Electric Ballroom, which sells vinyl and CDs on weekends and is also a music venue. The Inverness Street Market opposite sells similar garb to the Camden Market as well as a diminishing supply of fruit and vegetables. North, next to the railway bridge, you'll find crafts, clothes, trinkets and small curiosities with a Japanese pop culture influence at Camden Lock and Camden Lock Village. Just north is the Stables Market where you'll find some good vintage clothes shops. Finally, the Horse Hospital area (which once cared for horses injured while pulling barges) is good for second-hand clothing, food stands and designer furniture. Here, too, is Cyberdog, with probably London's wackiest-looking sales assistants – perfect if you've pink dreadlocks, Buffalos and piercings and need some 'rave toys' or day-glo clubware.

Jewish Museum

Raymond Burton House, 129-131 Albert Street, NW1 7NB (7284 7384, www.jewishmuseum. org.uk). Camden Town tube. **Open** 10am-5pm Mon-Thur, Sat, Sun; 10am-2pm Fri. **Admission** £7.50; £3.50-£6.50 reductions; free under-5s. **Credit** MC, V. **Map** p404 Y3.
Reopened in 2010, this expanded museum is a brilliant exploration of Jewish life in Britain since 1066. Access is free to the downstairs café, located beside an ancient ritual bath, and the shop you enter past. There is an entry fee for the galleries upstairs, but they're well worth the money, combining fun interactives – you can wield the iron in a tailor's sweatshop, sniff chicken soup, pose for a wedding photo or take part in some Yiddish theatre – with serious history. There's a powerful Holocaust section, using the testimony of a single survivor, Leon Greenman, to bring tight focus to the unimaginable horror of it all. Opposite, a beautiful room of religious artefacts,

---

INSIDE TRACK
CROWD CONTROL

Camden Market's crowds can be awful at the weekends – unfortunately, this is also the best time to visit. After you're done shopping, slip out sideways on to the canal and stroll five minutes to sedate **Primrose Hill** (*see p153*), the perfect place to recuperate and assess your purchases.

including a 17th-century synagogue ark and centre-piece chandelier of Hanukkah lamps, does an elegant job of introducing Jewish ritual.

Around Camden

Primrose Hill, to the west of Camden, is just as attractive as the actors and pop stars who frequent the gastropubs and quaint cafés along **Regent's Park Road** and **Gloucester Avenue**. On sunny Sunday mornings, there's no better spot to read the papers than the pavement tables in front of Ukrainian café **Trojka** (101 Regent's Park Road, 7483 3765). Other favourite hangouts on Regent's Park Road include the long-established **Primrose Pâtisserie** (no.136, 7722 7848) and upmarket Greek bistro **Lemonia** (no.89, 7586 7454). For a gastropub feed, head to Gloucester Avenue: both the **Engineer** (no.65, 7722 0950) and **Lansdowne** (no.90, 7483 0409) are here. On a clear day, the walk up the hill is a delight.

ST JOHN'S WOOD

St John's Wood or Swiss Cottage tube.

The woodland that gives St John's Wood its name was part of the great Middlesex Forest, before the land was claimed by the Knights of St John of Jerusalem. Areas of forest were cleared for private villas in the mid 19th century, and uncharacteristically sensitive redevelopment during the 1950s left the area smart and eminently desirable: even a modest semi can

cost £2 million. The expensive tastes of locals are reflected in the posh boutiques along the High Street. The main tourist attraction is **Lord's** cricket ground (*see below*), but a steady stream of music fans pay tribute to the Beatles by crossing the zebra crossing in front of **Abbey Road Studios** (3 Abbey Road). The studio, founded in 1931 by Sir Edward Elgar, is still used to record albums and film scores, including *The Lord of the Rings*.

Lord's Tour & MCC Museum

St John's Wood Road, NW8 8QN (7616 8595, www.lords.org). St John's Wood tube. **Open** *Tours* phone or check website for details. **Admission** £15; £9 reductions; free under 5s; £40 family. **Credit** AmEx, MC, V.

Lord's is more than just a famous cricket ground. As the headquarters of the Marylebone Cricket Club (MCC), it is official guardian of the rules – and self-appointed guardian of the elusive 'spirit' – of cricket. As well as staging Test matches and internationals, the ground is home to the Middlesex County Cricket Club (MCCC). Visitors can take an organised tour round the futuristic, pod-like JP Morgan Media Centre and the august, portrait-bedecked Long Room. Highlights of the museum include the tiny urn containing the Ashes (this coveted trophy never leaves Lord's, no matter how many times the Australians win it although, of course, England emphatically beat Australia on their last tour) and memorabilia celebrating the achievements of such legends of the game as WG Grace.

▶ *Lord's is the venue for Archery at the London 2012 Olympic Games.*

Kenwood House. See p155.

SIGHTS

HAMPSTEAD

Hampstead tube, or Gospel Oak or Hampstead Heath rail.

It may have been absorbed into London during the city's great Victorian expansion, but hilltop Hampstead still feels like a Home Counties' village. It has long been a favoured roost for literary and artistic types: Keats and Constable lived here in the 19th century, and sculptors Barbara Hepworth and Henry Moore took up residence in the 1930s. However, the area is now popular with City workers, who are among the only people able to afford what is some of London's priciest property.

The undisputed highlight of the district is **Hampstead Heath**, the relatively vast and in places wonderfully overgrown tract of countryside between Hampstead village and Highgate that is said to have inspired CS Lewis's Narnia. The heath covers 791 acres of woodland, playing fields, swimming ponds and meadows of tall grass that attract picnickers and couples in search of privacy. It will feel even more delightfully rural if the City of London Corporation's 'aspiration' to graze sheep on the heath as a flock of organic lawnmowers comes to fruition.

The south end of the heath is where you'll find dinky Hampstead village, all genteel shops and cafés, restaurants and lovely pubs such as the **Holly Bush** (*see p250*). While you're there, tour the gorgeous sunken gardens and antique collection at **Fenton House** (*see right*) or gaze at the stars from the **Hampstead Scientific Society Observatory** (Lower Terrace, 8346 1056, www.hampsteadscience.ac.uk/astro), open on clear Friday and Saturday evenings and Sunday lunchtimes from mid September to mid April. A stroll along nearby Judges Walk reveals a line of horse chestnuts and limes virtually unchanged since they appeared in a Constable painting from 1820. Constable was buried nearby at **St John-at-Hampstead Church** (7794 5808), as was the comedian Peter Cook. At the top of Hampstead, North End Way divides the main heath from the wooded West Heath, one of London's oldest gay cruising areas (but perfectly family-friendly by day). Just off North End Way is Hampstead's best-kept secret, the secluded and charmingly overgrown **Hill Garden & Pergola** (open 8.30am-dusk daily), which was built by Lord Leverhulme using soil from the excavation of the Northern line's tunnels.

East of Hampstead tube, a maze of postcard-pretty residential streets shelters **Burgh House** (New End Square, 7431 0144, www.burghhouse. org.uk), a Queen Anne house with a small local history museum and gallery. Also in the area are

Highgate Cemetery.

2 Willow Road (*see p155*), architect Ernö Goldfinger's self-designed 1930s residence, and **40 Well Walk**, Constable's home for the last ten years of his life. Downhill towards Hampstead Heath Overground station is **Keats House** (*see p155*). Further west, and marginally closer to Finchley Road tube, is the **Freud Museum** (*see below*), while the innovative contemporary art exhibitions of **Camden Arts Centre** are almost opposite Finchley Road & Frognal Overground station.

Fenton House

3 Hampstead Grove, NW3 6RT (7435 3471, www.nationaltrust.org.uk). Hampstead tube. **Open** *Mar-Oct* times vary; check website for details. **Admission** *House & gardens* £6.50; £3 reductions; £16 family; free under-5s. *Gardens* £2. *Joint ticket with 2 Willow Road* £9. **Credit** MC, V.

Set in a gorgeous garden, with a 300-year-old apple orchard, this manor house is notable for its 17th- and 18th-century harpsichords, virginals and spinets, which are still played at lunchtime and evening concerts (phone for details). Also on display are European and Chinese porcelain, Chippendale furniture and some artful 17th-century needlework.

Freud Museum

20 Maresfield Gardens, NW3 5SX (7435 2002, www.freud.org.uk). Finchley Road tube. **Open** noon-5pm Wed-Sun. **Admission** £6; £3-£4.50 reductions; free under-12s. **Credit** AmEx, MC, V.

Driven from Vienna by the Nazis, Sigmund Freud lived in this quiet suburban house in north London with his wife Martha and daughter Anna until his death in 1939. Now a museum with temporary exhibitions, the house displays Freud's antiques, art and therapy tools, including his famous couch. The building has two blue plaques, one for Sigmund and another for Anna, a pioneer in child psychiatry.

Keats House
Keats Grove, NW3 2RR (7332 3868, www.cityof london.gov.uk/keatshousehampstead). Hampstead tube, Hampstead Heath rail or bus 24, 46, 168. **Open** *Apr-Oct* 1-5pm Tue-Sun. *Nov-Mar* 1-5pm Fri-Sun. **Admission** £5; £3 reductions; free under-16s. **Credit** MC, V.

Reopened after refurbishment in 2009, Keats House was the Romantic poet's last British home before tuberculosis forced him to Italy and death at the age of only 25. A leaflet guides you through each room, starting from the rear, as well as providing context for Keats's life and that of his less famous friend and patron, Charles Brown. The 2009 renovation has ensured the decorative scheme is entirely accurate, down to the pale pink walls of Keats's humble bedroom. The garden, in which he wrote 'Ode to a Nightingale', is particularly pleasant.

★ FREE Kenwood House/ Iveagh Bequest
Hampstead Lane, NW3 7JR (8348 1286, www.english-heritage.org.uk). Hampstead tube, or Golders Green tube then bus 210. **Open** 11.30am-4pm daily. **Admission** free. *Tours* (for groups by appointment only) £5-£7. **Credit** AmEx, MC, V.

Set in lovely grounds at the top of Hampstead Heath, Kenwood House is every inch the country manor house. Built in 1616, the mansion was remodelled in the 18th century for William Murray, who made the pivotal court ruling in 1772 that made it illegal to own slaves in England. The house was purchased by brewing magnate Edward Guinness, who was kind enough to donate his art collection to the nation in 1927. Highlights include Vermeer's *The Guitar Player*, Gainsborough's *Countess Howe*, and one of Rembrandt's finest self-portraits (dating to c1663). Note: the house will be closed from April 2012 for renovation. *Photo p153.*

2 Willow Road
2 Willow Road, NW3 1TH (7435 6166, www.nationaltrust.org.uk). Hampstead tube or Hampstead Heath rail. **Open** *Mar-Oct* 11am-5pm Wed-Sun. *Tours* 11am, noon, 1pm, 2pm Wed-Sun. **Admission** £6; £3 children; free under-5s; £15 family. *Joint ticket with Fenton House* £9. **No credit cards.**

A surprising addition to the National Trust's collection of historic houses, this small modernist building was designed by Hungarian-born architect Ernö Goldfinger. The house was made to be flexible, with ingenious movable partitions and folding doors. Home to the architect and his wife until their deaths, it contains a fine, idiosyncratic collection of art by the likes of Max Ernst and Henry Moore. Goldfinger also designed Notting Hill's Trellick Tower (*see p127*).

HIGHGATE
Archway or Highgate tube.

Taking its name from the tollgate that once stood on the High Street, Highgate is inexorably linked with London's medieval mayor, Richard 'Dick' Whittington. As the story goes, the disheartened Whittington, having failed to make his fortune, fled the City as far as Highgate Hill, but turned back when he heard the Bow Bells peal out 'Turn again, Whittington, thrice Mayor of London'. Today, the area is best known for the atmospheric grounds of **Highgate Cemetery** (*see below*). Adjoining the cemetery is pretty **Waterlow Park**, created by low-cost housing pioneer Sir Sydney Waterlow in 1889, with ponds, a mini-aviary, tennis courts and a cute garden café in 16th-century **Lauderdale House** (8348 8716, www.lauderdalehouse.co.uk), former home of Charles II's mistress, Nell Gwynn. North of Highgate tube, shady **Highgate Woods** are preserved as a conservation area, with a nature trail, adventure playground and a café that hosts live jazz during the summer.

★ Highgate Cemetery
Swains Lane, N6 6PJ (8340 1834, www. highgate-cemetery.org). Archway tube. **Open** *East Cemetery* Mar-Oct 10am-5pm Mon-Fri; 11am-5pm Sat, Sun; Nov-Mar 10am-4pm Mon-Fri; 11am-4pm Sat, Sun. *West Cemetery* by tour only. **Admission** £3; £2 reductions. *Tours* £7; £5 reductions. **No credit cards.**

The final resting place of some very famous Londoners, Highgate Cemetery is a wonderfully overgrown maze of ivy-cloaked Victorian tombs and time-shattered urns. Visitors are free to wander through the East Cemetery, with its memorials to Karl Marx, George Eliot and Douglas Adams, but the most atmospheric part of the cemetery is the foliage-shrouded West Cemetery, laid out in 1839. Only accessible on an organised tour (book ahead, dress respectfully and arrive 30mins early), the shady paths wind past gloomy catacombs, grand Victorian pharaonic tombs, and the graves of notables such as poet Christina Rossetti, scientist Michael Faraday and poisoned Russian dissident Alexander Litvinenko.

INSIDE TRACK
WATER WALKING

If you fancy a walk, the **Regent's Canal** towpath runs all the way east from south of Angel tube past Hackney's trendily boho Broadway Market and the Olympic Park as far as the Thames.

SIGHTS

▶ *The cemetery closes during burials, so call ahead before you visit. Note that children under eight are not allowed in the West Cemetery.*

ISLINGTON

Angel tube or Highbury & Islington tube/rail.

Islington started life as a small country village beside one of Henry VIII's expansive hunting reserves. It soon became an important livestock market supplying the Smithfield meat yards, before being enveloped into Greater London. The 19th century brought industrial development along the Regent's Canal and later industrial decay, but locals kept up their spirits at the area's music halls, launchpads for such working-class heroes as Marie Lloyd, George Formby and Norman Wisdom. From the 1960s, there was a massive influx of arts and media types, who gentrified the Georgian squares and Victorian terraces and opened cafés, restaurants and boutiques around Upper Street and Essex Road. It is now a suburban bower of the *Guardian*-reading middle classes.

Close to the station on Upper Street, the popular **Camden Passage** antiques market (*see p278*) bustles with browsing activity on Wednesdays and Saturdays. The music halls have long gone, but local residents still take advantage of the celluloid offerings at the **Screen on the Green** (*see p307* **Everyman & Screen Cinemas**) and the stage productions at the **Almeida** theatre (*see p349*).

East of Angel, Regency-era **Canonbury Square** was once home to George Orwell (no.27) and Evelyn Waugh (no.17A). One of the handsome townhouses now contains the **Estorick Collection of Modern Italian Art** (*see right*). Just beyond the end of Upper Street is **Highbury Fields**, where 200,000 Londoners fled in 1666 to escape the Great Fire. The surrounding district is best known as the home of Arsenal Football Club, who abandoned the charming Highbury Stadium in 2006 for the gleaming 60,000-seater behemoth that is the **Emirates Stadium** (*see p337*). Fans can either tour the ground or just check out the memorabilia at the **Arsenal Museum** (7619 5000, www.arsenal.com).

★ Estorick Collection of Modern Italian Art

39A Canonbury Square, N1 2AN (7704 9522, www.estorickcollection.com). Highbury & Islington tube/rail or bus 271. **Open** 11am-6pm Wed-Sat; noon-5pm Sun. **Admission** £5; £3.50 reductions; free under-16s, students. **Credit** AmEx, MC, V.
Originally owned by American political scientist and writer Eric Estorick, this is a wonderful depository of early 20th-century Italian art. It is one of the world's foremost collections of futurism, Italy's brash and confrontational contribution to international modernism. The four galleries are full of movement, machines and colour, while the temporary exhibits meet the futurist commitment to fascism full on. There is also a shop and café.

DALSTON & STOKE NEWINGTON

Dalston Kingsland, Dalston Junction, Rectory Road, Stamford Hill or Stoke Newington rail.

Although scruffy, Dalston scores points for the vibrant African-flavoured market on Ridley Road, and the Turkish *ocakbaşı* (grill restaurants) along Stoke Newington Road, including excellent **Mangal II** (no.4, 7254 7888). Low property prices attracted a growing contingent of student types, who congregate at the appealingly urban **Dalston Jazz Bar** (4 Bradbury Street, 7254 9728) and the brilliant **Vortex Jazz Club** (*see p327*).

Neighbouring **Stoke Newington** is the richer cousin of Dalston and poorer cousin of Islington, home to a disproportionate number of journalists, TV news presenters and lesbians. At weekends, pretty **Clissold Park** (www.clissoldpark.com) is overrun with picnickers and mums pushing prams.

Most visitors head to Stoke Newington for bijou **Church Street**. This curvy road is lined with second-hand bookshops, cute boutiques and kids' stores, and superior cafés and restaurants – Keralan vegetarian restaurant **Rasa** (no.55, 7249 0344) is probably the best of them. Another local highlight is **Abney Park Cemetery** (7275 7557, www.abney-park.org.uk), a wonderfully wild, overgrown Victorian boneyard and nature reserve.

Screen on the Green.

SIGHTS

East London

Home of the 2012 Games and a million clubs, shops and galleries.

The planners of London 2012 chose well. For years, east London has been on the cultural cutting edge. Read the style mags, and it's hard to believe how recently the East End was notorious for its slums, petty gangsters and urban blight. It was also cursed with the smelliest and most unpleasant of London's dock-side industries.

How things change. East London now has some of London's most vital areas. Alongside the City, **Spitalfields** and **Brick Lane** are tourist must-visits, with markets, boutiques, restaurants and – as they shade into **Shoreditch** – art-student trendy nightlife. To the north, **Dalston** and **London Fields** drive the arts and fashion zeitgeist; eastwards, **Docklands** rivals the City for blue-chip institutions and **Stratford** is the gateway to the Olympic Park (*see pp52-58*).

| Map p 401 & p403 | Hotels pp210-212 |
| Pubs & bars pp251-253 | Restaurants & cafés pp234-237 |

Map p 401 & p403 Pubs & bars pp251-253 Hotels pp210-212 Restaurants & cafés pp234-237

SPITALFIELDS

Aldgate East tube/Liverpool Street tube/rail.

Approach this area from Liverpool Street Station, up Brushfield Street, and you'll know you're on the right track when the magnificent spiky spire of **Christ Church Spitalfields** (*see p158*) comes into sight. The area's other signature sight, **Spitalfields Market** (*see p263*), has emerged from redevelopment and the market stalls have moved back underneath the vaulted Victorian roof of the original building.

Outside, along Brushfield Street, the shops might look as if they're from Dickens's day, but most are recent inventions: the charming grocery shop **A Gold** (no.42, 7247 2487) was lovingly restored in the noughties; the owners of the **Market Coffee House** (nos.50-52, 7247 4110) put reclaimed wood panelling and creaky furniture into an empty shell; and the deli **Verde & Co** (no.40, 7247 1924) was opened by its owner, author Jeanette Winterson, inspired by the local food shops she found in – whisper it – France. It's a nice enough stroll, but for another perspective on Spitalfields head a few streets south on a Sunday to find the salt-of-the-earth **Petticoat Lane Market**, hawking knickers and cheap electronics around Middlesex Street. At the foot of Goulston Street, **Tubby Isaacs** seafood stall has sold whelks and cockles since 1919.

A block north of Spitalfields Market is **Dennis Severs' House** (*see p158*), while across from the market, on the east side of Commercial Street and in the shadow of Christ Church, the **Ten Bells** (84 Commercial Street, 7366 1721) is where one of Jack the Ripper's prostitute victims drank her last gin. On the next corner, Sandra Esqulant's **Golden Heart** pub (no.110, 7247 2158) has hosted every Young British Artist of note, ever since the day Gilbert & George decided to pop in on their new local. The streets between here and Brick Lane to the east are dourly impressive, lined with tall, shuttered Huguenot houses; **19 Princelet Street** (www.19princeletstreet.org.uk) is open to the public a few times a year. This unrestored 18th-century house was home first to French silk merchants and later Polish Jews who built a synagogue in the garden.

FREE Christ Church Spitalfields
Commercial Street, E1 6QE (7859 3035, www. christchurchspitalfields.org). Liverpool Street tube/rail or Shoreditch High Street rail. **Open** 11am-4pm Tue; 1-4pm Sun. **Admission** free. **No credit cards. Map** p401 S5.

SIGHTS

Spitalfields Market.
See p157.

Built in 1729 by architect Nicholas Hawksmoor, this splendid church has in recent years been restored to its original state (tasteless alterations had been made to the building following a lightning strike in the 19th century). Most tourists get no further than cowering before the wonderfully overbearing spire, but the revived interior is impressive too, its pristine whiteness in marked contrast to its architect's dark reputation. The formidable 1735 Richard Bridge organ is almost as old as the church. Regular concerts are held here, notably during the two annual Spitalfields festivals (*see p317*).

★ Dennis Severs' House

18 Folgate Street, E1 6BX (7247 4013, www. dennissevershouse.co.uk). Liverpool Street tube/ rail or Shoreditch High Street rail. **Open** noon-4pm Sun; noon-2pm Mon following 1st & 3rd Sun of mth; times vary Mon evenings. **Admission** £10 Sun; £7 noon-2pm Mon; £14 Mon evenings. **Credit** MC, V. **Map** p401 R5.

The ten rooms of this original Huguenot house have been decked out to recreate vivid snapshots of daily life in Spitalfields between 1724 and 1914. A tour through the compelling 'still-life drama', as American creator Dennis Severs dubbed it, takes you through the cellar, kitchen, dining room, smoking room and upstairs to the bedrooms. With hearth and candles burning, smells lingering and objects scattered apparently haphazardly, it feels as though the inhabitants have deserted the building only moments before you arrived.

BRICK LANE

Aldgate East tube.

Join the crowds flowing east from Spitalfields Market along Hanbury Street during the weekend, and the direction you turn at the end determines which Brick Lane you see. Turn right and you'll know you're in 'Banglatown', the name adopted by the ward back in 2002: until you hit the bland modern offices beside the kitsch Banglatown arch, it's almost all Bangladeshi cafés, curry houses, grocery stores, money transfer services and sari shops – plus the **Pride of Spitalfields** (3 Heneage Street, 7247 8933), an old-style East End boozer serving ale to all-comers.

Despite the street's global reputation for Indian food (there's even a Brick Lane restaurant in Manhattan), most of the food on offer in the street is disappointing, but nearby there are some good restaurants: try **Tayyabs** (*see p237*) or **Needoo Grill** (*see p236*). Alternatively, opt for Bengali sweets from the **Madhubon Sweet Centre** at no.42.

Between Fournier Street and Princelet Street, **Jamme Masjid Mosque** is a key symbol of Brick Lane's hybridity. It began as a Huguenot chapel, became a synagogue and was converted, in 1976, into a mosque – in other words, immigrant communities have been layering their experiences on this street at least since

1572, when the St Bartholomew's Day Massacre forced many French Huguenots into exile.

The newest layer is boho gentrification. On Sunday, there's the lively street market, complemented by the trendier UpMarket – superior, clothes-wise, to Spitalfields market – and Backyard Market (for arts and crafts), both held in the **Old Truman Brewery** (nos.91-95). Pedestrianised Dray Walk, full of hip independent businesses, is crowded every day. Heading north on Brick Lane, you'll find the **Vibe Bar** (7377 2899, www.vibe-bar.co.uk) and shops such as second-hand clothes store **Rokit** (nos.101 & 107, 7375 3864, 7247 3777). Further north, Cheshire Street is good for vintage fashion, too – the cavernous **Beyond Retro** (*see p268*) is the stand-out.

WHITECHAPEL

Aldgate East or Whitechapel tube.

Not one of the prettier thoroughfares to be found in London, busy but anonymous Whitechapel Road sets the tone for this area. One bright spot is **Whitechapel Gallery** (*see p168*), west from the foot of Brick Lane, while a little to the east, the **Whitechapel Bell Foundry** (nos.32 & 34, 7247 2599, www.whitechapelbellfoundry.co.uk) continues to manufacture bells, as it has since 1570. It famously produced Philadelphia's Liberty Bell and Big Ben. To join one of the fascinating Saturday tours you'll have to reserve a place (usually well in advance).

At Whitechapel's foremost place of worship, it isn't bells but a muezzin that summons the faithful each Friday: the **East London Mosque**, founded elsewhere in 1910 and now the focal point for the largest Muslim community in Britain, can accommodate 10,000 worshippers. Behind is Fieldgate Street and the dark mass of **Tower House**, a former doss house whose 700 rooms have, inevitably, been redeveloped into flats. This 'sought after' converted warehouse building' was a rather dismal – but decidedly cheaper – proposition when Joseph Stalin and George Orwell (researching his book *Down and Out in Paris and London*) kipped here for pennies. The red-brick alleys give a flavour of what Victorian Whitechapel must have been like.

East again is the Royal London Hospital and, in a small crypt on Newark Street, the **Royal London Hospital Archives & Museum** (7377 7608, closed Mon, Sat & Sun). Inside are reproduction letters from Jack the Ripper (including the notorious missive 'From Hell', delivered with an enclosed portion of human kidney) and information on Joseph Merrick, the 'Elephant Man', so named for his congenital deformities. Rescued by surgeon Sir Frederick Treves, Merrick was given his own room in the Royal London Hospital.

Behind the hospital is the brand new, high-tech **Centre of the Cell** (4 Newark Street, 7882 2562, www.centreofthecell.org), which gives visitors a lively, interactive insight into cell biology in a purpose-built pod, suspended over labs investigating cancer and tuberculosis.

SIGHTS

Whitechapel Gallery. *See p160.*

★ FREE Whitechapel Gallery

77-82 Whitechapel High Street, E1 7QX (7522 7888, www.whitechapelgallery.org). Aldgate East tube. **Open** 11am-6pm Tue, Wed, Fri-Sun; 11am-9pm Thur. **Admission** free. *Temporary exhibitions vary.* **Credit** MC, V. **Map** p403 S6.

This East End stalwart reopened in 2009, following a major redesign that saw the Grade II-listed building expand into the similarly historic former library next door – rather brilliantly, the architects left the two buildings stylistically distinct rather than trying to smooth out their differences. As well as nearly tripling its exhibition space, the Whitechapel gave itself a research centre and archives, plus a proper restaurant (*see p237*) and café. It looks set to improve a stellar reputation as a contemporary art pioneer built on shows of Picasso – *Guernica* was shown here in 1939 – Jackson Pollock, Mark Rothko and Frida Kahlo. With no permanent collection, there's a rolling programme of temporary shows. For London 2012 Festival, a new frontage by Rachel Whiteread is to be unveiled (1 June). *Photo p159.*

SHOREDITCH & HOXTON

Old Street tube/rail.

The story is familiar: in the 1980s, impecunious artists moved into the derelict warehouses in the triangle formed by Old Street, Shoreditch High Street and Great Eastern Street, and quickly turned it into the place to be. Rising rents have since driven many of the artists further east, but they've been replaced by the tech-hip denizens of 'silicon roundabout' – the area around Old Street roundabout has become a focus for digital start-ups – and this small patch clings on to some of its reputation as the city's most exciting arts and clubbing centre.

Nightlife permeates the area (linking conveniently to Brick Lane), with centres on Curtain Road, the lower end of Kingsland Road and around Hoxton Square. Nostalgists have to pencil in a visit to Old Street's **333** club (7739 5949, www.333mother.com) – no longer cutting edge, but a landmark nonetheless – but the final eviction in 2010 of squatters from scuzzy club the Foundry (84-86 Great Eastern Street) to make way for a luxury hotel may be a sign of things to come. Redchurch Street is a more hopeful emblem of the new East End (*see p273* **Style Street**), with its independent boutiques.

Apart from Hoxton Square galleries (**White Cube** – 48 Hoxton Square, N1 6PB, 7930 5373, www.whitecube.com – is here) and **Rivington Place** (*see p161*), the area's sole bona fide tourist attraction is the exquisite **Geffrye Museum** (*see p161*), a short walk north up Kingsland Road. The surrounding area is dense with good, cheap Vietnamese restaurants (try **Sông Quê**; *see p237*).

Geffrye Museum.

SIGHTS

Docklands. *See p163.*

★ FREE Geffrye Museum

*136 Kingsland Road, E2 8EA (7739 9893,
www.geffrye-museum.org.uk). Hoxton rail.* **Open**
10am-5pm Tue-Sat; noon-5pm Sun. *Almshouse
tours* 1st Sat, 1st & 3rd Wed of mth. **Admission**
free; donations appreciated. *Almshouse tours*
£2; free under-16s. **Credit** (shop) MC, V.
Map p401 R3.

Housed in a set of 18th-century almshouses, the
Geffrye Museum offers a vivid physical history of
the English interior. Displaying original furniture,
paintings, textiles and decorative arts, the museum
recreates a sequence of typical middle-class living
rooms from 1600 to the present. It's an oddly interesting way to take in domestic history, with any
number of intriguing details to catch your eye –
from a bell jar of stuffed birds to a particular decorative flourish on a chair. There's an airy restaurant overlooking the lovely gardens, which include
a walled plot for herbs and a chronological series
in different historical styles.

FREE Rivington Place

*Rivington Place, EC2A 3BA (7729 9616, www.
rivingtonplace.org). Old Street tube/rail or Shoreditch
High Street rail.* **Open** 11am-6pm Tue, Wed, Fri;
11am-9pm Thur; noon-6pm Sat. **Admission** free.
Credit (shop) MC, V. **Map** p401 R4.

Designed by David Adjaye and one of Shoreditch's
more exciting recent additions, this was London's
first new-built public gallery since the opening of
the Hayward in 1968. The programme champions
culturally diverse visual arts. Two project spaces
provide a platform for British and international
work, and there's a ground-floor café.

BETHNAL GREEN

*Bethnal Green tube/rail/Cambridge Heath
rail/Mile End tube.*

Once a gracious suburb of spacious
townhouses, by the mid 19th century
Bethnal Green was one of the city's poorest
neighbourhoods. As in neighbouring Hoxton,
a recent upturn in fortunes has in part been
occasioned by Bethnal Green's adoption as
home by a new generation of artists,
attracted by the low rents resulting from
the neihbourhood's long-standing misfortunes.
The **Maureen Paley** gallery (no.21) in Herald
Street remains the key venue, but the new
Bethnal Green is typified by places such as
Herald Street (no.2), just down the road,
and the arrival of the ambitious **Town Hall
Hotel** (*see p211*) and **Viajante** restaurant
(*see p237*). Take a seat at **E Pellicci** (*see
p236*), the exemplary traditional London
caff, for a taste of the old Bethnal Green.

The **V&A Museum of Childhood** (*see
p162*) is close to Bethnal Green tube station,
but the area's other main attraction is a bit of
a walk away. Nonetheless, a visit to the weekly
Columbia Road flower market (*see p260*) is
a lovely way to fritter away a Sunday morning.
A microcosmic retail community has grown up
around the market: **Treacle** (nos.110-112, 7729
0538) for groovy crockery and cup cakes;
Angela Flanders (no.96, 7739 7555) for
perfume; **Marcos & Trump** (no.146, 7739
9008) for vintage fashion.

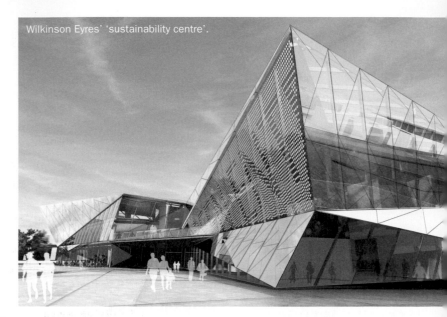

Wilkinson Eyres' 'sustainability centre'.

SIGHTS

FREE Ragged School Museum

*46-50 Copperfield Road, E3 4RR (8980 6405,
www.raggedschoolmuseum.org.uk). Mile End tube.*
Open 10am-5pm Wed, Thur; 2-5pm 1st Sun of
mth. *Tours* by arrangement; phone for details.
Admission free; donations appreciated. **No
credit cards**.

Ragged schools were an early experiment in public
education: they provided tuition, food and clothes
for destitute children. This one was the largest in
London, and Dr Barnardo himself taught here. It's
now a sweet local museum that contains complete
mock-ups of a ragged classroom and Edwardian
kitchen, with displays on vanished local history. The
events programme is increasingly lively.

★ FREE V&A Museum of Childhood

*Cambridge Heath Road, E2 9PA (8983 5235,
www.museumofchildhood.org.uk). Bethnal Green
tube/rail or Cambridge Heath rail.* **Open** 10am-
5.45pm daily. **Admission** free; donations
appreciated. **Credit** MC, V.

Home to one of the world's finest collections of children's toys, dolls' houses, games and costumes, the
Museum of Childhood shines brighter than ever after
extensive refurbishment, which has given it an
impressive entrance. Part of the Victoria & Albert
Museum (*see p149*), the museum has been amassing
childhood-related objects since 1872 and continues
to do so, with *Incredibles* figures complementing
bonkers 1970s puppets, Barbie Dolls and Victorian
praxinoscopes. The museum has lots of hands-on
stuff for kids dotted about the many cases of historic

artefacts. Regular exhibitions are held upstairs,
while the café in the centre of the main hall helps to
revive flagging grown-ups.

DOCKLANDS

London's docks were fundamental to the
prosperity of the British Empire. Between
1802 and 1921, ten separate docks were built
between Tower Bridge in the west and
Woolwich in the east. These employed tens
of thousands of people. Yet by the 1960s, the
shipping industry was changing irrevocably.
The new 'container' system of cargo demanded
larger, deep-draught ships, as a result of which
the work moved out to Tilbury, from where
lorries would ship the containers into the city.
By 1980, the London docks had closed.

The London Docklands Development
Corporation (LDDC), founded in 1981, spent
£790 million of public money on redevelopment
during the following decade, only for a
country-wide property slump in the early 1990s
to leave the shiny new high-rise offices and
luxury flats unoccupied. Nowadays, though, as
a financial hub, Docklands is a booming rival
to the City, with an estimated 90,000 workers
commuting to the area each day, on improved
transport links. For visitors, regular **Thames
Clippers** (0870 781 5049, www.thames
clippers.com) boat connections with central
London and the **Docklands Light Railway**
(DLR) make the area easily accessible.

Just a few stops from where the DLR starts at Bank station is Shadwell, south of which is **Wapping**. In 1598, John Stowe described Wapping High Street as 'a filthy strait passage, with alleys of small tenements or cottages, inhabited by sailors' 'victuallers'. This can still just about be imagined as you walk along it now, flanked by tall Victorian warehouses. The historic **Town of Ramsgate** pub (no.62, 7481 8000), dating to 1545, helps. Here 'hanging judge' George Jeffreys was captured in 1688, trying to escape to Europe in disguise as a woman. Privateer Captain William Kidd was executed in 1701 at Execution Dock, near Wapping New Stairs; the bodies of pirates were hanged from a gibbet until seven tides had washed over them. Further east, the **Prospect of Whitby** (57 Wapping Wall, 7481 1095) dates from 1520 and has counted Samuel Pepys and Charles Dickens among its regulars. It has good riverside terraces and a fine pewter bar counter. Opposite sits a rather more modern 'victualler': Wapping Food occupies an ivy-clad Victorian hydraulic power station.

East of here are the **Isle of Dogs** and Canary Wharf. The origin of the name 'Isle of Dogs' remains uncertain, but the first recorded use is on a map of 1588; one theory claims Henry VIII kept his hunting dogs here. In the 19th century, a huge system of docks and locks transformed what had been just drained marshland; in fact, the West India Docks cut right across the peninsula, so the Isle of Dogs did eventually become true to its name.

Almost all the interest for visitors is to be found in the vicinity of Cesar Pelli's dramatic **One Canada Square**, which was the country's tallest habitable building between 1991 and 2012, when it was overtopped by the Shard (*see p83*). The only slightly shorter HSBC and Citigroup towers joined it in the noughties, and clones are springing up thick and fast. Shopping options are limited to the mall beneath the towers (www.my canarywharf.com), but you'll find a soothing if slightly too crisp Japanese garden beside Canary Wharf tube station. Across a floating bridge over the dock to the north, there's the brilliant **Museum of London Docklands** (*see right*).

It's also well worth hopping on the DLR and heading south to **Island Gardens** station at the tip of the Isle of Dogs. From narrow Island Gardens park, there's a famous Greenwich view – and the entrance to the Victorian pedestrian tunnel. Nearby to the north, at **Mudchute Park & Farm** (Pier Street, 7515 5901, www.mudchute.org), a complete farmyard of animals ruminate in front of the skyscrapers.

Further east, the Lee River empties into the Thames at Bow Creek (*see p165* **Sounds**

of the Sea), for which your best stop is East India DLR. If you follow the Lee north, you'd eventually find yourself at the Olympic Park. A couple more stops give you access to London's grandest docks – Royal Victoria, Royal Albert and King George V – as well as the **ExCeL** conference centre, a major venue for events in the London 2012 Olympic and Paralympic Games (*see p58*). Wilkinson Eyre's £30m 'sustainability centre' is due to open here in early 2012. A footbridge from ExCeL, high above Royal Victoria Dock, takes you to the beautiful **Thames Barrier Park** (www. thamesbarrierpark.org.uk). Opened in 2001, this was London's first new park in half a century. It has a lush sunken garden of waggly hedges and offers perhaps the best views from land of the Thames Barrier (*see p174*). If you don't fancy walking, enter the park from Pontoon Dock DLR.

Unless you're checking in at **London City Airport** (*see p364*), keep on the DLR as far as King George V to get a free ferry (every 15mins daily, 8853 9400) that chugs pedestrians and cars across the river, or stay in your carriage as the DLR passes under the river all the way to its final stop at Woolwich Arsenal (*see p174*).

★ Museum of London Docklands

No.1 Warehouse, West India Quay, Hertsmere Road, E14 4AL (7001 9844, www.museumin docklands.org.uk). Canary Wharf tube or West

---

**INSIDE TRACK
OUTSIDE THE OLYMPIC PARK**

The best vantage point over the **Olympic Park** (*see p52*) – the **View Tube** (*see p166*) – will be inaccessible at Games Time, but a short walk north of the Park's south-west exit there are superb views across the Lee Navigation from Fish Island, where you'll find both the two-floor **Counter Café** (Stour Space, 7 Roach Road, E3 2PA, 07834 275920 mobile, www.thecounter cafe.co.uk) and **Forman's** (*see p235*). North again, Hackney Wick combines edgy gallery-studio spaces – www.timeout.com will list new exhibitions and openings – and the **Hackney Pearl** restaurant (*see p234*).

Through the main eastern exit are the sundry attractions of **Westfield Stratford City** (*see p259*), and beyond the mall and station, in central Stratford, is Gerry Raffles Square, with a cinema and the historic **Theatre Royal Stratford East** (*see p350*). The other key sightseeing opportunity is via the southernmost exit: a fine river walk takes you past **Three Mills Island** (*see p166*) and to the Thames beyond.

SIGHTS

India Quay DLR. **Open** 10am-6pm daily.
Admission free. *Temporary exhibitions* vary;
check website for details. **Credit** MC, V.
Housed in a 19th-century warehouse (itself a Grade
I-listed building), this huge museum explores the
complex history of London's docklands and the river
over two millennia. Displays spreading over three
storeys take you from the arrival of the Romans all
the way to the docks' 1980s closure and the area's
subsequent redevelopment. The Docklands at War
section is very moving, while a haunting new permanent exhibition sheds light on the dark side of
London's rise as a centre for finance and commerce,
exploring its involvement in the slave trade. You can
also walk through full-scale mock-ups of a quayside
and a dingy riverfront alley. Temporary exhibitions
are set up on the ground floor, where you'll also find
a café and a docks-themed play area for kids. Just
like its elder brother, the Museum of London (*see p95*
Profile), the MoLD has a great programme of
screenings and special events. Note: the museum will
be closed during the London 2012 Games.

HACKNEY & AROUND

*Hackney: London Fields or Hackney Central
rail. Dalston: Dalston Junction or Dalston
Kingsland rail. Victoria Park: Mile End tube,
then 277 bus.*

The opening of the East London Line in 2010
leaves even bus-averse visitors few excuses
to ignore this part of town. Hackney has few
blockbuster sights, but is one of London's
fastest changing areas, with a re-energised,
creative local life.

Hackney is a large borough. Its admistrative
centre is Town Hall Square on Mare Street,
where you'll find a century-old music hall, the
Hackney Empire (291 Mare Street, 8985
2424, www.hackneyempire.co.uk); an art deco
town hall; a multiscreen cinema in the old
Victorian library; and the fine little **Hackney
Museum** (1 Reading Lane, 8356 3500,
www.hackney.gov.uk/cm-museum.htm), in the
21st-century library. Within walking distance
to the east is the historic **Sutton House**.

The area of London Fields, to the west of
central Hackney, demonstrates the borough's
changing demographics. Once a failing fruit
and veg market, **Broadway Market** is now
brimming with young urbanites and trendy
families. The food and vintage garb market
on Saturdays has been joined by two eclectic
food and collectibles markets on Westgate
Street; the street is lined with browsable
boutiques, curiosity shops and modish boho
eating and drinking venues. The old days are
respectably represented by **F Cooke** (no.9, 7254
6458), a pie and mash place that's been here
since the early 1900s.

From the south end of Broadway Market,
you can walk east along the Regent's Canal to
Victoria Park. Opened in 1845 to give the
impoverished working classes access to green
space, this sprawling, 290-acre oasis was
designed by Sir James Pennethorne, a pupil of
John Nash, its elegant landscaping (complete
with rose garden and waterfowl lake) also
reminiscent of Nash's Regent's Park (*see p124*).
But the classicism is softened by a casual East
End vibe, including a cool waterfront café and
the occasional summer musical festival.

Across the dual carriageway at the eastern end
of the park, **Hackney Wick** is a mishmash of
post-industrial buildings, several occupied by
artists. Nearby Hackney Marshes are legendary
as a Sunday morning football venue, and will
have their moment in the London 2012 spotlight
as the venue for the Hackney Weekend festival
(*see p320*). The Marshes are right on the western
edge of the Olympic Park, which can be accessed
via Victoria Park.

Nearer to central London, Dalston is the
neighbourhood of Hackney that's been nominated
as London's latest hipster quarter. Occupying the
area around the junction of Balls Pond Road and
Kingsland Road, it's certainly atracting trend-
seekers, but also has a good deal of substance,
with a couple of dynamic new cultural venues,
Café Oto (*see p326*) and the **Arcola** theatre (see
see p350), and well-established Turkish and
African-Caribbean communities.

Sutton House

*2-4 Homerton High Street, E9 6JQ (8986 2264,
www.nationaltrust.org.uk). Bethnal Green tube
then bus 254, 106, D6, or Hackney Central rail.*
Open times vary; check website for details.
Admission £3; £1 reductions; £6.90 family; free
under-5s, National Trust members. **Credit** MC, V.
Built in 1535 for Henry VIII's first secretary of state,
Sir Ralph Sadleir, this red-brick Tudor mansion is
east London's oldest home. Now beautifully restored
in authentic original decor, with a real Tudor kitchen
to boot, it makes no secret of its history of neglect:
even some 1980s squatter graffiti has been preserved. The house closes for January each year.

LEA VALLEY

*Bromley-by-Bow tube or Stratford
tube/DLR/rail.*
The Lea River (also known as the Lee at points
along its length) wriggles south-east for 50 miles
from its source near Luton, Bedfordshire to join
the River Thames. Through history, it has been
a working river used for transport, irrigation,
infrastructure and industry: the latter turned its
lower reaches into a toxic wasteland that is now
being reclaimed as the site of the Olympic Park
for the London 2012 Games (*see p53*).

Sounds of the Sea

London's only lighthouse is a beacon of modern art.

Where the River Lee flows into the Thames, almost directly opposite the white, deflated balloon of the O2 Arena (*see p321*), **Trinity Buoy Wharf** (64 Orchard Place, E14 0JW, www.trinitybuoywharf.com) is pure incongruity. Built in the early 1800s – just as London's docks were entering their period of global dominance – it was a depot and repair yard for shipping buoys, and a maintenance dock for lightships. And it was here, in the 1860s, that James Douglass – designer 20 years later of the amazing fourth Eddystone Lighthouse in Devon – built London's only lighthouse.

The Experimental Lighthouse was used for training lighthouse keepers and trialling new light technology, but now it's literally a work of art. Open to the public every weekend from 11am to 4pm (5pm in summer), the lighthouse is the magnificent setting for a 'sound art' composition by Jem Finer, a founder member of Irish punk-folksters the Pogues. *Longplayer* (http://longplayer.org) is a piece of music that started playing on 1 January 2000 as part of the millennium exhibition. Performed on gongs and Tibetan singing bowls, this meditative piece is designed not to repeat itself during a continuous performance lasting exactly 1,000 years. It's a soothing soundtrack for the vast Thames, seen through the bars of the lantern room.

Longplayer isn't the only artistic project at the lighthouse. In September 2010, Marcus Vergette installed a *Time & Tide Bell*, one of a dozen he is gradually placing around the country, each of which is rung by tidal movements. The wharf is home to a lightship, interesting historical information boards and the brightly coloured Container City, offices and studios built from recycled ship containers by Urban Space Management (also behind the Olympic Park's View Tube; *see p166*).

Take it all in over pastrami and rye in the 1940s Fatboy's Diner (7987 4334, www.fatboysdiner.co.uk, open 10am-5pm Tue-Sun), shipped here from the States, or cakes at the Driftwood Café (8am-3pm Mon-Fri). The wharf is ten minutes' walk from East India DLR, round a small bird reserve where terns nest in summer; alternatively, get the 277 bus for Leamouth from near Mile End tube.

SIGHTS

The atmospheric **Lea Valley Walk** is 50 miles of waterside path following the length of the river. It provides a magical glimpse of hidden London and its suburbs; a mixture of bucolic greenery, bleak forgotten warehouses, moody marshland, wildlife sanctuaries, posh new-build flats – and the Olympic Park (though only ticket holders can enter). For more information, see www.leavalleywalk.org.uk. Many of the riverside paths have been improved as part of the London 2012 Games's sustainability programme, and when it re-emerges in legacy (*see p63* **Whatever Next?**), the Queen Elizabeth Olympic Park will offer beautifully landscaped routes along and over the river's several channels.

Get off the tube at Bromley-by-Bow and, once you've followed the signs past the thundering roads, you can explore the Lea's southern reaches around **Three Mills Island** (*see p166*), with its film and TV studio.

A little further up the river, at pretty **Old Ford Lock**, the river splits again into the straighter, artificial Lee Navigation and the windier river proper. If you turn left (west) off the Lea Navigation, by crossing the bridge just past the Olympic Stadium, you can get on to the towpath of the mile-long Hertford Union Canal. A pedestrian bridge, still in sight of the stadium, takes you on to **Fish Island**, an industrial park with the terrific **Counter Café** (*see p163* **Inside Track**) and **Forman's** salmon smokery, restaurant (*see p235*) and art gallery. Keep on the towpath and you'll cut past graffiti artists, a garden centre and a houseboat colony, eventually running alongside leafy Victoria Park (*see p164*) before joining up with Regent's Canal, which can take you through Hackney (including an exit at funky Broadway Market), Islington and Little Venice (about eight miles in total).

If you stay on the Lea Navigation north, the path heads along **Hackney Marshes**, passing the Olympic Park's Energy Centre, the Copper Box (*see p57*) and the International Broadcast Centre/Main Press Centre (the towpath is likely to be closed at Games Time).

As the path meanders north, it alternates between urban grit (soap factories), natural beauty (Tottenham Marshes is dotted with wild flowers), nature reserve/pitch and putt (WaterWorks Nature Reserve, Lammas Road, 8988 7566, open 8am-8pm or dusk daily) and, far to the north, historical splendour (Waltham Abbey, a fine Norman church). A few miles north of the abbey, the sluices of the **Lee Valley White Water Centre** (*see p64*) are already up and running.

Three Mills Island

Three Mill Lane, E3 3DU (8980 4626, www. housemill.org.uk). Bromley-by-Bow tube. **Tours** *May-Oct* 11am-4pm Sun. **Admission** £3; £1.50 reductions; free under-16s. **No credit cards**.
This pretty island in the River Lea takes its name from the mills that, until the 18th century, ground flour and gunpowder here. The House Mill, built in 1776, is the oldest and largest tidal mill in Britain and, though out of service, it is occasionally opened to the public. The island has pleasant walks that can feel quite rural. There's also a small café and, to puncture the idyll, one of the mills is a film and TV studio.

View Tube

The Greenway, Marshgate Lane, E15 2PJ (www.theviewtube.co.uk). Pudding Mill Lane DLR. **Open** 9am-5pm daily. **Admission** free.
Made out of recycled shipping containers painted a vivid yellow-green, the View Tube feels like it's in touching distance of the Olympic Stadium (*see p52*). Information boards help you figure out what's where and give interesting information about the site, and there's good coffee at the Container Café (*see p234*).
▶ *At Games Time, the View Tube will be within the Park perimeter, accessible only to ticket-holders.*

WALTHAMSTOW

Walthamstow Central tube/rail.

Quaint **Walthamstow Village**, a few minutes' walk east of the tube station, is centred on ancient St Mary's Church and the neat little **Vestry House Museum** (Vestry Road, 8496 4391, www.walthamforest.gov.uk; closed Mon, Tue), which contains one of the first motor cars and has a fine garden for picnics. Further north, near the junction of Hoe Street and Forest Road, is peaceful Lloyd Park; the grand Georgian house at its entrance is home to the **William Morris Gallery** (*see below*) – the Arts and Crafts pioneer was a Walthamstow boy.

FREE William Morris Gallery

Lloyd Park, Forest Road, E17 4PP (8496 4390, www.walthamforest.gov.uk/william-morris). Walthamstow Central tube/rail or bus 34, 97, 215, 275. **Open** 10am-5pm Wed-Sun. *Tours* phone for details. **Admission** free; donations appreciated. **Credit** (shop) MC, V.
Artist, socialist and source of flowery wallpaper, William Morris lived here between 1848 and 1856. There are plenty of designs in fabric, stained glass and ceramic on show, produced by Morris and his acolytes. The gallery – in 2010 awarded a £1.5m grant for improvements from the Heritage Lottery Fund – features the medieval-style helmet and sword the designer used as props for some of his murals, but there are also plenty of humble domestic objects: his coffee cup, for instance.
▶ *The gallery is closed until July 2012, when it will re-open with new features including improved display spaces and a tea room.*

South-east London

A World Heritage Site and several unjustly overlooked attractions.

Beyond the world-famous sights of Greenwich, south-east London used to be ignored by many tourists – largely because the absence of the Underground in this part of the city made it seem remote from the centre. Then the London Overground made the journey from trendy east London to Rotherhithe, Forest Hill and Crystal Palace simple. The wonderful **Horniman Museum** (*see p169*) and the sweet little **Brunel** (*see p170*) and **Crystal Palace** (*see p169*) museums are key beneficiaries of this new transport link.

Map p393 & p404	Hotels pp199-202
Pubs & bars p253	Restaurants & cafés pp237-238

In any case, the area's transport difficulties are relative. The most visited neighbourhood is still, deservedly, **Greenwich** (*see p170*), an area that rivals even South Kensington for historic cultural destinations. It's easily reached on the DLR from Bank. The superb **Imperial War Museum** (*see below*) always had a nearby tube station. And, in fact, the rest of south-east London benefits from an extensive bus and rail network: if you're prepared to use it, such delights as the **Dulwich Picture Gallery** (*see p169*) are yours to enjoy.

KENNINGTON & THE ELEPHANT

Kennington tube or Elephant & Castle tube/rail.

Even back in the 17th century, the **Elephant & Castle** (named, perhaps, after the ivory-dealing Cutlers Company, or maybe after Charles I's once-intended, the Infanta of Castille) was a busy place. In the early 20th century, it was a tram terminus and south London's West End, before losing its looks to World War II bombs and a grisly 1960s makeover. Regeneration of this ugly corner of town has been promised for nearly a decade without ever looking like it might happen, but then the most visible part of a £1.5bn, 170-acre redevelopment project appeared: the new Strata residential skyscraper (www.stratalondon.com) isn't much loved, but it is instantly recognisable – look for a black-and-white building shaped like a beard-trimmer, with three giant wind turbines set into the roof.

Behind the **Imperial War Museum** (*see right*), Kennington Road leads through an area once blighted by factory stink; the smell was young resident Charlie Chaplin's abiding memory of the place. Today, the area's smarter houses are favoured by second-home politicians and lawyers requiring easy access to the city. For many, Kennington means cricket, especially in the beery atmosphere of a Test match at the **Kia Oval** (*see p336*).

★ FREE Imperial War Museum

Lambeth Road, Elephant & Castle, SE1 6HZ (7416 5320, www.iwm.org.uk). Lambeth North tube or Elephant & Castle tube/rail. **Open** 10am-6pm daily. **Admission** free. *Special exhibitions prices vary.* **Credit** MC, V. **Map** p402 N10.
Antique guns, tanks, aircraft and artillery are parked in the main hall of this imposing edifice, built in 1814 as a lunatic asylum (the Bethlehem Royal Hospital, aka Bedlam). After the inmates were moved out in 1930, the central block became the war museum, only to be damaged by World War II air raids. Today, the museum gives the history of armed conflict, especially involving Britain and the Commonwealth, from World War I to today.

SIGHTS

Moving on from the more gung-ho exhibits on the ground floor, there are extensive galleries devoted to the two World Wars. The museum's tone darkens as you ascend. On the third floor, the Holocaust Exhibition (not recommended for under-14s) traces the history of European anti-Semitism and its nadir in the concentration camps. Upstairs, Crimes Against Humanity (unsuitable for under-16s) is a minimalist space in which a film exploring contemporary genocide and ethnic violence rolls relentlessly.

There is also the world's largest collection of Victoria Crosses (displayed from autumn 2010) and excellent, long-running temporary exhibitions that are suitable for children: 'Outbreak 1939', looks at ordinary lives as Britain declares war.

The major exhibitions for 2012 are 'Family In War' (from spring 2012), which tells the story of 92-year-old Harry Allpress, the last of ten siblings who all experienced World War II; and 'Cecil Beaton: the Theatre of War' (6 Sept-5 May 2013), an exhibition of Beaton's wartime photographs.

CAMBERWELL & PECKHAM

Denmark Hill or Peckham Rye rail.

The Camberwell Beauty butterfly is unlikely to be found again in the area where it was first identified, but there is a lively art scene, centring on the **Camberwell College of Arts** and the **South London Gallery** (*see p171* **Artistic Revival**).

East of here, **Peckham** is still unfairly associated with teenage gangs and dodgy traders, but regeneration schemes continue to spruce up the streets. Rye Lane looks like old Peckham; Will Alsop's award-winning and frankly odd-looking **Peckham Library**, in an area now known as **Peckham Square**, represents the new. Due south on Rye Lane is **Peckham Rye**, where poet-visionary William Blake saw his angels; it's now a prettily laid-out park with well-kept gardens – the 1908 Japanese Garden, restored in 2005, is lovely. Keep walking south from Peckham Rye (or take a P4 or P12 bus) to enjoy views over London and Kent from **Honor Oak** and **One Tree Hill**, where Elizabeth I picnicked with Richard Bukeley of Beaumaris in 1602.

DULWICH & CRYSTAL PALACE

Crystal Palace, East Dulwich, Herne Hill, North Dulwich or West Dulwich rail.

Dulwich is a little piece of rural England that fiercely guards its bucolic prosperity. Tasteful fingerposts offer directions: perhaps towards the attractive park (once a duelling spot), the historic boys' public school or the **Dulwich Picture Gallery** (*see p169*). It's a pleasant,

Imperial War Museum. *See p167.*

brisk half-hour's walk from the gallery across Dulwich Park and up Lordship Lane to the **Horniman Museum** (*see below*) in Forest Hill.

East and west of Dulwich sit **East Dulwich** and **Herne Hill**, the latter home to an exquisite art deco lido in Brockwell Park. The two areas represent the middle(-class) way: not as expensive or charismatic as Dulwich, but less challenging than the relentless pace of Brixton.

Crystal Palace is named in honour of Joseph Paxton's famous structure, built for the Great Exhibition in Hyde Park in 1851, moved here three years later and destroyed by fire in 1936. **Crystal Palace Park** contains arches and the sphinx from the Exhibition's Egyptian-themed display; the Dinosaur Park, a lake ringed by Benjamin Waterhouse-Hawkins's life-sized (and decidedly inaccurate) dinosaur statues; and the **National Sports Centre** (*see p336*). The **Crystal Palace Museum** (Anerley Hill, SE19 2BA, 8676 0700, www.crystalpalace museum.org.uk), opened by volunteers each weekend, has an 'exhibition of the Exhibition'.

★ Dulwich Picture Gallery

Gallery Road, Dulwich, SE21 7AD (8693 5254, www.dulwichpicturegallery.org.uk). North Dulwich or West Dulwich rail. **Open** 10am-5pm Tue-Fri; 11am-5pm Sat, Sun. **Admission** £5; free-£4 reductions. *Special exhibitions* £9; free-£8 reductions. **Credit** MC, V.

Lending weight to the idea that the best things come in small packages, this bijou gallery was designed by Sir John Soane in 1811 as the first purpose-built gallery in the UK. It's a beautiful space that shows off Soane's ingenuity with lighting effects, especially in the quiet mausoleum at the heart of the building where the gallery's founders rest. The gallery displays a small but outstanding collection of work by Old Masters, offering a fine introduction to the Baroque era through works by Rembrandt, Rubens, Poussin and Gainsborough. It also has some brilliant temporary exhibitions. From June to September 2012 it's showing Andy Warhol Portfolios: Life and Legends, over 60 pieces from the mid '60s to 1985. *Photo p170.*
▶ *For Sir John Soane's Museum, see p103.*

★ FREE Horniman Museum

100 London Road, Forest Hill, SE23 3PQ (8699 1872, www.horniman.ac.uk). Forest Hill rail or bus 122, 176, 185, 363, P4, P13. **Open** 10.30am-5.30pm daily. **Admission** free; donations appreciated. *Temporary exhibitions* prices vary. *Aquarium* £2; £1 reductions; £5 family; free under-3s. **Credit** MC, V.

South-east London's premier free family attraction, the Horniman was once the home of tea trader Frederick J Horniman. It's an eccentric-looking art nouveau building (check out the clocktower, which starts as a circle and ends as a square), with a main entrance that gives out on to extensive gardens.

The oldest section is the Natural History gallery, dominated by an ancient walrus (mistakenly over-stuffed by Victorian taxidermists) and now ringed by glass cabinets containing pickled animals, stuffed birds and insect models. Other galleries include the Nature Base, African Worlds and the Centenary Gallery, which focuses on world cultures. Downstairs, the Music Gallery contains hundreds of instruments: their sounds can be unleashed via touch-screen tables, while hardier instruments (flip-flop drums, thumb pianos) can be bashed with impunity.

The most popular part of the museum is its show-piece Aquarium, where a series of tanks and rock-pools cover seven distinct aquatic ecosystems. There are mesmerising moon jellyfish, strangely large British seahorses, starfish, tropical fish and creatures from the mangroves. It forms a key part of the Evolution 2010 project, which brought together the natural history collection, aquarium and gardens to explore biodiversity and the story of how life has evolved on earth.

ROTHERHITHE

Rotherhithe tube.

Once a shipbuilding village and, in the 17th and 18th centuries, a centre for London's whaling trade, the ghostly locale of Rotherhithe has long since seen its docks filled in. Go back in time at the **Brunel Museum** (*see p170*) or the mariners' church of **St Mary's Rotherhithe** (St Mary Church Street, SE16 4JE, www.stmaryrotherhithe.org), which contains maritime oddities; among them is a communion table and bishop's chair made from timber salvaged from the HMS *Temeraire*, immortalised by Turner (the painting is in the National Gallery; *see p134*). Captain Christopher Jones was buried here in 1622; his ship, the *Mayflower*, set sail from Rotherhithe in 1620. A waterside pub of the same name marks the spot from which the pilgrims are said to have embarked on their journey.

Rotherhithe's road tunnel takes cars across to Limehouse. At the mouth of the tunnel stands the **Norwegian Church & Seaman's Mission**, one of a number of Scandinavian churches in the area. There's also a Finnish church – with a sauna – at 33 Albion Street (7237 1261). Across Jamaica Road, **Southwark Park** has a gallery (7237 1230, www.cafe galleryprojects.com), an old bandstand, a lake and playgrounds.

Brunel Museum

Brunel Engine House, Railway Avenue, SE16 4LF (7231 3840, www.brunel-museum.org.uk). Rotherhithe rail. **Open** 10am-5pm Mon, Wed-Sun; 10am-9pm Tue. *Tours* by appointment only. **Admission** £2; £1 reductions; £5 family; free under-16s. **No credit cards**.

This little museum occupies the engine house where the father-and-son team of Sir Marc and Isambard Kingdom Brunel worked to create the world's first tunnel beneath a navigable river. The story of their achievement is told most entertainingly during guided tours, which can either start at the museum or include a walk along the river before descending into the Grand Entrance Hall at the start of the Thames Tunnel; see the website for details. There's a decent little shop, a café and outdoor space should you wish to picnic.

▶ *If you visit the museum using the Overground line from north of the river, you'll actually travel under the Thames through the master engineers' tunnel, still in perfect working order.*

GREENWICH

Cutty Sark for Maritime Greenwich DLR.

Riverside Greenwich is an irresistible mixture of maritime, royal and horological history, a combination that's earned it recognition as a UNESCO World Heritage Site. The permanent attractions are gathered around **Greenwich Park**, a handsome space with great views, which will provide a grand setting for the London 2012 Equestrian events (*see p57*).

Royalty has stalked the area since 1300, when Edward I stayed here. Henry VIII was born in Greenwich Palace; the palace was built on land that later contained Wren's Royal Naval Hospital, now the **Old Royal Naval College** (*see p172*). The College is now a very handy first port-of-call. Its Pepys Building not only contains the **Greenwich Tourist Information Centre** (0870 608 2000, www.greenwich.gov.uk), but is also the home of a new exhibition that provides a great overview of Greenwich's numerous attractions. A short walk away, shoppers swarm to **Greenwich Market**, still involved in battles over a controversial redevelopment.

If you keep the river to your left, you reach the Thames-lapped **Trafalgar Tavern** (6 Park Row, 8858 2909; *photo p173*), haunt of Thackeray and Dickens, and the **Cutty Sark Tavern** (4-6 Ballast Quay, 8858 3146), which dates to 1695. Near the DLR stop is Greenwich Pier; every 15 minutes (peak times), the popular and speedy **Thames Clipper** boats (0870 781 5049, www.thamesclippers.com) shuttle passengers to and from central London.

The pier from which the Thames Clipper service departs is beside the old sailing ship, the **Cutty Sark**. The domed structure by the river is the entrance to a Victorian **pedestrian tunnel** that emerges on the far side of the Thames in Island Gardens (*see p163*).

Dulwich Picture Gallery. See p169.

Artistic Revival

Forget about the East End – Camberwell is a real artistic heartland.

At first glance, Camberwell's blend of run-down Georgian buildings, ugly tower blocks and traffic-choked roads appears less than artful. However, its built-up environment have been a fertile ground for a flourishing cultural scene that dates back to Victorian times but has found new life in the 21st century.

In 1891, William Rossiter opened the pioneering South London Fine Art Gallery. A century later, renamed the **South London Gallery** (65 Peckham Road, 7703 6120, www.southlondongallery.org), it found new renown as the first exhibitor of *Everyone I Have Ever Slept With 1963-1995*, Tracey Emin's infamous tent. A beacon for Brit Art during the 1990s, the gallery remains one of London's leading contemporary art venues. Its new £1.8m extension, which swallowed up the three-storey Victorian townhouse next door in order to add a new café, two extra exhibition spaces and a resident artist's flat, should keep it on the cutting edge.

Next door sits the **Camberwell College of Arts** (45-65 Peckham Road, 7514 6302, www.camberwell.arts.ac.uk), where the likes of Pink Floyd's Syd Barrett and film director Mike Leigh once studied. Like the South London Gallery, it's been expanding. In 2010, Peckham Square welcomed the college's **Peckham Space** (7358 9645, www.peckhamspace.com), a new contemporary art venue that has added to the good programme of free public exhibitions and events staged at the college's Camberwell Space. Outside the college, its students continue to colonise Camberwell bars such as the **Sun & Doves** (61-63 Coldharbour Lane, 7733 1525, www.sunanddoves.co.uk) and the **Bear** (296A Camberwell New Road, 7274 7037, www.thebear-freehouse.co.uk).

The modern-day scene isn't limited to the visual arts: the railway arches are vital spaces for clubbing and other diversions. Under Loughborough Junction station, **Arch 468** (Unit 4, 209A Coldharbour Lane, 07973 302908, www.arch468.com) stages work by emerging playwrights and theatre companies, with regular free rehearsed readings of new pieces. The more established **Blue Elephant** theatre (*see p302*) continues to present a vibrant programme of new writing, classic plays, physical theatre and dance. And talent of all kinds goes into the melting pot each June for the **Camberwell Arts Festival** (www.camberwellarts.org.uk). Previous years have seen Queer Tango sessions and tea dances, while a 'stumble-on-and-hit-upon' orchestra got to play instruments built out of junk. In Camberwell, it seems, getting creative is unavoidable.

From the riverside, it's a ten-minute walk (or shorter shuttle-bus trip) up the steep slopes of Greenwich Park to the **Royal Observatory** (*see p173*). The building looks even more stunning at night, when the bright green Meridian Line Laser illuminates the path of the Prime Meridian across the London sky.

The riverside Thames Path leads past rusting piers and boarded-up factories to the **Greenwich Peninsula**, dominated by the **O2 Arena**. Designed by the Richard Rogers Partnership as the Millennium Dome, this once-maligned structure's fortunes have improved considerably since its change of use. Alongside the concerts and sporting events in the huge arena (*see p321*) and movies in the cineplex, attractions include restaurants, big exhibitions and the glossy, permanent **British Music Experience** (*see p172*). The Dome is also a key London 2012 venue (*see p61* **North Greenwich Arena**), with planning permission being sought for a cable car that would connect the east flank of the peninsula with Royal Victoria Dock on the north bank of the Thames, for easy access to ExCeL (*see p57*).

The Dome and its environs are all something of a contrast with the Greenwich Peninsula Ecology Park (www.urbanecology.co.uk), and with the nearby riverside walks that afford broad, flat, bracing views and works of art; you could hardly miss *Slice of Reality*, a rusting ship cut in half by Richard Wilson, and Antony Gormley's 100-foot *Quantum Cloud*.

To the south is grassy, upmarket **Blackheath**. Smart Georgian homes and a few stately pubs surround a heath on which some of the world's earliest sports clubs started; among them is the Royal Blackheath Golf Club, said to be the oldest golf club in the world. The heath hosted the week-long Climate Camp of 3,000 anti-capitalist and environmental protesters in August 2009, a conscious echo of Blackheath's long history of radical protest that runs back to the Peasants' Revolt in 1381.

National Maritime Museum.

British Music Experience

O2 Bubble, Millennium Way, SE10 0BB (8463 2000, www.britishmusicexperience.com). North Greenwich tube. **Open** 10am-7.30pm daily. **Admission** £15; £12 reductions; £40 family; free under-5s. **Credit** AmEx, MC, V.

The memorabilia on show on the top floor of the O2 Arena (*see p321*) includes David Bowie's Ziggy Stardust costume and Noel Gallagher's Union Jack guitar. The main focus, though, is on interactive exhibits: downloading archive music, trying your hand at guitar tutorials and so on. Workshops, lectures and concerts are also part of the experience.

Cutty Sark

King William Walk, SE10 9HT (8858 2698, www.cuttysark.org.uk). Cutty Sark DLR. Check website for opening times and prices. **Map** p405 X2.

The *Cutty Sark* is to reopen in spring 2012, fully patched up after surviving a serious fire in 2007. Built in Scotland in 1869, this tea clipper was the quickest in the business when it was launched in 1870, but steam soon overtook sail and it was retired in the 1950s to this dry dock. Despite the fire, the vessel will be 90% original, with figurehead, masts, rigging and coach house intact, and is to be raised ten feet above the ground, so visitors for the first time will enter from beneath.

★ FREE Discover Greenwich & the Old Royal Naval College

2 Cutty Sark Gardens, SE10 9LW (8269 4799, www.oldroyalnavalcollege.org.uk). Cutty Sark DLR or Greenwich DLR/rail. **Open** 10am-5pm daily. *Tours* 2pm daily; other times by arrangement. **Admission** free. *Tours* £6. **Credit** (shop) MC, V. **Map** p405 X1.

In March 2010, the Pepys Building (the block of the Naval College nearest to the *Cutty Sark*, the pier and Cutty Sark DLR) reopened as the excellent Discover Greenwich. It's full of focused, informative exhibits on architecture and building techniques of the surrounding buildings, the life of Greenwich pensioners, Tudor royalty and so forth, delivered with a real sense of fun: while grown-ups read about coade stone or scagliola (popular fake stone building materials), for example, the nippers can build their own chapel with soft bricks or try on a knight's helmet. There's also a well-stocked shop and a helpful Tourist Information Centre.

Designed by Wren in 1694, with Hawksmoor and Vanbrugh helping to complete the project, the Old Royal Naval College is a superb collection of buildings. It was originally a hospital for the relief and support of seamen and their dependants, with pensioners living here from 1705 to 1869, when the complex became the Royal Naval College. The Navy left in 1998, and the neoclassical buildings now house part of the University of Greenwich and Trinity College of Music. The public are allowed into the impressive rococo chapel, where there are free organ recitals, and Painted Hall, a tribute to William and Mary that took Sir James Thornhill 19 years to complete. Nelson lay in state in the Painted Hall for three days in 1806, before being taken to St Paul's Cathedral for his funeral.

There's a lively events programme in the grounds, ranging from comedy shows (*see p299* **Our Own Edinburgh?**) and early music (*see p317* **Festivals**) to weekend appearances from historic figures – costumed actors – ranging from Pepys and Sir James to the 'pirate queen' Grace O'Malley and Joe Brown, veteran of the Battle of Trafalgar.

▶ *Attached to Discover Greenwich, the Old Brewery is an ace bar-restaurant that serves own-brewed beers; see p238.*

Fan Museum

12 Crooms Hill, SE10 8ER (8305 1441, www.fan-museum.org). Cutty Sark DLR or Greenwich DLR/rail. **Open** 11am-5pm Tue-Sat; noon-5pm Sun. **Admission** £4; £3 reductions; £10 family; free under-7s. **Credit** MC, V. **Map** p405 X2.

The world's most important collection of hand-held fans is displayed in a pair of restored Georgian townhouses. There are about 3,500 fans, including some beauties in the Hélène Alexander collection, but not all are on display at any one time. For details of the regular fan-making workshops and temporary exhibitions, check the website.

★ FREE National Maritime Museum

*Romney Road, SE10 9NF (8858 4422,
information 8312 6565, www.nmm.ac.uk). Cutty
Sark DLR or Greenwich DLR/rail.* **Open** 10am-
5pm daily. *Tours* phone for details. **Admission**
free; donations appreciated. *Temporary exhibitions*
vary; check website for details. **Credit** MC, V.
Map p405 X2.

The world's largest maritime museum contains a
huge store of creatively organised maritime art, car-
tography, models and regalia. Ground-level galleries
include Explorers, which covers great sea expedi-
tions back to medieval times, and Maritime London,
which concentrates on the city as a port. The new
Sammy Ofer wing contains Nelson's uniform, complete with fatal bullet-hole, as well as the introduc-
tory Voyages gallery, temporary exhibitions, a café,
brasserie and shop. Upstairs are Your Ocean, which
reveals our dependence on the health of the world's
oceans. Level two holds the interactives: the Bridge
has a ship simulator, and All Hands lets children
load cargo, and you can even try your hand at a
ship's gunner. The Ship of War is the museum's collection of models; Oceans of Discovery commemorates the history of world exploration; and the
Atlantic World gallery looks at the relationship
between Britain, Africa and the Americas.
▶ *To celebrate the Queen's Diamond Jubilee
and its own 75th anniversary, the NMM will be
staging 'Royal River: Power, Pageantry and the
Thames', from 27 April to 9 Sept.*

FREE Queen's House

*Romney Road, SE10 9NF (8312 6565,
www.nmm.ac.uk). Cutty Sark DLR or Greenwich
DLR/rail.* **Open** 10am-5pm daily. *Tours* phone for
details. **Admission** free. *Tours* free. **No credit
cards. Map** p405 X2.

The art collection of the National Maritime Museum
is displayed in what was formerly the summer villa
of Charles I's queen, Henrietta Maria. Completed in
1638 by Inigo Jones, the house has an interior as
impressive as the paintings on the walls. As well as
the stunning 1635 marble floor, look for Britain's
first centrally unsupported spiral stair, and the fine
painted woodwork and ceilings. The collection
includes portraits of famous maritime figures and
works by Hogarth and Gainsborough, as well as
some wartime art from the 20th century and a room
of amazing pictures of exotic tropical islands painted
during Captain Cook's explorations.

Ranger's House

*Chesterfield Walk, SE10 8QX (8853 0035,
www.english-heritage.org.uk). Blackheath rail,
Cutty Sark DLR or bus 53.* **Open** *Apr-Sept* 11am-
5pm Sun. *Tours* 11.30am, 2.30pm Mon-Wed. *Oct*
group bookings only. **Admission** £6; £2.80-£5.10
reductions; free under-5s. **Credit** MC, V. **Map**
p405 Y4.

The house of the 'Ranger of Greenwich Park' (a post
that was held by George III's niece, Princess Sophia
Matilda, from 1815) now contains the collection of
treasure – medieval and Renaissance art, jewellery,
bronzes, tapestries, furniture, porcelain, paintings –
amassed by Julius Wernher, a German who made
his considerable fortune trading in South African
diamonds. His booty is displayed through a dozen
lovely rooms in this red-brick Georgian villa, the
back garden of which is the fragrant Greenwich
Park rose collection.

★ FREE Royal Observatory & Planetarium

*Greenwich Park, SE10 9NF (8312 6565,
www.rog.nmm.ac.uk). Cutty Sark DLR or
Greenwich DLR/rail.* **Open** 10am-5pm daily.
Tours phone for details. **Admission** prices
vary; check website for details. **Credit** MC, V.
Map p405 Y3.

SIGHTS

Trafalgar Tavern. *See p170.*

The northern section of this two-halved attraction chronicles Greenwich's horological connection. Flamsteed House, the observatory that was built in 1675 on the orders of Charles II, contains the apartments of Sir John Flamsteed and other Astronomers Royal, as well as the instruments that have been used in timekeeping since the 14th century. An onion dome houses the country's largest (28-inch) refracting telescope – it was completed in 1893.

The south site houses the Astronomy Centre, home to the Peter Harrison Planetarium and Weller Astronomy Galleries. The 120-seater planetarium's architecture cleverly reflects its astrological position: the semi-submerged cone tilts at 51.5 degrees, the latitude of Greenwich, pointing to the north star, and its reflective disc is aligned with the celestial equator. Daily and weekend shows include 'Black Holes: The Other Side of Infinity' and 'Starlife', a show describing the birth and death of stars.

► *In the courtyard of Flamsteed House is the Prime Meridian Line, star of a billion snaps of happy tourists with a foot carefully placed in each hemisphere.*

WOOLWICH ARSENAL & THE THAMES BARRIER

Woolwich Arsenal DLR/rail or Woolwich Dockyard rail.

Established by the Tudors as the country's main source of munitions, **Woolwich Arsenal** stretched 32 miles along the river by World War I, with its own internal railway system. Much of the land was sold off during the 1960s, but the main section has been preserved and is now home to **Firepower** (*see right*). To the south, **The Royal Artillery Barracks** has the longest Georgian façade in the country. It will host the Shooting for the London 2012 Games (*see p61*). The river is spanned by an architectural triumph that is the Barracks' modern equal: the **Thames Barrier** (*see below*).

This is a grim bit of London, but regeneration has begun to arrive in the form of an extension of the DLR from King George V station under the river to Woolwich Arsenal. More charismatic, though, is the ramshackle **Woolwich Ferry** (8853 9400), diesel-driven boats that take pedestrians (for free) and cars across the river every ten minutes daily. The **Woolwich Foot Tunnel** is closed for a longer-than-expected refurbishment. It should re-open in spring 2012.

Firepower
Royal Arsenal, Woolwich, SE18 6ST (8855 7755, www.firepower.org.uk). Woolwich Arsenal DLR/rail. **Open** 10.30am-5pm Wed-Sun. **Admission** £5.30; £2.50-£4.60 reductions; £12.50 family; free under-5s. **Credit** MC, V.

Occupying a series of converted arsenal buildings beside the river, Firepower bristles with preserved artillery pieces, some of them centuries old. 'Field of Fire' has four screens relaying archive film and documentary footage of desert and jungle warfare. Smoke fills the air, searchlights pick out the ordnance that surrounds you and exploding bombs shake the floor. Across the courtyard, another building contains a huge collection of trophy guns and the Cold War gallery, focused on the 'monster bits' (tanks and guns used from 1945 to the present). Army-obsessed kids can get shouted at by real soldiers when they take part in drill call; the website has details of this and other attractions. The on-site café becomes a bistro in the evening.

Thames Barrier Information & Learning Centre
1 Unity Way, Woolwich, SE18 5NJ (8305 4188, www.environment-agency.gov.uk/thamesbarrier). Woolwich Dockyard rail, or North Greenwich tube then bus 472. **Open** 10.30am-5pm daily. **Admission** £3.50; £2-£3 reductions; free under-5s. **Credit** MC, V.

This adjustable dam has been variously called a triumph of modern engineering and the eighth wonder of the world. The shiny silver fins, lined up across Woolwich Reach, are indeed an impressive sight. Built in 1982 at a cost of £535m, they've already saved London from flooding some 80 times. The barrier is regularly in action for maintenance purposes; check the website for a current timetable.

To learn more, pay £3.50 for a look around the recently refurbished learning centre, where you'll find an account of the 1953 flood that led to the barrier's construction, as well as displays on wildlife in the Thames and how a flood would affect London. There's a pleasant café with picnic benches.

► *Some of the best Barrier views are from north of the river in Thames Barrier Park; see p163.*

INSIDE TRACK RIVER ART

Planning to attend some London 2012 events at the North Greenwich Arena (*see p61*)? After a more entertaining journey to a gig at the O2 Arena (*see p321*) than the Jubilee Line? Take the River Bus (*see p366*) from central London and you'll pass a sliced-open sand dredger, docked beside the Greenwich Peninsula. Sculptor Richard Wilson's *Slice of Reality* is just off the Thames Path, round the back of the Dome. There's more art where you disembark: near the Thames Clipper pier, Antony Gormley's vast *Quantum Cloud* consists of a seemingly random cloud of steel sections, but look into it from a distance and you'll see a denser area at the centre in the shape of a human body.

South-west London

Deprivation, gentrification and the poshest of the posh.

Towards the Surrey border, south-west London starts to feel like a collection of villages rather than a single sprawling metropolis. In **Richmond**, **Barnes** and **Wimbledon**, pretty Georgian houses overlook quaint greens and expansive commons where the blessed clichés of Englishness – tea-drinking, cricket – still hold sway. The rich and royal took advantage of the area's leafy proximity to the central city a long time ago, with visitors able to enjoy their legacy in the form of world-class tourist attractions: **Kew Gardens** (*see p178*), **Hampton Court Palace** (*see p180*) and **Richmond Park** (*see p178*).

Map p388	Hotels p212
Pubs & bars pp255-256	Restaurants & cafés p238

Industrialisation and urban creep soon took over the fields. **Stockwell** and **Brixton** are now just like their south-east London neighbours: diverse, busy and vibrant, despite creeping gentrification.

Between them and the posh suburbs, **Wandsworth** and **Clapham** are a vision of the likely gentrified future: herds of young professionals picnic on the fine commons at weekends, fill the bars and restaurants, and fall asleep on Egyptian cotton sheets dreaming of an apartment beside the river in **Battersea**.

SIGHTS

VAUXHALL, STOCKWELL & BRIXTON

Stockwell tube, or Brixton or Vauxhall tube/rail.

The area now known as Vauxhall was, in the 13th century, home to a big house owned by one Falkes de Bréauté, a soldier rewarded for carrying out King John's dirtier military deeds. Over time, Falkes' Hall became Fox Hall and finally Vauxhall. Vauxhall's heyday was in the 18th century when the infamous Pleasure Gardens, built back in 1661, reached the height of their popularity. As described in William Thackeray's *Vanity Fair*, the wealthy mingled here with the not-so-wealthy, getting into all kinds of trouble on 'lovers' walks'.

The Gardens closed in 1859 and the area became reasonably respectable – all that remains is Spring Garden, behind popular gay haunt the Royal Vauxhall Tavern (aka **RVT**; *see p312*). For a glimpse of old Vauxhall head to lovely, leafy **Bonnington Square**. Down

on the river is the cream and emerald ziggurat designed by Terry Farrell for the Secret Intelligence Service. On the other side of the approach to Vauxhall Bridge, glitzy apartment complex **St George's Wharf** has justifiably been nicknamed the 'five ugly sisters'.

At the top end of the South Lambeth Road, **Little Portugal** – a cluster of Portuguese cafés, shops and tapas bars – is an enticing oasis. At the other end, **Stockwell** is prime commuter territory, with little to lure visitors except some charming Victorian streets: Albert Square, Durand Gardens, Stockwell Park Crescent and Hackford Road – no.87 was briefly home to Van Gogh.

South of Stockwell is **Brixton**, a lively hub of clubs and music. The town centre has been enjoying significant redevelopment, with Windrush Square completed at the end of Coldharbour Lane in 2010 (*see also p176* **Inside Track**). The square's name is significant: HMS *Windrush* was the boat that brought West Indian immigrants from

Jamaica in 1948. They were hardly welcomed, but managed to make Brixton a thriving community. As late as the 1980s, tensions were still strong, as the Clash song 'Guns of Brixton' famously illustrates. The rage of the persecuted black community, still finding themselves isolated and under suspicion decades after arriving, is better expressed by dub poet Linton Kwesi Johnson – try 'Sonny's Lettah (Anti-Sus Poem)' for starters. The riots of 1981 and 1985 around Railton Road and Coldharbour Lane left the district scarred for years.

Now, most visitors come to Brixton for Brixton Village Market (*see p257* **The World in a Village**). The two covered arcades date to the 1920s and '30s and were – with Market Row – Grade II-listed in 2010. The district's main roads are modern and filled with chain stores, but there's also some attractive architecture – check out the **Ritzy Cinema** (Brixton Oval, Coldharbour Lane, 0871 902 5739, www.picturehouses.co.uk), dating to 1911. Brixton's best-known street, **Electric Avenue**, got its name when, in 1880, it became one of the first shopping streets to get electric lights.

Minutes from Brixton's hectic centre, **Brockwell Park** (Brixton Water Lane, www.brockwellpark.com) is one of London's most underrated green spaces. Landscaped in the early 19th century for a wealthy glass maker, the park contains its Georgian country house – now a café – an open-air swimming pool, bowling green, walled rose garden and miniature railway. Each July, there's an enjoyable traditional country fair.

BATTERSEA

Battersea Park or Clapham Junction rail.

Battersea started life as an island in the Thames, but it was reclaimed when the surrounding marshes were drained. Huguenots settled here from the 16th century and, prior to the Industrial Revolution, the area was mostly farmland. The river is dominated by Sir Giles Gilbert Scott's magnificent four-chimneyed **Battersea Power Station** (www.battersea powerstation.org.uk), which can be seen close up from all trains leaving Victoria Station. Images of this iconic building have graced album covers (notably Pink Floyd's *Animals*) and films (among them Ian McKellen's *Richard III* and Michael Radford's *1984*), and its instantly recognisable silhouette pops up repeatedly as you move around the capital. Work started on what was to become the largest brick-built structure in Europe in 1929, and the power station was in operation through to the early 1980s. Too impressive to be destroyed, its future continues to be the subject

INSIDE TRACK
BLACK AND PROUD

Gathered over a quarter of a century, the **Black Cultural Archives** (www.bca heritage.org.uk) are getting a permanent new home. It will be housed in Britain's first black cultural centre, due to open in 2012 in the Grade II-listed Raleigh Hall on Windrush Square in Brixton (*see p175*).

of intense public debate – meanwhile, it's carved out a niche as a venue for circus spectaculars and extreme sports festivals.

Overlooking the river a little further west, **Battersea Park** (www.batterseapark.org) has beautiful lakes (one with a fine Barbara Hepworth sculpture) and gardens. Much of the park was relandscaped in 2004 according to the original 19th-century plans, albeit with some modern additions left in place: the Russell Page Garden, designed for the 1951 Festival of Britain; a Peace Pagoda, built by a Buddhist sect in 1985 to commemorate Hiroshima Day; a petting zoo (7924 5826; *see p295*); and an art gallery (the Pumphouse, 8871 7572, www.wandsworth.gov.uk/gallery). The park extends to the Thames; from the wide and lovely riverside walk you can see both the elaborate **Albert Bridge** and the simpler **Battersea Bridge**, rebuilt between 1886 and 1890 by sewer engineer Joseph Bazalgette.

West of the bridges, you'll find the beautiful church of **St Mary's Battersea** (Battersea Church Road); this was where poet William Blake was married and Benedict Arnold, who contrived to fight on both sides during the American War of Independence, is buried. From here, JMW Turner used to paint the river.

CLAPHAM & WANDSWORTH

Clapham Common tube, or Wandsworth Common or Wandsworth Town rail.

In the 18th and 19th centuries, **Clapham** was colonised by the wealthy upper classes and social reformers, notably abolitionist William Wilberforce's Clapham Sect. But the coming of the railways meant that the posh folk upped sticks, and from 1900 the area fell into decline. Nowadays, it is once again one of the capital's more desirable addresses. **Clapham Common** provides an oasis of peace amid busy traffic, with Holy Trinity Church, which dates from 1776, at its perimeter. From Clapham Common station, turn north into the **Pavement** – it leads to the pubs and shops of Clapham Old Town. Alternatively, head south to the smart shops and cafés of **Abbeville Road**. The area to the west of the common is known as 'Nappy Valley', because of the many young middle-class families who reside there. If you can fight your way between baby carriages, head for **Northcote Road** – especially on weekends, when a lovely little market sets up.

PUTNEY & BARNES

East Putney or Putney Bridge tube,
or Barnes or Putney rail.

If you want proof of an area's well-to-do credentials, count the rowing clubs: **Putney** has a couple of dozen. **Putney Bridge** is partly responsible, as its buttresses made it difficult for large boats to continue upstream, creating a stretch of water conducive to rowing. The **Oxford & Cambridge Boat Race** (*see p334*) has started in Putney since 1845. The river has good paths in either direction; heading west along the Putney side of the river will take you past the **WWT Wetland Centre** (*see right*), which lies alongside Barnes Common. The main road across the expanse, Queen's Ride, humpbacks over the railway line below. It was here, on 16 September 1977, that singer Gloria Jones's Mini drove off the road, killing her passenger (and boyfriend) T-Rex singer Marc Bolan. The slim trunk of the sycamore hit by the car is covered with notes, poems and declarations of love; steps lead to a bronze bust.

★ WWT Wetland Centre

Queen Elizabeth's Walk, Barnes, SW13 9WT (8409 4400, www.wwt.org.uk). Hammersmith tube then bus 283, Barnes rail or bus 33, 72, 209. **Open** *Mar-Oct* 9.30am-6pm daily. *Nov-Feb* 9.30am-5pm daily. **Admission** £10.55; £5.85-£7.85 reductions; £29.40 family; free under-4s. **Credit** MC, V.

Reclaimed from industrial reservoirs a decade ago, the 43-acre Wildfowl & Wetlands Trust Wetland Centre is four miles from central London, but feels a world away. Quiet ponds, rushes, rustling reeds and wildflower gardens all teem with bird life – some 150 species – as well as the now very rare water vole. Naturalists ponder its 27,000 trees and 300,000 aquatic plants and swoon over 300 varieties of butterfly, 20 types of dragonfly and four species of bat (now sleeping in a stylish new house designed by Turner Prize-winning artist Jeremy Deller). You can explore water-recycling initiatives in the new RBC Rain Garden or check out the new interactive section: pilot a submerged camera around a pond, learn about the life-cycle of a dragonfly or make waves in a digital pool. Traditionalists needn't be scared – plain old pairs of binoculars can be hired.

KEW & RICHMOND

Kew Gardens or Richmond tube/rail,
or Kew Bridge rail.

Much of Kew has a rarified air, with leafy streets that lead you into a quaint world of teashops, tiny bookstores and gift shops, a

SIGHTS

WWT Wetland Centre.

Hampton Court Palace. *See p180.*

sweet village green, ancient pubs and pleasant riverpaths. Kew's big appeal is its vast and glorious **Royal Botanic Gardens** (*see right*), but the **National Archives** – formerly the Public Records Office – are housed here too, a repository for everything from the Domesday Book to recently released government documents. The place is always full of people researching their family trees. Overlooking the gardens, **Watermans Arts Centre** (40 High Street, 8232 1010, www.watermans.org.uk) contains a gallery, cinema and theatre focusing on Brit-Asian and South Asian arts.

Originally known as the Shene, the wealthy area of **Richmond**, about 15 minutes' walk west down Kew Road, has been linked with royalty for centuries: Edward III had a palace here in the 1300s and Henry VII loved the area so much that in 1501 he built another (naming it Richmond after his favourite earldom); this was where Elizabeth I spent her last summers. Ultimately, the whole neighbourhood took the palace's name, although the building itself is long gone – pretty much all that's left is a small gateway on **Richmond Green**. On the east side of the green, medieval alleys (such as Brewer's Lane) replete with ancient pubs lead to the traffic-choked high street. The **Church of St Mary Magdalene**, on Paradise Road, blends architectural styles from 1507 to 1904.

A short walk away in Richmond's Old Town Hall, you'll find the small **Museum of Richmond** (Whittaker Avenue, 8332 1141, www.museumofrichmond.com, closed Mon & Sun). Nearby, the riverside promenade is eminently strollable and dotted with pubs; the **White Cross** (Water Lane, 8940 6844), which has been here since 1835, has a special 'entrance at high tide' – the river floods regularly. The 13 arches of **Richmond Bridge** date from 1774 – this is the oldest surviving crossing over the Thames and offers fine sweeping views.

Richmond Park is the largest of the Royal Parks, occupying some 2,500 acres. There are hundreds of red and fallow deer roaming free across it – presumably much happier without having to listen out for the 'View halloo!' of one of Henry VIII's hunting parties. Within the park's bounds is the Palladian splendour of White Lodge and Pembroke Lodge, childhood home to philosopher Bertrand Russell but now a café.

★ Royal Botanic Gardens (Kew Gardens)

Kew, Richmond, Surrey TW9 3AB (8332 5655, www.kew.org). Kew Gardens tube/rail, Kew Bridge rail or riverboat to Kew Pier. **Open** times vary; check website for details. **Admission** £13.90; £11.90 reductions; free under-17s. **Credit** AmEx, MC, V.

Kew's lush, landscaped beauty represents the pinnacle of our national gardening obsession. From the early 1700s until 1840, when the gardens were given to the nation, these were the grounds for two fine royal residences – the White House and Richmond Lodge. Early resident Queen Caroline, who was wife of George II, was very fond of exotic plants brought back by botanists voyaging to far-flung parts of the world. In 1759, the renowned 'Capability' Brown was employed by George III to improve on the work of his predecessors here, William Kent and Charles Bridgeman. Thus began the shape of the extraordinary garden that today attracts hundreds of thousands of visitors each year.

Covering half a square mile, Kew feels surprisingly big – pick up a map at the ticket office and follow the handy signs. Head straight for the 19th-century greenhouses, filled to the roof with plants – some of which have been here as long as the huge glass structures themselves. The sultry Palm House holds tropical plants: palms, bamboo, tamarind, mango and fig trees, not to mention fragrant hibiscus and frangipani. The Temperate House features *Pendiculata sanderina*, the Holy Grail for orchid hunters, with petals some 3ft long.

Also worth seeking out are the Princess of Wales Conservatory, divided into ten climate zones; the

Marine Display, downstairs from the Palm House (it isn't always open, but when it is you can see the delightful seahorses); the lovely, quiet indoor pond of the Waterlily House (closed in winter); and the exquisite Victorian botanical drawings found in the fabulous Marianne North Gallery. The Xstrata Treetop Walkway has been a hugely popular addition to the gardens, allowing you a completely different woodland walk 60ft up in the leaf canopy.
► *Britain's smallest royal palace is also within the gardens: Kew Palace (www.hrp.org.uk/KewPalace; closed Oct-Mar; £5.30, free-£4.50 reductions) dates all the way back to the 18th century.*

WIMBLEDON

Wimbledon tube/rail.

Beyond the world-famous tennis tournament, **Wimbledon** is little but a wealthy and genteel suburb. Turn left out of the station on to the uninspiring Broadway, and you'll wonder why you bothered. So turn right instead, climbing a steep hill lined with huge houses. At the top is **Wimbledon Village**, a trendy little enclave of posh shops, eateries and some decent pubs.

From here you can hardly miss **Wimbledon Common**, a huge, wild, partly wooded park, that is criss-crossed by paths and horse tracks. The windmill (Windmill Road, 8947 2825, www.wimbledonwindmill.org.uk; closed Nov-Mar) provides an eccentric touch: Robert Baden-Powell wrote *Scouting for Boys* (1910) here; it's now home to a tearoom and a hands-on milling museum.

East of the common lies **Wimbledon Park**, with its boating lake, and the **All England Lawn Tennis Club** and **Wimbledon Lawn Tennis Museum** (*see below*). Two other attractions are worth seeking out – Grade II-listed **Cannizaro Park** (www.cannizaropark. com) is lovely, as is the **Buddhapadipa Temple** (14 Calonne Road, Wimbledon Parkside, 8946 1357, www.buddhapadipa.org). When it was built in the early 1980s, this was the only Thai temple in Europe. The Shrine Room contains a golden statue of the Buddha, a copy of the Buddhasihing that is on show in Bangkok's National Museum.

Wimbledon Lawn Tennis Museum

Museum Building, All England Lawn Tennis Club, Church Road, SW19 5AE (8946 6131, www.wimbledon.org/museum). Southfields tube or bus 493. **Open** 10am-5pm daily; ticket holders only during championships. **Admission** (incl tour) £20; £12.50-£17 reductions; free under-5s. **Credit** MC, V.
Highlights at this popular museum on the history of tennis include a 200° cinema screen that allows you to find out what it's like to play on Centre Court and

a re-creation of a 1980s men's dressing room, complete with a 'ghost' of John McEnroe. Visitors can also enjoy a behind-the-scenes tour.
► *Wimbledon is the venue for the London 2012 Olympic Games Tennis competition; see p62.*

FURTHER SOUTH-WEST

Richmond tube/rail, or Hampton Court or St Margaret's rail.

If the water level allows, follow the river from Richmond west. You could stop at **Petersham**, home to the **Petersham Nurseries** with its garden café (Church Lane, off Petersham Road, 8940 5230, www.petershamnurseries.com), or take in a grand country mansion, perhaps **Ham House** (*see below*) or **Marble Hill House**, with the **Orleans House Gallery** (for both, *see p180*) right next door.

The river runs on past **Twickenham**, home to rugby's **Twickenham Stadium** (*see p180*), to the curious Gothic 'castle' **Strawberry Hill** (*see p180*). Several miles further along the Thames, the river passes beside the magnificent **Hampton Court Palace** (*see p180*). Few visitors will want to walk this far, of course – instead take a train from Waterloo or, for that extra fillip of adventure, a boat.

Ham House

Ham Street, Richmond, Surrey TW10 7RS (8940 1950, www.nationaltrust.org.uk/ hamhouse). Richmond tube/rail then bus 371. **Open** times vary; check website for details. **Admission** prices vary; check website for details. **Credit** MC, V.
Built in 1610 for one of James I's courtiers, Thomas Vavasour, this lavish red-brick mansion is full of period furnishings, rococo mirrors and ornate tapestries. Detailing is exquisite, down to a table in the dairy with sculpted cows' legs. The restored formal grounds also attract attention: there's a lovely trellised Cherry Garden and some lavender parterres. The tearoom in the old orangery turns out historic dishes (lavender syllabub, for instance) using ingredients from the Kitchen Gardens.
► *Between February and October (weekends only for the winter months), a ferry crosses the river to Marble Hill House; see p180.*

INSIDE TRACK CREEPY CASTLE

Chiming with the vogue for all things vampiric, the twilight and moonlight tours of Strawberry Hill (*see p180*), 18th-century home of proto-Goth Horace Walpole, show this folly of a house at its most theatrical, spooky best.

SIGHTS

SIGHTS

★ Hampton Court Palace

East Molesey, Surrey KT8 9AU (0844 482 7777, www.hrp.org.uk). Hampton Court rail, or riverboat from Westminster or Richmond to Hampton Court Pier (Apr-Oct). **Open** *Palace* Apr-Oct 10am-6pm daily; Nov-Mar 10am-4.30pm daily. *Park* dawn-dusk daily. **Admission** *Palace, courtyard, cloister & maze* £14.50; £7.25-£12 reductions; £39.50 family; free under-5s. *Maze only* £3.50; £2.50 reductions. *Gardens only* Apr-Oct £4.80; free-£4.50 reductions; Nov-Mar free. **Credit** AmEx, MC, V.

It may be a half-hour train ride from central London, but this spectacular palace, once owned by Henry VIII, is well worth the trek. It was built in 1514 by Cardinal Wolsey, the high-flying Lord Chancellor, but Henry liked it so much he seized it for himself in 1528. For the next 200 years it was a focal point of English history: Elizabeth I was imprisoned in a tower by her jealous and fearful elder sister Mary I; Shakespeare gave his first performance to James I in 1604; and, after the Civil War, Oliver Cromwell was so besotted by the building he ditched his puritanical principles and moved in to enjoy its luxuries.

Centuries later, the rosy walls of the palace still dazzle. Its vast size can be daunting, so it's a good idea to take advantage of the guided tours. If you do decide to go it alone, start with Henry VIII's State Apartments, which include the Great Hall, noted for its beautiful stained-glass windows and elaborate religious tapestries; in the Haunted Gallery, the ghost of Catherine Howard – Henry's fifth wife, executed for adultery in 1542 – can reputedly be heard shrieking. The King's Apartments, added in 1689 by Wren, are notable for a splendid mural of Alexander the Great, painted by Antonio Verrio. The Queen's Apartments and Georgian Rooms feature similarly elaborate paintings, chandeliers and tapestries. The Tudor Kitchens are great fun, with their giant cauldrons, fake pies and blood-spattered walls.

More extraordinary sights await outside, where the exquisitely landscaped gardens contain superb topiary, peaceful Thames views, a reconstruction of a 16th-century heraldic garden and the famous Hampton Court maze. In summer, there's a music festival and a flower show that rivals the more famous one at Chelsea; every winter, an ice rink is installed. *Photo p178.*

Marble Hill House

Richmond Road, Twickenham, Middx TW1 2NL (8892 5115, www.english-heritage.org.uk). St Margaret's rail or bus 33, 490, H22, R70. **Open** times vary; check website for details. **Admission** £5.30; £3.20-£4.80 reductions; £13.80 family; free under-5s. **Credit** MC, V.

King George II spared no expense to win the favour of his mistress, Henrietta Howard. Not only did he build this perfect Palladian house (1724) for his lover, he almost dragged Britain into a war while doing so: by using Honduran mahogany to construct the grand staircase, he managed to spark off a major

diplomatic row with Spain. Frankly, it was worth it. Picnickers are welcome to the grounds, as are sporty types (there are tennis, putting and cricket facilities). ▶ *A programme of concerts runs in summer, and ferries cross the river to Ham House; see p179.*

FREE Orleans House Gallery

Riverside, Twickenham, Middx TW1 3DJ (8831 6000, www.richmond.gov.uk/orleans_house_gallery). Richmond tube then bus 33, 490, H22, R68, R70, or St Margaret's or Twickenham rail. **Open** *Apr-Sept* 1-5.30pm Tue-Sat; 2-5.30pm Sun. *Oct-Mar* 1-4.30pm Tue-Sat; 2-4.30pm Sun. **Admission** free. **Credit** MC, V.

Secluded in pretty gardens, this Grade I-listed riverside house was constructed in 1710 for James Johnson, Secretary of State for Scotland. It was later named after the Duke of Orleans, Louis-Philippe, who lived in exile here from 1800 until 1817. Though partially demolished in 1926, the building retains James Gibbs's neoclassical Octagon Room. There are also regularly changing temporary exhibitions here. ▶ *The new café (Karmarama, open Wed-Sun) is a welcome addition, offering good coffee and snacks.*

Strawberry Hill

268 Waldegrave Road, Twickenham, Middx TW1 4ST (8744 1241, www.strawberryhillhouse.org.uk). Richmond tube then bus R68, or Strawberry Hill rail. **Open** *Apr-Oct* 2-4.30pm Mon-Wed; noon-4.30pm Sat, Sun. **Admission** £8; £7 reductions; £20 family; free under-5s. **Credit** MC, V.

Antiquarian and novelist Horace Walpole, who created the Gothic novel with his book *The Castle of Otranto*, was laying the groundwork for the Gothic Revival of Victorian times as early as the 18th century. This 'little Gothic castle' reopened to the public in autumn 2010 after a £9m restoration. Pre-booked tickets, timed at 20min intervals, will allow you to explore the crepuscular nooks and crannies of Walpole's 'play-thing house'.

World Rugby Museum/ Twickenham Stadium

Twickenham Rugby Stadium, Rugby Road, Twickenham, Middx TW1 1DZ (8892 8877, www.rfu.com). Hounslow East tube then bus 281, or Twickenham rail. **Open** *Museum* 10am-5pm Tue-Sat; 11am-5pm Sun. *Tours* 10.30am, noon, 1.30pm, 3pm Tue-Sat; 1pm, 3pm Sun. **Admission** £14; £8 reductions; £40 family; free under-5s. **Credit** AmEx, MC, V.

The impressive Twickenham Stadium is the home of English rugby union. Tickets for international matches are extremely hard to come by, but the Museum of Rugby is on the site to provide some compensation. Guided tours take in the England dressing room, the players' tunnel and the Royal Box. Memorabilia (a jersey from 1871, the Calcutta Cup) charts the game's development from the late 19th century, and there's a scrum machine.

West London

Old money and new peoples.

It's fitting that west London still has a distinct air of aristocash. This was, after all, the first of the city's frontiers to be developed, just outside the City of Westminster and out of the way of the westerly smog-carrying winds. Even today, the elegant Georgian townhouses of **Holland Park** and **Kensington** have retained their high status.

Unlike London's north, east and south, where the posher neighbourhoods are tucked away in more remote, leafier suburbs, the smartest parts of the west – chiefly Fulham, Kensington and Notting Hill – are conveniently central, while the working-class districts of **Southall** and **Wembley**, now the first stop for those who've arrived in the country via Heathrow, are further out.

Map p394	Hotels pp212-214
Pubs & bars	Restaurants &
p255	cafés pp238-240

KENSINGTON & HOLLAND PARK

High Street Kensington or Holland Park tube.

There are more millionaires per square mile in this corner of London than in any other part of Europe, a hangover from the days when Kensington was a semi-rural retreat for aristocrats. Just off **Kensington High Street**, one of London's smarter mainstream shopping stretches, an array of handsome squares are lined with grand 19th-century houses, many of which still serve as single-family homes. The houses here are not as ostentatiously grand as they are in, say, Belgravia, but nor is the wealth worn as lightly and subtly as it is in many corners of Mayfair. You're always aware that you're around money.

Linking with Notting Hill (*see p127*) to the north, **Kensington Church Street** has many antiques shops selling furniture so fine you would probably never dare use it. **St Mary Abbots** (7937 6032, www.stmaryabbots church.org), at the junction of Church Street and High Street, is a wonderful Victorian neo-Gothic church, built on the site of the 12th-century original by Sir George Gilbert Scott between 1869 and 1872. Past worshippers have included Isaac Newton and William

Wilberforce. As well as beautiful stained-glass windows, it has London's tallest spire (278 feet).

Across the road is a striking art deco building, once the department store Barkers but now taken over by Texan organic food giant **Whole Foods Market** (nos.63-97, 7368 4500, www.wholefoodsmarket.co.uk). South down Derry Street, past the entrance to the **Roof Gardens** – a restaurant and private members' club, which boasts flamingos and a stream, 100 feet above central London – is Kensington Square, which has one of London's highest concentrations of blue plaques. The writer William Thackeray lived at no.16 and the

INSIDE TRACK
TRAINS, TAXIS AND BUSES

Transport boffins and fans of design classics: the **London Transport Museum** (*see p112*) opens its Acton depot to visitors on a few weekends a year. The warehouse contains over 370,000 objects that wouldn't fit into the Covent Garden museum, including vehicles – a 1950s Routemaster bus prototype among them – and vintage posters and uniforms. See www.ltmuseum.co.uk for details.

Leighton House.

painter Edward Burne-Jones at no.41; at no.18, John Stuart Mill's maid made her bid for 'man from Porlock' status by using Carlyle's sole manuscript of *The French Revolution* to start the fire. The houses, though much altered, date from the development of the square in 1685, and – hard to believe now – were surrounded by fields until 1840.

Further to the west is one of London's finest green spaces: **Holland Park**. Along its eastern edge, Holland Walk is one of the most pleasant paths in central London, but the heart of the park is the Jacobean **Holland House**. Left derelict after World War II, it was bought by the London County Council in 1952; the east wing now houses the city's best-sited youth hostel (*see p214*). In summer, open-air theatre and opera are staged on the front terrace. Three lovely formal gardens are laid out near the house. A little further west, the Japanese-style Kyoto Garden has huge koi carp and a bridge at the foot of a waterfall. Elsewhere, rabbits hop about and peacocks stroll around with the confidence due to such supremely beautiful creatures. To the south of the park are another two historic houses: **Linley Sambourne House** and, reopened after extensive refurbishment in spring 2010, **Leighton House** (for both, *see right*).

★ Leighton House

12 Holland Park Road, W14 8LZ (7602 3316, www.rbkc.gov.uk). High Street Kensington tube. **Open** 10am-5.30pm Mon, Wed-Sun. *Tours* 3pm Wed (other times by appointment only). **Admission** £5; £3 reductions. **Credit** MC, V. **Map** p394 A9.

Behind its sternly Victorian red-brick façade, Leighton House has received a £1.6m refurbishment. In the 1860s, artist Frederic Leighton commissioned a showpiece house, which he filled with classical treasures from all over the world, as well as his own works and those of his contemporaries. Every inch of his house is decorated in high style: magnificent downstairs reception rooms designed for lavish entertaining; a dramatic staircase leading to a light-filled studio that takes up most of the first floor; and, above all, the 'Arab Hall', which showcases Leighton's huge collection of 16th-century Middle Eastern tiles. The only private space in the whole house is a tiny single bedroom.

Linley Sambourne House

18 Stafford Terrace, W8 7BH (information 7938 1295, tours 7602 3316, www.rbkc.gov.uk/linley sambournehouse). High Street Kensington tube. **Open** *Mid Sept-mid June* 11.15am, 2.15pm Wed; 11.15am, 1pm, 2.15pm, 3.30pm Sat, Sun. **Tours** £6; £1-£4 reductions. **Credit** MC, V. **Map** p394 A9.

The home of cartoonist Edward Linley Sambourne was built in the 1870s and has almost all of its original fittings and furniture. Tours last 90mins, with weekend tours led by an actor in period costume (except 11.5am tour).

▶ *If you enjoy the re-enactment tours here, note that something similar is offered at Benjamin Franklin House; see p114.*

EARL'S COURT & FULHAM

Earl's Court, Fulham Broadway or West Brompton tube.

Earl's Court sells itself short, grammatically speaking, since it was once the site of the courthouse of two earls: both the Earl of Warwick and the Earl of Holland. The 1860s saw Earl's Court move from rural hamlet to investment opportunity as the Metropolitan Railway arrived. Some 20 years later it was already much as we see it today, bar the fast food joints. The terraces of grand old houses are mostly subdivided into bedsits and cheap hotels; today, the transient population tends to be Eastern European or South American.

In 1937, the **Earls Court Exhibition Centre** was built, and in its day it was the largest reinforced concrete building in Europe. The centre hosts a year-round calendar of events, from trade shows to pop concerts (Pink Floyd built and tore down *The Wall* here), and will host the London 2012 Volleyball (*see p57*). The Exhibition Centre is close to the diverting little **Metropolitan Police Museum** (ground floor, Empress State Building, Empress Approach, Lillie Road, SW6 1TR, 7161 1234; open 10am-4pm Mon-Fri). Two minutes south down Warwick Road is a tiny venue, with an impressive pedigree: the **Troubadour** (263-267 Old Brompton Road, 7370 1434, www.troubadour.co.uk), a 1950s coffeehouse with a downstairs club that hosted Jimi Hendrix, Joni Mitchell, Bob Dylan and Paul Simon in the 1960s. While it's no longer at the cutting edge, it still delivers a full programme of music, poetry and comedy.

Heading west along Warwick Road you come to the gates of **Brompton Cemetery**. It's full of magnificent monuments to the famous and infamous, including suffragette Emmeline Pankhurst and, his grave marked by a lion, boxer 'Gentleman' John Jackson – 'Gentleman' John taught Lord Byron to box. The peace and quiet of the cemetery are regularly disturbed at its southern end by neighbouring **Stamford Bridge**, home of Chelsea FC. **Craven Cottage** (for both, *see p337*), the home of west London's other Premiership team, Fulham FC, is west of here, at the northern end of the park that surrounds **Fulham Palace** (*see right*).

FREE Fulham Palace & Museum

Bishop's Avenue, off Fulham Palace Road, SW6 6EA (7736 3233, www.fulhampalace.org). Putney Bridge tube or bus 14, 74, 220, 414, 430. **Open** *Museum & gallery* 1-4pm Mon-Wed, Sat, Sun. Gallery closes for functions; phone in advance. *Gardens* dawn-dusk daily. **Tours** 2pm 3rd Tue, 2nd & 4th Sun of mth. **Admission** free; under-16s must be accompanied by an adult. *Tours* £5; free under-16s. **No credit cards.**

Fulham Palace was the episcopal retreat of the Bishops of London. The present building was built in Tudor times, with later significant Georgian and Victorian additions. It would be more accurate to call it a manor house than a palace, but it gives a fine glimpse into the changing lifestyles and architecture of nearly 500 years, from the Tudor hall to the splendid Victorian chapel; try out the echo in the courtyard. There's also access to a glorious stretch of riverside walk, and the newly restored vineries and walled garden. Best of all, these delights still seem largely undiscovered by the majority of Londoners.

▶ *The Drawing Room Café has outdoor tables looking out over an expansive lawn.*

SHEPHERD'S BUSH

Goldhawk Road or Shepherd's Bush Market tube, or Shepherd's Bush tube/rail.

Shepherd's Bush was once west London's impoverished backwater, the setting for junkyard sitcom *Steptoe & Son*. Now, a couple of decades after house prices started going through the roof, there's visible evidence of gentrification. **Queens Park Rangers** (*see p337*), the underperforming local football team, has benefited from a huge cash injection from three of the world's richest businessmen, while Shepherd's Bush got a similar boost from the gargantuan **Westfield London** shopping mall (*see p259*). The **Bush** theatre (*see p349*) stages excellent leftfield drama, while **Bush Hall** (*see p323*), a beautifully restored former snooker hall, and the **O2 Shepherd's Bush Empire** (*see p321*), an old BBC theatre, have become essential destinations on the music scene. The bar at the **K West** hotel (Richmond Way, W14 0AX, 8008 6600, www.k-west.co.uk) is a good place if you're interested in spotting trendy bands after they've played the Empire.

BBC Television Centre

TV Centre, Wood Lane, W12 7RJ (0370 603 0304, www.bbc.co.uk/tours). White City or Wood Lane tube. **Open** by appointment only Mon-Sat. **Admission** £9.95; £7.75-£9.25 reductions; £30 family. No under-9s. **Credit** MC, V.

Half a mile north of Shepherd's Bush Green is the BBC TV Centre where, if you book in advance, you can catch a fascinating tour around the temple of

SIGHTS

British televisual history. Tours include visits to the news desk, the TV studios and the Weather Centre, though children and *Doctor Who* fans might be most excited about the TARDIS on display.

▶ *Fancy being part of a BBC television show audience? Apply for free tickets at www.bbc.co.uk/showsandtours/tickets or by phone on 0370 901 1227 (24hrs daily).*

HAMMERSMITH

Hammersmith tube.

Dominated by the grey concrete of its flyover, the centre of Hammersmith, **Hammersmith Broadway**, was once a grotty bus garage. It's now a shiny new shopping mall. Make it over the road and you'll find the **HMV Hammersmith Apollo** (*see p320*). Opened in 1932 as the Gaumont Palace, it entered rock legend as the Hammersmith Odeon, hosting pivotal gigs by such bands as the Beatles, Motörhead and Public Enemy.

Hammersmith Bridge, the city's oldest suspension bridge, is a green and gold hymn to the strength of Victorian ironwork. There's a lovely walk west along the Thames Path from here that takes in a clutch of historic pubs including the **Blue Anchor** (13 Lower Mall, W6 9DJ, 8748 5774); head in the opposite direction for cultural happenings at the **Riverside Studios** (*see p308*).

CHISWICK

Turnham Green tube or Chiswick rail.

Once a sleepy, semi-rural suburb, Chiswick is now one of London's swankiest postcodes, its residents including broadcasters, directors, actors, advertising bods and a smattering of rock 'n' roll royalty. In recent years, **Chiswick High Road**, its main thoroughfare, has developed a gastronomic reputation, with dozens of high-end eateries.

Chiswick also has a surprising number of sightseeing attractions. **Chiswick Mall** is a beautiful residential path that runs alongside the river from Hammersmith, and includes **Kelmscott House** (26 Upper Mall, 8741 3735, www.morrissociety.org.uk), once home to pioneering socialist William Morris but now a private house that opens to the public 2-5pm on Thursdays and Saturdays. From here, it's a short walk to **Fuller's Brewery** (*see right*) and **Hogarth's House** (*see right*), while the **Kew Bridge Steam Museum** (*see right*) and the **Musical Museum** (*see p185*) are only a bus ride away. It's possible to return to the river path after visiting **Chiswick House** (*see right*), and the wonderful Royal Botanic Gardens at Kew (*see p178*) are just over the bridge. Further upstream is **Syon House** (*see p185*).

Chiswick House
Burlington Lane, W4 2RP (8995 0508, www.chgt.org.uk). Hammersmith tube then bus 190, or Chiswick rail. **Open** *Apr-Oct* 10am-5pm Mon-Wed, Sun. **Admission** £5.50; £3.50-£5 reductions; free under-5s. **Credit** MC, V.
Richard Boyle, third Earl of Burlington, designed this lovely Palladian villa in 1725 as a place to entertain the artistic and philosophical luminaries of his day. The Chiswick House & Gardens Trust has restored the gardens to Burlington's original design. The restoration was greatly helped by details from the newly acquired painting *A View of Chiswick House from the South-west* by Dutch landscape artist Pieter Andreas Rysbrack (c1685-1748).
▶ *There's a good new café here (8995 6356, www.chiswickhousecafe.co.uk).*

Fuller's Brewery
Griffin Brewery, Chiswick Lane South, W4 2QB (8996 2000, www.fullers.co.uk). Turnham Green tube. **Open** *Tours* hourly 11am-3pm Mon-Fri, by appointment only. *Shop* 10am-8pm Mon-Fri; 10am-6pm Sat. **Admission** (incl tasting session) £10; £8 reductions. **Credit** MC, V.
Fuller Smith & Turner PLC is London's last family-run brewery. Most of this current building dates back to 1845 but there's been a brewery on this site since Elizabethan times. The two-hour tours need to be booked in advance, but – surprise – there is a pub next door if you can't get on a tour.
▶ *London Pride and ESB are the most popular Fuller's brews in London pubs.*

FREE Hogarth's House
Hogarth Lane, Great West Road, W4 2QN (8994 6757). Turnham Green tube or Chiswick rail. **Open** *Apr-Oct* 1-5pm Tue-Fri; 1-6pm Sat, Sun. *Nov, Dec, Feb, Mar* 1-4pm Tue-Fri; 1-5pm Sat, Sun. **Admission** free; donations appreciated. **No credit cards.**
Recently reopened – fittingly, by comedian, satirist and Chiswick resident Dara O'Brien – after refurbishment, this was the country retreat of the 18th-century artist and social commentator William Hogarth. On display are some famous engravings, including *Gin Lane, Marriage à la Mode* and a copy of *Rake's Progress*, and biographical information.

★ Kew Bridge Steam Museum
Green Dragon Lane, Brentford, Middx TW8 0EN (8568 4757, www.kbsm.org). Gunnersbury tube/rail or Kew Bridge rail. **Open** 11am-4pm Tue-Sun. **Admission** £9.50; £3.50-£8.50 reductions; free under-5s. **Credit** AmEx, MC, V.
One of London's most engaging small museums, this impressive old Victorian pumping station is a reminder that steam wasn't just used for powering

Syon House.

SIGHTS

trains but also for supplying enough water to the citizens of an expanding London. It's now home to an extraordinary collection of different engines. There are lots of hands-on exhibits for kids, a great dressing-up box and even a miniature steam train.

★ Musical Museum
399 High Street, Brentford, Middx TW8 0DU (8560 8108, www.musicalmuseum.co.uk). Kew Bridge rail or bus 65, 237, 267. **Open** 11am-5.30pm (last admission 4.30pm) Tue-Sun. **Admission** £8; £6.50 reductions; free accompanied under-16s. **Credit** MC, V.
Housed in a converted church, this museum contains one of the world's foremost collections of automatic instruments. From tiny Swiss musical boxes to the self-playing Mighty Wurlitzer, the collection has an impressive array of sophisticated pianolas, cranky barrel organs, spooky orchestrions, residence organs and violin players, as well as over 30,000 piano rolls.

Syon House
Syon Park, Brentford, Middx TW8 8JF (8560 0882, www.syonpark.co.uk). Gunnersbury tube/rail then bus 237, 267. **Open** *House* (mid Mar-Oct only) 11am-5pm Wed, Thur, Sun. *Gardens* (all year) 10.30am-dusk daily. *Tours* by arrangement. **Admission** *House & gardens* £10.50; £4-£8 reductions; £22 family; free under-5s. *Gardens only* £5.50; £2.50 £3.50 reductions; £11 family; free under-5s. *Tours* free. **Credit** MC, V.
The Percys, Dukes of Northumberland, were once known as 'the Kings of the North' such was their power in the land. Their old house is on the site of a

Bridgettine convent, suppressed by Henry VIII in 1534. The building was converted into a house in 1547 for the Duke of Northumberland, its neoclassical interior created by Robert Adam in 1761; there's an outstanding range of Regency portraits by the likes of Gainsborough. The gardens, which were designed by 'Capability' Brown, are enhanced by the splendid Great Conservatory and in winter you can take an evening walk through illuminated woodland.

SOUTHALL
Southall rail.

Immigrants used to enter London via the docks and settle in the East End. Now, though, they come via Heathrow and settle in the area around the airport: thus a huge arc of suburban west London – Hounslow, Hayes, Southall,

INSIDE TRACK ARTS HOUSE

Printer Emery Walker was a friend and colleague of William Morris, the founder of the Arts and Crafts Movement, and his house at 7 Hammersmith Terrace is a perfectly preserved time capsule of a perfectly realised Arts and Crafts home.

Tours take place every Saturday from April to September and by prior arrangement. See www.emerywalker.org.uk for further details.

SIGHTS

Harrow, Wembley, Neasden – has become home to Europe's biggest South Asian population. **Southall** is Britain's best-established immigrant community. From the 1950s onwards, Punjabi Sikhs flocked to the area to work at the Wolf Rubber Factory and in London Transport; the area soon developed a thriving Asian infrastructure of restaurants, shops and wholesalers that attracted Hindus, Muslims, Tamils, Indian Christians and, more recently, Somalis and Afghans. Take a 607 bus from Shepherd's Bush or a Great Western train from Paddington and, on arrival in Southall, you'll think you're in downtown Delhi – all pounding Bollywood hits, sari fabrics, pungent spices and freshly fried samosas.

Southall Broadway is well worth a visit if only to gawp at **Southall Market**, a unique mix of rural India and Cockney London, which until 2007 sold squawking poultry and horses. It still does a brisk trade in general bric-a-brac on Friday and, on Saturday, pretty much everything else. Equally worthy of diversion is the programme of movies at the three-screen **Himalaya Palace** (14 South Road, www.himalayapalacecinema.co.uk), a restored old movie house dedicated to Bollywood epics. But it's the food that makes Southall really special; you can hardly go wrong eating here.

A short walk south of Southall railway station, the **Gurdwara Sri Guru Singh Sabha Southall** (Havelock Road, 8574 4311, www.sgsss.org) is the largest Sikh place of worship outside India. Its golden dome is visible from the London Eye in the east and Windsor Castle to the west; it also provides vegetarian food free to all visitors from the *langar*, or communal kitchen. Non-Sikh visitors are welcome but must take off their shoes before entering, and women must wear a headscarf (they're provided, should you not have one to hand). Enthroned within is the Guru Granth Sahib, the Sikh scripture and supreme spiritual authority of Sikhism.

To the north, **Wembley** is home to a secular religion: British football has its home and heart at **Wembley Stadium** (*see p336*), stunningly redeveloped by Lord Foster. The distinctive arch has become a welcome sign of home-coming for Londoners driving back to the city from the West Country. The stadium will be hosting the Football for the London 2012 Games (*see p62*), while the nearby **Wembley Arena** (*see p322*) will be the venue for the Badminton and Rhythmic Gymnastics (*see p61*).

The neighbouring suburb of Neasden has its own claim to British Asian fame: the **Shri Swaminarayan Mandir** (105-119 Brentfield Road, 8965 2651, www.mandir.org), the largest Hindu temple outside India to have been built using traditional methods. To this end, nearly 5,000 tons of stone and marble were shipped out to India, where craftsmen carved it into the intricate designs that make up the temple. Then the temple was shipped, piece by piece, to England, where it was assembled on site. The shining marble temple stands incongruously close to one of IKEA's giant blue boxes.

Gurdwara Sri Guru Singh Sabha Southall.

Consume

Mark's Bar. *See p246.*

Hotels

Lots of new openings for London 2012 – but prices remain high.

London was short on hotel rooms when it was named Olympic host city – particularly on the east side – and the building frenzy that ensued has only just calmed down. A couple of major projects have been postponed until 2013, but dozens of new hotels have opened at all points on the spectrum, and many more have been restored, revamped or extended. Visit London is now confident of meeting demand during the 2012 Games (*see p69*) – though, as ever, the earlier you book the greater your choice will be: the most desirable and best-located properties will naturally fill up first. The extra capacity bodes well for visits outside Games Time: the choice and quality – no saggy beds! – will be unprecedented in this town.

Of the prestige hotels, the reopening of a glamorously refitted **Savoy** (*see p197*) in late 2010 was a major event – trumped by the **Dorchester** in 2011 with the opening of the all-new and très chic **45 Park Lane** (*see p203*). The W empire – which aims for urban hip and usually achieves it – has finally come to town in the form of **W London Leicester Square** (*see p197*). It's an impressive UK debut for the chain, but its boutique aspirations are better realised by the nearby **St John Hotel** (*see p198*), a 'with rooms' version of the landmark restaurant.

Catching a lot of buzz is the reopened hotel behind the Grade I-listed frontage of St Pancras Station, the **St Pancras Renaissance** (*see p192*). The restored historic grandeur is breathtaking, and open to all in the Booking Office bar.

Room prices remain high. Significantly, **Dean Street Townhouse** (*see p197*), its slightly younger sibling **Shoreditch Rooms** (*see p211*) and St John Hotel offer 'tiny' or 'post-supper' rooms at lower-than-you-might-fear rates. The popularity of hip new B&Bs (**Rough Luxe**, *see p194*; **40 Winks**, *see p211*) and no-frills hotel concepts (*see p212* **Inside Track**) speaks to the same need.

OUR LISTINGS

Hotels in this chapter are classified according to the average price of a double room. You can expect to pay more than £300 a night for hotels in the **Deluxe** category, £200-£300 for **Expensive** hotels, £100-£200 for **Moderate** properties and under £100 a night for hotels listed as **Budget**.

The rates we've listed are only for guidance. The variation within these room rates, top to bottom and over the course of the year, can be huge. As a rule, book as far ahead as possible, and always try hotels' own websites first: many offer special online deals throughout the year.

If you do arrive in town without a bed booked, staff at **Visit London** (1 Lower Regent Street, 0870 156 6366, www.visitlondon.com) will be happy to help you out. Room rates in this chapter include VAT (20%). Be aware that not all hotels include VAT in the rates they quote. And watch out for added extras. If you're bringing a car (not recommended), always check with the hotel before you arrive:

> ❶ Red numbers given in this chapter correspond to the location of each bar as marked on the street maps. See pp392-416.

few central hotels offer parking, and those that do charge steeply for it.

We've tried to indicate which hotels offer rooms adapted for disabled customers, but it's always best to confirm the precise facilities before you travel. Time Out's **Open London** guide makes several detailed recommendations.

THE SOUTH BANK & BANKSIDE
Moderate

Bermondsey Square Hotel
Bermondsey Square, Tower Bridge Road, SE1 3UN (0870 111 2525, www.bespokehotels.com). Borough tube or London Bridge tube/rail. **Rates** £109-£199 double. **Rooms** 80. **Credit** AmEx, MC, V. **Map** p403 Q10 ❶
This is a deliberately kitsch new-build on a newly developed square. Suites are named after the heroines of psychedelic rock classics (Lucy, Lily and so on), there are classic discs on the walls, and you can kick your heels from the suspended Bubble Chair at reception. But, although occupants of the Lucy suite get a multi-person jacuzzi (with a great terrace view), the real draw isn't the gimmicks – it's well-designed rooms for competitive prices. The restaurant-bar, which serves British food, is a bit hit-or-miss, but the hotel's pretty staff are happy and helpful. *Bar/café. Conference facilities. Internet: wireless (free). Restaurant. TV.*

Park Plaza County Hall
1 Addington Street, SE1 7RY (7021 1800, www.parkplaza.com). Waterloo tube/rail. **Rates** £120-£250 double. **Rooms** 398. **Credit** AmEx, MC, V. **Map** p399 M9 ❷
Park Plaza County Hall is an enthusiastically – if somewhat haphazardly – run new-build. Each room has its own kitchenette with microwave and sink, and room sizes aren't bad across the price range (the floor-to-ceiling windows help them feel bigger). There's a handsomely vertiginous atrium, enabling you to peer down into the central restaurant from the frustratingly infrequent glass lifts, and the ground-floor bar is buzzy with business types after work. The gargantuan Park Plaza Westminster Bridge (200 Westminster Bridge Road, SE1 7UT) has now opened nearby, at the southern end of Westminster Bridge. It's London's largest new-build hotel for four decades. *Bars/cafés (2). Concierge. Conference facilities. Disabled-adapted rooms. Gym. Internet: wireless (free). Parking: £20/day. Restaurant. Room service. Spa facilities. TV: pay movies.*

Premier Inn London County Hall
County Hall, Belvedere Road, SE1 7PB (0871 527 8648, www.premierinn.com). Waterloo tube/rail. **Rates** £69-£191 double. **Rooms** 314. **Credit** AmEx, DC, MC, V. **Map** p399 M8 ❸

Its position right by the London Eye, the Thames, Westminster Bridge and Waterloo Station is a gift for out-of-towners on a bargain weekend break. Extra points are garnered for its friendly and efficient staff, making this newly refurbished branch of the Premier Travel chain the acceptable face of budget convenience. Check-in is quick and pleasant; rooms are spacious, clean and warm with comfortable beds and decent bathrooms with very good showers. Breakfast, a buffet-style affair in a comfortable dining room, is extra but provides ballast for a day of sightseeing/shopping, or indeed meetings. But given the daily cost of the Wi-Fi, you're better off leaving the work at home. *Bars/café. Disabled-adapted rooms. Internet: wireless (£10/day). Restaurant. TV.*

THE CITY
Deluxe

Andaz Liverpool Street
40 Liverpool Street, EC2M 7QN (7961 1234, www.london.liverpoolstreet.andaz.com). Liverpool Street tube/rail. **Rates** £165-£315 double. **Rooms** 267. **Credit** AmEx, DC, MC, V. **Map** p403 R6 ❹
A faded railway hotel until its £70m Conran overhaul in 2000, the red-brick Great Eastern became in 2007 the first of Hyatt's new Andaz portfolio. The new approach means out with gimmicky menus, closet-sized minibars and even the lobby reception desk, and in with down-to-earth, well-informed service and eco-friendliness. The bedrooms still wear style-magazine uniform – Eames chairs, Frette

Bermondsey Square Hotel.

St Pancras Renaissance. *See p192.*

CONSUME

linens – but free services (local calls, wireless internet, healthy minibar) are an appreciated touch. *Bars/cafés (5). Business centre. Concierge. Disabled-adapted rooms. Gym. Internet: wireless & high-speed (free). Restaurants (5). Room service. Smoking rooms. TV.*

Expensive

★ Mint Tower of London
7 Pepys Street, EC3N 4AF (7709 1000, www.minthotel.com). Tower Hill tube. See website for rates and rooms. **Map** p403 R7 ❺
As you turn from the Tower of London and Tower Bridge among anonymous modern buildings to reach the new Mint, you might feel your heart sink. Keep your spirits up: the hotel has unexpectedly brilliant views. Even if you aren't lucky enough to stay in the spacious Thames suite, the 12th-floor SkyLounge bar, with its outside terrace, looks over the rooftops to provide a fine Thames vista. As at Mint Westminster, service is smooth and smiley, and the room technology and fittings top-class.

Threadneedles
5 Threadneedle Street, EC2R 8AY (7657 8080, www.theetoncollection.com). Bank tube/DLR. **Rates** £225-£525 double. **Rooms** 69. **Credit** AmEx, MC, V. **Map** p403 Q6 ❻
Threadneedles boldly slots some contemporary style into a fusty old dame of a building, formerly the grand Victorian HQ of the Midland Bank, bang next to the Bank of England and the Royal Exchange. The etched glass-domed rotunda of the lobby soars on columns over an artful array of designer furniture and shelving that looks like the dreamchild of some powerful graphics software – it's a calm space, but a stunning one. The bedrooms are individual, coherent and soothing examples of City-chic, in muted beige and textured tones, with limestone bathrooms and odd views of local landmarks: St Paul's, Tower 42 and the Lloyd's building. It's all well run and well thought out. *Bar/café. Concierge. Disabled-adapted rooms. Internet: wireless (free). Restaurant. Room service. TV: pay movies.*

Moderate

Apex London Wall
7-9 Copthall Avenue, EC2R 7NJ (7562 3030, www.apexhotels.co.uk). Bank tube or Moorgate tube/rail. **Rates** £130-£311 double. **Rooms** 89. **Credit** AmEx, MC, V. **Map** p403 Q6 ❼
The mini-chain's second London hotel shares the virtues of the first (Apex City of London, 1 Seething Lane, 7702 2020). The service is obliging, the rooms are crisply designed with all mod cons, and there are comforting details – rubber duck in the impressive bathrooms, free jelly beans, free local calls and internet, kettle and iron provided. The City of

London branch has the better location for tourists, a short walk from the Tower of London, but this one – tucked in among offices – is handier for business. From the suites, a terrace peers over commercial buildings, but the view from the restaurant – of the flamboyantly sculpted frieze on a business institute – is rather pleasing. *Bar/café. Disabled-adapted rooms. Gym. Internet: wireless (free). Restaurant. Room service. TV.*

Montcalm London City
52 Chiswell Street, EC1Y 4SD (7374 2988, www.themontcalmlondoncity.co.uk). Barbican tube or Moorgate tube/rail. **Rates** £118-£216 double. **Rooms** 235. **Credit** AmEx, DC, MC, V. **Map** p400 P5 ❽
Newly opened Montcalm London City stands on the former site of the 18th-century Whitbread brewery. The service is welcoming, the decor very much old meets new: brickwork and an original art deco staircase sit with Swarovski crystal chandeliers and spotlight flooring. All rooms have lime green and brown furnishings and are fitted with slick digital doorbell, housekeeping and privacy sensors. The furniture arrangement is a little cramped, but they are well equipped with mod cons, including media-hubs and flatscreen TVs. The hotel's modern restaurant and cocktail bar is filled with natural light and serves up a traditional British menu. The careful mix of heritage values and contemporary glamour makes for a luxurious and comfortable business hotel. *Bar. Conference rooms. Internet: wireless (free). Parking: £32/day, free for club and suite guests. Restaurant. Room service. TV.*

HOLBORN & CLERKENWELL
Expensive

Malmaison
Charterhouse Square, EC1M 6AH (7012 3700, www.malmaison.com). Barbican tube. **Rates** £265 double. **Rooms** 97. **Credit** AmEx, DC, MC, V. **Map** p400 O5 ❾
Malmaison is deliciously located, looking out on a lovely cobbled square on the edge of the Square Mile, near the bars, clubs and better restaurants of the East End. This being design-conscious Clerkenwell, it's no surprise that the decor throughout makes a cool statement (note the Veuve Cliquot ice buckets built into the love seats at reception). The rooms overlooking the square are the pick of the bunch, with the best of the views and morning sunshine that pours through large sash windows on to big, white firm beds. Gripes? The muted, business-friendly decor in the rooms is a bit of a let-down after the dark and sultry foyer. There's smiley service downstairs in the lovely basement brasserie, and internet usage is free. *Bars/cafés (2). Disabled-adapted rooms. Gym. Internet: wireless (free). Parking: £20/day. Restaurant. Room service. TV.*

CONSUME

INSIDE TRACK SAFARI CAMP

ZSL (*London Zoo; see p125*) is offering the ultimate camping break in May 2012. You'll stay in comfortable tents, eat and drink like a king and go on a torch-lit tour – lots of the inhabitants are more active at night. Call 7449 6269 to book. It costs £225-£250 each for two sharing and is for adults only.

★ **Rookery**
12 Peter's Lane, Cowcross Street, EC1M 6DS (7336 0931, www.rookeryhotel.com). Farringdon tube/rail. **Rates** £276-£300 double. **Rooms** 33. **Credit** AmEx, DC, MC, V. **Map** p400 O5 ⑩
Sister hotel to Hazlitt's (*see p198*), the Rookery has long been something of a celebrity hideaway deep in Clerkenwell. Its front door is satisfyingly hard to find, especially when the streets around are teeming with Fabric (*see p331*) devotees; the front rooms can be noisy on these nights, but the place is otherwise as creakily calm as a country manor house. Once inside, guests enjoy an atmospheric warren of rooms, each individually decorated in the style of a Georgian townhouse: huge clawfoot baths, elegant four-posters, brass shower fittings. There's an honesty bar in the bright and airy drawing room at the back, which opens on to a sweet little patio. The ground-floor suite has its own hallway, a cosy boudoir and a subterranean bathroom. Topping it all is the huge split-level Rook's Nest suite, which has views of St Paul's Cathedral (*see p90*).
Bar/café. Concierge. Internet: wireless (free). Room service. TV: DVD.

★ **Zetter**
86-88 Clerkenwell Road, EC1M 5RJ (7324 4444, www.thezetter.com). Farringdon tube/rail. **Rates** £185-£438 double. **Rooms** 59. **Credit** AmEx, MC, V. **Map** p400 O4 ⑪
Zetter is a fun, laid-back, modern hotel with some interesting design notes. There's a refreshing lack of attitude and a forward-looking approach, with friendly staff and firm eco-credentials (such as free Brompton bikes for guests' use). The rooms, stacked up on five galleried storeys around an impressive atrium, look into an intimate and recently refreshed bar area. They are smoothly functional, but cosied up with choice home comforts such as hot-water bottles and old Penguin paperbacks, as well as having walk-in showers with REN smellies. The superlative Bistrot Bruno Loubet (*see p218*) and new Zetter Townhouse in a historic building just across the square have only served to widen the place's already considerable appeal.
Bar/café. Concierge. Conference facilities. Disabled-adapted rooms. Internet: wireless (free). Restaurant. Room service. TV: DVD.

Moderate

★ **Fox & Anchor**
115 Charterhouse Street, EC1M 6AA (0845 347 0100, www.foxandanchor.com). Barbican tube or Farringdon tube/rail. **Rates** £150-£294 double. **Rooms** 6. **Credit** AmEx, MC, V. **Map** p400 O5 ⑫
Check in at the handsome attached boozer (*see p243*) and you'll be pointed to the separate front entrance, with its lovely floor mosaic, and a handful of well-appointed, atmospheric and surprisingly luxurious rooms. All are different, but the high-spec facilities (big flatscreen TV, clawfoot bath and drench shower) and quirky attention to detail (bottles of ale in the minibar, the 'Nursing hangover' privacy signs) are common throughout. Expect some clanking noise in the early mornings, but proximity to the historic Smithfield meat market also means you get a feisty fry-up in the morning in the pub.
Bar/café. Internet: wireless (free). Restaurant. TV: DVD.

BLOOMSBURY & FITZROVIA
Deluxe

Charlotte Street Hotel
15-17 Charlotte Street, W1T 1RJ (7806 2000, www.firmdale.com). Goodge Street or Tottenham Court Road tube. **Rates** £288-£312 double. **Rooms** 52. **Credit** AmEx, MC, V. **Map** p397 K5 ⑬
Now a fine exponent of Kit Kemp's much imitated fusion of flowery English and avant-garde, this gorgeous hotel was once a dental hospital. Public rooms have Bloomsbury Set paintings, by the likes of Duncan Grant and Vanessa Bell, while bedrooms mix English understatement with bold flourishes. The huge, comfortable beds and trademark polished granite and oak bathrooms are suitably indulgent, and some rooms have unbelievably high ceilings. The Oscar restaurant and bar are classy and busy with a smart crowd of media and ad people. At 5pm on Sundays the mini-cinema holds screenings.
Bar/café. Concierge. Disabled-adapted rooms. Gym. Internet: wireless (£20/day). Restaurant. Room service. Smoking rooms. TV: DVD.

★ **St Pancras Renaissance**
Euston Road, King's Cross, NW1 2AR (7841 3540, www.marriott.com). King's Cross tube/rail. **Rates** £396-£540. **Rooms** 245. **Credit** AmEx, DC, MC, V. **Map** p397 L3 ⑭
A landmark hotel in every sense of the word, the St Pancras Renaissance is the born-again Midland Grand, the pioneering railway hotel designed into the station's imposing Gothic Revival frontage. It opened in 1873 but fell into disuse in the 20th century (except for appearances as a Harry Potter backdrop and in the Spice Girls' Wannabe video, among other screen roles). The Renaissance group (fittingly) has

CONSUME

done a beautiful and painstaking job of restoring it to its breathtaking, Grade 1 listed best while adding modern comforts. The 120 rooms and suites in the historic hotel (there's a new wing, too) have high ceilings, original features and awesome views over the station concourse or forecourt. Facililties are high-spec – Bose stereo, Nespresso machines, REN toiletries, marble baths – furniture modern classic and design sensitive to the context, re-using motifs from the original decor in the carpets, for example. Public areas, including both restaurants (for the Ticket Office, *see p250*) and the gorgeous grand staircase, are similarly splendid. London loves it. *Photos p190*.
Bars/cafés (2). Concierge. Conference facilities. Disabled-adapted room. Gym. Internet: wireless (free & £15/day, depending on room). Restaurant (2). Room service. Spa facilities. Pool (indoor). TV.
▶ *For details of public tours, see p209* **The Grand Tour**.

Sanderson
50 Berners Street, W1T 3NG (7300 1400, www.morganshotelgroup.com). Oxford Circus tube. **Rates** £306-£654 double. **Rooms** 150. **Credit** AmEx, DC, MC, V. **Map** p416 V1 ⑮
No designer flash in the pan, the Sanderson remains a statement hotel, a Schrager/Starck creation that takes clinical chic in the bedrooms to new heights. Colour is generally conspicuous by its absence. The design throughout is all flowing white net drapes, gleaming glass cabinets and retractable screens. The residents-only Purple Bar sports a button-backed purple leather ceiling and fabulous cocktails; in par-

ticular, try the Vesper. The 'billiard room' has a purple-topped pool table, surrounded by strange tribal adaptations of classic dining room furniture.
Bars/cafés (2). Business centre. Concierge. Disabled-adapted rooms. Gym. Internet: wireless (£10/day). Parking: £40/day. Restaurant. Room service. Spa facilities. TV: DVD.

Expensive

Myhotel Bloomsbury (11-13 Bayley Street, WC1B 3HD, 7667 6000, www.myhotels.co.uk) is a grown-up, urban brother to Myhotel Chelsea (*see p206*), giving the trademark Asian touches a masculine, minimalist twist.

Academy Hotel
21 Gower Street, WC1E 6HG (7631 4115, www.theetoncollection.com). Goodge Street tube. **Rates** £230-£345 double. **Rooms** 49. **Credit** AmEx, MC, V. **Map** p397 K5 ⑯
he Academy goes for the country intellectual look to suit Bloomsbury's studious yet decadent history. It's made up of five Georgian townhouses, and provides in all its rooms a tranquil generosity of space that's echoed in the Georgian squares sitting serenely between the arterial traffic rush of Gower Street and Tottenham Court Road. There's a restrained country-house style in the summery florals and checks and a breath of sophistication in the handsome, more plainly furnished suites. The library and conservatory open on to fragrant walled gardens where drinks and breakfast are served in summer.
Bar/café. Internet: wireless (free). Restaurant. Room service. TV.

Moderate

Harlingford Hotel
61-63 Cartwright Gardens, WC1H 9EL (7387 1551, www.harlingfordhotel.com). Russell Square tube or Euston tube/rail. **Rates** £112-£120 double. **Rooms** 40. **Credit** MC, V. **Map** p397 L4 ⑰
An affordable hotel with bundles of charm in the heart of Bloomsbury, the perkily styled Harlingford has light airy rooms with evident boutique aspirations. The decor is lifted from understated sleek to quirky with the help of vibrant colour splashes from coloured glass bathroom fittings and mosaic tiles – overall, the hotel has something of a Scandinavian feel. The crescent it's set in has a lovely and leafy private garden where you can lob a tennis ball about or just dream under the trees on a summer's night.
Internet: wireless (free). TV.

Morgan
24 Bloomsbury Street, WC1B 3QJ (7636 3735, www.morganhotel.co.uk). Tottenham Court Road tube. **Rates** £125 double. **Rooms** 21. **Credit** MC, V. **Map** p397 K5 ⑱

Savoy. *See p197.*

CONSUME

This brilliantly located, comfortable budget hotel in Bloomsbury is tastefully done out in neutral shades. The rooms are well equipped and all are geared up for the electronic age with wireless, voicemail, flatscreen tellies with freeview and air-conditioning. A good, slap-up English breakfast is served in a good-looking room with wood panelling, London prints and blue and white china plates. The spacious flats are excellent value.
Internet: wireless (free). TV.

Rough Luxe
1 Birkenhead Street, WC1H 8BA (7837 5338, www.roughluxe.co.uk). King's Cross tube/rail. **Rates** £189-£289 double. **Rooms** 9. **Credit** AmEx, MC, V. **Map** p397 L3 ⑲

The latest thing in hotel design chic is – at least, according to the owners of this hotel – Rough Luxe. In a bit of King's Cross that's choked with ratty B&Bs and cheap chains, this Grade II-listed property has walls artfully distressed, torn wallpaper, signature works of art, old-fashioned TVs that barely work and even retains the sign for the hotel that preceded Rough Luxe: 'Number One Hotel'. Each room has free wireless internet, but otherwise have totally different characters: there's the one with the freestanding copper tub, the one with the rose motif and so on. The set-up is flexible too: rooms with shared bathrooms can be combined for group bookings, and the owners are more than happy to chat with guests over a bottle of wine in the back courtyard where a great breakfast is served. A place to stay if you're looking for somewhere different from the norm.
Internet: wireless (free).

Budget

Clink78
78 King's Cross Road, WC1X 9QG (7183 9400, www.clinkhostels.com). King's Cross tube/rail. **Rates** £65-£70 double; £17-£32 bed. **Beds** 717. **Credit** MC, V. **Map** p397 M3 ⑳

Located in a listed courthouse, the Clink set the bar high for party-style hosteldom when it opened a few years back. There was the setting: the hostel retains the superb original wood-panelled lobby and courtroom where the Clash once stood before the beak. Then there's the urban chic ethos that permeates the whole enterprise, from the streamlined red reception counter to the Japanese-style 'pod' beds. By the time this guide hits the shelves, a thorough redesign of the public areas and licensed bar downstairs should give things a new rock 'n' roll fillip, with street-art decor and more comfortable furniture to enhance the place's good-time vibe. Clink261 – a rebrand of the nearby Ashlee House, which has had its public areas pepped up in 2010 – might be a better choice for older and calmer hostellers.
Bar/café. Internet: shared terminal (£2/hr). TV. **Other locations** Clink261, 261-265 Gray's Inn Road, Bloomsbury, WC1X 8QT (7833 9400).

Jenkins Hotel
45 Cartwright Gardens, WC1H 9EH (7387 2067, www.jenkinshotel.demon.co.uk). Russell Square tube or Euston tube/rail. **Rates** £98 double. **Rooms** 12. **Credit** MC, V. **Map** p397 K3 ㉑

This well-to-do Georgian beauty has been a hotel since the 1920s. It still has an atmospheric, antique

W London Leicester Square. *See p197.*

Have Bike, Will Travel

More and more hotels are welcoming tourists on tourers.

Cyclists used to get short shrift at check-in, especially at high-end hotels. You'd secure your steed to nearby railings and prepare for a supercilious survey of your less-than-evening dress. But a sea change is in progress. Our hotel spy was recently at the **Dorchester** (*see p203*), and saw the door staff respectfully park a vintage fixie for a businessman in Lycra and a sit-up-and-beg for a woman who then changed in the ladies' room, no eyebrows raised. The Dorchester can also lend guests a Brompton folding bike – a UK design classic that you can carry on the tube. The Morgans hotel group, which includes the **Sanderson** (*see p193*) and **St Martins Lane** (*see p196*), also loans out cycles to residents, and can even pack you up an afternoon tea for a park picnic.

The **W London Leicester Square** (*see p197*) has espoused the style potential of the bicycle by commissioning a hip 'fixie' (fixed-wheel) version and then asking six designers, including Patrick Cox, Ron Arad and Alice Temperley, to customise it and suggest a ride for guests. The scheme ended in October 2011 when the bikes were auctioned off for charity, but something similar is expected for 2012. Meanwhile, guests who arrive on their own bikes will have them stored securely.

Aiming for substance over style, the **InterContinental London Park Lane** (1 Hamilton Place, W1J 7QY, 0871 423 4876, www.intercontinental.com) offers a one-night 'B-Spoke' package that includes a guided ride on London Cycle Hire bikes with well-known rider, writer and thinker Rob Penn.

W London Leicester Square.

air, although the rooms have mod cons enough – TVs, mini-fridges, tea and coffee. Its looks have earned it a role in *Agatha Christie's Poirot*, but it's not chintzy, just quite floral in the bedspread and curtain department. The breakfast room is handsome, with snowy cotton tablecloths and Windsor chairs. *Internet: wireless (free). TV.*

YHA London Central
104 Bolsover Street, W1W 5NU (0845 371 9154, www.yha.org.uk). Great Portland Street tube. **Rates** from £14.65 adult. **Beds** 307. **Credit** MC, V. **Map** p396 J5 **㉒**
The Youth Hostel Association's newest hostel is one of its best – as well as being one of the best hostels in London. The friendly and well-informed receptionists are stationed at a counter to the left of the entrance, in a substantial café-bar area. The basement contains a well-equipped kitchen and washing areas; above it, five floors of clean, neatly designed rooms, many en suite. Residents have 24hr access (by individual key cards) and the location is quiet but an easy walk from most of central London. *Bar/café. Internet: wireless (£5/day). TV.* **Other locations** throughout the city.

COVENT GARDEN & THE STRAND

Deluxe

★ Covent Garden Hotel
10 Monmouth Street, WC2H 9LF (7806 1000, www.firmdale.com). Covent Garden, Leicester

CONSUME

Montagu Place. *See p198.*

Square or Tottenham Court Road tube. **Rates**
£360-£414 double. **Rooms** 58. **Credit** AmEx,
MC, V. **Map** p416 X2 ㉓
The excellent location in the heart of London's theatre district and tucked-away screening room of this
Firmdale hotel ensure it continues to attract starry
customers, with anyone needing a bit of privacy
able to retreat upstairs to the lovely panelled private
library and drawing room. In the guest-rooms, Kit
Kemp's distinctive style mixes pinstriped wallpaper, pristine white quilts and floral upholstery with
bold, contemporary elements; each room is unique,
but each has the Kemp trademark upholstered man-
nequin and granite and oak bathroom. On the
ground floor, the 1920s Paris-style Brasserie Max
and its retro zinc bar retain their buzz – outdoor
tables give a perfect viewpoint on Covent Garden
boutique life in summer.
Bar/café. Concierge. Disabled-adapted rooms.
Gym. Internet: wireless (£20/day). Parking:
£37/day. Restaurant. Room service. Smoking
rooms. TV: DVD.

One Aldwych
1 Aldwych, WC2B 4RH (7300 1000,
www.onealdwych.com). Covent Garden or Temple
tube, or Charing Cross tube/rail. **Rates** £282-£474
double. **Rooms** 105. **Credit** AmEx, DC, MC, V.
Map p416 Z3 ㉔

You only have to push through the front door and
enter the breathtaking Lobby Bar to know that
you're in for a treat. Despite the building's weighty
history – the 1907 building was once the offices of
the *Morning Post* – One Aldwych is a thoroughly
modern establishment, with Frette linen, bathroom
mini-TVs and an environmentally friendly loo-
flushing system. Flowers and fruit are replenished
daily and a card with the next day's weather fore-
cast appears at turndown. The location is perfect
for the West End theatres and has become popular
with attendees of London Fashion Week, particularly since many of the events are now held nearby
in Somerset House. The three round corner suites
are very romantic, and a cosy screening room, excellent spa and a downstairs swimming pool where
soothing music is played may dissuade you from
ever stepping outside.
Bar/café. Concierge. Disabled-adapted rooms.
Gym. Internet: wireless, high-speed (free). Parking:
£45/day. Pool: indoor. Restaurants (2). Room
service. Spa facilities. TV: DVD & pay movies.

St Martins Lane Hotel
45 St Martin's Lane, WC2N 4HX (7300 5500,
www.morganshotelgroup.com). Leicester Square
tube or Charing Cross tube/rail. **Rates** £282-£564
double. **Rooms** 204. **Credit** AmEx, DC, MC, V.
Map p416 X4 ㉕

When it opened a decade ago, the St Martins was the toast of the town. The flamboyant, theatrical lobby was constantly buzzing, and guests giggled like schoolgirls at Philippe Starck's playful decor. The Starck objects – such as the giant chess pieces and gold tooth stools in the lobby – remain, but the space, part of the Morgans Hotel Group, lacks the impact of its heyday. There's still much to be impressed by: the all-white bedrooms have comfortable minimalism down to a T, with floor-to-ceiling windows, gadgetry secreted in sculptural cabinets and sleek limestone bathrooms with toiletries from the spa at sister property Sanderson (*see p193*).
Bar/café. Business centre. Concierge. Disabled-adapted rooms. Gym. Internet: wireless (£10/day). Parking: £45/day. Restaurant. Room service. TV: DVD & pay movies.

★ Savoy
Strand, WC2R 0EU (7836 4343, www.fairmont.com). Covent Garden or Embankment tube, or Charing Cross tube/rail. **Rates** £354-£642 double. **Rooms** 268. **Credit** AmEx, DC, MC, V. **Map** p416 Z4 **㉖**

The superluxe, Grade II-listed Savoy reopened after more than £100m of renovations in October 2010 – the numerous delays testimony to the difficulty of bringing a listed building, loved by generations of visitors for its discreet mix of Edwardian neoclassical and art deco, up to scratch as a modern luxury hotel. Built in 1889 to put up theatregoers from Richard D'Oyly Carte's Gilbert & Sullivan shows, the Savoy is the hotel from which Monet painted the Thames, where Vivien Leigh met Laurence Olivier, where Londoners learned to love the martini. The famous cul-de-sac at the front entrance now has a garden of new topiary and centrepiece Lalique crystal fountain, but the welcome begins before you arrive with a phone call to ascertain your particular requirements. There's a new tearoom with glass-roofed conservatory; the leather counter of the new Beaufort champagne bar is set on a stage that once hosted big bands for dinner dances; and the Savoy Grill is again under the control of Gordon Ramsay's company. Traditionalists can relax: the American Bar remains unchanged. *Photo p193.*
Bars (2). Concierge. Disabled-adapted rooms. Gym. Internet: wireless (£9.95/day). Pool (indoor). Restaurants (4). Room service. Spa facilities. TV: DVD & pay movies.

SOHO & LEICESTER SQUARE
Deluxe

Soho Hotel
4 Richmond Mews, W1D 3DH (7559 3000, www.firmdale.com). Piccadilly Circus or Tottenham Court Road tube. **Rates** £354-£552 double. **Rooms** 91. **Credit** AmEx, DC, MC, V. **Map** p416 W2 **㉗**

You'd hardly know you were in the heart of Soho once you're inside Firmdale's edgiest hotel: the place is wonderfully quiet, with what was once a car park now feeling like a converted loft building. The big bedrooms exhibit a contemporary edge, with modern furniture, industrial-style windows and nicely planned mod cons (digital radios as well as flatscreen TVs), although they're also classically Kit Kemp with bold stripes, traditional florals, plump sofas, oversized bedheads and upholstered tailor's dummies. The quiet drawing room and other public spaces feature groovy colours while Refuel, the loungey bar and restaurant, has an open kitchen and, yes, a car-themed mural.
Bar/café. Concierge. Disabled-adapted rooms. Gym. Internet: wireless & high-speed (£20/day). Restaurant. Room service. Smoking rooms. Spa facilities. TV: DVD.

W London Leicester Square
10 Wardour Street, Leicester Square, W1D 6QF (7758 1000, www.wlondon.co.uk). Leicester Square tube. **Rates** £335-£371 double. **Rooms** 192. **Credit** AmEx, DC, MC, V. **Map** p416 W4 **㉘**

The old Swiss Centre building on the edge of Leicester Square has been demolished and in its place is the UK's first W Hotel. The W brand has made its name with a series of hip hotels around the world that offer glamorous bars, classy food and functional but spacious rooms. The London W is no exception: Spice Market gets its first UK site within the hotel; Wyld is a large nightclub/bar space aiming to become the Met Bar for a new decade, and the W lounge aims to bring New York's cocktail lounge ethos to London. The rooms – 192 of them, across ten storeys – are well equipped and decent-sized, and SWEAT (the hotel's state-of-the-art fitness facility) offers fine views over Soho. Also of note is the W's gob-smacking exterior: the entire hotel is veiled in translucent glass, which is lit in different colours through the day. *Photo p194.*
Bar/café. Business centre. Concierge. Disabled-adapted rooms. Gym. Internet: wireless (£15/day). Parking: (£45/day). Restaurant. Room service. Smoking rooms. Spa facilities. TV.

Expensive

★ Dean Street Townhouse & Dining Room
69-71 Dean Street, W1D 3SE (7434 1775, www.sohohouse.com). Leicester Square or

---

**INSIDE TRACK
BUYER BEWARE!**

Many high-end hotels charge extra for services that some travellers assume will be free, most commonly internet access and breakfast. Always check in advance if you're blowing the budget for a treat.

CONSUME

Piccadilly Circus tube. **Rates** £90-£410 double. **Rooms** 39. **Credit** AmEx, MC, V. **Map** p416 W3 **29**

This Grade II-listed, 1730s townhouse has been converted into another winning enterprise from the people behind Soho House members' club, **Shoreditch Rooms** (*see p211*) and **High Road House** (*see p213*). To one side of a buzzy ground-floor restaurant are four floors of bedrooms that run from full-size rooms with early Georgian panelling and reclaimed oak floors to half-panelled 'Tiny' rooms that are barely bigger than their double beds – but can be had from the website for as little as £90. The atmosphere is gentleman's club cosy (there are cookies in a cute silver Treats container in each room), but modern types also get rainforest showers, 24hr room service, Roberts DAB radios, free wireless internet and big flatscreen TVs. Even the calm little library room behind reception manages to be both low-key and luxurious.

Bar/café. Disabled-adapted rooms. Internet: wireless (free). Restaurant. Room service. TV: DVD.

★ Hazlitt's

6 Frith Street, W1D 3JA (7434 1771, www.hazlittshotel.com). Tottenham Court Road tube. **Rates** £203-£311 double. **Rooms** 30. **Credit** AmEx, DC, MC, V. **Map** p416 W2 **30**

Four Georgian townhouses comprise this absolutely charming place, named after William Hazlitt, the spirited 18th-century essayist who died here in abject poverty. With flamboyance and staggering attention to detail the rooms evoke the Georgian era, all heavy fabrics, fireplaces, free-standing tubs and exquisitely carved half-testers, yet modern luxuries – air-conditioning, TVs in antique cupboards and double-glazed windows – have been subtly attended to as well. It gets creakier and more crooked the higher you go, culminating in enchanting garret single rooms with rooftop views. Of seven new bedrooms, the main suite is a real knock-out: split-level, with a huge eagle spouting water into the raised bedroom bath and a rooftop terrace with sliding roof, it's a joyous extravaganza. Entertainingly, from the back alley outside, the extension has been made to look like 1700s shopfronts.

Bar/café. Concierge. Conference facilities. Internet: wireless & high-speed (free). Room service. TV: DVD.

★ St John Hotel

1 Leicester Street, off Leicester Square, WC2H 7BL (7251 0848, www.stjohnhotellondon.com). Leicester Square or Piccadilly Circus tube. **Rates** (not incl breakfast) £240-£654 double. **Rooms** 15. **Credit** AmEx, DC, MC, V. **Map** p416 W4 **31**

When one of London's finest restaurants decides to move into the hotel trade, it's well worth taking notice. Co-owner Trevor Gulliver described the hotel as 'that rare thing – a hotel where people would actu-

ally want to eat'. To which end, the first floor, ground floor and basement are given over to a bar and restaurant (*see p219*); above them are 15 rooms and a three-bedroom rooftop suite – the bathroom's round window looks west to Big Ben. The decor is in keeping with the white, masculine, minimalist style of the Smithfield original.

Bar. Concierge. Disabled-adapted room. Internet: wireless (free). Restaurant. Room service. TV.

OXFORD STREET & MARYLEBONE

Expensive

Cumberland

Great Cumberland Place, off Oxford Street, W1H 7DL (0871 376 9014, www.guoman.com). Marble Arch tube. **Rates** £100-£400 double. **Rooms** 1,019. **Credit** AmEx, DC, MC, V. **Map** p393 F6 **32**

Perfectly located by Marble Arch tube (turn the right way and you're there in seconds), the Cumberland is a bit of a monster: in addition to the 900 rooms in the main block, there are another 119 in an annexe down the road. The echoing, rather chaotic lobby has some dramatic modern art and sculptures, as well as an impressive but somewhat severe waterfall. The rooms are minimalist, with acid-etched headboards, neatly modern bathrooms and plasma TVs – nicely designed, but rather small. The hotel's excellent dining room is the exclusive Rhodes W1, but there are also a bar-brasserie and boisterous, trash-industrial style, late-night DJ bar. Weekend breakfasts can feel like feeding the 5,000.

Bars/cafés (3). Concierge. Gym. Internet: wireless (£10/day), high-speed (£15/day). Restaurants (3). Room service. TV: pay movies.

Montagu Place

2 Montagu Place, W1H 2ER (7467 2777, www.montagu-place.co.uk). Baker Street tube. **Rates** £200-£260 double. **Rooms** 16. **Credit** AmEx, DC, MC, V. **Map** p396 G5 **33**

A small, fashionable townhouse hotel, Montagu Place fills a couple of Grade II-listed Georgian residences with sharply appointed rooms graded according to size. The big ones are entitled Swanky, and have king-size beds and big bathrooms – some have narrow front terraces. More modest in size, the Comfy category has queen-size beds and, being at the back of the building, no street views. All rooms have a cool and trendy look, with cafetières and ground coffee instead of Nescafé sachets, as well as flatscreen TVs. The decision to combine bar and reception desk (situated at the back of the house) means you can get a drink at any time and retire to the graciously modern lounge. Service is at once sharp and very obliging. *Photos p196.*

Bar/café. Internet: wireless & high-speed (free). Room service. TV: DVD.

CONSUME

Moderate

Sumner

54 Upper Berkeley Street, W1H 7QR (7723 2244,
www.thesumner.com). Marble Arch tube. **Rates**
(incl breakfast) £185-£258 double. **Rooms** 19.
Credit AmEx, MC, V. **Map** p393 F6 ④
The Sumner's cool, deluxe looks have earned it
many fans, not least in the hospitality industry,
where it has won a number of awards. You won't be
at all surprised when you get here: from the soft dove
and slatey greys of the lounge and halls you move
up to glossily spacious accommodation with brilliant
walk-in showers. The breakfast room feels soft and
sunny, with a lovely, delicate buttercup motif and
vibrant Arne Jacobsen chairs to cheer you on your
way to the museums, but the stylishly moody front
sitting room is also a cosy gem.
Concierge. Internet: wireless (free). TV.

22 York Street

22 York Street, W1U 6PX (7224 2990,
www.22yorkstreet.co.uk). Baker Street tube. **Rates**
£129 double. **Rooms** 10. **Credit** AmEx, MC, V.
Map p396 G5 ㉟
Bohemian French chic – white furniture, palest pink
lime-washed walls, mellow wooden floors, subtly
faded textiles and arresting *objets d'époque* – makes
this delightfully unpretentious bed and breakfast in
the heart of Marylebone a sight to behold. It doesn't
announce itself from the outside, so you feel as if
you've been invited to stay in someone's arty home,
especially when you're drinking good coffee at the
gorgeous curved table that dominates the breakfast
room-cum-kitchen. Guests are also given free rein
with the hot beverages in a lounge full of knick-
knacks upstairs, while a cluttered smaller room
downstairs has an internet station for those without
wireless. All rooms are a decent size and have en
suite baths, a rarity at this price and in this part of
town, but some are rather eccentrically arranged.
Bar/café. Internet: wireless (free). TV.

PADDINGTON & NOTTING HILL

Deluxe

Hempel

31-35 Craven Hill Gardens, W2 3EA (7298
9000, www.the-hempel.co.uk). Lancaster Gate or
Queensway tube or Paddington tube/rail. **Rates**
£215-£719 double. **Rooms** 50. **Credit** AmEx,
DC, MC, V. **Map** p392 C6 ㊱
Since the mid 1990s, the serried white stucco façades
of Craven Hill Gardens, a quiet backwater square in
Bayswater, have concealed a dramatic alternative
universe dreamed up by Anouska Hempel. The
vision still works. Though no longer under her ownership, this boutique hotel started a minimalist
design revolution. H is the logo and clinical the look:
the coffee tables sunk into the polished stone floor

Stylotel. *See p201.*

CONSUME

of the lobby; the empty expanses of magnolia paint on the walls; the green plastic turf in the 'Zen-like' garden. The rooms are all different, but defiantly minimal to the point of barely furnished. The upstairs restaurant serves a menu of European and Japanese fish dishes.

Bar/café. Concierge. Disabled-adapted rooms. Internet: wireless (free). Restaurant. Room service. TV: DVD & pay movies.

Expensive

Portobello Hotel

22 Stanley Gardens, W11 2NG (7727 2777, www.portobellohotel.com). Holland Park or Notting Hill Gate tube. **Rates** (incl breakfast) £234-£384 double. **Rooms** 21. **Credit** AmEx, MC, V. **Map** p404 Y5 ③

The Portobello is a hotel with approaching half a century of celebrity status, having hosted the likes of Johnny Depp, Kate Moss and Alice Cooper, who used his tub to house a boa constrictor. It remains a pleasingly unpretentious place, with a more civilised demeanour than its legend might suggest. There is now a lift to help rockers who are feeling their age up the five floors, but there's still a 24hr guest-only bar downstairs for those who don't yet feel past it. The rooms are themed – the superb basement Japanese Water Garden, for example, has an elaborate spa bath, its own private grotto and a small private garden – but all are stylishly equipped with a large fan, tall house plants and round-the-clock room service.

Bar/café. Internet: wireless (free). Restaurant. Room service. TV.

Moderate

Hotel Indigo London Paddington

16 London Street, W2 1HL (7706 4444, www.ichotelsgroup.com). Paddington tube/rail. **Rates** £203-£300 double. **Rooms** 64. **Credit** AmEx, DC, MC, V. **Map** p393 D6 ③

The first of four boutique properties planned for London from the people behind Crowne Plaza and Holiday Inn has a relaxed all-day bar-restaurant, sharp-witted and friendly staff, and rooms with all mod cons (excellent walk-in showers rather than

---

THE BEST NEW HOTELS

45 Park Lane
The Dorchester's high-style, high-tech younger brother. *See p203.*

St John Hotel
Eat well, sleep well. *See p198.*

St Pancras Renaissance
Reborn in magnificent style. *See p192.*

---

baths) – the smaller and cheaper attic rooms have most character. The decor is a bit try-hard: a clinical white foyer gives on to acid-bright striped carpets and wardrobe interiors that are an assault by psychedelic swirl. Photographs of Paddington past and ingenious ceiling strips of sky show how less could have been more. A second Hotel Indigo (142 Minories, EC3N 1LS, 7265 1014) opened in 2010 on the eastern edge of the City.

Bar/café. Disabled-adapted rooms. Internet: wireless (free). Restaurant. Room service. TV: pay movies.

New Linden

59 Leinster Square, W2 4PS (7221 4321, www.newlinden.co.uk). Bayswater tube. **Rates** £95-£149 double. **Rooms** 50. **Credit** AmEx, MC, V. **Map** p392 B6 ③

Modern, modish and moderately priced – that's the Mayflower Group for you. This is its Bayswater baby; it chooses to call the area 'trendy Notting Hill' on the website, but that's stretching the bounds of London geography a little far. It looks very cool, however, and it is a fantastically comfortable place to stay. The lobby and lounge are slick and glamorous – there's a beautiful teak arch in the lounge and the rooms are low key with some vibrant, twirly eastern influences. Some of the larger family rooms retain their elaborate period pillars and cornicing. The bathrooms are a symphony in marble; the walk-in showers have deluge heads. There's a pleasant little patio, upstairs at the back, for morning coffee and evening drinks.

Concierge. Internet: wireless (free). TV.

Vancouver Studios

30 Prince's Square, W2 4NJ (7243 1270, www.vancouverstudios.co.uk). Bayswater or Queensway tube. **Rates** £120-£155 double. **Rooms** 48. **Credit** AmEx, DC, MC, V. **Map** p392 B6 ④

Step into the hall or comfortably furnished sitting room of this imposing townhouse and it feels like the gracious home of a slightly dotty uncle, with decor in the public spaces comprising colonial swords and historic prints. The studio or apartment accommodation is more modern in tone. Each room has its own style – from cool contemporary lines to a softer, more homely feel – and all are well equipped with kitchen appliances so that guests can do a bit of self-catering, should they wish. Zeus the cat lords it over the building and can show you into the pretty garden with its fountain and heady scent of jasmine – a shady stunner.

Internet: wireless (free). TV: DVD.

Budget

Garden Court Hotel

30-31 Kensington Gardens Square, W2 4BG (7229 2553, www.gardencourthotel.co.uk).

Myhotel Chelsea. *See p206.*

Bayswater or Queensway tube. **Rates** (incl breakfast) £79-£125 double. **Rooms** 32. **Credit** MC, V. **Map** p392 B6 ④

Once people have discovered the Garden Court, they tend to keep coming back, says Edward Connolly, owner-manager of this long-established hotel, with quiet pride. There aren't many places this close to Hyde Park and Portobello Market that give such excellent value for money and impeccable service. The rooms in this grand Victorian terrace have a bright, modern look and plenty of space, and the lounge, with its wood floor, leather-covered furniture, sprightly floral wallpaper and elegant mantelpiece is a lovely place to linger. As the name suggests, there's a small walled garden, lushly planted, and laden guests might be cheered by the presence of a lift.
Internet: wireless (£2/day). TV.

Pavilion

34-36 Sussex Gardens, W2 1UL (7262 0905, www.pavilionhoteluk.com). Edgware Road tube, or Marylebone or Paddington tube/rail. **Rates** £85-£100 double. **Rooms** 29. **Credit** MC, V. **Map** p393 E5 ④

A hotel that describes itself as 'fashion rock 'n' roll' is never going to be staid, but Danny and Noshi Karne's Pavilion is quite mind-bogglingly excessive. The rooms have attention-grabbing names, such as 'Enter the Dragon' (Chinese themed), 'Flower Power' (blooming flowery) and 'Cosmic Girl' (way out there,

man) and are frequently used for fashion shoots: the website has an impressive list of celebrities who have rocked up here over the years. Bizarre and voluptuous choice of decor notwithstanding, this crazy hotel represents excellent value and has the usual amenities. You might be disappointed if you want cool contemporary elegance and poncey toiletries – the Pavilion's much more fun than that.
Internet: wireless (free). Parking: £10/day. TV: DVD.

★ **Stylotel**

160-162 Sussex Gardens, W2 1UD (7723 1026, www.stylotel.com). Edgware Road tube, or Marylebone or Paddington tube/rail. **Rates** £95 double. **Rooms** 39. **Credit** AmEx, MC, V. **Map** p393 E6 ④

Partly due to the young manager's enthusiasm, it's hard not to like this place. It's a retro-futurist dream: metal floors and panelling, lots of royal blue (the hall walls, the padded headboards) and pod bathrooms. But the real deal at Stylotel is its bargain studio and apartment (respectively, £120-£150 and £150-£200, breakfast £8 extra), around the corner above a pub. Designed – like the rest of the hotel – by the owner's son, they suggest he's calmed down with age. Here's real minimalist chic: sleek brushed steel or white glass wall panels, simply styled contemporary furniture upholstered in black or white. *Photos p199.* *Concierge. Internet: wireless (£2/hr). Parking: £15/day. TV.*

26 Hillgate Place

26 Hillgate Place, W8 7ST (7727 7717,
www.26hillgateplace.co.uk). Notting Hill Gate tube.
Rates £80-£115 double. **Rooms** 2. **No credit**
cards. Map p404 Y6 ④

Artist Hilary Dunne has furnished her B&B with
paintings of glossy-skinned, doe-eyed women inspired
by her travels in the West Indies, as well as the spoils
from her former life as a textiles importer. The ground-
floor room with its large en suite bathroom contains
some of the Caribbean collection; the smaller, more
colourful second room, with shared bathroom, is bright
with wall hangings and cushions from India. The overall effect is of a much-loved, warm and lived-in family
home. Breakfast is taken in a busy little space next to
the galley kitchen, with French windows opening on
to a tiny, ivy-clad courtyard. A slightly larger patio
upstairs, home to Hilary's extensive plant collection,
looks out over the gardens of Hillgate Place.
Internet: wireless (free). TV.

PICCADILLY CIRCUS & MAYFAIR

Deluxe

Brown's

Albemarle Street, W1S 4BP (7493 6020,
www.roccofortecollection.com). Green Park tube.
Rates £393-£705 double. **Rooms** 117. **Credit**
AmEx, DC, MC, V. **Map** p416 U4 ④

Brown's was opened in 1837 by James Brown, butler
to Romantic poet, hedonist and freedom-fighter Lord
Byron. The first British telephone call was made

from here in 1876, five years after Napoleon III and
Empress Eugenie took refuge in one of the considerable suites after fleeing the Third Republic.
Ethiopian Emperor Haile Selassie and Rudyard
Kipling were also guests. The bedrooms are all large
and extremely comfortable, furnished with original
art, collections of books and, in the suites, fireplaces;
the elegant, classic British hotel restaurant, Hix at
the Albemarle (*see p227*), gives a nod to modernity
with a series of contemporary British artworks,
including pieces by the likes of Tracey Emin, but the
public spaces of the hotel thrum with history. Non-
residents can visit: try the £37.50 afternoon tea in
the English Tea Room or sip a cocktail in the classily
masculine Donovan Bar.
Bar/café. Business centre. Concierge. Disabled-
adapted rooms. Gym. Internet: wireless & high-
speed (£15/day). Restaurant. Room service. Spa
facilities. TV: pay movies.

★ Claridge's

55 Brook Street, W1K 4HR (7629 8860,
www.claridges.co.uk). Bond Street tube. **Rates**
£359-£828 double. **Rooms** 203. **Credit** AmEx,
DC, MC, V. **Map** p396 H6 ④

Claridge's is sheer class and pure atmosphere, with
its signature art deco redesign still simply dazzling.
Photographs of Churchill and sundry royals grace
the grand foyer, as does an absurdly over-the-top
Dale Chihuly chandelier. Without departing too far
from the traditional, Claridge's bars and restaurant
are actively fashionable – Gordon Ramsay is the in-
house restaurateur, and the A-listers can gather for
champers and sashimi in the bar. The rooms divide

45 Park Lane.

CONSUME

evenly between deco and Victorian style, with period touches such as deco toilet flushes in the swanky marble bathrooms. Bedside panels control the mod-con facilities at the touch of a button. If money's no object, opt for a David Linley suite, done out in gorgeous duck-egg blue and white, or lilac and silver. *Bars/cafés (2). Business centre. Concierge. Disabled-adapted rooms. Gym. Internet: wireless (free). Restaurants (2). Room service. Smoking rooms. Spa facilities. TV: DVD & pay movies.*

★ Connaught

Carlos Place, W1K 2AL (7499 7070, www.the-connaught.co.uk). Bond Street tube. **Rates** £490-£650 double. **Rooms** 119. **Credit** AmEx, DC, MC, V. **Map** p398 H7 ⑰
This isn't the only hotel in London to provide butlers, but there can't be many that offer 'a secured gun cabinet room' for hunting season. This is traditional British hospitality for those who love 23-carat gold leaf trimmings and stern portraits in the halls, but all mod cons in their room, down to flatscreens in the en suite. Too lazy to polish your own shoes? The butlers are trained in shoe care by the expert cobblers at John Lobb. Both of the bars – gentleman's club cosy Coburg and cruiseship deco Connaught (*see p247*) – and the Hélène Darroze restaurant are very impressive. In the new wing, which doubled the number of guestrooms, there's a swanky spa and 60sq m swimming pool. *Bars/cafés (2). Concierge. Disabled-adapted rooms. Gym. Internet: wireless (free). Pool: indoor. Restaurants (2). Room service. Smoking rooms. Spa facilities. TV: DVD.*

★ Dorchester

53 Park Lane, W1K 1QA (7629 8888, www.thedorchester.com). Hyde Park Corner tube. **Rates** £354-£720 double. **Rooms** 250. **Credit** AmEx, DC, MC, V. **Map** p398 G7 ⑱
A Park Lane fixture since 1931, the Dorchester's interior may be thoroughly, opulently classical, but the hotel is cutting edge in attitude, providing an unrivalled level of personal service. With the grandest lobby in town, amazing views of Hyde Park, state-of-the-art mod cons and a magnificent spa, it's small wonder the hotel continues to welcome movie stars (the lineage stretches from Elizabeth Taylor to Tom Cruise) and political leaders (Eisenhower planned the D-Day landings here). You're not likely to be eating out, either: the Dorchester employs 90 full-time chefs at the Grill Room, Alain Ducasse and the wonderfully atmospheric China Tang. There's even an angelic tearoom in the new spa: the Spatisserie. The Dorchester opened an entirely new hotel, 45 Park Lane (*see p203*), early in 2011 in the former Playboy club premises, almost opposite the entrance to its predecessor. *Bar/café. Concierge. Disabled-adapted rooms. Gym. Internet: wireless & high-speed (£19.50/day). Parking: £50/day. Restaurants (5). Room service. Smoking rooms. Spa facilities. TV: DVD & pay movies.*

THE BEST BARGAIN BEDS

40 Winks
First choice for creative types. *See p211.*

Hoxton Hotel
Pioneer of cheap, quality rooms. *See p211.*

Shoreditch Rooms
Superb value and supercool. *See p211.*

★ 45 Park Lane

45 Park Lane, W1K 1PN (7493 4545, www.45parklane.com). Hyde Park Corner tube. **Rates** from £510 double. **Rooms** 45. **Credit** AmEx, MC, V. **Map** p398 G8 ⑲
Offspring of the Dorchester, which it faces across a twinkly-treed forecourt, 45 Park Lane opened in late 2011 to immediate acclaim in the style and travel press. It had succeeded resoundingly in the task it had set itself: to translate the famously high standards of the Dorchester into a buzzier, boutiquier, even blingier form. Where the Dorchester offers liveried concierges, 45 PL allocates guests a personal host sharply suited in grey; where the Dorchester can arrange a limo, so can 45 – or lend you a folding bike. Wolfgang Puck brings informal glamour and high-end steaks to The Cut restaurant. Rooms are standard rectangles given character by well-chosen art, quality furnishings, great views (ask for an upper floor) and considered touches such as a yoga mat, designer glassware and in-safe electrical outlet. Technology is state of the art; enormous flatscreens swing out from the walls; a TV is embedded in the bathroom mirror (to watch from the giant marble bath); and touchscreens control room functions electronically (or will do, once early glitches are smoothed out). Breakfasts are awesome. *Bar. Concierge. Disabled-adapted rooms. Gym. Internet: wireless (free). Restaurant. Room service. TV: DVD.*

Haymarket Hotel

1 Suffolk Place, SW1Y 4BP (7470 4000, www.firmdale.com). Piccadilly Circus tube. **Rates** £312-£408 double. **Rooms** 50. **Credit** AmEx, DC, MC, V. **Map** p416 W5 ⑳
A terrific addition to Kit Kemp's Firmdale portfolio, this block-size building was designed by John Nash, the architect of Regency London. The public spaces are a delight, with Kemp's trademark combination of contemporary arty surprises and plump, floral sofas. Wow-factors include the bling basement swimming pool and bar (shiny sofas, twinkly roof) and the central location. Rooms are generously sized (as are bathrooms), individually decorated and discreetly stuffed with facilities, and there's plenty of attention from the switched-on staff. The street-side bar and restaurant are top-notch, the breakfast exquisite.

CONSUME

Bar/café. Concierge. Disabled-adapted rooms. Gym. Internet: wireless (£20/day). Pool: indoor. Restaurant. Room service. Smoking rooms. Spa facilities. TV: DVD.

Metropolitan
19 Old Park Lane, W1K 1LB (7447 1000, www.metropolitan.como.bz). Hyde Park Corner tube. **Rates** £275-£510 double. **Rooms** 150. **Credit** AmEx, DC, MC, V. **Map** p398 H8 ⑤
The flashier little sister of the Halkin (*see p207*), the Metropolitan may have had its fashion heyday in the 1990s, but it still retains a buzzy, relaxed sense of cool. The Met bar and Nobu restaurant continue to attract celebrities and models, bands such as Kings of Leon still rock up, and many mere mortals drop by to rubberneck. The hotel itself is bright and uncluttered. The rooms are a little clinical and appear ever-so-slightly dated, but pear-wood furnishings, super-soft mattresses and suede throws keep things very comfortable, and the toiletries in the bathrooms are a cut above the usual chuck-away fodder. The hotel's greatest asset, however, is the prime location, overlooking a corner of Hyde Park. *Bar/café. Business centre. Concierge. Disabled-adapted rooms. Gym. Internet: wireless, high-speed & shared terminal (free). Parking: £45/day. Restaurant. Room service. Smoking rooms. Spa facilities. TV: DVD & pay movies.*

Ritz
150 Piccadilly, W1J 9BR (7493 8181, www.theritzlondon.com). Green Park tube. **Rates** £300-£495 double. **Rooms** 136. **Credit** AmEx, DC, MC, V. **Map** p398 J8 ⑤
If you like the idea of a world where jeans and trainers are banned and jackets must be worn by gentlemen when dining (the requirement is waived for breakfast), the Ritz is the place for you. Founded by hotelier extraordinaire César Ritz, the hotel is deluxe *in excelsis*. The show-stopper is the ridiculously ornate, vaulted Long Gallery, an orgy of chandeliers, rococo mirrors and marble columns, but all the high-ceilinged, Louis XVI-style bedrooms have been painstakingly renovated to their former glory in restrained pastel colours. But amid the old-world luxury, there are plenty of mod cons including free wireless in most rooms, large TVs and a gym. An elegant afternoon tea in the Palm Court (book ahead) is the way in for interlopers. *Bar/café. Concierge. Gym. Internet: high-speed (£26/day); wireless (£26/day). Restaurant. Room service. Smoking rooms. Spa facilities. TV: DVD.*

Expensive

No.5 Maddox Street
5 Maddox Street, W1S 2QD (7647 0200, www.living-rooms.co.uk). Oxford Circus tube. **Rates** £324-£492 double. **Rooms** 12. **Credit** AmEx, MC, V. **Map** p416 U2 ⑤

This bolthole just off Regent Street is perfect for visiting film directors looking to be accommodated in a chic apartment at a reasonable long-term rate. Here they can shut the discreet brown front door, climb the stairs and flop into a home from home with all contemporary cons, including new flatscreen TVs. The East-meets-West decor is classic 1990s minimalist, but very bright and clean after a gentle refurbishment. Each apartment has a fully equipped kitchen, but room service will shop for you as well as providing usual hotel amenities. There's no bar, but breakfasts and snacks are served, and there's a Thai restaurant (Patara) on the ground floor. *Concierge. Internet: wireless & high-speed (£10/day, £50/wk). Room service. TV: DVD.*

WESTMINSTER & ST JAMES'S
Deluxe

Royal Horseguards
2 Whitehall Court, SW1A 2EJ (0871 376 9033, www.guoman.com). Embankment tube or Charing Cross tube/rail. **Rates** £300-£400 double. **Rooms** 280. **Credit** AmEx, MC, V. **Map** p399 L8 ⑤
The Royal Horseguards occupies a French château that is discreetly located off Whitehall. The building was designed by Alfred 'Natural History Museum' Waterhouse for the National Liberal Club in 1887, and the club's founder, William Gladstone, the great reformer that he was, probably would have approved of the recent refurbishment of the interior by the Guoman group. It's immaculately clean, 'classic but modern' in style, with welcoming staff. The bedrooms have useful dressing tables, iPod docks and wonderfully comfortable Hypnos beds, and bathrooms come with flatscreen TV and Guoman toiletries. The buffet-style breakfasts are ordinary, but from the upper floors the river views of County Hall and the London Eye – whisper it – rival those of the Savoy (*see p197*). *Bars/cafés (2). Business centre. Concierge. Disabled-adapted rooms. Gym. Internet: wireless (free). Restaurant. Room service. TV.*

INSIDE TRACK
STRATFORD SLEEPS

The new Westfield City Mall development bordering the Olympic Park will contain three accommodation options offering, in total, 617 beds. First to open was a Premier Inn (www.premierinn.com), with a Holiday Inn (www.holidayinn.com) and Staybridge Suites (www.staybridge.com) due in time for the London 2012 Olympic and Paralympic Games. Rooms were already selling out at press time.

CONSUME

Boundary. *See p210.*

Expensive

Eccleston Square Hotel

37 Eccleston Square, SW1V 1PB (3489 1000, www.ecclestonsquarehotel.com). Pimlico tube or Victoria tube/rail. **Rates** *£330-£450.* **Rooms** *39.* **Credit** AmEx, MC, V. **Map** p398 H11 ⑤⑤

This Grade II-listed Georgian house has been transformed to the tune of £6.5m into an ultra-modern boutique hotel. The focus is on high-spec technology – with 46in 3D flatscreens, an iPad2 to control the room environment and electronically adjustable Hastens beds in each of the 39 rooms.

Bar/café. Concierge. Conference facilities. Internet: wireless (free). Restaurant. Room service. TV: DVD.

Trafalgar

2 Spring Gardens, Trafalgar Square, SW1A 2TS (7870 2900, www.thetrafalgar.com). Charing Cross tube/rail. **Rates** *£282-£407 double.* **Rooms** 129. **Credit** AmEx, DC, MC, V. **Map** p416 X5 ⑤⑥

The Trafalgar is part of the Hilton chain of hotels, but you'd hardly notice. The mood is young and dynamic at the chain's first 'concept' hotel, for all that it's housed in the imposing edifice that was once the headquarters of Cunard (this was where the *Titanic* was conceived). To the right of the open reception is the Rockwell Bar, boisterous at night,

although thick walls should prevent sound leaking up to the rooms; breakfast downstairs is accompanied by gentler music, sometimes played live. It's the none-more-central location, however, that's the hotel's biggest draw – the handful of corner suites look directly into the square (prices reflect location). Those without their own view can always avail themselves of the little rooftop bar, which is now open to the public.

Bars/cafés (2). Business centre. Concierge. Disabled-adapted rooms. Gym. Internet: wireless & high-speed (£15/day). Restaurant. Room service. TV: DVD & pay movies.

Moderate

B+B Belgravia

64-66 Ebury Street, SW1W 9QD (7259 8570, www.bb-belgravia.com). Victoria tube/rail. **Rates** (incl breakfast) £135 double. **Rooms** 17. **Credit** AmEx, MC, V. **Map** p398 H10 ⑤⑦

How do you make a lounge full of white and black contemporary furnishings seem cosy and welcoming? Hard to achieve, but the owners have succeeded at B+B Belgravia, which takes the B&B experience to a new level. It's fresh and sophisticated without being hard-edged: there's nothing here that will make the fastidiously design-conscious wince (leather sofa, arty felt cushions, modern fireplace), but nor is it overly precious. A gleaming espresso machine provides 24/7 caffeine, and there's a large but somewhat dark garden to sit out in at the rear. *Disabled-adapted rooms. Internet: wireless (free). TV.*

Windermere Hotel
142-144 Warwick Way, SW1V 4JE (7834 5163, www.windermere-hotel.co.uk). Victoria tube/rail. **Rates** (incl breakfast) £145-£175 double. **Rooms** 19. **Credit** AmEx, MC, V. **Map** p398 H11 ⑤⑧
Heading the procession of small hotels that are strung out along Warwick Way, the Windermere is a comfortable, traditionally decked-out London hotel with, thankfully, no aspirations to boutique status. The decor may be showing its age a bit in the hall, but you'll receive a warm welcome and excellent service – there are over a dozen staff for just 19 rooms. There's a cosy basement restaurant-bar, where the breakfasts are top-notch.
Bar/café. Internet: wireless (free). Restaurant. Room service. TV.

Budget

Morgan House
120 Ebury Street, SW1W 9QQ (7730 2384, www.morganhouse.co.uk). Pimlico tube or

Victoria tube/rail. **Rates** (incl breakfast) £78-£98 double. **Rooms** 11. **Credit** MC, V. **Map** p398 G10 ⑤⑨
The Morgan has the understated charm of the old family home of a posh but unpretentious English friend: a pleasing mix of nice old wooden or traditional iron beds, pretty floral curtains and coverlets in subtle hues, the odd chandelier or big gilt mirror over original mantelpieces, and padded wicker chairs and sinks in every bedroom. Though there's no guest lounge, guests can sit in the little patio garden, and for Belgravia, the prices are a steal.
Internet: wireless (free). TV.

CHELSEA
Expensive

Myhotel Chelsea
35 Ixworth Place, SW3 3QX (7225 7500, www.myhotels.com). South Kensington tube. **Rates** £167-£348 double. **Rooms** 45. **Credit** AmEx, DC, MC, V. **Map** p395 E11 ⑥⓪
The Chelsea Myhotel feels a world away from its sleekly modern Bloomsbury sister (*see p193*). The Sloane Square branch has an aesthetic that is softer and decidedly more English – with a floral sofa and

40 Winks. *See p211.*

plate of scones in the lobby, and white wicker headboards, velvet cushions and Bee Kind toiletries in the guestrooms. These feminine touches contrast nicely with the mini-chain's feng shui touches, its Eastern-inspired treatment room, and its sleek aquarium. The modernised country farmhouse feel of the bar-restaurant works better for breakfast than it does for a boozy cocktail, but the central library, which is done out conservatory style, is simply wonderful. Just pick up a book, sink into one of the ample comfy chairs and listen to the tinkling water feature. *Photo p201. Bar/café. Business centre. Concierge. Internet: wireless & high-speed (free). Restaurant. Room service. TV: DVD.*
Other locations 11-13 Bayley Street, Bloomsbury, WC1B 3HD (7667 6000).

San Domenico House

29-31 Draycott Place, SW3 2SH (7581 5757, www.sandomenicohouse.com). Sloane Square tube. **Rates** £306-£432 double. **Rooms** 16. **Credit** AmEx, MC, V. **Map** p395 F11 ⑥
Along a quiet terrace of late 19th-century red-stone buildings just off Sloane Square, San Domenico owes much of its tasteful, historic look to previous owner Sue Rogers, the interior designer who transformed this former private residence into a boutique hotel masterpiece. All the categories of guestroom, including the split-level gallery suites and a new junior suite, feature original furnishings or antiques. Royal portraits, Victorian mirrors and Empire-era travelling cases are complemented by fabrics of similar style and taste, offset by contemporary touches to bathrooms. The spacious bedrooms enjoy wide-angle views of London, some from little balconies. Breakfasts are taken up to guests or laid out in the room downstairs, while main meals may be taken in the sumptuous coffee room by the lobby.
Bar/café. Internet: wireless (free). Room service. TV.

KNIGHTSBRIDGE & SOUTH KENSINGTON

Deluxe

Blakes

33 Roland Gardens, SW7 3PF (7370 6701, www.blakeshotels.com). South Kensington tube. **Rates** £318-£450 double. **Rooms** 48. **Credit** AmEx, MC, V. **Map** p395 D11 ⑥
As original as when Anouska Hempel opened it in 1983 – the scent of oranges and the twittering of a pair of lovebirds fill the dark, oriental lobby – Blakes and its maximalist decor have stood the test of time, a living casebook for interior design students. Each room is in a different style, with influences from Italy, India, Turkey and China. Exotic antiques picked up on the designer's travels – intricately carved beds, Chinese birdcages, ancient trunks – are set off by sweeping drapery and piles of plump cush-

ions. Downstairs, the Eastern-influenced restaurant caters for a celebrity clientele enticed by the hotel's discreet, residential location.
Bar/café. Business centre. Concierge. Internet: wireless & high-speed (free). Parking: £50/day. Restaurant. Room service. TV: DVD & pay movies.

Gore

190 Queen's Gate, SW7 5EX (7584 6601, www.gorehotel.com). South Kensington tube. **Rates** £216-£528 double. **Rooms** 50. **Credit** AmEx, MC, V. **Map** p395 D9 ⑥
This fin-de-siècle period piece was founded by descendants of Captain Cook in two grand Victorian townhouses. The lobby and staircase are close hung with old paintings, and the bedrooms all have fantastic 19th-century carved oak beds, sumptuous drapes and shelves of old books. The suites are spectacular: the Tudor Room has a huge stone-faced fireplace and a minstrels' gallery, while tragedy queens should plump for the Venus room and Judy Garland's old bed (and replica ruby slippers). Bistrot 190 provides a casually elegant setting for great breakfasts, while the warm, wood-panelled 190 bar is a charming setting for cocktails.
Bar/café. Concierge. Internet: wireless & high-speed (£20/day). Restaurant. Room service. TV.

Halkin

Halkin Street, SW1X 7DJ (7333 1000, www.halkin.como.bz). Hyde Park Corner tube. **Rates** £540 double. **Rooms** 41. **Credit** AmEx, DC, MC, V. **Map** p398 G9 ⑥
Set up by Singaporean fashion mogul Christina Ong (who also owns the Metropolitan; *see p204*), the Halkin marries Eastern charm, style and food with a central and quiet location in Knightsbridge. The rooms, all located off black curved, almost trompe l'oeil wooden corridors, are comfortable and full of Asian artefacts and clever gadgetry (a touch-screen bedside panel controls everything from the air-con to the 'do not disturb' sign on the door). Bathrooms are well equipped and heavy on the marble, and come stocked with a range of products from Ong's Shambhala spa. The Michelin-starred Thai restaurant Nahm (*see p231*), a gastronomic sensation, is on the ground floor.
Bar/café. Concierge. Disabled-adapted rooms. Gym. Internet: wireless & high-speed (free). Parking: £45/day. Restaurant. Room service. TV: DVD & pay movies.

★ Lanesborough

1 Lanesborough Place, SW1X 7TA (7259 5599, www.lanesborough.com). Hyde Park Corner tube. **Rates** £475-£675 double. **Rooms** 93. **Credit** AmEx, DC, MC, V. **Map** p398 G8 ⑥
Generally considered one of London's more historic luxury hotels, the Lanesborough was in fact redeveloped – impressively – only in 1991. Occupying

CONSUME

an 1820s Greek Revival building that was designed as a hospital by William Wilkins (the man behind the National Gallery; *see p134*), its luxurious guestrooms are traditionally decorated with thick fabrics, antique furniture and lavish Carrera-marble bathrooms. Electronic keypads control everything from the air-conditioning to the superb 24hr room service at the touch of a button. As luxury hotels go, the Lanesborough's rates are unusually inclusive: high-speed internet access, movies and calls within the EU and to the USA are complimentary, as are personalised business cards stating your residence. The Library Bar and the cigar and cognac lounge are excellent.

Bar/café. Business centre. Concierge. Disabled-adapted rooms. Gym. Internet: wireless & high-speed (free). Parking: £6/hr. Restaurant. Room service. Spa facilities. TV: DVD & pay movies.

Milestone Hotel & Apartments

1-2 Kensington Court, W8 5DL (7917 1000, www.milestonehotel.com). High Street Kensington tube. **Rates** £300-£432 double. **Rooms** 57. **Credit** AmEx, DC, MC, V. **Map** p392 C8 ⑤

Wealthy American visitors make annual pilgrimages here, their arrival greeted by the comforting, gravel tones of their regular concierge, as English as roast beef, and the glass of sherry in the room. Yet amid old-school luxury (butlers on 24hr call) thrives inventive modernity (the resistance pool in the spa). Rooms overlooking Kensington Gardens feature the inspired decor of South African owner Beatrice Tillman: the Safari suite contains tent-like draperies and leopard-print upholstery; the Tudor Suite has an elaborate inglenook fireplace, minstrels' gallery and a pouffe concealing a pop-up TV.

Bar/café. Business centre. Concierge. Disabled-adapted rooms. Gym. Internet: wireless & high-speed (free). Pool: indoor. Restaurant. Room service. Smoking rooms. Spa facilities. TV: DVD & pay movies.

Expensive

★ Number Sixteen

16 Sumner Place, SW7 3EG (7589 5232, www.firmdale.com). South Kensington tube. **Rates** £246-£348 double. **Rooms** 41. **Credit** AmEx, DC, MC, V. **Map** p395 D10 ⑥

This may be Kit Kemp's most affordable hotel but there's no slacking in style – witness the fresh flowers and origami-ed birdbook decorations in the comfy drawing room. Bedrooms are generously sized, bright and very light, and carry the Kemp trademark mix of bold and traditional. The whole place has an appealing freshness about it, enhanced by a delicious, large back garden with its central water feature. By the time you finish breakfast in the sweet conservatory, you'll have forgotten you're in the city.

Concierge. Internet: wireless & high-speed (£20/day). Parking: £45/day. Room service. TV: DVD.

Moderate

Aster House

3 Sumner Place, SW7 3EE (7581 5888, www.asterhouse.com). South Kensington tube. **Rates** (incl breakfast) £180-£300 double. **Rooms** 13. **Credit** MC, V. **Map** p395 D11 ⑥

This swish, thoroughly archetypal white-terraced South Kensington street is a great setting for a hotel. But Aster House has not just relied on location; it's become an award-winner through attention to detail (such as impeccable housekeeping, the mobile phone guests can borrow, and the introduction of wireless internet and flatscreen TVs) and the warmth of its managers, Leona and Simon Tan. It's all low-key, comfortably soothing creams with touches of dusty rose and muted green. Star of the show is the plant-filled conservatory that serves as a breakfast room and guest lounge – star, that is, after Ollie and Cordelia, the resident ducks.

Internet: wireless (free). TV.

★ Lux Pod

38 Gloucester Road, SW7 4QT (7460 3171, www.theluxpod.com). Gloucester Road tube. **Rates** (min 3-night stay) £129 double. **Rooms** 1. **No credit cards. Map** p394 C9 ⑥

This marvellously eccentric little hideaway is the pride and joy of its owner, Judith Abraham, with many of the features purpose-designed for the hotel. Little is the operative word: it's a tiny space that ingeniously packs in a bathroom, slide-top kitchenette and lounge, with the comfy bed high up above the bathroom and accessible only by ladder. All is shiny and modern, and the room is packed with gadgets (iPod dock with fine B&O speakers, flatscreen TV, funky cooker hobs and lighting arrangements, electronic curtains) and high-style details (leather flooring, hip chairs). The tight space is ideal for one, a little fiddly to get round for two, but terrific fun for any design fan.

Internet: wireless (free). TV: DVD.

Vicarage Hotel

10 Vicarage Gate, W8 4AG (7229 4030, www.londonvicaragehotel.com). High Street Kensington or Notting Hill Gate tube. **Rates** (incl breakfast) £102-£130 double. **Rooms** 17. **Credit** AmEx, MC, V. **Map** p392 B8 ⑦

Scores of devotees return regularly to this tall Victorian townhouse, which has a great location, tucked in a quiet leafy square just off High Street Ken, hard by Kensington Gardens. It's a comfortable, resolutely old-fashioned establishment – and that's what the punters come for. The refurbished entrance hall is wonderfully grand, with red and gold striped wallpaper, a huge gilt mirror and chandelier. A sweeping staircase ascends from there to an assortment of good-sized rooms, furnished in pale florals and nice old pieces of furniture.

Internet: wireless (free). TV.

The Grand Tour

Visit the apotheosis of the Victorian Age.

You don't have to stay in the gorgeous **St Pancras Renaissance** (*see p192*) in order to appreciate its beauty (though admittedly it would be nice). In recognition of its considerable historical and architectural worth as a pioneering Victorian railway hotel, the Renaissance (then the St Pancras Grand) employs a dedicated historian. Royden Stock leads regular tours of the uniquely beautiful public areas – and if you're lucky, he'll also let you sneak a peek into the luxury rooms and suites.

Royden has been associated with the building for 15 years, dating back to before its lavish £150 million renovation (it launched on 5 May 2011, 138 years to the day after its original opening), so he knows

what he's talking about, and does so with passion, expertise and humour.

En route you'll learn how the architect, George Gilbert Scott, poured his frustrated creative energies into the project, having been overruled on his designs for the Foreign and Commonwealth Office; about the unique demands of station architecture past and present; and how the hotel pioneered, among other things, the revolving door, the electric lift and the women's smoking room. Tours end with questions and refreshments in the Booking Office café-bar.

To book, contact Royden Stock by phone on 7841 3540, or via email at royden.stock@renaissancehotels.com). Tours cost £20 per person.

CONSUME

NORTH LONDON
Expensive

York & Albany
127-129 Parkway, Camden, NW1 7PS (7387 5700, www.gordonramsay.com). Camden Town tube. **Rates** £156-£348 double. **Rooms** 9. **Credit** AmEx, DC, MC, V. **Map** p404 X3 **71**
Overcommitment to TV and transatlantic enterprises might have knocked a little gloss off Gordon Ramsay's restaurants, but his only hotel is still going strong. Housed in a grand John Nash building that was designed as a coaching house but spent the recent past as a pub, it consists of a restaurant (split over two levels), bar and delicatessen downstairs; above them a selection of nine rooms, handsomely designed by Russell Sage in mellow shades. The decor is an effective mix of ancient and modern, sturdy and quietly charismatic furniture married to modern technology; if you're lucky, you'll have views of Regent's Park from your bedroom window.
Bar/café. Disabled-adapted rooms. Internet: wireless (free). Restaurant. Room service. TV: DVD.

Moderate

Colonnade
2 Warrington Crescent, Little Venice, W9 1ER (7286 1052, www.theetoncollection.com). Warwick Avenue tube. **Rates** £168-£258 double. **Rooms** 43. **Credit** AmEx, MC, V. **Map** p392 C4 **72**
Housed in an imposingly sited white mansion, the Colonnade has been lushly done up in interior-designer traditional – lots of swagged curtains, deep opulent colours, luxurious fabrics and careful arrangements of smoothly upholstered furniture. Some of the larger high-ceilinged rooms have had mezzanine floors added. Note that the hotel no longer has a restaurant or bar, although it still serves breakfast to guests in the old restaurant space.
Internet: wireless (free). Parking: £20/day. Room service. TV.

Rose & Crown
199 Stoke Newington Church Street, N16 9ES (7923 3337, www.roseandcrownn16.co.uk). Bus 73. **Rates** (incl breakfast) £132-£197 double. **Rooms** 6. **Credit** MC, V.
The Rose has always been popular as a pub, but now a separate entrance leads to a contemporary B&B range. Landscape gardener Will, who with Diane runs the place, transformed three floors to create individually and tastefully styled guestrooms (drench showers, quality smellies and furnishings), a breakfast room and a sun-catching roof terrace with a large table, a couple of loungers, a patio heater and a view across to central London from the illuminated glow of 13th-century St Mary's Church alongside. Pricier rooms feature a stand-alone bathtub, and the suite by the breakfast room is vast.

Truman Brewery touches from yesteryear remain: the pub sign lettering, a finely carved pre-war stair rail and the Mystery Arrow games machine.
Internet: wireless (free). TV.

Budget

Hampstead Village Guesthouse
2 Kemplay Road, Hampstead, NW3 1SY (7435 8679, www.hampsteadguesthouse.com). Hampstead tube or Hampstead Heath rail. **Rates** £80-£125 double. **Rooms** 9. **Credit** AmEx, MC, V.
Owner Annemarie van der Meer loves to point out all the quirky space-saving surprises as she shows you round her wonderful and idiosyncratic bed and breakfast: here's the folding sink, there's the bed that pops out of an antique wardrobe... The special atmosphere at this double-fronted Victorian house, set on a quiet Hampstead street, means that guests return year after year. Each room is uniquely decorated with eclectic furnishings – such as the French steel bathtub in one room – and there's a self-contained studio with its own kitchen. All guests may make use of a range of home comforts, from hot-water bottles to mobile phones, as well as a laptop to borrow. Breakfast (£7) may be taken in the garden that surrounds this lovely property on all four sides.
Internet: wireless (free). Parking: £15/day. TV.

66 Camden Square
66 Camden Square, Camden, NW1 9XD (7485 4622, rodgerdavis@btinternet.com). Camden Town tube or Camden Road rail. **Rates** (incl continental breakfast) £100 double. **Rooms** 2. **No credit cards. Map** p404 Z1 **73**
A world away from the Eurobustle of Camden Market, lovely 66 Camden Square isn't actually on Camden Square – it's on Murray Street, behind 1 Camden Square, an easy no.29 bus hop to town. A radical design by co-owner/architect Rodger Davis allows natural light to flood through the open-plan interior. Breakfast, taken in the expansive living room or on the terrace, is overseen by Rodger's hospitable other half Sue and a colourful parrot by the name of Peckham. The two guestrooms (one double, one single) are upstairs, convivial and comfortable. Neither is en suite, and the owners are keen to point out that they wouldn't have strangers sharing the bathroom. The double room costs £100 per night, the single is £60, there's a £5 supplement for one-nighters and a maximum stay of one week. A foot path will get you to St Pancras International in 15 minutes.
Internet: wireless (free). TV.

EAST LONDON
Expensive

Boundary
2-4 Boundary Street, Shoreditch, E2 7DD (7729 1051, www.theboundary.co.uk). Liverpool Street

CONSUME

tube/rail or Shoreditch High Street rail. **Rates** £204-£264 double. **Rooms** 17. **Credit** AmEx, DC, MC, V. **Map** p401 R4 🟤

Design mogul Sir Terence Conran's Boundary Project warehouse conversion was a labour of love. Its restaurants – which include Albion (*see p234*), one of the best openings of 2009, a downstairs fine-dining establishment and a rooftop bar – are high quality but relaxed, and all 17 bedrooms are beautifully designed. Each has a wet room and handmade bed, but are otherwise individually furnished with classic furniture and original art. The five split-level suites range in style from the bright and sea-salt fresh Beach to a new take on Victoriana by Polly Dickens, while the remaining rooms (the slightly larger corner rooms have windows along both external walls) are themed by design style: Mies van der Rohe, Eames, Shaker. There's also a charming Heath Robinson room, decorated with the cartoonist's sketches of hilariously complex machines. *Photo p205.*
Bar/café. Concierge. Disabled-adapted rooms. Internet: wireless (free). Restaurant. Room service. TV: DVD.

Town Hall Hotel

Patriot Square, Bethnal Green, E2 9NF (7871 0460, www.townhallhotel.com). Bethnal Green tube. **Rates** £312-£384 double. **Rooms** 98. **Credit** AmEx, MC, V.

In 2010, a grand, Grade II-listed, early 20th-century town hall was transformed into a classy modern aparthotel – despite its location between a council estate and a scruffy row of shops. The decor is minimal, retaining many features (walnut panelling and marble for the interior, Portland stone outside, stained glass and fire hoses on old brass reels scattered about) that would be familiar to the bureaucrats who used to toil here, but jazzed up with contemporary art and a patterned aluminium 'veil' that covers the new floor at the top of the building. The pale-toned, spacious apartments are well equipped for self-catering, but hotel luxuries such as free wireless internet and TV/DVD players are also in place. The De Montfort suite is the size of most houses, stretching over three floors, with a living room as big as a council chamber, and Viajante restaurant (*see p237*), is one of the hottest in town. Under a conservatory roof, there's a narrow basement swimming pool with sparkly tiles.
Bar/café. Business centre. Concierge. Disabled-adapted rooms. Gym. Internet: wireless (free). Restaurant. Room service. Pool (indoor). TV: DVD.

Moderate

★ 40 Winks

109 Mile End Road, Stepney, E1 4UJ (7790 0259, 07973 653944, www.40winks.org). Stepney Green tube. **Rates** (incl breakfast) £175 double. **Rooms** 2. **No credit cards.**

Opposite a housing estate and cheap Somali diners, the family home of an interior designer has become the B&B of choice for movie stars and fashion movers. The 'micro-boutique hotel' looks extraordinary (kitchen frescoes, a music room with Beatles drumkit, a lion's head tap in the bath), but each stay is made individual by owner David Carter's commitment to his guests, making them feel they're staying with a fabulous friend rather than just renting a room. Too late to book? Intriguing soirées such as Bedtime Stories (for which everyone must wear pyjamas) open the house to a wider audience. It's flamboyant, fashionable and very cool. *Photos p206.*
Internet: wireless (free). Parking: free.

Hoxton Hotel

81 Great Eastern Street, Shoreditch, EC2A 3HU (7550 1000, www.hoxtonhotels.com). Old Street tube/rail. **Rates** (incl breakfast) £49-£199 double. **Rooms** 208. **Credit** AmEx, MC, V. **Map** p401 Q4 🟤

Famous for its low rates (including some publicity-garnering £1-a-night rooms), the Hoxton deserves credit for many other things. First, there's the hip Shoreditch location – hip enough for Soho House to have taken over the downstairs bar-brasserie a few years ago. Then there are the great design values (the foyer is a sort of postmodern country lodge, complete with stag's head). Finally, the rooms are well thought out, if mostly rather small, with lots of nice touches – free milk in the fridges, a cold snack for breakfast, free wireless internet. Nowadays, there are even three individually designed suites. The downside? The hotel's popularity. If you don't book well in advance and plan to visit during the week rather than at the weekend, you could pay as much as at one of the big chains.
Bar/café. Business centre. Disabled-adapted rooms. Internet: wireless (free). Restaurant. Room service. TV: pay movies.

★ Shoreditch Rooms

Ebor Street, Shoreditch, E1 6AW (7739 5040, www.shoreditchhouse.com). Shoreditch High Street rail. **Rates** £75-£225 double. **Rooms** 26. **Credit** AmEx, MC, V. **Map** p401 S4 🟤

The most recent hotel opening from Soho House members' club (*see also p197* **Dean Street Townhouse**; *p213* **High Road House**) might even be the best, perfectly catching the local atmosphere with its unfussy, slightly retro design. The rooms feel a bit like urban beach huts, with pastel-coloured tongue-and-groove, shutters and swing doors to the en suite showers. They feel fresh, bright and comfortable, even though they're furnished with little more than a bed, an old-fashioned phone and DAB radio, and a big, solid dresser (minibar, hairdryer and treats within, flatscreen TV on top). Guests get access to the fine eating, drinking and fitness facilities (yes, a gym, but more importantly an excellent rooftop pool) in the members' club next

CONSUME

door. Everything's put together with a light touch, from the 'Borrow Me' bookshelf by the lifts (jelly beans, umbrellas and boardgames) to the room nomenclature: Tiny (from just £75), Small and Small+ (with little rooftop balconies and loungers from which to survey the grey horizon).
Bar/café. Disabled-adapted room. Gym. Internet: wireless (free). Restaurants (2). Pool: outdoor. TV.

SOUTH-EAST LONDON
Moderate

Church Street Hotel
29-33 Camberwell Church Street, Camberwell, SE5 8TR (7703 5984, www.churchstreethotel.com). Denmark Hill rail or bus 36, 436. **Rates** (incl breakfast) £120-£170 double. **Rooms** 31. **Credit** AmEx, MC, V.
Craftsman José Raido is behind this attractive and original family-run hotel, near Camberwell Green. Funky bathroom tiles in the bright, high-ceilinged bedrooms, for example, come from Guadalajara, and are thus a perfect match for Mexicana such as imported film posters, while the bed frames were forged by José himself. The colours are as vivid as a Mexican sunset. Bathroom products are organic, as are the pastries and cereals served for breakfast

---

INSIDE TRACK NO FRILLS

Chain hotels aren't covered in this chapter, unless they're new, especially well located (**Premier Inn London County Hall**; *see p189*) or otherwise unusually praiseworthy. This is simply because the internal logic of chain hotels is that one should be as similar as possible to another, with reliability one major virtue – and price the other. You can find double rooms for around £100 at **Holiday Inn** and **Holiday Inn Express** (www.ichotelsgroup. com), **Ibis** (www.ibishotel.com) and **Travelodge** (www.travelodge.co.uk).

A relatively new development has been the 'no frills' approach – very low rates, with nothing inessential included. Airline-offshoot **EasyHotel** (www.easyhotel.com) was the first, but it now has a challenger: the first British hotel from **Tune** (www.tunehotels.com) is located not far inland from the South Bank, across the river from the Houses of Parliament. Rooms are usually about £50 a night.

If you've got an awkward departure time from Gatwick or Heathrow, consider the neat and funky 'pod' rooms at a **Yotel** (www.yotel.com). A four-hour stay will cost £45.

---

in an icon-filled dining room that also operates as a 24hr honesty bar. You pay only £90 for a double with shared bathroom, which is a real bargain, and the hotel tapas restaurant, Angels & Gypsies, has been a big hit locally since opening in 2009.
Bar/café. Internet: wireless (free). Restaurant. TV.

SOUTH-WEST LONDON
Expensive

★ Bingham
61-63 Petersham Road, Richmond, Surrey TW10 6UT (8940 0902, www.thebingham.co.uk). Richmond tube/rail. **Rates** £190-£285 double. **Rooms** 15. **Credit** AmEx, DC, MC, V.
Quality boutique hotel, destination restaurant (under Shay Cooper's award-winning supervision) and sun-filled cocktail bar in one, the Bingham makes excellent use of its superb riverside location by Richmond Bridge. Six of its individually styled and high-ceilinged rooms overlook the Thames; all of them are named after a poet, in honour of the Bingham's artistic past (lesbian aunt-and-niece couple Katherine Harris Bradley and Edith Emma Cooper lived here in the 1890s, regularly hosting members of the Aesthetic Movement while they were in residence). Each room accommodates an ample bathtub and shower, art deco touches to the furnishings and irresistibly fluffy duck-and-goose feather duvets. Run by the Trinder family for the last 25 years, the Bingham manages to feel both grand and boutique. A treat.
Bar/café. Internet: wireless (free). Parking: £10/day. Restaurant. Room service. TV: DVD.

WEST LONDON
Moderate

Base2Stay
25 Courtfield Gardens, Earl's Court, SW5 0PG (7244 2255, www.base2stay.com). Earl's Court tube. **Rates** £123-£141 double. **Rooms** 67. **Credit** AmEx, MC, V. **Map** p394 B10 ⓱
Base2Stay looks good, with its modernist limestone and taupe tones, and keeps prices low by removing inessentials: no bar, no restaurant. Instead, there's the increasingly popular solution of a 'kitchenette' (microwave, sink, silent mini-fridge, kettle), but here with all details carefully attended to (not just token cutlery, but sufficient kitchenware with corkscrew and can opener, and guidance about where to shop). The rooms, en suite (with power showers) and air-conditioned, are as carefully thought out, with desks, modem points and flatscreens, but the single/bunkbed rooms are small. Discount vouchers for nearby chain eateries are supplied by the friendly duo on 24hr reception duty.
Disabled-adapted rooms. Internet: wireless (free). Parking: £30/day. TV: pay movies.

Shoreditch Rooms. *See p211.*

ing, unadorned, white Shaker Modern with little fizzes of colour (and little hidden treats), the bathrooms well stocked with Cowshed products. *Bars/cafés (2). Disabled-adapted rooms. Internet: wireless (free). Restaurants (2). Room service. TV: DVD & pay movies.*

★ Mayflower Hotel

26-28 Trebovir Road, Earl's Court, SW5 9NJ (7370 0991, www.mayflower-group.co.uk). Earl's Court tube. **Rates** (incl continental breakfast) £109-£150 double. **Rooms** 46. **Credit** AmEx, MC, V. **Map** p394 B11 ⑦

After fighting on the frontlines of the Earl's Court budget-hotel style revolution, the Mayflower's taken the struggle to other parts of London (New Linden; *see p200*). But this is where the lushly contemporary house style evolved, proving affordability can be opulently chic. The recent complete refurbishment of the hotel, involving public areas and all the guestrooms, shows that it's not resting on its laurels. Hand-carved Asian artefacts complement the richly coloured fabrics. The facilities, too, are well up to scratch, featuring marble bathrooms, Egyptian cotton sheets and CD players in the rooms. *Internet: wireless (free). Parking: £30/day. TV.*

★ Garret

Troubadour, 263-267 Old Brompton Road, Earl's Court, SW5 9JA (7370 1434, www. troubadour.co.uk). West Brompton tube/rail. **Rates** £175 double. **Rooms** 1. **Credit** AmEx, MC, V. **Map** p394 B11 ⑦

This idiosyncratic attic apartment is an absolute treat. High above the Troubadour, a 1960s counterculture café that still hosts poetry and music events, it's unjustly named: yes, the rooms are in the attic and have charming pitched roofs, but there are acres of space for two – and even enough for a small family, if the kids sleep on the pull-out sofa in the loungekitchen. The huge, high main bed lies under a skylight and there's a writing desk, but any thought of poetic torment is banished by the well-executed Arts & Crafts decor and fully equipped kitchen area, right down to the cafetière and wines. *Bar/café. Internet: wireless (free). Room service. TV: DVD.*

Rockwell

181-183 Cromwell Road, Earl's Court, SW5 0SF (7244 2000, www.therockwell.com). Earl's Court tube. **Rates** £160-£200 double. **Rooms** 40. **Credit** AmEx, MC, V. **Map** p394 B10 ⑧

The Rockwell aims for relaxed contemporary elegance – and succeeds magnificently. The listed premises mean there are no identikit rooms here: they're all different sizes and individually designed, but share gleaming woods and muted glowing colours alongside more sober creams and neutrals. Among the rooms, pleasing eccentricities include a pair of central single rooms with skylights, and basement garden rooms that have tiny patios, complete with garden furniture, looking up at the ground-level bridge that leads on to the garden terrace proper from the handsome bar-restaurant. Each room has a power shower, Starck fittings and bespoke cabinets in the bathrooms, and triple-glazing ensures you never notice the noisy road just outside. *Bar/café. Concierge. Internet: wireless (free). Restaurant. TV: pay movies.*

High Road House

162 Chiswick High Road, Chiswick, W4 1PR (8742 1717, www.highroadhouse.co.uk). Turnham Green tube. **Rates** £145-£205 double. **Rooms** 14. **Credit** AmEx, MC, V.

This west London outpost of Nick Jones's ever-fashionable Soho House stable (*see also p197* **Dean Street Townhouse**; *p211* **Shoreditch Rooms**) features guestrooms designed by Ilse Crawford, and a members' bar and restaurant above the buzzing ground-floor brasserie. Serving a modern British menu, this has a retro sophisticated-Parisian-bistromeets-Bloomsbury feel and, as you might expect, the food and service are excellent. Guestrooms are sooth-

Twenty Nevern Square

20 Nevern Square, Earl's Court, SW5 9PD (7565 9555, www.twentynevernsquare.co.uk). Earl's Court tube. **Rates** (incl breakfast) £90-£150 double. **Rooms** 25. **Credit** AmEx, MC, V. **Map** p394 A11 ⑧

Only the less-than-posh location of this immaculate boutique hotel keeps the rates reasonable. Tucked away in a private garden square, it feels far from its locale. The modern-colonial style was created by its well-travelled owner, who personally sourced many

CONSUME

of the exotic and antique furnishings (as well as those in sister hotel the Mayflower; *see p213*). In the sleek marble bathrooms, toiletries are tidied away in decorative caskets, but the beds are the real stars: from elaborately carved four-posters to Egyptian sleigh styles, all with luxurious mattresses. The vaguely Far Eastern feel extends into the lounge and the airy conservatory, with its dark wicker furniture. *Bar/café. Internet: wireless & high-speed (free). Parking: £30/day. Room service. TV: DVD.*

APARTMENT RENTAL

Holiday Serviced Apartments (0845 060 4477, www.holidayapartments.co.uk) and **Palace Court Holiday Apartments** (7727 3467, www.palacecourt.co.uk) specialise in holiday lets. **London Holiday Accommodation** (7265 0882, www.london holiday.co.uk) offers half a dozen decent-priced self-catering options in the West End and on the South Bank. For serviced apartments, try the South Bank or Earl's Court 'campuses' run by **Think Apartments** (3465 9100, www.think-apartments.com). **Accommodation Outlet** (7287 4244, www.outlet4holidays.com) is a recommended lesbian and gay agency that has some excellent properties across London in general and in Soho in particular.

CAMPING & CARAVANNING

If putting yourself at the mercy of English weather in a far-flung suburban field doesn't put you off, the difficult transport links into central London might do the job instead. Still, you can't really beat the prices.

Crystal Palace Caravan Club *Crystal Palace Parade, Crystal Palace, SE19 1UF (8778 7155). Crystal Palace rail or bus 3.* **Open** *Mar-Sept* 9am-6pm daily. *Oct-Jan* 9.30am-5.30pm daily.

STAYING WITH THE LOCALS

Several agencies can arrange for individuals and families to stay in Londoners' homes. They include **At Home in London** (8748 1943, www.athomeinlondon.co.uk), **Host & Guest Service** (7385 9922, www.host-guest.co.uk), **London Bed & Breakfast Agency** (7586 2768, www.londonbb.com) and **London Homestead Services** (7286 5115, www.lhslondon.co.uk). There is usually a minimum length of stay.

UNIVERSITY RESIDENCES

During vacations, much of London's dedicated student accommodation is available to visitors. Central locations can make these a bargain.

International Students House *229 Great Portland Street, Marylebone, W1W 5PN (7631 8300, www.ish.org.uk). Great Portland Street tube.* **Open** *Reception* 7.45am-10.30pm Mon-Fri; 8am-10.30pm Sat, Sun. **Rates** £19 (per person) dormitory; £39 single; £34 twin. **No credit cards. Map** p396 H4 🙲
King's College Conference & Vacation Bureau *Strand Bridge House, 138-142 Strand, Covent Garden, WC2R 1HH (7848 1700, www.kcl.ac.uk/kcvb). Temple tube.* **Rates** £24-£44 single; £48-£65 twin. **No credit cards. Map** p416 Z3 🙲
LSE *Bankside House, 24 Sumner Street, Bankside, SE1 9JA (7107 5750, www.lsevacations.co.uk). London Bridge tube.* **Rates** £32-£59 single; £59-£77 twin/double. **Credit** MC, V. **Map** p402 O8 🙲
The LSE has vacation rentals across town, but Bankside House is the best located.

YOUTH HOSTELS

For Youth Hostel Assocation venues, you can get extra reductions on the rates detailed below if you're a member of the IYHF (International Youth Hostel Federation): you'll pay £3 less a night. Joining costs only £15.95 (£9.95 for under-25s), and can be done on arrival or through www.yha.org.uk prior to departure. All under-18s receive a 25 per cent discount, in any case. YHA hostel beds are arranged either in dormitories or in twin rooms. Our favourite hostels are reviewed (**YHA London Central**, *see p195*; **Clink78**, *see p194*), but those listed below are all handily located across town.

Earl's Court *38 Bolton Gardens, Earl's Court, SW5 0AQ (7373 7083, www.yha.org.uk). Earl's Court tube.* **Open** 24hrs daily. **Rates** £16.95-£67. **No credit cards. Map** p394 B11 🙲
Holland Park *Holland Walk, South Kensington, W8 7QU (7937 0748, www.yha.org.uk). High Street Kensington tube.* **Open** 24hrs daily. **Rates** £14.65-£22.65. **Credit** MC, V. **Map** p392 A8 🙲
Meininger *Baden-Powell House, 65-67 Queen's Gate, South Kensington, SW7 5JS (7590 6910, www.meininger-hostels.com). Gloucester Road or South Kensington tube.* **Rates** £15-£40. **Credit** AmEx, MC, V. **Map** p395 D10 🙲
Oxford Street *14 Noel Street, Soho, W1F 8GJ (7734 1618, www.yha.org.uk). Oxford Circus tube.* **Open** 24hrs daily. *Reception* 7am-11pm daily. **Rates** £22-£70. **Credit** MC, V. **Map** p416 V2 🙲
St Pancras *79-81 Euston Road, King's Cross, NW1 2QE (7388 9998, www.yha.org.uk). King's Cross tube/rail.* **Open** 24hrs daily. **Rates** £15-£69. **Credit** MC, V. **Map** p397 L3 🙲
St Paul's *36 Carter Lane, the City, EC4V 5AB (7236 4965, www.yha.org.uk). St Paul's tube or Blackfriars rail.* **Open** 24hrs daily. **Rates** £14-£72. **Credit** MC, V. **Map** p402 O6 🙲

CONSUME

Restaurants & Cafés

London continues to cook up a storm.

It took a decade or more, but British cuisine has moved from being a national embarrassment to a commonplace, with regional dishes, local ingredients and hitherto unfashionable cuts thoroughly rehabilitated. The best kitchens – Fergus Henderson's pioneering **St John** (*see p219*), still-hot **Hix** (*see p227*) and gastropub exponents such as **Anchor & Hope** (*see p216*) – continue to serve immaculate food, but there are now also an increasing number of Brit-by-numbers places best avoided. These do not include **Dinner by Heston Blumenthal** (*see p229*), one of the landmark haute-cuisine openings of 2010/11.

Other big-name newcomers include Jason Atherton's **Pollen Street Social** (*see p224*) and Gordon Ramsay's new **Bread Street Kitchen** (www.gordonramsay.com) in the City, which was due to open as this chapter went to press. It promises a less formal but still foodie approach.

Another celebrity name ploughing this buzzy, food-savvy furrow is Jamie Oliver (www.jamieoliver.com), whose fun and worthwhile **Jamie's Italian** chain (*see p235*) is flourishing in new developments across town, including both Westfield malls. His **Union Jack's** in Covent Garden opens in late 2011, offering the Jamie take on British food. Small – but multiplying – independents such as **Spuntino** (*see p225*) and **Brawn/Terroirs** (*see p234*) are also flourishing in this niche. The south-of-stupid price point is key: the recession has affected trade substantially, often visibly (in portion size and ingredient choice). The strongest are surviving, along with this new mid-range.

While you're here, be sure to take advantage of the culinary riches London's many immigrants have brought here. Fine Indian, Moroccan, Lebanese, Turkish and Vietnamese restaurants are listed here, as are top-notch exponents of the cuisines of France, Italy, Japan, Spain, China and Thailand. And also welcome the coffee revolution: finally, some genuine conoisseurship is going into selecting and serving the bean – and, this being England, the cake alongside.

ESSENTIAL INFORMATION

Try to book a table in advance. At many establishments, booking is vital; at a select few restaurants, you may need to book far in advance. Smoking is banned in all restaurants and cafés. Tipping is standard practice: ten to 15 per cent is usual. Many restaurants add this charge as standard to bills; some do so but still present the credit card slip as 'open', cheekily encouraging the customer to tip twice. Always check the bill.

We've listed a range of meal prices for each establishment that we've listed. However, restaurants often change their menus, so treat these prices only as guidelines. Budget venues are marked **£**. For good places to eat with children, *see pp294-295*.

About the reviews

This chapter is compiled from Time Out's annual London Eating & Drinking *guide (£11.99), available from www.timeout.com. Time Out reviews anonymously and pays for all meals.*

> ❶ Blue numbers given here correspond to the location of each restaurant and café on the street maps. *See pp392-416.*

THE SOUTH BANK & BANKSIDE

Borough Market (*see p272*), full of stalls selling all kinds of wonderful food, is a superb forage for gourmet snackers. **Tate Modern Café: Level 2** (*see p295*) is great for those with children, as are the neighbouring outposts of chains **Wagamama** and **Giraffe** under the Royal Festival Hall.

Anchor & Hope

36 The Cut, SE1 8LP (7928 9898). Southwark tube or Waterloo tube/rail. **Open** 5-11pm Mon; 11am-11pm Tue-Sat; 12.30-5pm Sun. **Main courses** £12-£20. **Credit** MC, V. **Map** p402 N8 ❶ **Gastropub**

The most common complaint about this relaxed Waterloo gastropub is the no-booking policy. Those who end up having to wait at the bar can salivate over the seasonal British menu on the blackboard, but choose carefully: despite good sourcing, not all dishes are equally successful. Arbroath smokie is a good bet if it's available; other dishes might include cold roast beef and dripping on toast. There's a single sitting on Sundays.

Baltic

74 Blackfriars Road, SE1 8HA (7928 1111, www.balticrestaurant.co.uk). Southwark tube. **Open** noon-3pm, 5.30-11.15pm Mon-Sat; noon-10.30pm Sun. **Main courses** £10.50-£17. **Credit** AmEx, MC, V. **Map** p402 N8 ❷ **Eastern European**

This stylish spot remains the brightest star on London's east European restaurant scene. The menu combines the best of east European cuisine – from Georgian-style lamb with aubergines to Romanian sour cream *mamaliga* (polenta) – with a light, modern European twist. Great cocktails, a wide choice of vodkas, an eclectic wine list and friendly service add to the appeal. In the high-ceilinged restaurant, gaze up at hundreds of shards of golden amber in the stunning chandelier.

Canteen

Royal Festival Hall, Belvedere Road, SE1 8XX (0845 686 1122, www.canteen.co.uk). Embankment tube or Waterloo tube/rail. **Open** 8am-11pm Mon-Fri; 9am-11pm Sat, Sun. **Main courses** £8.50-£14.50. **Credit** AmEx, MC, V. **Map** p399 M8 ❸ **British**

Furnished with utilitarian tables and booths, this branch of Canteen is tucked into the back of the Royal Festival Hall. No surprise, then, that it's often busy. Dishes range from a bacon sandwich and

afternoon jam scones to full roast dinners. Classic breakfasts (eggs benedict, welsh rarebit) are served throughout the day, joined by the likes of macaroni cheese or sausage and mash from lunchtime. Quality can be variable.

Other locations 2 Crispin Place, off Brushfield Street, Spitalfields, E1 6DW; Park Pavilion, 40 Canada Square, Docklands, E14 5FW; 55 Baker Street, Marylebone, W1U 8EW.

Magdalen

152 Tooley Street, SE1 2TU (7403 1342, www.magdalenrestaurant.co.uk). London Bridge tube/rail. **Open** noon-2.30pm, 6.30-10pm Mon-Fri; 6.30-10pm Sat. **Main courses** £13.50-£20. **Set lunch** £15.50 2 courses, £18.50 3 courses. **Credit** AmEx, MC, V. **Map** p403 Q8 ❹ **British**

The atmosphere at Magdalen is low-key and quite romantic, with tea lights flickering on white-clothed tables and classical music playing quietly. The menu may be short, but it is creative. Ingredients are chosen with evident care and treated with respect, neither too fussily nor too plainly. Service is friendly and suitably unfussy. Magdalen is excellent value at dinner and the set lunch is a bargain.

£ M Manze

87 Tower Bridge Road, SE1 4TW (7407 2985, www.manze.co.uk). Bus 1, 42, 188. **Open** 11am-2pm Mon; 10.30am-2pm Tue-Thur; 10am-2.30pm Fri; 10am-2.45pm Sat. **Main courses** £2.75-£5.20. **No credit cards. Map** p403 Q10 ❺ **Pie & mash**

Manze's is the finest remaining purveyor of the dirt-cheap traditional foodstuff of London's working classes. It's the oldest pie shop in town, established in 1902, with tiles, marble-topped tables and worn wood benches. Orders are simple: minced beef pies or, for braver souls, stewed eels with mashed potato and liquor (a thin parsley sauce).

Roast

Floral Hall, Borough Market, Stoney Street, SE1 1TL (7940 1300, www.roast-restaurant.com). London Bridge tube/rail. **Open** 7-11am, noon-2.45pm, 5.30-11pm Mon, Tue; 7-11am, noon-3.45pm, 5.30-11pm Wed-Fri; 8-11.30am, noon-3.45pm, 6-11pm Sat; 11.30am-3pm, 4-9.45pm Sun. **Main courses** £16.50-£35. **Set meal** (Sun) £28 2 courses, £32 3 courses. **Credit** AmEx, MC, V. **Map** p402 P8 ❻ **British**

A big airy restaurant by Borough Market, Roast gets crammed on market days, but staff cope admirably. The same, bracingly pricey but extensive carte is served at lunch and dinner; set-price menus aren't much of a bargain either. Portions, though, are hearty. Cold poached Devon sea trout with wild garlic salad cream is typical, with Neal's Yard cheeses and trad desserts for afters. Add to this an impressive drinks list, including a fine roster of teas, and you have a great all-rounder.

CONSUME

Tapas Brindisa.

Tapas Brindisa
*18-20 Southwark Street, SE1 1TJ (7357 8880,
www.brindisa.com). London Bridge tube/rail.*
Open 11am-3pm, 5.30-11pm Mon-Thur; 9-11am,
noon-4pm, 5.30-11pm Fri, Sat; noon-10pm Sun.
Tapas £4-£12.90. **Credit** AmEx, MC, V. **Map**
p402 P8 ⑦ **Spanish**
Top-quality ingredients have always been the key
at Brindisa, but its genius lies in the ability to assemble them into eminently tempting tapas. The set-up
is equally simple: a bar area at one end dotted with
high tables, and a close-packed, concrete-floored dining room at the other. Both are generally thronged.
Behind the bar is a hatch into the kitchen which produces a succession of deceptively simple dishes.
Other locations 7-9 Exhibition Road, South
Kensington, SW7 2HE (7590 0008); 46 Broadwick
Street, Soho, W1F 7AF (7534 1690).

Zucca
*184 Bermondsey Street, SE1 3TQ (7378 6809,
www.zuccalondon.com). London Bridge tube/rail or
Bermondsey tube.* **Open** 12.30-3pm, 6.30-10pm
Tue-Sat; 12.30-3pm Sun. **Main courses** £14.50-
£14.95. **Credit** MC, V. **Map** p403 Q9 ⑧ **Italian**
If only more restaurants had Zucca's approach: good
food at great prices, served by interested staff with
a genuine regard for diners. It sounds so simple, yet
it's pretty rare. The modern Italian menu is partnered by an all-Italian wine list, and the staff are
happy to help or enlarge upon both. The restaurant
is open-plan, with the kitchen completely exposed to
view. Decor is white with splashes of intense orange.

THE CITY
In several parts, the City remains a working-
hours kind of place, with venues shut in the
evenings and at weekends. Pretty much
everywhere is busiest for weekday lunches.

Bodean's
*16 Byward Street, EC3R 5BA (7488 3883,
www.bodeansbbq.com). Tower Hill tube.* **Open**
noon-11pm Mon-Sat; noon-10.30pm Sun. **Main
courses** £6.25-£18.95. **Credit** AmEx, MC, V.
Map p403 R7 ⑨ **American**
Bodean's has five branches: Soho, Fulham, Clapham
and, very handy for the Tower of London (*see p101*),
here. The schtick remains unchanged at each of
them: Kansas City barbecue, with a small informal
upstairs and bigger, smarter downstairs with US
sport on TV. The food is decent, generous and very,
very meaty – bring an appetite. US sport is screened.
Other locations throughout the city.

£ Fish Central
*149-155 Central Street, EC1V 8AP (7253 4970,
www.fishcentral.co.uk). Old Street tube/rail or bus
55.* **Open** 11am-2.30pm Mon-Sat; 5-10.30pm
Mon-Thur; 5-11pm Fri, Sat. **Main courses**
£9.55-£18.95. **Credit** MC, V. **Map** p400 P3
⑩ **Fish & chips**
A large photograph on the wall shows Fish Central
as it was pre-makeover: just your everyday chippy.
Today, it's quite a lively, trendy set-up. The specials
board contains the likes of warm squid salad, but
tradition-seekers won't be disappointed. Good chips
and mushy peas, decent wines and a welcome choice
of tap beers make this a fine local.

Restaurant at St Paul's
*St Paul's Cathedral, St Paul's Churchyard, EC4M
8AD (7248 2469, www.restaurantatstpauls.co.uk).
St Paul's tube.* **Open** *Café* 9am-5pm Mon-Sat;
10am-4pm Sun. *Restaurant* noon-4.30pm daily.
Set lunch £21.50 2 courses, £25.95 3 courses.
Credit MC, V. **Map** p402 O6 ⑪ **British**
This is a really rather dull moniker for a handsome,
light-filled space in the crypt of the great cathedral,

THE BEST OF BRITISH

Dinner by Heston Blumenthal
Art and history on a plate. *See p229.*

Fish Central
Our favourite fish 'n' chip shop in London.
See above.

St John
A pioneer that still sets the standard.
See p219.

THE BEST TREAT EATS

Bistrot Bruno Loubet
Pure dining delight. *See below.*

Hawksmoor Seven Dials
Steak 'n' chips on another level. *See p221.*

Pollen Street Social
Jason Atherton delivers in his new venture. *See p224.*

with very sensuous and textural decor; it's perfect for a restaurant, a little surprising beneath a place of worship. Seasonality and provenance are the focus of the menu, and the excellent food reveals a deft pair of hands in the kitchen. We've enjoyed the likes of summery asparagus and poached Gressingham duck egg, treacle-cured salmon with watercress, Trigger Farm barnsley chop and portobello mushroom wellington.

▶ *The restaurant is closed in the evening, but there are good alternatives in Paternoster Square: try the Paternoster Chop House (Warwick Court, EC4M 7DX, 7029 9400) or Corney & Barrow wine bar.*

Sweetings
39 Queen Victoria Street, EC4N 4SA (7248 3062). Mansion House tube. **Open** 11.30am-3pm Mon-Fri. **Main courses** £15-£33. **Credit** AmEx, MC, V. **Map** p402 P6 ⓬ **Fish & seafood**
No-nonsense British food served in a quintessentially English setting. Diners at the communal tables at the rear can survey walls hung with old cartoons, photos and cricket mementos. Specials might include gull's eggs and smoked salmon pâté while the 'bill of fare' proffers traditional dishes. Sweetings opens only for lunch, takes no bookings, and is full soon after noon, so order a silver pewter mug of Guinness and enjoy the wait.

HOLBORN & CLERKENWELL

Home to pioneers of the two huge trends in contemporary London food – modern British at **St John**, the gastropub at the **Eagle** – this is where you'll find a surprising proportion of London's best eating options.

★ Bistrot Bruno Loubet
St John's Square, 86-88 Clerkenwell Road, EC1M 5RJ (7324 4455, www.bistrotbrunoloubet.com). Farringdon tube/rail. **Open** 7-10.30am, noon-2.30pm, 6-10.30pm Mon-Fri; 7.30-11am, noon-3pm, 6-10.30pm Sat; 7.30-11am, noon-3pm, 6-10pm Sun. **Main courses** £13.50-£21.50. **Credit** AmEx, MC, V. **Map** p400 O4 ⓭ **French**
Bruno Loubet has completely reinvigorated the restaurant at the Zetter hotel (*see p192*). The menu

is short, but reads like a dream: beetroot ravioli, fried breadcrumbs and sage with rocket salad; soused mackerel, watercress salad and buckwheat bread with prawn butter; quail with spinach and egg yolk raviolo; braised beef with mango and herb salad. The room is fairly plain, with quirky touches (including a waiters' station made from refashioned furniture, and retro lamps). Tables are squeezed into the slightly awkward space, but huge windows look straight into St John's Square and there's a buzz of happy diners. A restaurant with a real wow factor.

★ £ Caravan
11-13 Exmouth Market, EC1R 4QD (7833 8115, www.caravanonexmouth.co.uk). Farringdon tube/rail. **Open** 8am-10.30pm Mon-Fri; 10am-10.30pm Sat; 10am-4pm Sun. **Main courses** £4.50-£16. **Credit** AmEx, MC, V. **Map** p400 N4 ⓮ **International**
Caravan has slotted easily into the Exmouth Market dining scene. The casual vibe and industrial-funky design – rough wooden tables, white pipework, light fittings made from old-fashioned cow-milking bottles – are part of the appeal, but it's the food that's the draw. Expect a parade of unusual, international tastes: peanut butter and blue cheese wontons, salt beef fritters with green beans. Young staff zip between tables, but are never too rushed to smile.

Le Comptoir Gascon
61-63 Charterhouse Street, EC1M 6HJ (7608 0851, www.comptoirgascon.com). Farringdon

Modern Pantry.

tube/rail. **Open** noon-2.15pm, 7-9.45pm Tue, Wed; noon-2.15pm, 7-10.45pm Thur, Fri; 9am-3pm, 7-10pm Sat. **Main courses** £10-£15. **Credit** AmEx, MC, V. **Map** p400 O5 ⓯ **French**

The bistro offshoot of Club Gascon is a deservedly popular spot. A small, convivial brick-lined room that doubles as a deli, it offers the over-30s refuge on a street lined with raucous bars. Even more importantly, the food is great and nicely priced. Splendid, taste-packed mains of grilled lamb and beef onglet are excellent; sides are worth the extra, especially mighty french fries cooked in duck fat. Try the own-made ice-creams for dessert.

▶ *The smarter, similarly excellent Club Gascon (57 West Smithfield, EC1A 9DS, 7796 0600, www.clubgascon.com) is across the meat market.*

Eagle

159 Farringdon Road, EC1R 3AL (7837 1353). Farringdon tube/rail. **Open** noon-11pm Mon-Sat; noon-5pm Sun. *Meals served* 12.30-3pm, 6.30-10.30pm Mon Fri; 12.30 3.30pm, 6.30 10.30pm Sat; 12.30-3.30pm Sun. **Main courses** £5-£15. **Credit** MC, V. **Map** p400 N4 ⓰ **Gastropub**

Widely credited with being the first gastropub (it opened in 1991), the Eagle is still recognisably a pub with quality food: noisy, often crowded (you'll usually be sharing a table), with no-frills service. The room is dominated by a giant open range at which T-shirted cooks toss earthy grills in theatrical bursts of flame. The kitchen takes up one half of the long bar, with the hearty Med-influenced menu chalked up above it. A short wine list is available by glass or bottle; there are also real ales on tap.

Hix Oyster & Chop House

36-37 Greenhill Rents, off Cowcross Street, EC1M 6BN (7017 1930, www. hixoysterandchophouse.co.uk). Farringdon tube/rail. **Open** noon-3pm, 5.30-11pm Mon-Fri; 5.30-11pm Sat; noon-9pm Sun. **Main courses** £16.50-£36.50. **Credit** AmEx, MC, V. **Map** p400 O5 ⓱ **British**

Although the name tells diners what to expect, there's more to Mark Hix's place than chops and oysters: free-range Goosnargh chicken with wild garlic sauce (for two), for example. But oysters (such as Helford natives or Colchester rocks), chops and steaks feature prominently; accordingly, most diners are male. Puddings are nicely retro, but usually with an imaginative modern twist.

▶ *The superb Hix (66-70 Brewer Street, W1F 9UP, 7292 3518, www.hixsoho.co.uk) opened in Soho, with Mark's Bar (see p246) downstairs.*

★ Modern Pantry

47-48 St John's Square, EC1V 4JJ (7250 0833, www.themodernpantry.co.uk). Farringdon tube/rail. **Open** *Café* 8-11am, noon-10pm Mon; 8-11am, noon-11pm Tue-Fri; 9am-4pm, 6-11pm Sat; 10am-4pm, 6-10pm Sun. *Restaurant* noon-

3pm, 6-11pm Tue-Fri; 6-11pm Sat; 10am-4pm Sun. **Main courses** £15-£22.50. **Credit** (both) AmEx, MC, V. **Map** p400 O4 ⓭ **International**

A culinary three-parter spread across two Georgian townhouses, the Modern Pantry feels savvy and of the moment. The venue is fashionable without being annoying, and service is spot on. Both pantry (takeaway) and café (informal) are at street level; upstairs are adjoining dining rooms (still reasonably informal). Each of Anna Hansen's dishes is a complex fusion of all kinds of fine ingredients, in such multiplicity it seems they could never work together – and yet they never seem to fail. The weekend brunch is popular, so be sure to book.

★ Moro

34-36 Exmouth Market, EC1R 4QE (7833 8336, www.moro.co.uk). Farringdon tube/rail or bus 19, 38, 341. **Open** 12.30-10.30pm Mon-Sat. **Main courses** £15.50-£19. *Tapas* £3.50-£14.50. **Credit** AmEx, DC, MC, V. **Map** p400 N4 ⓭ **North African**

A meal that excites the senses is a rarity, but Sam and Sam Clark's Moro often manages to produce just that. For a restaurant with a big reputation, its decor is unpretentious, the centrepiece being a simple view of the kitchen's big wood-fired oven. You can enjoy tapas at the bar or sit down for a more leisurely wander through the Moorish menu, with inspiration from Egypt to Portugal, Spain to the Lebanon. The drinks list is a point of pride: almost all the wines, sherries and cava come from the Iberian peninsula.

▶ *Next door, Morito (no.32, EC1R 4QE, 7278 7007, closed Sun) is a fine no-booking tapas bar offshoot.*

★ St John

26 St John Street, EC1M 4AY (7251 0848, www.stjohnrestaurant.com). Barbican tube or Farringdon tube/rail. **Open** noon-3pm, 6-11pm Mon-Fri; 6-11pm Sat; 1-3pm Sun. **Main courses** £13.50-£23.80. **Credit** AmEx, DC, MC, V. **Map** p400 O5 ⓴ **British**

Chef-patron Fergus Henderson opened the daddy of new-wave British restaurants in the shell of a Smithfield smokehouse in 1995, and hasn't looked back since. The focus is on seasonal and unusual British produce, simply cooked. Although it's a world-famous restaurant, it's completely unstuffy: staff are approachable as well as highly competent and the French wine list won't frighten anyone. While prices aren't low, they're not excessive for the quality; if you are a bit strapped for cash, having a snack in the airy bar is even cheaper.

▶ *St John has a hotel too; see p198.*

BLOOMSBURY & FITZROVIA

Just next door to Benito's Hat, classy **Salt Yard** (*see p223* **Dehesa**) provides superb Spanish-Italian tapas.

£ Benito's Hat

56 Goodge Street, W1T 4NB (7637 3732, www.benitos-hat.com). Goodge Street tube. **Open** 11.30am-10pm Mon-Wed, Sun; 11.30am-11pm Thur-Sat. **Main courses** £5.50-£6.40. **Credit** MC, V. **Map** p396 J5 **㉑ Mexican**

Tex-Mex eateries are currently ten a peso in London, but the Benito's Hat production line serves some of the best burritos in town. Try the slow-cooked pork, wrapped in a soft, floury tortilla along with fiery salsa brava (made several times daily) and black beans authentically flavoured with avocado leaves. If you're having a drink, the margaritas are suitably merciless. The counter, facing the entrance, serves lots of takeaways, but there are tables on the pavement, window perches and proper seating in the rear. **Other locations** 19 New Row, Covent Garden, WC2N 4LA (7240 5815); 12 Great Castle Street, Fitzrovia, W1W 8LR (7636 6560).

Camino

3 Varnishers Yard, Regents Quarter, N1 9FD (7841 7331, www.camino.uk.com). King's Cross tube/rail. **Open** *Restaurant* 8-11.30am, noon-3pm, 6.30-11pm Mon-Fri; 8-11.30am, noon-4pm, 6-11pm Sat; 8-11.30am, noon-4pm Sun. *Bar* noon-4pm, 4.30-11pm Mon-Fri; noon-4pm, 4.30-11pm Sat, Sun. **Main courses** £2.75-£39.50. **Credit** AmEx, MC, V. **Map** p397 L3 **㉒ Tapas**

Camino's cavernous premises contain sleek bar and restaurant areas, and, outside, a courtyard where drinkers sip iced Cruzcampo and nibble plump, golden-crumbed croquetas. The tapas list, dotted with regional specialities, can be eaten anywhere, but the full menu of classic Iberian fare with some modern European forays has to be eaten in the restaurant, where the self-consciously modern, stripped-down aesthetic is softened by muted candlelight and the hum of conversation.

▶ *Camino's Bar Pepito just across the courtyard serves a superb selection of sherries.*

★ Giaconda Dining Room

9 Denmark Street, WC2H 8LS (7240 3334, www.giacondadining.com). Tottenham Court Road tube. **Open** noon-2.15pm, 6-9.15pm Tue-Fri; 6-9.15pm Sat. **Main courses** £12-£14. **Cover** £1.50. **Credit** AmEx, MC, V. **Map** p416 X2 **㉓ Modern European**

Giaconda is a thoroughly likeable restaurant. The decor is nothing special and the room is a bit cramped, but the food served is what most people want to eat most of the time: the Australian owners describe it as French-ish with a bit of Spain and Italy, but there are also big-flavoured grills, fish of the day and any number of intriguing assemblages (chorizo, chicken liver, trotters and tripe, for instance).

Hakkasan

8 Hanway Place, W1T 1HD (7927 7000, www.hakkasan.com). Tottenham Court Road tube. **Open** *Restaurant* noon-3pm, 6-11pm Mon-Wed; noon-3pm, 6pm-midnight Thur, Fri; noon-4pm, 6pm-midnight Sat; noon-4pm, 6-11pm Sun. *Bar* noon-12.30am Mon-Wed; noon-1.30am Thur-Sat; noon-midnight Sun. **Main courses** £9.50-£58. *Dim sum* £3-£20. **Credit** AmEx, MC, V. **Map** p416 W1 **㉔ Chinese**

Creator Alan Yau sold this esteemed restaurant to an Abu Dhabi-based company a few years back, but the changes it's made are minimal. Why mess with brilliance? It's hard not to be enamoured by the sultry enclave of chinoiserie that is this underground restaurant, where sleek staff glide out of the shadows carrying all manner of elegantly presented modern Chinese fare. To dine on dim sum here is a pleasure, the sweet scallop *siu mai* with glistening flying-fish roe a highlight. **Other locations** 17 Bruton Street, Mayfair, W1J 6QB (7907 1888).

£ Lantana

13 Charlotte Place, W1T 1SN (7637 3347, www.lantanacafe.co.uk). Goodge Street tube. **Open** 8am-6pm Mon, Tue; 8am-10.30pm Wed-Fri; 9am-5pm Sat, Sun. **Main courses** £5-£12.50. **Credit** MC, V. **Map** p396 J5 **㉕ Café**

This cheerful but busy Aussie café is open for breakfast through to lunch (dinner at the end of the week). Sweetcorn fritters with crispy bacon or smoked salmon with lime aïoli is one highlight, the delicious banana bread another. The combination of Monmouth beans and a La Marzocco espresso machine ensures flawless coffee every time.

Paramount

32nd floor, Centre Point, 101-103 New Oxford Street, WC1A 1DD (7420 2900, www.paramount.uk.net). Tottenham Court Road tube. **Open** 8-10.30am, noon-3pm, 6-11pm Mon-Fri; 11.30am-3pm, 6-11pm Sat; noon-3pm Sun. **Main courses** £14.50-£25.50. **Credit** AmEx, MC, V. **Map** p416 X1 **㉖ Modern European**

A private members' club opened on the 32nd floor of the landmark Centre Point building – almost exactly a month after the 2008 recession began in earnest. So, in 2010, owners Pierre and Kathleen Condou hired an excellent chef and opened it as a smart restaurant. The handsome Tom Dixon-designed interior is upstaged by the superb view, but Colin Layfield's menu manages to hold its own, with carefully constructed dishes that appeal to the eye and the tongue. The attached bar is open only to members or diners.

▶ *If dinner prices are too vertiginous, check out the surprisingly reasonable breakfast menu.*

COVENT GARDEN

£ Abeno Too

17-18 Great Newport Street, WC2H 7JE (7379 1160, www.abeno.co.uk). Leicester Square tube.

Open noon-11pm Mon-Sat; noon-10.30pm Sun.
Main courses £9-£24. **Credit** MC, V. **Map**
p416 X3 **㉗** Japanese
The tables and counter at Abeno Too are all fitted
with hot plates for cooking the *okonomiyaki* (pancakes with nuggets of vegetables, seafood, pork and
other titbits added to a disc of noodles) that are the
speciality of this small chain. The lovely staff cook
the pancakes to order, right in front of you: hearty,
comforting stuff it is too. If *okonomiyaki* doesn't suit
your mood, choose from *katsu* curries, sashimi, salads, rice and noodle dishes and *teppanyaki*.
Other locations 47 Museum Street, Bloomsbury,
WC1A 1LY (7405 3211).

£ Dishoom
*12 Upper St Martin's Lane, WC2H 9FB (7420
9320, www.dishoom.com). Covent Garden or
Leicester Square tube.* **Open** 8am-11pm Mon-Fri;
10am-11pm Sat; 10am-10pm Sun. **Main courses**
£1.70-£10.50. **Credit** AmEx, MC, V. **Map** p416 X3
㉘ Pan-Indian
Dishoom has got the look of a Mumbai 'Irani' café
(the cheap, cosmopolitan eateries that were set up
by Persian immigrants in the 1900s) spot on. Solid
oak panels, antique mirrors and ceiling fans say
'retro grandeur'; a web of black cables for the pendant lights says 'contemporary and fun'. A fascinating display of old magazine covers, nostalgic
adverts and fading photos of Indian families adorns
the walls. Parts of the menu are familiar street
snacks (a terrific *pau bhaji*), but chocolate fondant,
classy cocktails and intriguing lassi flavours move
things more upmarket.

£ Food for Thought
*31 Neal Street, WC2H 9PR (7836 9072). Covent
Garden tube.* **Open** noon-8.30pm Mon-Sat; noon-
5pm Sun. **Main courses** £4.90-£8. **No credit
cards**. **Map** p416 Y2 **㉙** Vegetarian café
Taking the stairs to this old basement café, where
sharing tables is the norm, is like making a steady
descent to the 1970s. Of its type, the food is excellent,
fresh and with big, well-considered flavours. Prices
are persuasive, but service can be sloppy.

THE BEST VALUE

Arbutus
Set menus offer couture cooking at
diffusion prices. *See p222.*

Great Queen Street
Great main courses; modestly priced
accoutrements. *See p221.*

Jamie's Italian
Special occasion atmosphere, everyday
prices. *See p235.*

★ Great Queen Street
*32 Great Queen Street, WC2B 5AA (7242 0622).
Covent Garden or Holborn tube.* **Open** *Restaurant*
noon-2.30pm, 6-10.30pm Mon-Sat; noon-3pm Sun.
Bar 5-11.30pm Tue-Sat. **Main courses** £10.80-
£22. **Credit** MC, V. **Map** p416 Z2 **㉚** British
The staff at this casual eaterie are a helpful young
bunch. The ex-pub premises have been tarted up,
but not too much, and the food is direct and robust;
expect the likes of hare with noodles and giant pies
to share. Other plus points: desserts are taken seriously, and wines come in glass, carafe and bottle
sizes. In the basement, drinks and snacks are served.
As you'd expect, booking is essential – but later
drop-ins can sometimes be accommodated.

★ Hawksmoor Seven Dials
*11 Langley Street, WC2H 9JJ (7856 2154,
www.thehawksmoor.co.uk). Covent Garden tube.*
Open noon-3.30pm, 5.30-10.30pm Mon-Sat; noon-
4.30pm Sun. **Main courses** £15-£30. **Credit**
AmEx, MC, V. **Map** p416 Y3 **㉛** Steakhouse
Hawksmoor is a carnivore's paradise, a homage to
British beef. But it's not just a steakhouse. Starters
focus on British fish and it also has a gorgeous bar
serving cocktails of high pedigree and reasonable
cost. The emphasis is very much on carefully chosen
ingredients, served simply, so the meat all comes
from excellent, Yorkshire-based butcher Ginger Pig.
The clued-up staff are keen to advise on the various
cuts of meat and the lengthy wine list. The worthy
original is based in Spitalfields (157 Commercial
Street, E1 6BJ, 7247 7392, www.thehawksmoor.
co.uk), and a new branch has opened in the City. The
buzz just won't go away.
▶ *Hawksmoor Seven Dials won the award for best
new restaurant in Time Out's Eating & Drinking
Awards 2011.*

Icecreamists
*Market Building, Covent Garden Market, WC2E
8RF (8616 0721, www.theicecreamists.com).
Covent Garden tube.* **Open** noon-10.30pm daily.
Credit MC, V. **Map** p416 Y3 **㉜** Ice-cream
Although the black and electric-pink decor, thumping music and neon signage is more sex shop than
ice-cream parlour, the Icecreamists isn't all garish
style over substance. The gimmick-laden gelatos are
actually pretty good, with the sea salt lacing 'Sex,
Drugs & Choc 'n' Roll' giving the creamy milk chocolate a superb lift.

£ Rock & Sole Plaice
*47 Endell Street, WC2H 9AJ (7836 3785). Covent
Garden tube.* **Open** 11.30am-10.30pm Mon-Sat;
noon-9.30pm Sun. **Main courses** £9-£12. **Credit**
MC, V. **Map** p416 Y2 **㉝** Fish & chips
Exactly when the Rock & Sole Plaice (or its predecessor) started battering fish is in dispute; some say
1871, others maintain that it opened just after World
War II. Either way, this small corner chippy near

CONSUME

CONSUME

Drury Lane continues to thrive. West End theatre posters line the interior, but, on warmer days, you'll do best to try to squeeze on to one of the inevitably busy roadside tables.

£ Scoop

40 Shorts Gardens, WC2H 9AB (7240 7086, www.scoopgelato.com). Covent Garden tube. **Open** noon-10.30pm daily. Times may vary, phone to check. **Ice-cream** £2.50-£3/scoop. **Credit** AmEx, MC, V. **Map** p416 Y2 ㉔ **Ice-cream**
The peak-time queues are testament to the quality of the ice-creams, even the dairy-free health versions, at this Italian artisan's shop. Flavours include ricotta and fig, and a very superior Piedmont hazelnut type. **Other locations** 53 Brewer Street, Soho, W1F 9UJ (7494 3082).

★ J Sheekey

28-34 St Martin's Court, Leicester Square, WC2N 4AL (7240 2565, www.j-sheekey.co.uk). Leicester Square tube. **Open** noon-3pm, 5.30pm-midnight Mon-Sat; noon-3.30pm, 6-11pm Sun. **Main courses** £13.50-£39.50. **Credit** AmEx, DC, MC, V. **Map** p416 X4 ㉟ **Fish & seafood**
Unlike many of London's period-piece restaurants (which this certainly is, having been chartered in the mid 19th century), Sheekey's buzzes with fashionable folk and famous faces. And it seldom turns out a dud from a menu that runs from sparklingly simple seafood platters to dishes that are interesting without being elaborate. You'll pay for the privilege of dining here, and booking ahead is essential, but the rewards are worth both expense and effort.
▶ *Next door, the J Sheekey Oyster Bar (nos.33-34, WC2N 4AL) serves a similar menu to customers sitting casually at the counter, and with an expanded choice of oysters.*

£ Wahaca

66 Chandos Place, WC2N 4HG (7240 1883, www.wahaca.co.uk). Covent Garden or Leicester Square tube. **Open** noon-11pm Mon-Sat; noon-10.30pm Sun. **Main courses** £6-£10. **Credit** AmEx, MC, V. **Map** p416 Y4 ㊱ **Mexican**
Wahaca has many points in its favour: a central location, colourful and casually fashionable decor, a trendy Mexican menu and pretty comfortable prices. It's run by celebrity chef of sorts: Thomasina Miers, a former winner of BBC's *MasterChef*, appears frequently on TV and in the recipe press. The kitchen's aim is to marry locally sourced ingredients with Mexican-inspired recipes: a laudable aim, but some substitutions are better than others.
Other locations throughout the city.

SOHO & CHINATOWN

Chinatown stalwarts such as **Mr Kong** (21 Lisle Street, 7437 7341) and **Wong Kei** (41-43 Wardour Street, 7437 8408) still ply their reliable Anglo-Cantonese trade, but there's more gastronomic excitement offered by the newer likes of **Barshu** (*see below*) or, on Ganton Street a little to the west, **Cha Cha Moon** (*see p223*).

★ Arbutus

63-64 Frith Street, W1D 3JW (7734 4545, www.arbutusrestaurant.co.uk). Tottenham Court Road tube. **Open** noon-2.30pm, 5-11pm Mon-Thur; noon-2.30pm, 5-11.30pm Fri, Sat; noon-3pm, 5.30-10.30pm Sun. **Main courses** £14-£19.95. **Credit** AmEx, MC, V. **Map** p416 W2 ㊲ **Modern European**
Providing very fine cooking at very fair prices isn't an easy trick, but Anthony Demetre makes it look easy. Although it's not cheap to eat à la carte, the set lunch (three courses £16.95) and 'pre-theatre' dinner (three courses £18.95) are famously good value. The restaurant pioneered 250ml carafes for sampling the wines from the well-edited list; try a carafe of macabeo with a juicy, herby mullet with gnocchi, spinach and clams.
▶ *Sister restaurant to Arbutus, Wild Honey (12 St George Street, W1S 2FB, 7758 9160, www.wildhoneyrestaurant.co.uk), is great value for lunch.*

Barshu

28 Frith Street, W1D 5LF (7287 6688, www.barshu.co.uk). Leicester Square or Tottenham Court Road tube. **Open** noon-11pm Mon-Thur, Sun; noon-11.30pm Fri, Sat. **Main courses** £8.90-£28.90. **Credit** AmEx, MC, V. **Map** p416 W3 ㊳ **Chinese**
Since opening in 2006, Barshu has done much to popularise Sichuan cuisine in London. Its owners now run two other restaurants nearby, but the cooking continues to thrill and it is still an exceedingly charming venue, its decor modelled on that of an old Beijing teahouse. A dive into the large menu with its helpful illustrations reveals a number of 'blood and guts' dishes: the likes of crunchy ribbons of jellyfish with a dark vinegar sauce and sesame oil.
▶ *For more unusual (and cheap) Chinese food in Soho, try Barshu's siblings Ba Shan (24 Romilly Street, W1D 5AH, 7287 3266) and Baozi Inn (25 Newport Court, WC2H 7JS, 7287 6877).*

INSIDE TRACK CHINATOWN

For atmosphere, drop in for a 'bubble tea' (sweet, icy, full of balls of jelly and slurped up with a straw) at late-night fave **HK Diner** (22 Wardour Street, 7434 9544). If you need to eat especially late, Cantonese old-stager the **New Mayflower** (68-70 Shaftesbury Avenue, 7734 9207) is open nightly until 4am.

Dehesa.

Bocca di Lupo

12 Archer Street, W1D 7BB (7734 2223,
www.boccadilupo.com). Piccadilly Circus tube.
Open 12.30-3pm, 5.30-11pm Mon-Sat; noon-4pm
Sun. **Main courses** £7-£25. **Credit** AmEx, MC,
V. **Map** p416 W3 **39 Italian**
This busy, informal Italian restaurant has a lively
open kitchen and tapas-style menu of regional specialities. Select one small dish from several different
categories on the menu (raw and cured, fried, pastas
and risottos, soups and stews, roasts, and so on) and
you should enjoy a fairly balanced meal; for those
who prefer not to share, large portions of each dish
are also offered.
▶ *The same team runs the fine gelateria*
Gelupo, down the road at no.7 (7287 5555,
www.gelupo.com).

£ Cha Cha Moon

15-21 Ganton Street, W1F 9BN (7297 9800,
www.chachamoon.com). Oxford Circus tube. **Open**
11.30am-11pm Mon-Thur; 11.30am-11.30pm Fri,
Sat; 11.30am-10.30pm Sun. **Main courses** £7-£8.
Credit AmEx, MC, V. **Map** p416 U3 **40 Chinese**
Like Wagamama before it, Alan Yau's Cha Cha
Moon offers fast food of mixed Asian inspiration at
low prices, served on long cafeteria-style tables in a
sleek room. The main focus is on excellent noodle
dishes, hailing from Hong Kong, Shanghai and elsewhere in China, clocking in at a bit over £6 each.

★ Dehesa

25 Ganton Street, W1F 9BP (7494 4170). Oxford
Circus tube. **Open** noon-11pm Mon-Sat; noon-5pm
Sun. **Tapas** £3.75-£10.50. **Credit** AmEx, MC, V.
Map p416 U3 **41 Spanish/Italian tapas**
This informal yet sophisticated spot now takes
bookings, which makes it easier to enjoy its Spanish-
Italian tapas. The black-footed Ibérico pig (the place
is named after its woodland home) appears in nutty-
flavoured ham and other charcuterie, but local sourc-
ing comes to the fore in tapas such as confit of Old
Spot pork belly with cannellini beans. Staff are
bright, well informed and efficient.
▶ *North of Oxford Street in Fitzrovia, Salt Yard*
is another excellent choice for tapas (54 Goodge
Street, W1T 4NA, 7637 0657).

★ £ Hummus Bros

88 Wardour Street, W1F 0TH (7734 1311,
www.hbros.co.uk). Oxford Circus or Tottenham
Court Road tube. **Open** noon-10pm Mon-Wed,
Sun; noon-11pm Thur-Sat. **Main courses** £6.65-
£8.45. **Credit** AmEx, MC, V. **Map** p416 W3
42 Café
The simple and hugely successful formula at this
café-takeaway is to serve houmous as a base for a
selection of toppings, which you scoop up with excellent, pillowy pitta bread that's toasted while you wait.
That's it. There's are two or three sweet things for
pudding, plus some hot and cold drinks, but the key
attraction is quick, tasty, nutritious, filling and great-
value food, whether you eat in or take away.
Other locations 37-63 Southampton Row,
Bloomsbury, WC1B 4DA (7404 7079); 128
Cheapside, the City, EC2V 6BT (7726 8011).

£ Maison Bertaux

28 Greek Street, W1D 5DQ (7437 6007).
Leicester Square tube. **Open** 9am-10pm Mon-
Sat; 9am-8pm Sun. **Main courses** £3.60-£4.75.
No credit cards. Map p416 X3 **43 Café**
Oozing arty, bohemian charm, this café dates back
to 1871 when Soho was London's little piece of the
Continent. Battered old bentwood tables and chairs
add to the feeling of being in a pâtisserie in rural

France, albeit one with a bit of additional camp Soho flamboyance. The provisions (cream cakes, greasy pastries, pots of tea) are really beside the point.

★ Manchurian Legends

12 Macclesfield Street, W1D 5BP (7437 8785). Leicester Square or Piccadilly Circus tube. **Open** noon-11pm daily. **Main courses** £7.50-£12.80. **Credit** MC, V. **Map** p416 W3 ㉔ **Chinese**

Manchurian Legends specialises in food from, er, Manchuria. Expect rich, warming, slow-cooked dishes, and plenty of pork belly. Some dishes are a major departure from standard Chinatown fare, such as the sweet, sticky sauce covering a crispy, fatty lamb skewer sprinkled with cumin seeds and dried chilli. Service is friendly and geared up for those unfamiliar with the cuisine, with cutlery offered instead of chopsticks and doggy bags for those who over-order.
▶ *Manchurian Legends won the award for best new cheap restaurant in Time Out's Eating & Drinking Awards 2011.*

★ Pollen Street Social

8 Pollen Street, W1S 1NQ (7290 7600, www.pollenstreetsocial.com).Oxford Circus tube. **Open** noon-midnight Mon-Sat. **Main courses** £21-£24.50. **Credit** AmEx, MC, V. **Map** p416 U2 ㊺ **Modern European**

Jason Atherton, formerly of Maze, has certainly put Pollen Street on the map. The site comprises lounge bar and restaurant areas, a dessert bar, a private dining room, showcase kitchen, glass-walled wine cellar and meat-ageing room. Overall, PSS is a must-visit for fans of fine dining, though we've yet to decide if the take-home gift is charming or smarmy.

★ £ Princi

135 Wardour Street, W1F 0UF (7478 8888, www.princi.co.uk). Leicester Square or Tottenham Court Road tube. **Open** 7am-midnight Mon-Sat; 8.30am-10pm Sun. **Main courses** £5-£12. **Credit** AmEx, MC, V. **Map** p416 W3 ㊻ **Bakery-café**

Chef's Table

Where London's best cooks go to eat.

Spuntino.

John Torode is well known in Britain for his work on *MasterChef*, and also runs the Luxe (*see p236*). 'My favourite restaurant is the River Café (*see p240*),' he says. 'I think it's an extraordinary institution. The food changes depending on what's in season: whenever you walk in the door, you know you're going to eat very good food.' And after a day in the kitchen, Torode says he's taken by the tapas approach to dining. 'When you work in the sort of environment we do, you don't want heavy meals. You want to go somewhere and eat something very tasty, but not very much of it. I love Bocca di Lupo (*see p223*). The sort of place you can go late at night, get a lovely glass of wine – perfect. I'm certainly not going out for seven-course degustation menus.'

Thomasina Miers, executive chef and co-founder of the Wahaca (*see p222*) chain of restaurants and writer on Mexican cooking, recommends the welsh rarebit at the Soho Hix (*see p219*), and in keeping with the 'grazing and sharing' trend, a visit to nearby Spuntino (*see p225*) for deep-fried olives and sliders. 'It only has 26 covers, and serves delicious New York-style food. It's perfect for an early supper or late lunch: the atmosphere is great and so are the cocktails. I also love the laid-back cooking at Hereford Road (*see p232*), the luxury of the River Café (*see p240*) and the great, seasonal food at Corrigan's (*see p227*).'

CONSUME

Asian-cuisine supremo Alan Yau teamed up with a prestigious Italian bakery chain for this popular venture. The premises consist of a huge L-shaped granite counter and communal seating, a stylish variation on his much-copied Wagamama noodle bar concept. As well as cakes, tiramisu and pastries, there's a vast range of savoury dishes. The big slices of pizza have a springy base, the margherita variety pungent with fresh thyme; caprese salad comes with creamy balls of buffalo mozzarella and big slices of beef tomato. Princi can get hectic, but it's a solid option for inexpensive snacks.

Spuntino

61 Rupert Street, W1D 7PW (no phone, www.spuntino.co.uk). Piccadilly Circus tube. **Open** 11am-midnight Mon-Sat; noon-11pm Sun. **Main courses** £5.50-£10. **Credit** AmEx, MC, V. **Map** p416 W3 ④ **Italian**

You can spot this speakeasy-like eaterie by the queue snaking out the door – the signage certainly

isn't clear. The narrow, dimly lit space is artfully contrived to look semi-derelict, and the loud retro rock soundtrack is reminiscent of college radio stations, but the overall effect is very pleasant. Food is Italian with an American flavour and reasonably good value. Be prepared to arrive early (before 7pm) or you'll have to join the queue.

▶ *Owner Russell Norman also runs the excellent Da Polpo in Covent Garden (6 Maiden Lane, WC2E 7NW, 7836 8448, www.dapolpo.co.uk).*

Yauatcha

15 Broadwick Street, W1F 0DL (7494 8888). Piccadilly Circus or Tottenham Court Road tube. **Open** noon-11.45pm Mon-Sat; noon-10.30pm Sun. **Dim sum** £4-£15. **Credit** AmEx, MC, V. **Map** p416 V2 ④ **Dim sum/tearoom**

Serving dim sum day and night over two floors, Yauatcha happily cocks a snook at traditionalists who believe the treats to 'touch the heart' (the meaning of *dim sum*) should never be served past 5pm.

It's the lucky Londoner who doesn't have to travel far to a favourite restaurant, and Marcus Wareing, chef patron of the Gilbert Scott in the St Pancras Hotel, is among them. 'I love Chez Bruce (2 Bellevue Road, Wandsworth, SW17 7EG, 8672 0114, www.chezbruce.com) – I can walk there, it's got a Michelin star but is very relaxed, and the quality of food is always high.'

Yotam Ottolenghi's London restaurant/takeaways are acclaimed for their sleek design and fresh, inventive, Mediterranean-influenced cooking, and he's recently opened NOPI (21 Warwick Street, W1B 5NE, 7494 9584, www.nopi-restaurant.com) in Soho. But he's another chef who prefers the down-to-earth over the starry when eating out. 'One place I really like going to is Mangal Ocakbasi (*see p233* **Inside Track**), a Turkish place in Dalston. I love the grilled lamb chops and the mixed salad with tomato and cucumber.'

Bocca di Lupo.

Much is made of the unusually good (and lengthy) tea list, and the choice of dim sum dishes is extended with congee, noodles and some intriguing stir-fries. The place's popularity shows no sign of easing.

OXFORD STREET & MARYLEBONE

L'Autre Pied
5-7 Blandford Street, W1U 3DB (7486 9696, www.lautrepied.co.uk). Baker Street tube. **Open** noon-2.30pm, 6-10.30pm Mon-Sat; noon-3.30pm. **Main courses** £21.50-£27.95. **Credit** AmEx, MC, V. **Map** p396 G5 ❹ **Modern European**
For a far less eye-watering outlay than a meal at older sibling Pied à Terre, L'Autre Pied offers nuanced cooking in handsome rooms. With a light touch and subtle use of herbs, chef Marcus Eaves doesn't stint on the dairy, as demonstrated by an intensely creamy mushroom and leek risotto. Despite the trappings of somewhere that takes food very seriously, L'Autre Pied is accessible and relaxing. The kitchen doesn't put a foot wrong.

★ £ Busaba Eathai
8-13 Bird Street, W1U 1BU (7518 8080, http://busaba.com). Bond Street tube. **Open** noon-11pm Mon-Thur; noon-11.30pm Fri, Sat; noon-10pm Sun. **Main courses** £6.20-£10.90. **Credit** AmEx, MC, V. **Map** p396 G6 ❺ **Thai**
All the branches of this handsome Thai fast food canteen are excellent and busy, but this one is superbly located for Oxford Street shoppers. The interior combines shared tables and bench seats with a touch of dark-toned oriental mystique, and the dishes are always intriguing.
Other locations throughout the city.

Fairuz
3 Blandford Street, W1U 3DA (7486 8108, www.fairuz.uk.com). Baker Street or Bond Street tube. **Open** noon-11.30pm Mon-Sat; noon-11pm Sun. **Main courses** £12-£19.95. *Set meze* £19.95. *Cover* £1.50. **Credit** AmEx, MC, V. **Map** p396 G5 ❺ **Middle Eastern**
The combination of Lebanese food, neighbourhood-taverna surroundings and West End location has proved enduringly popular for this long-standing Marylebone favourite. Its collection of meze – smooth houmous, zingy *fuul moukala* (broad beans with olive oil, lemon and coriander), tabouleh, spinach *fatayer* – is brilliantly executed.

£ La Fromagerie
2-6 Moxon Street, W1U 4EW (7935 0341, www.lafromagerie.co.uk). Baker Street or Bond Street tube. **Open** 8am-7.30pm Mon-Fri; 9am-7pm Sat; 10am-6pm Sun. **Main courses** £6-£15. **Credit** AmEx, MC, V. **Map** p396 G5 ❺ **Café**
There aren't many cafés in London where Herefordshire snails cooked in garlic butter make

the menu, but Patricia Michelson's high-end deli-café has always ploughed its own, very stylish, culinary furrow, and its communal tables are often packed with devotees. The basic menu, which includes a classy ploughman's lunch, is supplemented by a separate breakfast offer (own-made baked beans, granola with posh French yoghurt) and a 'kitchen menu' from 12.30pm.
Other locations 30 Highbury Park, Highbury, N5 2AA (7359 7440).

£ Golden Hind
73 Marylebone Lane, W1U 2PN (7486 3644). Bond Street tube. **Open** noon-3pm, 6-10pm Mon-Fri; 6-10pm Sat. **Main courses** £6.30-£10.50. **Credit** AmEx, MC, V. **Map** p396 G5 ❻ **Fish & chips**
The Golden Hind's walls are lined with old black and white photos and a blackboard listing the names of owners back as far as 1914. The current Hellenic ownership is reflected in a menu that places mixed Greek pickles and deep-fried feta alongside standard starters such as fish cakes. Try for a seat on the ground floor so you can gawp at the stunning art deco fryer (sadly, no longer used). Staff are jovial and service is quick.

PICCADILLY CIRCUS & MAYFAIR

Lunch at **Wild Honey** (*see p222* **Arbutus**), the sister establishment to Anthony Demetre's Arbutus restaurant, is a great option for an affordable treat.

★ Bentley's Oyster Bar & Grill
11-15 Swallow Street, W1B 4DG (7734 4756, www.bentleysoysterbarandgrill.co.uk). Piccadilly Circus tube. **Open** *Oyster Bar* 7.30-10.30am, noon-11pm Mon-Fri; noon-11pm Sat; noon-9.30pm Sun.

Restaurant noon-2.30pm, 5.30-10.30pm Mon-Fri; 5.30-10.30pm Sat. **Main courses** *Oyster Bar* £8.75-£36. *Restaurant* £18.95-£38. **Credit** AmEx, MC, V. **Map** p416 V4 ⬛ **Fish & seafood**
There's something timeless about Richard Corrigan's restoration of this classic oyster house. World War I was raging when Bentley's first opened, but the suited gents who flock here today enjoy their seafood with the same gusto as their great-grandfathers before them. While the first-floor dining rooms are more sedate and well mannered, the downstairs oyster bar is where the action is.
▶ *Corrigan also runs the estimable Corrigan's Mayfair (28 Upper Grosvenor Street, W1K 7EH, 7499 9943).*

Chisou
4 Princes Street, W1B 2LE (7629 3931, www.chisou.co.uk). Oxford Circus tube. **Open** noon-2.30pm, 6-10.15pm Mon-Sat. **Main courses** £12-£23.50. **Credit** AmEx, MC, V. **Map** p416 T2 ⬛ **Japanese**
Chisou looks quiet enough from the outside; inside, though, this modestly fashionable restaurant hums with purposeful activity. Friendly waitresses keep things moving at the blond-wood tables, while to the rear is a fun sushi bar. Salted belly pork, and the pure *ume cha* (rice in a light hot broth with pickled plum) are highlights, and there's a serious saké and shochu list. Next door is Chisou's excellent noodle and *donburi* bar.

★ Hibiscus
29 Maddox Street, W1S 2PA (7629 2999, www.hibiscusrestaurant.co.uk). Oxford Circus tube. **Open** noon-2.30pm, 6.30-10pm Mon-Thur; noon-2.30pm, 6-10pm Fri, Sat. **Set meals** £33.50-£80 3 courses; £100 tasting menu. **Credit** AmEx, MC, V. **Map** p416 U3 ⬛ **Haute cuisine**
Tables in this simple Mayfair dining room are arranged around a large central workstation topped with an extravagant floral display. The crowd is well heeled and rather businesslike, even when their intentions are social. Many stick with the set lunch (as usual, far cheaper than the equivalent dinner menu), on which you might find the moussaka of Elwy Valley mutton with feta and anchovy jus that has become something of a signature dish for Hibiscus. For dessert, try clafoutis with almonds and an unusually rich pistachio ice-cream.

Hix at the Albemarle
Brown's, 33-34 Albemarle Street, W1S 4BP (7493 6020, www.thealbemarlerestaurant.com). Green Park tube. **Open** noon-3pm, 5.30-11pm Mon-Sat, 12.30-4pm, 7-10.30pm Sun. **Main courses** £14.50-£32.50. **Credit** AmEx, DC, MC, V. **Map** p416 U4 ⬛ **British**
The modern art-strewn dining room at Brown's (*see p202*) is much more enticing than most hotel restaurants. A blend of period and modern furnishings,

comfortable chairs and charming staff makes for a relaxed and enjoyable meal – even before you get to the excitement of the menu. Seasonal British ingredients are used throughout. Vegetarians get their own menu, and there's a great-value set meal – on Sunday, this includes the roast.

Momo
25 Heddon Street, W1B 4BH (7434 4040, www.momoresto.com). Piccadilly Circus tube. **Open** noon-5.30pm, 6.30pm-midnight Mon-Sat; 6.30-midnight Sun. **Main courses** £17-£28. **Credit** AmEx, DC, MC, V. **Map** p416 U3 ⬛ **North African**
The ornate Momo, opened in 1997, made Algerian-born restaurateur Mourad Mazouz's reputation. Carved screens, tasselled cushions, brass lanterns and low tables transport diners to Morocco's most fashionable imaginary club. Tables are tightly packed, adding to a lively mood; come during the day for a more serene vibe. The alfresco terrace evokes riad-cool and offers shisha pipes; downstairs is Mô Café (mint tea, wraps, meze) and Bazaar (books, CDs, furniture), plus the luxurious Kemia bar. The menu ranges from harira and chicken tagine with preserved lemons and olives, mint and potatoes with quince marmalade to, well, rump of lamb with jerusalem artichoke purée, garlic and rosemary jus.

Parlour
1st floor, Fortnum & Mason, 181 Piccadilly, W1A 1ER (7734 8040, www.fortnumandmason.co.uk). Green Park or Piccadilly Circus tube. **Open** 10am-8pm Mon-Sat; noon-5.30pm Sun. **Ice-cream** £8-£15. **Credit** AmEx, MC, V. **Map** p416 V5 ⬛ **Ice-cream**
David Collins's quirky design for this café is all ice-cream and chocolate tones, with retro kitchenette seating. It's a great place to meet friends, though prices are high. The best option is an ice-cream 'flight': you'll get three scoops of your choice, served with wonderfully silky Amedei dark- or milk-chocolate sauce for £10.

Sketch: The Parlour
9 Conduit Street, W1S 2XJ (0870 777 4488, www.sketch.uk.com). Oxford Circus tube. **Open** 10am-9pm Mon-Sat. *Tea served* 1-6.30pm Mon-Sat. **Main courses** £4-£8.50. *Set tea* £10.50-£27. **Credit** AmEx, MC, V. **Map** p416 U3 ⬛ **Café**
Of the three parts of Pierre Gagnaire's legendarily expensive Sketch, which also includes destination dining at the Gallery and the Lecture Room's haute-beyond-haute cuisine, Parlour appeals the most for its tongue-in-cheek sexiness. Saucy nudes illustrate the chairs, and the chandelier appears to be covered with pairs of red fishnet tights. Gagnaire's menu includes simple hearty dishes and quirky high-concept creations, such as the club sandwich with red and green bread and a layer of stencilled jelly on top; it's mostly air-dried ham with tiny flecks of grapefruit.

£ Tibits
12-14 Heddon Street, W1B 4DA (7758 4110,
www.tibits.co.uk/e). Oxford Circus tube. **Open**
9am-midnight Mon-Sat; 11.30am-10.30pm Sun.
Buffet £2-£2.20/100g. **Credit** MC, V. **Map** p416
U3 ③ **Vegetarian café**
Designers Guild fabrics in raspberry and lime contrast with a black ceiling and smart wicker chairs
at this modern take on the buffet restaurant. Part of
a small Swiss chain, Tibits may be vegetarian but
it's not puritanical. Fill your plate from the salads
and hot dishes in the central 'boat' and take it to the
counter for weighing. There are organic Freedom
lagers on tap, plus a handful of wines, and coffees.

★ Wolseley
160 Piccadilly, W1J 9EB (7499 6996,
www.thewolseley.com). Green Park tube. **Open**
7am-midnight Mon-Fri; 8am-midnight Sat, Sun.
Tea served 3-6.30pm Mon-Fri; 3.30-5.30pm Sat;
3.30-6.30pm Sun. **Main courses** £6.75-£28.75.
Set tea £9.75-£21. *Cover* £2. **Credit** AmEx, DC,
MC, V. **Map** p416 U5 ② **Brasserie**
An interpretation of the grand cafés of Europe, the
Wolseley serves breakfast, lunch, tea and dinner to
a smart set of Londoners and visitors in its opulent
dining room. Huge bronze doors open up to an art
deco dining room, while an entrance table displays
a selection of the day's choices. No one comes here
just for the food, but breakfast at the Wolseley is a
failsafe treat. Attention to detail suggests the place
is under no threat of losing its iconic status.

WESTMINSTER & ST JAMES'S

Cinnamon Club
Old Westminster Library, 30-32 Great
Smith Street, SW1P 3BU (7222 2555,
www.cinnamonclub.com). St James's Park or
Westminster tube. **Open** 7.30-9.30am, noon-
2.45pm, 6-10.45pm Mon-Fri; noon-2.45pm, 6-
10.45pm Sat. **Main courses** £14-£32. **Credit**
AmEx, DC, MC, V. **Map** p399 K9 ③ **Indian**
Aiming to create a complete Indian fine-dining expe-
rience, Cinnamon Club provides cocktails, fine
wines, tasting menus, breakfasts (Indian, Anglo-
Indian, British), private dining rooms and all attendant flummery in an impressive, wood-lined space.
Executive chef Vivek Singh devises innovative
dishes, including a well-priced set meal.
Other locations Cinnamon Kitchen, 9
Devonshire Square, the City, EC2M 4WY
(7626 5000, www.cinnamonkitchen.co.uk).

Inn the Park
St James's Park, SW1A 2BJ (7451 9999,
www.innthepark.com). St James's Park tube. **Open**
8-11am, noon-3pm, 6-8.30pm Mon-Fri; 9-11am,
noon-4pm, 6-8.30pm Sat, Sun. *Tea served* 3-5pm
Mon-Fri; 4-5pm Sat, Sun. **Main courses** £10.50-
£18.50. **Credit** MC, V. **Map** p399 K8 ④ **British**
It's all about the location at this beautifully
appointed and designed café-restaurant. The seasonal British cooking isn't always up to expectations, especially given the prices, but there is plenty
on the plus side: staff are lovely, and the setting
(overlooking the duck lake, with trees all around and
the London Eye in the distance) is really wonderful.

National Dining Rooms
Sainsbury Wing, National Gallery,
Trafalgar Square, WC2N 5DN (7747 2525,
www.thenationaldiningrooms.co.uk). Charing
Cross tube/rail. **Open** *Bakery* 10am-5.30pm
Mon-Thur, Sat, Sun; 10am-8.30pm Fri. *Restaurant*
noon-3.15pm Mon-Thur, Sat, Sun; noon-3.15pm,
5-7pm Fri. **Main courses** *Bakery* £8-£12.
Restaurant £18. **Credit** AmEx, MC, V.
Map p416 X4 ⑤ **British**
Oliver Peyton's restaurant in the Sainsbury Wing of
the National Gallery (*see p134*) offers far better food
than the unpleasant fare museum diners have
become accustomed to, albeit at a price: oak-smoked
Cornish duck, pea shoots with quince jelly and aval
fries, perhaps, followed by wild wood pigeon with
currant and beetroot glaze. The few window seats
have prized views over Trafalgar Square, and the
bakery side of the operation ably fulfils the cakes-
and-a-cuppa role of the traditional museum café.

Saké No Hana
23 St James's Street, SW1A 1HA (7925 8988).
Green Park tube. **Open** noon-3pm Mon-Fri; noon-
3pm, 6-11.30pm Mon-Sat. **Main courses** £4-£40.
Credit AmEx, MC, V. **Map** p398 J8 ⑥ **Japanese**
The food presentation at Alan Yau's upmarket venture is unmistakably high-end, as are the smart
staff's black uniforms and architect Kengo Kuma's
cool tatami and cedar design. Sashimi and sushi
account for much of the menu, but pricier cooked
dishes such as miso Chilean sea bass in houba leaf
make menu-perusing more interesting. The saké and
shochu list is substantial.

CHELSEA

Gallery Mess
Saatchi Gallery, Duke of York's HQ, King's Road,
SW3 4LY (7730 8135, www.saatchi-gallery.co.uk).
Sloane Square tube. **Open** 10am-9.30pm Mon-Sat;
10am-6.30pm Sun. **Main courses** £11-£18.50.
Credit AmEx, MC, V. **Map** p395 F11 ⑦
Brasserie
The Saatchi Gallery (*see p144*) welcomed this fabulous brasserie shortly after opening. You can sit inside
surrounded by modern art, but the grounds outside
– littered with portable tables until 6pm, if the
weather's fair – can be a better option in summer.
There's a simple breakfast menu of pastries, eggs and
toast or fry-up served until 11.30am, then lunch and
dinner take over, with the expected salads, pastas and
burgers joined by more ambitious daily specials: per-

Bar Boulud.

haps steamed salmon served in a yellow 'curry' broth or saddle of lamb drizzled with a zig-zag of yoghurt. Of the desserts, knickerbocker glory is a triumph.

★ Tom's Kitchen
27 Cale Street, SW3 3QP (7349 0202, www.tomskitchen.co.uk). Sloane Square or South Kensington tube. **Open** 8-11am, noon-3pm, 6-11pm Mon-Fri; 10am-4pm, 6-11pm Sat, Sun. **Main courses** £14.50-£29.50. **Credit** AmEx, MC, V. **Map** p395 E11 ❻❽ **Brasserie**
White-tiled walls, vast expanses of marble and a busy open kitchen ensure Tom Aikens' place sounds full even when it isn't – for weekend lunches it can often be packed. The big draw here is the pancake: well over an inch thick and almost as big as the serving plate, it's categorically London's best, filled with blueberries and drizzled with maple syrup. Lunch and dinner menus make the most of the wood-smoked oven, spit-roast and grill. Expect hearty, big-tasting comfort food.
▶ *For similar food and prices that match the superb river views, try Tom's Kitchen & Terrace at Somerset House.*

KNIGHTSBRIDGE & SOUTH KENSINGTON

Amaya
Halkin Arcade, Motcomb Street, SW1X 8JT (7823 1166, www.amaya.biz). Knightsbridge tube. **Open** 12.30-2.15pm, 6.30-11.30pm Mon-Sat; 12.45-2.45pm, 6.30-10.30pm Sun. **Main courses** £19-£24. **Credit** AmEx, DC, MC, V. **Map** p398 G9 ❻❾ **Indian**
Slinky by night, when its black leather seating, modish chandeliers and soundtrack of cool beats attract smooching couples, Amaya is light and breezy by

day. From the open kitchen, black-aproned chefs display consummate skill at the tawa griddle, the tandoor oven and at the house-speciality charcoal grill.

★ Bar Boulud
Mandarin Oriental Hyde Park, 66 Knightsbridge, SW1X 7LA (7201 3899, http://danielnyc.com/barboulud_hub.html). Knightsbridge tube. **Open** noon-2.30pm, 3.30-5pm, 5.30-10.30pm daily. **Main courses** £12-£28. *Set meals* £22 3 courses. **Credit** AmEx, MC, V. **Map** p393 F8 ❼❶ **Brasserie**
Daniel Boulud, a French chef rated one of the best restaurateurs in New York, has brought over some Big Apple style and French polish. The menu points to Lyon, the heart of French gastronomy, with amazing charcuterie and refined country classics, and to New York with three types of burger. The service is well informed, well mannered and utterly professional, and the atmosphere refreshingly informal, with children genuinely welcomed.

★ Dinner by Heston Blumenthal
Maandarin Oriental Hyde Park, 66 Knightsbridge, SW1X 7LA (7201 3833, www.dinnerbyheston.com). Knightsbridge tube. **Open** noon-2.30pm, 6.30-10.30pm daily. **Main courses** £26.50-£72. *Set lunch (Mon-Fri)* £28 3 courses. **Credit** AmEx, DC, MC, V. **Map** p393 F8 ❼❶ **British**
With Heston Blumenthal now a fully-fledged celebrity, this warm, relaxing room is an international hotspot attracting high-profile clientele. Worth noting, though, that dinner is not actually by Blumenthal, but under the command of Ashley Palmer-Watts, executive head chef of the Fat Duck group. The pair developed the menu together, taking inspiration from British culinary history, though the dishes are rendered in modern (rather than revolutionary) haute cuisine style.

CONSUME

Geales. *See p232.*

£ Lido Café
South side of the Serpentine, Hyde Park, W2 2UH (7706 7098, www.companyofcooks.com). Hyde Park Corner or Marble Arch tube. **Open** 8am-5.30pm daily (times may vary). **Main courses** £6.50-£13.50. **Credit** MC, V. **Map** p393 E8 **⑫ Café**

The Lido Café is a year-round haven with a menu ranging from summery calamari to warming slow-cooked shoulder of lamb with creamed flageolet – and plenty of outdoor seating. The mace-flavoured brown shrimp salad with soft-boiled egg is a delight. Children's plates include pizzettas, fish fingers and home-made orange jelly. A jolly choice of wines starts at £3.95 per glass; speciality beers include Theakston Old Peculier and London's own Meantime pale ale, and the cocktail list features tempting breakfast options.

▶ *At the eastern end of the lake, the Serpentine Bar & Kitchen (7706 8114, www.serpentine barandkitchen.com) also has great lakeside tables.*

Madsen
20 Old Brompton Road, SW7 3DL (7225 2772, www.madsenrestaurant.com). South Kensington tube. **Open** noon-11pm Mon-Thur; noon-midnight Fri, Sat; noon-5pm Sun. **Main courses** £11.50-£17.50. **Credit** MC, V. **Map** p395 D10 **⑬**
Scandinavian

Danes might feel frustrated that this chic, serene and very friendly café-cum-restaurant doesn't reflect the excitement that is currently surrounding Copenhagen's food scene, but the straightforward home cooking on offer – chicken breast fillet with horseradish cream sauce and roast root vegetables, *stegt rødspætte* (pan-fried plaice with melted butter and carrots) – is pleasing enough. Skip the brief, international wine list in favour of the wonderful speciality Danish beers from Ærø.

Min Jiang

Royal Garden Hotel, 2-4 Kensington High Street, W8 4PT (7361 1988, www.minjiang.co.uk). High Street Kensington tube. **Open** noon-3pm, 6-10.30pm daily. **Main courses** £10-£48. **Credit** AmEx, MC, V. **Map** p392 B8 ⑦ **Chinese**
Located on the tenth floor of the hotel, Min Jiang has fabulous views over Kensington Gardens. Much money has been spent on ensuring the interior is suitably swish, with lattice screens and faux-Ming pottery, but the food is also pretty good. Invest in an authentic Beijing duck and you'll get a chance to admire the carving skills of the chef at your table.

Nahm

Halkin, Halkin Street, SW1X 7DJ (7333 1234, www.nahm.como.bz). Hyde Park Corner tube. **Open** noon-2.30pm, 7-10.45pm Mon-Fri; 7-10.45pm Sat; 7-9.45pm Sun. **Main courses** £17.50-£26.50. **Credit** AmEx, MC, V. **Map** p398 G9 ⑦ **Thai**
Done out in gold and bronze tones, the elegant dining room at the Halkin (*see p207*) feels opulent yet unfussy. Tables for two look out over a manicured garden, and the opportunity to share rare dishes of startling flavour combinations from Australian-born David Thompson's kitchen always makes for a memorable meal. He seeks to interpret historic Thai cooking, yet flashes of inspiration bring the dishes firmly into the modern era: for example, a chicken and banana-flower salad unusually, but successfully, includes samphire and palourdes clams. Presentation is exquisite.

Racine

239 Brompton Road, SW3 2EP (7584 4477). Knightsbridge or South Kensington tube. **Open** noon-3pm, 6-10.30pm Mon-Fri; noon-3.30pm, 6-10.30pm Sat; noon-3.30pm, 6-10pm Sun. **Main courses** £12.50-£20.75. **Credit** AmEx, MC, V. **Map** p395 E10 ⑦ **French**
Heavy curtains inside the door allow diners to make a grand entrance into Racine's warm, vibrant 1930s retro atmosphere. The clientele seems to have become less varied in recent times, feeling more male and moneyed than before, but there's still plenty to enjoy from the menu: try a starter such as garlic and saffron mousse with mussels, or, for dessert, a clafoutis with morello cherries in kirsch.

★ Yashin

1A Argyll Road, W8 7DB (7938 1536, www.yashinsushi.com). High Street Kensington tube. **Open** noon-2.30pm, 6-11pm daily. **Set meals** £12.50-£60. **Credit** AmEx, MC, V. **Map** p394 B9 ⑦ **Sushi**
Soy sauce is unnecessary here. Individual seasonings and garnishes are paired with each piece to bring out the flavours of the seafood or the meat; some are lightly blowtorched, resulting in contrasting textures and a smoky flavour. A meal at Yashin is expensive but it's worth saving up the money for an unbeatable experience.
▶ *Yashin won the award for best sushi bar in Time Out's Eating & Drinking Awards 2011.*

★ Zuma

5 Raphael Street, SW7 1DL (7584 1010, www.zumarestaurant.com). Knightsbridge tube. **Open** *Restaurant* noon-2.45pm, 6-10.45pm Mon-Fri; 12.30-3.15pm, 6-10.45pm Sat; 12.30-3.15pm, 6-10.15pm Sun. *Bar* noon-11pm Mon-Fri; 12.30-11pm Sat; 12.30-10.30pm Sun. **Main courses** £14.80-£70. **Credit** AmEx, DC, MC, V. **Map** p395 F9 ⑦ **Japanese**
Zuma has established itself as a must-go destination for every rich visitor to London. The stylishly displayed bottles, skilful lighting and slickly presented sushi and robata bars still impress, and kitchen standards are as high as ever. Two things stand out: the quality of raw ingredients, and the imaginative flavour combinations, such as ginger, lime and coriander on the *tataki* (seared raw beef).

PADDINGTON & NOTTING HILL

Assaggi

1st floor, 39 Chepstow Place, W2 4TS (7792 5501). Bayswater, Notting Hill Gate or Queensway tube. **Open** 12.30-2.30pm, 7.30-11pm Mon-Fri; 1-2.20pm, 7.30-11pm Sat. **Main courses** £18-£24. **Credit** MC, V. **Map** p404 Z5 ⑦ **Italian**
This Notting Hill icon fills the first floor of a Georgian house above the Chepstow pub. The dining room has a mere dozen tables, so it's clamorous when full – as it usually is. The effusive greeting and uncompromising menu, both entirely in Italian, that once gave an exciting sense of place, now come across as a bit clichéd, but Assaggi remains delightful for Saturday lunch. Although pricey, the Sardinian food and wine here are better value than at London's other fashionable Italian restaurants.

★ Le Café Anglais

8 Porchester Gardens, W2 4DB (7221 1415, www.lecafeanglais.co.uk). Bayswater tube. **Open** noon-3.30pm, 6.30-10.30pm Mon-Thur; noon-3.30pm, 6.30-11pm Fri, Sat; noon-3.30pm, 6.30-10pm Sun. **Main courses** £14.50-£22. *Cover* £1.85. **Credit** AmEx, MC, V. **Map** p392 B6 ⑧ **Modern European**
Chef-proprietor Rowley Leigh's fine restaurant opened to great acclaim and remains very popular – an all-day café-oyster bar was a welcome addition in 2010. Despite its location in Whiteleys shopping centre, the big, art deco-style room is glamorous, with floor-to-ceiling leaded windows on one side, and the open kitchen, rotisserie and bar opposite. It's a see-and-be-seen place with a menu perfect for grazers.

CONSUME

Geales

*2 Farmer Street, W8 7SN (7727 7528,
www.geales.com). Notting Hill Gate tube.* **Open**
6-10.30pm Mon; noon-3pm, 6-10.30pm Tue-Fri;
noon-10.30pm Sat; noon-9.30pm Sun. **Main
courses** £8-£29.50. **Credit** AmEx, MC, V.
Map p404 Z6 ㉛ **Fish & seafood**
Don't come here looking for exotic species of fish or
fancy cooking: Geales is all about good, classic
dishes, competently served in simple but smart
premises. The chef's only glance beyond these
shores is towards the Continent, with steamed mussels and a tomatoey fish soup. Otherwise it's oysters, smoked salmon, prawn cocktail and firm, white
fish in faultlessly crisp batter. Puddings confirm the
place's fine British pedigree. *Photos p230.*
Other locations 1 Cale Street, Chelsea, SW3 3QT
(7965 0555).

Hereford Road

*3 Hereford Road, W2 4AB (7727 1144,
www.herefordroad.org). Bayswater tube.* **Open**
noon-3pm, 6-10.30pm Mon-Fri; noon-3.30pm,
6-10.30pm Sat; noon-4pm, 6-10pm Sun. **Main
courses** £9.50-£14.50. **Credit** AmEx, MC, V.
Map p404 Z5 ㉜ **British**
Hereford Road has the assurance of somewhere
that's been around much longer than it actually has.
It's an easy place in which to relax, with a mixed
crowd and a happy buzz. Starters include the likes
of (undyed) smoked haddock with white beans and
leeks, while mains might feature mallard with
braised chicory and lentils.

Hereford Road.

Ledbury

*127 Ledbury Road, W11 2AQ (7792 9090,
www.theledbury.com). Westbourne Park tube.*
Open 6.30-10.30pm Mon; noon-2.30pm, 6.30-
10.30pm Tue-Sat; noon-3pm, 7-10pm Sun. **Set
meals** £27.50-£90. **Credit** AmEx, MC, V.
Map p404 Y4 ㉝ **French**
The cheeriness that defines a midweek lunch in this
residential backwater is testament to the reputation
of Brett Graham's cooking. The imaginative, meticulous dishes are never overwrought, the sourcing is
impeccable and the drinks list is exceptional. The
comfort and noise level, service and food seamlessly
knit together to produce unruffled pleasure.

£ Taqueria

*139-143 Westbourne Grove, W11 2RS (7229
4734, www.taqueria.co.uk). Notting Hill Gate tube.*
Open noon-11pm Mon-Thur; noon-11.30pm Fri,
Sat; noon-10.30pm Sun. **Main courses** £3.90-
£8.75. **Credit** MC, V. **Map** p404 Z4 ㉞ **Mexican**
Pop-art prints of iconic Mexican insurrectionist
Emiliano Zapata adorn the walls of this classy can-
tina. The food isn't exactly revolutionary – classic
Mexican street food of tacos, tortas and tostadas, for
the most part – but the standard is sound, and
Taqueria's traditional Mexican hot chocolate is
every bit as spicy and frothy as it should be.
▶ *Nearby García (246 Portobello Road, 7221
6119, W11 1LL, www.cafegarcia.co.uk) is an
excellent traditional Spanish café.*

NORTH LONDON

★ £ Chin Chin Laboratorists

*49-50 Camden Lock Place, Camden, NW1 8AF
(www.chinchinlabs.com). Camden Town tube.*
Open noon-7pm Tue-Sun. **No credit cards**.
Map p404 X2 ㉟ **Ice-cream**
The 'laboratorists' are husband-and-wife duo
Ahrash Akbari-Kalhur and Nyisha Weber. In their
ice-cream parlour, which looks like a mad scientist's
lab, they use liquid nitrogen to make ice-cream on
demand. Gimmicky? Of course, but Chin Chin
Laboratorists is run without pretension and is a
whole lot of fun. And its ice-cream, frozen so fast no
coarse ice-crystals can form, is wonderfully smooth.
The practical application of science has never been
cooler or tastier.

Haché

*24 Inverness Street, Camden, NW1 7HJ (7485
9100, www.hacheburgers.com). Camden Town
tube.* **Open** noon-10.30pm Mon-Wed; 10.30am-
11pm Thur-Sat; noon-10pm Sun. **Main courses**
£6.95-£12.95. **Credit** AmEx, MC, V. **Map** p404
Y2 ㊱ **Burgers**
There's a wide choice of gourmet burgers on the
menu at Haché, ranging from duck and venison to a
welcome vegetarian selection. But the place also
excels at top-notch basic burgers, such as steak au

Taqueria.

naturel and lamb au naturel – portions are large and the meat first-rate, and sides of frites, potato wedges or salad shouldn't disappoint.
Other locations 329 Fulham Road, Chelsea, SW10 9QL (7823 3515); 153 Clapham High Street, Clapham, SW4 7SS (7738 8760).

Horseshoe
28 Heath Street, Hampstead, NW3 6TE (7431 7206). Hampstead tube. **Open** 10am-11pm Mon-Thur; 10am-midnight Fri, Sat; 10am-10.30pm Sun. **Main courses** £8-£15. **Credit** AmEx, MC, V.
Gastropub
The kitchen at this gastropub cooks with real flair and, pleasingly, the pub has stayed true to its ancestry by serving excellent beer. It brews its own ales downstairs, but the homebrew is supplemented by a great range of bottled options and a pretty decent winelist. Service can be a bit too laid-back, but if you're happy to chill, the Horseshoe makes a relaxing stop for the likes of refreshing artichoke, tomato, basil and ragstone cheese salad or Heveningham Hall lamb loin with white beans in marjoram pesto.

Manna
4 Erskine Road, Chalk Farm, NW3 3AJ (7722 8028, www.mannav.com). Chalk Farm tube or bus 31, 168. **Open** 6.30-10.30pm Tue-Fri; noon-3pm, 6.30-10.30pm Sat, Sun. **Main courses** £10-£18. **Credit** AmEx, MC, V. **Map** p404 W2 **⑥⑦**
Vegetarian
Going strong after upwards of 40 years, Manna appears to have settled into a more mature style. The dining space consists of a tiny conservatory and a cosy, curtained snug for more intimate encounters. The menu picks and chooses from around the world, with the popular chef's salad (beetroot, avocado, balsamic-marinated onions, pumpkin seeds and protein from a selection of halloumi, feta or crispy tofu) always a feature.

Market
43 Parkway, Camden, NW1 7PN (7267 9700, www.marketrestaurant.co.uk). Camden Town tube. **Open** noon-2.30pm, 6-10.30pm Mon-Sat; 1-3.30pm Sun. **Main courses** £13-£16. **Credit** AmEx, DC, MC, V. **Map** p404 Y2 **⑧⑧** **British**
Parkway doesn't have a reputation as a foodie destination, so hats off to Market for succeeding on this very tricky Camden thoroughfare. Behind an unassuming black frontage, a wide demographic of groups, couples, families and lone diners lap up the good-value, broadly British fare, with occasional European flourishes (gazpacho, say, or gnocchi with peas, broad beans and ragstone cheese). Service is brisk, but comes with a smile.

★ Ottolenghi
287 Upper Street, Islington, N1 2TZ (7288 1454, www.ottolenghi.co.uk). Angel tube or Highbury & Islington tube/rail. **Open** 8am-10pm Mon-Wed; 8am-10.30pm Thur-Sat; 9am-7pm Sun. **Main courses** £5.50-£12. **Credit** AmEx, MC, V. **Map** p400 O1 **⑧⑨** **Bakery-café**
Ottolenghi is more than an inviting bakery. Behind the pastries piled in the window is a comparatively prim deli counter with lush salads, available day and evening, eat-in or take away. This is a brilliant and stylish daytime café, but people book well in advance for dinner too – the inventive fusion menu (currently only available at this branch) is fabulous.

INSIDE TRACK EAT TURKISH

From Dalston Kingsland station north to Stoke Newington Church Street is the Turkish and Kurdish heart of Hackney: both **19 Numara Bos Cirrik** (34 Stoke Newington Road, N16 7XJ, 7249 0400) and **Mangal Ocakbaşı** (10 Arcola Street, E8 2DJ, 7275 8981, www.mangal1.com) serve superb grilled meats, marinated and cooked to perfection.

CONSUME

Other locations 1 Holland Street, Kensington, W8 4NA (7937 0003); 63 Ledbury Road, Notting Hill, W11 2AD (7727 1121); 13 Motcomb Street, Belgravia, SW1X 8LB (7823 2707).

EAST LONDON

Spitalfields, Shoreditch and Hoxton are key nightlife districts and well furnished with bars; see pp251-253. The curry restaurants of Brick Lane rarely live up to their reputation.

★ £ Albion

2-4 Boundary Street, Shoreditch, E2 7DD (7729 1051, www.albioncaff.co.uk). Shoreditch High Street rail. **Open** 8am-11pm daily. **Main courses** £8-£12. **Credit** AmEx, MC, V. **Map** p401 R4 ⑩ **Café**
Almost every new London restaurant seems to be mining the vein of nostalgia for traditional British cuisine these days, but few have pulled it off as well as Terence Conran's stand-out 'caff'. You get platters of cupcakes and doorstop-thick slices of battenberg, baked on-site, and mains such as toad in the hole or devilled kidneys. The English breakfast is superb, with buttery scrambled eggs and juicy mushrooms.
► *For the hotel upstairs, see p210* **Boundary**.

Brawn

49 Columbia Road, E2 7RG (7729 5692, www.terroirswinebar.com). Hoxton rail or bus 48, 55. **Open** noon-3pm, 6-11pm Mon-Sat; noon-4pm Sun. **Main courses** £16-£27.50. **Credit** MC, V. **Map** p401 S3 ⑪ **Modern European**

INSIDE TRACK
PARK PERSPECTIVES

Made out of recycled metal shipping containers and painted a vivid yellow-green, the View Tube (www.theview tube.co.uk) was constructed on a ridge a short walk from Pudding Mill Lane DLR to provide the best possible vantage on the Olympic Park as it developed – the Olympic Stadium looks close enough putt a shot at. At ground level, it houses the **Container Café** (*see right*), with floor-to-ceiling picture windows. During the Games, it will be inside the Olympic Park perimeter – for a Games Time alternative, *see p163* **Inside Track**.

There's a posh option available as well. On the west side of the Park, **Forman's Restaurant** (*see p235*) serves house-cured smoked salmon in a lovely room with wonderful views across the River Lea to the Olympic Stadium. Again, it's advisable to check availability before visiting at Games Time.

As the name suggests, the menu here is a robust affair, with a whole section of the list simply labelled 'pig' (brawn, prosciutto di parma, terrine, rillettes and so on). When things are good here, they're very good, though there is the occasional misfire, and prices sometimes seem high. Brawn is an offshoot of the popular West End wine bar Terroirs (*see p245*); though the vibe here is altogether cooler, it exhibits the same passion for organic or biodynamic 'natural' wines. Bread is scrumptious (Hackney Wild sourdough from London Fields' e5 bakery), and typical of the careful sourcing at work here.

★ £ Brick Lane Beigel Bake

159 Brick Lane, E1 6SB (7729 0616). Liverpool Street tube/rail or bus 8. **Open** 24hrs daily. **Main courses** £1.95-£5.95. **No credit cards. Map** p401 S4 ⑫ **Jewish**
This little East End institution rolls out perfect bagels (egg, cream cheese, salt beef, at seriously low prices), good bread and moreish cakes. Even at 3am, fresh-baked goods are pulled from the ovens at the back; no wonder the queue for bagels trails out the door when the local bars and clubs close.

£ Container Café

View Tube, the Greenway, Marshgate Lane, E15 2PJ (07702 125081, www.theviewtube.co.uk). Pudding Mill Lane DLR (closed at Games Time). **Open** 9am-4.30pm daily. **Main courses** £4-£7. **Credit** AmEx, MC, V. **Café**
Right opposite the Olympic Stadium, and on the Greenway walking and cycling route, this is a perfect location from which to view the Olympic Park (*see left* **Inside Track**). It's also no slouch on the refreshments front, offering toothsome cakes, snacks and sandwiches and properly made coffees in an attractive wood-furnished room. At Games Time, the Container Café will be within the perimeter of the Olympic Park, so only ticket-holders will be able to visit – Pudding Mill Lane DLR will also be inaccessible to the general public.

★ Eyre Brothers

70 Leonard Street, Shoreditch, EC2A 4QX (7613 5346, www.eyrebrothers.co.uk). Old Street tube/rail. **Open** noon-2.45pm, 6.30-10.45pm Mon-Fri; 7-11pm Sat. **Main courses** £15-£27.50. **Credit** AmEx, DC, MC, V. **Map** p401 Q4 ⑬ **International**
This long, attractive room is extremely popular with City gents and the media crowd. Robert and David Eyre have taken the food of the Iberian peninsula into their heart and soul, and reproduce it in a form that's true to its rustic roots yet sophisticated enough to compete with top-level French or Italian cooking. The tapas are sensational.

Hackney Pearl

11 Prince Edward Road, Hackney Wick, E9 5LX (8510 3605, www.thehackneypearl.com). Hackney

CONSUME

Wick rail. **Open** 8am-11pm Tue-Fri; 10am-11pm Sat, Sun. **Main courses** £10-£14. **Credit** MC, V. **Café-bar**
Very sure of itself, Hackney Pearl perfectly fits the brief for a friendly neighbourhood hangout, with the owners having made something special out of not very much. Two former shop units in a post-industrial enclave between Victoria Park and the Lea Navigation have been enlivened by furniture that seems to have been salvaged from a groovy thrift shop – colourful rugs, Formica tables and old dressers. The compact menu lists simple but imaginative food, with an eastern European slant.

Forman's Restaurant

Stour Road, Fish Island, E3 2NH (8525 2365, www.formans.co.uk/restaurant). Pudding Mill Lane DLR (closed at Games Time) or Hackney Wick rail. **Open** *Restaurant* 7-11pm Thur, Fri; 10am-2pm, 7-11pm Sat; noon-5pm Sun. *Gallery Bar* 5-9pm Thur, Fri; noon-5pm, 7-11pm Sat; noon-5pm Sun. **Main courses** £13-£21.50. **Credit** MC, V. **British**
Come here to enjoy a truly local speciality in a truly amazing setting. Forman's invented London-cure smoked salmon and has been manufacturing in the East End since 1905. The firm's original factory closed to make way for the Olympic Park, but the café-bar and restaurant at these new premises have a superb Olympic Stadium view and food to match, plus a gallery overlooking the smokery. In addition to the salmon, served with buckwheat blinis, seasonal British produce on offer includes Hampshire buffalo mozzarella and smoked eel. Call to check opening times before visiting during the Games.

Jamie's Italian

Unit 17, 2 Churchill Place, Canary Wharf, E14 5RB (3002 5252, www.jamieoliver.com). Canary Wharf tube/DLR. **Open** 11.30am-11pm Mon-Fri; noon-11pm Sat; noon-10.30pm Sun. **Main courses** £9.85-£15.95. **Credit** AmEx, DC, MC, V.
Jamie Oliver has got everything right at his chain of mid-priced restaurants designed to compete with the likes of Carluccio's, Giraffe and Strada. It certainly leaves those last two in the shade. Staff are almost improbably nice, in a Jamie-ly perky way. We chose small portions of pasta so that we could try the enticing antipasti too, but you can also order pasta dishes in main-course sizes; in addition, there's a choice of fish or meat dishes, such as steaks, fish stew and whole roasted sea bass. Prawn linguine and a spring vegetable pasta dish were both full of flavour, and several different varieties of chips were right on the money. No wonder the chain is packed.
Other locations throughout the city.

Hackney Pearl.

Sông Quê.

CONSUME

Luxe

*109 Commercial Street, Spitalfields, E1 6BG
(7101 1751, www.theluxe.co.uk). Liverpool Street
tube/rail or Shoreditch High Street rail.* **Open**
Restaurant noon-3pm, 6-10.45pm Mon-Fri;
6-10.45pm Sat; noon-4pm Sun. *Café-bar* 8.30am-
4.30pm Mon-Sat; 9.30am-4.45pm Sun. **Main
courses** *Restaurant* £13-£15. *Café-bar* £7.50-
£11.50. **Credit** AmEx, MC, V. **Map** p401 S5
🈴 **Modern European**
This restaurant in Spitalfields' Grade II-listed Old
Flower Market building provides customers with a
different eating and drinking experience on each
floor. The centrepiece is a premium-priced first-floor
dining room with a show kitchen – white marble
bar cut out and filled with logs – and deft combinations of ingredients (Japanese glazed mackerel with
pickled cucumber and sesame, for example). The
bustling ground-floor café-bar and its charming rear
terrace are great places to take breakfast or to go
for a casual lunch, while the basement bar and
music venue is dark and moody.

£ Needoo Grill

*87 New Road, Whitechapel, E1 1HH (7247 0648,
www.needoogrill.co.uk). Whitechapel tube.* **Open**
11.30am-11.30pm daily. **Main courses** £6-£6.50.
Credit AmEx, MC, V. **Pakistani**
Needoo Grill, with its lively and boisterous mix of
young families and groups of friends, has the vibe
of a community meeting place. It offers meaty
Pakistani-Punjabi staples but also earthy vegetarian dishes, made with care. Past the grill near the
entrance, the decor of the main seating area is as
big and bold as the cooking.

★ £ E Pellicci

*332 Bethnal Green Road, Bethnal Green, E2
0AG (7739 4873). Bethnal Green tube/rail or
bus 8.* **Open** 7am-4pm Mon-Sat. **Main courses**
£6.40-£8.20. **No credit cards**. **Café**
This hive of humanity, a family business to the core,
has been trading since 1900. It's an aesthetic delight:
the art deco wood-panelled interior holds Grade II-
listed status. The menu features sandwiches, rolls
and ciabattas; big breakfasts; steak pies and
lasagnes; and boarding-school classic desserts.
Although it's been trading for 110 years, the prices
remain firmly rooted in the old East End.

Pizza East

*56 Shoreditch High Street, Shoreditch, E1 6JJ
(7729 1888, www.pizzaeast.com). Shoreditch High
Street rail.* **Open** noon-11pm Mon-Wed; noon-
midnight Thur; noon-1am Fri, 10am-1am Sat;
10am-11pm Sun. **Main courses** £8-£17. **Credit**
AmEx, MC, V. **Map** p401 R4 🈴 **Pizza**
There's an Italian-American slant to the pizzas, such
as a New England speciality clam pizza that comes
garnished with cherry tomatoes, garlic and pecorino.
The vibe is cool, but friendly and relaxed, with
beams and concrete indicating its industrial past.
Other locations 310 Portobello Road, Ladbroke
Grove, W10 5TA (8969 4500).

▶ *Downstairs in the lower basement, Concrete serves up food, booze and varied club nights until midnight (1am or 2am at weekends).*

Princess of Shoreditch
76-79 Paul Street, EC2A 4NE (7729 9270, www.theprincessofshoreditch.com). Old Street tube/rail or bus 55. **Open** noon-11pm Mon-Sat; noon-10pm Sun. **Main courses** £11.50-£19. **Credit** AmEx, MC, V. **Map** p401 Q4 ⑳
Gastropub
The Princess has new owners, but the gentle refurb wisely didn't monkey about with the historic decor – the place was built in 1742. It is indeed a princess among gastropubs, somewhere you'll feel equally comfortable scoffing or quaffing (local cask ales, a respectable list of wines by the glass, bottle and carafe, bloody marys), a combination of attributes that won it our award for Best Gastropub in 2010.

£ Sông Quê
134 Kingsland Road, Shoreditch, E2 8DY (7613 3222). Hoxton rail. **Open** noon-3pm, 5.30-11pm Mon-Sat; 12.30-11pm Sun. **Main courses** £4.80-£14.80. **Credit** MC, V. **Map** p401 R3 ⑳
Vietnamese
North-east London retains its monopoly on the capital's most authentic Vietnamese restaurants, several of which cluster on this street. Sông Quê, which was the key pioneer, remains the benchmark for all of them. It's an efficient, canteen-like operation to which diners of all types are attracted – be prepared to share tables at busy times, and ready to taste the fresh herby kick of proper Viet soups and noodles.

£ Tayyabs
83 Fieldgate Street, Whitechapel, E1 1JU (7247 9543, www.tayyabs.co.uk). Aldgate East or Whitechapel tube. **Open** noon-11.30pm daily. **Main courses** £6.50-£25.80. **Credit** AmEx, MC, V. **Pakistani**
Behind the green frontage of a former pub, Tayyabs is a bright, modern Pakistani café that bucks up this down-at-heel backstreet. Droves of City suits are attracted for lunch, along with students and locals. The upbeat mood is accentuated by Bollywood beats, a crimson, ochre and mustard colour scheme and the bustle from an open kitchen. Expect to queue at busy times – this has become a cult favourite.

★ Viajante
Town Hall Hotel, Patriot Square, Bethnal Green, E2 9NF (7871 0461, www.viajante.co.uk). Bethnal Green tube/rail or Cambridge Heath rail. **Open** 6-9.30pm Mon, Tue; noon-2pm, 6-9.30pm Wed-Sun. **Set lunch** £28-£70. **Set dinner** £65-£90 6 courses. **Credit** AmEx, MC, V. **Pan-Asian & fusion**
Globetrotting culinary adventurer Nuno Mendez is chef-patron at Viajante, still a must-visit destination for style-conscious gastronauts following its stellar

debut in 2010. A meal here doesn't come cheap, but it's a fun ride through extraordinary combinations of flavour and texture, no doubt influenced by Mendez's spell at El Bulli. His newer Corner Room, in the same hotel, is a no-booking, lower-price exponent of the same inquiring spirit, whose quietly arty, first-floor corner space belies its provocative flavours. Service can occasionally be overrun. *Photos p239.*

Whitechapel Gallery Dining Room
Whitechapel Gallery, 77-82 Whitechapel High Street, E1 7QX (7522 7888, www.whitechapelgallery.org/dine). Aldgate East tube. **Open** noon-3pm Tue; noon-3pm, 6-9.30pm Wed-Sat; noon-3.45pm Sun. **Main courses** £10.50-£14.95. **Credit** AmEx, MC, V. **Map** p403 S6 ㊳
Modern European
In an attractive former library, with ceiling-height windows and tall mirrors to bring in much-needed light, this is a small but vibrant art gallery restaurant. The menu is largely British, with hints of Italian influence. Cheerful staff and customers who range from East End arty to posh arty create a pleasant atmosphere.

Yi-Ban
London Regatta Centre, Dockside Road, E16 2QT (7473 6699, www.yi-ban.co.uk). Royal Albert DLR. **Open** noon-11pm Mon-Sat; 11am-10.30pm Sun. **Main courses** £4-£30. **Credit** AmEx, MC, V. Chinese
Yi-Ban is one of the few places in London where the food is as good as the view. Granted, it's a view of London City Airport, but that has its own charm. The long, spacious room takes cues from hotel dining areas and Chinese wedding banquets – gold lamé in particular makes an amusing appearance – but the food doesn't have to follow crispy duck and sweet-and-sour pork clichés. Experiment instead with the daytime dim sum, west lake soup or Cantonese-style crispy roast pork belly. The staff are a charming and efficient bunch.

SOUTH-EAST LONDON

Amid the over-styled bistros and high-street chain restaurants, Greenwich still lacks stand-out eateries. **Inside**, the **Old Brewery** and some solid boozers (*see p253*) are pretty much it.

Inside
19 Greenwich South Street, Greenwich, SE10 8NW (8265 5060, www.insiderestaurant.co.uk). Greenwich rail/DLR. **Open** noon-2.30pm, 6.30-11pm Tue-Fri; 6.30-11pm Sat; noon-3pm Sun. **Main courses** £12.95-£18.95. **Credit** AmEx, MC, V. **Map** p405 W3 ㊴ **Modern European**
There are too few neighbourhood restaurants in south-east London that tantalise you with fresh flavours, however often or seldom you dine there. With proficient, unobtrusive service, a smart little

CONSUME

interior and reasonable prices, Inside manages to do this, with careful and imaginative sourcing matched by lively combinations of ingredients: roasted cod, Spanish paprika, white bean and chorizo cassoulet with steamed leeks and tomato coulis was a recent hit. Desserts are good enough to convert even the usually pudding-averse.

Old Brewery

Pepys Building, Old Royal Naval College, Greenwich, SE10 9LW (3327 1280, www.old brewerygreenwich.com). Cutty Sark DLR. **Open** 11am-11pm daily. **Main courses** £6-£17.50. **Credit** MC, V. **Map** p405 X1 ⓤ **British**
By day, the Old Brewery is a café; by night, a restaurant. There's a small bar, with tables outside in a large walled courtyard – a lovely spot in which to test the 50-strong beer list – but most of the action is in the vast, high-ceilinged main space, beneath a wave-like structure of empty bottles and a wall of shiny copper vats – handsome enough to net our award for Best Design in 2010. The short menu highlights provenance and seasonality, with matching beers suggested for each dish.

£ Pavilion Tea House

Greenwich Park, Blackheath Gate, SE10 8QY (8858 9695, www.companyofcooks.com). Blackheath rail or Greenwich rail/DLR. **Open** 9am-5.30pm Mon-Fri; 9am-6pm Sat, Sun. **Main courses** £4.95-£6.60. **Credit** MC, V. **Map** p405 Y3. ⓤ **Café**
Diagonally opposite the Royal Observatory, set in its own pretty, fenced-in grounds, the Pavilion Tea House provides a convivial cake-and-a-break for weary parents. If you're stuck for breakfast or a proper hot meal, it also punches above its weight, and the salads, snacks and sandwiches are all a notch above average.

SOUTH-WEST LONDON

Earl Spencer

260-262 Merton Road, SW18 5JL (8870 9244, www.theearlspencer.co.uk). Southfields tube. **Open** 11am-11pm Mon-Thur; 11am-midnight Fri, Sat; noon-10.30pm Sun. **Main courses** £8.50-£14. **Credit** AmEx, MC, V. **Gastropub**
The Earl Spencer was a gastropub pioneer and has continued on the same path, with a short, chalkboard menu, scrubbed wooden tables, good ales and friendly, laid-back staff. The Earl is a popular local pitstop, keeping regulars happy with salt beef sandwiches or big bowls of Thai-spiced mussels.

★ £ Franco Manca

4 Market Row, Electric Lane, Brixton, SW9 8LD (7738 3021, www.francomanca.co.uk). Brixton tube/rail. **Open** noon-5pm Mon-Wed; noon-9pm Thur-Sat; noon-4pm Sun. **Main courses** £5-£7.50. **Credit** MC, V. **Pizza**

Inside one of the arches in Brixton Market, with a dining area that mixes indoor and outdoor seating, Franco Manca has been showered with acclaim. The menu is precise (just six pizzas) and cheap, but the pizzas are among London's best: key to their success are the sourdough bases, thin and flavoursome. The organic lemonade is nearly as unmissable. A delight. **Other locations** 144 Chiswick High Road, Chiswick, W4 1PU (8747 4822).

Lawn Bistro

67 High Street, Wimbledon, SW19 5EE (8947 8278, www.thelawnbistro.co.uk). Wimbledon tube/rail/tram. **Open** noon-2.30pm, 6.30-10.30pm Mon-Sat; noon-3pm Sun. **Credit** MC, V. **French**
Chef Ollie Couillaud runs this modern French restaurant in the heart of Wimbledon Village. Flavours are adventurous, without being too crazy, so sea bass was served on a risotto with crayfish and chorizo, the advertised 'coriander' restricted to a seed-sprout garnish, so the pungent flavour didn't overwhelm the rest of the dish. All around us, Lawn Bistro was packed with well-heeled locals - many of them couples relishing the chance to try a baked alaska for two, old flames relit at the table.

WEST LONDON

Clarke's

124 Kensington Church Street, Kensington, W8 4BH (7221 9225, www.sallyclarke.com). Notting Hill Gate tube. **Open** 12.30-2pm, 6.30-10pm Mon-Fri; noon-2pm, 6.30-10pm Sat; noon-2pm Sun. **Main courses** £18.50-£24. **Set dinner** £40.50 3 courses. **Credit** AmEx, DC, MC, V. **Map** p404 Z6 ⓤ **Modern European**
Chef-proprietor Sally Clarke has been espousing the 'seasonal and local' ethic since the mid 1980s. The food at this stylishly low-key restaurant shows influences from western Europe, executed with a deft hand, and the wine list has some very good bottles. Don't miss the breads, for which the deli next door (& Clarke's) is justly famed.

★ Gate

51 Queen Caroline Street, Hammersmith, W6 9QL (8748 6932, http://thegaterestaurants.com). Hammersmith tube. **Open** noon-2.30pm, 6-10.30pm Mon-Sat. **Main courses** £10.50-£15.50. **Credit** AmEx, MC, V. **Vegetarian**
West London's most prominent vegetarian restaurant continues to impress with its innovative dishes and atmospheric, high-ceilinged dining room. The mood is casual and pleasantly noisy with the clatter of cutlery and the chatter of meat-avoiders. Dishes can feature a bewildering number of flavours from around the world. Desserts are equally tempting.

Harwood Arms

Corner of Walham Grove & Farm Lane, Fulham, SW6 1QP (7386 1847, www.harwoodarms.com).

Viajante. See p237.

Fulham Broadway tube. **Open** 5.30-11pm Mon; noon-11pm Tue-Fri; noon-midnight Sat; noon-10pm Sun. **Main courses** £16.50-£18. **Credit** AmEx, MC, V. **Map** p394 A13 ⑩ **Gastropub**
Snagging a table has become far more difficult since a Michelin star was awarded to this terrific gastropub – a source of frustration, surely, for the locals who saw it as a neighbourhood watering hole that happened to serve brilliant food. The posh-country feel is created via rustic design details: hessian napkins, linen bags in place of a bread basket, slabs of wood for presentation. Service is smart-shirted, but laid-back and friendly.

£ Masala Zone
147 Earl's Court Road, Earl's Court, SW5 9RQ (7373 0220, www.masalazone.com). Earl's Court tube. **Open** 12.30-3pm, 5.30-11pm Mon-Fri; 12.30-11pm Sat; 12.30-10.30pm Sun. **Main courses** £7.75-£13. **Credit** MC, V. **Map** p394 B10 ⑩ **Indian**
Branches of this smart, clever chain are popping up faster than mustard seeds in a hot pan of ghee. Each outlet is decorated with a different theme – this branch has striking work by tribal artists. The mood is both vibrant and relaxed – as cheering to singletons having a thali for supper, as it is to family groups and couples. Good food at good prices. **Other locations** throughout the city.

Mesopotamia
115 Wembley Park Drive, Wembley, Middx HA9 8HG (8453 5555, www.mesopotamia.ltd.uk). Wembley Park tube. **Open** 5.30pm-midnight Mon-Sat. **Main courses** £8-£15.50. **Credit** AmEx, DC, MC, V. **Iraqi**
Outside is traffic-clogged Wembley; inside is Middle Eastern romance. Under a ceiling of billowing silk, Mesopotamia's long, dimly lit interior is decorated with an intricately carved dresser, a wall frieze of Babylonian beasts and palms in relief, and dark, metallic light fittings. It's an enchanting spot, helped along by kindly service (although proceedings can slow during busy spells). Special set dinners are served before events at Wembley Stadium.

Mohsen
152 Warwick Road, Earl's Court, W14 8PS (7602 9888). Earl's Court tube or Kensington (Olympia) tube/rail. **Open** noon-midnight daily. **Main courses** £12-£15. Unlicensed. Corkage no charge. **No credit cards. Map** p394 A10 ⑩ **Iranian**
It is consistency, not evolution, that has kept this establishment among our favourite Iranian restaurants for so long. Some of its Kensington contemporaries have meddled with their formula – diluting their all-Iranian staff, employing belly dancers and catering to hordes of late-night kebab-seekers – but Mohsen has retained the family atmosphere that remains its biggest draw.

CONSUME

River Café

Thames Wharf, Rainville Road, Hammersmith,
W6 9HA (7386 4200, www.rivercafe.co.uk).
Hammersmith tube. **Open** 12.30-5pm, 7-11pm
Mon-Sat; 12.30-5pm Sun. **Main courses** £30-£37.
Credit AmEx, DC, MC, V. **Italian**
River Café continues on its tranquil way. Inside is all cool, calming blues, white and steel with the occasional splash of bright yellow; outside is a pretty little herb and vegetable garden. Staff are young, friendly and dressed just a little more fashionably than the core Fulham and Kensington customer base. The food is simple, usually brilliantly so, but costly.

£ Sakonis

129 Ealing Road, Wembley, Middx HA0 4BP
(8903 9601, www.sakonis.co.uk). Alperton tube.
Open noon-10pm Mon-Fri; 9-11am, noon-10pm
Sat, Sun. **Main courses** £2-£4.99. **Credit** MC, V.
Gujarati vegetarian
A mainstay of the Ealing Road Indian dining scene, Sakonis attracts hordes of shoppers at the weekend. It's a sizeable, utilitarian café with tiled walls, melamine tableware and easy-wipe tables. At the front is a snack counter, a well-liked source of takeaways, while to the rear is a buffet popular with South Asian families. We particularly rate the street food.

Hot Coffee

Where dedicated followers of the bean go.

In the last couple of years, London has got very serious about its coffee, with local roasteries springing up (the best known is Square Mile) and a new wave of passionate and knowledgeable barista-proprietors trading in carefully sourced beans and sophisticated production methods. On the side: wireless, large slices of cake and a distinctly non-chain atmosphere.

Brill

27 Exmouth Market,
EC1R 4QL (7833 9757).
Map p400 N4 **106**
Superior coffees –
Union Hand Roasted's
Revelation espresso
blend – plus CDs and
Brick Lane bagels.

Climpson & Sons

67 Broadway Market,
E8 4PH (7812 9829,
www.climpsonandsons.com).
Macchiato, piccolo, zola, gibraltar… you can have it all in this charming coffee-geek haven.

Federation Coffee

Unit 46, Brixton Village Market,
Coldharbour Lane, SW9 8PS (no
phone, www.federationcoffee.com).
A groovy little coffee shop serving a range of coffees from Nude Espresso.

Fernandez & Wells

16A St Anne's Court, W1F 0BG (7494
4242, www.fernandezandwells.com).
Map p416 W2 **107**
Invigorating triple ristretto shots are served at the 'espresso bar' branch of F&W.

Flat White

17 Berwick Street, W1F 0PT (7734 0370,
www.flatwhitecafe.com). **Map** p416 V2 **108**
Flat White's shabby chic resembles cafés found on the central New South Wales coast; its namesake coffee is good and strong.

Leila's Shop

15-17 Calvert Avenue,
E2 7JP (7729 9789).
Map p401 R4 **109**
Leila McAlister's
eclectic deli-café is a
long-time favourite for
consistantly excellent
coffee.

Prufrock

23-25 Leather
Lane, EC1N 7TE
(07852 243470,
www.prufrockcoffee.com).
Map p400 N5 **110**
Gwilym Davies is a demi-god among those who take their cup of joe seriously; test his wares here.

Scootercaffè

132 Lower Marsh, SE1 7AE (7620 1421).
Map p399 M9 **111**
A coffee shop in a former Vespa repair garage, employing a vintage Faema espresso machine.

Tapped & Packed

26 Rathbone Place, W1T 1JD (7580 2163,
www.tappedandpacked.co.uk). **Map** p416
W1 **112**
Choose your method – siphon, Aeropress, cafetière – as well as your bean.

CONSUME

Pubs & Bars

The grape, the grain and the swizzle stick – London loves them all.

Every visitor to London has a perfect mind's-eye vision of the traditional pub – polished brass, etched mirrors, ale pumps and a roaring fire. The truth is more complex. The UK is losing its locals at a rate of knots, and nowhere more so than in the capital. But the best exponents, scattered through the sidestreets, continue to do a roaring trade, and they have been supplemented by a vast range of other thriving drinks dispensaries of all styles and sizes, from spirits specialists to gastropubs, well-curated wine bars to fashionista cocktail bars both shabby and chic.

The last few years have seen a surge in interest in craft beers from home and abroad, and there has been a remarkable flowering of brewing in London. When Youngs moved out of its Wandsworth premises in 2006, there were only three breweries that we know of left in town (the largest of them Fullers, maker of London Pride). Thanks to the fashion for all things local and hand-made, abetted by some new tax breaks and a fall in the price of commercial property, the number had risen to ten by 2010 and a couple of dozen by the end of 2011 (*see p255* **Something's Brewing**). This has had the pleasing effect of ensuring that some of the new 'beer bars' in town are really pubs by any other name – thus compensating in a small way for the decline of the local.

CONSUME

THE SOUTH BANK & BANKSIDE

If top-quality beer is your priority when choosing a pub, then you could do much worse than the superb ranges at the tiny **Rake** (14A Winchester Walk, SE1 9AG, 7407 0557), in Borough Market, and at a branch of **Draft House** (206-208 Tower Bridge Road, SE1 2UP, 7924 1814, www.drafthouse.co.uk; *see p254*), at the south side of Tower Bridge.

★ Gladstone Arms
64 Lant Street, SE1 1QN (7407 3962). Borough tube. **Open** noon-11pm Mon-Thur; noon-midnight Fri, Sat; noon-10.30pm Sun. *Food served* noon-10pm daily. **Credit** MC, V. **Map** p402 P9 ❶
While the Victorian prime minister still glares from the massive mural on the outer wall, inside is now funky, freaky and candlelit. Gigs (blues, folk, acoustic, five nights a week) take place at one end of a cosy space; opposite, a bar dispenses ales and lagers. Pies provide sustenance. Retro touches include an old-fashioned 'On Air' studio sign and a communist-style railway clock.

Skylon
Royal Festival Hall, Belvedere Road, SE1 8XX (7654 7800, www.danddlondon.com). Waterloo tube/rail. **Open** 11am-midnight daily. *Food served* noon-11pm daily. **Credit** AmEx, MC, V. **Map** p399 M8 ❷
There can't be many better views than this in town. Sit at the cocktail bar (between the two restaurant areas), and gaze at trains trundling out of Charing Cross, cars and buses whizzing across Waterloo Bridge, and boats and cruisers pootling along the Thames. Drinks include ten bellinis, a large range of liqueurs and a list of classics (manhattans, sidecars, negronis), all at a price.

Wine Wharf
Stoney Street, SE1 9AD (7940 8335, www.winewharf.co.uk). London Bridge tube/rail.

❶ Green numbers given in this chapter correspond to the location of each pub or bar on the street maps. *See pp392-416.*

CONSUME

Open 4-11.30pm Mon, Tue; noon-11.30pm Wed-Sat. *Food served* 5.30-10pm Mon, Tue; noon-3pm, 5.30-10pm Wed-Sat. **Credit** AmEx, DC, MC, V. **Map** p402 P8 ❸

Part of the Vinopolis complex, Wine Wharf inhabits two storeys of a reclaimed Victorian warehouse, all exposed brickwork and high-ceilinged industrial chic. You could drink very well indeed here: the 250-bin list stretches to 1953 d'Yquem and some very serious prestige cuvée champagnes. But with nearly half the wines available by the glass, there's a great opportunity to experiment.

Other locations Brew Wharf, Stoney Street, SE1 9AD (7378 6601, www.brewwharf.com).

THE CITY

Artillery Arms
102 Bunhill Row, EC1Y 8ND (7253 4683). Moorgate or Old Street tube/rail. **Open** noon-11pm Mon-Sat; noon-10.30pm Sun. *Food served* noon-3pm, 6-9pm Mon-Fri; noon-9pm Sat, Sun. **Credit** AmEx, MC, V. **Map** p400 P4 ❹

Close to the Barbican and opposite Bunhill Fields, this small tucked-away pub has an agreeably local feel, as post-work City folk mix easily with neighbourhood stalwarts at the sturdy, immovable bar. It has a slightly austere feel, but is an easy place to lose track of an evening, aided by the local vibe and the predictably fine Fuller's beers: easygoing Chiswick, toothsome London Pride and potent ESB.

Vertigo 42
Tower 42, 25 Old Broad Street, EC2N 1HQ (7877 7842, www.vertigo42.co.uk). Bank tube/DLR or Liverpool Street tube/rail. **Open** noon-4.30pm, 5-11pm Mon-Fri; 5-11pm Sat. *Food served* noon-2.30pm, 5-9.30pm Mon-Fri; 5-9.30pm Sat. **Credit** AmEx, DC, MC, V. **Map** p403 Q6 ❺

Stretching out across the City, the views from this 42nd-floor bar are breathtaking. So, too, are the prices (house wine, £9 a glass). Food is more down to earth: options include wild mushroom tart with artichoke salad, and seared peppered tuna steak. Seating is arranged so everyone can enjoy the 360° panorama; for the privilege, you must book ahead, promise a minimum £10 spend and then undergo airport-style security.

▶ *Vertigo has some competition for the high-life: nearby Heron Tower, the City's newest tallest building, is due to open a bar/restaurant up top in the first half of 2012. Outdoor terraces and a private glass elevator are promised.*

Worship Street Whistling Shop
63 Worship Street, EC2A 2DU (7247 0015, www.whistlingshop.com). Old Street tube/rail. **Open** noon-1am Mon-Thur; noon-2am Fri, Sat. *Food served* noon-10pm Mon-Sat. **Credit** MC, V. **Map** p401 Q4 ❻

Worship Street venerates all things Victorian (with the possible exception of Victorian musical taste, as the soundtrack owes more to the 1980s than to the 1880s). The U-shaped space feels like a Dickensian drinking den with its gas lamps and Chesterfield sofas – even the staff wear period clobber. The cocktail list applies modern molecular mixology techniques to Victorian recipes. The line between authentic and a little bit silly blurs somewhat, but the drinks and staff are terrific.

HOLBORN & CLERKENWELL

Clerkenwell has a compelling claim to being the birthplace of the now ubiquitous gastropub: the **Eagle** (*see p219*) kicked things off. Other food pioneers that provide great drinking are **St John**, **Le Comptoir Gascon** (*for both, see p219*) and **Caravan** (*see p218*).

Café Kick
43 Exmouth Market, EC1R 4QL (7837 8077). Angel tube or Farringdon tube/rail. **Open** noon-11pm Mon-Thur; noon-midnight Fri, Sat; 1-10.30pm Sun. *Food served* noon-3pm, 6-10pm Mon-Thur; noon-3pm, 6-10.30pm Fri, Sat; 1-10pm Sun. **Credit** AmEx, MC, V.

Clerkenwell's most likeable bar is this table-football themed gem. The soccer paraphernalia is authentic, retro-cool and mainly Latin (you'll find a Zenit St

Terroirs.
See p245.

Petersburg scarf amid the St Etienne and Lusitanian gear); bar staff, beers and bites give the impression you could be in Lisbon. A modest open kitchen ('we don't microwave or deep-fry') dishes out tapas, sandwiches and charcuterie platters.
Other locations Bar Kick, 127 Shoreditch High Street, Shoreditch, E1 6JE (7739 8700).

★ Fox & Anchor
115 Charterhouse Street, EC1M 6AA (7250 1300, www.foxandanchor.com). Barbican tube or Farringdon tube/rail. **Open** 7am-11pm Mon-Thur; 7am-1am Fri; 8.30am-1am Sat; 8.30am-10pm Sun. *Food served* 7am-11am, noon-9.45pm Mon-Fri; 8.30am-11am, noon-9.45pm Sat; 8.30am-11am, noon-4pm, 6-9pm Sun. **Credit** AmEx, MC, V. **Map** p400 O5 ❽
Pristine mosaic tiling and etched glass paired together indicate 'sensitive refurbishment' at this Smithfield treasure. The dark wood bar is lined with pewter tankards; to the back is the Fox's Den, a series of intimate rooms used for both drinking and dining. Local sourcing is a priority and a pleasure: in addition to the own-label ale, cask beers might include Red Poll and Old Growler from Suffolk's fine Nethergate brewery. There are plenty more delights among the bottles.

Three Kings of Clerkenwell
7 Clerkenwell Close, EC1R 0DY (7253 0483). Farringdon tube/rail. **Open** noon-11pm Mon-Sat. *Food served* noon-3pm, 6.30-10pm Mon-Fri. **No credit cards. Map** p400 N4 ❾
Rhinoceros heads, Egyptian felines and photos of Dennis Bergkamp provide the decorative backdrop against which a regular bunch of discerning bohos glug Scrumpy Jack, Beck's Vier, Old Speckled Hen or London Pride, and tap the well-worn tables to the Cramps and other gems from an outstanding jukebox that is crammed with fabulous old platters.

28°-50° Wine Workshop & Kitchen
140 Fetter Lane, EC4A 1BT (7242 8877, www.2850.co.uk). Farringdon tube/rail. **Open** noon-midnight Mon-Fri. **Food served** noon-2.30pm, 6-9.30pm Mon-Fri. **Credit** AmEx, MC, V. **Map** p402 N6 ❿
This venture, named between the latitudes between which wine is produced, is at once serious and relaxed. Serious, in that the wines – a changing roster available by the glass and a distinctive collector's list – are assembled with specialist knowledge; relaxed in that the staff are great communicators and not at all wine-snobby. They offer flights (minimum glass size is a sensible 75ml) to sample a particular style or theme, and ensure that the seasonal menu complements the wines nicely – though the food isn't just second fiddle: there's a good palate at work here too, ensuring distinctive tastes in the French-influenced menu. It's a pleasant basement space with a modern-rustic feel.

THE BEST BUZZ BARS

Mason & Taylor
New in 2011, and instantly popular with the boutique-beer crowd. *See p253.*

Hawksmoor
This stellar steak-and-cocktail joint has made Covent Garden fashionable all over again. *See p221X.*

Worship Street Whistling Shop
Costumed barstaff, steampunk clientele and veeeery serious spirits. *See p242.*

Vinoteca
7 St John Street, EC1M 4AA (7724 7288, www.vinoteca.co.uk). Barbican tube or Farringdon tube/rail. **Open** noon-11pm Mon-Sat; noon-5pm Sun. *Food served* noon-3pm, 6-10pm Mon-Sat; noon-5pm Sun. **Credit** MC, V. **Map** p400 O5 ⓫
Inspired in name and approach by the Italian *enoteca* (a blend of off-licence and wine bar, with snacks thrown in), Vinoteca is more of a serious gastropub in spirit. But even if you're not in the mood for much more than a plate of bread and olive oil, it's worth heading here for the impressive 200-bottle wine list, of which 25 are available by the glass. Bonus: all wines are available to take away at retail price.
Other location 15 Seymour Place, W1H 5BD (7724 7288).

★ Zetter Townhouse
49-50 St John's Square, EC1V 4JJ (7324 4545, www.thezettertownhouse.com). Farringdon tube/rail. **Open** 10am-midnight Mon-Thur, Sun; 10am-1am Fri, Sat. **Food served** noon-5pm, 6-10.30pm daily. **Credit** AmEx, MC, V. **Map** p400 O4 ⓬
Head barman and all-round cocktail obsessive Tony Conigliaro has dug out many forgotten British libationary techniques (and created a number of his own), so you'll see intriguing ingredients such as 'port evaporation', nettle cordial and gunpowder tea tinctures on the list. The menu's simple descriptions belie the attention to detail – a dainty coupe is the receptacle for a Koln martini, the standard gin and martini combo brought dazzlingly to life with a pipette of own-make citrus aromatics. Decor recalls an eccentric antiques shop, but perfectly mannered staff give this the lie.

BLOOMSBURY & FITZROVIA

For sheer style, try the bar at **Hakkasan** (*see p220*). In King's Cross, **Camino** (*see p220*) added a dedicated sherry bar called Pepito, while the **Big Chill House** (*see p331*) is a great place for boozy music fans to stop at.

CONSUME

CONSUME

All Star Lanes

*Victoria House, Bloomsbury Place, WC1B 4DA
(7025 2676, www.allstarlanes.co.uk). Holborn tube.*
Open 5-11.30pm Mon-Wed; 5pm-midnight Thur;
noon-2am Fri; 11am-2am Sat; 11am-11pm Sun.
Food served 5-10pm Mon-Thur; noon-10pm Thur,
Fri; 11am-10pm Sat; 11am-9.30pm Sun. *Bowling*
£7.75-£8.75/person per game. **Credit** AmEx, MC,
V. **Map** p397 L5 ⑬
Of Bloomsbury's two subterranean bowling dens,
this is the one with aspirations. Walk past the lanes
and smart, diner-style seating, and you'll find yourself in a comfortable, subdued side bar with chilled
glasses, classy red furnishings, an unusual mix of
bottled lagers (try Anchor Steam) and some impressive cocktails. There's an American menu and, at
weekends, a range of DJs.
Other locations Whiteleys, 6 Porchester
Gardens, Bayswater, W2 4DB (7313 8363);
Old Truman Brewery, 91 Brick Lane, E1 6QL
(7426 9200).
▶ *Nearby, Bloomsbury Bowling Lanes (Bedford
Way, 7183 1979, WC1H 9EU, www.bloomsbury
bowling.com) offers a pints-and-worn-carpets take
on the game – and private karaoke booths.*

Bradley's Spanish Bar

*42-44 Hanway Street, W1T 1UT (7636 0359).
Tottenham Court Road tube.* **Open** noon-11pm
Mon-Sat; 3-10.30pm Sun. **Credit** MC, V. **Map**
p416 W1 ⑭
There's something of the Barcelona dive bar about
the place, and San Miguel or Cruzcampo on draught,
but Bradley's isn't really very Spanish. A hotchpotch
of local workers, shoppers and foreign exchange students fill the cramped two-floor space, or enrage taxi
drivers by spilling on to the narrow street, unper-
turbed by the routinely unpleasant toilets. After all,
there's a good jukebox and good atmosphere – what
more could anyone want?

Lamb

*94 Lamb's Conduit Street, WC1N 3LZ (7405
0713, www.thelamblondon.co.uk).* Holborn or
Russell Square tube. **Open** noon-11.30pm Mon-
Wed; noon-12.30am Thur-Sat; noon-10.30pm Sun.
Food served noon-9pm daily. **Credit** AmEx, MC,
V. **Map** p397 M4 ⑮

INSIDE TRACK POP-UP BARS

From arty Frank's Campari Bar in a
Peckham multi-storey car park to the
gin cocktails served from a retro Citröen
van beside the Serpentine Bar & Kitchen,
London summers are these days all about
the pop-up bar. To catch the hottest
new ones before they close, check
www.timeout.com and sign up for the blog.

The standard range of Young's beers is dispensed
from a central horseshoe bar in this 280-year-old
pub, around which are ringed original etched-glass
snob screens, used to prevent Victorian gentlemen
from being seen when liaising with 'women of dubi-
ous distinction'. A sunken back area gives access to
a convenient square of summer patio.

Long Bar

*Sanderson, 50 Berners Street, W1T 3NG (7300
1400, www.sandersonlondon.com). Goodge Street
or Oxford Circus tube.* **Open** 11am-midnight Mon-
Wed; 11am-1am Thur-Sat; noon-10.30pm Sun.
Food served noon-11.30pm Mon-Wed; noon-
12.30pm Thur-Sat; 1-10pm Sun. **Credit** AmEx,
DC, MC, V. **Map** p396 J5 ⑯
Its early noughties celeb-infested glory days may
now only be a faded memory, but the Long Bar still
has plenty of easy glamour. The long bar in question
is a thin onyx affair, though despite its length, nab-
bing one of the eyeball-backed stools is an unlikely
prospect. A better bet is the lovely courtyard, where
table service, candlelight and watery features make
a much nicer setting for the fine cocktails. Bar
snacks are priced high.

Shochu Lounge

*Basement, Roka, 37 Charlotte Street, W1T
1RR (7580 9666, www.shochulounge.com).
Goodge Street or Tottenham Court Road tube.*
Open 5.30pm-midnight Mon-Sat; 5.30-11pm
Sun. *Food served* 5.30-11.30pm Mon-Sat; 5.30-
10.30pm Sun. **Credit** AmEx, DC, MC, V.
Map p396 J5 ⑰
Beneath landmark Japanese restaurant Roka, the
chic Shochu Lounge offers drinks based on the
vodka-like distilled spirit of the same name. Shochu
is often overlooked for its better-known and more
widespread counterpart, saké, but it's here used in
healthy tonics, in cocktails, and sold by the 50ml
measure. With a 13.5% service charge, drinks run
to around £10. The full Roka menu is available if
you're hungry.

COVENT GARDEN & THE STRAND

★ **Gordon's Wine Bar**
*47 Villiers Street, Strand, WC2N 6NE (7930
1408, www.gordonswinebar.com). Embankment
tube or Charing Cross tube/rail.* **Open** 11am-11pm
Mon-Sat; noon-10pm Sun. *Food served* noon-10pm
Mon-Sat; noon-9pm Sun. **Credit** AmEx, MC, V.
Map p416 Y5 ⑱
Gordon's Wine Bar was established in its present
form as long ago as 1890, but the atmospheric
exposed brickwork and flickering candlelight make
this basement feel older still. Although this is the
definitive old-school wine bar, it gets packed with
a young and lively crowd, half of whom seem to be
on first dates. The wine list is surprisingly modern;

Mark's Bar. *See p246.*

still, in such surroundings, it seems a shame not to drink the fortified wines, which are drawn directly from casks behind the bar.

Lamb & Flag
33 Rose Street, WC2E 9EB (7497 9504). Covent Garden tube. **Open** 11am-11pm Mon-Thur; 11am-11.30pm Fri, Sat; noon-10.30pm Sun. *Food served* noon-3pm Mon-Fri; noon-4.30pm Sat, Sun. **Credit** MC, V. **Map** p416 Y3 ⑲

This dog-leg alleyway used to be a pit of prostitution and bare-knuckle bashes, the latter hosted at this historic, low-ceilinged tavern back when it was called the Bucket of Blood; poet John Dryden was beaten up here in 1679. Space is always at a premium, hence the pavement cluster on summer evenings. Two centuries of mounted cuttings and caricatures amplify the sense of character.
▶ *If it's too busy, try the Benelux-themed beer-café Lowlander (36 Drury Lane, WC2B 5RR, 7379 7446, www.lowlander.com).*

★ Terroirs
5 William IV Street, WC2N 4DW (7036 0660, www.terroirswinebar.com). Charing Cross tube/rail. **Open/food served** noon-11pm Mon-Sat. **Credit** AmEx, MC, V. **Map** p416 Y4 ⑳

Now extending over two floors, Terroirs is a superb and very popular wine bar that specialises in the new generation of exorganic and biodynamic, sulphur-, sugar- or acid-free wines. The list of wines is only slightly shorter than the Bible and almost as profound, with tasting notes that are honest to a fault – a wine like a hedgehog? All in all, a place for oenophiliac adventure. The line-up of Calvados and Armagnac bottles is impressive and the food terrific: a tapas-style selection of French bar snacks, charcuterie and seafood. *Photo p242.*

SOHO & LEICESTER SQUARE

Soho is a focus for gay nightlife; *see pp310-313.*

Dog & Duck
18 Bateman Street, W1D 3AJ (7494 0697, www.nicholsonspubs.co.uk). Tottenham Court Road tube. **Open** 10am-11pm Mon-Thur; 10am-11.30pm Fri, Sat; noon-10.30pm Sun. *Food served* 10am-10pm Mon-Sat; noon-9pm Sun. **Credit** AmEx, MC, V. **Map** p416 W2 ㉑

This Soho landmark is known for its literary heritage, vintage interior (etched mirrors, carved mahogany) and ever-changing selection of good ales, ranging from the familiar likes of London Pride to an altogether rarer range of beers from the Newman Brewery. Sausages are another feature. The George Orwell room upstairs, where the writer sometimes drank, offers more space; downstairs, punters spill out on to the pavement.

★ Experimental Cocktail Club
13A Gerrard Street, W1D 5PS (7434 3559, www.chinatownecc.com). Leicester Square tube. **Open/food served** 6pm-3am Mon-Sat; 5pm-midnight Sun. **Map** p416 W3 ㉒

Quite fancy, a little French and fairly flipping phenomenal, the London outpost of Paris's ECC is a stylish (sort of) speakeasy. The main, first-floor bar is classic, slightly colonial and cosy; there's an equally impressive and intimate bar upstairs. The cocktails aren't cheap but these lads know their liquids. A less-bitter twist on the negroni uses lavender-infused gin; rare vintage gins and vodkas, served in classic cocktails for £150, offer a bling imbibing experience. The wine list is strong; beer a baffling blind spot; food is French and simple – boards of bread, cheese and charcuterie.

Purl.

CONSUME

French House

49 Dean Street, W1D 5BG (7437 2799,
www.frenchhousesoho.com). Leicester Square or
Piccadilly Circus tube. **Open** noon-11pm Mon-Sat;
noon-10.30pm Sun. *Food served* noon-3pm, 5.30-
11pm Mon-Sat. **Credit** AmEx, DC, MC, V.
Map p416 W3 ㉓

Through the door of this venerable Gallic establishment have passed many titanic drinkers of the pre-
and post-war era, the Bacons and the Behans. The
venue's French heritage also enticed de Gaulle to run
a Resistance operation from upstairs – it's now,
incongruously, a tiny Venetian-style restaurant. De
Gaulle's image survives behind the bar, where beer
is served in half-pints and litre bottles of Breton cider
are still plonked on the famed back alcove table.
▶ *The little upstairs restaurant, Polpetto (7734*
1969, www.polpetto.co.uk), is the first offshoot of
the popular Polpo – and every bit as crammed.

★ LAB

12 Old Compton Street, W1D 4TQ (7437
7820, www.labbaruk.com). Leicester Square or
Tottenham Court Road tube. **Open** 4pm-midnight
daily. *Food served* 4-10pm daily. **Credit** MC, V.
Map p416 X2 ㉔

Newer spots have overtaken the '70s-meets-'90s
decor, but few can match the sheer enthusiasm and
knowledge of the staff at the London Academy of
Bartending. Cocktails are king here, and many original combinations are mixed using LAB's own infu-
sions and syrups (chorizo tequila, anyone?). Pull up
a chair and let one of the ultra-helpful mixologists
guide you through the menu. The unashamed party
vibe means this place fills up early.

Lucky Voice

52 Poland Street, W1F 7LR (7439 3660,
www.luckyvoice.co.uk). Oxford Circus tube.
Open/food served 5.30pm-1am Mon-Thur;
3pm-1am Fri, Sat; 3-10.30pm Sun. **Credit** AmEx,
MC, V. **Map** p416 V2 ㉕

There are nine rooms at this karaoke venue, each of
them with space for between four and 12 singers;
some come with props such as hats, wigs and inflatable electric guitars. A drinks menu includes cocktails (£7), saké and spirits, brought to your room
when you press the 'thirsty' button; food is limited to
pizzas and snacks. The perfect place to discover your
inner Susan Boyle.

Other locations 173-174 Upper Street, Islington,
N1 1RG (7354 6280).

★ Mark's Bar

66-70 Brewer Street, W1F 9UP (7292 3518,
www.marksbar.co.uk). Piccadilly Circus tube.
Open/food served noon-1am Mon-Sat;
11am-11pm Sun. **Credit** AmEx, MC, V.
Map p416 V3 ㉖

In the basement under Mark Hix's fine Soho restaurant, this is a sort-of subterranean speakeasy without the smugness. There's a low zinc bar, retro rugs
and comfy Chesterfields slouched next to a bar billiards table. Service is flawless and the drinks menu
crafted by an all-star cocktail dream-team, led by
Nick Strangeway. The 150-strong wine list might be
expected in a restaurant bar, but it's rare to find such
an enlightened beer menu. You have to order some
food (it's part of the licence requirement), but that's
no hardship: it includes the entire à la carte menu
from upstairs and lovely bar snacks. *Photo p245.*

★ Milk & Honey

61 Poland Street, W1F 7NU (7065 6841, www.mlkhny.com). Oxford Circus tube. **Open** *Non-members* 6-11pm Mon-Sat (2hrs max, last admission 9pm). *Members* 6pm-3am Mon-Sat. **Credit** AmEx, DC, MC, V. **Map** p416 V2 **27**

You could walk past the inconspicuous door of this semi-mythical, dimly lit Soho speakeasy every day and never know it was here, and that's probably just how they like it. It's members-only most of the time, but mere mortals can book a table until 11pm, although even then you're not likely to get a table later on in the week. While the place may not be at its best earlier in the evening, what it then lacks in atmosphere it more than makes up for with its outstanding cocktails.

OXFORD STREET & MARYLEBONE

★ Purl

50 Blandford Street, W1U 7HX (7935 0835, www.purl-london.com). Bond Street tube. **Open** 5-11.30pm Mon-Thur; 5pm-midnight Fri, Sat. **Credit** AmEx, MC, V. **Map** p396 G5 **28**

This new cocktail bar has a speakeasy/Prohibition feel. There's even a (working) retro phone booth. The four young chaps behind it claim inspiration from the golden age of bartending. Accordingly, a lot of effort goes into each drink: for Mr Hyde's Fixer Upper (£9), a Smoking Gun hand-held food smoker pipes applewood smoke into a flask of rum, cola reduction and orange bitters. The flask is then sealed with candlewax before being served with a silver goblet.

PADDINGTON & NOTTING HILL

★ Lonsdale

48 Lonsdale Road, W11 2DE (7727 4080, www.thelonsdale.co.uk). Ladbroke Grove or Notting Hill Gate tube. **Open** 6pm-midnight Mon-Thur; 6pm-1am Fri, Sat. *Food served* 6-11pm Mon-Sat. **Credit** AmEx, MC, V. **Map** p404 Y4 **29**

It's been a fair few years since he mixed drinks here, but bartender Dick Bradsell's influence is still felt in the outstanding modern cocktails: try the elderflower fizz (elderflower cordial, lemon juice and champagne). Comprising a sun-catching front terrace, a long bar counter and a wide, candlelit seating area at the back, the Lonsdale treats cocktail history with reverence; drinks invented in London between 1914 and 1934 are a specialist subject.

Portobello Star

171 Portobello Road, W11 2DY (7229 8016, www.portobellostarbar.co.uk). Ladbroke Grove or Notting Hill Gate tube. **Open** 11am-11pm Mon-Thur; 11am-12.30am Fri; 10am-12.30am Sat; 11am-11.30pm Sun. **Credit** MC, V. **Map** p404 X4 **30**

This 'cocktail tavern' deftly blends discerning bar and traditional boozer. The bountifully stocked bar

is manned by friendly staff thoroughly educated in the art of adult refreshment; 'Drink less but better' is the mantra of leading mixologist Jake Burger. His impeccable, approachable directory of discerning drinks is the last word on sophisticated intoxication. If you want to mix drinking with music, there are DJs on Friday and Saturday nights.

PICCADILLY CIRCUS & MAYFAIR

★ Connaught Bar

Connaught, Carlos Place, W1K 2AL (7499 7070, www.the-connaught.co.uk). Bond Street tube. **Open** 4pm-1am Mon-Sat. **Credit** AmEx, DC, MC, V. **Map** p398 H7 **31**

The main bar of the swish Connaught hotel (*see p203*) is grown-up, darkly elegant and reminiscent of a cruise liner, with unobtrusive lighting and a deco feel. The expensive drinks and the service have a lot to live up to in the surroundings, but they do so. The Connaught martini is worth ordering for the tableside theatre alone and the staff are faultless – slightly formal, but never standoffish.

▶ *Across the lobby, the hotel's discreet Coburg Bar is both smart and unpretentious.*

Galvin at Windows

London Hilton, Park Lane, W1K 1BE (7208 4021, www.galvinatwindows.com). Hyde Park Corner tube. **Open** 11am-1am Mon-Wed; 11am-3am Thur, Fri; 3pm-3am Sat; 11am-10.30pm Sun. *Food served* 11am-12.30am Mon-Wed; 6pm-12.30am Thur-Sat. **Credit** AmEx, DC, MC, V. **Map** p398 G8 **32**

There's suddenly no shortage of rooftop venues in London, but the location of Windows is still superb. It offers remarkable panoramic views from the 28th floor of the Park Lane Hilton. Add a sleek interior that mixes art deco glamour with a hint of 1970s petrodollar kitsch, and you can't go wrong. The wine and cocktails don't come cheap, but the drinks are assembled with care, and the service is attentive without being obsequious.

WESTMINSTER & ST JAMES'S

Albannach

66 Trafalgar Square, WC2N 5DS (7930 0066, www.albannach.co.uk). Charing Cross tube/rail. **Open** noon-1am Mon-Sat; noon-7pm Sun. *Food served* noon-11pm Mon-Sat; noon-6.30pm Sun. **Credit** AmEx, DC, MC, V. **Map** p416 X5 **33**

Right on Trafalgar Square, Albannach (as opposed to 'sassanach') specialises in Scotch whiskies and cocktails thereof. A map in the menu details the origins of these Highland and Island malts, the pages brimming with 17-year-old Glengoynes, 12-year-old Cragganmore and 29-year-old Auchentoshan. That said, kilted staff, illuminated reindeer and too many loud office groups detract from the quality on offer.

CONSUME

Boisdale.

Boisdale
13-15 Eccleston Street, SW1W 9LX (7730 6922,
www.boisdale.co.uk). Victoria tube/rail. **Open/**
food served noon-1am Mon-Fri; 6pm-1am Sat.
Admission £5 before 10pm, then £12. **Credit**
AmEx, DC, MC, V. **Map** p398 H10 ㉞
There's nowhere quite like this posh, Scottish-
themed enterprise, and that includes its sister branch
in the City. If you're here to drink, you'll be drinking
single malts from a terrific range. That said, the outstanding wine list is surprisingly affordable, with
house selections starting at under £20. Additional
appeal comes from live jazz (six nights a week) and
a heated cigar terrace.
Other locations Boisdale of Bishopsgate,
Swedeland Court, 202 Bishopsgate, the City,
EC2M 4NR (7283 1763); Cabot Place, E14 4QT
(7715 5818).

★ Dukes Bar
35 St James's Place, SW1A 1NY (7491 4840,
www.campbellgrayhotels.com). Green Park tube.
Open 2pm-midnight Mon-Thur, Sun; noon-
midnight Fri, Sat. **Credit** AmEx, DC, MC, V.
Map p398 J8 ㉟
This titchy bar looks like an upper-class Georgian
sitting room. The martinis, mixed formally at your
table, are among the best in London, and priced
accordingly. Sipping one amid the polite murmur of
the very adult clientele, while munching on complimentary nuts and Puglian olives, is a soothing experience. Alternatives include nearly a dozen good
wines by the glass.

St Stephen's Tavern
10 Bridge Street, SW1A 2JR (7925 2286,
www.hall-woodhouse.co.uk). Westminster tube.
Open 10am-11.30pm Mon-Thur, Sat; 10am-
12.15pm Fri; 10.30am-11pm Sun. *Food served*
noon-10pm daily. **Credit** MC, V. **Map**
p399 L9 ㊱
Done out with dark woods, etched mirrors and Arts
and Crafts-style wallpaper, this is a lovely old pub.
The food is reasonably priced and the ales are excellent, but drinks can be expensive. Opposite Big Ben,
its location is terrific, yet it's neither too touristy nor
too busy. If the downstairs bars are full, head
upstairs and look for a seat on the mezzanine.
▶ *St Stephen's nearest rival is the Red Lion (48*
Parliament Street, SW1A 2NH, 7930 5826), by
tradition the politicians' favourite.

CHELSEA

★ Cadogan Arms
298 King's Road, SW3 5UG (7352 6500,
www.thecadoganarmschelsea.com). Sloane Square
tube then bus 19, 22, 319. **Open** 11am-11pm
Mon-Sat; 11am-10.30pm Sun. *Food served* noon-
3.30pm, 6-10.30pm Mon-Fri; noon-10.30pm Sat;
noon-9pm Sun. **Credit** AmEx, DC, MC, V.
Map p395 E12 ㊲
In 2009, this 19th-century Chelsea pub was given a
major rebuild by its new owners, the Martin brothers. It now has a countrified look, complete with
stuffed animals and fly-fishing displays, and
remains a proper boozer, with top-quality real ales,
notwithstanding the snug and smoothly run dining
area, where great food is on offer. *Photo p251.*
▶ *On Sloane Square, the Martin brothers'*
Botanist (no.7, 7730 0077) provides a similar
mix of fine booze and hearty food.

KNIGHTSBRIDGE & SOUTH KENSINGTON

Anglesea Arms
15 Selwood Terrace, SW7 3QG (7373 7960,
www.capitalpubcompany.com). South Kensington
tube. **Open** 11am-11pm Mon-Sat; noon-10.30pm

The Gin Craze

The crack cocaine of the 18th century has returned – in high style.

London is occasionally convulsed by events that are breathtakingly sordid, and the early 18th-century Gin Craze is one of them. Captured in brutal detail by Hogarth's famously dystopian *Gin Lane* (1751), the reality wasn't far removed from his imaginings: Andrew Barr's *Drink: A Social History* tells of the mother who reclaimed her two-year-old from the workhouse, strangled him for his new clothes, and sold them for a tot of gin.

It was war with France – specifically an attempt by William III to get one over on the Frogs by taxing popular imports of their brandy out of existence – that gave impetus to gin-drinking, previously little known. Local distillers could start making the stuff merely by posting notice of their intention to do so ten days in advance. By 1694, the spirit was cheaper than Britain's age-hallowed staple, beer. Barr notes that when William acceded to the throne in 1688, 500,000 gallons of gin were drunk a year; by 1742, it was 19 million gallons – ten times the amount now consumed in the country by ten times more people, and far higher in alcohol. A series of Acts of Parliament failed to address the problem, until legislation combined with a grain shortage to drive up prices. By the 1750s, the Gin Craze was over.

Gin's steep decline in popularity did not mean its career was over. In the 1830s the industrial working class of the city were supping in 'gin palaces' (such as the Lamb; *see p244*), pubs where the drinkers stood at a counter to encourage them to swiftly knock back short measures of strong liquor, rather than relaxing at a table steadily quaffing a pint.

Gin's more recent forays into the city's drinking culture have been more glamorous. London Dry Gin – which adds to the juniper distinctive citrus botanicals and spices, but never colourings or sugar – was a bedrock spirit for the classic cocktails that fuelled the flappers through the Roaring Twenties. Since then, London Dry Gin has maintained its popularity, but not its legion of local distillers. Only **Beefeater** (www.beefeater gin.com) remained into the 21st century, and even that was considered rather unfashionable. But taken over in 2005 by Pernod Ricard – French revenge for the brandy tax, perhaps – the distiller has been reborn: its premium Beefeater 24 took gold at the prestigious San Francisco World Spirits Competition in 2010. A number of boutique local distillers have followed: **Sipsmith** (www.sipsmith.com) is the best reputed after Beefeater, but **Sacred** (www.sacredspiritcompany.com) is among several micro-distilleries producing 'hand-crafted' and 'small batch' London Dry Gin.

Of course, these are connoisseur snifters – and as such, best enjoyed in appropriate surroundings. Fusing the Shoreditch fashion for steam-punk Victoriana with gourmet tippling, the new **Worship Street Whistling Shop** (*see p242*) and the bar at on-trend **Bistrotheque** (23-27 Wadeson Street, E2 9DR, 8983 7900, www.bistrotheque.com), refitted as the Gin Den in 2011, are just two of the bars combining 'dram shop' atmospherics with superluxe booze.

CONSUME

Worship Street Whistling Shop.

Sun. *Food served* noon-3pm, 6-10pm Mon-Fri; noon-5pm, 6-10pm Sat; noon-5pm, 6-9.30pm Sun. **Credit** AmEx, MC, V. **Map** p395 D11 ⑧

Formerly the local of both Charles Dickens and DH Lawrence, this old boozer is packed tight on summer evenings, the front terrace and main bar filled with professional blokes chugging ale, and their female equivalents putting bottles of Sancerre on expenses. But the Anglesea has always had more aura than the average South Kensington hostelry; perhaps it's the link with the Great Train Robbery, reputedly planned here.

Blue Bar
Berkeley, Wilton Place, SW1X 7RL (7235 6000, www.the-berkeley.co.uk). Hyde Park Corner tube. **Open** 4pm-1am Mon-Sat; 4-11pm Sun. **Credit** AmEx, DC, MC, V. **Map** p398 G9 ㊴

It isn't just a caprice: this David Collins-designed bar really lives up to its name. The sky-blue bespoke armchairs, the deep-blue ornate plasterwork and the navy-blue leather-bound menus combine with discreet lighting to striking effect. It's more a see-and-be-seen place than somewhere to kick back, but don't let the celeb-heavy reputation put you off: staff treat everyone like royalty, and the cocktails are a masterclass in sophistication.

NORTH LONDON

The **Lock Tavern** (*see p331*) and **Proud** (*see p332*) are excellent Camden DJ bars, while the **Blues Kitchen** (*see p323*) and scuzzy indie-den the **Dublin Castle** (94 Parkway, NW1 7AN, 7485 1773) supply live music. In Islington, the boisterous **Old Queen's Head** (*see p331*) is a boisterous and lively pub. The **Horseshoe** (*see p233*) in Hampstead is an excellent gastropub which doesn't disappoint on the own-brewed ale front.

Booking Office
St Pancras Renaissance London Hotel, NW1 2AR (7841 3540, www.bookingofficerestaurant.com). King's Cross or St Pancras tube/rail. **Open** 6.30am-2.45am daily. **Credit** AmEx, DC, MC. **Map** p397 L3 ㊵

Superlatives come easily when describing the Booking Office: epic, soaring, magnificent. As part of Sir Gilbert Scott's 1873 Midland Grand Hotel, it was designed to instil in passengers a sense of awe at the power of the railways. These days, it serves as an awe-inspiring bar, and the refit has made the most of the Victorian splendour while introducing the comforts expected in a modern five-star hotel.

Bull & Last
168 Highgate Road, NW5 1QS (7267 3641, www.thebullandlast.co.uk). Kentish Town tube or Gospel Oak rail. **Open** noon-11pm Mon-Thur; noon-midnight Fri, Sat; noon-10.30pm Sun. **Food** served noon-3pm, 6.30-10pm Mon-Fri; 12.30-3.30pm, 6.30-10pm Sat; 12.30-3.30pm, 7-9pm Sun. **Credit** MC, V.

The Bull & Last's location on the Parliament Hill side of Hampstead Heath, along with its home-made ice-cream, generous fireplace and hearty menu, make it a natural choice for refreshment after a spot of outdoor activity. It's far better than it needs to be, with great, seasonal cooking (notable are the meats and chips), well-priced ales and serious ales. Not suprisingly, it's often packed. *Photo p253.*

Driver
2-4 Wharfdale Road, King's Cross, N1 9RY (7278 8827, www.driverlondon.co.uk). King's Cross tube/rail. **Open** noon-midnight Mon-Fri; 5pm-midnight Sat; noon-6pm Sun. *Food served noon-3pm, 6-10pm Mon-Fri; 6-10pm Sat; noon-6pm Sun.* **No credit cards. Map** p397 M2 ㊹

Spread over five floors, with decor alternating from urban to intricate, this soaring yet svelte Swiss army knife of a venue encompasses a pub-style restaurant, a small roof terrace, a members' bar, a lounge and a dining room that, later, transforms *Bugsy Malone*-style into a dancefloor with decks. There's a living plant wall on the outside.

★ Holly Bush
22 Holly Mount, Hampstead, NW3 6SG (7435 2892). Hampstead tube or Hampstead Heath rail. **Open** noon-11pm Mon-Sat; noon-10.30pm Sun. *Food served* noon-3pm, 6-10pm Mon-Fri; noon-4pm, 6-10pm Sat; noon-5pm, 6-9pm Sun. **Credit** (over £10) MC, V.

As the trend for gutting old pubs claims yet more Hampstead boozers, this place's cachet increases. Located on a quiet hilltop backstreet, it was built as a house in the 1790s and used as the Assembly Rooms in the 1800s, before becoming a pub in 1928. A higgledy-piggledy air remains, with three low-ceilinged bar areas and one bar counter at which are poured decent pints. Sound food and a good choice of wines by the glass are further draws. *Photo p254.*

★ 69 Colebrooke Row
69 Colebrooke Row, Islington, N1 8AA (07540 528593, www.69colebrookerow.com). Angel tube. **Open** 5pm-midnight Mon-Wed; 5pm-1am Thur; 5pm-2am Fri, Sat. **Credit** AmEx, MC, V. **Map** p400 O2 ㊷

Tucked away on a side street, 69 Colebrooke Row is a cocktail bar of distinction. With just a handful of tables supplemented by a few stools at the bar, it may be smaller than your front room, but the understated, intimate space proves a fine environment in which to enjoy the pristine cocktails (liquorice whisky sours, raspberry and rosehip bellinis, gimlets with own-made rhubarb cordial, depending on the season), mixed with quiet ceremony. Impeccably attired staff, handwritten bills and tall glasses of water poured from a cocktail shaker also elevate it from the pack.

CONSUME

Cadogan Arms.
See p248.

EAST LONDON

Late-night **Charlie Wright's International Bar** (*see p327*) is as much about drinking as it is about music; there's music, food and booze at Concrete, beneath **Pizza East** (*see p236*). Shoreditch has a thriving gay scene, *see pp310-315*; for nightclubs, *see pp332-333*.

Callooh Callay

65 Rivington Street, Shoreditch, EC2A 3AY (7739 4781, www.calloohcallaybar.com). Old Street tube/rail or Shoreditch High Street rail. **Open/food served** 6pm-midnight Mon-Wed, Sun; 6pm-1am Thur-Sat. **Credit** MC, V. **Map** p401 R4 ⓭

Only a pair of intertwined Cs divulges Callooh Callay's location. Inside, it's warm and whimsical; the neo-Victorian decor is as eclectic as 'Jabberwocky', the poem by Lewis Carroll from which the bar gets its name. A laid-back lounge, a mirrored bar and loos tiled in old cassettes lie behind an oak Narnia wardrobe. Stake out seats here to people-watch: lots of vintage fabrics and fixed-gear cyclists.

Carpenter's Arms

73 Cheshire Street, Brick Lane, E2 6EG (7739 6342, www.carpentersarmsfreehouse.com). Liverpool Street tube/rail. **Open** 4-11.30pm Mon; noon-11.30pm Tue-Thur, Sun; noon-12.30am Fri, Sat. *Food served* 5-10pm Mon; 1-10pm Tue-Sun. **Credit** MC, V. **Map** p401 S4 ⓮

At one time, this cosy boozer took centre stage in East End gangsterland. It was bought by the Kray twins in 1967 for their dear old mum, and it was here that Ronnie tanked up on dutch courage before murdering Jack 'the Hat' McVitie. Today, Hoxtonites, fashionistas, the odd ironic moustache and a few ambitious hats fill the snug space. The drinks selection is great, and the cut-above food (boards of cheese, Sunday roasts) isn't sold at stupid prices.

Commercial Tavern

142 Commercial Street, Spitalfields, E1 6NU (7247 1888). Liverpool Street tube/rail or Shoreditch High Street rail. **Open** 5-11pm Mon-Fri; noon-11pm Sat; noon-10.30pm Sun. **Credit** AmEx, MC, V. **Map** p401 R5 ⓯

The inspired chaos of retro-eccentric decor and warm, inclusive atmosphere make this landmark flat-iron corner pub very likeable. It seems to have escaped the attentions of the necking-it-after-work masses, perhaps because of the absence of wall-to-wall lager pumps in favour of some proper real ale. The bar is made up of colourful art deco tiles, and there's a distinct decorative playfulness throughout; it's a great example of how a historic pub can be lit up with new life.

▶ *Just down the street, the fabulous, every-busy Golden Heart (no.110, E1 6LZ, 7247 2158) is a famous nursery for East End artists.*

CONSUME

Grapes

76 Narrow Street, Limehouse, E14 8BP (7987 4396). Westferry DLR. **Open** noon-3pm, 5.30-11pm Mon-Wed; noon-11pm Thur-Sat; noon-10.30pm Sun. *Food served* noon-2.30pm, 7-9.30pm Mon-Sat; noon-3.30pm Sun. **Credit** AmEx, MC, V. If you're trying to evoke the feel of the Thames docks before their Disneyfication into Docklands, these narrow, ivy-covered and etched-glass 1720 riverside premises are a good place to start: the downstairs is all wood panels and nautical jetsam; the upstairs plainer, but it's easier to find seats for Sunday lunch. It's a fairly blokey pub: expect good ales and a half-dozen wines of each colour by glass and bottle, plus jugs of kir royale or strawberry fizz for summer and port for winter. There's a tiny terrace too.

▶ *Nearby, Gordon Ramsay's gastropub, the Narrow (44 Narrow Street, E14 8DQ, 7592 7950, www.gordonramsay.com), serves some great bar snacks.*

Sofa Sport

Where to watch the London 2012 Games in a sporting atmosphere.

The London 2012 Games will be broadcast on TV, but that doesn't mean you have to view at home. Experience the passion of the home crowd by watching in a bar that attracts a partisan sporting clientele. For an electric atmosphere, choose an event in which Team GB is expected to do well, such as Cycling, Rowing or Equestrian.

For Cycling, the best port of call is the wonderful café/bar **Look Mum No Hands** (49 Old Street, EC1V 9HX, 7253 1025, www.lookmumnohands.com). As well as the excellent snacks and light meals provided by the kitchen – and good-quality coffee – the workshop fixes bikes and a big screen shows cycle sports live.

Rowers are a sociable bunch and, since they have a professional interest in water, their watering holes are usually situated on riverbanks. In London, this means the Thames around Putney and Hammersmith – key locations for the annual Boat Race and home to many rowing clubs. Venues include, in Putney, the **Duke's Head** (8 Lower Richmond Road, SW15 1JN, 8788 2552, www.dukesheadputney.com), the **Coat & Badge** (8 Lacy Road, SW15 1NI, 8788 4900, www.geronimo-inns.co.uk) and the **Boathouse** (Brewhouse Lane, SW15 2JX, 8789 0476, www.boathouse putney.co.uk), and, in Hammersmith, the **Rutland Arms** (15 Lower Mall, W6 9DJ, 8748 5586, www.taylor-walker.co.uk).

If it's Equestrian that floats your boat, **Hemingways Lounge Bar** (57 High Street, SW19 5EE, 8944 7722, www.hemingways bar.co.uk) is so horsey that it has named its booths after the four-legged occupants of Wimbledon Village Stables. **PJ's Bar & Grill** (52 Fulham Road, SW3 6HH, 7581 0025, www.pjsbarandgrill.co.uk) is a popular venue with polo players in particular, while soldiers from the Household Cavalry and members of the Civil Service Riding Club often take up residence in the **Paxtons Head** (153 Knightsbridge, SW1X 7PA, 7589 6627, www.taylor-walker.co.uk) after a gallop.

CONSUME

Look Mum No Hands.

★ Mason & Taylor
*51 Bethnal Green Road, Shoreditch, E1 6LA
(7749 9670, www.masonandtaylor.co.uk).
Liverpool Street tube/rail or Shoreditch High Street
rail.* **Open** 5pm-midnight Mon-Thur; 5pm-2am
Fri; noon-2am Sat; noon-midnight Sun. *Food
served* 5-10pm Mon-Thur; 5-10.30pm Fri; noon-
10.30pm Sat; noon-9pm Sun. **Credit** AmEx, MC,
V. **Map** p401 S4 ⓐ
This two-floor, somewhat urban/industrial space
showcases boutique beers. Behind a concrete bar, a
dozen draught taps draw both the obscure and the
accessible: Brooklyn Lager, De Koninck and a milk
stout from Colorado. The friendly staff are happy to
advise on putting together a taster flight. Tapas-
style small plates have a British bent and on Sunday
it's all about the roasts. It can get pretty busy.

SOUTH-EAST LONDON

Dartmouth Arms
*7 Dartmouth Road, Forest Hill, SE23 3HN (8488
3117, www.thedartmoutharms.com). Forest Hill
rail or bus 122, 176, 185.* **Open** noon-11pm Mon-
Thur, Sun; noon-1am Fri, Sat. *Food served* noon-
3.30pm, 6.30-10pm Mon-Fri; noon-10pm Sat;
12.30-4pm, 5-9pm Sun. **Credit** MC, V.
This gastropub is ideally located for the Horniman
Museum. The front bar is now a well-aired, sepia-
tinted space perfect for relaxing with the papers or
the free Wi-Fi; there's also an adjoining 'snug bar'
(the red walls of which boast exhibitions by local
artists) and a rear dining room. Cocktails are just
£5.50-£6.25, and there's a long wine list, but beers
are limited: Brakspear and Bombardier,
Staropramen and Kronenbourg.

Gipsy Moth
*60 Greenwich Church Street, Greenwich,
SE10 9BL (8858 0786, www.thegipsymoth
greenwich.co.uk). Cutty Sark DLR.* **Open** noon-
11pm Mon-Thur; noon-midnight Fri, Sat; noon-
10.30pm Sun. *Food served* noon-10pm Mon-Fri;
noon-10pm Sat; noon-9.30pm Sun. **Credit**
AmEx, MC, V. **Map** p405 W2 ⓐ
The split-level garden and roomy interior at this
moderately funky pub are ideal for a sit-down after
roaming around Greenwich. The pub offers an
impressive number of beers (Früli, Budvar, Paulaner
and at least six others), well-priced wines and pretty
decent food, from full breakfasts through bar snacks
(olives, pistachios, pork crackling) to solid mains
such as pork sausage and sage mash.
► *In good weather, the riverside seats of Cutty
Sark Tavern (4-6 Ballast Quay, SE10 9PD, 8858
3146, www.cuttysarktavern.co.uk) are popular.*

Greenwich Union
*56 Royal Hill, Greenwich, SE10 8RT (8692 6258,
www.greenwichunion.com). Greenwich rail/DLR.*
Open noon-11pm Mon-Fri; 11am-11pm Sat;

Bull & Last. *See p250.*

11.30am-10.30pm Sun. *Food served* noon-10pm
Mon-Fri; 11am-10pm Sat; 11am-9pm Sun. **Credit**
MC, V. **Map** p405 W3 ⓐ
Decorated with framed covers of the *Picture Post*,
this tidy operation is the spiritual home of Alistair
Hook's mission to bring his Meantime Brewery's
German-style beers to the British public. Six tap
options complement a couple of dozen bottled international beers, and food runs from a humble bacon
butty to chargrilled steaks. Coffee, tea and a small
front terrace make it a decent option for non-drink-
ing visitors to Greenwich's many attractions.
► *Near the Thames – and on the premises of the
Old Royal Naval College – the Old Brewery (see
p238) is Meantime's flagship bar-restaurant.*

CONSUME

Holly Bush. *See p250.*

SOUTH-WEST LONDON

Draft House
94 Northcote Road, Battersea, SW11 6QW (7924 1814, www.drafthouse.co.uk). Clapham South tube or Clapham Junction rail. **Open** 11am-11pm Mon-Fri; 10am-11pm Sat; 10am-10.30pm Sun. *Food served 11am-10pm Mon-Sat; 10am-9pm Sun.* **Credit** AmEx, MC, V.

This attractive beer bistro is clad in wood, warmed by candlelight and brightened with pop art and green furniture. The curved bar sports 17 shiny draught fonts and there are three-dozen bottles in the fridge. Served in third, half and full pints, the beers range across Europe and as far as the craft breweries of the United States, while ale-friendly tucker includes ham hock salad and a succulent roquefort burger.

Other locations 206-208 Tower Bridge Road, the City, SE1 2UP (7378 9995); 74-76 Battersea Bridge Road, Battersea, SW11 3AG (7228 6482).

▶ *The bar also offers tours of the Sambrook's Brewery in nearby Battersea.*

Effra
38A Kellet Road, Brixton, SW2 1EB (7274 4180). Brixton tube/rail. **Open** noon-11pm Mon-Thur; noon-midnight Fri; 10am-midnight Sat; 10am-10.30pm Sun. *Food served noon-10pm Mon-Fri; 11am-10pm Sat; 11am-9.30pm Sun.* **No credit cards**.

This old-school pub has more of an Afro-Caribbean community feel than many Brixton watering holes. The daily changing menu offers the likes of sea-weed callaloo and jerk pork, and palm fronds tower over drinkers in the cosy patio garden. One look at the fading Victorian splendour of the gold-corniced ceiling and pretty domed glass lamps, and it's no wonder locals pack the place out each night.

Lost Angel
339 Battersea Park Road, Battersea, SW11 4LF (7622 2112, www.lostangel.co.uk). Battersea Park rail. **Open** 5-11pm Tue, Wed; 5pm-1am Thur; 4pm-2am Fri; noon-2am Sat; noon-11pm Sun. *Food served 5-10pm Tue-Thur; 4-10pm Fri; noon-10pm Sat, Sun.* **Credit** AmEx, MC, V.

You might not expect to find a bar as likeable as this along such a sorry-looking stretch of the Battersea Park Road. The range of drinks covers most bases: the three ales may include Wandle from nearby Sambrook's Brewery, while the cocktail list is split between classics, reinventions and shouldn't-work-but-do corruptions. They're all served within an eye-catching interior that falls pleasingly between corner pub and modish bar (trombones on the ceiling, white phone box). The kitchen offers poshed-up bar food and entertainment runs from DJs to quiz nights.

▶ *Not far away, the same owners run the buzzworthy bar-restaurant Lost Society (697 Wandsworth Road, SW8 3JF, 7652 6526, www.lostsociety.co.uk).*

Something's Brewing

A fresh flush of microbreweries is refreshing London.

Ask any hipster who was drinking only canned lagers two years ago: relief from bad beer has arrived in the form of London microbreweries. The new beers are packaged in stylish bottles, taste exciting and come with the right local artisan credentials. But why is this happening in London, and why now?

Then chancellor Gordon Brown's 2002 progressive beer duty relief – which meant smaller breweries paid proportionally less tax – paved the way for new, start-up microbreweries, but London was slow to catch up. In the early 20th century, the city had scores of breweries, but even as recently as 2008, most of London's fonts were supplied by a handful of companies making beer in industrial quantities.

The last few years have seen a huge increase in the number of enterprising beer buffs moving their ale production out of the bathtub and into commercial premises all over the city. We haven't seen diversity like it since Victorian times.

Look out for these beers in select local pubs and independent off-licences around the city, or at brewery open days. Breweries to look for include Old Brewery (*see p238*),

London Fields Brewery (374 Helmsley Place, E8 3SB, 07917 322550, www. londonfieldsbrewery.co.uk), Redchurch Brewery (273 Poyser Street, E2 9RF, www.theredchurchbrewery.com) and Kernel Brewery (98 Druid Street, SE1 2HQ, 07757 552636, www.thekernelbrewery.com).

Old Brewery.

CONSUME

★ White Horse

1-3 Parsons Green, Parsons Green, SW6 4UL (7736 2115, www.whitehorsesw6.com). Parsons Green tube. **Open** 9.30am-11.30pm Mon-Wed, Sun; 9.30am-midnight Thur-Sat. *Food served* 10am-10.30pm daily. **Credit** AmEx, MC, V.

Only a lack of ceiling fans stops the main bar of this renowned hostelry from feeling like something from the days of the Raj. Although they might lack fans, the Victorian ceilings are nevertheless airily high, and wide windows with wooden venetian blinds let in plenty of light. Chesterfield-style sofas surround huge tables, though the umbrella-covered pavement tables are most coveted. Expect plenty of turned-up collars, rugby shirts and pashminas, although the mix of customers is wider than you might imagine. There are usually six to eight handpumped ales alongside the 135 bottled beers.

WEST LONDON

Botanist on the Green

3-5 Kew Green, Kew, Surrey TW9 3AA (8948 4838, www.thebotanistkew.com). Kew Gardens tube/rail or bus 65, 391. **Open** noon-11pm Mon-Thur; noon-2am Fri, Sat; noon-10.30pm Sun.

Food served noon-3pm, 6-10pm Mon-Thur; noon-3pm, 6-9pm Fri; noon-9pm Sat, Sun. **Credit** AmEx, MC, V.

The name is a nod to its floral neighbour, the Royal Botanic Gardens; certainly, this pub's position on the corner of Kew Green makes it a perfect place for a relaxing pint after a mooch around the gardens. The space has little nooks – one with a fabulous double-sided fireplace – and raised areas that give it a more intimate feel.

Ladbroke Arms

54 Ladbroke Road, Holland Park, W11 3NW (7727 6648, www.capitalpubcompany.com). Holland Park tube. **Open** 11.30am-11pm Mon-Sat; noon-10.30pm Sun. *Food served* noon-2.30pm, 7-9.30pm Mon-Fri; 12.30-2.45pm, 7-9.30pm Sun. **Credit** AmEx, MC, V. **Map** p404 Y6 ⓭

The Ladbroke caters to moneyed fortysomethings sinking Sancerre on the front terrace and to ale aficionados after a pint of Sharp's Cornish Coaster. The decor in the light main bar is noteworthy, with an original 1920s poster for Fap'Anis on one side and a pre-war French ad for olive oil on the other. A back room fills with middle-aged chatter, while a narrow corridor behind provides peace for bookreaders.

Shops & Services

Lifestyle boutiques, vintage emporiums and department stores.

In its celebration of both tradition and cutting-edge style, the recent revamp of one of London's signature department store's, **Liberty** (*see p258*), captured everything that's great about the capital's shopping scene. For each fashion-forward new opening and pop-up store in the city – east London's **Redchurch Street** (*see p273* **Style Street**) has been particularly lively over the past couple of years – you'll find a classic independent that's still going strong after centuries in operation (take a bow, umbrella specialists **James Smith & Sons**; *see p275*).

Between those extremes lies a changing kaleidoscope of places in which to part with your cash: multicultural street markets, deluxe department stores, design-led homewares stores, flashy food shops and, of course, chain-store flagships. You'll also find some of the best places in Europe to buy books, records and second-hand clothes. Despite credit crunches and chopped-up bank cards, London is still one of the world's most exciting, exhaustive and exhausting retail centres.

CONSUME

SHOPPING IN LONDON

The listings in this chapter concentrate on British brands and shops that are not only unique to the city, but also relatively central. For the key shopping areas around London, *see 263* **Where to Shop**.

Most goods – with the notable exceptions of books, food and children's clothes – are subject to value added tax (VAT), which is almost always included in the prices advertised by shops. VAT is currently levied at 20 per cent. Some shops operate a scheme allowing visitors from outside the European Union to claim back VAT when leaving the country.

Central London shops stay open late (until 7pm or 8pm) one night a week – it's Thursday in the West End, and Wednesday in Chelsea and Knightsbridge.

General

DEPARTMENT STORES

High-street favourite for undies, sandwiches and ready meals, **Marks & Spencer** (www.marksandspencer.co.uk) also offers several reliable fashion ranges, including its designer Autograph collection for men and women, and the younger, trend-led Per Una line and Limited Collection.

Fortnum & Mason

181 Piccadilly, St James's, W1A 1ER (7734 8040, www.fortnumandmason.co.uk). Green Park or Piccadilly Circus tube. **Open** 10am-8pm Mon-Sat; noon-6pm Sun. **Credit** AmEx, DC, MC, V. **Map** p416 V4.

Fortnum & Mason is one of London's most inspiring department stores, and, in business for over 300 years, it's as historic as it is inspiring. A sweeping spiral staircase soars through the four-storey building, while light floods down from a central glass dome. The iconic eau de nil blue and gold colour scheme with flashes of rose pink abound on both the store design and the packaging of the fabulous ground-floor treats, such as the chocolates, biscuits, teas and preserves. The five restaurants are equally impressive, with a new ice-cream parlour a welcome addition. A food hall in the basement has a good range of fresh produce; and beehives installed on top of the building mean that Fortnum's Bees honey is as local as it gets. The shop is redolent of a time when luxury meant the highest degree of comfort rather than ostentation, but that's not to say it's beyond the means of a modest budget. The famous hampers start from £40 – though they rise to a whopping £5,000 for the most luxurious. The Diamond Jubilee hamper, at £200, draws on F&M's beguiling commemorative range, which comes in highly collectable packaging.

Harrods

87-135 Brompton Road, Knightsbridge, SW1X 7XL (7730 1234, www.harrods.com). Knightsbridge tube. **Open** 10am-8pm Mon-Sat; noon-6pm Sun (browsing from 11.30am). **Credit** AmEx, DC, MC, V. **Map** p395 F9.

All the glitz and marble can be a bit much, but in the store that boasts of selling everything, it's hard not to leave with at least one thing. In fact, it even sold itself in 2010: former owner Mohammed Al Fayed received a reported £1.5bn from Qatar Holdings for the place. It's on the fashion floors that Harrods really comes into its own, with a 10,000sq ft Designer Studio on the first floor, featuring well-edited collections from the heavyweights, including a revamped Chanel boutique. There's also an excellent lingerie section, a luxury pet department and a top-notch sport section. The legendary food halls and restaurants range from a branch of 18th-century Venetian coffee bar Caffè Florian to a Xin Dim Sum bar. *Photo p258.*

▶ *Nearby Harvey Nichols (109-125 Knightsbridge, SW1X 7RJ, 7235 5000, www.harveynichols.com) is coasting a little these days, but you'll still find a worthy clutch of unique fashion brands, plus a belle époque-style champagne bar.*

The World in a Village

There's a cornucopia of flavours to be tried at Brixton Village.

It feels like fiesta time. A Brazilian band is belting out bossa nova in the alley; a mixed crowd is laughing, chatting and browsing; the narrow passageways are lined with diners spilling out of tiny cafés. African fabric shops sit cheek-by-jowl with butchers' displays. The holiday mood is hard to place – it's not immediately clear which country you're in. But this is Brixton Village.

In the 1980s, the market was only kept going by a few resilient African and Caribbean stores, but by the late noughties most units were empty.

Granville Arcade, as it was known then, was bought for redevelopment in 2008 – the plan being to knock down the original 1930s building with its high, glass-ceilinged 'arcades'. But, in 2010, it was declared a listed building. This prompted the new owners to think laterally.

One of the first shops was Cornercopia, a café and corner shop selling local produce. Space Makers, a non-profit organisation, asked for locals – business people, entrepeneurs and artists – to come up with ideas for transforming the empty units into places that could be environmentally and economically sustainable, and sociable.

Another new arrival was Bellantoni's, an Italian trattoria, run by chef proprietor Dario Bellantoni, from Genoa. 'My staff are all Italian. We do a lot of vegetarian dishes, we make our own pasta here, we do a lot of Ligurian and Neapolitan dishes.'

Adding to the international flavour is Elephant, a tiny Pakistani café, containing barely half a dozen small tables. Chef proprietor Imran Bashir's story is not uncommon for many of the newer traders.

'A Colombian friend brought me here [Brixton Village] for dinner, and it was just amazing – lots of new restaurants, lots of things going on, and units to let. So I put my name down on the waiting list, and got Elephant. Ever since then, I've just been really busy.'

Thursday night has become the big night at Brixton Village, in part because of the live music. But any day of the week, the market offers flavours from around the world, to eat in or take home and cook.

For listings and review, *see p258*.

CONSUME

Harrods. See p257.

CONSUME

★ Liberty

Regent Street, Soho, W1B 5AH (7734 1234, www.liberty.co.uk). Oxford Circus tube. **Open** 10am-9pm Mon-Sat; noon-6pm Sun. **Credit** AmEx, DC, MC, V. **Map** p416 U2.

Charmingly idiosyncratic, Liberty is housed in a 1920s mock Tudor structure. The store was given a major revamp in early 2009, with new lines and the creation of a dedicated scarf room. The expanded beauty hall on the ground floor goes from strength to strength, with a perfumerie selling scents from cult brands such as Le Labo and Byredo, skincare from the much-celebrated Egyptian Magic, and a new Margaret Dabbs Sole Spa, for pedicures, polishing and shaping. At the main entrance to the store you'll find Wild at Heart's exuberant floral concession, and just off from here you'll find yourself in a room devoted to the store's own label. Fashion brands focus on high-end British designers, such as Vivienne Westwood and Christopher Kane. But despite being up with the latest fashions, Liberty still respects its dressmaking heritage with an extensive range of cottons in the third-floor haberdashery department. Stationery also pays homage to the traditional, with beautiful Liberty of London notebooks, address books and diaries embossed with the art nouveau 'Ianthe' print, while the interiors departments showcase new furniture designs alongside a dazzling collection of 20th-century classics. Artful and arresting window displays, exciting new collections and luxe labels make it an experience to savour.

★ Selfridges

400 Oxford Street, Marylebone, W1A 1AB (0800 123 400, www.selfridges.com). Bond Street or Marble Arch tube. **Open** 9.30am-8pm Mon-Wed, Fri, Sat; 9.30am-9pm Thur; noon-6pm Sun (browsing from 11.30am). **Credit** AmEx, DC, MC, V. **Map** p396 G6.

With its plethora of concession boutiques, store-wide themed events and collections from all the hottest brands, Selfridges is as dynamic as a department store could be. Although the store changes regularly, the useful floor plans make navigating the place easy-peasy. While the basement is chock-full of hip home accessories and stylish kitchen equipment, it's Selfridges' fashion floors that really get hearts racing. With a winning combination of new talent, hip and edgy labels, high-street brands and luxury high-end designers, the store stays ahead of the pack. Highlights include the huge denim section, and the extensive Shoe Galleries, the world's biggest women's footwear department, while Selfridges' 3rd Central initiative is where you'll find the hippest brands of the day. Level 4 hosts the new Toy Shop. Regularly changing pop-up and special events keep customers on their toes, with recent highlights including the Tracey Emin Concept Store and the Mimi Holliday lingerie pop-up. There are plenty of new draws in the food hall, too, with great deli produce from London-based Baker & Spice.

SHOPPING CENTRES & ARCADES

The **Royal Arcades** in the vicinity of Piccadilly are a throwback to shopping past – the Burlington Arcade (*see 259*) is both the largest and grandest, but the Piccadilly Arcade, opposite it, and the Royal Arcade, at 28 Old Bond Street, are also worth a visit.

★ Brixton Village

Corner of Coldharbour Lane & Brixton Station Road, SW9 8PR (7274 2990, http://spacemakers.org.uk/brixton). Brixton tube/rail. **Open** 6am-6pm Mon-Wed; 6am-10pm Thur-Sat; 8am-5pm Sun; check website for opening hours of individual shops. **Credit** AmEx, MC, V.

Once almost forgotten, Granville Arcade has found a new lease of life. It originally opened in 1937, when it was proclaimed 'London's Largest Emporium', and later became a Caribbean market in the 1960s. But by the 1990s, many of the arcade's units were unoccupied and its old art deco avenues were falling into a dilapidated state. In 2009, Lambeth Council called in urban regeneration agency Spacemakers, which launched a competition whereby local entrepreneurs could apply for a unit. It then awarded the best initiatives a place on site, and renamed the space Brixton Village, in line with its eclectic, locally minded new contents – from bijoux bakeries and vintage boutiques to international eateries and fledgling fashion labels. Highlights from the shops here include Margot Waggoner's Leftover, with its Marseille lace and vintage sailor dresses, and Binkie and Tabitha's Circus (unit 70), which juxtaposes retro glassware with an assortment of socialist literature. *See p257* **The World in a Village**.

★ Burlington Arcade
Piccadilly, St James's, W1 (7630 1411, www.burlington-arcade.co.uk). Green Park tube. **Open** 8am-6.30pm Mon-Sat; 11am-5pm Sun. **No credit cards. Map** p408 U4.

In 1819, Lord Cavendish commissioned Britain's very first shopping arcade. Nearly two centuries later, the Burlington is still one of London's most prestigious shopping 'streets', patrolled by 'beadles' decked out in top hats and tailcoats. Highlights include collections of classic watches at David Duggan, established British fragrance house Penhaligon's, British luxury luggage brand Globe-Trotter (*see p270*) and Sermoneta, selling Italian leather gloves in a range of bright colours. High-end food shops come in the form of Luponde Tea and Ladurée; head to the latter

for exquisite Parisian macaroons. Burlington also houses a proper shoe-shine boy working with waxes and creams for just £4. *Photo p261*.

One New Change
New Change Road, the City, EC4M 9AF (7002 8900, www.onenewchange.com). Mansion House or St Paul's tube or Bank tube/DLR. **Open** varies; check website for opening hours of individual shops. **Credit** AmEx, MC, V. **Map** p402 P6.

This new development, a short stroll from St Paul's Cathedral, is a sprawling shopping mall designed by Jean Nouvel, and featuring a warren of high-street retailers, office buildings and restaurants (Jamie Oliver's Barbecoa and Gordon Ramsay's Bread Street Kitchen among the latter). Nicknamed the 'stealth building' due to the structure's resemblance to a stealth bomber, the place is unsurprisingly popular with City workers on their lunchbreaks or on post-work spending sprees. Highlights from the shops include Banana Republic, Topshop and Bea's of Bloomsbury bakery.

Westfield Stratford City
Great Eastern Road, Stratford, E20 (8221 7300, www.westfield.com/stratfordcity). Stratford tube/rail/DLR. **Open** 10am-9pm Mon-Fri; 9am-9pm Sat; 11am-5pm Sun; check website for opening hours of individual shops. **Credit** AmEx, MC, V.

The 'city within a city', Westfield's £1.45bn retail behemoth snakes through the London 2012 site, with 300 retail units – the cornerstones of which are gigantic versions of high-street brands John Lewis, Marks & Spencer and Waitrose – 70 restaurants, bars and cafés, and a 17-screen digital cinema. There's no denying that it's a mega-mall, but Stratford City has at least attempted to reflect the diversity and creative vibe of its neighbourhood, with local artists and creatives creating uniforms, lighting systems, public art and environmental projects. And the food market, the Great Eastern Market, looks set to give opportunities to small, independent producers enjoying a guaranteed customer base: Westfield has projected a phenomenal footfall of 10 million during the Games in 2012 – in a stroke of planning genius, the route to the stadium passes right through the centre of Westfield Stratford City.

▶ *Westfield London (www.westfield.com/london) sits on the other side of town in Shepherd's Bush, on the site of the 1908 Olympic Games. Hailed as Europe's largest city shopping centre when it opened in autumn 2008, it houses some 265 shops and 50 restaurants.*

MARKETS

London's neighbourhood markets are a great place to sample street life while picking up bargains. Below is a selection of the best; for

Selfridges.

CONSUME

tourist mecca, **Camden Market**, *see p151*; for food markets, *see p272. See also p258* **Brixton Village**.

Bermondsey Square Antiques Market

Corner of Bermondsey Street & Long Lane, Bermondsey, SE1 (www.bermondseysquare. co.uk/antiques.html). Borough tube or London Bridge tube/rail. **Open** 5am-1pm Fri. **No credit cards.**

Following the redevelopment of Bermondsey Square, the ancient antiques market – which started in 1855 in north London – continues in an expanded space that now accommodates 200 stalls. Traditionally good for china and silverware, as well as furniture and glassware (with items from Georgian, Victorian and Edwardian eras), there are now also food, fashion and crafts stalls. Browsing here is a bit like going through Fagin's gang's loot, and, indeed, the market is famous for being the spot where, back in the day, thieves could sell their goods with impunity. It's half car boot sale, half chic Parisian fleamarket. Insider tip: get there early – lunchtime arrivals will be disappointed to find grouchy antiques sellers (well, they did start work at 4am) packing up.

★ Columbia Road Market

Columbia Road, Bethnal Green, E2. Hoxton rail or bus 26, 48, 55. **Open** 8am-2pm Sun. **Map** p401 S3.

CONSUME

East Meets Westfield

The mall that's almost as big as the London 2012 Games opens.

It's alive! Westfield Stratford City, London's £1.45billion retail monster, opened in autumn 2011. Overlooking the Olympic Park, within the newly minted E20 postcode (also that of *EastEnders'* fictional Walford), Europe's most ambitious, ballsy shopping development boasts 300 retail units, 70 restaurants, bars and cafés, a 17-screen cinema and 1,600-tonne bridge soaring over 11 railway lines.

So far, so mega-mall, but Westfield Stratford City has at least attempted to be led by its east London neighbours, looking inwards to the immediate area and the creative hubs of Shoreditch and Hoxton, rather than outwards to Romford and Billericay. Much has been made of programmes such as Studio East – an industry panel that includes Richard Mouret, Tracey Emin and Erin O'Connor – giving young British creatives the chance to design uniforms, lighting systems and public art.

But don't these indie-edged community projects confuse what Stratford City is? Is it an incubator for underground design, fledgling fashion labels and east London subcultures – or a consumerist theme park with a veneer of altruism? And how does the on-site Aspers mega-casino fit into this vision? One thing is obvious. Westfield Stratford City has started to transform one of the UK's most econonically deprived areas, with some of the lowest employment figures in the country. Approximately a fifth of the burly construction crew was local and now it's completed, some 8,500 permanent jobs have been created.

For listings, *see p259*.

On Sunday mornings, this unassuming East End street is transformed into a swathe of fabulous plant life and the air is fragrant with blooms and the shouts of old-school Cockney stallholders (most offering deals for 'a fiver'). But a visit here isn't only about flowers and pot plants: alongside the market is a growing number of shops selling everything from pottery, Mexican glassware and arty prints to cupcakes and perfume; don't miss Ryantown's delicate paper cut-outs at no.126 (7613 1510). Get there early for the pick of the crops, or around 2pm for the bargains; refuel at Jones Dairy (23 Ezra Street, 7739 5372, www.jonesdairy.co.uk).

Portobello Road Market
Portobello Road, Notting Hill, W10 (www.portobelloroad.co.uk). Ladbroke Grove or Notting Hill Gate tube. **Open** *General* 8am-6pm Mon-Wed; 9am-1pm Thur; 7am-7pm Fri, Sat. *Antiques* 6am-4pm Fri, Sat. **No credit cards**. **Map** p404 Y4.
Best known for antiques and collectibles, this is actually several markets rolled into one: antiques start at the Notting Hill end; further up are food stalls; under the Westway and along the walkway to Ladbroke Grove are emerging designer and vintage clothes on Fridays (usually marginally less busy) and Saturdays (invariably manic). For the excellent vintage buys of Portobello Green Market, *see p126* **Inside Track**.

Specialist
BOOKS & MAGAZINES

Central branches of the big bookselling chains, where any bibliophile could happily waste an hour, include the **Waterstone's** flagship (203-206 Piccadilly, SW1Y 6WW, 7851 2400, www.waterstones.co.uk), which has a fine bar-café and an on-site branch of the Trailfinders travel agency, and the academic bookseller **Blackwell** (100 Charing Cross Road, WC2H 0JG, 7292 5100, www.blackwell.co.uk).

General

★ Daunt Books
83-84 Marylebone High Street, Marylebone, W1U 4QW (7224 2295, www.dauntbooks.co.uk). Baker Street tube. **Open** 9am-7.30pm Mon-Sat; 11am-6pm Sun. **Credit** AmEx, MC, V. **Map** p396 G5.
This beautiful Edwardian shop's elegant three-level back room – complete with oak balconies, viridian-green walls and stained-glass window – houses a much praised travel section featuring row upon row of guidebooks, maps, language reference, travelogues and related fiction. Travel aside, Daunt is also a first-rate stop for literary fiction, biography, gardening and much more.

Burlington Arcade. *See p259.*

Other locations 158-164 Fulham Road, Chelsea, SW10 9PR (7373 4997); 112-114 Holland Park Avenue, Holland Park, W11 4UA (7727 7022); 51 South End Road, Hampstead, NW3 2QB (7794 8206); 193 Haverstock Hill, Belsize Park, NW3 4QL (7794 4006); 61 Cheapside, EC2V 6AX (7248 1117).

Foyles
113-119 Charing Cross Road, Soho, WC2H 0EB (7437 5660, www.foyles.co.uk). Tottenham Court Road tube. **Open** 9.30am-9pm Mon-Sat; noon-6pm Sun. **Credit** AmEx, MC, V. **Map** p416 X2.
Probably the single most impressive independent bookshop in London, Foyles built its reputation on the sheer volume and breadth of its stock: there are 56 specialist subjects covered here, in the flagship store. The music, gay-interest, foreign fiction, law and philosophy sections are especially strong. The shop's five storeys accommodate several concessions, too, including Unsworth's antiquarian booksellers, the new Grant & Cutler foreign-language bookstore, and, on the third floor, Ray's Jazz (*see p278*). The popular first-floor café hosts readings from the likes of Douglas Coupland and Sebastian Faulks, as well as occasional gigs and other events.
Other locations Southbank Centre, Riverside, SE1 8XX (7440 3212); St Pancras International, Euston Road, N1C 4QL (3206 2650); Westfield, W12 7GE (3206 2656).
► *Foyles is set to get even bigger in 2013, when it's due to move into the huge space that currently houses the Central Saint Martins art school, just down the road from its current site.*

Lutyens & Rubinstein
21 Kensington Park Road, Notting Hill, W11 2EU (7229 1010). Ladbroke Grove tube. **Open** 10am-6pm Mon-Sat; noon-6pm Sun. **Credit** AmEx, DC, MC, V. **Map** p404 X4.

Founded in 2009 by literary agents, Lutyens & Rubinstein sells a beautifully arranged selection of literary fiction and general non-fiction. The core stock of titles was put together by the owners canvassing hundreds of readers on which books they would most like to find in a bookshop; thus every book stocked is sold because somebody has recommended it. The result is an appealing alternative to the homogeneous chain bookshops, with some unusual titles available. As well as books, the shop stocks a small range of stationery, greetings cards, paperweights, local honey and literary-inspired scents from CB I Hate Perfume.

Specialist

Artwords

20-22 Broadway Market, Hackney, E8 4QJ (7923 7507, www.artwords.co.uk). London Fields rail. **Open** 10.30am-6.30pm Mon-Fri; 10am-6pm Sat; noon-6pm Sun. **Credit** AmEx, MC, V.
Artwords has its finger firmly on the pulse when it comes to contemporary visual arts publications. Stock relating to contemporary fine art dominates, but there are also plenty of architecture, photography, graphic design, fashion, advertising and film titles on display, plus an excellent range of industry and creative magazines. **Other locations** 65A Rivington Street, Shoreditch, EC2A 3QQ (7729 2000).

Gosh!

1 Berwick Street, Soho, W1F 0DR (7636 1011, www.goshlondon.com). Oxford Circus or Tottenham Court Road tube. **Open** 10.30am-7pm daily. **Credit** MC, V. **Map** p416 V3.
There's never been a better time to take up reading comics – and there's nowhere better to bolster your collection than at this Soho specialist. There's a huge selection of Manga comics, but it's graphic novels that take centre stage, from early classics such as *Krazy Kat* to Alan Moore's Peter Pan adaptation *Lost Girls*. Classic children's books, of the *This is London* vein, are also a strong point.

Stanfords

12-14 Long Acre, Covent Garden, WC2E 9LP (7836 1321, www.stanfords.co.uk). Covent Garden or Leicester Square tube. **Open** 9am-7.30pm Mon-Fri; 10am-8pm Sat; noon-6pm Sun. **Credit** MC, V. **Map** p416 Y3.
Three floors of travel guides, travel literature, maps, language guides, atlases and magazines. The basement houses the full range of British Ordnance Survey maps; you can plan your next trip over Fairtrade coffee in the Natural Café.

Used & antiquarian

Bookended by Charing Cross Road and St Martin's Lane, picturesque **Cecil Court** (www.cecilcourt.co.uk) is known for its antiquarian book, map and print dealers. Notable residents include children's specialist **Marchpane** (*see below*), 40-year veteran **David Drummond of Pleasures of Past Times** (no.11, 7836 1142), the 100-year-old mystical and spiritual specialist **Watkins** (nos.19 & 21, 7836 2182) and weclome newcomer **Natalie Galustian** (no.22, 7240 6822, www.nataliegalustian.com), specialising in books about poker, and early gay literature.

Marchpane

16 Cecil Court, Covent Garden, WC2N 4HE (7836 8661, www.marchpane.com). Leicester Square tube. **Open** 11am-6pm Mon-Sat. **Credit** MC, V. **Map** p416 X4.
This specialist in classic children's books is on bookshop passageway Cecil Court (*see above*), and a perfect fit for its locale. Stock includes titles such as *Winnie-the-Pooh* and *The Wind in the Willows*, but the shop's forte is Lewis Carroll, with a collection of illustrated editions of *Alice's Adventures in Wonderland*. A BBC Dalek and a Scalextric track in the basement add to the nostalgia.

Quinto/Francis Edwards

72 Charing Cross Road, Covent Garden, WC2H 0BB (7379 7669). Leicester Square tube. **Open** 9am-9pm Mon-Sat. **Credit** AmEx, MC, V. **Map** p416 X3.
This stalwart among the Charing Cross Road bookshops completely changes its stock of antiquarian, rare, second-hand and collectable books once a month, when it brings thousands of titles down from its base in Hay-on-Wye.

Skoob

Unit 66, The Brunswick, Bloomsbury, WC1N 1AE (7278 8760, www.skoob.com). Russell Square tube. **Open** 10.30am-8pm Mon-Sat; 10.30am-6pm Sun. **Credit** MC, V. **Map** p397 L4.
A back-to-basics basement beloved of students from the nearby University of London, Skoob showcases some 50,000 titles covering virtually every subject, from philosophy and biography to politics and the occult. Prices are very reasonable.

CHILDREN
Fashion

In addition, try baby superstore **Mamas & Papas** (256-258 Regent Street, W1B 3AF, 0845 268 2000, www.mamasandpapas.co.uk).

Aravore Babies

31 Park Road, Crouch End, N8 8TE (8347 5752, www.aravore-babies.com). Archway tube then bus 41 or Finsbury Park tube/rail then bus W7. **Open** 10am-5.30pm Mon-Sat; noon-4.30pm Sun. **Credit** AmEx, MC, V.

Where to Shop

London's best shopping neighbourhoods in brief.

COVENT GARDEN & SOHO

The famous former flower market is choked with chains and crowds, but **Neal Street** and the streets radiating off **Seven Dials** rule for streetwear, while new shopping enclave **St Martin's Courtyard** (www.stmartinscourtyard.co.uk), between Long Acre and Upper St Martin's Lane, is good for quality brands such as Jaeger and Twenty8Twelve. Another urbanwear centre is Soho's pedestrianised **Carnaby Street**, as well as **Newburgh Street** and **Kingly Street**, which run parallel on either side of Carnaby Street. **Berwick Street** is the new central London hotspot for vintage clothing shops, as well as a few surviving record shops, while **Charing Cross Road** and **Cecil Court** are prime browsing territory for bookish types.

OXFORD STREET & AROUND

London's commercial backbone, **Oxford Street** is positively heaving with department stores and big chains, which spill over on to elegant **Regent Street**. At its eastern end is **Tottenham Court Road**, known for its electronics shops. **Marylebone**, north-west of Oxford Street, has a villagey atmosphere and small shops that sell everything from designer jewellery to artisan cheeses. Venture further north to **Church Street** for antiques.

NOTTING HILL

Best known for its antiques market on **Portobello Road**, Notting Hill also has an impressive cache of posh boutiques around the intersection of **Westbourne Grove** and **Ledbury Road** – a laid-back alternative to the West End and Chelsea. The area is also good for rare vinyl and vintage clothes.

MAYFAIR & ST JAMES'S

The traditional home of tailors (**Savile Row**) and shirtmakers (**Jermyn Street**), this patch also retains venerable specialist hatters, cobblers and perfumers. **Bond Street** glitters with jewellers and designer stores,

while the reinvigorated **Mount Street** is the place for niche upmarket labels.

CHELSEA & KNIGHTSBRIDGE

King's Road is pretty bland these days, but punctuated with some interesting shops. An up-and-coming nearby sidestreet is **Pavilion Road**, now home to a clutch of ultra-feminine boutiques. Designer salons line **Sloane Street** and mix with chains on **Knightsbridge**, which is anchored by deluxe department stores.

KENSINGTON

Once a hub of hip fashion, **Kensington High Street** has surrendered to the chains, but it's still worth exploring the backstreets leading up to Notting Hill Gate. Rarefied antiques shops gather on **Kensington Church Street**. In South Ken, **Brompton Cross** has glossy contemporary furniture showrooms and designer boutiques.

EAST LONDON

East London is great for quirkier shops and some of the city's best markets; go there on a Sunday for **Columbia Road** and Spitalfields markets. Head to **Brick Lane** and its offshoots, especially **Redchurch Street**, for clothing, accessories and home goods that have been made or adapted by idiosyncratic young designers, and heaps of vintage fashion. **Shoreditch** and **Hoxton** have hip boutiques, furniture stores and bookshops, while Hackney's **Broadway Market** hosts a Saturday farmers' market as well as a clutch of cool indie stores.

NORTH LONDON

The grungy markets of **Camden** are best left to the under-25s, but nearby **Primrose Hill** has an exquisite selection of small shops selling, among other things, quirky lingerie and vintage clothes. Antiques dealers are thinning out on Islington's **Camden Passage**, but there's a growing number of other indies, including gourmet chocolatier Paul A Young and lifestyle boutique Smug.

CONSUME

Distinctive fashions for babies from Aravore aren't cheap, but they'll be much appreciated as gifts for new parents. The crocheted and knitted organic clothes go up to age five, and offer much to coo over, including beautiful merino wool mittens and booties.

Sasti

6 Portobello Green Arcade, 281 Portobello Road, Notting Hill, W10 5TZ (8960 1125, www.sasti.co.uk). Ladbroke Grove tube. **Open** 10am-6pm Mon-Sat; noon-5pm Sun. **Credit** AmEx, MC, V. **Map** p404 Y4.

This affordable children's boutique sells delightfully fun clothes for little girls and boys. Perennial best-sellers include the bunny dresses, flower-covered skirts, bus pyjamas, nursery rhyme blouses and kitten scarves. Apart from its own-label clothes, Sasti also stocks items from Ubang and Pixie Dixie.

Toys

Selfridges (*see p258*) and **Harrods** (*see p257*) have dedicated toy departments. **Hamley's** (188-196 Regent Street, W1B 5BT, 0871 704 1977, www.hamleys.com) has all the must-have toys but is a noisy experience.

Benjamin Pollock's Toy Shop

44 The Market, Covent Garden, WC2E 8RF (7379 7866, www.pollocks-coventgarden.co.uk). Covent Garden tube. **Open** 10.30am-6pm Mon-Sat; 11am-4pm Sun. **Credit** AmEx, MC, V. **Map** p416 Z3.

Best known for its toy theatres (from £6.50 for a Miniature Regency Theatre to about £70 for the more elaborate models), Pollock's is also superb for traditional toys, such as knitted animals, china tea sets, masks, glove puppets, cards, spinning tops and fortune-telling fish.

► *There is another branch of the shop at the associated toy museum; see p110.*

Three Potato Four

Alliance House, 44-45 Newington Green, Newington Green, N16 9QH (7704 2228, www.threepotatofour.co.uk). Canonbury rail. **Open** 10am-5pm Mon-Fri; 9.30am-6pm Sat; 11am-5pm Sun. **Credit** MC, V. **Map** p404 Y4.

This unique children's boutique manages to appeal to both children and adults, through blending a child-focused fun factor with a pleasing dose of nostalgia. Among the new and vintage toys for sale are Olive & Moss soft toys, Schleich plastic animals and dinosaurs, and old Fisher Price items. Stylish children's clothes, lunchboxes and books are also stocked in the retro-inspired interior.

Playlounge

19 Beak Street, Soho, W1F 9RP (7287 7073, www.playlounge.co.uk). Oxford Circus or Piccadilly Circus tube. **Open** 11am-7pm Mon-Sat; noon-5pm Sun. **Credit** AmEx, MC, V. **Map** p416 V3.

Compact but full of fun, this groovy little shop has action figures, gadgets, books and comics, e-boy posters, T-shirts and clothes that appeal to kids and adults alike. Those nostalgic for illustrated children's literature shouldn't miss the Dr Seuss PopUps and *Where the Wild Things Are* books.

ELECTRONICS & PHOTOGRAPHY
General

Ask

248 Tottenham Court Road, Fitzrovia, W1T 7QZ (7637 0353, www.askdirect.co.uk). Tottenham Court Road tube. **Open** 10am-7pm Mon-Wed, Fri, Sat; 10am-8pm Thur; noon-6pm Sun. **Credit** AmEx, DC, MC, V. **Map** p397 K5.

Some shops on Tottenham Court Road feel gloomy and claustrophobic, but Ask has four capacious, well-organised floors that give you space to browse. Stock, spanning digital cameras, MP3 players, laptops, hi-fis and TVs , concentrates on the major consumer brands. Prices are competitive.

Specialist

Behind its grand façade, the **Apple Store** (235 Regent Street, 7153 9000, www.apple.com) offers all the services you'd expect, including the trademark 'Genius Bar' for technical support. Another – arguably even grander – branch opened in Covent Garden (1-7 The Piazza, 7447 1400) in August 2010. There are lots of electronics shops on **Tottenham Court Road**, with several offering laptop repairs. **Adam Phones** (2-3 Dolphin Square, Edensor

Road, W4 2ST, 8742 0101, www.adam phones.com) offers mobile phone handsets for hire at reasonable rates. For film processing, try **Snappy Snaps** (www.snappysnaps.co.uk) and **Jessops** (www.jessops.com); the latter also has a wide range of photography equipment for sale.

Aperture Photographic
44 Museum Street, Bloomsbury, WC1A 1LY (7242 8681, www.apertureuk.com). Holborn or Tottenham Court Road tube. **Open** 11am-7pm Mon-Fri; noon-7pm Sat. **Credit** AmEx, MC, V. **Map** p397 L5.
This camera shop-cum-café has a great atmosphere. The photographic side centres on an excellent selection of new and vintage, manual and autofocus Nikons, Leicas, Canons and Hasselblads, along with a sprinkling of other makes, at reasonable prices. The café is frequented by paparazzi and camera enthusiasts. Staff are happy to answer questions.

FASHION
Multi-label boutiques

The following shops stock garments for both women and men.

b store
24A Savile Row, Mayfair, W1S 3PR (7734 6846, www.bstorelondon.com). Oxford Circus tube. **Open** 10.30am-6.30pm Mon-Fri; 10am-6pm Sat. **Credit** AmEx, MC, V. **Map** p416 U3.
A platform for cutting-edge designers in the heartland of traditional tailoring, b store is the place to preview next big things, with pieces from recent fashion graduates sitting alongside established iconoclasts such as Peter Jensen and Opening Ceremony. The eponymous own label, offering stylish basics and shoes, is going from strength to strength.

Browns
23-27 South Molton Street, Mayfair, W1K 5RD (7514 0000, www.brownsfashion.com). Bond Street tube. **Open** 10am-6.30pm Mon-Wed, Fri, Sat; 10am-7pm Thur. **Credit** AmEx, MC, V. **Map** p396 H6.
Among the 100-odd designers jostling for attention in Joan Burstein's five interconnecting shops (menswear is at no.23) are Chloé, Christopher Kane, Marc Jacobs, Balenciaga and Todd Lynn, with plenty of fashion exclusives. No.24 now also houses Shop 24, selling 'staple items you can't live without'. Browns Focus is younger and more casual; Labels for Less is loaded with last season's leftovers. Browns celebrated its 40th anniversary in 2010.
Other locations Browns Focus, 38-39 South Molton Street, W1K 5RL (7514 0000); Browns Labels for Less, 50 South Molton Street, W1K 5RD (7514 0000); Browns Bride, 11-12 Hinde

Street, W1U 3BE (7514 0056); 6C Sloane Street, SW1X 9LE (7514 0040); Vera Wang at Browns, 59 Brook Street, W1K 4HS (7514 0000).

Folk
53 Lamb's Conduit Street, Bloomsbury, WC1N 3NG (8616 4191, www.folkclothing.com). Holborn tube. **Open** 11am-7pm Mon-Sat; noon-5pm Sun. **Credit** AmEx, MC, V. **Map** p397 M4.
While the menswear store at no.49 (7404 6458) concentrates on the stylish own-label (albeit with additional pieces from Scandinavian brands Our Legacy and Han Kjøbenhavn), this branch of Folk is a godsend for women with a penchant for Scandinavian labels such as Won Hundred and Acne, as well as boutique faves Sessùn and Humanoid. Bags from Ally Capellino provide some tasty icing on a thoroughly fashion-forward cake.

Goodhood
41 Coronet Street, Hoxton, N1 6HD (7729 3600, www.goodhood.co.uk). Old Street tube/rail. **Open** 11am-7pm Mon-Fri; 11am-6.30pm Sat. **Credit** AmEx, MC, V. **Map** p401 R3.
A first stop for East End trendies, Goodhood is owned by streetwear obsessives Kyle and Jo. Japanese independent labels are well represented, while other covetable brands include Pendleton, Norse Projects and Wood Wood.

Single-label boutiques

Margaret Howell
34 Wigmore Street, Marylebone, W1U 2RS (7009 9009, www.margarethowell.co.uk). Bond Street tube. **Open** 10am-6pm Mon-Wed, Fri, Sat; 10am-7pm Thur; noon-5pm Sun. **Credit** AmEx, DC, MC, V. **Map** p396 H5.
Margaret Howell's wearable clothes are made in Britain with an old-fashioned attitude to quality. These principles combine with her elegant designs to make for the best 'simple' clothes for sale in London. Her pared-down approach means prices seem steep, but these are clothes that last and seem only to get better with time.

Preen
5 Portobello Green, 281 Portobello Road, Ladbroke Grove, W10 5TZ (8968 1542, www.preen.eu). **Open** 10am-6pm Thur-Sat. **Credit** AmEx, DC, MC, V. **Map** p404 X4.
Preen – the hip British label from Justin Thornton and Thea Bregazzi – brings imaginative takes to traditional silhouettes. Collections are characterised by urban, minimalist shapes and interesting splashes of colour. Look out for a great range of bags and shoes, plus an accessories range.

Supreme
2-3 Peter Street, Soho, W1F 0AA (7437 0493, www.supremenewyork.com). Piccadilly Circus or

CONSUME

Oxford Circus tube. **Open** 11am-7.30pm Mon-Sat; noon-6pm Sun. **Credit** AmEx, MC, V. **Map** p416 W3.

Europe's first Supreme store opened in September 2011, to much excitement among the city's skaters and streetwear fans. The standalone Soho store – which feels more like a gallery than a shop – stocks the entire collection of the cool New York brand's clothing, footwear and boards.

Sunspel

7 Redchurch Street, Shoreditch, E2 7DJ (7739 9729, www.sunspel.com). Shoreditch High Street rail. **Open** 11am-7pm Mon-Sat; noon-6pm Sun. **Credit** AmEx, MC, V. **Map** p401 S4.

It may look like a trendy east London newcomer, but Sunspel is actually a classic British label, which has been producing quality menswear for over 150 years. It even claims to have introduced boxer shorts to the UK. This corner space is the brand's first retail outlet, showcasing the range of underwear, T-shirts, merino wool knitwear and polo shirts, as well as the new smaller line of equally pared-down womenswear.

YMC

11 Poland Street, Soho, W1F 8QA (7494 1619, www.youmustcreate.com). Oxford Circus tube. **Open** 11am-7pm Mon-Sat. **Credit** AmEx, MC, V. **Map** p416 V2.

Impeccably designed staples are the forte of this London label, which opened its first store in 2010. It's the place to head to for simple vest tops and T-shirts, stylish macs and duffle coats, tasteful knits and chino-style trousers, for both men and women. **Other locations** 23 Hanbury Street, E1 6QR (3432 3010).

Lifestyle boutiques & concept stores

Lifestyle boutiques and concept stores are interchangeable terms that signal shops selling a wide range of covetable and exclusive items, covering fashion, accessories, homewares and gift-type items. The underlying idea is to provide a shopping 'experience' rather than just a marketplace.

Anthropologie

158 Regent Street, W1B 5SW (7529 9800, www.anthropologie.co.uk). Piccadilly Circus tube. **Open** 10am-7pm Mon-Wed, Fri, Sat; 10am-8pm Thur; noon-6pm Sun. **Credit** AmEx, MC, V. **Map** p416 U3.

Anthropologie, the romantically inclined elder sister to fellow US brand Urban Outfitters, opened the doors of its first European store in autumn 2009. Stock is of a feminine bent, with delicate necklaces and soft-knit cardies, while the store's signature large-scale window displays and 1,500sq ft living

wall of plants are worth the trip alone. A second store opened on the King's Road in spring 2010. **Other locations** 131-141 King's Road, Chelsea, SW3 4PW (7349 3110).

Darkroom

52 Lamb's Conduit Street, Bloomsbury, WC1N 3LL (7831 7244, www.darkroomlondon.com). Holborn or Russell Square tube. **Open** 11am-7pm Mon-Fri; 11am-6pm Sat; noon-5pm Sun. **Credit** AmEx, MC, V. **Map** p397 M5.

This shop is quite literally dark (with black walls and lampshades), creating a striking backdrop for the carefully chosen selection of unisex fashion, accessories and interiors items for sale. Stock includes Fleet Ilya bags, DMK glassware and Solomia ceramics. The space doubles up as a gallery, with art displays intermingling with a range of sculptural jewellery.

★ Dover Street Market

17-18 Dover Street, Mayfair, W1S 4LT (7518 0680, www.doverstreetmarket.com). Green Park tube. **Open** 11am-6.30pm Mon-Wed; 11am-7pm Thur-Sat; noon-5pm Sun. **Credit** AmEx, MC, V. **Map** p398 J7.

Comme des Garçons designer Rei Kawakubo's ground-breaking six-storey space combines the edgy energy of London's indoor markets – concrete floors, tills inside corrugated iron shacks, Portaloo dressing rooms – with a fine range of rarefied labels. All 14 of the Comme des Garçons collections are here, alongside exclusive lines from such designers as Lanvin and Azzedine Alaïa.

Shop at Bluebird

350 King's Road, Chelsea, SW3 5UU (7351 3873, www.theshopatbluebird.com). Sloane Square tube. **Open** 10am-7pm Mon-Sat; noon-6pm Sun. **Credit** AmEx, MC, V. **Map** p395 D12.

Part lifestyle boutique and part design gallery, the Shop at Bluebird offers a shifting showcase of clothing for men, women and children (Emma Cook, Peter Jensen, Marc Jacobs), accessories, furniture, books and gadgets. The shop has a retro feel, with vintage furniture, reupholstered seating and hand-printed fabrics. The menswear range is particularly strong.

Smug

13 Camden Passage, Islington, N1 8EA (7354 0253, www.ifeelsmug.com). Angel tube. **Open** 11am-6pm Wed, Fri, Sat; noon-7pm Thur; noon-5pm Sun. **Credit** MC, V. **Map** p400 O2.

Graphic designer Lizzie Evans has decked out this lovely lifestyle boutique with all her favourite things. You'll be treated to a well-edited selection of home accessories (owl ceramic candlesticks, say); vintage homewares (Welsh blankets, 1960s Formica furniture); colourful cushions; Pixie make-up; home-made brooches; old-fashioned notebooks; retro Casio watches and a range of graphic-print men's T-shirts.

CONSUME

THE BEST FASHION

Dover Street Market
Edgy capsule collections. *See p266.*

Goodhood
London's best boutique for ultra-hip mid-range labels. *See p265.*

Selfridges
London's most fashion-forward department store. *See p258.*

High-end designer

Key British designers include **Vivienne Westwood** (44 Conduit Street, W1S 2YL, 7439 1109, www.viviennewestwood.com); **Paul Smith** (Westbourne House, 120 Kensington Park Road, W11 2EP, 7727 3553, www.paulsmith.co.uk); **Alexander McQueen** (4-5 Old Bond Street, W1S 4PD, 7355 0088, www.alexandermcqueen.com), headed by Sarah Burton since the designer's death; and **Stella McCartney** (30 Bruton Street, W1J 6QR, 7518 3100, www.stellamccartney.com). Those after some Parisian style should head to the luxurious **Louis Vuitton Maison** flagship (17-20 New Bond Street, W1S 2UE, 7399 3856, www.louisvuitton.com), or the more pared-down but equally fashion-forward **Vanesso Bruno** boutique (1A Grafton Street, W1S 4EB, 7499 7838, www.vanessabruno.com), the designer's first London store.

Discount

Tussle with teens for bargains at cheap-as-chips **Primark** (499-517 Oxford Street, 7495 0420, www.primark.co.uk). Grown-ups might prefer **Browns Labels for Less** (*see p265*).

Burberry Factory Shop

29-31 Chatham Place, Hackney, E9 6LP (8328 4287). Hackney Central rail. **Open** 10am-6pm Mon-Thur; 9am-7pm Fri, Sat; 11am-5pm Sun. **Credit** AmEx, MC, V.
This warehouse space showcases seconds and excess stock reduced by 50% or more. Classic men's macs can be had for around £199 or less.

Paul Smith Sale Shop

23 Avery Row, Mayfair, W1X 9HB (7493 1287, www.paulsmith.co.uk). Bond Street tube. **Open** 10.30am-6.30pm Mon-Wed, Fri, Sat; 10.30am-7pm Thur; noon-6pm Sun. **Credit** AmEx, DC, MC, V. **Map** p398 H7.
Samples and previous season's stock at a 30-50% discount. Stock includes clothes for men, women and children, as well as a range of accessories.

High street

The best of the high-street chains are designer-look **Reiss** (Kent House, 14-17 Market Place, Fitzrovia, W1H 7AJ, 7637 9112, www.reiss.co.uk); **Banana Republic** (224 Regent Street, W1B 3BR, 7758 3550, www.bananarepublic.eu) – a recent arrival to British shores, which now has several branches in the city; H&M's upmarket sibling **COS** (222 Regent Street, W1B 5BD, 7478 0400, www.cosstores.com); **Whistles** (12-14 St Christopher's Place, W1U 1NH, 7487 4484, www.whistles.co.uk) for high-quality but on-trend womenswear; and **Urban Outfitters** (200 Oxford Street, W1D 1NU, 7907 0815, www.urbanoutfitters.co.uk), with a great range of boutique labels. **Topshop**'s (*see below*) massive, throbbing flagship continues to push the envelope, while branches of US casualwear brand **American Apparel** (www.americanapparel.net) can now be found across the city.

★ Topshop

214 Oxford Street, W1W 8LG (0844 848 7487, www.topshop.com). Oxford Circus tube. **Open** 9am-9pm Mon-Wed, Fri; 9am-10pm Thur; 11.30am-6pm Sun. **Credit** AmEx, DC, MC, V. **Map** p416 U2.
Topshop has been the queen of the British high street for the past decade, and walking into the busy Oxford Street flagship, it's easy to see why. Spanning three huge floors, the place lays claim to being the world's largest fashion shop, and is always buzzing with fashion-forward teens and twenty-somethings keen to get their hands on the next big trends. The store covers a huge range of styles and sizes, and includes free personal shoppers, boutique label concessions, capsule collections, a Daniel Hersheson Blow Dry Bar (*see p275*), Nails Inc manicures, a Metalmorphosis tattoo parlour, a café and sweet shop. Topman is as on-the-ball and innovative as its big sister, stocking niche menswear labels such as Garbstore, and housing a trainer boutique, a suit section, and a new personal shopping suite, featuring consultation rooms, Xbox 360s and an exhibition space. Both shops are even more of a hive of activity than normal during London Fashion Week, when a series of special events are held.
Other locations throughout the city.

Tailors

Chris Kerr

31 Berwick Street, Soho, W1F 8RJ (7437 3727, www.eddiekerr.co.uk). Oxford Circus tube. **Open** 9am 5.30pm Mon Fri; 9am 1pm Sat. **Credit** AmEx, MC, V. **Map** p416 V2.
Chris Kerr, son of legendary 1960s tailor Eddie Kerr, is the man to visit if Savile Row's prices or attitude aren't to your liking. The versatile Kerr has no house

CONSUME

style; instead, he makes every suit to each client's exact specifications, and those clients include Johnny Depp and David Walliams. A good place to get started with British tailoring.

▶ *For the tailors of Savile Row, see p130.*

Timothy Everest
35 Bruton Place, Mayfair, W1J 6NS (7629 6236, www.timothyeverest.co.uk). Bond Street tube. **Open** 10am-6pm Mon-Fri; 11am-5pm Sat. **Credit** AmEx, MC, V. **Map** p398 H7.
One-time apprentice to the legendary Tommy Nutter, Everest is a star of the latest generation of London tailors. He's well known for his relaxed 21st-century definition of style.

Used & vintage

East London, and particularly the area around Brick Lane, is still an excellent place to find vintage fashion shops. In the past year, however, Soho has upped its game, with a wave of new vintage shop openings on and around **Berwick Street**.

Beyond Retro
112 Cheshire Street, Shoreditch, E2 6EJ (7613 3636, www.beyondretro.com). Shoreditch High Street rail. **Open** 10am-7pm Mon-Wed, Fri, Sat; 10am-8pm Thur; 10am-6pm Sun. **Credit** MC, V. **Map** p403 S4.
This enormous palace of second-hand clothing and accessories is the starting point for many an expert stylist, thrifter or fashion designer on the hunt for bargains and inspiration. The 10,000 items on the warehouse floor include 1950s dresses, cowboy boots and denim hot pants, many under £20. In-store events, such as live bands, add to the lively and supremely east London vibe. An equally massive new branch opened in Dalston in autumn 2011. **Other locations** 58-59 Great Marlborough Street, Soho, W1F 7JY (7434 1406); Simpson House, 92-100 Stoke Newington Road, N16 7XB (7613 3636).

★ Lucy in Disguise
48 Lexington Street, Soho, W1F 0LR (7434 4086, www.lucyindisguiselondon.com). Oxford Circus or Piccadilly Circus tube. **Open** 10am-7pm Mon-Wed, Fri, Sat; 10am-8pm Thur. **Credit** AmEx, MC, V. **Map** p416 V3.
The vintage store of Lily Allen and half-sister Sarah Owen has really come into its own since moving to this fabulous Lexington Street space. The shiny chequered floor, big 1950s-style TV and vintage chandeliers create a cool and glamorous vibe in which to shop for good-quality vintage, from dresses and tops by Pierre Cardin and Christian Dior, to silk scarves and beautiful leather handbags. The Lucy in Disguise own-label – new dresses inspired by vintage designs – is also a real draw.

Beyond Retro.

Vintage Emporium
14 Bacon Street, Brick Lane, E1 6LF (7739 0799, www.vintageemporiumcafe.com). Shoreditch High Street rail. **Open** 10am-7pm daily. **Credit** AmEx, MC, V. **Map** p401 S4.
With a well-edited range of clothing (in the basement) from the Victorian era to the 1950s, this café-shop's vintage time frame is somewhat tighter than that of its nearby rivals, but maybe all the better for it. Beautiful lace blouses, 1950s dresses, a great selection of hats, and top-notch accessories are all for sale, and, considering the age of most of the items, prices are very reasonable.

FASHION ACCESSORIES & SERVICES
Clothing hire

Lipman & Sons
22 Charing Cross Road, Soho, WC2H 0HR (7240 2310, www.lipmanandsons.co.uk). Leicester Square tube. **Open** 9am-6pm Mon-Wed, Fri, Sat; 9am-8pm Thur. **Credit** AmEx, DC, MC, V. **Map** p416 X4.
Lipman & Sons is a reliable, long-serving formal-wear specialist.

Cleaning & repairs

British Invisible Mending Service
32 Thayer Street, Marylebone, W1U 2QT (7935 2487, www.invisible-mending.co.uk). Bond Street tube. **Open** 8.30am-5.30pm Mon-Fri; 10am-1pm Sat. **No credit cards. Map** p396 G5.
A 24-hour service is offered.

CONSUME

Celebrity Cleaners
*9 Greens Court, Soho, W1F 0HJ (7437 5324).
Piccadilly Circus tube.* **Open** 8.30am-6.30pm Mon-
Fri. **No credit cards. Map** p416 W3.
Dry-cleaner to West End theatres and the ENO.
Other locations Neville House, 27 Page Street,
Pimlico, SW1P 4JJ (7821 1777).

Fifth Avenue Shoe Repairers
*41 Goodge Street, Fitzrovia, W1T 2PY (7636
6705). Goodge Street tube.* **Open** 8am-6pm Mon-
Fri; 10am-6pm Sat. **Credit** AmEx, MC, V.
Map p396 J5.
High-calibre, speedy shoe repairs.

Hats

For bold hats by the king of couture headgear,
head to **Philip Treacy** (69 Elizabeth Street,
SW1 9PJ, 7730 3992, www.philiptreacy.co.uk).

Bernstock Speirs
*234 Brick Lane, Brick Lane, E2 7EB (7739 7385,
www.bernstockspeirs.com). Shoreditch High Street
rail.* **Open** 11am-6pm Tue-Fri; 11am-5pm Sat,
Sun. **Credit** AmEx, MC, V.
Paul Bernstock and Thelma Speirs's unconventional
hats for men and women have a loyal following,
being both wearable and fashion-forward. Past
ranges have included collaborations with Peter
Jensen and Emma Cook.

Jewellery

There are also some lovely pieces for sale in
Contemporary Applied Arts (*see p274*).

ec one
*41 Exmouth Market, Clerkenwell, EC1R 4QL
(7713 6185, www.econe.co.uk). Farringdon
tube/rail.* **Open** 10am-6pm Mon-Wed, Fri; 11am-
7pm Thur; 10.30am-6pm Sat. **Credit** MC, V.
Map p400 N4.
Husband-and-wife team Jos and Alison Skeates have
a magpie's eye for good design, which makes for
delightfully varied browsing at this stylish
Clerkenwell shop. Over 50 designers are showcased:
temptingly inexpensive trinkets include colourful
lucite bangles and sweet little heart necklaces.
Among the slightly pricier standouts are Celestine
Soumah's beguilingly simple silver designs.
Other locations 56 Ledbury Road, Notting Hill,
W11 2AJ (7243 8811).

Garrard
*24 Albemarle Street, Mayfair, W1S 4HT (0870
871 8888, www.garrard.com). Bond Street or
Green Park tube.* **Open** 10am-6pm Mon-Fri; 10am-
5pm Sat. **Credit** AmEx, MC, V. **Map** p416 U5.
The Crown Jeweller's diamond-studded designs
have appealed to a new generation of bling-seekers

since the brand was modernised by Jade Jagger. It's
now in the hands of London-based jeweller Stephen
Webster, who took over as creative director in 2009.

Kabiri
*18 The Market, The Piazza, Covent Garden,
WC2E 8RB (7240 1055, www.kabiri.co.uk).
Covent Garden tube.* **Open** 10am-6.30pm Mon-
Sat; noon-5pm Sun. **Credit** AmEx, MC, V. **Map**
p416 Y3.
The work of more than 100 jewellery designers,
from emerging talent to established names, is
showcased at Kabiri's flagship in Covent Garden.
Innovation and sophistication are both highly
prized, and the pieces cover a good range of price
categories. Several designers are exclusive to
Kabiri, including K Brunini and Roberto Marroni.
There's a smaller shop on Marylebone High Street.
Other locations 37 Marylebone High Street,
Marylebone, W1U 4QE (7224 1808).

Lingerie & underwear

Agent Provocateur is now a glossy
international chain, but the original outpost
of the shop that went on to popularise high-
class kink around the world is still in Soho
(6 Broadwick Street, W1F 8HL, 7439 0229,
www.agentprovocateur.com). For a serious
bespoke service, royal corsetière **Rigby &
Peller** (22A Conduit Street, W1S 2XT, 0845
076 5545, www.rigbyandpeller.com) is in
Mayfair. Erotic emporium **Coco de Mer**
(*see p274*) also has a small selection of
boudoir-esque lingerie.

Bordello
*55 Great Eastern Street, EC2A 3HP (7503 3334,
www.bordello-london.com). Old Street or Liverpool
Street tube/rail.* **Open** 11am-7pm Tue-Sat. **Credit**
MC,V. **Map** p401 R4.
Bordello, opened by Michele Scarr in 2008, offers a
touch of decadent, old-school naughtiness and glamour in Shoreditch. Inspired by the burlesque scene,
the sumptuous boudoir, with its red-painted walls
and antique chandeliers, is the place to head to for
some saucy vintage-inspired smalls by the likes of
Damaris, Mimi Holliday, Lascivious and Fifi
Chachnil, as well as a host of corsetry, sleepwear and
swimwear. There's a beautiful range of bridal and
maternity lingerie, as well as some choice vintage
pieces. Bordello also stocks boudoir furniture, sex
toys, scented candles and erotic literature.

Myla
*74 Duke of York Square, King's Road, Chelsea,
SW3 4LY (7730 0700, www.myla.com). Sloane
Square tube.* **Open** 10am-6.30pm Mon-Sat; noon-
5pm Sun. **Credit** AmEx, MC, V. **Map** p395 F11.
Luxury lingerie brand Myla has acquired a devoted
following. There are now five London stores and var-

CONSUME

CONSUME

Ally Capellino.

▶ *Looking for luggage that's a solution rather than an investment? Marks & Spencer (www.marksandspencer.co.uk) does reliable basics.*

Shoes

Among the best footwear chains is **Office** (57 Neal Street, Covent Garden, WC2H 4NP, 7379 1896, www.office.co.uk), which offers funky styles for guys and girls at palatable prices. **Kurt Geiger** (198 Regent Street, W1B 5TP, 3238 0044, www.kurtgeiger.com) and **Russell & Bromley** (24-25 New Bond Street, W1S 2PS, 7629 6903, www.russellandbromley.co.uk) both turn out classy takes on key trends for both sexes; and **Clarks** (476 Oxford Street, W1C 1LD, 0844 499 9302, www.clarks.co.uk) has shed its school-shoe image and gone on to be known as the inventor of Wallabes.

Carnaby Street is a great place for trainers, with branches of **Size?** (nos.33-34, www.size.co.uk), **Puma** (nos.52-55, www.puma.com) and **Vans** (no.47, www.vans.eu) among the options.

Black Truffle
4 Broadway Market, Hackney, E8 4QJ (7923 9450, www.blacktruffle.co.uk). London Fields rail or bus 394. **Open** 11am-6pm Tue-Fri; 10am-6pm Sat; noon-6pm Sun. **Credit** AmEx, MC, V.
This firm Hackney favourite sells quirky, stylish yet wearable footwear for women, men and children from its deceptively large space on the canal end of Broadway Market. Look out in particular for shoes by Melissa, Vialis, F Troupe and Falke, knee-high boots by Alberto Fermani and bags from Ally Capellino and Matt & Nat.
Other locations 52 Warren Street, Fitzrovia, W1T 5NJ (7388 4547).

Kate Kanzier
67-69 Leather Lane, Holborn, EC1N 7TJ (7242 7232, www.katekanzier.com). Chancery Lane tube or Farringdon tube/rail. **Open** 8.30am-6.30pm Mon-Fri; 11am-4pm Sat. **Credit** AmEx, MC, V. **Map** p400 N5.
Adored for great-value directional footwear for women, Kate Kanzier is the place to visit for brogues (£30), ballerinas (£20), sandles and leather boots in a huge range of colours. Sexy high-heeled pumps in patent, suede, leather and animal prints are characterised by vintage designs. Handbags and clutches are also stocked in the spacious Holborn shop.

Oliver Spencer
37 Lamb's Conduit Street, WC1N 3NG (7831 4898, www.oliverspencer.co.uk). Russell Square tube. **Open** 11am-7pm Mon-Sat. **Credit** AmEx, MC, V. **Map** p397 M4.
This new shop showcases Spencer's Northampton-made men's footwear. The Oliver Spencer range com-

ious concessions around town, which makes getting one's hands on the label's stylish, high-quality bras, knickers, toys and accessories a breeze.

Luggage & bags

Harrods (*see p257*), **John Lewis** (*see p275*) and **Selfridges** (*see p258*) have excellent selections of luggage and bags.

★ Ally Capellino
9 Calvert Avenue, Shoreditch, E2 7JP (7613 3073, www.allycapellino.co.uk). Shoreditch High Street rail. **Open** 11am-6pm Tue-Sat; 11am-5pm Sun. **Credit** AmEx, MC, V. **Map** p401 R4.
This shop stocks the full range of Ally Capellino's stylishly understated unisex leather and waxed cotton bags, satchels, wallets, purses and laptop cases. Prices start at around £40 for a cute leather coin purse, rising to over £300 for larger, more structured models.
Other locations 312 Portobello Road, W10 5RU (8964 1022).

Globe-Trotter
54-55 Burlington Arcade, Mayfair, W1J 0LB (7529 5950, www.globe-trotterltd.com). Green Park tube. **Open** 10am-6pm Mon-Sat. **Credit** AmEx, MC, V. **Map** p398 J7.
Globe-Trotter's indestructible steamer-trunk luggage, available here in various sizes and colours, accompanied the Queen on honeymoon. Iconic Mackintosh coats share the shop space.

prises classic, hand-stitched shoes and boots with a contemporary twist, with a focus on brogues, desert boots and deck shoes. The quality of the materials (mainly leather and suede) and craftsmanship is high, and some of the newer models feature a comfortable Dainite sole, which has a superior grip. Prices start at around the £140 mark, going up to around £280. Spencer Footwear is the more affordable diffusion line, and the shop also sells men's accessories.

FOOD & DRINK

Bakeries

Konditor & Cook
22 Cornwall Road, Waterloo, SE1 8TW (7261 0456, www.konditorandcook.com). Waterloo tube/rail. **Open** 7.30am-6.30pm Mon-Fri; 8.30am-2.30pm Sat. **Credit** AmEx, MC, V. **Map** p402 N10.
Gerhard Jenne caused a stir when he opened this bakery on a South Bank sidestreet in 1993, selling gingerbread people for grown-ups and lavender-flavoured cakes. Success lay in lively ideas such as magic cakes that spell the recipient's name in a series of individually decorated squares. Quality prepacked salads and sandwiches are also sold. The brand is now a mini-chain, with several branches. **Other locations** throughout the city.

Primrose Bakery
69 Gloucester Avenue, Primrose Hill, NW1 8LD (7483 4222, www.primrosebakery.org.uk). Chalk Farm tube. **Open** 8.30am-6pm Mon-Sat; 10am-5.30pm Sun. **Credit** AmEx, MC, V. **Map** p404 X2.
Catch a serious sugar high from Martha Swift's pretty, generously sized cupcakes in vanilla, coffee and lemon flavours. The tiny, retro-styled shop also sells peanut butter cookies and layer cakes. **Other locations** 42 Tavistock Street, Covent Garden, WC2E 7PB (7836 3638).

Drinks

★ Algerian Coffee Stores
52 Old Compton Street, Soho, W1V 6PB (7437 2480, www.algcoffee.co.uk). **Open** 9am-7pm Mon-Wed; 9am-9pm Thur, Fri; 9am-8pm Sat. **Credit** AmEx, DC, MC, V. **Map** p416 W3.
For over 120 years, this unassuming little shop has been trading over the same wooden counter. The range of coffees is broad, with house blends sold alongside single-origin beans, and some serious teas and brewing hardware are also available.
▶ *Passing? Take away a single or double espresso for £1, or a cappuccino or a latte for £1.20.*

Berry Bros & Rudd
3 St James's Street, Mayfair, SW1A 1EG (7396 9600, www.bbr.com). Green Park tube. **Open** 10am-6pm Mon-Fri; 10am-5pm Sat. **Credit** AmEx, DC, MC, V. **Map** p398 J8.

Britain's oldest wine merchant has been trading on the same premises since 1698, and its heritage is reflected in its panelled sales and tasting rooms. Burgundy- and claret-lovers will drool at the hundreds of wines, but there are also decent selections from elsewhere in Europe and the New World. Prices are generally fair.

Cadenhead's Whisky Shop & Tasting Room
26 Chiltern Street, Marylebone, W1U 7QF (7935 6999, www.whiskytastingroom.com). Baker Street tube. **Open** 10.30am-6.30pm Mon-Fri; 10.30am-6pm Sat. **Credit** DC, MC, V. **Map** p416 Z3.
Cadenhead's is a survivor of a rare breed: the independent whisky bottler. And its shop is one of a kind, at least in London. Cadenhead's selects barrels from distilleries all over Scotland and bottles them without filtration or any other intervention.
▶ *For a wider range of spirits – the widest to be found in London, according to the staff – try Gerry's (74 Old Compton Street, Soho, W1D 4UW, 7734 4215, www.gerrys.uk.com). It's not far from Milroy's (3 Greek Street, Soho, W1D 4NX, 7437 2385, www.milroys.co.uk), another whisky specialist.*

Primrose Bakery.

★ Postcard Teas

*9 Dering Street, Mayfair, W1S 1AG (7629 3654,
www.postcardteas.com). Bond Street or Oxford
Circus tube.* **Open** 10.30am-6.30pm Mon-Sat.
Credit AmEx, MC, V. **Map** p396 H6.

The range in Timothy d'Offay's exquisite little shop
is not huge, but it is selected with great care: for
instance, some of its Darjeeling teas (£3.50-
£9.95/50g) are currently sourced from the Glenburn
estate, regarded as one of the best in the region.
There's a central table for those who want to try a
pot; or book in for one of the tasting sessions held
on Saturdays between 10am and 11am. Tea-ware
and accessories are also sold.

General

You'll find branches of Britain's most
popular supermarkets, **Sainsbury's**
(www.sainsburys.co.uk) and **Tesco**
(www.tesco.com), throughout the city. Superior-
quality **Waitrose** (www.waitrose.com) has
central branches on Tottenham Court Road,
Marylebone High Street and in Bloomsbury's
Brunswick Centre (www.brunswick.co.uk).
For a more ethical type of supermarket
shopping, head to Lamb's Conduit Street
for the **People's Supermarket** (nos.72-78,
WC1N 3LP, 7430 1827, www.peoples
supermarket.org), a co-operative that
focuses on locally sourced produce.

Whole Foods Market

*63-97 Kensington High Street, South Kensington,
W8 5SE (7368 4500, www.wholefoodmarket.com).
High Street Kensington tube.* **Open** 8am-10pm
Mon-Sat; 10am-6pm Sun. **Credit** AmEx, DC,
MC, V.

Postcard Teas.

The London flagship of the American health-food
supermarket chain occupies the handsome deco
department store that was once Barkers. There are
several eateries on the premises.

Markets

The farmers' markets in the capital reflect
Londoners' concern over provenance and green
issues. Two central ones are in **Marylebone**
(Cramer Street car park, corner of Moxton
Street, off Marylebone High Street, 10am-2pm
Sun) and **Notting Hill** (behind Waterstone's,
access via Kensington Place, W8, 9am-1pm Sat).
For a fashion show and farmers' market in one,
head to Hackney's **Broadway Market** on
Saturday. Contact **London Farmers'
Markets** (7833 0338, www.lfm.org.uk).

★ Borough Market

*Southwark Street, Borough, SE1 (7407 1002,
www.boroughmarket.org.uk). London Bridge
tube/rail.* **Open** 11am-5pm Thur; noon-6pm Fri;
8am-5pm Sat. **No credit cards**. **Map** p402 P8.

The food hound's favourite market is also London's
oldest, dating back to the 13th century. It's the
busiest, too, occupying a sprawling site near London
Bridge. Gourmet goodies run the gamut, from fresh
loaves from Flour Station to chorizo and rocket rolls
from Spanish specialist Brindisa, plus rare-breed
meats, fish and game, fruit and veg, cakes and all
manner of preserves, oils and teas; head out hungry
to take advantage of the numerous free samples. The
market is now also open on Thursdays, when it tends
to be quieter than on always-mobbed Saturdays. A
rail viaduct planned for above the space is still going
ahead, despite a campaign against it, but a recent
plan for the market to expand into the adjacent
Jubilee Market area means that the space shouldn't
be lost (even if some Grade II-listed structures are).
▶ *Over the past year, Borough Market's trade has
been challenged by former stallholders who have
set up camp under the railway arches on nearby
Maltby Street in Bermondsey (www.maltbystreet.
com); head here on a Saturday morning (9am-
2pm) for Monmouth coffees (Arch 34), delicious
raclette from Kappacasein (no.1), and the city's
finest custard doughnuts, courtesy of the St John
Bakery (Arch 72).*

Specialist

Daylesford Organic

*44B Pimlico Road, Belgravia, SW1W 8LJ (7881
8060, www.daylesfordorganic.com). Sloane Square
tube.* **Open** 8am-8pm Mon-Sat; 10am-4pm Sun.
Credit AmEx, MC, V. **Map** p398 G11.

Goods include ready-made dishes, staples such as
pulses, pastas, cakes and breads, and cheeses.
Other locations 208-212 Westbourne Grove,
Notting Hill, W11 2RH (7313 8050); Selfridges.

Style Street

Redchurch Street is leading the way with its funky independent shops.

London's fashion- and experience-led shopping scene has been thriving over the past couple of years, with exciting new independents, concept stores and pop-up shops appearing all over town. One shabby Shoreditch cut through has undergone a particularly dramatic transformation, now finding itself at the centre of London cool. Redchurch Street is now a strong contender for the capital's best shopping street.

Vintage homewares specialist **Caravan** (no.3, 7033 3532, www.caravanstyle.com), which relocated from Spitalfields Market in 2009, led the charge. Selling an assortment of homely oddities, such as vintage cushions, retro desk lamps and plastic birds that tweet, it's a first-port-of-call for stylists. This end of the street then saw a flurry of openings. One of our favourites is **Aesop** (no.5A, 7613 3793, www.aesop-europe.com), the botanical beauty shop from the Aussie luxury skincare brand. The geranium leaf body balm is an exquisitely scented, paraben-free treat. There's also a really lovely new fashion boutique at no.7: **Sunspel** (www.sunspel.com). The first retail outlet of the classic British menswear-makers, it specialises in quality underwear, T-shirts and polo shirts.

For goods that are equally English, but edible rather than sartorial, head to **Albion** (*see p234*), the café-shop that's part of Terence Conran's Boundary Project (*see p210*), on the corner of Redchurch and Boundary streets. You'll find a wealth of home-grown brands in the shop, from HP Sauce to Daylesford Organic via Neal's Yard. The buzz surrounding Redchurch Street was intensified by the hullabaloo that greeted Boundary and nearby members' club **Shoreditch House** (*see p211*), which houses an open-to-all branch of the Cowshed spa (7749 4531; *see p277*). A little further up Boundary Street, new womenswear boutique **11 Boundary** (no.11, 7033 0330, www.11boundary.com) sells floaty bits from Wildfox and tailoring from Twenty8Twelve.

Further up Redchurch Street, there are more exciting new shops. **Hostem** (nos.41-43, 7739 9733, www.hostem.co.uk) is a darkly lit menswear shop with a well-edited selection from the likes of Philip Lim. Decadent **Maison Trois Garçons** (no.45,

Labour & Wait.

7613 1924, www.lestroisgarcons.com) deals in interiors. The **Painted Lady** (no.65, 7729 2154), a cute hair salon and nail bar, specialises in vintage-style up-dos and offers great-value manicures. There's even a grungy thrift shop, **Sick** (no.105, 7033 2961), run by the founders of cult 1980s label Boy, which specialises in 1990s, for want of a better word, vintage.

Two of the highest-profile arrivals are capacious British concept store **Aubin & Wills** (nos.64-66), where you can buy men's, women's and homeware lines in a sort of grown-up collegiate style reminiscent of Abercrombie & Fitch, as well as catching a film in the small luxury cinema or some art in the gallery, and the large new premises of the much-loved Cheshire Street homeware shop **Labour & Wait** (*see p278*).

After this style overload, you may need some light refreshment. Head to the **Owl & the Pussycat** (no.34, 7613 3628) for a good pint of bitter. Despite a recent revamp, this is still a proper boozer, one of the few reminders of this happening street's former self.

CONSUME

THE BEST
TALKING-POINT SOUVENIRS

Coco de Mer
A bit of London sauce. *See p274.*

London 2012 Shop
All your Games memorabilia. *See p275.*

Luna & Curious
Arty jewellery and homewares. *See p275.*

Hope & Greenwood
*1 Russell Street, Covent Garden, WC2B 5JD
(7240 3314, www.hopeandgreenwood.co.uk).
Covent Garden tube.* **Open** 11am-7.30pm Mon-Fri;
10.30am-7.30pm Sat; noon-6pm Sun. **Credit** MC, V.
Map p416 Z3.
Saturday queues are almost inevitable at this small
vacuum for pocket money. Everything from chocolate gooseberries to sweetheart candies is prettily
displayed in plastic beakers, cellophane bags, glass
jars, illustrated boxes, porcelain bowls and cake tins.
Relive sweet childhood memories by indulging in a
bag of sherbert Flying Saucers, gobstoppers or
rhubarb and custard 'rations', as well as Double
Dips, sugar mice, Curly Wurlys, Love Hearts and
lots more. Posher chocolates are also available,
including the delicious-sounding lavender and geranium truffles. Gift possibilities include retro gumball
machines, and the refills for them. Ice-cream is available in the warmer months.
Other locations 20 Northcross Road, East
Dulwich, SE22 9EU (8613 1771).

Lina Stores
18 Brewer Street, Soho, W1F 0SH (7437 6482).
Open 8.30am-6.30pm Mon-Fri; 8am-5.30pm Sat.
Credit AmEx, MC, V. **Map** p416 W3.
Behind the 1950s green ceramic Soho frontage and
crowded windows is an iconic family-run Italian deli
that's been in business for over half a century. A
recent modernisation has taken away some of the
old-school character, but a new coffee machine goes
some way to making up for it. Besides dried pastas,
there's a deli counter chock-full of cured meats,
hams, salamis, olives, pesto, cheeses, marinated arti-
chokes and fresh pastas. Lina is also one of the best
places to buy truffles when they are in season.

★ Neal's Yard Dairy
*17 Shorts Gardens, Covent Garden, WC2H 9UP
(7240 5700, www.nealsyarddairy.co.uk). Covent
Garden tube.* **Open** 11am-7pm Mon-Sat. **Credit**
MC, V. **Map** p416 Y2.
Neal's Yard buys from small farms and creameries
and matures the cheeses in its own cellars until
they're ready to sell in peak condition. Names such
as Stinking Bishop and Lincolnshire Poacher are as

evocative as the aromas in the shop. It's best to walk
in and ask what's good today: you'll be given tasters
by the well-trained staff. There's a shop in Borough
Market too (6 Park Street, SE1 9AB, 7367 0799).
▶ *There are more great cheeses at Marylebone's
La Fromagerie (see p226), and Paxton &
Whitfield (93 Jermyn Street, SW1Y 6JE, 7930
0259, www.paxtonandwhitfield.co.uk), which has
been on its site near Green Park since 1894.*

Paul A Young Fine Chocolates
*33 Camden Passage, Islington, N1 8EA (7424
5750, www.payoung.net). Angel tube.* **Open** 10am-
6.30pm Tue-Thur, Sat; 10am-7pm Fri; noon-5pm
Sun. **Credit** AmEx, MC, V. **Map** p400 O2.
A gorgeous boutique with almost everything –
chocolates, cakes, ice-cream – made in the downstairs kitchen and finished in front of customers.
Young is a respected pâtissier as well as a chocolatier and has an astute chef's palate for flavour combinations: the white chocolate with rose masala is
divine, as are the salted caramels.
Other locations 143 Wardour Street, Soho,
W1F 8WA (7437 0011); 20 Royal Exchange,
Threadneedle Street, the City, EC3V 3LP
(7929 7007).
▶ *England's oldest chocolatier, Prestat (14
Princes Arcade, St James's, SW1Y 6DS, 0800
021 3023, www.prestat.co.uk) offers unusual and
traditional flavours in brightly coloured gift boxes.*

GIFTS & SOUVENIRS

★ Coco de Mer
*23 Monmouth Street, Covent Garden, WC2H
9DD (7836 8882, www.coco-de-mer.com). Covent
Garden tube.* **Open** 11am-7pm Mon-Wed, Fri, Sat;
11am-8pm Thur; noon-6pm Sun. **Credit** AmEx,
MC, V. **Map** p416 Y2.
London's most glamorous erotic emporium sells a
variety of tasteful books, toys and lingerie, from
glass dildos that double as objets d'art to a Marie
Antoinette costume of crotchless culottes and corset.
Trying on items can be fun as well: the peepshow-
style velvet changing rooms allow your lover to peer
through and watch you undress from a 'confession
box' next door.

Contemporary Applied Arts
*2 Percy Street, Fitzrovia, W1T 1DD (7436 2344,
www.caa.org.uk). Goodge Street or Tottenham
Court Road tube.* **Open** 10am-6pm Mon-Sat.
Credit AmEx, MC, V. **Map** p397 K5.
This airy gallery, run by a charitable arts organisation, represents more than 300 makers. The work
embraces the functional – jewellery, tableware,
textiles – but also includes unique, purely decorative
pieces. The ground floor hosts exhibitions by individual artists, or themed by craft; in the basement
shop, you'll find pieces for all pockets. Glass is
always exceptional here.

CONSUME

James Smith & Sons.

and welovekaoru, as well as the fabulous hand-stitched creatures by Finch, and jewellery by Rheanna Lingham, who uses ceramics, feathers and old embroidery to make necklaces, earrings and headbands. Also adorning the walls are taxidermy gulls by Jane Howarth, while the unique Paperself patterned paper eyelashes, based on Chinese paper-cut designs, have been selling thick and fast. In a new space since February 2011, Luna & Curious now also doubles up as a gallery space.

HEALTH & BEAUTY
Complementary medicine

Hale Clinic
7 Park Crescent, Marylebone, W1B 1PF (7631 0156, www.haleclinic.com). Great Portland Street or Regent's Park tube. **Open** 8.30am-9pm Mon-Fri; 9am-5pm Sat. **Credit** MC, V. **Map** p396 H4.
Around 100 practitioners are affiliated to the Hale Clinic, which was founded with the aim of integrating complementary and conventional medicine and opened by the Prince of Wales in 1988. The treatment list is an A-Z of alternative therapies, while the shop stocks supplements, skincare products and books.

Hairdressers & barbers

If the options listed below are out of your range, try a branch of **Mr Topper's** (7631 3233; £9 men, £20 women).

Daniel Hersheson
45 Conduit Street, Mayfair, W1F 2YN (7434 1747, www.danielhersheson.com). Oxford Circus tube. **Open** 9am-6pm Mon-Wed, Sat; 9am-8pm Thur, Fri. **Credit** AmEx, MC, V. **Map** p416 U3.

James Smith & Sons
53 New Oxford Street, Holborn, WC1A 1BL (7836 4731, www.james-smith.co.uk). Holborn or Tottenham Court Road tube. **Open** 9.30am-5.15pm Mon-Fri; 10am-5.15pm Sat. **Credit** AmEx, MC, V. **Map** p416 Y1.
More than 175 years after it was established, this charming shop, with Victorian fittings still intact, is holding its own in the niche market of umbrellas and walking sticks. The stock here isn't the throwaway type of brolly that breaks at the first sign of bad weather. Lovingly crafted 'brellas, such as a classic City umbrella with a Malacca Cane handle at £120, are built to last. A repair service is also offered.

London 2012 Shop
Unit 2A, St Pancras International, Pancras Road, King's Cross, NW1 2QP (7837 8558, http://shop.london2012.com). King's Cross tube/rail. **Open** 7.30am-9pm Mon-Fri; 8am-7pm Sat; 11am-6pm Sun. **Credit** V. **Map** p397 L3.
If you want to browse for Games merchandise in person rather than online, drop in at the dedicated shop. You'll find everything from collectable pin badges, mugs and die-cast models of cabs or double-decker buses to Stella McCartney-designed sportswear. **Other locations** John Lewis (5th floor), 300 Oxford Street, W1A 1EX (7629 7711, www.johnlewis.com).

Luna & Curious
24-26 Calvert Avenue, E2 7JP (3222 0034, www.lunaandcurious.com). Old Street tube/rail or Shoreditch High Street rail. **Open** 11am-6pm daily. **Credit** AmEx, MC, V. **Map** p401 R4.
The stock here is put together by a collective of young artisans. Look out for the quintessentially English teacups and ceramics from Polly George

INSIDE TRACK
LONDON 2012 SHOPS

If you want something to help remember the 2012 Games, browse the shelves at an official London 2012 Shop (http://shop.london2012.com). Perhaps the handiest is the standalone shop in St Pancras International Station (Pancras Road, NW1 2QP, 7837 8558), but there are also outlets at Canary Wharf's Jubilee Place, Paddington Station, Stansted Airport and airside at Heathrow's Terminals 3 and 5. Further London 2012 Shops are to be found in the John Lewis stores on Oxford Street (no.300, W1A 1EX, 7629 7711, www.johnlewis.com) and in Stratford City. You'll find everything from collectable pin badges and mugs to Stella McCartney-designed sportswear.

CONSUME

Despite its location in the heart of upmarket Mayfair, this modern two-storey salon isn't at all snooty, with a staff of very talented cutters and colourists. Prices start at £55 (£40 for men), though you'll pay £300 for a cut with Daniel (£150 for men). There's also a menu of therapies; the swish Harvey Nichols (*see p257*) branch has a dedicated spa. Hersheson's Blow Dry Bars are located at Topshop (*see p267*; 7927 7888 to book), Westfield London (*see p259*; 8743 0868) and One New Change (*see p259*; 7248 6225).

★ F Flittner

86 Moorgate, the City, EC2M 6SE (7606 4750, www.fflittner.com). Moorgate tube/rail. **Open** 8am-6pm Mon-Wed, Fri; 8am-6.30pm Thur. **Credit** AmEx, MC, V. **Map** p403 Q6.

In business since 1904, Flittner seems not to have noticed that the 21st century has begun. Hidden behind beautifully frosted doors (marked 'Saloon') is a simple, handsome room, done out with an array of classic barber's furniture that's older than your gran. Within these hushed confines, up to six black coat-clad barbers deliver straightforward haircuts (dry cuts £16-£20, wet cuts £24-£30) and shaves.

▶ *For a modern take on the art of the wet shave, try Murdock (340 Old Street, Shoreditch, EC1V 9DS, 7729 2288, www.murdocklondon.com).*

Tommy Guns

65 Beak Street, Soho, W1F 9SN (7439 0777, www.tommyguns.com). Oxford Circus or Picadilly Circus tube. **Open** 10am-8pm Mon-Fri; 10am-6pm Sat. **Credit** AmEx, MC, V.

Now over a decade old, and with new branches on Brewer Street and all the way over in New York City, Tommy Guns remains a very cool prospect indeed. This original Soho space, complete with retro fittings, is filled with youthful colourists and cutters and there's a friendly, relaxed buzz to the place most days. Men's cuts start from £39.95, and women's cuts can be had from £49.95.

Other locations 49 Charlotte Road, Shoreditch, EC2A 3QT (7739 2244); 65 Brewer Street, Soho, W1F 9TQ (7287 0011).

Opticians

Dollond & Aitchison (www.danda.co.uk) and **Specsavers** (www.specsavers.com) are chains with branches on most high streets.

Cutler & Gross

16 Knightsbridge Green, Knightsbridge, SW1X 7QL (7581 2250, www.cutlerandgross.com). Knightsbridge tube. **Open** 9.30am-7pm Mon-Sat; noon-5pm Sun. **Credit** AmEx, MC, V. **Map** p395 F9.

C&G celebrated its 40th anniversary in 2009, and its stock of handmade frames is still at the cutting edge of optical style. Stock runs from Andy Warhol-inspired glasses to naturally light buffalo-horn

Cutler & Gross.

frames, and recent collaborations have included frames with trend-leaders Comme des Garçons. Vintage eyewear from the likes of Ray-Ban and Courrèges is at the sister shop down the road.

Other locations 7 Knightsbridge Green, Knightsbridge, SW1X 7QL (7590 9995).

▶ *For cool vintage frames and sunglasses, check out Covent Garden's Opera Opera (98 Long Acre, WC2E 9NR, 7836 9246, www.operaopera.net), which has operated from the same corner site for over three decades.*

Pharmacies

National chain **Boots** (www.boots.com) has branches across the city, offering dispensing pharmacies and photo processing. The store on Piccadilly Circus (44-46 Regent Street, W1B 5RA, 7734 6126) is open until midnight (except Sunday, when it closes at 6pm).

DR Harris

29 St James's Street, St James's, SW1A 1HB (7930 3915, www.drharris.co.uk). Green Park or Piccadilly Circus tube. **Open** 8.30am-6pm Mon-Fri; 9.30am-5pm Sat. **Credit** AmEx, MC, V. **Map** p398 J8.

Founded in 1790, this venerable chemist has a royal warrant. Wood-and-glass cabinets are filled with bottles, jars and old-fashioned shaving brushes and manicure kits. The smartly packaged own-brand products such as the bright blue Crystal Eye Gel have a cult following.

Shops

Eco pioneer **Neal's Yard Remedies** (15 Neal's Yard, Covent Garden, WC2H 9DP, 7379 7222, www.nealsyardremedies.com) has several

CONSUME

central London branches, offering organic products and a herbal dispensary. Beauty chain **Space NK** (8-10 Broadwick Street, Soho, W1F 8HW, 7734 3734, www.spacenk.com) has also expanded in recent years, and is a great source of niche skincare and make-up brands.

Liz Earle Naturally Active Skincare

38-39 Duke of York Square, Chelsea, SW3 4LY (7730 9191, http://uk.lizearle.com). Sloane Square tube. **Open** 10am-7pm Mon, Wed-Sat; 10.30am-7pm Tue; 11am-5pm Sun. **Credit** AmEx, MC, V. **Map** p395 F11.

The London flagship of Liz Earle's botanical skincare range is housed in a large, light, fresh space in Chelsea's Duke of York Square, and stocks the full range of pleasingly gimmick-free and affordable products based on a regime of cleansing, toning and moisturising. Highlights among the products include the Instant Boost Skin Tonic and Superskin Moisturiser. 'Minis' and essentials packs are a great introduction (£13 for a starter kit).

▶ *Niche Aussie skincare brand Aesop (www. aesop-europe.com) now has three standalone London boutiques, on Mayfair's Mount Street, Westbourne Grove and east London's Redchurch Street (see p273* **Style Street***).*

Lost in Beauty

117 Regent's Park Road, Primrose Hill, NW1 8UR (7586 4411, www.lostinbeauty.com). Chalk Farm tube. **Open** 10am-6.30pm Mon-Sat; noon-5pm Sun. **Credit** AmEx, MC, V. **Map** p404 W2.

Kitted out with vintage shop fittings, this chic Primrose Hill boutique stocks a well-edited array of cult beauty brands, including Phyto, Becca, Caudalie, Dr Hauschka, Environ, Art of Hair and Butter London nail polish. Jimmyjane candles and Belmacz Oyster Pearl translucent face powder are also stocked. Illuminated theatre mirrors are perfect for sampling products, while the friendly staff are on hand to offer advice. There's also a choice selection of vintage jewellery.

Miller Harris

21 Bruton Street, Mayfair, W1J 6QD (7629 7750, www.millerharris.com). Bond Street or Green Park tube. **Open** 10am-6pm Mon-Sat. **Credit** AmEx, MC, V. **Map** p398 H7.

Grasse-trained British perfumer Lyn Harris's scents, in lovely floral packaging, are made with natural extracts and oils. Noix de Tubéreuse, a lighter and more palatable tuberose scent than many on the market, is a perennial favourite, while Fleurs de Bois evokes a traditional English garden. Newcomers to the range include La Fumée and La Pluie, reflecting the characteristics of smoke and rain respectively. Prices aren't cheap – between £85 and £110 for 100ml – but you'll be paying for top-quality ingredients. This flagship branch, which has recently been refurbished, also has a tea room.

Other locations 14 Needham Road, Notting Hill, W11 2RP (7221 1545); 14 Monmouth Street, Covent Garden, WC2H 9HB (7836 9378).

Spas & salons

Many of London's luxury hotels – including the **Sanderson** (*see p193*) and the **Dorchester** (*see p203*) – make their excellent spa facilities available to the public.

Cowshed

119 Portland Road, Notting Hill, W11 4LN (7078 1944, www.cowshedclarendoncross.com). Holland Park tube. **Open** 9am-8pm Mon-Fri; 9am-7pm Sat; 10am-5pm Sun. **Credit** AmEx, MC, V. **Map** p404 X6.

The London branch of Cowshed (from Somerset's renowned Babington House's) does its country cousin proud. The chic, white ground floor is buzzy, with a tiny café area on one side, and a manicure/pedicure section on the other. For facials, massages and waxing, head downstairs.

Other locations 31 Fouberts Place, Soho, W11 7QG (7534 0870); Ebor Street, Bethnal Green, E1 6AW (7749 4531); 162 Chiswick High Road, Chiswick, W4 1PR (8987 1607).

Elemis Day Spa

2-3 Lancashire Court, Mayfair, W1S 1EX (7499 4995, www.elemis.com). Bond Street tube. **Open** 9am-9pm Mon-Sat; 10am-6pm Sun. **Credit** AmEx, MC, V. **Map** p396 H6.

This leading British spa brand's exotic, unisex retreat is tucked away down a cobbled lane off Bond Street. The elegantly ethnic treatment rooms are a lovely setting in which to relax and enjoy a spot of pampering, from wraps to facials.

Miller Harris.

HOUSE & HOME
Antiques & second-hand

Although boutiques have encroached on their
territory, there are still some quirky dealers
on Islington's **Camden Passage** (off Upper
Street, 7359 0190, www.camdenpassage
antiques.com); try the Pierrepont Arcade.
Marylebone's **Church Street** is now a major
area for vintage homewares, and host to Alfie's
Antique Market (*see below*), but **Portobello
Road** (*see p261*) and **Bermondsey Square
Antiques Market** (*see p260*) remain the
best-known markets for antiques.

Alfie's Antique Market
*13-25 Church Street, Marylebone, NW8 8DT
(7723 6066, www.alfiesantiques.com). Edgware
Road tube or Marylebone tube/rail.* **Open** 10am-
6pm Tue-Sat. **No credit cards. Map** p393 E4.
Alfie's hosts more than 100 dealers in vintage furniture and fashion, art, books, maps and the like.
Check out Dodo Posters for 1920s and '30s ads.

Core One
*Gas Works, 2 Michael Road, Fulham, SW6 2AD
(7823 3900). Sloane Square tube then bus 11, 19,
22, 319, 211.* **Open** 10am-6pm Mon-Fri; 11am-
4pm Sat. **No credit cards.**
A group of antiques and 20th-century dealers has
colonised this industrial building in Fulham, including Dean Antiques (7610 6997, www.deanantiques.
co.uk) for dramatic pieces, and De Parma (7736 3384,
www.deparma.com) for elegant mid-century design.

Grays Antique Market & Grays in the Mews
*58 Davies Street, W1K 5LP & 1-7 Davies
Mews, Mayfair, W1K 5AB (7629 7034,
www.graysantiques.com). Bond Street tube.*
Open 10am-6pm Mon-Fri; 11am-5pm Sat.
Credit AmEx, MC, V. **Map** p396 H6.
More than 200 dealers in this smart covered market
sell everything from antique furniture and rare
books to vintage fashion and jewellery.

Two Columbia Road
*2 Columbia Road, E2 7NN (7729 9933,
www.twocolumbiaroad.com). Hoxton or Shoreditch
High Street rail.* **Open** noon-7pm Tue-Fri; noon-
6pm Sat; 10am-3pm Sun. **Credit** MC, V. **Map**
p401 S3.
Well-selected 20th-century pieces are the order of the
day here, whether it's 1970s chrome pendant lights,
Danish 1960s rosewood desks, or collectable Charles
Eames wooden chairs. The appealing corner site is
owned by Tommy Roberts and is run by his son
Keith. Expect to find well-known names such as
Arne Jacobsen and Willy Rizzo among the stock as
well as more affordable pieces.

General

Heals (196 Tottenham Court Road, W1T 7LQ,
7636 1666, www.heals.co.uk) is a good source of
mid-range modern design.

Conran Shop
*Michelin House, 81 Fulham Road, Fulham,
SW3 6RD (7589 7401, www.conran.co.uk). South
Kensington tube.* **Open** 10am-6pm Mon, Tue, Fri;
10am-7pm Wed, Thur; 10am-6.30pm Sat; noon-
6pm Sun. **Credit** MC, V. **Map** p395 E10.
Sir Terence Conran's flagship store in the Fulham
Road's beautiful 1909 Michelin Building showcases
furniture and design for every room in the house as
well as the garden; as well as design classics, such
as the Eames Dar chair, there are plenty of portable
accessories, gadgets, books, stationery and toiletries
that make great gifts or souvenirs.
Other locations 55 Marylebone High Street,
Marylebone, W1U 5HS (7723 2223).

★ Labour & Wait
*85 Redchurch Street, Shoreditch, E2 7DJ (7729
6253, www.labourandwait.co.uk). Shoreditch High
Street rail.* **Open** 11am-6pm Tue-Sun. **Credit** MC,
V. **Map** p401 S4.
This retro-stylish store, now on London's ultra-
trendy Redchurch Street (*see p273* **Style Street**),
sells the sort of things everybody would have had
in their kitchen or pantry 60 years ago: functional
domestic goods that have a timeless style. Spend any
time here and you'll be filled with the joys of spring
cleaning. For the kitchen there are some great simple
classics such as enamel milk pans in retro pastels,
and lovely 1950s-inspired Japanese teapots, and you
can garden beautifully with ash-handled trowels.
Vintage Welsh wool blankets, classic toiletries, and
some great old-fashioned gifts, such as a pinhole
camera kit and a lovely range of handmade notebooks from Portugal, make it hard to leave empty
handed. Labour & Wait also has a space at concept
store Dover Street Market (*see p266*).

MUSIC & ENTERTAINMENT
CDs, records & DVDs

Oxford Street's last music megastore, **HMV**
(www.hmv.co.uk), offers a comprehensive line-
up of CDs and DVDs, plus some vinyl. Serious
music browsers, however, head south into
Soho, where independent record stores are
still clinging on around Berwick and
D'Arblay streets.
   Ray's Jazz, London's least beardy jazz
shop, is to be found on the third floor of Foyles
bookshop (*see p261*) on Charing Cross Road. The
predominantly CD-based stock contains a good
selection of blues, avant-garde, gospel, folk and
world, but modern jazz is the main draw.

Flashback

*50 Essex Road, Islington, N1 8LR (7354 9356,
www.flashback.co.uk). Angel tube then bus 38, 56,
73, 341.* **Open** 10am-7pm Mon-Sat; 11.30am-6pm
Sun. **Credit** AmEx, MC, V. **Map** p400 O1.
Stock is scrupulously organised at this second-hand
treasure trove. The ground floor is dedicated to CDs,
while the basement is vinyl-only: an ever-expanding
jazz collection jostles for space alongside soul, hip
hop and a carpal tunnel-compressing selection of
library sounds. A range of rarities is pinned in plastic sleeves to the walls.

Harold Moores Records

*2 Great Marlborough Street, Soho, W1F 7HQ
(7437 1576, www.hmrecords.co.uk). Oxford Circus
tube.* **Open** 10am-6.30pm Mon-Sat. **Credit** AmEx,
MC, V. **Map** p416 V2.
Harold Moores is not your stereotypical classical
music store: young, open-minded staff and an expansive stock of new and second-hand music bolster its
credentials. This collection sees some great old masters complemented by a range of eclectic contemporary music. There's a suitably studious basement
dedicated to second-hand classical vinyl, including
an excellent selection of jazz music.

Honest Jon's

*278 Portobello Road, Notting Hill, W10 5TE
(8969 9822, www.honestjons.com). Ladbroke
Grove tube.* **Open** 10am-6pm Mon-Sat; 11am-5pm
Sun. **Credit** AmEx, MC, V. **Map** p404 X4.
Honest Jon's found its way to Notting Hill in 1979,
and the owner helped James Lavelle set up Mo'Wax
records. You'll find jazz, hip hop, soul, broken beat,
reggae and Brazilian music on the shelves.

★ Rough Trade East

*Dray Walk, Old Truman Brewery, 91 Brick
Lane, Spitalfields, E1 6QL (7392 7788,
www.roughtrade.com). Liverpool Street tube/rail.*
Open 8am-9pm Mon-Thur; 8am-8pm Fri; 10am-
8pm Sat; 11am-7pm Sun. **Credit** AmEx, DC, MC,
V. **Map** p401 S5.
Celebrating its 35th birthday in 2011, this infamous
temple to indie music has never looked more upbeat,
its new-found impetus provided by the 2007 opening
of Rough Trade East. The 5,000sq ft record store,
café and gig space offers a dizzying range of vinyl
and CDs, spanning punk, indie, dub, soul, electronica
and more. With 16 listening posts and a stage for
live sets, this is close to musical nirvana.
Other locations 130 Talbot Road, Notting Hill,
W11 1JA (7229 8541).

Sounds of the Universe

*7 Broadwick Street, Soho, W1F 0DA (7734 3430,
www.soundsoftheuniverse.com). Tottenham Court
Road tube.* **Open** 11am-7.30pm Mon-Sat. **Credit**
AmEx, MC, V. **Map** p416 V2.
This stylish sound store has universal appeal. Its
affiliation with reissue kings Soul Jazz records
means its remit is broad. This is especially true on
the ground floor (new vinyl and CDs), where grime
and dubstep 12-inches jostle for space alongside new
wave cosmic disco, electro-indie re-rubs and
Nigerian compilations, while the second-hand vinyl
basement is big on soul, jazz, Brazilian and alt-rock.

Musical instruments

Site of the legendary recording studio Regent
Sounds in the 1960s, **Denmark Street**, off
Charing Cross Road, is now a hub for music
shops, especially those selling guitars.

Chappell of Bond Street

*152-160 Wardour Street, Soho, W1F 8YA (7432
4400, www.chappellofbondstreet.co.uk). Tottenham
Court Road tube.* **Open** 9.30am-6pm Mon-Fri;
10am-5.30pm Sat. **Credit** AmEx, MC, V.
Map p416 V2.

CONSUME

Rough Trade East.

It's retained its old name, but Chappell recently moved from Bond Street (its home for nearly 200 years) to this amazing three-storey musical temple. This is the leading Yamaha stockist in the UK, and the collection of sheet music (classical, pop and jazz) is reputedly the largest in Europe.

SPORTS & FITNESS

Harrods (*see p257*) has a good fitness department. Bike chains **Evans Cycles** (www.evanscycles.com) and **Cycle Surgery** (www.cyclesurgery.com) each have a number of branches across the city. London's skaters now have a home branch of cult New York brand **Supreme** (*see p265*), selling the full range of boards and apparel. For the best places to find fashion trainers, *see p270*.

Bobbin Globe Store

23 Arlington Way, EC1R 1UY (7998 0356, www.bobbinglobestore.co.uk). Angel tube. **Open** noon-6pm Tue-Fri; noon-6pm Sat. **Credit** call for details. **Map** p400 N3.
If your preference is for the more elegant days of cycle touring, rather than the modern penchant for squeezing into lycra, then Bobbin is the shop for you. Now in a new space, the shop stocks the full range of Bobbin Bicycles (www.bobbinonline.co.uk) as well as the slightly sportier Globe bikes.

Decathlon

Canada Water Retail Park, Surrey Quays Road, Rotherhithe, SE16 2XU (7394 2000, www.decathlon.co.uk). Canada Water tube. **Open** 9am-9pm Mon-Fri; 9am-7pm Sat; 11am-5pm Sun. **Credit** MC, V.
The warehouse-sized London branch of this French chain offers London's biggest single collection of sports equipment. You'll find a vast array of reasonably priced equipment and clothing for all mainstream racket and ball sports as well as swimming, running, surfing, fishing, skiing and more.

INSIDE TRACK POP-UP SHOPS

Pop-up shops have proved to be more than a fleeting trend, and are now an established part of London's shopping scene. They range from innovative two-day events by arty east London independents, to month-long temporary concessions by high-end brands in the city's department stores. A five-year 'pop-up mall' has stretched the concept to its limit – **Boxpark** (www.boxpark.co.uk) opened in Shoreditch in autumn 2011, housing a range of streetwear shops – as well as a branch of Finnish lifestyle brand Marimekko – in a series of shipping containers.

Ellis Brigham

Tower House, 3-11 Southampton Street, WC2E 7HA (7395 1010, www.ellis-brigham.com). Covent Garden tube. **Open** 10am-8pm Mon-Fri; 9.30am-6.30pm Sat; 11.30am-5.30pm Sun. **Credit** AmEx, MC, V. **Map** 416 Z3.
This is the largest of the mountain sports shops on Southampton Street. It also houses London's only ice-climbing wall, 8m (26ft) high.
Other locations Unit 2003, Westfield Shopping Centre, W12 7GF (8222 6300); 178 Kensington High Street, W8 7RG (7937 6889); 6 Cheapside Passage, EC2V 6AF (3170 8746); Unit 2092, Westfield Stratford City, W12 7GF (8740 3790).

Run & Become

42 Palmer Street, Victoria, SW1H 0PH (7222 1314, www.runandbecome.com). St James's Park tube. **Open** 9am-6pm Mon-Wed, Fri, Sat; 9am-8pm Thur. **Credit** MC, V. **Map** p398 J9.
The experienced staff here, most of them enthusiastic runners, will find the right pair of shoes for your physique and running style. The gamut of running kit, from clothing to speed monitors, is available.

TICKETS

For London performances, whether musical, theatrical or in some other cultural orbit, it's worth booking ahead – surprisingly obscure acts sell out, and high-profile gigs and sporting events can do in seconds. It's almost always cheaper to bypass ticket agents and go direct to the box office: agents charge booking fees that often top 20 per cent. If you have to use an agent, booking agencies include **Ticketmaster** (0844 844 0444, www.ticketmaster.co.uk), **Stargreen** (7734 8932, www.stargreen.com), **Ticketweb** (0844 477 1000, www.ticketweb.co.uk), **See Tickets** (0871 220 0260, www.seetickets.com) and **Keith Prowse** (3137 7420, www.keithprowse.com). However, there are several ways to save money on tickets. For specific tips on where to get tickets (and how to keep the cost down) for the theatre, *see p343*; for gigs and concerts, *see p320 and p316*.

TRAVELLERS' NEEDS

Independent travel specialist **Trailfinders** (European travel 0845 050 5945, worldwide flights 0845 058 5858, www.trailfinders.com) has several branches in the capital, including in the Piccadilly Waterstone's (nos.203-206, SW1Y 6WW, 0843 290 8549, www.waterstones.co.uk).

Excess Baggage Company

4 Hannah Close, Great Central Way, Wembley, Middx NW10 0UX (0800 524 4822, www.excess-baggage.com). **Credit** AmEx, MC, V.
Ships goods to over 300 countries and territories.

Arts & Entertainment

Calendar

Wherever and whenever – the lowdown on what's going on.

Forget about British reserve. Lots of Londoners like nothing more than finding a crowd and making fools of themselves. Festivals and events play ever more elaborate variations on the age-old themes of parading and dancing, nowadays with ever-larger sprinklings of often-innovative arts and culture.

The event of the year, of course, if not the century, is the London 2012 Olympic and Paralympic Games, which kick off in late July and late August respectively (*see pp41-73* for a complete guide). These will be a feast not only of sport but of arts and culture too. The national Cultural Olympiad programme is already up and running; on 21 June 2012 the flagship London 2012 Festival swings into action (*see p289* **London 2012 Festival**).

INFORMATION

The weekly *Time Out London* magazine, in print and online (www.timeout.com/london), is the definitive authority on everything that matters in the capital's cultural calendar; get instant news of key events mainstream and underground via the blog, Twitter and facebook.

Always confirm details well in advance – events can be cancelled and dates may change with little notice, especially during the Games.

The main cultural festivals in all genres are included in this chapter; a series of boxes throughout the Arts & Entertainment section details more specialist events.

ALL YEAR ROUND

For the **Changing of the Guard**, *see p290* **Standing on Ceremony**.

Ceremony of the Keys

Tower of London, Tower Hill, the City, EC3N 4AB (0844 482 7777, www.hrp.org.uk). Tower Hill tube or Tower Gateway DLR. **Date** 9.30pm daily (advance bookings only). **Map** p403 R7.
Join the Yeoman Warders after-hours at the Tower of London as they ritually lock the fortress's entrances in this 700-year-old ceremony. You enter the Tower at 9.30pm and it's all over just after 10pm, but places are hotly sought after – apply at least two months in advance; full details are on the website.

Gun Salutes

Green Park, Mayfair & St James's, W1, & Tower of London, the City, EC3. **Dates** 6 Feb (Accession Day); 21 Apr & 16 June (Queen's birthdays); 2 June (Coronation Day); 10 June (Duke of Edinburgh's birthday); 16 June (Trooping the Colour); State Opening of Parliament (*see p291*); 10 Nov (Lord Mayor's Show); 11 Nov (Remembrance Sunday); also for state visits. **Map** p398 H8.
There are gun salutes on many state occasions – see the list of dates given above for a complete breakdown of when the cannons roar out. A cavalry charge features in the 41-gun salutes mounted by the King's Troop Royal Horse Artillery in Hyde Park at noon (it takes place opposite the Dorchester Hotel; *see p203*), whereas, on the other side of town, the Honourable Artillery Company ditches the ponies and piles on the firepower with its 62-gun salutes (1pm at the Tower of London). If the dates happen to fall on a Sunday, the the salute is held on the following Monday.

JANUARY-MARCH

This is a good time of year for dance events, among them **Resolution!** at the Place; *see p302* **Festivals**. For the **London Lesbian & Gay Film Festival**, *see p306*.

Joseph Grimaldi Memorial Service

Pentonville Road, Islington, N1 9JE (www. clowns-international.co.uk). King's Cross tube/rail. **Date** 5 Feb.

Join hundreds of motley-clad 'Joeys' for their annual service commemorating the legendary British clown, Joseph Grimaldi (1778-1837).

★ Chinese New Year Festival
Around Gerrard Street, Chinatown, W1, Leicester Square, WC2, & Trafalgar Square, WC2 (7851 6686, www.londonchinatown.org). Leicester Square or Piccadilly Circus tube. **Date** 29 Jan. **Map** p416 W3.
Launch the Year of the, er, Dragon in style at celebrations that engulf Chinatown and Leicester Square. Dragon dancers writhe alongside a host of impressive acts in the grand parade to Trafalgar Square, while the restaurants of Chinatown get even more packed than usual.

Pancake Day Races
Great Spitalfields *Dray Walk, off Brick Lane, E1 6QL (7375 0441, www.alternativearts.co.uk). Liverpool Street tube/rail.*
Poulters Annual *Guildhall Yard, the City, EC2P 2EJ (www.poulters.org.uk). Bank tube/DLR or Moorgate tube/rail.*
Both Date 21 Feb.
Shrove Tuesday brings out charity pancake racers. Don a silly costume and join the Great Spitalfields Pancake Race (register in advance) or watch City livery companies race in full regalia at the event organised by the Worshipful Company of Poulters.

Who Do You Think You Are? Live
Olympia, Hammersmith Road, Kensington, W14 8UX (www.whodoyouthinkyouarelive.co.uk). Kensington Olympia tube/rail. **Date** 24-26 Feb.

Pancake Day Races.

A spin-off from the hugely successful BBC TV series that keeps Brits glued to the box watching weepy celebs uncover their ancestry, this enormous family history event could help you trace yours.

★ Kew Spring Festival
For listings, *see p178* **Royal Botanic Gardens**. **Date** early Feb-Mar.
Kew Gardens is at its most beautiful in spring, with five million flowers carpeting the grounds.

National Science & Engineering Week
0870 770 7101, www.britishscience association.org/nsew. **Date** 9-18 Mar.
From the weirdly wacky to the profound, this annual series of events engages the public in celebrating science, engineering and technology.

St Patrick's Day Parade & Festival
7983 4000, www.london.gov.uk. **Date** 17 Mar.
Join the London Irish out in force for this huge annual parade through central London followed by toe-tapping tunes in Trafalgar Square.

APRIL-JUNE

Early summer is a terrifi time for outdoor events. There's excellent alfresco theatre at the **Greenwich & Docklands International Festival** and, on the South Bank, **Watch This Space** (for both, *see p349* **Festivals**). Fans of sport can go racing (**Royal Ascot**, the **Epsom Derby**), queue for **Wimbledon** tickets or watch a football playoff; for all, *see p334.* For classical music at the **City of London Festival** and the **Hampton Court Palace Festival,** *see p317* **Festivals**; for rockier fare at the **Camden Crawl**, the **Wireless Festival** and the **Somerset House Summer Series,** *see p322* **Festivals**.

Oxford & Cambridge Boat Race
River Thames, from Putney to Mortlake (www.theboatrace.org). Putney Bridge tube, or Barnes Bridge, Mortlake or Putney rail. **Date** 7 Apr.
Blue-clad Oxbridge students race each other in a pair of rowing eights, watched by tens of millions

ARTS & ENTERTAINMENT

Happy and Glorious

Queen Elizabeth II celebrates her Diamond Jubilee.

Hang the expense. The Golden Jubilee of 2002 was a year-long celebration of queen and country: classical concerts, exhibitions, a new footbridge to adorn the Thames. A decade later and organisers have outdone themselves; the long holiday weekend (2-5 June) celebrating HM's 60th year in the job will showcase entertainment of sublime extravagance.

The official festivities commence at 2pm on Sunday with the Thames River Pageant; a 1,000-strong flotilla of boats led by the Queen in the Royal Barge. Replete with flag-waving citizenry, music boats, daylight fireworks and a floating belfry, the fleet will drift steadily downriver from Battersea to the Tower of London.

The double bank holiday weekend continues on Monday with a concert at Buckingham Palace (broadcast live by the BBC), after which Her Majesty will light a beacon in The Mall, completing a network of 2,012 similar beacons spanning the country. The entertainment begins to wind down on Tuesday as the Queen attends a thanksgiving service at St Paul's Cathedral, with a formal carriage procession taking place afterwards.

From 10 to 13 May, Windsor Castle hosts the Diamond Jubilee Pageant (tickets from £30), an event that promises 'a journey to the seven corners of the earth'. With a majestic line-up including over 800 international performers and 500 horses, the spectacle will present dance, music and displays both military and equestrian.

Several exhibitions complement the celebrations, showing rare treasures from the Royal Collection that will impress the hardest-line republican.

Diamonds: A Jubilee Celebration
Buckingham Palace (see p140). **Date** Aug-Sept.
An unprecedented display of the Queen's diamonds, which have been passed down through the royal line.

Leonardo da Vinci: Anatomy
The Queen's Gallery, Buckingham Palace (see p140). **Date** 4 May-7 Oct.
The largest ever exhibition of Da Vinci's treatise, *Anatomy*, the artist-scientist-inventor's pioneering work on the human form, which was lost for four centuries.

National Portrait Gallery.

The Queen: Sixty Photographs for Sixty Years
The Drawings Gallery, Windsor Castle. **Date** Feb 2012-January 2013.
Royal Rota photographers present a compilation of photo-portraits capturing fleeting moments from Elizabeth's reign.

Treasures from the Queen's Palaces
The Queen's Gallery, Palace of Holyroodhouse, Edinburgh. **Date** 16 Mar-16 Sept.
One hundred of the finest treasures from the Royal Collection. Paintings by Rembrandt and Monet. Drawings by Michelangelo and Raphael. Imperial Easter Eggs by Fabergé. Unmissable.

The Queen: Art and Image
National Portrait Gallery (see p135). **Date** 17 May-21 Oct).
The National Portrait Gallery is bringing together 60 of the most remarkable images – from press pictures to works by contemporary artists – of Elizabeth II. Artists and photographers include Cecil Beaton, Andy Warhol, Lucian Freud and Pietro Annigoni, and works will be accompanied by archival material from film footage to postage stamps.

ARTS & ENTERTAINMENT

worldwide. Experience the excitement from the riverbank (along with 250,000 other fans) for the 158th instalment of the historic race.

Shakespeare's Birthday
For listings, *see p346* **Shakespeare's Globe**.
Date wknd closest to 23 Apr.
To celebrate the Bard's birthday, the Globe Theatre throws open its doors for a series of events.

★ Virgin London Marathon
Greenwich Park to the Mall via the Isle of Dogs, Victoria Embankment & St James's Park (7902 0200, www.virginlondonmarathon.com). Blackheath & Maze Hill rail (start), or Charing Cross tube/rail (end). **Date** 22 Apr.
One of the world's elite long-distance races, the London Marathon is also one of the world's largest fundraising events – nearly 80% of participants run for charity, so zany costumes abound among the 35,000 starters. If you haven't already applied to run, you're too late: just go along to watch.

Sundance London 2012
O2 Arena, Millennium Way, North Greenwich, SE10 0BB (www.sundance-london.com). **Date** 26-29 Apr.
Robert Redford's mini-version of the Sundance Film Festival, his annual celebration of independent film.

Covent Garden May Fayre & Puppet Festival
Garden of St Paul's Covent Garden, Bedford Street, Covent Garden, WC2E 9ED (7375 0441, www.punchandjudy.com/coventgarden.htm). Covent Garden tube. **Date** 12-13 May.
Map p416 Y4.
All-day puppet mayhem (10.30am-5.30pm) devoted to celebrating Mr Punch at the scene of his first recorded sighting in England in 1662 (making 2012 the 350th anniversary). Mr P takes to the church's pulpit at 11.30am.

Chelsea Flower Show
Royal Hospital, Royal Hospital Road, Chelsea, SW3 4SR (www.rhs.org.uk). Sloane Square tube. **Date** 22-26 May. **Map** p395 F12.
Elbow past the crowds to admire perfect blooms, or get ideas for your own plot. The first two days are reserved for Royal Horticultural Society members and tickets for the open days are hard to come by. The show closes at 5.30pm on the final day, with display plants being sold off from around 4.30pm.

Coin Street Festival
Bernie Spain Gardens (next to Oxo Tower Wharf), South Bank, SE1 9PH (7021 1600, www.coinstreet.org). Southwark tube or Waterloo tube/rail. **Date** June-Aug. **Map** p402 N8.
Celebrating London's cultural diversity, this free, summer-long Thames-side festival features a series of music-focused events, usually involving a few guest musicians or theatre groups from across the world, as well as local talent. Food stalls too.

World Naked Bike Ride
www.worldnakedbikeride.org. **Date** mid June.
Help expose the problem of pollution caused by motor vehicles by exposing yourself in honour of the World Naked Bike Ride. Cyclists across the globe strip off and saddle up to mark the occasion.

Open Garden Squares Weekend
www.opensquares.org. **Date** 9-10 June.
Secret – and merely exclusive – gardens are thrown open to the public. You can visit roof gardens, prison gardens and children-only gardens, as well as a changing selection of those tempting oases railed off in the middle of the city's finest squares. Some charge an entrance fee.

Art Car Boot Fair
www.artcarbootfair.com. **Date** tbc.
Cheaper and certainly more fun than your average art fair, this afternoon event is an opportunity to purchase specially made, usually humorous pieces by the likes of Gavin Turk, Peter Blake, Bob and Roberta Smith, and Pam Hogg.

Marylebone Summer Fayre
www.marylebonesummerfayre.com. **Date** mid June.
Streets in the Marylebone Village neighbourhood are closed to traffic and filled with market stalls and entertainment, including a farmers' market and a fairground, in aid of the Teenage Cancer Trust.

Exhibition Road Music Day
Exhibition Road, South Kensington, SW7 (www.exhibitionroad.com). South Kensington tube. **Date** 21 June. **Map** p395 D9.
London's counterpart to France's midsummer Fête de la Musique ranges through institutions that border Exhibition Road and spills into Hyde Park. With Imperial College and the Ismaili Centre among the participants, you can expect anything from experimental, electronic music to Sufi chants.

INSIDE TRACK
LONDON 2012 LOCAL

The five London 2012 host boroughs will be devising their own programmes of Games-related events throughout 2012. Track events as they are announced on www.hackney.gov, www.greenwich. gov.uk, www.towerhamlets.gov.uk, www.newham.com/summer and www.walthamforestbig6.co.uk. Clue: some may involve the Olympic Torch...

Greenwich & Docklands International Festival

Various venues (www.festival.org). **Date** 21-30 June. This annual festival of outdoor arts, theatre, dance and family entertainment is consistently spectacular. Events take place at the Old Royal Naval College and other sites in Greenwich including St Alfege Park, also Canary Wharf, the Isle of Dogs, Woolwich and Mile End Park.

Southbank Centre's Poetry Parnassus

Southbank Centre, Belvedere Road, London, SE1 8XX (7969 4200, www.southbankcentre.co.uk). **Date** 26 June-1 July. **Map** p399 M8.
Set to be the largest poetry festival ever staged in the UK, the Southbank Centre's Poetry Parnassus brings together poets from all the nations competing in the London 2012 Olympic Games and includes readings, worskhops and a gala finale event.

JULY-SEPTEMBER

The long-awaited London 2012 Olympic and Paralympic Games and their attendant cultural Festival dominate the agenda for summer. For the sporting action, including schedules, see *pp41-73* **London 2012**; and for Festival 2012, *see p289* **London Festival 2012**.

In addition, summer sees some of the most important music festivals of the year – namely, the **BBC Sir Henry Wood Promenade Concerts** (more commonly, the Proms), the **Lovebox Weekender**, the **English Heritage Picnic Concerts** at Kenwood

House and the teenager-friendly **Underage** festival (for all, *see p317 and p322* **Festivals**) – as well as the city's major gay event, **Pride London** (*see p311* **Festivals**). There are also two cutting-edge dance events, the **Place Prize** and **Dance Umbrella** (for both, *see p302* **Festivals**).

Create Festival

http://createlondon.org. **Date** July.
Multi-arts festival in the five boroughs to host the 2012 Olympic and Paralympic Games.

Shoreditch Festival

www.shoreditchfestival.org.uk. **Date** tbc.
Last year's event saw screenings, music, dance, art commissions, fashion, spoken word, walks and food markets on tow paths, green spaces, basins, bridges and other venues adjacent to Regent's Canal between Shoreditch Park, N1, and Victoria Park, E3.

London Literature Festival

Southbank Centre, Belvedere Road, SE1 8XX (0844 847 9939, www.londonlitfest.com). Waterloo *tube/rail.* **Date** 1st 2wks of July. **Map** p399 M8.
The London Literature Festival combines superstar writers with stars from other fields: architects, comedians, sculptors and cultural theorists examining anything from queer literature to migration.

★ Chap Olympiad

www.thechap.net. **Date** 14-15 July.
English eccentrics are in full cry at this annual event mounted by the *Chap* magazine, which starts with the

---

Please, Sir, Can We Have Some More?

Dickens to your heart's content.

The year of 2012 marks the 200th anniversary of the birth of Charles Dickens (on 7 February) – an author who represented the quintessence of 19th-century London. With their social justice paradigm of harsh industrialism versus goodness of the heart, his literary works remain relevant, and his bicentenary is being celebrated not only in London but also worldwide, in a series of events throughout the year. Visit www.dickens 2012.org for more details.

There are tributes from several branches of the arts. In January, BFI Southbank (*see* p308) is screening a Dickens season, drawing on its extensive collection of Dickens-related works on film and TV; and the Barbican (*see* p316) is hosting silent film adaptations of his novels for its regular silent film season. The Museum of London

(*see* p93) offers a Dickens and London exhibtion (to 10 June), recreating Victorian life in the capital in celebration of the author's connection to the city through sound, projections, photographs and rare manuscripts. The supernatural element of Dickens's writing is brought to life up to 4 March at the British Library (*see* p109), which explores the ghoulish references the writer makes in his works.

Dickens's relatively unknown narrative *The Life of Our Lord* makes its theatrical premiere in the West End in spring 2012 as a one-man play, with royalties going to Dickens and theatre charities. From 8-10 June, venture out of London to Kent for the popular annual Rochester Dickens Festival (www.rochesterdickensfestival.org.uk) combining all things Victorian, from music and dance to costume and street theatre.

Chap Olympiad.

Two million people stream in to Notting Hill to Europe's largest street party, full of the smells, colours and music of the Caribbean. Massive mobile sound systems dominate the streets with whatever bass-heavy party music is currently hip, but there's plenty of tradition from the West Indies too: calypso music and a spectacular costumed parade.

▶ *For sightseeing in Notting Hill, see p127.*

Great River Race
River Thames, from Millwall Docks, Docklands E14, to Ham House, Richmond, Surrey TW10 (8398 9057, www.greatriverrace.co.uk). **Date** 15 Sept.
The alternative Boat Race (*see p283*) is much more fun, with an exotic array of around 300 traditional rowing boats from across the globe racing the 22 miles from Richmond to Greenwich. Hungerford Bridge, the Millennium Bridge and Tower Bridge all provide good viewpoints.

Mayor's Thames Festival
Between Westminster Bridge & Tower Bridge (7928 8998, www.thamesfestival.org). Waterloo tube/rail or Blackfriars rail. **Date** 8-9 Sept. **Map** p402 N7.
A giant party along the Thames, this is the largest free arts festival in London. It's a spectacular and family-friendly mix of carnival, pyrotechnics, art

lighting of the Olympic Pipe. 'Sports' include cucumber sandwich discus and hop, skip and G&T. Check the venue closer to the time: it has been held in Bloomsbury for the last few years.

Carnival del Pueblo
Various locations from City Hall to Burgess Park (www.carnavaldelpueblo.co.uk). Elephant & Castle tube/rail. **Date** 19 Aug.
This vibrant outdoor parade and festival is more than just a loud-and-proud day out for South American Londoners: it attracts people from all walks of life (as many as 60,000, most years) looking to inject a little Latin spirit into the weekend.

Great British Beer Festival
Olympia, Hammersmith Road, Kensington, W14 8UX (01727 867201, www.camra.org.uk). Kensington Olympia tube/rail. **Date** 7-11 Aug.
Real ale is the star at this huge event devoted to the finest in British brews, including cider and perry (that's a pear cider for the uninitiated). Foreign beers and lagers get a look-in at what's been called 'the biggest pub in the world'.

London Mela
Gunnersbury Park, Ealing, W3 (7387 1203, www.londonmela.org). Acton Town or South Ealing tube. **Date** 19 Aug.
Thousands flock to west London for this exuberant celebration of Asian culture, dubbed the Asian Glastonbury. You'll find urban, classical and experimental music, circus, dance, visual arts, comedy, children's events, and great food.

★ Notting Hill Carnival
Notting Hill, W10, W11 (7727 0072, www.thenottinghillcarnival.com). Ladbroke Grove, Notting Hill Gate or Westbourne Park tube. **Date** 26-27 Aug. **Map** p404 Z4.

London Celebrates
Kicking off in style.

London 2012 venues are guaranteed to be alive with atmosphere at Games Time. But how about the rest of town – will the spirit of the event sweep all of London in its wake? The answer is, very likely, yes. The Games action will be relayed to large screens around town (*see p64* **Live Sites**), which will also act as focal points for other entertainments. Organisers are hoping that the excitement will also be recreated in homes across the country. They're designating Opening Ceremony night (27 July) 'The Big Night In' and are encouraging families and friends to gather to view at home – and employers to let workers out a few hours early to build the atmosphere. 'Local leaders' are being recruited to make sure the party atmosphere extends into every street and neighbourhood, and with the current vogue for street parties the bunting should be out in force – especially if Team GB grabs a medal or three. To find out what's on near you, consult www.london2012.com/joinin.

London Fashion Week.

installations, river events and live music alongside craft and food stalls. The highlight is the last-night lantern procession and firework finale – Blackfriars Bridge provided a stunning viewpoint last year.

London Fashion Week
Somerset House, the Strand, WC2R 1LA (7759 1999, www.londonfashionweek.co.uk). Charing Cross tube/rail or Embankment tube. **Date** 21-26 Sept.
The biannual showcase embellishes London's reputation for cutting-edge street style and sartorial innovation. Until recently, it was considered the least significant of the big four trade shows, behind New York, Milan and Paris. Not any more.

Mayor of London's Skyride
www.goskyride.com. **Date** early Sept.
Each year since 2007, this cycling festival has encouraged around 50,000 people to don branded fluorescent vests and ride a traffic-free route from Buckingham Palace to the Tower of London, as well as any number of subsidiary routes. Enjoy music, car-less roads and the chance to meet sports stars on the way.

★ Open-City London
3006 7008, www.open-city.org.uk. **Date** 22-23 Sept.

INSIDE TRACK
TRAFALGAR SQUARE

Among ex-mayor Ken Livingstone's most popular initiatives was pedestrianising the north side of Trafalgar Square, and then programming almost weekly events in it. Even under budget-slashing Boris, various entertainments happen here – music, film, theatre, dance – and usually for free. For details, check www.london.gov.uk/ trafalgarsquare.

Londoners' favourite opportunity to snoop round other people's property: more than 500 palaces, private homes, corporate skyscrapers, pumping stations and bomb-proof bunkers, many of which are normally closed to the public. Along with the building openings, there's a programme of debates on architecture, plus the 20-mile London Night Hike.

Great Gorilla Run
Mincing Lane, the City, EC3 (7916 4974, www.greatgorillas.org/london). Monument or Tower Hill tube, or Fenchurch Street rail. **Date** 22 Sept. **Map** p403 R7.
Go ape with a 600-strong pack of gorilla-suited runners, who take on a 7km course through the City in aid of gorilla conservation.

Pearly Kings & Queens Harvest Festival
St Martin-in-the-Fields, Trafalgar Square, Westminster, WC2N 4JJ (7766 1100, www.pearlysociety.co.uk). Leicester Square tube or Charing Cross tube/rail. **Date** late Sept/early Oct. **Map** p416 Y4.
London's Pearly Kings and Queens assemble for their annual thanksgiving service dressed in spangly (and colossally heavy) Smother Suits covered in hundreds of pearl buttons. These sensational outfits evolved from Victorian costermongers' love of decorating their clothes with buttons, and remain a cherished Cockney tradition.

OCTOBER-DECEMBER

Along with the launch of the Turner Prize, the **Frieze Art Fair** and **Zoo** are huge art events. The **London Film Festival** (*see p306* **Festivals**) takes place in October, and this is also the season for the **London Jazz Festival** (*see p327* **Festivals**) and the winter instalment of the **Spitalfields Festival** (*see p317* **Festivals**).

Big Draw

8351 1719, www.campaignfordrawing.org.
Date 1-31 Oct.
Engage with your inner artist at the Big Draw, a nationwide frenzy of drawing using anything from pencils to vapour trails. The British Library's Big Picture Party brings out heavy art hitters.

Bloomsbury Festival

www.bloomsburyfestival.org.uk. **Date** late Oct.
Around 150 events for art-lovers, music fans, shopaholics, literature buffs, young people and families in venues across Bloomsbury. Last year's event included a lantern-lit procession in Russell Square Gardens and a street party on Lamb's Conduit Street.

Diwali

Trafalgar Square, Westminster, WC2 (7983 4100, www.london.gov.uk). Charing Cross tube/rail. **Date** 13 Nov. **Map** p416 X5.
A vibrant celebration of the annual Festival of Light by London's Hindu, Jain and Sikh communities. There are fireworks, food, music and dancing.

London to Brighton Veteran Car Run

Serpentine Road, Hyde Park, W2 2UH (01327 856024, www.lbvcr.com). Hyde Park Corner tube. **Date** 1st Sun of Nov (3-4 Nov 2012). **Map** p393 E8.
The London to Brighton is not so much a race as a sedate procession southwards by around 500 pre-1905

London 2012 Festival

There's more to the Olympic Games than sport.

The **London 2012 Festival** (21 June-9 Sept) is the culmination of the Cultural Olympiad. It's a nationwide extravaganza offering a rich and varied programme of performances, exhibitions, art commissions, festivals and participation events that will have London dancing in the streets – and then stopping by the opera in the evening. It offers both innovation and cultural clout, with the likes of Cate Blanchett, Damon Albarn, Juliet Binoche, Lucien Freud, Pina Bausch, Rachel Whiteread and Olafur Eliasson all featuring.

Highlights of the 160 or so 2012 Festival and Cultural Olympiad events in London are scattered throughout this book, in the appropriate chapter (look out for the boxes with a pink title). Below is a sampling of the events that can't be so easily classified. For more information, and to book tickets (though many events are free), see http://festival.london2012.com.

(This is also the contact for any events below listed without an individual website.)

Turner Prize winner Martin Creed's **All the Bells** heralds the start of the Olympic Games themselves at 8am on the morning of 27 July. The work is subtitled 'All the bells in a country rung as quickly and as loudly as possible for three minutes' – which just about sums it up. If you're interested in participating, go to http://allthebells.com.

Another participation event is the **Big Dance** (7-15 July), which plugs into the street-to-stage dance boom with classes, workshops, courses, performances, flashmobs in unusual locations, world record attempts and pop-up cinema. Find more details at www.bigdance2012.com.

As part of the Southbank Centre's (*see p318*) stimulating and extensive programme, Baba Maal's **Africa Utopia** (1-29 July) conducts an in-depth examination of what Africa has to offer the world, using performance, debate and film. Musicians, artists, writers and activists, and 300 young people share the forum.

The Rose Theatre in Kingston-upon-Thames presents the biggest children's opera ever written (the cast numbers 6,000). **Ring Round the World** (21 June-20 July; www.rosetheatrekingston.org) tells – and sings – stories gathered by children from the world's 220 major nations.

The six UK exhibitions that comprise **The English Flower Garden** (1 May-17 September) between them display 15,000 individually made ceramic flowers. It's a moving sight that you can catch, in London, at the Southbank Centre, the House of Commons and Chiswick Gardens.

Standing on Ceremony

London is a past master when it comes to parades and ceremonials.

On alternate days from 10.45am (www.royal.gov.uk/RoyalEventsandCeremonies/ChangingtheGuard/Overview.aspx has the details), one of the five Foot Guards regiments lines up in scarlet coats and tall bearskin hats in the forecourt of Wellington Barracks; at exactly 11.27am, the soldiers start to march to **Buckingham Palace** (*see p137*), joined by their regimental band, to relieve the sentries there in a 45-minute ceremony for the **Changing of the Guard**.

Not far away, at **Horse Guards Parade** in Whitehall, the Household Cavalry mount the guard daily at 11am (10am on Sunday). Although this ceremony isn't as famous as the one at Buckingham Palace, it's more visitor-friendly: the crowds aren't as thick as they are at the palace, and spectators aren't held far back from the action by railings. After the old and new guard have stared each other out in the centre of the parade ground, you can nip through to the Whitehall side to catch the departing old guard perform their hilarious dismount choreography, a synchronised, firm slap of approbation to the neck of each horse before the gloved troopers all swing off.

As well as these near-daily ceremonies, London sees other, less frequent parades on a far grander scale. The most famous is **Trooping the Colour**, staged to mark the Queen's official birthday on 13 June (her real one's in April). At 10.45am, the Queen rides in a carriage from Buckingham Palace to Horse Guards Parade to watch the soldiers, before heading back to Buckingham Palace for a midday RAF flypast and the impressive gun salute from Green Park.

Also at Horse Guards, on 3-4 June, a pageant of military music and precision marching begins at 7pm when the Queen (or another royal) takes the salute of the 300-strong drummers, pipers and musicians of the Massed Bands of the Household Division. This is known as **Beating the Retreat** (7414 2271, tickets 7839 5323).

Horse Guards Parade.

cars. The first pair trundles off at sunrise (7-8.30am), but you can catch them a little later crossing Westminster Bridge or view them in lovingly polished repose on a closed-off Regent's Street the day before the event (11am 3pm).

Bonfire Night
Date 5 Nov & around.
Diwali pyrotechnics segue seamlessly into Britain's best-loved excuse for setting off fireworks: the celebration of Guy Fawkes's failure to blow up the Houses of Parliament in 1605. Try Battersea Park, or Alexandra Palace for fireworks, or pre-book a late ride on the London Eye (*see p71*).

★ Lord Mayor's Show
Through the City (7332 3456,
www.lordmayorsshow.org). **Date** 10 Nov.
This big show marks the traditional presentation of the new Lord Mayor for approval by the monarch's justices. The Lord Mayor leaves Mansion House in a fabulous gold coach at 11am, along with a colourful procession of floats and marchers, heading to the Royal Courts of Justice (*see p83*). There he makes his vows, and is back home easily in time for afternoon tea. At 5pm, there's a fireworks display launched from a Thames barge.
▶ *The Lord Mayor is a City officer, elected each year by the livery companies and with no real power outside the City of London; don't confuse him with the Mayor of London, Boris Johnson.*

Remembrance Sunday Ceremony
Cenotaph, Whitehall, Westminster, SW1. Charing Cross tube/rail. **Date** 11 Nov. **Map** p399 L8.
Held on the Sunday nearest to 11 November – the day World War I ended – this solemn commemoration honours those who died fighting in the World Wars and later conflicts. The Queen, the Prime Minister and other dignitaries lay poppy wreaths at the Cenotaph (*see p132*). A two-minute silence at 11am is followed by a service of remembrance.

State Opening of Parliament
Palace of Westminster, Westminster, SW1A 0PW (7219 4272, www.parliament.uk). Westminster tube. **Date** Nov. **Map** p399 L9.
Pomp and ceremony attend the Queen's official reopening of Parliament after its summer recess. She arrives and departs in the state coach, accompanied by troopers of the Household Cavalry.

Christmas Celebrations
Covent Garden (0870 780 5001, www.coventgardenlondonuk.com); Bond Street (www.bondstreetassociation.com); St Christopher's Place (7493 3294, www.stchristophersplace.com); Marylebone High Street (7580 3163, www. marylebonevillage.com); Trafalgar Square (7983 4100, www.london.gov.uk). **Date** Nov-Dec.

Christmas in Trafalgar Square.

Of the big stores, Fortnum & Mason (*see p256*) still creates enchantingly old-fashioned Christmas windows, and Harvey Nichols (*see p257*) usually produces show-stopping displays. Otherwise, though, skip the commercialised lights on Oxford and Regent's streets and head, instead, for smaller shopping areas such as St Christopher's Place, Bond Street, Marylebone High Street and Covent Garden. It's traditional to sing carols beneath a giant Christmas tree in Trafalgar Square (*see p133*) – an annual gift from Norway in gratitude for Britain's support during World War II – but you can also join in a mammoth singalong at the Royal Albert Hall (*see p317*) or an evocative carol service at one of London's historic churches. London's major cathedrals all, naturally, celebrate Christmas with splendid liturgies and music.

New Year's Eve Celebrations
Date 31 Dec.
The focus of London's public celebrations has officially moved from overcrowded Trafalgar Square (though it's still sure to be packed) to the full-on fireworks display launched from the London Eye and rafts on the Thames. The best view is from nearby bridges, but you'll have to get there early. The 2012 event will include a 'ring-based spectacular' to kick off celebrations for the London 2012 Olympic and Paralympic Games. Those with stamina can take in the New Year's Day Parade in central London the following day (www.londonparade.co.uk).

ARTS & ENTERTAINMENT

Children

Strongholds, family-friendly museums and great playgrounds.

London's museums go out of their way to engage the minds of children. The capital also has gorgeous parks, brilliant theatres and world-famous attractions to keep kids stimulated. Many key attractions, such as the **Natural History Museum** (*see p147*) and the **Science Museum** (*see p148* **Profile**), are free; many of those that aren't, such as the **Tower of London** (*see p101*), give you a lot of fun for your entry fee.

Plan carefully, but don't try to cram too much in one day. Sometimes, the most fun happens in the gaps between the official itinerary.

For children's festivals, *see pp282-291*. For weekly event listings, check the Around Town pages in *Time Out* magazine. For useful tips, visit the Mayor's site at www.london.gov.uk/young-london.

WHERE TO GO
South Bank & Bankside (pp76-85)

This is one of the all-time favourite spots for a family day out in London. Just strolling along the wide riverside promenade will lead you past skateboarders, street artists, installations, book stalls and, often, free performances. The expensive end is around **London Eye** (*see p77*), **London Aquarium** (*see p78*) and **London Film Museum** (*see p77*). Moving east, visit the **Southbank Centre** (*see p73 and p318*), where free shows and workshops take place in holidays and weekends in the Clore Ballroom. Don't miss Jeppe Hein's 'Appearing Rooms' play fountains in summer. Next, the **National Theatre** (*see p344*) offers free entertainment during summer.

Keep going along the riverbank, past Gabriel's Wharf, a riverside cluster of shops and restaurants. Until redevelopment of Blackfriars Station is complete in 2012, you have to head briefly inland to get to **Tate Modern** (*see p82*). Tate Modern is a day out in itself, with its dramatic Turbine Hall entrance, free family trails and a Bloomberg Learning Zone on Level Five. At weekends and in school holidays, age-appropriate activity packs are available from Level 3. (There's a boat service from here to **Tate Britain**; *see p83*.)

Once you've emerged, pick up the Bankside Walk, ducking under the southern end of Southwark Bridge. Walk down cobbly Clink Street towards the **Golden Hinde** (*see p81*) and **Southwark Cathedral** (*see p84*), having passed the **Clink Prison Museum** (*see p81*), a cheaper alternative to the **London Dungeon** (*see p84*) and **London Bridge Experience** (*see p83*). From Tooley Street, march through Hays Galleria to regain the riverside path, which takes you to the warship museum **HMS Belfast** (*see p85*) and on, past the dancing fountains, to **City Hall** and **Tower Bridge** (*see p101*).

The City (pp86-101)

It seems pricey, but the **Tower of London** (*see p101*) is a top day out for all ages. If it is free stuff you're after, though, the **Museum of London** (*see p95* **Profile**) is superb. Its new Galleries of Modern London put interactivity

---

THE BEST LONDON LESSONS

For history
Museum of London. *See p95.*

For geography
Prime Meridian Line. *See p174.*

For English literature
Shakespeare's Globe. *See p82.*

and drama at the heart of exciting exhibits, and there are lots of regular child-friendly storytelling sessions and workshops. Nearby, the **Bank of England Museum** (*see p97*) is a surprising hit with bullion-obsessed youth, who can try to lift a gold bar.

Bloomsbury (pp105-109)

Children are captivated by the mummies at the **British Museum** (*see p106*). However, the size of the collection can make it overwhelming. The beautifully produced and well-conceived free trails for different ages take a theme and lead families around an edited selection (available in the Paul Hamlyn Library). Alternatively, there are regular events and workshops or free backpacks for kids, filled with puzzles and games. For weekends and school holidays, the Ford Centre for Young Visitors provides a picnic-style eating area.

Central London's best playground, **Coram's Fields** (*see p297*), is close, and the **Foundling Museum** (*see p108*) is well worth a visit.

Covent Garden & the Strand (pp111-115)

At the lively **London Transport Museum** (*see p112*), children can make believe they are driving a bus or riding in a horse-drawn carriage. They love the numbered stamp trail too. The museum also has a programme of school-holiday events. Across the Piazza, the acts pulling in crowds in front of **St Paul's Covent Garden** (*see p112*) are worth watching. On the south side of the Strand, **Somerset House** (*see p114*) allows kids to play outside among the fountains in summer and skate on the winter ice rink. There are also regular art workshops.

Trafalgar Square (pp133-135)

London's central square (www.london.gov.uk/trafalgarsquare) has been a free playground for children since time immemorial – those lions beg to be clambered on. Festivals take place most weekends. Even if all is quiet in the square, the **National Gallery** (*see p134*) has paper trails and audio tours, as well as regular kids' and teens' workshops and storytelling sessions for under-fives. For three- to 12-year-olds, the **National Portrait Gallery** (*see p135*) runs Family Art Workshops at weekends and during the school holidays.

Just nearby, **St Martin-in-the-Fields** (*see p135*) has London's only brass-rubbing centre (kids are transfixed by this absorbing activity) as well as a fine café that does plenty of the type of food that goes down well with children.

South Kensington (pp146-149)

Top of any Grand Day Out itinerary is this cultural goldmine. The **Science Museum** (*see p148* **Profile**) offers heaps of excitement, with six play zones for all ages, from the Garden in the basement for under-sixes to the new Atmosphere gallery upstairs, where children can use touchscreens to learn about climate change. Dinosaur fans won't rest until they've visited the **Natural History Museum** (*see p147*), and seen the animatronic beasties in action. A butterfly tunnel in summer and ice rink in winter also draw the crowds. The **Victoria & Albert Museum** (*see p149*) marks interactive displays on its floorplan. Its free weekend and school holiday drop-in family events (featuring trails, activity-based backpacks, and interactive workshops) provide great ways of focusing on the collection. Educational resources are available in the Sackler Centre studios and the Theatre & Performance Galleries. (Its sister gallery, Bethnal Green's **V&A Museum of Childhood**, *see p162*, has an excellent programme of events for children.)

Greenwich (pp170-174)

Magical Greenwich provides a lovely day out away from the mayhem of the West End. Arrive by boat to appreciate its riverside charms, then take time to get the latest on the restorations to the **Cutty Sark** (due for completion in 2012)

National Maritime Museum. *See p294.*

ARTS & ENTERTAINMENT

That Place on the Corner.

and to explore the excellent new **Discover Greenwich** (*see p172*). Then head to the very child-friendly **National Maritime Museum** (*see p173, photo p293*) and visit the new Sammy Ofer Wing. From here it's a pleasant leg-stretch in the Royal Park for views from the very top of the hill, crowned by the spectacular **Royal Observatory & Planetarium** (*see p173*). When the stars come out, keep an eye out for the luminous green Meridian Line that cuts across the sky towards the city.

EATING & DRINKING

Of the venues listed in the Restaurants & Cafés chapter, **Inn the Park** (*see p228*) and **Masala Zone** (*see p239*) are particularly suitable for children.

Big Red Bus

30 Deptford Church Street, SE8 4RZ (3490 8346, www.thebigredpizza.com). Deptford Bridge DLR. **Open** 5-11pm Tue-Fri; noon-11pm Sat; noon-9pm Sun. **Main courses** £6-£9. **No credit cards.**
Kids will love this new pizzeria – set inside an old double decker bus in Deptford. It's beside the DLR, so you can travel here in style. Just around the corner is Deptford's Creekside Centre (www.creeksidecentre.org.uk), if you want to combine food with an excursion. Either sit at the exciting tables inside the bus, or make the most of the large and pretty decked terrace out back.

Frizzante@Hackney City Farm

1A Goldsmith's Row, Hackney, E2 8QA (7739 2266, www.frizzanteltd.co.uk). Hoxton rail. **Open** 10am-4pm Tue, Wed, Fri-Sun; 10am-4pm, 7-11pm Thur. **Main courses** £5-£17. **Credit** MC, V.
Once you've trotted around visiting pigs, poultry and sheep outside on the farm, you can settle down

to eat their relatives (or stick to vegetarian options). The oilcloth-covered tables heave with families tucking into healthy nosh, including farm breakfasts.

Gracelands

118 College Road, NW10 5HD (8964 9161, www.gracelandscafe.com). Kensal Green tube/rail. **Open** 8.30am-5pm Mon-Fri; 9am-4.30pm Sat; 9.30am-3.30pm Sun. **Main courses** £7-£12.95. **Credit** AmEx, MC, V.
While many places claim to be child-friendly, this café really means it, with its toy-filled play area, a healthy tots-own menu (£3.70 for the likes of pasta bolognese or sausage and mash). and chefs cooing at high-chair diners from the open-plan kitchen. For grown-ups, the burger, made from 21-day matured beef, has proper foodie pedigree and the salads are unfailingly excellent.

Mudchute Kitchen

Mudchute Park & Farm, Pier Street, Isle of Dogs, Docklands, E14 3HP (3069 9290, www.mudchute.org). Mudchute DLR. **Open** 9.30am-4.50pm Tue-Sun. **Main courses** £2.50-£9. **Credit** MC, V.
A farm fenced in by skyscrapers is an amusing place for anyone to eat lunch, but Mudchute is ideal for families. You can eat at farmhouse kitchen tables in the courtyard, while your babies roll around on a big futon or in the toy corner, or in the spacious interior. Frizzante (*see left*) took over in 2011, which means the food is excellent.

Rainforest Café

20 Shaftesbury Avenue, Piccadilly, W1D 7EU (7434 3111, www.therainforestcafe.co.uk). Piccadilly Circus tube. **Open** noon-10pm Mon-Fri; 11.30am-8pm Sat; 11.30am-10pm Sun. **Main courses** £12.95-£18.90. **Credit** AmEx, MC, V. **Map** p416 W4.

This themed restaurant is designed to thrill children with animatronic wildlife, cascading waterfalls and accompanying jungle sound-effects. The menu has lots of family-friendly fare, from 'paradise pizza' and 'Bamba's bangers' to a host of amusing dishes for grown-ups. The children's menu costs £11.95 for two courses.

★ Tate Modern Café: Level 2

Tate Modern, Sumner Street, Bankside, SE1 9TG (7401 5014, www.tate.org.uk). Southwark tube or London Bridge tube/rail. **Open** 10am-5.30pm Mon-Thur, Sun; 10am-9.30pm Fri; 10am-7.30pm Sat. **Main courses** £9.95-£10.50. **Credit** AmEx, MC, V. **Map** p402 O7.

In addition to views from the windows framing the busy River Thames, there are literacy and art activities on the junior menu, handed out with a pot of crayons. Children can choose haddock fingers with chips, pasta bolognese with parmesan or a ham and cheese bake with foccacia, finished off with ice-cream or a fruit salad, for £5.20; a free children's main is offered when an adult orders a regular main. There is also a 'teen menu' of reduced-price dishes from the adult menu.

That Place on the Corner

1-3 Green Lanes, Stoke Newington, N16 9BS (7704 0079, www.thatplaceonthecorner.co.uk). Canonbury rail then bus 73, 141, 341. **Open** 9.15am-6pm Mon-Thur; 9.30am-8pm Fri; 9.30am-3pm Sat; 10.30am-3pm Sun. Closes Sat, Sun for functions; phone ahead. **Main courses** £4-£8.25. **Credit** MC, V.

London's only child-friendly café that won't let in unaccompanied grown-ups. There's a library, puppet theatre and dressing-up corner, as well as baking, dance and music classes. The menu sticks to the trusted pasta/panini/big breakfast formula, with brasserie staples such as fish cakes.

ENTERTAINMENT
City farms & zoos

There's always something new at **ZSL London Zoo** (*see p125*); Penguin Beach is the latest big addition. The admission charge seems high, but it's a guaranteed winner. Easier on the budget is the adorable **Battersea Park Children's Zoo** (www.batterseaparkzoo.co.uk), where ring-tailed lemurs, giant rabbits, inquisitive meerkats, playful otters and kune kune pigs are among the inhabitants.

City farms all over London charge nothing to get in. Try **Freightliners City Farm** (www.freightlinersfarm.org.uk) and **Kentish Town City Farm** (www.aapi.co.uk/cityfarm) or, in the east, **Mudchute City Farm** (www.mudchute.org) and **Hackney City Farm** (www.hackneycityfarm.co.uk), both of which have terrific cafés (for both, *see opposite*).

ARTS & ENTERTAINMENT

Meet the Mascots

Let us introduce you to London 2012's sport-crazy cheerleaders.

There's more to the official London 2012 mascots than meets the eye, or at least the ear. The name of Wenlock – the orange and silver one with a little 'W' above its eye – is inspired by Much Wenlock, the Shropshire town where the 'Olympian Games' that so enthused De Coubertin still take place (*see pp43-47* **Olympic City**). Mandeville – blue and silver, with an 'M' – is named after Stoke Mandeville, the birthplace of the Paralympic Games (*see p47* **Birth of the Paralympic Games**).

The story of their creation, written by the acclaimed children's author Michael Morpurgo (you can see the story, animated beautifully, at www.london2012.com/mascots), tells how they were crafted in Bolton from two drops of British steel, the last ones left after the girders that hold up the Olympic Stadium were finished. They then came to life, full of a can-do enthusiasm for getting involved with Olympic and Paralympic sports. Just as well, really: they've got a busy programme of school events, festivals and opening weekends to get through over the coming months.

Puppets

★ Little Angel Theatre

*14 Dagmar Passage, off Cross Street, Islington,
N1 2DN (7226 1787, www.littleangeltheatre.com).
Angel tube or Highbury & Islington tube/rail.*
Open *Box office* 10am-6pm Mon-Fri; 10am-4pm
Sat, Sun. **Tickets** £5-£13. **Credit** MC, V.
Map p400 O1.

London's only permanent puppet theatre is set in a
charming old Victorian temperance hall and stages
diverse productions. All aspects of puppetry are covered, with themes, styles and stories drawn from a
broad array of traditions. There's a Saturday Puppet
Club and a youth puppet theatre. Shows are often
for fives and above.

Puppet Theatre Barge

*Opposite 35 Blomfield Road, Little Venice, W9
2PF (07836 202745 summer, 7249 6876 winter,
www.puppetbarge.com). Warwick Avenue tube.*
Open *Box office* 10am-6pm daily. **Tickets** £10;
£8.50 reductions. **Credit** AmEx, MC, V.

This intimate waterborne stage is the setting for
quality puppet shows that put a modern twist on traditional tales, such as *Mr Rabbit meets Brer Santa*
and *The Flight of Babuscha Baboon*. The barge is
moored here between October and July; shows themselves are held at 3pm on Saturday and Sunday, and
daily during school holidays, plus some matinées.
The barge also holds performances in Richmond.

Science & nature

Creekside Centre

*14 Creekside, Greenwich, SE8 4SA (8692 9922,
www.creeksidecentre.org.uk). Deptford Bridge or
Greenwich DLR, or bus 53, 177, 188.* **Open**
phone for details. **Admission** free, walks vary;
check for details.

Deptford Creek is a tributary of the Thames and this
centre allows visitors to explore its surprisingly
diverse wildlife and rich heritage. Low tide walks
take place on selected weekend days for accompanied eight-year-olds and above and there's also a programme of puppet theatre.

★ WWT Wetland Centre

*Queen Elizabeth's Walk, Barnes, SW13
9WT (8409 4400, www.wwt.org.uk/london).
Hammersmith tube then bus 33, 72, 209 (alight
at Red Lion pub).* **Open** *Summer* 9.30am-6pm
daily. *Winter* 9.30am-5pm daily. **Tours** 11am,
2pm daily. *Feeding tours* 3pm daily. **Admission**
£10.55; £7.85 reductions; £5.85 4-16s; free under-
4s; £29.40 family (2+2). *Tours* free. **Credit** MC, V.

This wetland reserve is one of London's best-kept
secrets. If you can get children past the giant snakes
and ladders game (with giant dice), there are 104
acres for them to stretch their legs in, along paths
that take them past the main lake, reed beds, ponds
and wetland meadows, as well as one of the best playgrounds in London. A series of interactive exhibits
exploring the environment was added in 2010.

Theatre

Polka Theatre

*240 Broadway, Merton, SW19 1SB (8543 4888,
www.polkatheatre.com). South Wimbledon tube or
Wimbledon tube/rail, then bus 57, 93, 219, 493.*
Open *Box office* (by phone) 9.30am-4.30pm Mon;
9.30am-5.30pm Tue-Fri; 10am-4.30pm Sat; (in
person) 9.30am-4.30pm Tue-Fri; 10am-4.30pm Sat.
Tickets £9-£16. **Credit** MC, V.

This children's theatre pioneer has been up and running since 1979. Daily shows are staged by touring
companies in the main auditorium, while shorter
works for babies and toddlers take over at the
Adventure Theatre once a week.

Coram's Fields.

INSIDE TRACK ON THE BUS

Tours too expensive? An economical way of doing London as a family is by bus, since everyone under the age of 20 currently travels free (over-11s do need different types of ID; see p365). Good routes for sightseeing are the 7, 8, 11 and 12 (all double-deckers). For a riverside route, take the RV1 (Tower Hill to South Bank); for a taste of the traditional open-backed London red bus, look out for Routemasters 9 and 15 (for details, see p134 **Get There Greener**).

Unicorn Theatre

147 Tooley Street, Bankside, SE1 2HZ (7645 0560, www.unicorntheatre.com). London Bridge tube/rail. **Open** *Box office* 9.30am-6pm Mon-Fri; 10am-6pm Sat; noon-5pm Sun. **Tickets** £9-£22; £7-£13 reductions. **Credit** MC, V. **Map** p403 Q8.
This light, bright building near Tower Bridge, with its huge white unicorn in the foyer, has two performance spaces. Its small ensemble company of actors performs in all Unicorn shows and focuses on an outreach programme for local children.

Theme parks

There are several theme parks within easy reach of London. Heading out west., **Legoland** (Winkfield Road, Windsor, Berks SL4 4AY, 0870 504 0404, www.legoland.co.uk) is always a hit with youngsters, with rides including the wet 'n' wild Viking's River Splash, and the extraordinary Miniland London, made of 13 million Lego bricks. **Thorpe Park** (Staines Road, Chertsey, Surrey KT16 8PN, 0871 663 1673, www.thorpepark.com) has the fastest rollercoaster in Europe, called Stealth, and the terrifying horror-movie ride, Saw; it's best for older kids and teens. And **Chessington World of Adventures** (Leatherhead Road, Chessington, Surrey KT9 2NE, 0871 663 4477, www.chessington.com) is a gentler option. This theme park, open since the 1930s, is partly a zoo, and children can pay to be zoo keeper for a day.

For a day with less of an adrenaline rush, try **Bekonscot Model Village** (Warwick Road, Beaconsfield, Bucks HP9 2PL, 01494 672919, www.bekonscot.com), a haven of vintage miniature villages with a ride-on train that takes you around the site. To the north, the fast-developing **Butterfly World** (Miriam Lane, Chiswell Green, Herts AL2 3NY, 01727 869203, www.butterflyworldproject.com) is designed to look like an enormous butterfly head from the air with a 330ft diameter walk-through biome (the butterfly's eye) opening in autumn 2012.

There's plenty to see before then with a large walk-through butterfly tunnel and the butterfly breeding house showing kids all the incredible stages of a butterfly's life cycle.

Likely to be on any child's visiting wishlist is the new Harry Potter studio tour near Watford, a short journey north of town. *See p359* **Warner Bros Studio Tour London**.

SPACES TO PLAY

London's parks are lovely. **Hyde Park** (*see p149*) and **St James's Park** (*see p140*) are very central, but it isn't much further to **Regent's Park** (*see p124*), and **Greenwich Park** (*see p170*) is easily reached by river.

FREE Coram's Fields

93 Guilford Street, Bloomsbury, WC1N 1DN (7837 6138, www.coramsfields.org). Russell Square tube. **Open** *Apr-Sept* 9am-7pm daily. *Oct-Mar* 9am dusk daily. **Admission** free (adults only admitted if accompanied by child under 16). **No credit cards. Map** p397 L4.
No adult can enter the amazing Coram's Fields without a child. The historic site dates to 1747, when Thomas Coram established the Foundling Hospital, but only opened as a park in 1936. It has sandpits, a small petting zoo, ride-on toys and playgrounds for different age groups.
▶ *For the museum now located in the Foundling Hospital, see p108.*

★ FREE Diana, Princess of Wales Memorial Playground

Near Black Lion Gate, Broad Walk, Kensington Gardens, South Kensington, W8 2UH (7298 2141, www.royalparks.gov.uk). Bayswater or Queensway tube. **Open** *Summer* 10am-6.45pm daily. *Winter* 10am-dusk daily. **Admission** free; adults only admitted if accompanied by under-12s. **No credit cards. Map** p393 E8.
Bring buckets and spades, if you can, to this superb playground: the huge, central pirate ship is moored in a sea of sand. Other attractions include a tepee camp and a treehouse encampment, and excellent provision is made for children with special needs.

Discover Children's Story Centre

383-387 High Street, Stratford, E15 4QZ (8536 5555, www.discover.org.uk). Stratford tube/rail/DLR. **Open** 10am-5pm Tue-Fri; 11am-5pm Sat, Sun. *School holidays* 10am-5pm Mon-Fri; 11am-5pm Sat, Sun. **Admission** £4.50; £16 family; free under-2s. **Credit** MC, V.
The UK's first creative learning centre for children is committed to promoting diversity and providing learning opportunities for socially and economically disadvantaged children. The main floor offers all sorts of imaginative exploration, while downstairs houses temporary interactive exhibitions. The garden is fun.

Comedy

It's a laugh a minute in the UK's comedy capital.

London is the best city in Britain, and one of the best in the world, for comedy. New talents are constantly arriving in town, hoping for their own BBC show or – failing that – work writing for one of the capital's innumerable production companies. The result is around 250 gigs a week, ranging from open-mic nights in pubs all the way up to arena tours, and a weight of competition that ensures the comedians here stay at the top of their game.

Where to begin? Probably at the purpose-built **Comedy Store**, fail-safe home of alternative laughs. Bit don't stop there. Explore dingy pubs and clubs where skills are honed; arenas and theatres for the finished acts. London's comedy scene gets a bit quieter during the exodus to Edinburgh every August. For weekly line-ups, check *Time Out* magazine and www.timeout.com.

CENTRAL

Amused Moose Soho

Moonlighting, 17 Greek Street, Soho, W1D 4DR (7287 3727, www.amusedmoose.com). Leicester Square or Tottenham Court Road tube. **Shows** *Oct-Mar* 7.30pm Sat. **Admission** £10-£14. **Credit** MC, V. **Map** p416 W2.

Hils Jago's rosters are always strong, with names such as Bill Bailey and Eddie Izzard continuing to justify the club's multi-award-winning status. Jago has a lot of special guests who can't be named – in other words, really top names trying out new material – and runs the Amused Moose Laugh Offs; finalists have included Jimmy Carr and Simon Amstell.

Comedy Store

1A Oxendon Street, Soho, SW1Y 4EE (0844 871 7699, www.thecomedystore.co.uk). Leicester Square or Piccadilly Circus tube. **Shows** phone for details Mon; 8-10.30pm Tue-Thur, Sun; 8pm & midnight Fri, Sat. **Admission** £14-£20. **Credit** AmEx, MC, V. **Map** p416 W4.

Alternative line-ups at this, the daddy of British comedy clubs, helped launch jokers such as Alexei Sayle, Dawn French and Paul Merton. The legendary gong show, in which would-be stand-ups are given only as much time on stage as the audience will allow, is on the last Monday of the month.

About the author

Ben Williams is editor of the Comedy section of Time Out London.

Funny Side of Covent Garden

The George, 213 the Strand, WC2R 1AP (0844 478 0404, www.thefunnyside.info). Covent Garden tube or Leicester Square tube. **Shows** 8pm Fri, Sat. **Admission** £12.50. **Credit** MC, V. **Map** p399 M6.

This is an enjoyable club upstairs in a mock Tudor pub, but calling it 'Covent Garden' is a bit of a stretch, geographically speaking – it's on the fringes of the City near the Royal Courts of Justice (*see p87*). Well-known comedians such as Felix Dexter, Josie Long, Tom Wrigglesworth and Phil Kay have all performed here.

Other locations the Spectator (downstairs), 6 Little Britain, the City, EC1A 7BX; Café Koha, 11 St Martin's Court, the City, WC2N 4AJ.

Leicester Square Theatre

Leicester Square Theatre, 6 Leicester Place, Leicester Square, Soho, WC2H 7BX (0844 873 3433, www.leicestersquaretheatre.com). Leicester Square tube. **Shows** vary; check website for details. **Admission** £6-£10. **Credit** MC, V. **Map** p416 X4.

With a mixture of mixed-bill shows and solo offerings, the Leicester Square Theatre programmes comedy names in the main house, and rising stars in the basement. A favourite of many big-name American comics, the list of names who play here is getting better and better.

Soho Theatre

For listings, *see p350*.

Our Own Edinburgh?

The Greenwich Comedy Festival brings the laughs to south-east London.

Over a long weekend in early September, the lawns of the Old Royal Naval College and **Up the Creek** play host to London's biggest and best comedy festival, with a big top, pavilions and a temporary bar pitching up against one of the most beautiful backdrops in the city – the Thames on one side, Wren's serenely beautiful colonnades on the other. Add light shows, jugglers, dance troupes and musicians and the Greenwich Comedy Festival (www. greenwichcomedyfestival.co.uk) might rub the August smugness off Edinburgh's face.

Even in its first year, the festival had sufficient pulling power to be able to feature headline names such as Russell Howard and Jo Brand. By 2011, the roster included Angelos Epithemiou (*Shooting Stars*), *Father Ted*'s Ardal O'Hanlon, *Never Mind the Buzzcocks* stalwart Phill Jupitus, Edinburgh Comedy Award winner Tim Key and even musical comic turned rock 'n' roll superstar Tim Minchin. Performances in the big top are ticketed, but pop down with a picnic and you can enjoy plenty of events on the college lawns for nothing.

The Soho Theatre is one of the best places to see comics break out of their normal club sets to perform more substantial solo shows. There's always a good mix of home-grown and international talent.

Boat Show

Tattershall Castle, Kings Reach, Victoria Embankment, SW1A 2HR (07932 658895, www.boatshowcomedy.co.uk). Embankment tube. **Shows** 8.30pm 1st Mon of mth; 8pm Fri, Sat. **Admission** £10, £8 reductions Mon; £13, £11 reductions Fri, Sat. **No credit cards.** **Map** p399 L8.
The line-ups aboard this floating comedy club situated opposite the London Eye are consistently strong. Ticket prices are reasonable, and for those wishing to party into the small hours, a nightclub follows the comedy every Friday and Saturday at no extra charge.

Feature Spot

The 100 Club, 100 Oxford Street, Soho, W1D 1LL (07956 834135, www.featurespot.co.uk). Oxford Circus or Tottenham Court Road tube. **Shows** vary; check website for details. **Admission** £10-£15. **Credit** AmEx, MC, V. **Map** p416 V1.
Feature Spot's comedy nights often feature in critics' choices lists. Previous acts include Russell Howard, Stephen Merchant, Adam Buxton and Tim Minchin. But whoever's on the bill, you're guaranteed an excellent show. Check the website for upcoming shows.

NORTH LONDON

Downstairs at the King's Head

2 Crouch End Hill, Crouch End, N8 8AA (8340 1028, www.downstairsatthekingshead.com). Finsbury Park tube/rail then bus W7. **Shows** 8pm Thur, Sat, Sun. **Admission** £4-£9. **No credit cards.**

Founded in what seems like the comedic pre-history of 1981, this venue is still run with huge enthusiasm by its immensely knowledgeable promoter Pete Grahame. It's an easygoing, comfortable place where comedians can experiment and play around with new material and routines in complete freedom. It's popular with comics wanting to do warm-up shows for TV and tours.

Hen & Chickens

109 St Paul's Road, Highbury Corner, Islington, N1 2NA (7704 2001, www.henandchickens.com). Highbury & Islington tube/rail. **Shows** times vary. **Admission** £5-£12.50. **No credit cards.**
This dinky, black-box theatre above a cosy Victorian corner pub is well known as the place to see great solo shows, especially those warming up for a tour. Acts have included Jenny Eclair, Frankie Boyle, Rhona Cameron and Jimmy Carr.

Fat Tuesdays

Compass, 58 Penton Street, Islington, N1 9PZ (www.tiernandouieb.co.uk/fattuesday.htm). Angel tube. **Shows** 8pm alternate Tue. **Admission** £7-£8. **No credit cards.** **Map** p440 N2.
Charming compere Tiernan Douieb previously ran this intimate Islington gig, establishing it as one of the most welcoming comedy clubs in London. It's now in the hands of comedian Nish Kumar, and this

INSIDE TRACK THE BEST MEDAL-CEREMONY SONGS

As voted for by 55 Olympians...
1 **We Are the Champions** (Queen)
2 **Jerusalem** (Parry/Blake)
3 **Land of Hope and Glory** (Elgar/Benson)
4 **Eye of the Tiger** (Survivor)
5 **Don't Stop Me Now** (Queen)

ARTS & ENTERTAINMENT

tiny room above the Compass pub still hosts consistently brilliant line-ups, with wonderfully varied bills and headliners at the top of their game.

Hampstead Comedy Club

Pembroke Castle, 150 Gloucester Avenue, Chalk Farm, NW1 8JA (7633 9539, www. hampsteadcomedy.co.uk). Chalk Farm tube. **Shows** 8.30pm Sat. **Admission** £10; £8.50 reductions. **No credit cards. Map** p404 W2.
Veteran comedian and show promoter Ivor Dembina hosts this intimate Saturday night comedy club a few minutes from Chalk Farm tube. Dembina puts the quality of the show over everything else, booking a mixture of well-established circuit comics, hotly tipped newbies and the occasional TV favourite. An interesting night is well-nigh certain.

Etcetera Theatre

The Oxford Arms, 256 Camden High Street, Camden, NW1 7BU (7482 4857, www.etcetera theatre.com). Camden Town tube. **Shows** vary; check website for details. **Admission** £5-£10. **No credit cards. Map** p404 Y2.
This intimate black box theatre above the Oxford Arms pub on bustling Camden High Street is a great place to catch Edinburgh previews, comedy in August's Camden Fringe, and occasionally big names warming up for tours, which in the past have included Russell Brand and We Are Klang.

EAST LONDON

Comedy Café

66-68 Rivington Street, Shoreditch, EC2A 3AY (7739 5706, www.comedycafe.co.uk). Liverpool Street or Old Street tube/rail. **Shows** 9pm Wed-Sat. **Admission** £10-£16; free Wed. **Credit** MC, V. **Map** p401 R4.
The Comedy Café is another purpose-built club set up by a comedian. Noel Faulkner, who worked on trawlers and was wanted by the FBI in his time, now

---

Scipmylo

East London's comedy festival.

The impressive Scipmylo Festival (http://scipmylo.co.uk) made its debut in east London in September 2011 with a strong line-up that included not only TV names such as Ed Byrne, Andrew Maxwell and Stephen K Amos, but also circuit favourites such as Tiernan Douieb and Hal Cruttenden presenting their solo tours. The festival is centred around Shoreditch Town Hall and will be back for 2012 (check website for dates and details) – and, we hope, thereafter.

---

mainly keeps to the back room but, with the emphasis on inviting bills and satisfied punters, his influence can still be felt. The atmosphere is fun and food is an integral part of the experience.

SOUTH LONDON

Banana Cabaret

The Bedford Arms, 77 Bedford Hill, Balham, SW12 9HD (8682 8940, www.bananacabaret. co.uk). Balham tube/rail. **Shows** 9pm Fri, Sat. **Admission** £4-£16. **Credit** MC, V.
Satisfaction is pretty much guaranteed every Friday and Saturday at this exciting, long-running club in the big roundhouse setting of the Bedford Arms pub. A safe bet for a good night out.

Up the Creek

302 Creek Road, Greenwich, SE10 9SW (8858 4581, www.up-the-creek.com). Greenwich DLR/rail. **Shows** 7.30pm Thur; 9pm Fri; 8.30pm Sat, Sun. **Admission** £4 Thur; £11, £7 reductions Fri; £15, £12 reductions Sat; £6, £4 reductions Sun. **Credit** AmEx, MC, V. **Map** p405 W2.
Set up by the late and legendary Malcolm Hardee ('To say that he has no shame is to drastically exaggerate the amount of shame he has,' quipped one critic), this purpose-built club has been around since the 1990s, and it remains to this day one of the best places to see live comedy. It's renowned for its lively, not to say bearpit atmosphere, but there's a more chilled out feel to the 'Sunday Special Club' (www.sundayspecial.co.uk).

WEST LONDON

Headliners

George IV, 185 Chiswick High Road, Chiswick, W4 2DR (7221 4450, www.headlinerscomedy. com). Turnham Green tube. **Shows** 9pm Fri, Sat. **Admission** £12-£14. **No credit cards.**
West London isn't blessed with many good comedy nights, but Headliners does what it can to redress the balance from its purpose-designed warehouse tucked behind the pub. Past acts include Ed Byrne and Steve Coogan. The experienced Simon Randall, who also ran Ha Bloody Ha, is at the helm.

Canal Café Theatre

Delamere Terrace, Little Venice, W2 6ND (7289 6054, www.canalcafetheatre.com). Royal Oak or Warwick Avenue tube. **Shows** 9.30pm Thur-Sat; 9pm Sun. **Admission** £10-£11.50. **Credit** MC, V. **Map** p392 C4.
This charming little theatre, perched on the edge of a canal in Little Venice, offers a number of shows a week. Past performers include Stewart Lee and Pete Firman, and it's a good place to catch young comics and sketch acts, as well as NewsRevue, who have a residency performing their topical sketches and songs every Thursday to Sunday.

Dance

London dances to its own tune.

London is a hub for dance in a way few other cities can match. Stylistically (as well as geographically), it lies somewhere between the experimental, cerebral European scene and the eye-pleasing pure dance stylings of the US, with a truly international roster of choreographers and dancers choosing to make the city their base. As befits a famously creative and cosmopolitan city, there's plenty of cross-cultural, cross-artform pollination going on, and some cutting-edge ideas. Even the 80-year-old **Royal Ballet** is now producing groundbreaking new work, thanks to resident choreographer Wayne McGregor.

There are also plenty of chances to get moving yourself. Look out for the city's tea dances, tango milongas and swing nights, and the new freestyle dance jams that are popping up in more hipster parts of town. For information on upcoming events and classes, pick up *Time Out* magazine or see www.timeout.com/london/dance.

DANCE COMPANIES

There are two long-established classical dance companies. The **Royal Ballet**, founded in 1931 and resident at the Royal Opera House (*see p302*), is a company of global stature, whose 100 or so dancers include such global guest stars as Carlos Acosta. The only slightly less prestigious **English National Ballet** is a touring company, founded in 1950, that performs most often at the Coliseum (*see p318*) and, for the regular *Swan Lake* 'in the round', at the Royal Albert Hall (*see p317*). Its principals include Londoner Begoña Cao.

Israel-born **Hofesh Shechter** (www.hofesh.co.uk) is probably the hottest thing in UK dance right now, with his full-throttle approach to dance and music bringing a rock gig feel to the stage. Another popular name is **Matthew Bourne** (www.new-adventures.net), who reimagines classic tales (from *Swan Lake* to *Edward Scissorhands*) with great sets and plenty of humour. And although the **Rambert Dance Company** (www.rambert.org.uk) has been around since before World War II, a regular turnover of great dancers and new works keeps the troupe fresh, and its programmes of contemporary dance are always accessible.

The career of **Michael Clark** (www.michael clarkcompany.com) has had its controversial moments, but he's now reconciled his classical roots and punk spirit. **New Art Club**'s (www. newartclub.org) work lies between contemporary dance, theatre and stand-up comedy.

Many London choreographers absorb cross-cultural influences. **Akram Khan**

INSIDE TRACK PINA BAUSCH

German choreographer Pina Bausch's profile has never been higher, despite her sudden death in 2009, just before her 70th birthday. For the London 2012 Festival, the troupe she led for four decades – Tanztheater Wuppertal Pina Bausch – will dance the new commission 'World Cities 2012' (6 June-9 July 2012) at Sadler's Wells and the Barbican. Made up of pieces individually premièred across the globe over the last two decades, 'World Cities 2012' uses the company's characteristic combination of everyday gestures and the abstractions of contemporary dance to explore Hong Kong, Los Angeles, Santiago in Chile, Rome, Saitama, São Paulo, Kolkata, Istanbul, Palermo and Budapest.

About the author
Lyndsey Winship is the dance editor of Time Out *magazine.*

Festivals Dance

What to see, when.

London's three general dance festivals are the well-established **Dance Umbrella** (Oct, www.danceumbrella.co.uk, multiple venues) and the Place's **Resolution!** festival (Jan-Feb, www.theplace.org.uk), staging the work of young choreographers, and the **Place Prize** (biennial in even years, Sept, www.theplaceprize.com) choreography competition. Niche festivals include the four-day, Thames-side **London International Tango Festival** (Nov, www.tangoinlondon.com), the **Flamenco Festival** (Feb, www.sadlerswells.com) and hip hop weekend **Breakin' Convention** (May, www.breakinconvention.com). If you'd rather take part, the UK-wide **Big Dance** (July, www.bigdance2012.com), part of the London 2012 Festival, offers classes, workshops and performances in everything from disco to folk dance.

(www.akramkhancompany.net) combines north Indian kathak, contemporary dance and clever storytelling in powerful works around the theme of cultural identity, and **Shobana Jeyasingh** (www.shobanajeyasingh.co.uk) and Nina Rajarani's **Srishti** (www.srishti.co.uk) also work to varying degrees with South Asian dance.

MAJOR VENUES

Barbican Centre

For listings, see p316.

Conceived in the 1960s and completed in 1982, the Barbican attracts and nurtures experimental dance, especially in the perfectly intimate Pit Theatre. The year-round Barbican International Theatre Events series (BITE; www.barbican.org.uk/theatre) offers plenty of noteworthy dance performances.

★ Place

17 Duke's Road, Bloomsbury, WC1H 9PY (7121 1100, www.theplace.org.uk). Euston tube/rail. **Box office** noon-6pm Mon-Sat; noon-8pm on performance days. **Tickets** £9-£20. **Credit** MC, V. **Map** p399 K3.

For genuinely emerging dance, look to the Place. The theatre is behind the biennial Place Prize for choreography, which rewards the best in British contemporary dance as well as regular seasons of new work such as Resolution! (short works; Jan/Feb) and Spring Loaded (Apr/May).

★ Royal Opera House

For listings, see p320.

For the full ballet experience, nothing beats the Royal Opera House, home of the Royal Ballet. The current incarnation of the building is an appropriately grand space in which to see dreamy ballerinas including Alina Cojocaru and Tamara Rojo. Tours of the building sometimes take in a ballet rehearsal. There's edgier fare in the Linbury Studio Theatre and the Clore Studio Upstairs.

★ Sadler's Wells

Rosebery Avenue, Finsbury, EC1R 4TN (0844 412 4300, www.sadlerswells.com). Angel tube. **Box office** In person & by phone 10am-8pm Mon-Sat. **Tickets** £10-£60. **Credit** AmEx, MC, V. **Map** p402 N3.

Purpose-built in 1998 on the site of a 17th-century theatre of the same name, this dazzling complex is home to impressive local and international performances. The Lilian Baylis Studio offers smaller-scale new works and works-in-progress, and the Peacock Theatre (on Portugal Street in Holborn) operates as a satellite venue.

Siobhan Davies Dance Studios

85 St George's Road, Southwark, SE1 6ER (7091 9650, www.siobhandavies.com). Elephant & Castle tube/rail. **Box office** 10am-6pm Mon-Fri; 10am-5pm Sat, Sun (varies). **Tickets** £3-£10. **Credit** MC, V. **Map** p402 N10.

This award-winning studio was designed in consultation with dancers, ensuring it met their needs. As well as being home to Davies's own company, the studio hosts talks and performances at the more experimental end of the scale. The performance programme is sporadic: check details before setting out.

Southbank Centre

For listings, see p318.

From international contemporary dance to hip hop to physical theatre to South Asian dance, there's an eclectic programme at the cluster of venues collectively known as the Southbank Centre: the mammoth RFH, the medium-sized Queen Elizabeth Hall, the intimate Purcell Room and the riverside terrace.

OTHER VENUES

Blue Elephant

59A Bethwin Road, Camberwell, SE5 0XT (7701 0100, 0844 477 1000 tickets, www.blue elephanttheatre.co.uk). Oval tube. **Box office** In person 1hr before performance. By phone 24hrs. **Tickets** free-£12.50. **No credit cards.**

Hidden away in south London, the Blue Elephant Theatre is a little off the beaten path but it hosts occasional contemporary dance performances alongside its programme of theatre and other performance.

Greenwich Dance

Borough Hall, Royal Hill, Greenwich, SE10 8RE (8293 9741, www.greenwichdance.org.uk).

Greenwich DLR/rail. **Open** *Box office* 9.30am-9pm Mon-Thur; 9.30am-5.30pm Fri; 10am-3pm Sat. **Tickets** £7-£15. **Credit** MC, V. **Map** p405 W3. This art deco venue in Greenwich hosts classes and workshops and a regular tea dance, as well as unique cabaret nights, which deliver entertaining dance performances in short bursts.

Laban Centre

Creekside, Deptford, SE8 3DZ (8691 8600, 8469 9500 tickets, www.laban.org). Deptford DLR or Greenwich DLR/rail. **Open** 10am-8pm Mon-Sat. **Tickets** £6-£15. **Credit** MC, V.

Originally founded (in Manchester) by the innovative and influential movement theoretician Rudolf Laban (1879-1958), in 2005 the Laban Centre joined forces with Trinity College of Music to create the first ever UK conservatoire for music and dance. The centre was designed by Herzog & de Meuron of Tate Modern fame and features a curving, multi-coloured glass frontage. The stunning premises include a 300-seat auditorium and are home to Transitions Dance Company.

► *Also in Deptford, the Albany (Douglas Way, SE8 4AG, 8692 4446, www.thealbany.org.uk) specialises in hip hop theatre.*

Private View

Peek behind the scenes at the Royal Ballet.

Held around once a month, generally on Monday evenings, Royal Ballet in Rehearsal sessions at the Royal Opera House (*see p302*) offer a rare – and thrillingly close-up – glimpse behind the scenes at this most venerable of companies. The 90-minute sessions are held in the Linbury Studio Theatre or the Clore Studio Upstairs, with capacities of 400 and 170 respectively. This is ballet at its most stripped down: no sets, no exquisite costumes and no grand stage. Instead, there's just the piano, the squeak of shoes on the scuffed grey floor, and the intense concentration of the dancers.

The casting is generally only revealed on the night, and the old hands eagerly scan the programme to find out who will be rehearsing. It could be the leads practising an elaborate pas de deux, or new recruits from the corps de ballet learning the steps to *Swan Lake* or *Nutcracker* for the first time. 'We wait until the night to reveal the programme as things often change due to dancer injury, and we don't want to raise false expectations,' says Insight programme manager Tom Nelson, who co-ordinates the sessions. 'It's also a nice surprise to turn up and find out you've got two principals.'

Watching a work in progress like this, rather than a polished final performance, brings home the sheer physicality and meticulous timing demanded by each sequence, jump and entrance – and it's hard graft. The sessions invariably sell out.

ARTS & ENTERTAINMENT

Film

London's screening scene is ever more inventive.

It isn't until you stroll round London that you realise how often the city itself has played a starring role in films, with both its iconic sights (rampaging mummies at the British Museum) and characterful neighbourhoods (a floppy-haired bookseller in Notting Hill) giving visitors a visual preview of the capital. There's a lively and varied culture of screenings too. Giant picture palaces hosting red-carpet premières attended by A-list actors? Check out the **Odeon Leicester Square** (*see p307*). Cheap-as-chips repertory cinema? The **Prince Charles** (*see p308*) is right around the corner. 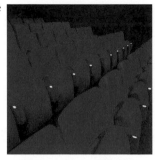 Refurbished art deco gems? Try the gorgeous, historic **Phoenix** (*see p307*). A world-class film festival? Happens every autumn. Outdoor screenings in remarkable settings, ciné clubs, film seasons devoted to every genre and national cinema under the sun? Yes, yes and yes. Get some popcorn and sit yourself down.

WHERE TO GO

Leicester Square underwent a major and much-needed facelift in 2011 and has the biggest first-run cinemas and stages most of the big-budget premières – but it also has the biggest prices. By contrast, the independents provide a cheaper and often more enjoyable night out, and they often show films that wouldn't come within a million miles of a red carpet.

Among the rep cinemas, the British Film Institute's flagship venue gets top billing. **BFI Southbank** (*see p308*) screens seasons exploring and celebrating various genres of cinema and TV. After the BFI, London's best repertory cinema is found at the **Riverside Studios** (*see p308*), where you'll find special seasons and film events. Despite the loss of two of the three screens at the **Barbican** (*see p306*), it's always worth checking out the self-explanatory Directorspective strand.

Unexpected venues for film-viewing include the big museums and galleries. The **British Museum** (*see p106*), **National Gallery** (*see p134*), **Imperial War Museum** (*see p166*) and **Tate Modern** (*see p82*) all have regular screenings themed to their temporary exhibitions, the **Museum of London** (*see p95* **Profile**) screens a classic London film each month, and even **St Paul's Cathedral** (*see p90*) has carved out a niche for silent movies with live organ soundtracks. Several luxury hotels open their screening rooms to the public; those at the **Soho Hotel** (*see p197*) and **One Aldwych** (*see p196*) are favourites.

Outdoor summertime screens have popped up across the capital. The most glamorous is the **Somerset House Summer Screen** (www.somersethouse.org.uk/film), for which recent blockbusters and old classics are run in a magnificent Georgian courtyard, and Park Nights at the **Serpentine Gallery** (*see p150*), where you can watch films in the annual temporary, starchitect-built pavilion. Fans of memorabilia can check out the enjoyable **London Film Museum** (*see p77*), but the latest trend is to mix cinema with other forms of entertainment, and to screen the films in a range of unusual locations (*see right* **Who Needs a Cinema?**).

The lowdown

Consult *Time Out* magazine's weekly listings or visit www.timeout.com/film for full details of what's on and performance times; note that the programmes change on a Friday. Films released in the UK are classified as follows: **U** – suitable for all ages; **PG** – open to all, parental guidance is advised; **12A** – under-12s only admitted with an over-18; **15** – no one under 15 is admitted; **18** – no one under 18 is admitted.

Who Needs a Cinema?

It's not just about the film any more: screenings are getting increasingly creative.

At unusual locations
Free Film Festivals
www.freefilmfestivals.org
This enterprising community project puts on free outdoor screenings in interesting public spaces in south-east London: *Battleship Potemkin* on the roof of a Peckham multistorey car park, say.

On a rooftop
Rooftop Film Club *Queen of Hoxton, 1-5 Curtain Road, EC2A 3JX, 7422 0958, www.rooftopfilmclub.com*
In summer, the rooftop garden at this bar/club/arts collective screens around five films a week. Everyone is issued with wireless headphones, and you can sip a beer or order some food while you watch.

In architectural splendour
Summer Screen at Somerset House
The Strand, WC2R 1LA, 7845 4600, www.somersethouse.org.uk/film
This summer season takes place in the lovely neoclassical courtyard of Somerset House; tickets sell out way in advance. Bring a picnic and plenty of cushions.

Thames-side
More London Free Festival
www.morelondon.com
A sunken outdoor amphitheatre by City Hall, the Scoop hosts a series of free film events in summer. The 2011 schedule included *The King's Speech* and *True Grit*.

On a barge
Floating Cinema *http://floatingcinema.info*
In summer 2011 the Floating Cinema plied London's waterways with screenings and events. Check the website for future events.

Bike-powered
Magnificent Revolution
www.magnificentrevolution.org
Audience members are encouraged to take a turn on the saddle of the eight or 20 stationary bikes that power screenings of eclectic films at eclectic venues.

On the QT
Secret Cinema *www.secretcinema.org*
Venue and film are announced just 24 hours before curtain-up at these immersive club-like experiences, with dress code.

Rooftop Film Club.

ARTS & ENTERTAINMENT

FIRST-RUN CINEMAS

Central London

Barbican

Silk Street, the City, EC2Y 8DS (7638 8891, www.barbican.org.uk). Barbican tube or Moorgate tube/rail. Tickets £10.50; £7.50-£8.50 reductions; £5 Mon. **Screens** 1. **Credit** AmEx, MC, V. **Map** p400 P5.

The closure of tiny Screens 2 and 3 at the huge concrete art centre (*see p93*) in 2010 has meant a single screen now shows the Barbican's excellent film programme – no matter, the raked seats always made Screen 1 the best of the three. Expect new releases of quality world and independent films, and surveys of the likes of Werner Herzog and Ingmar Bergman in the Directorspective strand.

Curzon Cinemas

Chelsea *206 King's Road, SW3 5XP (0871 703 3990). Sloane Square tube then bus 11, 19, 22, 319.* **Screens** 1. **Map** p395 E12.
Mayfair *38 Curzon Street, W1J 7TY (0871 703 3989). Green Park or Hyde Park Corner tube.* **Screens** 2. **Map** p398 H8.

Soho *99 Shaftesbury Avenue, W1D 5DY (0871 703 3988). Leicester Square tube.* **Screens** 3. **Map** p416 X3.
All *www.curzoncinemas.com.* **Tickets** £9.50-£12.50; £6-£8.50 reductions. **Credit** MC, V.

Expect a superb range of shorts, rarities, double-bills and seasons alongside new international releases across the small Curzon chain. There's 1970s splendour in Mayfair (it's sometimes used for premières) and comfort in Chelsea, which is perfect for a Sunday screening after a King's Road brunch. But the coolest of the bunch is the Soho outpost, which has a buzzing café, a decent basement bar and themes its eating and drinking spaces to tie in to event releases such as Pedro Almodóvar's *The Skin I Live In*.

★ ICA Cinema

Nash House, the Mall, SW1Y 5AH (7930 0493, 7930 3647 tickets, www.ica.org.uk). Charing Cross tube/rail. **Tickets** £7-£10; £8 reductions. **Screens** 2. **Credit** MC, V. **Map** p399 K8.

London's small contemporary arts centre (*see p141*) has met its brief not only by screening an eclectic range of cinema, but by distributing some of the most noteworthy films of recent years. After an uninspiring few years, there are signs of a renais-

---

Festivals Film

What not to miss this year.

There's a film festival taking place in the capital on pretty much any given week throughout the year, but the **London Film Festival** (www.bfi.org.uk/lff, Oct) is far and away the most prestigious. Nearly 200 new British and international features are screened, mainly at the BFI Southbank and Leicester Square's Vue West End. It's preceded by the scrappy but leftfield **Raindance Festival** (www.raindance.co.uk), which includes a terrific shorts programme. New for 2012, and in the big league, is a London offshoot of Robert Redford's Sundance Festival (www.sundance-london.com), in April.

Highlighting the importance of the city's LGBT communities, the **London Lesbian & Gay Film Festival** (7928 3232, www.bfi. org.uk/llgff, late Mar) is the UK's third largest film festival. Also taking place in spring are **Human Rights Watch International Film Festival** (7713 1995, www.hrw.org/iff, mid-late Mar) and the **East End Film Festival** (www.eastendfilmfestival. com, late Apr), which explores cinema's potential to cross cultural boundaries, reserving a special place for films starring London – in summer 2011, the festival

hosted special events near the Olympic Park, with films shown on a makeshift screen built of fridges and projected from a narrow boat on the River Lea.

Several festivals screen the output of a particular foreign territory. Among them are the Polish Cultural Institute's **Kinoteka** (www.kinoteka.org.uk, Mar); the **London Turkish Film Festival** (www.ltff.org.uk), the wonderful **Mosaïques** festival (Ciné Lumière, June); and the **French Film Festival** (www.frenchfilmfestival.org.uk, Ciné Lumière, Nov), which shows the best of new French cinema.

Short films are featured at the **London Short Film Festival** (www.shortfilms.org.uk) in the new year, while August's **London International Animation Festival** (www.liaf.org.uk) screens 300 or more animated shorts from around the globe. The **Portobello Film Festival** (www.porto bellofilmfestival.com, early Sept) offers an eclectic programme of free screenings, while a noble addition to the schedule since June 2011 is the **Open City London Documentary Festival** (www.opencitylondon.com, June), which is organised by and takes place mainly at UCL.

Screen on the Green.

sance under new leadership. Serious types can often be seen discussing the evening's programme afterwards in the ICA Café.

Odeon Leicester Square
Leicester Square, WC2H 7LQ (0871 224 4007, www.odeon.co.uk). Leicester Square tube. **Tickets** vary; check website for details. **Screens** 6. **Credit** AmEx, MC, V. **Map** p416 X4.
You'll often find the red carpets and crush barriers up outside this art deco gem – it's the city's leading site for star-studded premières and hosts the opening and closing nights of the London Film Festival. If you're lucky, you might catch one of the silent film screenings, with accompaniment on a 1937 Compton organ. Otherwise, it's big-volume mainstream hits.

Outer London

Electric Cinema
191 Portobello Road, Notting Hill, W11 2ED (7908 9696, www.electriccinema.co.uk). Ladbroke Grove or Notting Hill Gate tube. **Tickets** £12.50-£14.50; £8-£10.50 Mon. **Screens** 1. **Credit** AmEx, MC, V. **Map** p404 X4.
The Electric has gone from past-it fleapit to luscious luxury destination with leather seats and sofas, footstools and a bar inside the auditorium. It also has a fashionable brasserie next door.

Everyman & Screen Cinemas
Everyman *5 Hollybush Vale, Hampstead, NW3 6TX. Hampstead tube.* **Tickets** £13-£16; £7.50 reductions. **Screens** 2.
Screen on the Green *83 Upper Street, Islington, N1 0NP. Angel tube.* **Tickets** £11-£13.50; £7.50 reductions. **Screens** 2. **Map** p400 O2.
Both *0871 906 9060, www.everymancinema.com.* **Credit** MC, V.

London's most elegant cinema, the Everyman has a glamorous bar and two-seaters (£30) in its 'screening lounges', complete with foot stools and wine coolers. Everyman now also owns three former Screen cinemas, of which the Islington's Screen on the Green is the best – carefully refurbished in late 2009, it lost seats to make space for the more comfortable kind, gained an auditorium bar and a stage for live events, but kept its lovely exterior neon sign.

Hackney Picturehouse
270 Mare Street, Hackney, E8 1HE (0871 902 5734, www.picturehouses.co.uk). Hackney Central or London Fields rail. **Tickets** check website for details. **Screens** 4. **Credit** AmEx, MC, V.
Opened in autumn 2011, this new four-screener carved from the remains of the old Ocean music venue is set to become the flagship cinema for a borough woefully served for film. As well as showing new releases and hosting festivals and seasons geared towards the diverse local community, the Picturehouse will also feature an art gallery and café space that opens on to the street.

★ Phoenix
52 High Road, East Finchley, N2 9PJ (8444 6789, www.phoenixcinema.co.uk). East Finchley tube. **Tickets** £6-£9.50; £6 reductions. **Screens** 1. **Credit** MC, V.
Built in 1910 and revamped in the 1930s, the Grade II-listed Phoenix reopened in autumn 2010, restored to its copper and gold, art deco glory, at a cost of £1.1m. It has real old-fashioned glamour, and is London's oldest cinema to have remained in continuous operation. Owned by a charitable trust enjoying strong community support, it runs a varied programme including live theatre and opera transmissions, and now has a café-bar on the premises. The best cinema in north London.

Rio Cinema
107 Kingsland High Street, Dalston, E8 2PB
(7241 9410, www.riocinema.org.uk). Dalston
Kingsland rail. **Tickets** £9; £7 reductions.
Screens 1. **Credit** AmEx, MC, V.
Another great deco survivor, restored to its original
sleek lines, the Rio is east London's finest independent. Alongside mainstream releases, the Rio is well
known for its Turkish and Kurdish film festivals,
catering to strong local communities.

Vue Westfield London
Westfield London, Shepherd's Bush, W12 7GF
(0871 224 0240, www.myvue.com). White City
or Wood Lane tube, or Shepherd's Bush tube/rail.
Tickets check website for details. **Screens** 14.
Credit MC, V.
This Vue multiplex was a great addition to the vast
shopping centre (*see p259*). All the screens are
digital, with five 3D-ready and two 18m by 10m
whoppers. The main rooms are functional black
boxes with good sightlines, but you can also fork out
for over-18s 'Scene' screens: you get reclining chairs
and access to a private bar and a cloakroom. There's
a branch at the new Westfield centre in Stratford.
Other locations throughout the city.

REPERTORY CINEMAS

Several first-run cinemas also offer rep-style fare
– check *Time Out* magazine for locations.

★ BFI Southbank
South Bank, SE1 8XT (7928 3535, 7928 3232
tickets, www.bfi.org.uk). Embankment tube or
Waterloo tube/rail. **Tickets** £9.50; £6.75
reductions; £6.50 Tue. **Screens** 4. **Credit**
AmEx, MC, V. **Map** p399 M8.
In 2007, the expanded, former National Film Theatre
gained a new name, a destination bar-restaurant
(from museum-caterers Benugo) and the superb
Mediatheque. Since then the deathlessly popular

INSIDE TRACK GET HITCHED

As part of the London 2012 Festival,
the BFI Southbank (*see above*) will be
showing newly restored prints of some
of east Londoner Alfred Hitchcock's
early, rarely-seen silent films. Landmark
one-off screenings will be accompanied by
specially commissioned orchestral scores
by leading contemporary musicians: pick
of the bunch is *The Lodger: A Story of the
London Fog* (1926), set to the music of
Nitin Sawhney. If you miss out on tickets,
don't despair: BFI Southbank is also
planning to mount a major Hitchcock
autumn retrospective.

---

promenade-facing café-bar has also been improved
by Benugo, but the BFI's success is still built on its
core function: providing thought-provoking seasons
that give film-hungry locals the chance to enjoy rare
and significant British and foreign films. In summer
2011, the venue's three screens were given an impressive spruce-up, including brand new seats. Budget
cuts mean its short-lived gallery space is now closed.
► *Mediatheque gives you free access to the BFI's
huge film and documentary archive.*

Ciné Lumière
Institut Français, 17 Queensberry Place,
South Kensington, SW7 2DT (7073 1350,
www.institut-francais.org.uk). South Kensington
tube. **Tickets** £8-£10; £6-£8 reductions; £8 Mon.
Screens 1. **Credit** MC, V. **Map** p395 D10.
Ciné Lumière reopened in early 2009 with better
seating and a refreshed art deco interior. No longer
screening French films only (there are still, however,
regular French previews and classics), the Lumière
is a standard-bearer for world cinema in the capital.

Prince Charles
7 Leicester Place, off Leicester Square, WC2H
7BY (0870 811 2559, www.princecharles
cinema.com). Leicester Square tube. **Tickets**
£6.50-£10; £4-£6 reductions. **Screens** 2. **Credit**
MC, V. **Map** p416 X3.
Central and cheap, the Prince Charles is just up an
alley from the pricey Leicester Square monsters, but
even films on the new screen are a bargain. Perfect
for catching up on still-fresh films you missed first
time round, it is renowned for riotous singalong
screenings and cult programming such as *The
Room*, billed as 'the worst film ever made' and
shown to a packed house once a month.

★ Riverside Studios
Crisp Road, Hammersmith, W6 9RL (8237 1111,
www.riversidestudios.co.uk). Hammersmith tube.
Tickets £8.50; £7.50 reductions. **Screens** 1.
Credit MC, V.
The Riverside offers a superb programme of films
and has become well known in recent years for its
inventive double-bills. The café-bar and riverside
terrace are usually packed with a voluble mix of
film- and theatregoers.

IMAX

BFI IMAX
1 Charlie Chaplin Walk, South Bank, SE1
8XR (0870 787 2525, www.bfi.org.uk/imax).
Waterloo tube/rail. **Tickets** £10-£18.50; £8.50-
£15 reductions. **Screens** 1. **Credit** AmEx, MC, V.
Map p399 M8.
London's biggest screen mixes made-for-IMAX fare
and scenery-heavy documentaries with mainstream
blockbusters, such as *Harry Potter*, shown either
very big – or very big and in disorienting 3D.

Gay & Lesbian

Where the out go out.

Sydney's got the sun, New York City and San Francisco have the history and Rio's got the bodies, but – despite some grumbling among spoilt locals – London's got the buzz. Whatever your taste in music, from thunderous indie to thumping disco, you'll find a gay club that specialises in it, on a nightlife scene that runs around the clock and throughout the week. Add in an array of cabaret nights and literary salons, a handful of cafés and restaurants, a major gay and lesbian film festival and the World Pride celebrations in 2012, and there should be something to keep you busy.

THE GAY SCENE IN LONDON

Roughly speaking, London's gay scene is split into three distinct zones: **Soho**, **Vauxhall** and **east London**. Each of these three districts has its own character: in a nutshell, Soho is the most mainstream, Vauxhall is the most decadent and east London is the most outré.

Centred on Old Compton Street, the Soho scene continues to attract the crowds. Luvvies take in a singalong at the **Green Carnation**, fit freaks work out at **Sweatbox** and everyone else mills around the plethora of gay-slanted bars and cafés. And just down the road, close to Charing Cross Station, sits the legendary **Heaven**, home to **G-A-Y**. If your dream has always been to see Madonna or Kylie in a club, here's your chance – the list of singers who've done live PAs here reads like a *Who's Who* of squeal-tastic gay pop icons.

Down south, Vauxhall is more hedonistic. You could arrive in London on a Friday evening and dance non-stop here for an entire weekend before flying out of town again. But it's not all about going wild: venues such as the **RVT** and the Eagle (home to the superb **Horse Meat Disco**) draw pilgrims from far and wide.

The most alternative and creative of the capital's queer scenes is in east London. In the likes of the **George & Dragon** and the **Dalston Superstore**, you'll be rubbing shoulders with fashion and music's movers and shakers, to soundtracks built by ferociously underground DJs. With so much coolness going on, it can get a little snooty, but a lot of the bars and clubs round Shoreditch and Dalston are also properly mixed, which makes the area ideal for a night out with straight mates.

Keen to cut to the chase? **Chariots** is the sauna chain of choice, although **Vault 139** and **Pleasuredrome** (Arch 124, Cornwall Road, Waterloo, SE1 8XE, 7633 9194, www.pleasuredrome.com) also have their followers. Most regular bars don't have backrooms, but some club nights in Vauxhall can get raunchy. The monthly **Hard On** (www.hardonclub.co.uk) is the top pick on the calendar for lovers of fetish and leather.

For lesbians, clubby **Candy Bar** is the key venue. For bars, **Green** and Monday or Wednesday at **Retro** are good choices. The women-only **Glass Bar**, having survived threats of closure, is back in vogue. New stand-alone nights pop up all the time, but Duckie and Bar Wotever at **RVT** (*see p312*), Bird Club at the **Bethnal Green Working Men's Club** (*see p332*), exclusive Code at **Green Carnation**

see p312, *see p332*

INSIDE TRACK
BADGE OF HONOUR

If you're here for the Games and keen to show your true colours, invest in one of the official Olympics Games pin badges. The £6 pins are part of a campaign promoting six strands of diversity, and form part of a broad drive to get different communities involved in the Games. Olympic and Paralympic versions are available at official London 2012 Shops (*see p275*) and http://shop.london2012.com (search for 'rainbow pride').

RVT. *See p312.*

(*see p314*), Ruby Tuesdays at **Ku** (*see p315*) and Twat Boutique at **Dalston Superstore** (*see p313*) are recommended. Over the last decade, **100% Babe** in the basement at the Roxy (3-5 Rathbone Place, Fitzrovia, W1P 1DA, 7636 1598, www.theroxy.co.uk) has become an institution. Happening every Sunday night before a bank holiday, expect popular house music, feel-good floorfillers and a party mood.

Craving queer culture that's a little more cerebral? Try out London's new breed of queer salons, essentially literary or cultural get-togethers – events from the **House of Homosexual Culture** (on Facebook), **Tart Women's Salon** (www.tartsalon.co.uk/home.php) and **Polari** (www.myspace.com/polarigaysalon) are all recommended.

Lastly, special mention should go to the **NYC Downlow**, a travelling homo disco straight out of '70s New York that you can catch at festivals across the country (http://thedownlowradio.com/the-downlow/) including Lovebox (*see p211* **Festivals**).

RESTAURANTS & CAFÉS

More or less every café and restaurant in London welcomes gay custom. Certainly nowhere in or around Soho will so much as bat an eyelid at you and your other half having a romantic dinner; **J Sheekey** (*see p222*), the **Wolseley** (*see p228*) and **Arbutus** (*see p222*) have particularly enthusiastic gay followings. For thirtysomething lesbians, there are fun cocktail evenings amid the mom-and-pop Italian vintage decor of **Star at Night** (22 Great Chapel

Street, Soho, W1F 8FR, 7494 2488, www.thestaratnight.com, open 6-11.30pm Tue-Sat) – by day, it's just an old greasy spoon.

Balans

60 Old Compton Street, Soho, W1D 4UG (7439 2183, www.balans.co.uk). Leicester Square or Piccadilly Circus tube. **Open** 7.30am-5am Mon-Thur, Sun; 7am-6am Fri, Sat. **Admission** £2.50 after midnight Mon-Sat. **Credit** AmEx, MC, V. **Map** p416 W3.

The gay café-restaurant of choice for many years, Balans is all about location, location, location (plus hot waiters, decent food and ridiculous opening hours). Situated across from Compton's bar and next door to Clone Zone, it's the beating heart of the Soho scene. The nearby Balans Café (no.34) serves a shorter version of the menu. Both are open almost all night and are good for a post-club bite. **Other locations** throughout the city.

NIGHTCLUBS

London's club scene is particularly subject to change: venues close, nights end and new soirées start. Check *Time Out* magazine or www.timeout.com for details on what's on when you're here.

If you want to stay up all night and next day as well, head to Vauxhall. At **Fire** (South Lambeth Road, SW8 1UQ, www.fireclub.co.uk), popular nights include midweek urban music stalwart Work!, and popular funky house parties Beyond and Orange, which keep dancers going from Friday morning through until Tuesday. Other clubs in the area include

Union (no.66, www.clubunion.co.uk) and **Area** (nos.67-68, www.areaclublondon.com), on the Albert Embankment.

★ Candy Bar
4 Carlisle Street, Soho, W1D 3BJ (7287 5041, www.candybarsoho.com). Tottenham Court Road tube. **Open** 1pm-3am Mon-Sat; 1pm-12.30am Sun. **Admission** free; £5 after 9pm Fri, Sat. **Credit** MC, V. **Map** p416 W2.
Opened in 1996, the Candy Bar was London's first full-time drinking den for lesbians. It made a splash with its location – in Soho, right at the heart of boys-town – and entertainment: female strippers and lapdances for lesbians, and it has since gone on to become the location for a reality TV show, *Candy Bar Girls*. There is still stripping on the first Friday and third Saturday of the month – but you can do your own dancing in the basement (DJs spin everything from house and R&B to electro and old school). The crowd varies from lipstick lesbian to butch, from student to professional, and men must be accompanied by at least two women.

Club Kali
Dome, 1 Dartmouth Park Hill, Tufnell Park, N19 5QQ (7272 8153, www.clubkali.com). Tufnell Park tube. **Open** 10pm-3am 3rd Fri of mth. **Admission** £8; £5 reductions. **No credit cards.**
The world's largest LGBT Asian dance club offers Bollywood, bhangra, Arabic tunes, R&B and dance classics spun by DJs Ritu, Riz & Qurra.

Exilio Latin Dance Club
Guy's Bar, Boland House, St Thomas Street, Bankside, SE1 9RT (07931 374391, www.exilio.

co.uk). London Bridge tube/rail. **Open** 9.30pm-2.30am every other Sat. **Admission** £8-£12. **No credit cards. Map** p399 M6.
This is London's principal queer Latino spot, with girls and guys getting together for merengue, salsa, cumbia and reggaeton.

Heaven
Underneath the Arches, Villiers Street, Covent Garden, WC2N 6NG (7930 2020, www.heaven-london.com). Embankment tube or Charing Cross tube/rail. **Open** hrs vary. **Admission** prices vary. **No credit cards. Map** p416 Y5.
London's most famous gay club is a bit like *Les Misérables* – it's camp, it's full of history and tourists love it. Popcorn (Mon) has long been a good bet, but it's really all about G-A-Y (Thur-Sat). For years, divas with an album to flog (Madonna, Kylie, Girls Aloud) have turned up to play here at the weekend.

★ Horse Meat Disco
Eagle London, 349 Kennington Lane, Vauxhall, SE11 5QY (7793 0903, www.horsemeatdisco. co.uk). Vauxhall tube/rail. **Open** 9pm-3am Sun. **Admission** £6. **No credit cards.**
Not your average gay club. Skinny Soho boys and fashionistas rub shoulders with scally lads and bears in a traditional old boozer. The hip soundtrack is an inspired mix of Studio 54, New York punk and new wave. As one *Time Out* critic put it: 'if you ever wished you could hang out in a club like the one in *Beyond the Valley of the Dolls* or *Scarface*, you'll love Horse Meat Disco'. A must.
▶ *When Horse Meat isn't in residence, the Eagle is a hub for those wishing to try a bit of leather without a strict dress code.*

ARTS & ENTERTAINMENT

Festivals Gay & Lesbian
Key dates in the queer year.

July 2012 will see the usual Pride London (www.pridelondon.org) event turned into **World Pride**, an international celebration set to attract an extra million visitors to the capital. A two-week cultural festival precedes the big day.

Soho Pride (www.sohopride.net) sees the same West End streets overrun in late summer (though possibly not in 2012). In Regent's Park, **Black Pride** (www.ukblackpride.org.uk), a queer alternative to the Notting Hill Carnival – which still, sadly, has zero gay presence – continues to grow every year. Out east, the Sunday of Victoria Park's **Lovebox** festival has turned into a huge homo knees-up (www.lovebox.net). In spring, there's the annual **London Lesbian & Gay Film Festival**

(*see p306* **Festivals**), with an emphasis on edgier fare in the wake of *Brokeback Mountain*. Also worth checking out is July's **London Literature Festival** (*see p286*), which often hosts gay-oriented readings and talks.

Pride London.

Popstarz

The Den, 18 West Central Street, Covent Garden, WC1A 1JJ (7240 1864, www.popstarz.org). Holborn or Tottenham Court Road tube. **Open** 10pm-4am Fri. **Admission** free before 11pm, then £5-£8. **Credit** MC, V. **Map** p416 Y1.
What G-A-Y is to cheese, Popstarz is to indie. It's studenty, drunken, attitude-free and popular – so popular, in fact, that the club has spawned imitators from New York to Paris. There are also occasional PAs from in-demand acts – Gossip, say.

★ RVT

Royal Vauxhall Tavern, 372 Kennington Lane, Vauxhall, SE11 5HY (7820 1222, www.rvt.org. uk). Vauxhall tube/rail. **Open** 7pm-midnight Mon, Wed, Thur; 6pm-midnight Tue; 7pm-2am Fri; 9pm-2am Sat; 2pm-midnight Sun. **Admission** £5-£7. **Credit** MC, V.
This pub-turned-legendary-gay-venue, a much-loved stalwart on the scene for years, operates an anything-goes booking policy. The most famous fixture is Saturday's queer performance night Duckie

One-off Parties

Where it's at, out east.

Trailer Trash.

The east London gay scene has gone from strength to strength over the last few years, but many of its best queer club nights are hard-to-track-down, irregular parties that advertise little and change location a lot. To navigate the scene successfully, you'll need some pointers.

Cheap entry (rarely exceeding a fiver) and armies of Facebook fans can often mean mammoth queues, so get there super-early or super-late – and download discount fliers in advance. It's a scene that runs the gamut from the almost menacingly trendy to the lighthearted and silly. Falling into the former category (but still genuinely friendly) is the deeply dancey, girly-focused **Bastard Batty Bass** (www.battybass.com). Here you'll catch female MCs spitting over bassy electro to a midweek crowd that clearly isn't working tomorrow – on a good night this is one of the capital's most exciting clubs, gay or otherwise.

Trailer Trash (www.clubtrailertrash.com) comes from roughly the same stable and pulls in an equally fashion-forward pack of partiers for local up-and-coming DJ talent and internationally renowned stars such as Green Velvet and Switch – though the DJs' limelight is regularly stolen by a hilarious crew of trannies. **Dick and Fanny** (www.dick andfanny.tumblr.com) also tends to get

occasional big-name DJ guests such as Kim Ann Foxman of Hercules and Love Affair and is a hit with both boys and girls, straight and gay. Meanwhile, **Hot Boy Dancing Spot** (www.hotboydancingspot.com) is deservedly popular with everyone from art school undergrads to beary professionals who pack its warehouse bashes and dive bar parties for superlative DJing from residents the Lovely Jonjo and Hello Mozart! The vibe is deeply trendy – don't bother turning up if you're on a hen do.

A little more indie – and mixed – is **Unskinny Bop** (www.unskinnybop.co.uk) at the Bethnal Green Working Men's Club (*see p332*). Here you can expect to hear music from Mariah to Riot Grrrl anthems. You'll find a similar crowd, too, around the corner at the Star of Bethnal Green (www.starof bethnalgreen.com) with newcomer **Music, Paper, Scissors** (www.musicpaperscissors. com). This time, though, it's more about 1980s and '90s tunes – think Don Henley's 'Boys of Summer' and Whitney and Chaka classics. Not your bag? No problem; try **Club Motherfu*ker** (www.clubmotherfucker.com), which is often out east and pulls in a clued-up crowd for acts like Bloc Party, Simian Mobile Disco and Friendly Fires – years before anyone else has heard of them.

(www.duckie.co.uk), with Amy Lamé hosting performances at midnight that range from strip cabaret to porn puppets; Sunday's Dame Edna Experience drag show, from 5pm, is also essential, drawing quasi-religious devotees. The aim is always to please the crowd of regulars, reliably vocal with their feedback. Punters verge on the bear, but the main dress code is 'no attitude'. *Photo p310.*

Vogue Fabrics
66 Stoke Newington Road, Dalston, N16 7XB (http://voguefabricsdalston.com/club). Dalston Junction or Dalston Kingsland rail. **Open** 10pm-3am Fri, Sat. **Admission** £3-£5 Fri, Sat. **No credit cards.**
Small, sweaty and seemingly illegal (but in fact perfectly legitimate), Vogue Fabrics is the place to come if you like your nights messy and your men of the bear and otter variety. While the regular parties come and go, the electro-, disco-, Italo-pumpin' Dirtbox remains a favourite.
▶ *A little boy heavy? The guys behind Dirtbox run Dick and Fanny (see p312 One-off Parties).*

XXL
The Arches, 51-53 Southwark Street, Borough, SE1 1RU (7403 4001, www.xxl-london.com). London Bridge tube/rail. **Open** 10pm-3am Wed; 10pm-6am Sat. **Admission** £3-£15. **No credit cards. Map** p402 P8.
The world's biggest club – naturally! – for bears and their friends, XXL is nirvana for chubbier, hairier and blokier gay men and their twinky admirers. True to its name, the venue is bigger than average, with two dancefloors, two bars and even an outdoor beer garden.

PUBS & BARS

Unless otherwise stated, the pubs and bars listed here are open to both gay men and lesbians. The bar at **Ku** (*see p315*) is another good option if you're in the West End.

Barcode Vauxhall
Arch 69, Goding Street, Vauxhall, SE11 4AD (7582 4180, www.bar-code.co.uk). Vauxhall tube. **Open** 4pm-1am Mon-Wed; 4pm-2am Thur; 4pm-5am Fri; 4pm-7am Sat; 5pm-1am Sun. **Admission** £4 after 10pm Fri; £5 after 10pm Sat. **Credit** MC, V.
Prior to the arrival of Barcode Vauxhall, Vauxhall was mostly for clubbing, with those oh-so-necessary pre-dance drinks to be enjoyed anywhere-else-but here. Now those pre-dancing punters are joined by folks just after a drink at this massive, lavish venue, which generally attracts a blokey-ish crowd despite its shiny, sparkly surfaces.
▶ *BCV's forerunner Barcode, off Shaftesbury Avenue, hosts the mostly gay Comedy Camp night (www.comedycamp.co.uk).*

Dalston Superstore.

★ Dalston Superstore
117 Kingland High Street, Dalston, E8 2PB (7254 2273). Dalston Kingsland rail. **Open** noon-2am Mon; 10am-2am Tue-Thur; 10am-3am Fri, Sat; 10am-2am Sun.* **Credit** MC, V.
The opening of this gay arts space-cum-bar a few years back cemented Dalston's status as the final frontier of the East End's gay scene. Come during the day for the café grub, Wi-Fi and art exhibitions on the walls; at night, you can expect queues for an impressive roster of guest DJs spinning anything from garage to pop. Twat Boutique, Body Talk and the regular quiz nights are all nights thoroughly worth sticking in your diary.

Freedom Bar
66 Wardour Street, Soho, W1F 0TA (7734 0071, www.freedombarsoho.com). Leicester Square or Piccadilly Circus tube. **Open** 4pm-3am Mon-Thur; 2pm-3am Fri, Sat; 2-11.30pm Sun. **Admission** £5 after 10pm Fri, Sat. **Credit** MC, V. **Map** p416 W3.
A glitzy cocktail lounge and DJ bar, spread over two floors. The glam ground-floor bar attracts a fashion-conscious crowd, who sip cocktail among chandeliers, zebra-print banquettes and Venetian mirrors. A few 'strays' and dolled-up gal pals add colour. The large basement club and performance space hosts weekday cabaret and gets busy with the gay party crowd over the weekend.
▶ *In winter, the cosy alcoves of nearby retro-styled basement bar Friendly Society (no.79, 7434 3804) are great for cocktails and first dates.*

G-A-Y Bar
30 Old Compton Street, Soho, W1D 4UR (7494 2756, www.g-a-y.co.uk). Leicester Square or Tottenham Court Road tube. **Open** noon-midnight daily. **Credit** MC, V. **Map** p416 W3.

The G-A-Y night at Heaven (*see p311*) gets the celebrity cameos, but this popular bar is still a shrine to queer pop idols, with nightly drinks promos every time they play a video from the current diva du jour. There's also a women's bar in the basement, called (delightfully) Girls Go Down – popular with flirty, studenty lesbians, loathed by most older women.
▶ *G-A-Y bar's plush late-night sibling, G-A-Y Late, is round the corner on 5 Goslett Yard.*

George & Dragon

2 Hackney Road, Bethnal Green, E2 7NS (7012 1100). Old Street tube/rail or Hoxton rail. **Open** 6pm-midnight daily. **Credit** MC, V. **Map** p401 S3.
The trendy location of this mini-pub ensures a stylish and up-for-it clientele, while the decor (a wall-mounted horse's head, creepy puppets, random garbage) keeps the vibe fun. The music here – pop, indie and accessible electronica – is often delivered with a healthy sense of humour. Gay pub or not, this is one of London's best boozers.
▶ *Wondering where everyone went at closing time? To the Joiners Arms, of course (see right).*

Green Carnation

4-5 Greek Street, Soho, W1D 4DB (8123 4267, www.greencarnationsoho.co.uk). Tottenham Court Road tube. **Open** 4pm-2am Mon-Sat; 4pm-12.30am Sun. **Admission** £5 after 11pm Mon-Sat. **Credit** AmEx, MC, V. **Map** p416 W2.
The Green Carnation had a major refit a couple of years back, to spectacular effect. Head upstairs for cocktails in posh surroundings, with chandeliers and piano music to heighten the senses and raise the tone. There's a bar and a dancefloor downstairs. It's a haven for West End Wendies, always on hand to belt out a minor Sondheim in the wee hours.

Hoist

Arches 47B & 47C, South Lambeth Road, Vauxhall, SW8 1RH (7735 9972, www.the hoist.co.uk). Vauxhall tube/rail. **Open** 10pm-3am Fri; 10pm-4am Sat; 2-8pm, 10pm-2am Sun. **Admission** £6 Fri, Sun; £2-£10 Sat. **No credit cards**.
One of two genuine leather bars in town, this club sits under the arches and makes the most of its underground and industrial setting. The Sunday afternoon event SBN (Stark Bollock Naked) gives you the tone; leather, uniforms, rubber, skinhead or boots are the dress code. Strictly no trainers.

Joiners Arms

116-118 Hackney Road, Bethnal Green, E2 7QL (www.joinershoreditch.com). Old Street tube/rail or Hoxton rail. **Open** 5pm-2am Mon-Wed; 5pm-3am Thur; 5pm-4am Fri, Sat; 2pm-2am Sun. **Credit** MC, V. **Map** p401 S3.
Love it or loathe it, come midnight this is where all the gays in Shoreditch end up. A mix of fashion types, queer East End geezers and tourists cabbing it from Soho get down to pop, house and electro. The queue for the loos is obscene and the vibe can be obnoxiously trendy but on the whole it's friendly, drunken and fun. Word to the wise: Sunday nights are often where it's at.

KW4

77 Hampstead High Street, Hampstead, NW3 1RE (7435 5747, www.kingwilliamhampstead. co.uk). Hampstead tube or Hampstead Heath rail. **Open** 11am-11pm Mon-Thur; 11am-midnight Fri-Sun. **Credit** AmEx, MC, V.
The perfect evening ending (or beginning) to time spent on the heath, this fabulous old local – the King

Shadow Lounge.

William IV, or King Willy to those with longer memories – attracts a very Hampstead crowd (read: well-off and ready for fun). On summer weekends, the cute little beer garden tends to fill up with a mix of gay and straight punters keen to put down their shopping bags. The pub is more popular with lesbians in summer, too, as a stop-off after a dip in the heath's women's bathing pond.

★ Ku

30 Lisle Street, Chinatown, WC2H 7BA (7437 4303, www.ku-bar.co.uk). Leicester Square tube. **Open** *Bar* noon-11.30pm Mon-Sat; noon-10.30pm Sun. *Club* 10pm-3am Mon-Sat. **Credit** MC, V. **Map** p416 X3.

Voted London's best central gay bar by the readers of *Boyz* and *Pink Paper*, Ku must be doing something right. Formerly known as West Central, it has morphed from a mediocre space into a popular bar and club that offers everything from film nights to comedy. The sheer variety of club nights (held in the basement) is impressive, from Sandra D's Ruby Tuesdays for lesbians to the poptastic O-Zone on Fridays, hosted by veteran drag DJ Dusty O.

▶ *Ku has recently opened a three-floor bar-club in the heart of the local scene, on the corner of Frith Street and Old Compton Street. Serious competition for G-A-Y, then (see p311).*

Retro Bar

2 George Court, off the Strand, Covent Garden, WC2N 6HH (7839 8760). Charing Cross tube/rail. **Open** noon-11pm Mon-Fri; 2-11pm Sat; 2-10.30pm Sun. **Credit** MC, V. **Map** p416 Y4.

Iggy Pop and Kate Bush are on the walls of this bar of the Popstarz ilk (*see p312*), where nights are dedicated to indie rock and Eurovision hits. The crowd here is mixed in every sense: gay/straight, gay/lesbian and scene queen/true eccentric. Quiz nights are popular, and the bar on occasions even relinquishes control of the music and lets punters be the DJ – bring your iPod.

Shadow Lounge

5 Brewer Street, Soho, W1F 0RF (7287 7988, www.theshadowlounge.co.uk). Leicester Square or Piccadilly Circus tube. **Open** 10pm-3am Mon-Sat; 7pm-midnight Sun. **Admission** £5 after 11pm Tue-Thur, Sun; £10 after 11pm Fri, Sat. **Credit** AmEx, MC, V. **Map** p416 W3.

For celebrity sightings, suits, cuties and fancy boots, this is your West End venue. Expect a hefty cover charge and a queue on the weekends, but there's often a sublime atmosphere inside.

Yard

57 Rupert Street, Soho, W1V 7BJ (7437 2652, www.yardbar.co.uk). Piccadilly Circus tube. **Open** 4-11.30pm Mon-Thur; 4pm-midnight Fri; 2pm-midnight Sat; 2-10.30pm Sun. **Credit** AmEx, MC, V. **Map** p416 W3.

Come for the courtyard in summer, stay for the Loft Bar in winter. This unpretentious bar offers a great open-air courtyard in a central location, attracting pretty boys, blokes and lesbians in equal measure.

ADULT CLUBS & SAUNAS

Chariots

1 Fairchild Street, Shoreditch, EC2A 3NS (7247 5333, www.gaysauna.co.uk). Liverpool Street tube/rail or Shoreditch High Street rail. **Open** noon-9am daily. **Admission** £16; £14 reductions. **Credit** AmEx, MC, V. **Map** p401 R4.

Chariots is a sauna chain with outlets all over town. The original is this one in Shoreditch, the biggest and busiest, although not necessarily the best. That accolade probably goes to the one on the Albert Embankment at Vauxhall (nos.63-64, 7247 5333). The Waterloo branch (101 Lower Marsh, 7401 8484) has the biggest sauna in the UK. **Other locations** throughout the city.

★ Sweatbox

Ramillies House, 1-2 Ramillies Street, Soho, W1F 7LN (3214 6014, www.sweatboxsoho.com). Oxford Circus tube. **Open** noon-2am Mon-Thur, Sun; noon-7am Fri, Sat. **Admission** £19 day pass; £15 spa only; £10 under-25s. **Credit** MC, V. **Map** p416 U2.

Sweatbox Soho looks more like a nightclub than a typical gym, with the sleek design offset by friendly staff. Though small, the space is well laid out, with a multigym and a free weights room. Qualified masseurs offer treatments. If that doesn't do the trick, there's a sauna downstairs.

Vault 139

139B-143 Whitfield Street, Fitzrovia, W1T 5EN (7388 5500, www.vault139.com). Warren Street tube. **Open** 4pm-1am Mon-Sat; 1pm-1am Sun. **No credit cards. Map** p396 J4.

Hidden away on a quiet backstreet, Vault 139 is London's most central cruise bar – and it's classy, too, with plush sofas, TV screens and a DJ booth.

Music

Classical clout and bubbling creativity in every other genre.

The current crop of London-based musicians seems to be unusually open-minded. There are classical nights in rock clubs and electronica gigs in classical auditoriums. Street-wise dubstep producers rub shoulders with free-jazz hippies. Grime artists rap with indie rockers, and classical conductors check out the nightclubs with drum 'n' bass DJs. There are few cities that can rival London's music scene for diversity and choice, with the city continuing to exert a magnetic pull on the world's top musicians in all genres. But as well as this prevailing mix-and-match aesthetic, passionate

purists remain. With scenes fiercely dedicated to everything from cosy folk music to grubbily low-brow indie, the capital can service any musical fancy. Check *Time Out* magazine or www.timeout.com to get the weekly picture.

Classical & Opera

London's classical scene has never looked or sounded more current, with the **Southbank Centre** (*see p318*), the **Barbican Centre** (*see right*) and **Kings Place** (*see p317*) all working with strong programmes, and youthful music directors such as Edward Gardner at the **English National Opera** (*see p318*) keen to retain a spirit of adventure.

Tickets & information

Tickets for most classical and opera events are available direct from the venues, online or by phone. It's advisable to always book ahead. Several venues, such as the Barbican and the Southbank Centre, operate standby schemes, offering unsold tickets at cut-rate prices just before the show.

INSIDE TRACK
DR DEE

A jewel in the London 2012 Festival crown, this darkly magical new opera features the music of Damon Albarn and the life of Dr John Dee, a 16th-century practitioner of the dark arts. It runs from 25 June to 2 July at ENO's Coliseum (*see p318*).

CLASSICAL VENUES

In addition to the major venues below, you can hear what tomorrow's classical music might sound like at the city's music schools, which stage regular concerts by pupils and visiting professionals. Check the websites of the **Royal Academy of Music** (7873 7300, www.ram.ac.uk), the **Royal College of Music** (7589 3643, www.rcm.ac.uk), the **Guildhall School of Music & Drama** (7628 2571, www.gsmd.ac.uk) and **Trinity College of Music** (8305 4444, www.tcm.ac.uk).

★ Barbican Centre
Silk Street, the City, EC2Y 8DS (7638 4141 information, 7638 8891 tickets, www.barbican.org.uk). Barbican tube or Moorgate tube/rail. **Box office** 10am-8pm Mon-Sat; 11am-8pm Sun. **Tickets** £7-£32. **Credit** AmEx, MC, V. **Map** p400 P5.
Europe's largest multi-arts centre is easier to navigate than ever after a renovation. And the programming remains rich: alongside the London Symphony Orchestra, guided by principal conductor Valery Gergiev, and the BBC Symphony Orchestra, under Jiří Belohlávek, the Great Performers series presents recitals from major musicians, and there's a laudable amount of contemporary classical music.

Cadogan Hall
5 Sloane Terrace, off Sloane Street, Chelsea, SW1X 9DQ (7730 4500, www.cadoganhall.com).

ARTS & ENTERTAINMENT

Festivals Classical

What not to miss this year.

The **BBC Proms** – officially, the BBC Sir Henry Wood Promenade Concerts (0845 401 5040, www.bbc.co.uk/proms) – overshadow all other classical music festivals in the city. Held between mid July and mid September at the Royal Albert Hall (*see below*), with a few supplementary events at other venues, the season includes around 70 concerts, covering everything from early music recitals to orchestral world premières. You can buy tickets in advance, but many prefer to queue on the day for £5 'promenade' tickets, which allow entry to the standing-room stalls or the gallery at the very top of the auditorium.

Held in June and July, the **City of London Festival** (0845 120 7502, www.colf.org) presents a wide array of concerts in a variety of genres, with an emphasis on classical music and jazz. Many concerts are held in unusual venues (historic churches, handsome courtyards, ancient livery companies); there's always a strong programme of free events. Close by, the **Spitalfields Music Summer Festival** (www.spitalfieldsmusic.org.uk) stages a series of concerts in June based at the local Christ Church, Shoreditch Church and Spitalfields Market.

The height of summer sees concerts held in the grounds of various palaces and stately homes: the **English Heritage Picnic Concerts** at Kenwood House (www.picnicconcerts.com; *see p155*) are excellent fun. Another brilliant annual alfresco event is **Opera Holland Park** (0300 999 1000, www.operahollandpark.com), which sees a canopied theatre host a season of opera, with only occasional contributions from the ornate park's resident peacocks.

Then, in winter, the **Greenwich International Early Music Festival** in mid November (www.earlymusicfestival.com) takes place in the lovely setting of the Old Royal Naval College (*see p172*). Not forgetting the **Spitalfields Music Winter Festival**, and starry choral **Christmas Festival** at St John's, Smith Square, both in December.

Sloane Square tube. **Box office** *Non-performance days* 10am-6pm Mon-Sat. *Performance days* 10am-8pm Mon-Sat; 3-8pm Sun. **Tickets** £10-£39. **Credit** MC, V. **Map** p398 G10.

Jazz groups and rock bands have been attracted by the acoustics in this renovated former Christian Science church. However, the programming at the austere yet comfortable 900-seat hall is dominated by classical music. The Royal Philharmonic Orchestra are resident; other orchestras also perform, and there's regular chamber music.

★ Kings Place

90 York Way, King's Cross, N1 9AG (0844 264 0321, www.kingsplace.co.uk). King's Cross tube/rail. **Box office** 10am-8pm Mon, Wed-Sat; 10am-6pm Tue; noon-7pm Sun (performance days only). **Tickets** £6.50-£34.50. **Credit** MC, V. **Map** p397 L2.

For review, *see p319* **Profile**.

LSO St Luke's

161 Old Street, the City, EC1V 9NG (7490 3939 information, 7638 8891 tickets, www.lso.co.uk/lsostlukes). Old Street tube/rail. **Box office** 10am-8pm Mon-Sat; 11am-8pm Sun. **Tickets** free-£32. **Credit** AmEx, MC, V. **Map** p400 P4.

This Grade I-listed church, built by Nicholas Hawksmoor in the 18th century, was beautifully converted into a performance and rehearsal space by the LSO several years ago. The orchestra occasionally welcomes the public for open rehearsals (book ahead); the more formal side of the programme takes in global sounds and some pop alongside classical music, including lunchtime concerts every Thursday that are broadcast on BBC Radio 3.

► *Hawksmoor also designed Christ Church Spitalfields; see p157.*

Royal Albert Hall

Kensington Gore, South Kensington, SW7 2AP (7589 3203 information, 7589 8212 tickets, www.royalalberthall.com). South Kensington tube or bus 9, 10, 52, 452. **Box office** 9am-9pm daily. **Tickets** £5-£275. **Credit** AmEx, MC, V. **Map** p395 D9.

In constant use since opening in 1871, the Royal Albert Hall continues to host a wide array of events. The classical side of the programming is dominated by the BBC Proms, which runs every night for two months in summer and sees a wide array of orchestras and other ensembles battling a far-from-ideal acoustic. Otherwise, rock and pop dominate.

St James's Piccadilly

197 Piccadilly, Piccadilly, W1J 9LL (7381 0441, www.st-james-piccadilly.org). Piccadilly Circus tube. **Box office** 10am-6pm Mon-Sat. **Tickets** free-£30. **No credit cards. Map** p416 V4.

ARTS & ENTERTAINMENT

INSIDE TRACK AVOID THE FEES

You can avoid the brutal booking fees levied by many major venues by buying your tickets in cash from two box offices. Tickets for shows at the **Borderline** (see p323), the **HMV Apollo** (see p320), the **HMV Forum** (see p321), the **Jazz Café** (see p324) and the **Relentless Garage** (see p324) cost face value if purchased with cash at the Jazz Café's box office (10.30am-5.30pm Mon-Sat). And tickets for the **O2 Academy Brixton** (see p321), the **O2 Academy Islington** (see p321) and the **O2 Shepherd's Bush Empire** (see p321) can be bought for face value at the O2 Academy Islington's box office (noon-4pm Mon-Sat).

This community-spirited Wren church holds free lunchtime recitals (Mon, Wed, Fri at 1.10pm) and offers regular evening concerts in a variety of fields.

St John's, Smith Square
Smith Square, Westminster, SW1P 3HA (7222 1061, www.sjss.org.uk). Westminster tube. **Box office** 10am-5pm Mon-Fri. **Tickets** £5-£50. **Credit** MC, V. **Map** p399 K10.
This curiously shaped 18th-century church – it is said the four-turret design was the result of Queen Anne's demand that architect Thomas Archer make it look like a footstool that she had kicked over – hosts concerts more or less nightly. Down in the crypt are two bars for interval drinks and the Smith Square Bar & Restaurant. A notable recurring event is the **Rosenblatt Recitals** series for opera singers.

St Martin-in-the-Fields
Trafalgar Square, Westminster, WC2N 4JJ (7766 1100, www.stmartin-in-the-fields.org). Charing Cross tube/rail. **Box office** In person 10am-5pm Mon, Tue; 10am-9pm Wed; 10am-8.30pm Thur-Sat. *By phone* 10am-5pm Mon-Sat. **Tickets** free-£28. **Credit** MC, V. **Map** p416 X4.
This church is one of the capital's most amiable and populist venues, hosting performances of the likes of Bach, Mozart and Vivaldi by candlelight, jazz in the crypt's café and lunchtime recitals (Mon, Wed, Fri) from young musicians. The interior has been beautifully restored.
▶ *For more on the church, see p135.*

★ Southbank Centre
Belvedere Road, South Bank, SE1 8XX (7960 4200 information, 0844 875 0073 tickets, www.southbankcentre.co.uk). Embankment tube or Waterloo tube/rail. **Box office** In person 10am-8pm daily. *By phone* 9am-8pm daily. **Tickets** £7-£75. **Credit** AmEx, MC, V. **Map** p399 M8.

A £90m renovation has improved the Royal Festival Hall, externally and acoustically. There are three main halls here: the Royal Festival Hall, which holds nearly 3,000 seats and counts the London Philharmonic, Philharmonia and the Orchestra of the Age of Enlightenment as residents; the Queen Elizabeth Hall, which has room for around 900 concertgoers; and the 365-capacity Purcell Room. Programming is rich in variety; the same is true of the foyer stage, which hosts hundreds of free concerts every year.

★ Wigmore Hall
36 Wigmore Street, Marylebone, W1U 2BP (7935 2141, www.wigmore-hall.org.uk). Bond Street tube. **Box office** In person 10am-8.30pm daily. *By phone* 10am-7pm daily. **Tickets** £10-£75. **Credit** AmEx, DC, MC, V. **Map** p396 G6.
Built in 1901 as the display hall for Bechstein Pianos, this world-renowned, 550-seat concert venue has perfect acoustics for the 400 concerts that take place each year. Music from the classical and romantic periods are mainstays, usually performed by major classical stars, but under artistic director John Gilhooly there has been a broadening in the remit: more baroque, a young composer-in-residence (Luke Bedford) and increased (mostly unamplified) jazz, including late-night gigs. Monday lunchtime recitals are broadcast live on BBC Radio 3.

OPERA VENUES

In addition to the two big venues below, look out for performances at the **Linbury Studio**, downstairs at the Royal Opera House, **Cadogan Hall** (see p316), summer's **Opera Holland Park** (see p317 **Festivals**), sporadic appearances by **English Touring Opera** (www.englishtouringopera.org.uk) and much promising work, often directed by big names, at the city's music schools. A small but lively fringe opera scene has sprung up in Islington with **OperaUpClose** branching out from its King's Head Theatre base on Upper Street, (www.kingsheadtheatre.com), to play up west at Soho Theatre; and the **Charles Court Opera** company doing fine operetta at its Rosemary Branch home on Shepperton Road, N1. (www.charlescourtopera.com).

English National Opera, Coliseum
St Martin's Lane, Covent Garden, WC2N 4ES (0871 911 0200 tickets, www.eno.org). Leicester Square tube or Charing Cross tube/rail. **Box office** In person 10am-6pm Mon-Sat. *By phone* 24hrs daily. **Tickets** £19-£99. **Credit** AmEx, MC, V. **Map** p416 X4.
Built as a music hall in 1904, the home of the English National Opera (ENO) is in fine condition following a renovation in 2004. And after a shaky period several years ago, ENO itself is in solid shape under the

Profile Kings Place

Hear all of London's musical enthusiasms in one place.

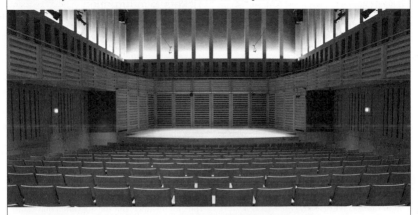

Scruffy and neglected, the streets around King's Cross Station have rarely had much to recommend them. However, the renovation of St Pancras Station has coincided with other new developments, of which the most impressive is tucked away up York Way.

Aware that office blocks are an 'unfriendly building type', property developer Peter Millican wanted **Kings Place** (for listings, *see p317*) to be different from the norm. The building, designed by Dixon Jones, is tidily integrated with the adjacent canal basin.

Above the airy lobby, the top seven floors of the building are given over to offices; the *Guardian* newspaper is the most high-profile resident. There's a gallery, a restaurant and a café on the ground floor. But the real appeal lies in the basement.

With just over 400 seats, the main hall is a subterranean beauty, dominated by wood carved from a single, 500-year-old oak tree and ringed by invisible rubber pads that kill unwanted noise which might interfere with the immaculate acoustic. There's also a versatile second hall and a number of smaller rooms, given over to workshops and lectures.

And the programming, overseen by Millican himself, is tremendous. It consists of long-weekend mini-series on diverse, classical-dominated themes. An innovation is the year-long sporadic concert series around a single composer (2012 sees Brahms Unwrapped). Other strands include chamber music on Sundays, and experimental music on Mondays, as well as the annual Kings Place Festival in September: 100 events in just four days. It's all part of an ethos that dares to be different.

**INSIDE TRACK
HACKNEY WEEKEND**

Leona Lewis and Plan B will perform, along with 80 other UK and international stars, before 100,000 spectators at BBC Radio 1's Hackney Weekend 2012. The festival will take place on Hackney Marshes and most of the tickets will go to residents of Hackney and the surrounding boroughs. Runs 23-24 June 2012.

---

youthful stewardship of music director Edward Gardner, with the last few years having offered some fascinating collaborations (such as with physical theatre troupe Complicité) and rare contemporary works (a flamboyant version of Ligeti's *Le Grand Macabre*). All works are in English, and prices are cheaper than at the Royal Opera.

★ **Royal Opera, Royal Opera House**
Covent Garden, WC2E 9DD (7304 4000, www.roh.org.uk). Covent Garden tube. **Box office** 10am-8pm Mon-Sat. **Tickets** £10-£210. **Credit** AmEx, MC, V. **Map** p416 Z3.
Thanks to a refurbishment at the start of the century, the Royal Opera House has once again taken its place among the ranks of the world's great opera houses. Critics sometimes suggest that the programming can be a little spotty, especially so given the famously elevated ticket prices, and not all of chief executive Tony Hall's attempts to win a new audience seem dignified (the recent *Anna Nicole* by Mark-Anthony Turnage for instance). But there are still many fine productions here, often taking place under the baton of Antonio Pappano. Productions take in favourite composers (Donizetti, Verdi) and some modern (Harrison Birtwistle, Thomas Adès).
▶ *It's not just music at the Opera House. The Royal Ballet is also based here. For more on the famous troupe, see p301.*

Rock, Pop & Roots

The longtime London cliché of indie bands playing in a sticky dive endures, but the capital's rock and pop scene is far from predictable. Close your eyes and stick a pin in *Time Out*'s weekly gig listings, and you might find yourself watching an American country star in a tiny basement, an African group under a railway arch or a torch singer in an ancient church.
Of late, big firms from outside the industry – record retailer HMV, phone company O2 – have been investing in many of the capital's large venues. The results of their involvement have been both welcome (improved sound systems, smarter decor) and undesirable (overpriced

bars, edgeless ambience). Regardless of who runs the venues, the range of acts playing in them is as good as it's ever been.

Tickets & information

Your first stop should be *Time Out* magazine, which lists hundreds of gigs every week. Most venues' websites detail future shows. Check ticket availability before setting out: venues large and small can sell out weeks in advance. The main exceptions are pub venues, which sell tickets only on the day. Prices vary wildly: you could pay £150 to see Madonna or see a superb singer-songwriter for free. Many venues offer tickets online via their websites, but beware: most online box offices are operated by ticket agencies, which add booking fees that can raise the ticket price by as much as 30 per cent. Try to pay cash in person if possible; for details of London's ticket agencies, *see p280*.
There's often a huge disparity between door times and stage times; the Jazz Café opens at 7pm, for instance, but the gigs often don't start until after 9pm. Some venues run club nights after the gigs, which means the show has to be wrapped up by 10.30pm; but at other venues, the main act won't even start until 11pm. If in doubt, call ahead.

MAJOR VENUES

In addition to the venues below, the **Barbican Centre** (*see p316*), the **Southbank Centre** (*see p318*) and the **Royal Albert Hall** (*see p317*) stage regular gigs.

HMV Forum
9-17 Highgate Road, Kentish Town, NW5 1JY (7428 4099 information, 0844 847 2405 tickets, http://venues.meanfiddler.com). Kentish Town tube/rail. **Box office** *In person* 4-8pm performance days. *By phone* 24hrs daily. **Tickets** £5-£30. **Credit** MC, V. **Map** p400 N2.
Built as a cinema in 1934, this somewhat cramped, 2,000-capacity art deco hall is now co-owned by HMV, part of the music retailer's attempt to shore up its business by diversifying into the increasingly lucrative live market. The high calibre of bands who play here (Public Enemy, Kasabian, White Lies) is a sign of its strong pulling power.
▶ *The time-honoured choice for a pre-gig pint is the nearby Bull & Gate, which also stages gigs.*

HMV Hammersmith Apollo
45 Queen Caroline Street, Hammersmith, W6 9QH (8563 3800 information, 0844 844 4748 tickets, http://venues.meanfiddler.com). Hammersmith tube. **Box office** *In person* 4-8pm performance days. *By phone* 24hrs daily. **Tickets** £10-£35. **Credit** MC, V.

This 1930s cinema doubles as a 3,600-capacity all-seater theatre (popular with big comedy acts and children's shows) and a 5,000-capacity standing-room-only gig space, hosting shows by major rock bands and others not quite ready for the O2.

IndigO2

For listings, see right **O2 Arena**.
The little brother of the vast O2 Arena (*see right*) is really only little in comparison with the huge expanses of its elder sibling; with a capacity of 2,350 (part-standing room, part-amphitheatre seating, sometimes part-table seating), IndigO2 is impressive in its own right. Its niche roster of MOR acts is dominated by soul, funk, pop-jazz and wearied old pop acts, though it also hosts after-show parties for those headlining at the O2.

★ Koko

1A Camden High Street, Camden, NW1 7JE (0870 432 5527 information, 0844 847 2258 tickets, www.koko.uk.com). Mornington Crescent tube. **Box office** *In person* noon-5pm Mon-Fri (performance days only). *By phone* 24hrs daily. **Tickets** £3-£25. **Credit** AmEx, MC, V. **Map** p404 Z3.
Avoid standing beneath the sound-muffling overhang downstairs and you may find that this former music hall, formerly the Camden Palace, is among London's finest venues. The 1,500-capacity hall stages weekend club nights and gigs by indie rockers, from the small and cultish to those on the up.

★ O2 Academy Brixton

211 Stockwell Road, Brixton, SW9 9SL (7771 3000 information, 0844 477 2000 tickets, www.o2academybrixton.co.uk). Brixton tube/rail. **Box office** *In person* 2hrs before doors on performance days. *By phone* 24hrs daily. **Tickets** £10-£40. **Credit** AmEx, MC, V.
Brixton is still the preferred venue for metal, indie and alt-rock bands looking to play their triumphant 'Look, ma, we've made it!' headline show. Built in the 1920s, this ex-cinema is the city's most atmospheric big venue. And with its sloping floor, everyone's guaranteed a decent view.

O2 Academy Islington

N1 Centre, 16 Parkfield Street, Islington, N1 0PS (7288 4400 information, 0844 477 2000 tickets, www.o2academyislington.co.uk). Angel tube. **Box**

INSIDE TRACK BOAT TO THE O2

You can get to the **O2 Arena** (*see above*) and **IndigO2** (*see above*) by tube, but it's more fun to take the 20min river ride on Thames Clipper (*see p366*) from London Bridge or Waterloo.

---

office *In person* noon-4pm Mon-Sat. *By phone* 24hrs daily. **Tickets** £10-£25. **Credit** AmEx, MC, V. **Map** p400 N2.
Located in the heart of a shopping mall, this 800-capacity room was never likely to be London's edgiest venue. Still, as a stepping stone between the pubs of Camden and the city's larger venues, it's a good place to catch fast-rising indie acts and re-formed '80s bands, not least because of the great sound system. The adjacent Bar Academy plays host to smaller bands.

★ O2 Arena

Millennium Way, North Greenwich, SE10 0BB (8463 2000 information, 0844 856 0202 tickets, www.theo2.co.uk). North Greenwich tube. **Box office** *In person* noon-7pm daily. *By phone* 24hrs daily. **Tickets** £10-£100. **Credit** AmEx, MC, V.
Since its launch in 2007, this conversion of the former Millennium Dome has been a huge success, taking over from Wembley Arena (*see p322*) and Earls Court as the arena venue of choice. With outstanding sound, unobstructed sightlines and the potential for artists to perform 'in the round', shows from even the world's biggest acts (Britney, Led Zep) don't feel very far away. IndigO2 (*see left*) is on the same site.
▶ *The O2 will be hosting London 2012 Games events as the North Greenwich Arena.*

O2 Shepherd's Bush Empire

Shepherd's Bush Green, Shepherd's Bush, W12 8TT (8354 3300 information, 0844 477 2000 tickets, www.o2shepherdsbushempire.co.uk). Shepherd's Bush Market tube or Shepherd's Bush tube/rail. **Box office** *In person* 4-8pm performance days. *By phone* 24hrs daily. **Tickets** £8-£40. **Credit** AmEx, MC, V.
Holding 2,000 standing or 1,300 seated, this former BBC theatre is a fine mid-sized venue. Sightlines are good, the sound is decent (with the exception of the alcove behind the stalls bar and the scarily vertiginous top floor) and the roster of shows is quite varied, with acts at the poppier end of the scale joined by everyone from folkies to grizzled '70s rockers.

★ Roundhouse

Chalk Farm Road, Camden, NW1 8EH (7424 9991 information, 0844 482 8008 tickets, www.roundhouse.org.uk). Chalk Farm tube. **Box office** *In person* 11am-6pm Mon-Sat. *By phone* 9am-7pm Mon-Fri; 9am-4pm Sat; 9.30am-4pm Sun. **Tickets** £5-£50. **Credit** MC, V. **Map** p404 W1.
The main auditorium's supporting pillars mean there are some poor sightlines, but this one-time railway turntable shed, used for hippie happenings in the 1960s before becoming a famous rock (and punk) venue in the '70s, has been a fine addition to London's music venues since its reopening in 2006. Expect a mix of arty rock gigs, dance performances, theatre and multimedia events.

Festivals Rock, Pop & Roots

What not to miss this year.

Both Camden and Shoreditch are home to a handful of rock and pop 'microfestivals', which are a cross between a pub crawl and a music festival. Buy a ticket (usually a coloured wristband) and you get access to a multitude of gigs in proximate venues over a couple of days. May's two-day **Camden Crawl** (www.thecamdencrawl.com) is the original, presenting a mix of hip indie acts. In May in Shoreditch, look out for the indie-friendly **Stag & Dagger** (www.staganddagger.com, late May).

As the weather improves, outdoor events take over for the summer. The Olympics are unofficially opened with the **River Of Music** festival (July 21 & 22), with artists from the five competing continents playing three stages at points along the Thames. As well as one-off mega gigs, Hyde Park hosts heritage-rock weekender **Hard Rock Calling** (www.hardrockcalling.co.uk) and the poppier, more contemporary **Wireless Festival** (www.wirelessfestival.co.uk) in late June. In June, Victoria Park is home to the leftfield **Field Day** (www.fielddayfestivals.com), the under-18s only **Underage Festival** (www.underagefestivals.com), family-friendly Apple Cart Festival (www.theapplecart festival.com) and Groove Armada's **Lovebox Weekender** (www.lovebox.net). And Clapham Common lords it over the August Bank Holiday with its **SW4** rave-up (www.southwestfour.com).

There's more mainstream fare for the **Radio One Hackney Weekend** (23 & 24 June), a six-stage showcase for international pop acts. If you're after something more salubrious, there's **Somerset House Summer Series**, during which Somerset House (*see p114*) welcomes an array of big and generally pretty mainstream acts for roughly ten days of open-air shows. And in summer, the Southbank Centre (*see p318*) invites a guest artist to curate **Meltdown**, a fortnight of gigs, films and other events. David Bowie, Ornette Coleman, Patti Smith and Richard Thompson are among the previous curators.

Other events are limited to a single genre. The best of them include the Southbank Centre's **London African Music Festival** (7328 9613, www.londonafricanmusic festival.com, Sept); **La Linea** (8693 1042, www.comono.co.uk, early Apr), a fortnight of contemporary Latin American music; and the terrific, ever-changing series of thematic folk and world events at the **Barbican** (*see p316*).

Scala

275 Pentonville Road, King's Cross, N1 9NL (7833 2022, www.scala-london.co.uk). King's Cross tube/rail. **Box office** 10am-6pm Mon-Fri. **Tickets** £8-£15. **Credit** MC, V. **Map** p397 L3.
Built as a cinema after World War I, the TARDIS-like, multi-floored Scala stages an agreeably broad range of indie, electronica, hip hop and folk, and is a frequent destination for one-off superparties. Its chilly air-con isn't rivalled anywhere in London – but the cheesy ballads of the Ultimate Power night are anything but cool. You can also check out rock, metal and punk at Freedom or the University of Dub.

Wembley Arena

Arena Square, Engineers Way, Wembley, HA9 0DH (8782 5566 information, 0844 815 0815 tickets, www.livenation.co.uk/wembley). Wembley Park tube. **Box office** *In person* 10.30am-4.30pm Mon-Fri; noon-4.30pm Sat (performance days only); 1hr before performance start Sun (performance days only). *By phone* 24hrs daily. **Tickets** £5-£100. **Credit** AmEx, MC, V.
Wembley Arena may have seen its commercial hey-day end with the arrival of the O2 (*see p321*). It's hardly anyone's favourite venue, not least because the food and drink could be cheaper and better, but most Londoners have warm memories of at least one Arena megagig, and a £30m refurbishment has improved this 12,500-capacity venue.
► *During the London 2012 Olympic Games, Wembley Arena will be hosting the Rhythmic Gymnastics and Badminton. See p62.*

CLUB & PUB VENUES

In addition to the venues listed below, a handful of London nightclubs also stage gigs. Try the **Notting Hill Arts Club** (*see p333*), **Madame JoJo's** (*see p331*), **Proud** (*see p332*) and the **ICA** (*see p141*).

Barfly

49 Chalk Farm Road, Chalk Farm, NW1 8AN (7688 8994 information, 0870 907 0999 tickets, www.barflyclub.com). Chalk Farm tube. **Open** 3pm-2am Mon, Thur; 3pm-1am Tue, Wed; 3pm-3am Fri, Sat; 3pm-midnight Sun. *Shows* from 7.30pm daily. **Admission** £5-£20. **Credit** MC, V. **Map** p404 X1.

Scala.

As other similarly sized venues open with smarter decor and less conventional booking policies, this 200-capacity venue's star was beginning to fade until the kicking London Sessions moved in. The venue is part of London's indie-rock fabric, a key player in the fusion of indie guitars and electro into an unholy, danceable row.

Bloomsbury Bowling Lanes

Basement, Tavistock Hotel, Bedford Way, Bloomsbury, WC1H 9EU (7183 1979, www.bloomsburybowling.com). Russell Square tube. **Open** 1pm-midnight Mon-Wed, Sun; 1pm-2am Thur; 1pm-3am Fri; noon-3am Sat. **Admission** varies. **Credit** AmEx, MC, V. **Map** p397 K4.

Offering a late-night drink away from Soho, BBL has been putting on live bands and DJs for a while now – and the range of activities make it like a playground for grown-ups. As well as the eight lanes for bowling, there's pool by the hour, table football, karaoke booths and, beside the entrance, a small cinema. Live music and club nights tend to be vintage: try 'We, Like You', 'Work it Versus Livin' Proof' and 1950s rock 'n' roll night 'Rock A Hula'.

★ Borderline

Orange Yard, off Manette Street, Soho, W1D 4JB (0844 847 2465, http://venues.meanfiddler.com). Totteham Court Road tube. **Open** hrs vary. **Admission** £3-£20. **Credit** AmEx, MC, V. **Map** p416 W2.

A small, sweaty dive bar-slash-juke joint right in the heart of Soho, the Borderline has long been a favoured stop-off for touring American bands of the country and blues varieties, though you'll also find a range of indie acts and singer-songwriters going through their repertoire here. Be warned, though, that it can get very, very cramped.

Blues Kitchen

111 Camden High Street, Camden, NW1 7JN (7387 5277, www.theblueskitchen.com). Camden Town or Mornington Crescent tube. **Open** noon-midnight Mon, Tue; noon-1am Wed; noon-2am Thur; noon-3am Fri; 11am-3am Sat; 11am-1am Sun. **Admission** free; £4 after 9pm Fri; £5 after 9pm Sat. **Map** p404 Y3.

The Blues Kitchen combines credible live music (roots blues, rockabilly and so on) with a rather high-end interior. The food is spicy New Orleans fare and there's a huge range of American bourbon for sippin'. All in all, it makes for a pleasant Sunday afternoon hangout as well as a late-opening gig venue.

★ Bush Hall

310 Uxbridge Road, Shepherd's Bush, W12 7LJ (8222 6955, www.bushhallmusic.co.uk). Shepherd's Bush Market tube. **Open** hrs vary. *Shows* from 7.30pm. **Tickets** £6-£20. **Credit** MC, V.

Over the years, this handsome room has been a dance hall, a soup kitchen and a snooker club. But now, with its original fittings intact, it plays host to big bands performing stripped-down shows, top folk outfits and rising indie rockers.

Corsica Studios

Elephant Road, Elephant & Castle, SE17 1LB (7703 4760, www.corsicastudios.com). Elephant & Castle tube/rail. **Open** hrs vary. **Tickets** £5-£15. **No credit cards. Map** p402 O10.

Corsica Studios is an independent, not-for-profit arts complex whose ethos is to breed creativity and culture. The flexible performance space is increasingly being used as one of London's most adventurous live music venues and clubs, supplementing bands with sundry poets, live painters and lunatic projectionists. Main nights here include Baba Yaga's Hut, which showcases a selection of both established and up-and-coming bands, and Trouble Vision, a mashing of different genres of dance music.

Green Note

106 Parkway, Camden, NW1 7AN (7485 9899, www.greennote.co.uk). Camden Town tube. **Open** 7-11pm Wed, Thur, Sun; 7pm-midnight Fri; 6.30pm-midnight Sat. *Shows* 9pm daily. **Tickets** £4-£15. **Credit** MC, V. **Map** p404 X3.

A stone's throw from Regent's Park, this cosy little venue and vegetarian café-bar was a welcome addi-

---

**INSIDE TRACK
LISZT FOR LUNCH**

London's classical music students provide many of the fine lunchtime recitals, held on weekdays at historic churches around the City. Admission is usually free or by small donation only; there's a monthly guide published online at **www.cityevents.co.uk**.

tion to the city's roots circuit back in 2005. Singer-songwriters, folkies and blues musicians make up the majority of the gig roster, with a handful of big names in among the listings.

Hoxton Square Bar & Kitchen

2-4 Hoxton Square, Shoreditch, N1 6NU (7613 0709, www.hoxtonsquarebar.com). Old Street tube/rail or Shoreditch High Street rail. **Open** 10.30am-midnight Mon; 10.30am-1am Tue-Thur; 10.30am-2am Fri, Sat; 10.30am-12.30am Sun. **Tickets** £5-£12. **Credit** AmEx, MC, V. **Map** p401 R3.

This 450-capacity venue is more than just a place to be seen: the venue's finger-on-the-pulse line-ups are always cutting edge and fun, with the venue often hosting a band's first London outing. Get there early or be prepared for a long queue.

★ 100 Club

100 Oxford Street, Soho, W1D 1LL (7636 0933, www.the100club.co.uk). Oxford Circus tube. **Open** Shows vary; check website for details. **Tickets** £6-£20. **Credit** MC, V. **Map** p416 V1.

Perhaps the most adaptable venue in London, this wide, famous, 350-capacity basement room has long provided a home for trad jazz, pub blues, northern soul and, famously, punk: the venue staged a historic show in 1976 that featured the Sex Pistols, the Clash and the Damned. These days, it offers jazz, indie acts and ageing rockers.

▶ *The 100 Club also hosts the monthly Limelight (http://londonlimelight.co.uk) – concert hall-quality classical music in a relaxed environment.*

Jazz Café

5 Parkway, Camden, NW1 7PG (7688 8899 information, 0844 847 2514 tickets, http://venues.meanfiddler.com). Camden Town tube. **Box office** *In person* 10.30am-5.30pm Mon-Sat. *By phone* 24hrs daily. **Tickets** £10-£30. **Credit** MC, V. **Map** p404 Y2.

While there is some jazz on the schedule, this two-floor club does tend to belie its name by dealing more in soul, R&B and hip hop these days. It's become the first port of call for soon-to-be-huge US acts: Mary J Blige, John Legend and the Roots all played their first European dates here.

★ Lexington

96-98 Pentonville Road, Islington, N1 9JB (7837 5371, www.thelexington.co.uk). Angel tube. **Open** noon-2am Mon-Thur, Sun; noon-4am Fri, Sat. **Tickets** free-£10. **Credit** AmEx, MC, V. **Map** p400 N2.

A lot of thought has gone into the Lexington. Downstairs, there's a lounge bar with a vast array of US beers and bourbons, above-par bar food and a Rough Trade music quiz (every Monday). And upstairs is a 200-capacity venue, with a superb sound system in place for the leftfield indie bands that dominate the programme.

★ Nest

36-44 Stoke Newington Road, Dalston, N16 7XJ (7354 9993, www.ilovethenest.com). Dalston Kingsland rail. **Open** hrs vary. **Tickets** free-£10. **Credit** AmEx, MC, V.

Formerly the site of the beloved Dalston hipster institution Bardens Boudoir, the Nest retains much of its predecessor's eclectic, forward-looking booking policy, with the benefit of a big money 'distressed industrial' refurbishment and, crucially, much improved toilets

93 Feet East

150 Brick Lane, Spitalfields, E1 6QL (7770 6006, www.93feeteast.co.uk). Aldgate East tube. **Open** 5-11pm Mon-Thur; 5pm-1am Fri; noon-1am Sat; noon-10.30pm Sun. *Shows* vary. **Admission** free-£10. **Credit** MC, V. **Map** p401 S5.

With three rooms, a balcony and a wrap-around courtyard that's great for barbecues, 93 Feet East manages by its breadth of programme to overcome its not very late licence. You can expect tech-house DJs, a mix of indie-dance bands and various art-rockers, plus short films and arty happenings.

Relentless Garage

20-22 Highbury Corner, Highbury, N5 1RD (7619 6720 information, 0844 847 1678 tickets, http://venues.meanfiddler.com). Highbury & Islington tube/rail. **Box office** *By phone* 24hrs daily. **Tickets** £3-£20. **Credit** AmEx, MC, V.

This 650-capacity alt-rock venue reopened in 2009 after three years of impressive refurbishment. It now books an exciting and surprisingly wide-ranging calendar of indie and art-rock gigs, from ancient punk survivors such as the Pop Group and Sham 69 to the poppier end of the indie singer-songwriter scale (Fran Healy in the smaller Upstairs, for example).

12 Bar Club

22-23 Denmark Place, Soho, WC2H 8NL (7240 2622, www.12barclub.com). Tottenham Court Road tube. **Open** *Café* 8am-7pm Mon-Sat; noon-7pm Sun. *Bar* 7pm-3am Mon-Sat; 7-12.30am Sun. *Shows* from 7.30pm; nights vary. **Admission** £3-£13. **Credit** MC, V. **Map** p416 X2.

A London treasure, this easy-to-miss hole-in-the-wall venue among the guitar shops of Denmark Street books a grab-bag of low-key stuff, though its tiny size (audience capacity of 100, minuscule stage) dictates a predominance of singer-songwriters.

Underworld

174 Camden High Street, Camden, NW1 0NE (7734 1932, www.theunderworldcamden.co.uk). Camden Town tube. **Box office** *In person* 11am-11pm Mon-Sat; noon-10.30pm Sun. *By phone* 24hrs daily. **Shows** hrs vary. **Admission** £5-£20. **No credit cards**. **Map** p404 Y2.

A dingy maze of pillars and bars below Camden, this subterranean oddity is an essential for metal and

ARTS & ENTERTAINMENT

Sounds and Pictures

Ten album covers that show various corners of the capital.

ABBEY ROAD
THE BEATLES (1969)
Abbey Road, NW8
You probably know this one already.

MEATY BEATY BIG AND BOUNCY
THE WHO (1971)
Railway Hotel, Railway Approach, HA3
The cover of this greatest-hits compilation shows seminal mod hangout the Railway Hotel in Harrow. It's now the site of four blocks of flats, each named after a member of the Who.

THE RISE AND FALL OF ZIGGY STARDUST AND THE SPIDERS FROM MARS
DAVID BOWIE (1972)
Heddon Street, W1
The red telephone box was returned to its original location in Heddon Street's recent makeover. The K West sign is long gone.

NEW BOOTS AND PANTIES!!
IAN DURY (1977)
Vauxhall Bridge Road, SW1
The title referred to the only clothes a thrifty Dury wouldn't buy from charity shops. The cover was shot outside a now-defunct clothing store called Axford's; the kid is Baxter Dury, Ian's son.

THIS IS THE MODERN WORLD
THE JAM (1977)
Under the Westway, W10
Behind Paul Weller, Rick Buckler and Bruce Foxton rise the towers of the Silchester West council estate, not far from Latimer Road tube station.

ANIMALS
PINK FLOYD (1977)
Battersea Power Station, east of Chelsea Bridge, SW8
During the photo shoot, the inflatable pig came loose from its moorings and disappeared into the London sky.

PARKLIFE
BLUR (1994)
Walthamstow Stadium, 300 Chingford Road, E4
A visual hymn to the East End. The album was launched at the stadium, with Blur sponsoring a race.

(WHAT'S THE STORY) MORNING GLORY
OASIS (1995)
Berwick Street, W1
The two men passing each other on this Soho street are believed to be Oasis art director Brian Cannon and DJ Sean Rowley.

ORIGINAL PIRATE MATERIAL
THE STREETS (2002)
Kestrel House, City Road, EC1
The photograph was taken in 1995 by German snapper Rut Blees Luxemburg, the same photographer who supplied the cover shot for Bloc Party's *A Weekend in the City*.

BURIAL
BURIAL (2006)
Wandsworth, SW18
William Bevan's dystopian dubstep is coloured by his life in south London. This shot looks down from the sky towards Wandsworth Prison.

INSIDE TRACK
RIVER OF MUSIC

River of Music is a massive celebration of the music of the world's continents. Stages will be set up in Battersea Park (Asia), Jubilee Gardens (Africa), Trafalgar Square and Somerset House (Europe), the Tower of London (the Americas) and Greenwich Old Royal Naval College (Oceania). Acts appearing include Scissor Sisters, Baaba Maal and Zakir Hussain. Runs 21-22 July 2012.

hardcore fans who want their ears bludgeoned by bands with names such as the Atomic Bitchwax, Skeletonwitch and Decrepit Birth.

Union Chapel
Compton Terrace, Islington, N1 2XD (7226 1686, www.unionchapel.org.uk). Highbury & Islington tube/rail. **Open** hrs vary. **Tickets** free-£40. **No credit cards.**
This Victorian Gothic church still holds services each Sunday, but it's also one of London's most atmospheric gig venues, booking acts such as Judie Tzuke, bits and bobs of contemporary classical or electronica, and classy intimate shows from bigger artists such as Paloma Faith. Look out for its many thematic series, as well as free Daylight gigs on Sundays.

★ Windmill
22 Blenheim Gardens, Brixton, SW2 5BZ (8671 0700, www.windmillbrixton.co.uk). Brixton tube/rail. **Open** *Shows* 8-11pm Mon-Thur; 8pm-1am Fri, Sat; 5-11pm Sun. **Admission** free-£10. **Credit** MC, V.
If you can live with the iffy sound and the amusingly taciturn barflies, you might think this pokey little L-shaped pub is one of the city's best venues. Mark it down to the adventurous bookings (punk, country, techno, folk, metal) and cheap admission.

Jazz

The international big hitters keep on visiting London, but these are exciting times, too, for the city's homespun jazz scene. Inspired by freewheeling attractions at the **Vortex** (*see p327*) and the sporadic, unhinged **Boat-Ting Club** nights (www.boat-ting.co.uk), acts such as Portico Quartet, Led Bib and Kit Downes Trio have won Mercury Prize nominations with recent albums, and the F-IRE and Loop Collectives are busy nurturing future stars.

In addition to the venues below, the **100 Club** (*see p324*) hosts trad groups, while the **Spice of Life** at Cambridge Circus (6 Moor Street, W1D 5NA, 7437 7013, www.spiceof lifesoho.com) has solid mainstream jazz. The **Jazz Café** (*see p324*) lives up to its name from time to time; there's a good deal of very good jazz at the excellent **Kings Place** (*see p317*); and both the **Barbican** (*see p316*) and the **Southbank Centre** (*see p318*) host dozens of big names. For the increasingly excellent **London Jazz Festival**, *see p327* **Festivals**.

Bull's Head
373 Lonsdale Road, Barnes, SW13 9PY (8876 5241, www.thebullshead.com). Barnes Bridge rail. **Open** noon-midnight daily. *Shows* 8.30pm Mon-Sat; 1-3.30pm, 8.30-11pm Sun. **Admission** £5-£12. **Credit** MC, V.
This venerable, ancient Thames-side pub won a reputation for hosting modern jazz in the 1960s but today specialises in mainstream British jazz and swing. Regular guests include ace veteran pianist Stan Tracey and sax maestro Peter King.

★ Café Oto
18-22 Ashwin Street, Dalston, E8 3DL (7923 1231, www.cafeoto.co.uk). Dalston Junction or Dalston Kingsland rail. **Open** 9.30am-1am Mon-Fri; 10.30am-midnight Sat, Sun. *Shows* from 8pm; days vary. **Admission** £3-£10. **No credit cards.**

Ronnie Scott's

Opened in 2008, this 150-capacity café and music venue can't easily be categorised, though its website offers the tidy definition that it specialises in 'creative new music that exists outside of the mainstream'. That means Japanese noise rockers ('Oto' is Japanese for 'sound'), electronica pioneers, improvising noiseniks and artists from the stranger ends of the rock, folk and classical spectrums.

★ Charlie Wright's International Bar
45 Pitfield Street, Hoxton, N1 6DA (7490 8345, www.charliewrights.com). Old Street tube/rail. **Open** noon-1am Mon-Wed; noon-4am Thur, Fri; 5pm-4am Sat; 5pm-2am Sun. *Shows* from 8.30pm daily. **Admission** free-£10. **Credit** MC, V. **Map** p401 Q3.

When Zhenya Strigalev and Patsy Craig began programming the line-up here in 2006, London's jazz fans were given a reason to visit what had previously been merely a rather good after-hours boozer. Now this agreeably scruffy venue stages a fine jazz programme on every night of the week except Saturday. Gigs don't usually start until 10pm, and run late on Thursdays and Fridays.

Forge & Caponata
3-7 Delancey Street, Camden, NW1 7NL (7383 7808, www.forgevenue.org). Camden Town or Mornington Crescent tube. **Open** hrs vary. **Admission** free-£15. **Credit** AmEx, MC, V. **Map** p404 Y3.

Run by a non-profit community organisation, this innovative music/restaurant space incorporates a stunning atrium, and hosts concerts of various sizes and formalities thanks to the flexible nature of its layout. The booking policy is skewed heavily to jazz, but the programme also features a carefully curated selection of roots and classical shows. There's a worthwhile on-site Italian restaurant, Caponata: you can dine while you listen at some performances, and there's an interesting Sunday brunch programme.

Pizza Express Jazz Club
10 Dean Street, Soho, W1D 3RW (0845 602 7017, www.pizzaexpresslive.com). Tottenham Court Road tube. **Shows** 8.30-10.30pm Mon-Thur; 9-11pm Fri, Sat; 8-10pm Sun. **Admission** £15-£25. **Credit** AmEx, DC, MC, V. **Map** p416 W2.

The upstairs restaurant (7437 9595) is jazz-free, but the 120-capacity basement is one of the best mainstream jazz venues in town. Singers such as Kurt Elling and Lea DeLaria join instrumentalists from home and abroad on the nightly bills.

★ Ronnie Scott's
47 Frith Street, Soho, W1D 4HT (7439 0747, www.ronniescotts.co.uk). Leicester Square or Tottenham Court Road tube. **Shows** 7.30pm-1am Mon-Sat; 6.30pm-late Sun. **Admission** (non-members) £20-£40. **Credit** AmEx, MC, V. **Map** p416 W2.

Opened (on a different site) by the British saxophonist Ronnie Scott in 1959, this jazz institution was completely refurbished in 2006. The capacity was expanded to 250, the food got better and the bookings became drearier. Happily, though, Ronnie's has got back on track, with jazz heavyweights dominating in place of the mainstream pop acts who held sway for a while. Perch by the rear bar or get table service at the crammed side-seating or more spacious (but noisier) central tables in front of the stage.

606 Club
90 Lots Road, Chelsea, SW10 0QD (7352 5953, www.606club.co.uk). Imperial Wharf rail or bus 11, 211. **Shows** 8.30pm Mon, Thur, Sun; 7.30pm Tue, Wed; 9.30pm Fri, Sat. **Admission** (non-members) £8-£12. **Credit** AmEx, MC, V.

Since 1976, Steve Rubie has run this spot, which relocated to this 150-capacity club in 1987. Alongside its Brit-dominated bills, expect informal jams featuring musos who've come from gigs elsewhere. There's no entrance fee as such; bands are funded from a music charge added to bills at the end of the night.

★ Vortex Jazz Club
Dalston Culture House, 11 Gillet Street, Dalston, N16 8JN (7254 4097, www.vortexjazz.co.uk). Dalston Kingsland rail. **Shows** 8.30pm daily. **Admission** free-£12. **Credit** MC, V.

Before Café Oto (*see p326*) joined the musical fray, the Vortex was the capital's centre for leftfield jazz, avant-garde and other marginalised talent, and it retains a fearsome reputation. Since relocating to Dalston in 2005, the venue has gone from strength to strength, hosting its own strand of the London Jazz Festival (*see below* **Festivals**) and various other forward-thinking events. The bar stays open late.

Festivals Jazz

What not to miss this year.

Showcasing London's thriving jazz scene while simultaneously welcoming an array of big names from abroad, November's excellent **London Jazz Festival** (7324 1880, www.londonjazzfestival.org.uk) covers most bases, from trad to free improv. It's comfortably the biggest jazz festival of the year, though you may also find some interesting events at the all-free, open-air **Ealing Jazz Festival** (8825 6064, www.ealing.gov.uk, July). For something edgier, look out for occasional showcases organised by the **Loop Collective** (www.loopcollective.org) and the **F-IRE Collective** (www.f-ire.com), which feature some of the best young talents in the country.

Nightlife

Travelling hopefully is the new necessity for the city's clubbers.

Years ago, many of London's most popular venues were large and centrally located. You could rely on them for a memorable, cutting-edge clubbing experience. But recent times have seen the closure of many of the capital's historic nightlife venues. The loss of Turnmills, the Cross and the End is already ancient history when measured in clubbing years, but the loss in spring 2010 of both Matter, which had been the newest beacon for the superclub-sized party crowd, and Shoreditch favourite T Bar began to feel a little apocalyptic.

Today, although London is still at the forefront of the world's forward-thinking nightlife and dance music, finding the best clubs requires a little effort. Not least because the merry-go-round of parties sees no need to stick to just one club. This lack of consistently excellent venues means that you can often stumble across the greatest nights bubbling out of pub-clubs such as the **Lock Tavern**, car parks and warehouse spaces such as **Corsica Studios**, polysexual bars such as the notorious **Dalston Superstore** (*see p313*) or makeshift clubs in the restaurant basements and former shops along Stoke Newington High Street.

SOUNDS OF THE CITY

What's hot? Big, beefy, speakerstack-destroying bass. Always. Dubstep is huge – and heavy – its reverberating beats sending dancefloors wild across the capital as it continues to morph through urban genres such as funky, future house, bassline, dancehall and 2step. The popularity of disco is tailing off, but you can still find its progeny at the latest wave of parties influenced by labels Wolf + Lamb, Crosstown Rebels, Hot Natured and their crisp, deep disco-tech sound, such as Kubicle (www.myspace.com/kubicle) and Krankbrother (www.krankbrother.com) and often in room three at Fabric on a Saturday night (*see p331*). Meanwhile, Berlin-influenced deep and glitchy sounds still work a treat at either seminal seasonal nights such as Secretsundaze (www.secretsundaze.net) and bank holiday mini-festivals such as Eastern Electrics (www.easternelectrics.com).

VENUES

Fabric remains the capital's best-loved club but Shoreditch is the hub of the capital's nightlife scene, especially around Brick Lane

(which offers plenty of late-night bars at the northern end of the strip) and across towards Hoxton Square. It is, however, becoming more and more commercialised (witness the trails of hen and office parties between Old Street and Spitalfields). Its latest live space and club **XOYO** is especially welcome.

The city's cool kids now take the bus north up the Kingsland Road from Shoreditch into Dalston and further on into Stoke Newington. The former has much-improved transport connections to the rest of the city since the London Overground arrived at Dalston Junction station, but it can be difficult to find the clubs – even more so what's happening in them. Spend a few moments browsing the Clubs section of *Time Out* magazine or www.timeout.com/clubs or hunting on Facebook and you'll unearth fabulous happenings at the likes of **Dalston Superstore** (*see p313*) and hipster-magnet Alibi (91 Kingsland High Street, E8 2PB, 7249 2733, www.thealibilondon.co.uk) next door.

With the demise of the End and the nearby Astoria, the appeal of clubbing in the West End has steeply declined; with the exception of **Madame JoJo's**, there's little here besides

All Dressed Up?

Here's where to go.

Bizarre Ball
Bizarre magazine (www.bizarremag.com)
stages twice-yearly balls celebrating the
zany, fetishistic and just plain weird. Wild
bands entertain the swathes of crazily
dressed people, interspersed by burlesque
and cabaret with a freakshow slant.

Blitz Party
Don 1940s thriftstore threads, period glam
or home-front uniform to swing at these
World War II-themed parties (www.theblitz
party.com). Expect big band tunes,
performers and DJs.

Candlelight Club
A dazzling, clandestine cocktail bar with a
1920s speakeasy flavour, lit by flickering
candles (www.thecandlelightclub.
com). There's live music, period
shellac spun by DJs, guest
cabaret acts and monthly
themes. Dress for the Jazz
Age: think flappers, good
grooming, LBDs and DJs.

Die Freche Muse
Promising decadent
cabaret in the grand
European tradition, host
Baron Von Sanderson invites
you to this soirée in a Dalston
venue (www.diefrechemuse.co.uk).
The dress code is 1920s to '40s,
jeans and trainers strictly verboten.

Gangbusters
Tim's Jumpin' Jive hosts this great club
at the Lexington on the first Sunday of the
month (www.hellzapoppin.co.uk). There's
a lindy hop dance class before DJs spin
1920s to 1950s swing, early jazz, jump
blues and more.

Last Tuesday Society
'The future belongs to the dandy,' say
these party organisers par excellence,
whose one-off soirées are masked,
decadent and not a little kinky
(www.thelasttuesdaysociety.org).

Magic Theatre
Forget a theme: you can dress up any
which way you want at Magic Theatre
(www.magic-theatre.co.uk) – so long as

you make an effort. The evening is based
around a live band, with blues and retro
dance DJs to follow. It's held at the Rivoli,
London's only intact '50s ballroom.

Prohibition
It's back to the 1920s for these Prohibition-
era themed parties (www.prohibition1920s.
com), boasting jazz bands, tap and
Charleston dancers, gambling tables and
silent movie screenings. The dress code
is stylish '20s (think flapper dresses,
feathered headbands, tuxedos, top hats
and spats), and the location secret.

Shore Leave
Sailor boys and girls wring the last drop
of rum from their remaining hours on dry
land at this itinerant evening
(www.shoreleave.co.uk).
There are bawdy bands and
burlesque, DJs spinning
sounds from far-flung ports
and a tattoo shack. Wear
vintage nautical attire.

Volupté's Vintage Ball
Every third Saturday
of the month at Volupté
(www.volupte-lounge.com),
'The Most Decadent Little
Supper Club in Town', the Black
Cotton Club (www.myspace.com/
blackcottonclub) hosts the Vintage
Ball. Book a table for the early evening
burlesque dinner show, or arrive from 9pm
for dancing until late. Dress for Prohibition.

White Blackbird
The country house party is alive and
highkicking at the White Blackbird
(www.thewhiteblackbird.com). It's held at
Stoke Place, a 17th-century mansion-turned-
hotel near Stoke Poges: stay overnight, or
join the coach party from central London.
Take your costume seriously, and dress to
theme; previous soirées include a 'Tainted
Love' Valentine's ball.

White Mischief
If White Mischief (www.whitemischief.info)
is behind it, you can count on a cabaret
extravaganza, with a Victorian/steampunk
ethos infusing everything from poster
design, decor and dress to theme.

Candlelight Club.

ARTS & ENTERTAINMENT

The Host with the Most

Welcome to the world of DIY music.

The wonderful world of the Dean Rodney Singers, resident at the Southbank Centre as part of the London 2012 Festival, is an interactive sound and visual experience created by singer and performance artist Dean Rodney. Dean has collaborated with 72 performers across the world in making 25 songs with video; the installation encourages the audience to create their own music, beats and video inspired by Dean's vision. If this sounds terribly high-flown, we should also say: it will be a LOT of fun. As the man says: 'People can find out how the project came together and then get the chance to take part themselves – remix a track, appear in a video – we just want everyone to come away having had a good time'. Anyone who's seen Dean sing will take that as a given.

Dean Rodney.

The event is produced by London-based Heart n Soul (www.heartnsoul.co.uk), a pioneering arts organisation with learning disability at its heart. As well as giving thousands of people the chance to participate in the arts and train and work as artists, Heart n Soul has revolutionised nightlife for disabled people, through its Beautiful Octopus Club, London's longest-running multimedia club night. This was the first inclusive cultural event to be run by artists with a learning disability and has helped to spawn 50 similar clubs around the UK and worldwide.

The Dean Rodney Experience runs from 1-9 September at the Southbank Centre (*see p318*) and is free to all. On 7 September, the Beautiful Octopus Club will also be in residence.

bars, pubs and a still bustling gay scene. To the north, up in King's Cross, **Egg** (200 York Way, N7 9AP, 7871 7111, www.egglondon.net) and the **Big Chill House** are all that remain of a former clubbing nexus lost to redevelopment. Though, the arrival of the **Star of Kings** pub-club (126 York Way, N1 0AX, 7278 9708, www.starofkings.co.uk) in December 2010, from the team behind the Star of Bethnal Green and underground club night Mulletover, and with its late licence and killer sound system, signifies that the area has still got hedonistic potential.

Further north, Camden is still very popular – especially with tourists. Indie student hangout **Proud**, teeny pub-rave spot the **Lock Tavern** and new bourbon-soaked gig haunt the **Blues Kitchen** (*see p323*) offer credible nights for London party people too.

There's more of interest to the south. The gay village in Vauxhall is just as welcoming to open-minded, straight-rolling types, with club promoters looking towards south-of-the-river venues such as **Area** (67 Albert Embankment, SE1 7TP, 3242 0040, www.areaclublondon.com) and **Hidden** (100 Tinworth Street, SE11 5EQ, 7820 6613, www.hiddenclub.co.uk) as occasional homes for their (largely drum 'n' bass and electronic) parties. The calendar is even fuller at **Cable** and **Corsica Studios**.

Across town, the cabaret juggernaut rolls on, smashing through into mainstream clubland. To see the best, head to **Volupté**, which hosts opulent burlesque nights; the always interesting **Bethnal Green Working Men's Club**; and the even more alternative **RVT** (*see p312*). Again, many of the best cabaret nights are one-off parties in a range of formal and informal venues – wherever you party, bring an open mind.

London rewards those who are willing to chance something new, but not all risks are worth taking. Before you head out, find which night bus gets you home and where you need to catch it (the tube doesn't start until around 7am on Sundays). If the bus network proves too mind-boggling at stupid o'clock, then check out our guide to catching a cab (*see p332 and p333* **Inside Track**). Always make sure that your cab is licensed; to find out how to tell, and for more on public transport, *see pp365-368*.

CENTRAL

Cable

33A Bermondsey Street, Borough, SE1 2EG (7403 7730, www.cable-london.com). London Bridge tube/rail. **Open** 10pm-6am Fri; 10pm Sat-1pm Sun. **Admission** £5-£15. **Credit** MC, V.

ARTS & ENTERTAINMENT

All old-style brickwork and industrial air-con ducts, this new spot has a similar feel to Fabric. The venue has two dance arenas, a bar with a spot-and-be-spotted mezzanine, plenty of seating and a great covered smoking area out the back. It has swiftly become a home for the capital's bass-hungry kids as nights with names like Ergh, DNB Noize and Licked Beatz take over the weekends and shake the speaker stacks.

Fabric
77A Charterhouse Street, Clerkenwell, EC1M 3HN (7336 8898, www.fabriclondon.com). Farringdon tube/rail. **Open** 10pm-6am Fri; 11pm-8am Sat; 11pm-6am Sun. **Admission** £8-£20. **Credit** AmEx, MC, V. **Map** p400 O5.
Fabric is the club that most party people come to see in London, with good reason. Located in a former meatpacking warehouse, it has a well-deserved reputation as the capital's biggest and best club. The line-ups are legendary. Fridays belong to the bass: guaranteed highlights include DJ Hype, who takes over all three rooms once a month for his drum 'n' bass and dubstep night Playaz, plus Andy C's Ram Records takeover and Caspa's Dub Police label nights. Saturdays descend into techy, minimal, deep house territory, with the world's most-famous DJs regularly making appearances. Be warned: the queues are also legendary. Blag on to the guestlist or buy tickets in advance to avoid a three-hour wait.

Madame JoJo's
8-10 Brewer Street, Soho, W1F 0SD (7734 3040, www.madamejojos.com). Leicester Square or Piccadilly Circus tube. **Open** 8pm-3am Tue-Thur, Sun; 6.30pm-3am Fri; 7pm-3am Sat. **Admission** £4-£10. **Credit** AmEx, MC, V. **Map** p416 W3.
The red and slightly shabby basement space at JoJo's is a beacon for those seeking to escape the West End's post-work chain pubs. The most treasured nights tend towards variety – Kitsch Cabaret is every Saturday night – but its long-running Tuesday nighter, White Heat, still books up-and-coming bands and DJs for a largely indie and student crowd.

The Social
5 Little Portland Street, Marylebone, W1W 7JD (7636 4992, www.thesocial.com). Oxford Circus tube. **Open** noon-midnight Mon-Wed; noon-1am Thur-Sat. **Admission** free-£10. **Credit** AmEx, MC, V. **Map** p416 U1.
A discreet, opaque front hides this daytime diner and DJ bar of supreme quality, set up by Heavenly Records. After drinks upstairs, its clientele of music industry workers, alt-rock nonebrities and other scenesters shamble down to an intimate basement space rocked by DJs six nights a week. The weekly Hip Hop Karaoke is always packed out.

Volupté
7-9 Norwich Street, Holborn, EC4A 1EJ (7831 1622, www.volupte-lounge.com). Chancery Lane tube. **Open** 5pm-1am Tue-Thur; 5pm-3am Fri; 1pm-3am Sat; 1-6pm Sun. **Admission** free-£30. **Credit** MC, V. **Map** p416 N5.
Expect to suffer wallpaper envy as you enter the ground-floor bar and then descend to the club. Punters enjoy some of the best cabaret talent and retro nights in town, from tables set beneath absinthe-inspired vines. It's daytime soirée, Afternoon Tease, coupled with scones and cream teas, is near-legendary.

NORTH LONDON

Better known as gig venues, **Koko** (*see p321*) and **Barfly** (*see p322*) have good reputations for feisty club nights, and the live music at the **Blues Kitchen** (*see p323*) can really rock.

Big Chill House
257-259 Pentonville Road, King's Cross, N1 9NL (7427 2540, www.bigchill.net). King's Cross tube/rail. **Open** 9am-midnight Mon-Wed; 9am-1am Thur; 9am-2am Fri; 11am-2am Sat; 11am-midnight Sun. **Admission** free. **Credit** MC, V. **Map** p397 M3.
A festival, a record label, a bar and now also a club venue, the Big Chill empire rolls on. A good thing too, if it keeps offering such interesting things as this three-floor space. The programme is constantly being reworked and its daytime barbecue bashes from the Heatwave, Five Easy Pieces and Reggae Roast make the most of its wonderful terrace in the warmer months.

Lock Tavern
35 Chalk Farm Road, Chalk Farm, NW1 8AJ (7482 7163, www.lock-tavern.co.uk). Chalk Farm tube. **Open** noon-midnight Mon-Thur; noon-1am Fri, Sat; noon-11pm Sun. **Admission** free. **Credit** AmEx, MC, V. **Map** p404 X1.
A favourite of artfully distressed rock urchins, it teems with aesthetic niceties inside (cosy black couches and warm wood panels downstairs; open-air terrace on the first floor), but it's the unpredictable after-party vibe that packs in the punters, with big-name DJs regularly providing the tunes.

Old Queen's Head
44 Essex Road, Islington, N1 8LN (7354 9993, www.www.theoldqueenshead.com). Angel tube. **Open** noon-midnight Mon-Wed, Sun; noon-1am Thur; noon-2am Fri, Sat. **Admission** £4 after 8pm Fri, Sat. **Credit** AmEx, MC, V. **Map** p400 O1.
Pulling in fun-seekers since its relaunch way back in 2006, the Old Queen's Head is another place with long queues at the weekends. There are two floors and outside seating front and back, and during the week you can lounge on the battered sofas. Weekends are for dancing, minor league celeb-spotting and chatting up the bar staff, or trying out the all-new private karaoke room.

ARTS & ENTERTAINMENT

Proud

*Horse Hospital, Stables Market, Camden, NW1
8AH (7482 3867, www.proudcamden.com). Chalk
Farm tube.* **Open** 11am-1.30am Mon-Wed; 11am-
2.30am Thur-Sat; 11am-12.30pm Sun. **Admission**
free-£10. **Credit** AmEx, MC, V. **Map** p404 W2.
The north London guitar-slingers have given way
to dubstep, rock 'n' rave and drum 'n' bass, but the
action at this former equine hospital is still rock 'n'
roll. Draping yourself – cocktail in hand – over the
luxurious textiles in the individual stable-style
booths (you must book in advance), sink into
deckchairs on the outdoor terrace, or spin around in
the main band room at its naughtily themed nights.

EAST LONDON

East London is now the heart of London's
clubland, with most venues of note based in
Hoxton, Shoreditch and Dalston. In addition to
the venues below, check out gay hangout the
Dalston Superstore (*see p313*).

Bethnal Green Working Men's Club

*42-44 Pollard Row, Bethnal Green, E2 6NB (7739
7170, www.workersplaytime.net). Bethnal Green
tube.* **Open** hrs vary; check website for details.
Admission free-£8. **Credit** AmEx, MC, V.
Sticky red carpet and broken lampshades perfectly
suit the programme of quirky lounge, retro rock 'n'
roll and fancy-dress burlesque parties here. You
might get to watch a spandex-lovin' dance duo or
get hip with burlesque starlets on a 1960s dancefloor.
The mood is friendly, the playlist upbeat and the air
full of artful, playful mischief.

Book Club

*100-106 Leonard Street, Shoreditch, EC2A
4RH (7684 8618, www.wearetbc.com). Old
Street tube/rail.* **Open** 8am-midnight Mon-Wed;
8am-2am Thur, Fri; 10am-2am Sat; noon-midnight
Sun. **Admission** free-£5. **Credit** AmEx, MC, V.
Map p401 Q4.
The Book Club aims to fuse lively creative events,
table tennis (there's a ping pong table upstairs and
regular tournaments) and late-night drinking seven
nights a week. Events range from Electro-Swing, the
night that started a huge trend in mashing up vintage
sounds with electro beats, to arty think-and-drink
workshops that give the nerds a good night out.

East Village

*89 Great Eastern Street, Shoreditch, EC2A
3HX (7739 5173, www.eastvillageclub.co.uk).
Old Street tube/rail.* **Open** times vary Thur-Sun;
check website for details. **Admission** free-£10.
Credit AmEx, MC, V. **Map** p401 Q4.
Stuart Patterson, one of the Faith crew who've been
behind all-day house-music parties across London
for more than a decade (they started in 1999), has
transformed what was once the Medicine Bar into

According to Dimi, a local cab driver,
'You'll always catch a cab where Bethnal
Green Road meets Shoreditch High Street,
by the members' club Shoreditch House.
You can also find cabs at the junction of
Hackney Road and Kingsland Road, next-
door to Browns.

this 'real house' bar-club that punches above its
weight. The top-notch DJs should suit any sophisticated clubber – it's had everyone from Juan Atkins
to David Rodigan on its basement decks in the past
year. Meanwhile, upstairs, the newly transformed
Villain Bar boasts more laid-back beats.

Nest

*36-44 Stoke Newington Road, Dalston, N16
7XJ (7354 9993, www.ilovethenest.com).
Dalston Junction rail.* **Open** 9pm-4am Fri,
Sat. **Admission** £5-£6. **Credit** MC, V.
RIP Bardens Boudoir. Long live the Nest! The
beloved red-and-orange chipboard den of affable
iniquity has – after a serious interior overhaul – been
replaced. The Nest now boasts an industrial chic
look and (mercifully) more salubrious toilets, but its
music programme mines the dancefloor-focused
disco, electro and house coalface.

Old Blue Last

*38 Great Eastern Street, Shoreditch, EC2A
3ES (7739 7033, www.theoldbluelast.com).
Liverpool Street or Old Street tube/rail.* **Open**
noon-midnight Mon-Wed; noon-12.30am Thur,
Sun; noon-1.30am Fri, Sat. **Admission** free-£10.
Credit AmEx, MC, V. **Map** p401 R4.
Klaxons, Arctic Monkeys and Lily Allen have all
played secret shows to the high-fashion rock 'n'
rollers in the sauna-like upper room at this two-floor
Victorian boozer. These days it's less shabby after a
refit, with a new and improved live space, and you're
more likely to find cutting-edge electronic and heavy
rock bands there than the pop pin-ups of tomorrow.

Plastic People

*147-149 Curtain Road, Shoreditch, EC2A 3QE
(7739 6471, www.plasticpeople.co.uk). Old Street
tube/rail.* **Open** 9.30pm-2am Thur; 10pm-4am Fri,
Sat; 11pm-4am 2nd Sun of mth. **Admission** free-£15.
Credit MC, V. **Map** p403 R4.
The long-established and ever-popular Plastic
People subscribes to the old-school line that all you
need for a kicking party is a dark basement and a
sound system. The programming remains true to
form: deep techno to house, all-girl DJ line-ups and
many a star DJ (Thom Yorke, anyone?) squeezing
through the doors for a secret gig.

Shacklewell Arms

71 Shacklewell Lane, Dalston, E8 2EB (7249 0810, www.shacklewellarms.com). Dalston Junction rail. **Open** 5pm-midnight Mon-Thur; 5pm-3am Fri; noon-3am Sat; noon-11pm Sun. **Admission** free-£6. **Credit** MC, V.

The latest contender on the Dalston club scene is a magnet for leftfield music. Live bands and DJs come from the electronic, lo-fi, chillwave and post-dubstep arenas, contrasting brilliantly with the shabby interior of this former Afro-Caribbean hotspot.

XOYO

32-37 Cowper Street, Shoreditch, EC2A 4AP (7729 5959, www.xoyo.co.uk). Old Street tube/ rail. **Open/admission** varies; check website for details. **Credit** AmEx, MC, V. **Map** p401 Q4.

A truly taste-making team is behind Shoreditch's latest club, XOYO. John 'Johnno' Burgess (who runs Bugged Out), acid house scene innovator Cymon Eckel, Marcus Weedon, the founder of Field Day, and Tom Baker, head of Eat Your Own Ears, clubbed together in 2010 to set up the 800-capacity venue. The Victorian loft-style space now provides the sort of effortlessly cool programming you might expect from a club with such credentials.

SOUTH LONDON

Corsica Studios

4-5 Elephant Road, Elephant & Castle, SE17 1LB (7703 4760, www.corsicastudios.com). Elephant & Castle tube/rail. **Open** 8pm-2am Mon-Thur; 10pm-6am Fri, Sat; 8pm-midnight Sun. **Admission** free-£15. **Credit** MC, V.

An independent warehouse-styled complex Corsica aims to breed creativity and culture in areas of regeneration. It's certainly rough around the edges with its makeshift bars and toilets but its club nights are second-to-none: flagship night Trouble Vision boasts the best of bass and, up until recently, a silent disco room, while cult online radio platform the Boiler Room hosts invite-only shows on Tuesdays.

Electric Brixton

Town Hall Parade, Brixton, SW2 1RJ (7274 2290, www.electricbrixton.com). Brixton tube/rail. **Open** times vary Thur-Sun; check website for details. **Admission** £10-£25. **Credit** MC, V.

The Fridge in Brixton was a rave paradise in the early '90s, a stomping ground for the rare groove scene, funky jazz-house and, later, hard dance and psy-trance beats. In 2011, however, it underwent a £1m refit, with new management, and was reborn as Electric Brixton, with mash-up night Get Loaded, from the Clapham festival of the same name, and dubstep/D&B heavy-hitter Spectrum on the books.

Ministry of Sound

103 Gaunt Street, off Newington Causeway, Elephant & Castle, SE1 6DP (7740 8600, www.ministryofsound.com). Elephant & Castle tube/rail. **Open** 10.30pm-6am Fri; 11pm-7am Sat. **Admission** £10-£20. **Credit** AmEx, MC, V. **Map** p402 O10.

Ministry of Sound was once the epitome of warehouse cool and is still possibly the UK's best-known clubbing venue. Laid out across four bars, five rooms and three dancefloors there's lots to explore. Long-running trance night the Gallery has made its home at Ministry of Sound on Fridays, while Saturday nights boast big-name DJ takeovers from the likes of Afrojack, Laidback Luke, Roger Sanchez and Erick Morillo.

Plan B

418 Brixton Road, Brixton, SW9 7AY (7733 0926, www.plan-brixton.co.uk). Brixton tube/rail. **Open** times vary Fri-Sun; check website for details. **Admission** £5-£12.50. **Credit** AmEx, MC, V.

It may be small, but Plan B is very cool. Having been refurbished after a fire, it reopened in late 2009 and the flow of great nights resumed, now with weekly block party Bump and irregular '90s R&B and hip hop night Supa Dupa Fly.

WEST LONDON

Notting Hill Arts Club

21 Notting Hill Gate, Notting Hill, W11 3JQ (7460 4459, www.nottinghillartsclub.com). Notting Hill Gate tube. **Open** hours vary, but around 7pm-2am Wed-Fri; 4pm-2am Sat; 6pm-1am Sun. **Admission** free-£8. **Credit** MC, V. **Map** p404 Y4.

Notting Hill Arts Club almost single-handedly keeps this side of town on the radar thanks to its mid-weekers YoYo! and Death2Disco, plus new nights such as heavy rocker Raw Power and future-thinking electronic bash Talking At Me.

Paradise

19 Kilburn Lane, Kensal Green, W10 4AE (8969 0098, www.theparadise.co.uk). Kensal Green tube or Kensal Rise rail. **Open** 4pm-midnight Mon-Wed; 4pm-1am Thur; 4pm-2am Fri; noon-2am Sat; noon-midnight Sun. **Admission** £4 after 9pm Fri, Sat. **Credit** MC, V.

This is a star among the legion of pub-clubs, thanks to its alternative programme of art auctions, burlesque life drawing and late-night club nights, making it more than just a good local spot.

INSIDE TRACK
GETTING HOME FROM BRIXTON

Getting back to your hotel in central London from Brixton isn't easy. 'It can be tough to get a cab here, so pick a night when there's a big gig on at the Brixton Academy (*see p321*),' says one driver.

ARTS & ENTERTAINMENT

Sport & Fitness

The run-up to the 2012 Games has sent the capital sport crazy.

Right now, you can't discuss London sport without discussing the London 2012 Olympic and Paralympic Games (*see pp41-74* **London 2012**). The venues are ready, the tickets allocated and the competitors trained to peak performance. The event has enthused grass-roots sport throughout the capital and country, and major legacy and volunteering initiatives have ensured that young people are engaged and inspired not just locally but worldwide. London sports fans are excited not only by the event itself but by the prospect of inheriting some world-class venues and facilities.

Most of the purpose-built venues, and the Olympic Park, will be open only to ticket-holders on the day of the event. (For ticketing details, *see p69*.) But you may be able to get a sneak preview at a test event (*see p335*). Otherwise, there are plenty of opportunities to get a feel for the Games: key venues outside the Olympic Park, including **Wimbledon** (*see p335*), **Lord's** (*see p337*) and **Wembley Stadium** (*see p336*), will be hosting regular sporting events in the run-up to London 2012.

Even setting the London 2012 Games aside, London has a busy sporting life, with week-in week-out matches featuring professional teams and a calendar dotted with major one-off events. It also offers the UK's best facilities for participating in sport and fitness activities.

Spectator Sports

THE SPORTING YEAR

Below is a list of major sporting events from spring 2012. For all events held in enclosed spaces (basically, everything except the Boat Race, the London Marathon and the cycling events), you'll have to book tickets in advance.

Spring

Rugby Union: Six Nations
Twickenham (see p338). **Date** 25 Feb, 17 Mar.
England take on Wales (25 Feb) and Ireland (17 Mar) at Twickenham in this tournament, which also features France, Scotland and Italy.

Football: Carling Cup Final
Wembley Stadium (see p336). **Date** 26 Feb.
The League Cup is less prestigious than the FA Cup, but the winners play in the UEFA Europa League.

★ **Rowing: The Boat Race**
River Thames. **Date** 7 Apr.
Blue-clad Oxbridge students race each other in a pair of rowing eights, watched by tens of millions worldwide and around 250,000 people on the riverbank. This is the 158th instalment of the historic race, which was first held in 1829.

★ **Athletics: Virgin London Marathon**
Around London. **Date** 22 Apr.
One of the world's elite long-distance races – and a huge participation event, with 35,000 starters. If you haven't applied to run, you're too late, but it costs nothing to watch the spectacle.

Summer

★ **Cricket: Internationals**
Kia Oval (see p336). **Dates** *Test* 19-23 July: Eng v South Africa. *One-day Internationals* 19 June: Eng v West Indies. 1 July: Eng v Australia. 31 Aug: Eng v South Africa. *Lord's (see p337).* **Date** *Tests* 17-21 May:

Rugby Union.

Eng v West Indies. 16-20 Aug: Eng v South Africa. *One-Day Internationals* 29 June: Eng v Australia. 2 Sept: Eng v South Africa.

England play a series of Test matches (the classic five-day format – most spectators only attend one day's play during the course of the match) and One-Day Internationals (50 overs per side.)

Football: 131st FA Cup Final
Wembley Stadium (see p336). **Date** 12 May.
The world's oldest domestic knockout tournament. In 2011, Manchester United beat Stoke City.

★ Horse Racing: Epsom Derby
Epsom Racecourse (see p338). **Date** 1-2 June.
The world's most famous flat race, run over one and a half miles.

Tennis: Aegon Championships
Palliser Road, West Kensington, W14 9EQ (7386 3400, www.queensclub.co.uk). Barons Court tube. **Date** 11-17 June.
The pros tend to treat this grass-court tournament as a summer warm-up to Wimbledon (*see below*).

Horse Racing: Royal Ascot
Ascot Racecourse (see p338). **Date** 19-23 June.
Major races include the Ascot Gold Cup on the Thursday, which is Ladies' Day. Expect sartorial extravagance and fancy hats.

★ Tennis: The Championships at Wimbledon
All England Lawn Tennis Club, Church Road, Wimbledon, SW19 5AE (8971 2700, www.wimbledon.org). Southfields tube. **Date** 25 June-8 July.
Getting into Wimbledon requires forethought. Seats on the show courts are distributed by a ballot, which closes the previous year; enthusiasts who queue on the day may gain entry to the outer courts. You can also turn up later in the day and pay reduced rates for seats vacated by spectators who've left early.

▶ *Wimbledon (see p62) will be hosting the tennis competition during the 2012 Games.*

Rowing: Henley Royal Regatta
Henley Reach, Henley-on-Thames, Oxon RG9 2LY (01491 572153, www.hrr.co.uk). Henley-on-Thames rail. **Date** 27 June-1 July.
First held in 1839, and under royal patronage since 1851, Henley is a posh, five-day affair .

Athletics: Aviva London Grand Prix
Crystal Palace National Sports Centre (see right). **Date** 13-14 July.
Big names gather in a last chance to impress before the Olympic Games.

Rugby Union: Heineken Cup Final 2012
Twickenham (see p338). **Date** 19 May.
The climax to the European Club season.

INSIDE TRACK
TEST EVENTS

The London Prepares series (www.londonprepares series.com) of test events gives the public a chance to see inside the Olympic Park well in advance of the Games. The hot tickets are for the showpiece venues: Track Cycling (17-19 Feb) in the gorgeous Velodrome; Diving (20-26 Feb) and Synchronised Swimming (18-22 Apr) under the swooping roof of Zaha Hadid's Aquatics Centre; and, in the Olympic Stadium itself, Athletics (4-7 May) and Paralympic Athletics (8 May). You can also watch Hockey (Riverbank Arena, 2-6 May) and Wheelchair Tennis (Eton Manor, 3-6 May). Tickets will be sold by Ticketmaster.

Rugby League: Carnegie Challenge Cup Final

Wembley Stadium (see right). **Date** late Aug.
Rugby league is mainly played in the north of the country, but for the Challenge Cup Final the north heads south, bringing boisterous, convivial crowds to Wembley Stadium.

Autumn

Cycling: Tour of Britain

Around London. **Date** mid Sept.
Join thousands on the streets for a stage of British cycling's biggest outdoor event. See the rising stars of arguably Britain's fastest growing sport.

American Football: NFL

Wembley Stadium (see right). **Date** Oct.
The NFL took a regular-season fixture out of North America for the first time in 2007, and plans to do so every year until 2012.

Winter

★ Darts: PDC World Championship

Alexandra Palace (www.pdcworldchampionship. co.uk). **Date** Dec-Jan.
The raucous, good-humoured PDC Championships are widely regarded as being of greater stature than the rival BDO tournament in January at Frimley Green (www.bdodarts.com).

Horse Racing: William Hill Winter Festival

Kempton Park (see p338). **Date** 26-27 Dec.
The King George VI three-mile chase on Boxing Day is the highlight of this festival, a Christmas staple for racing fans.

INSIDE TRACK FOOTBALL FUN

If you fail to get tickets to a Premiership game, you can still see the inside of a football stadium by going on a tour. However, you'll need to decide who to support: **Chelsea** (0871 984 1955, www.chelseafctours.com), **West Ham** (0871 222 2700, www.whufc.com), **Tottenham Hotspur** (0844 844 0102, www.tottenhamhotspur.com) and **Arsenal** (7619 5000, www.arsenal.com) all offer tours. But perhaps you'd do best instead to tour **Wembley Stadium** (0844 800 2755,www.wembleystadium.com/ Wembley-Tours; *see also p335*) – it's not only the home of English football, but the site for numerous games during the Football competition in the London 2012 Games (*see p62*).

MAJOR STADIUMS

The most important new stadiums in London are all rapidly nearing completion in the **Olympic Park** (*see p53*) near Stratford, in the east of the city. The 2012 Games will, however, also be making use of several pre-built venues across London (*see p57-62*). These include the **O2 Arena** (*see p321*), which hosts sporadic sporting events such as ice hockey and basketball each year; **Wembley Arena** (*see p322*), used for boxing, snooker, basketball and show jumping; and **Wembley Stadium**.

Crystal Palace National Sports Centre

Ledrington Road, Crystal Palace, SE19 2BB (8778 0131, www.gll.org). Crystal Palace rail.
This Grade II-listed building and leisure centre is the major athletics venue in the country (with the exception, for 2012, of the Olympic Stadium), and hosts popular summer Grand Prix events.

★ Wembley Stadium

Stadium Way, Wembley, Middx HA9 0WS (0844 980 8001, www.wembleystadium.com). Wembley Park tube or Wembley Stadium rail.
The new incarnation of Britain's most famous sports venue opened in 2007 after a famously expensive redevelopment. Designed by Lord Foster, the 90,000-capacity stadium is some sight, its futuristic steel arch now an imposing feature of the skyline (though less so from within). England football internationals and cup finals are played here, as are a number of one-off sporting events. Guided tours offer alternative access. A small aside: shame there's so little cycle parking.
▶ *Wembley Stadium will host the finals of the Football for London 2012; see p62. The original stadium also hosted the Opening Ceremony and many of the events in the 1948 Games.*

INDIVIDUAL SPORTS

Cricket

Typically, the English national team hosts Test and one-day series against two international sides each summer. (Test matches are the classic five-day format; one-day internationals last 50 overs a side.) For this summer's international fixtures, *see p334*. Seats are easier to come by for county games, both four-day and one-day matches. The season runs from April through to September. Surrey play at the Kia Oval and Middlesex at Lord's, which is hosting the Archery for London 2012; *see p61*.

Kia Oval *Kennington Oval, Kennington, SE11 5SS (0871 246 1100, www.kiaoval.com). Oval tube.* **Tickets** *International £53-£92. County £10-£20.*

Chelsea.

★ **Lord's** *St John's Wood Road, St John's Wood, NW8 8QN (7432 1000, www.lords.org). St John's Wood tube.* **Tickets** *International call for details. County £5-£15.*

Football

Playing in the lucrative Barclays Premier League, **Arsenal**, **Tottenham** and **Chelsea** are the city's major players. Arsenal, who play a slick-moving, quick-passing game but have won few trophies of late, are based in the 60,000-capacity Emirates Stadium. The team is under considerable pressure to deliver a trophy this year. **Chelsea**, with young Portuguese manager Andre Villas-Boas, are once again looking like title contenders. Their main London challenge will be from Tottenham Hotspur if they can produce a little more consistency. Other London-based Premier League sides are popular **Fulham** and the financially gifted **Queens Park Rangers**. For football stadium tours, *see left* **Inside Track**.

Tickets for Premier League games can be hard to obtain, but a visit to Fulham is a treat: a superb setting by the river, a historic ground, a life-size statue of Michael Jackson and seats in the 'neutral' section often available on the day. For clubs in the lower leagues (the Championship, Football Leagues 1 and 2), tickets are cheaper and easier to obtain. Prices given are for adult non-members.

The English national team plays its home fixtures at **Wembley Stadium** (*see p336*). Tickets can be hard to come by.

Arsenal *Emirates Stadium, Ashburton Grove, Highbury, N7 7AF (0844 277 3625, www.arsenal.com). Arsenal tube.* **Tickets** *£35-£100. Premier League.*

Brentford *Griffin Park, Braemar Road, Brentford, Middx TW8 0NT (0845 345 6442, www.brentfordfc.co.uk). Brentford rail.* **Tickets** *£20-£22. League 1.*

Charlton Athletic *The Valley, Floyd Road, Charlton, SE7 8BL (8333 4000, www.cafc.co.uk). Charlton rail.* **Tickets** *£18-£25. League 1.*

Chelsea *Stamford Bridge, Fulham Road, Chelsea, SW6 1HS (0871 984 1905, www.chelseafc.com). Fulham Broadway tube.* **Tickets** *£41-£87. Premier League.*

Crystal Palace *Selhurst Park, Whitehorse Lane, South Norwood, SE25 6PU (0871 200 0071, www.cpfc.co.uk). Norwood Junction or Selhurst rail or bus 468.* **Tickets** *£15-£30. Championship.*

Dagenham & Redbridge *Victoria Road, Dagenham, Essex RM10 7XL (8592 1549, www.daggers.co.uk). Dagenham East tube.* **Tickets** *£15-£22. League 2.*

Fulham *Craven Cottage, Stevenage Road, Fulham, SW6 6HH (0870 442 1234, www.fulhamfc.com). Putney Bridge tube.* **Tickets** *£20-£60. Premier League.*

Leyton Orient *Matchroom Stadium, Brisbane Road, Leyton, E10 5NF (8926 1111, www.leytonorient.com). Leyton tube.* **Tickets** *£21-£40. League 1.*

Millwall *The Den, Zampa Road, Bermondsey, SE16 3LN (7232 1222, www.millwallfc.co.uk). South Bermondsey rail.* **Tickets** *£24-£30. Championship.*

Queens Park Rangers *Loftus Road Stadium, South Africa Road, Shepherd's Bush, W12 7PA (0870 112 1967, www.qpr.co.uk). White City or Wood Lane tube.* **Tickets** *£45-£70. Premier League.*

Tottenham Hotspur *White Hart Lane Stadium, 748 High Road, Tottenham, N17 0AP (0844 844 0102, www.tottenhamhotspur.com). White Hart Lane rail.* **Tickets** *£31-£80. Premier League.*

West Ham United *Upton Park, Green Street, West Ham, E13 9AZ (0871 222 2700, www.whufc.com). Upton Park tube.* **Tickets** *£32-£47. Championship.*

Greyhound racing

In the continuining, much-lamented absence of Walthamstow Stadium, which was sold for development in 2008 (although campaigners are still working to save it for dog racing), **Wimbledon** (Plough Lane, 0870 840 8905, www.lovethedogs.co.uk) is the most central dog track, holding some of the year's most prestigious events. Further afield, head to buzzing **Romford** (London Road, 01708 762345, www.romfordgreyhoundstadium.co.uk) or **Crayford** (Stadium Way, 01322 557836, www.crayford.com). For more, visit www.thedogs.co.uk.

Horse racing

The racing year is roughly divided into the flat-racing season, from April to September, and the National Hunt season over jumps, from October to April. Racing is currently experiencing major changes in an effort to attract more followers. For more information about the 'sport of kings', visit www.britishhorseracing.com.

The Home Counties around London are liberally sprinkled with a fine variety of courses, each of which offers an enjoyable day out from the city. Impressive **Epsom** hosts the Derby in June, while **Royal Ascot** offers the famous Royal Meeting in June and the King George Day in July; book ahead for them all. **Sandown Park** hosts the Whitbread Gold Cup in April and the Coral Eclipse Stakes in July. There's also high-quality racing at popular **Kempton Park** and delightful **Windsor**.

Epsom *Epsom Downs, Epsom, Surrey KT18 5LQ (01372 726311 information, 0844 848 0195 tickets, www.epsomdowns.co.uk). Epsom Downs or Tattenham Corner rail.* **Admission** £15-£50.
Kempton Park *Staines Road East, Sunbury-on-Thames, Middx TW16 5AQ (01932 782292, www.kempton.co.uk). Kempton Park rail.* **Admission** from £15.
★ **Royal Ascot** *Ascot Racecourse, Ascot, Berks SL5 7JX (0870 727 1234, www.ascot.co.uk). Ascot rail.* **Admission** phone for details.
Sandown Park *Portsmouth Road, Esher, Surrey KT10 9AJ (01372 464348, www.sandown.co.uk). Esher rail.* **Admission** £18-£30.
Windsor *Maidenhead Road, Windsor, Berks SL4 5JJ (01753 498400, www.windsor-racecourse. co.uk). Windsor & Eton Riverside rail.* **Admission** £13-£23.

Motorsport

Every Sunday, bangers, hot rods and stock cars come together at **Wimbledon Stadium** (01252 322920, www.spedeworth.co.uk) for family-oriented mayhem. London's last Elite Speedway team are the **Lakeside Hammers** (www.lakesidehammers.co.uk) based at the Arena-Essex Raceway in Thurrock. **Rye House Stadium** (01992 440400) in Hoddesdon, on the northern edge of London, also hosts speedway, providing a home for the **Rye House Rockets** (www.ryehouserockets.co).

Rugby

For more than a century, there have been two rival rugby 'codes', each with their own rules and traditions: rugby union and rugby league.

Rugby union dominates in the south of England. The Guinness Premiership runs from early September to May; most games are played on Saturday and Sunday afternoons. Look out, too, for matches in the Heineken Cup, a pan-European competition. The local Premiership teams are listed below. Many more teams in the lower leagues are based close to central London; for a full list of clubs, contact the Rugby Football Union (0871 222 2120, www.rfu.com).

The English national team's home games in the Six Nations Championship (Jan-Mar; *see p334*) are held at **Twickenham** (Rugby Road, Twickenham, Middx 8892 2000, www.rfu.com), the home of English rugby union. Tickets are difficult to get hold of, but other matches are more accessible. There are also internationals in October and November.

Rugby league's heartland is in the north of England: London's sole Super League club is **Harlequins RL**. For 2012 they are being rebranded with a new name. In late summer, the sport moves south as Wembley hosts the Challenge Cup final; *see p336*.

Harlequins *Stoop Memorial Ground, Langhorn Drive, Twickenham, Middx TW2 7SX (8410 6000 information, 0871 527 1315 tickets, www. quins.co.uk). Twickenham rail.* **Tickets** £20-£42.
Harlequins Rugby League *Stoop Memorial Ground, Langhorn Drive, Twickenham, Middx TW2 7SX (8410 6000 information, 0871 527 1315 tickets, www.quinsrl.co.uk). Twickenham rail.* **Tickets** £15-£35.
London Irish *Madejski Stadium, Shooters Way, Reading, Berks RG2 0FL (0844 249 1871, www.london-irish.com). Reading rail then £2 shuttle bus.* **Tickets** £20-£40.
London Wasps *Adams Park, Hillbottom Road, High Wycombe, Bucks HP12 4HJ (0844 225 2990, www.wasps.co.uk). High Wycombe rail.* **Tickets** £15-£45.
Saracens *Vicarage Road Stadium, Watford, Herts WD18 0EP (01727 792800, www.saracens.com). Watford High Street rail.* **Tickets** £20-£65.

Tennis

For **Wimbledon**, *see p335*; for the **Aegon Championships**, *see p335*.

INSIDE TRACK ROLLER GIRLS

When it was founded in 1996, the London Roller Girls was Europe's first roller league. Six teams, with names like Ultraviolet Femmes and Suffra Jets, play in halls around the city. Don't let the fun names mislead you: this is a tough, fast and skilful sport, and great to watch. See www.londonrollergirls.com for details.

Participation & Fitness

CYCLING

Cycling in London is more popular than ever, especially with the introduction of the City Hall-sponsored bike rental scheme (*see p336*). Those in need of longer-term rental should try **Velorution**, which rents out folding bikes, with local delivery; and the South Bank-located **London Bicycle Tour Company**.

Sports riders currently have two options (pending the redevelopment of the Olympic Park's cycling venues into the much-anticipated Velopark). Track cyclists can try the outdoor track at the beautiful **Herne Hill Velodrome** (Burbage Road, Herne Hill, SE24 9HE, www.hernehillvelodrome. com), the world's oldest cycling circuit and the only single-sport venue to have survived from the 1948 Games. For road riders, there's the **Redbridge Cycle Centre** (Forest Road, Hainault, Essex IG6 3HP, 8500 9359, www.vision-rcl.org. uk), which has a road circuit, a mountain bike track and seven different circuit combinations.

Time Out's *Cycle London* book contains lots of advice and information plus 32 specially commissioned rides around town.

London Bicycle Tour Company *1A Gabriel's Wharf, 56 Upper Ground, South Bank, SE1 9PP (7928 6838, www.londonbicycle.com). Southwark tube.* **Open** 10am-6pm daily. **Hire** £3.50/hr; £20/1st day, then £5-£10/day. *Deposit* with credit card, or £180 cash. **Credit** AmEx, MC, V. **Map** p402 N7.

Velorution *93 Great Portland Street, Fitzrovia, W1W 7NX (7637 4004, www.velorution.biz). Oxford Circus tube.* **Open** 8.30am-6.45pm Mon-Fri; 10.30am-6.30pm Sat. **Hire** £20/day. **Credit** AmEx, MC, V. **Map** p396 J5.

GOLF

You don't have to be a member to play at public courses in the London area, but you will need to book. Courses are listed at www.englishgolfunion. org; two beauties are the lovely **Dulwich & Sydenham Hill Golf Club** in Dulwich (8693 8491, www.dulwichgolf.co.uk, £35-£45, members only Sat & Sun) and the testing **North Middlesex Golf Club** near Arnos Grove (8445 1604, www.northmiddlesexgc.co.uk, £18-£32, members only before 1pm Sat & Sun).

GYMS & SPORTS CENTRES

A lot of London hotels have gym facilities, some of very high quality. But if you're looking for something more serious than your hotel can offer, many health clubs and sports centres admit non-members and allow them to join classes. Some of the best are listed below; for a list of all venues in Westminster, call 7641 1846, or for Camden, call 7974 1542. Note that last entry is normally 45-60 minutes before the listed closing times. For more independent spirits, **Hyde Park/Kensington Gardens** (*see p149*) and **Battersea Park** (*see p176*) have good jogging trails.

Boom! Cycle

2 Scrutton Street, Shoreditch, EC2A 4RT (7426 0702, www.boommybody.com). Old Sreet tube/rail. **Open** 6.30am-9pm Mon-Fri; 9am-noon Sat. **Map** p401 Q4.

As one of the first purpose-built indoor cycling gyms to open in London, the loud music and flashing lights make this 2,500sq ft studio feel more like a nightclub than a gym. With workouts available for all skill levels, instructors aim to create a highly energised, fun and motivational class environment.

Frame

29 New Inn Yard, Shoreditch, EC2A 3EY (7033 1855, www.moveyourframe.com). Shoreditch High Street rail. **Open** 6.30am-10pm Mon-Fri; 9am-6.30pm Sat; 9.30am-6.30pm Sun. **Map** p401 R4.

This dance, fitness, yoga and Pilates studio has adopted the refreshing ethos that exercise doesn't have to be a chore. The 'Bend it like Barbie' and 'Jane Fonda Tribute' class are among the sessions on offer.

Jubilee Hall Leisure Centre

30 The Piazza, Covent Garden, WC2E 8BE (7836 4007, www.jubileehallclubs.co.uk). Covent Garden tube. **Open** 6.45am-10pm Mon-Fri; 9am-9pm Sat; 10am-5pm Sun. **Map** p416 Z3.

A reliable and very central venue that provides calm surroundings for workouts, Jubilee Hall also provides a selection of therapies and treatments. There are other centres in Southwark, Westminster and Hampstead.

Westway Sports Centre

1 Crowthorne Road, Ladbroke Grove, W10 6RP (8969 0992, www.westwaysportscentre.org). Ladbroke Grove or Latimer Road tube. **Open** 7am-10pm Mon-Fri; 8am-8pm Sat; 8am-10pm Sun.

A smart sports centre: all-weather pitches, tennis courts, a swim centre and gym, plus the largest indoor climbing facility in the country are on offer.

ICE SKATING

There's a permanent indoor rink in Bayswater: **Queens Ice & Bowl** (17 Queensway, Bayswater, W2 4QP, 7229 0172, www.queensiceandbowl.co.uk). But at Christmas, a variety of temporary rinks spring up all over town. **Somerset House** (*see p114*)

ARTS & ENTERTAINMENT

Ride the Rapids

Whitewater rapids in north London? Kathryn Miller braves the waves.

One of the most exciting legacies of the London 2012 Games will be the Lee Valley White Water Centre, venue for the Canoe Slalom. Costing £35 million to build, it was the first new Olympic Games venue to open to the public, in spring 2011. We were among the lucky few to raft down it (it's now closed to the public until after the Games).

The day before my visit, I spoke to GB slalom kayaker and 2012 hopeful Huw Swetnam. He helped to develop the Lee Valley course, and trains there every day. 'The centre's the best [artificial] whitewater facility in Britain and one of the best in the world,' he told me. 'It imitates some of the best natural whitewater rivers, such as the Etive in Scotland, the Grandtully course on the Tay, and the Tryweryn in Wales.' The course is particularly special because it can be altered to make it harder or easier.

Having been kitted out with wetsuits and given a safety briefing, I climbed on to the raft with three other guinea pigs and our instructor, Paskell Blackwell. Our first run was a straightforward top-to-bottom to make us feel at ease and get us used to the water. But for the second run, Paskell, who captains the GB rafting team, thought we needed to up the adrenaline and took us 'surfing'. We paddled towards the rapids, the boat span 360 degrees, and we all got drenched and shrieked a lot.

The Canoe Slalom course for the Games is 300m from start to finish, and has a 5.5m drop. Five powerful machines pump up to 15,000 litres of water per second, so there's plenty of white froth. The rapids are equivalent to a grade three or four river, but because the course isn't as long as a river, rafting sessions involve four or five runs that take about an hour and a half. A giant conveyer shuttles you and your craft back up to the starting pool. During these moments of calm, Paskell enthused about the opportunities the new facility will bring to the South-east. 'Slalom paddlers are traditionally from places like Scotland and Wales, where the best courses are. Now we've got this fantastic centre, it opens up the possibility of a watercourse champion from inner-city London.'

For the last run I sat in the 'party seat' on the floor at the front of the boat, facing backwards. I had nothing to hold on to, and as we zipped through the rapids I thought I'd be catapulted in. I managed to stay safely in the boat, but I did get thoroughly soaked, and had a lot of fun – without *quite* as much fear as on a natural river.

Lee Valley White Water Centre
Station Road Waltham Cross, Herts EN9 1AB (08456 770 606, www.leevalley park.org.uk/whitewaterrafting).

set the trend; it's since been followed by **Hampton Court Palace** (*see p180*), the **Tower of London** (*see p101*) and the **Natural History Museum** among others. Check *Time Out* magazine or www.timeout.com for a full list.

RIDING

There are various stables in and around the city; for a list, see www.bhs.org.uk. Those below run classes for all ages and abilities.

Hyde Park & Kensington Stables *63 Bathurst Mews, Paddington, W2 2SB (7723 2813, www.hydeparkstables.com). Lancaster Gate tube.* **Map** p393 D6.

Mudchute Equestrian Centre *Mudchute Park & Farm, Pier Street, Isle of Dogs, E14 3HP (7515 0749, www.mudchute.org). Crossharbour or Mudchute DLR.*

STREET SPORTS

Under the Westway in Acklam Road, W10, **Baysixty6 Skate Park** (www.baysixty6.com) has a large street course and four halfpipes, all wooden and covered. **Stockwell Skate Park** (Stockwell Park Road, SW9) is one of the city's most popular outdoor parks; it's rivalled by **Cantelowes Skatepark** (Cantelowes Gardens, Camden Road, Camden, NW1, www.cantelowesskatepark.co.uk) and **Mile End Skatepark** (corner of Burdett Road and St Pauls Way, E3), which opened in May 2009. Many skateboarders and BMXers prefer unofficial street spots such as the **South Bank** under the Royal Festival Hall. The unofficial centre of inline skating is Hyde Park, where you can find rides and lessons (see, for example, www.citiskate.co.uk). For rental nearby, try **London Skate Centre** (27 Leinster Terrace, W2, 7706 8769, www.lonskate.com).

SWIMMING

There are indoor pools scattered all over London. The **Oasis Sports Centre**'s indoor and outdoor pools are both worth a visit, but the historic **Marshall Street** baths, reopened in 2010, are certainly the best located and most beautiful – the impressively restored building dates back to 1931. To find your nearest pool, see www.activeplaces.co.uk. For pools suited to children, check www.swimming.org/britishswimming.

If alfresco swimming is more your thing, there are open-air lidos at **Parliament Hill Fields**, the **Serpentine**, **Tooting Bec**, **Brockwell Park** and **London Fields** (heated, and of Olympic proportions at 50m long). All are rammed in summer.

Marshall Street Leisure Centre *15 Marshall Street, Soho, W1F 7EL (7871 7222, www.gll.org). Oxford Circus or Piccadilly Circus tube.* **Open** 6.30am-10pm Mon-Fri; 8am-8pm Sat, Sun. **Map** p416 V2.

Oasis Sports Centre *32 Endell Street, Covent Garden, WC2H 9AG (7831 1804, www.gll.org). Holborn tube.* **Open** *Indoor and Outdoor* 6.30am-9.00pm Mon-Fri; 9.30am-5pm Sat, Sun. **Map** p416 Y2.

TENNIS

Many parks around the city have council-run courts that cost little or nothing to use; keener players should try the indoor and outdoor courts at the **Islington Tennis Centre**, though non-members may only book up to five days ahead. For grass courts, phone the Lawn Tennis Association's Information Department (8487 7000, www.lta.org.uk).

Islington Tennis Centre *Market Road, Islington, N7 9PL (7700 1370, www. aquaterra.org). Caledonian Road tube.* **Open** 7am-11pm Mon-Thur; 7am-10pm Fri; 8am-10pm Sat, Sun. **Court rental** £10-£24/hr.

TEN-PIN BOWLING

For a classier take on bowling, dine and drink cocktails while you strike at the branches of **All Star Lanes** (*see p244*).

Queens Ice & Bowl *17 Queensway, Bayswater, W2 4QP (7229 0172, www.queensiceandbowl. co.uk). Bayswater or Queensway tube.* **Open** 10am-11pm daily. **Bowling** £6.50/game. **Lanes** 12. **Map** p392 C7.

Rowans Bowl *10 Stroud Green Road, Finsbury Park, N4 2DF (8800 1950, www.rowans.co.uk). Finsbury Park tube/rail.* **Open** 10.30am-12.30am Mon-Thur, Sun; 10.30am-2.30am Fri, Sat. **Bowling** £3.70-£4.90. **Lanes** 24.

YOGA & PILATES

For something more than a quick stretch in your hotel room or the nearest park, check out the yoga activities and classes, and Pilates studio at Triyoga. You may also want to consult the **British Wheel of Yoga** (www.bwy.org.uk).

Triyoga *6 Erskine Road, Primrose Hill, NW3 3AJ (7483 3344, www.triyoga.co.uk). Chalk Farm tube.* **Open** 6am-9.30pm Mon-Fri; 8.00am-7.45pm Sat; 8.30am-9.00pm Sun. **Admission** £13-£15/session. **Other locations** Wallacespace, 2 Dryden Street, Covent Garden, WC2E 9NA (7483 3344); Kingly Court, Soho, W1B 5PW (use main number); 372 King's Road, Chelsea, SW3 5UZ (use main number).

ARTS & ENTERTAINMENT

Theatre

Even in the West End, variety is the spice of London theatrical life.

With the highest concentration of playhouses in the world, London's West End is a beacon for lovers of stage performance, drawing more theatregoers in an average year than Broadway. The biggest attractions remain the indomitable Shaftesbury Avenue musicals, some of which have been running for two decades. However, straight plays have been making something of a comeback; productions tend to be conservative but frequently attract the biggest names in showbiz from both sides of the Atlantic. And away from the commercial sector, political debate and formal innovation are mainstays at a handful of subsidised venues and a broad variety of fringe theatres, fed by the capital's multicultural influences and cross-pollination of its various arts scenes.

THEATRE IN LONDON

Escapism thrives when times are tough, so it's no surprise that the West End has retained its rosy glow into and through the recession. Broadway import *Wicked* scooped the 2010 Olivier for most popular musical. Yet the downturn also encouraged musical producers to stick safely to the Yellow Brick Road. Golden oldies such as *Crazy for You*, *Singin' in the Rain* and Andrew Lloyd Webber's rejigged *The Wizard of Oz* joined long-runners like **Billy Elliot** (*see p346*). And *Ghost the Musical* and *Shrek* proved that the film-to-stage vehicle is still trending in the West End.

INSIDE TRACK DIVA FEVER 1

The Barbican is pulling out all the stops for the Cultural Olympiad – and it's well worth checking out the entire programme (not least Toni Morrison's *The Desdemona Project* and Philip Glass and Robert Wilson's *Einstein on the Beach*). But *Gross und Klein* may be the hottest ticket of them all, as Sydney Theatre Company comes to town with artistic director Cate Blanchett in tow. She will star in a new translation of Botho Strauss's surreal 1978 drama about a pathologically awkward woman searching for a meaningful human connection. Runs 13-29 Apr.

Drama producers continue to rely on star casting as they fight to hold the line against the overwhelming tide of big-budget musicals and a general price hike that is over compensated by the burgeoning discount ticket market. The **Donmar Warehouse** (*see p349*) traditionally lures high-profile film stars to perform at its tiny Earlham Street home, while appearances by Kevin Spacey and his stellar chums at the **Old Vic** (*see p344*) have put bums on seats there.

Shows that start life at the **National Theatre** (*see p344*) regularly transfer to the West End, where James Corden vehicle *One Man Two Guvnors* joins Michael Morpurgo's unstoppable *War Horse* (*see p347*). On a smaller scale, Off-West End houses such as the Young Vic and the BAC continue to produce some of London's most exciting, best-value theatre. The Haymarket continues its unique practice of operating as a producing house: Trevor Nunn's season was remarkable for topnotch revivals of plays by Tom Stoppard and Terence Rattigan. The **Barbican Centre** (*see p343*), continues to programme visually exciting and physically expressive work from around the world.

For details of what's on when you're in town, see the Theatre section of the weekly *Time Out* magazine, which offers reviews and full listings information for all notable shows.

Theatre districts

In strictly geographical terms, the **West End** refers to London's traditional theatre district, a

National Theatre. *See p344.*

busy area bounded by Shaftesbury Avenue, Drury Lane, the Strand and the Haymarket. Most major musicals and big-money dramas run here, alongside transfers of successful smaller-scale shows. However, the 'West End' appellation is now also applied to other major theatres elsewhere in town, including subsidised venues such as the Barbican Centre (in the City), the National Theatre (on the South Bank) and the Old Vic (near Waterloo).

Off-West End denotes theatres with smaller budgets and smaller capacities. These venues, many of them sponsored or subsidised, push the creative envelope with new writing, often brought to life by the best young acting and directing talent. The Bush is good for up-and-coming writers, while the Almeida and Donmar Warehouse offer elegantly produced shows with the occasional big star.

One rung below these venues is the **Fringe** (*see p350* **Inside Track**), a disparate collection of small theatres within which quality and style vary wildly, but enthusiasm is a given.

Buying tickets

If there's a specific show you want to see, aim to book ahead. And, if possible, always try to do so at the theatre's box office, at which booking fees are generally smaller than they are with agents such as Ticketmaster (*see p280*). Shop around: different agencies offer different ticket prices and discounts.

If you're more flexible about your choice of show, consider buying from one of the **Tkts** booths or taking your chances with standby seats (for both, *see p344* **The Cheap Seats**).

THE WEST END
Major theatres

Barbican Centre
Silk Street, the City, EC2Y 8DS (7638 8891, www.barbican.org.uk). Barbican tube or Moorgate tube/rail. **Box office** *In person* 9am-9pm Mon-Sat; noon-9pm Sun. **Tickets** £7-£32. **Credit** AmEx, MC, V. **Map** p400 P5.
The annual BITE (Barbican International Theatre Events) season continues to cherry-pick exciting and

---

INSIDE TRACK DIVA FEVER 2

Also at the Barbican, French actress Juliette Binoche is set to star in *Mademoiselle Julie*, August Strindberg's scandalous 1888 classic. The production looks to inject a contemporary relevance into the Swedish dramatist's naturalistic play, relocating the action to the present day and tackling afresh issues of class, sex and social power. In an added twist, the play is to be performed in French with English surtitles. Runs 20-29 Sept.

---

eclectic theatre companies from around the globe. 2012 programme highlights include *Gross und Klein* in April, Martin Crimp's play starring Cate Blanchett. And new works by Complicite, Ninagawa Company and You Me Bum Bum Train are scheduled. Watch out, too, for imaginatively leftfield family-friendly theatre and installations during school holidays.

▶ *The Barbican is an all-round arts complex. For music there, see p316.*

★ National Theatre

South Bank, SE1 9PX (information 7452 3400, tickets 7452 3000, www.nationaltheatre.org.uk). Embankment or Southwark tube, or Waterloo tube/rail. **Box office** 9.30am-8pm Mon-Sat. **Tickets** *Olivier & Lyttelton* £12-£45. *Cottesloe* £12-£32. **Credit** AmEx, MC, V. **Map** p399 M8.
This concrete monster is the flagship venue of British theatre, and no theatrical tour of London is complete without a visit. Three auditoriums allow for different kinds of performance: in-the-round, promenade, even classic proscenium arch. Nicholas Hytner's artistic directorship, with landmark successes such as Alan Bennett's *The History Boys* and current cash cow *War Horse*, has shown that the state-subsidised

---

The Cheap Seats

Getting the most out of the box office.

At the two **Tkts** booths (Clocktower Building, Leicester Square, Soho, WC2H 7NA, www.officiallondon theatre.co.uk/tkts; or Brent Cross Shopping Centre in north-west London), anybody can buy tickets for big shows at much-reduced rates, either on the day or up to a week in advance. You can find the best seats for blockbusters sold at half-price. The Leicester Square branch opens at 10am (11am on Sundays); you can check which shows are available on any given day by checking the website. Before buying, be sure you're at the correct booth, in a stand-alone building on the south side of Leicester Square – the square is ringed with other ticket brokers, where the seats are worse and the prices are higher.

Many West End theatres also offer their own reduced-price tickets for shows that haven't sold out on the night; these are known as **'standby' seats**. Some standby deals are limited to those with student ID. The time these tickets goes on sale varies from theatre to theatre: check before setting out. And if you're buying online, shop around for discounts and watch out for very varied booking fees.

---

home of British theatre can turn out quality drama at a profit. The Travelex season ensures a widening audience by offering tickets for £12, £20 and £30, as does the free outdoor performing arts stage, Watch This Space, every summer. *Photo p343.*

★ Old Vic

The Cut, Waterloo, SE1 8NB (0844 871 7628, www.oldvictheatre.com). Southwark tube or Waterloo tube/rail. **Box office** *In person* 10am-7.30pm Mon-Sat. *By phone* 9am-10pm Mon-Sat; 10am-8pm Sun. **Tickets** £10-£49.50. **Credit** AmEx, MC, V. **Map** p402 N9.
The combination of Oscar-winner Kevin Spacey, who's been the artistic director here since 2003, and producer David Liddiment continues to be a commercial success; it's sometimes a critical hit as well, especially when Spacey himself or one of his stellar Hollywood chums takes to the stage. The Old Vic is a beautiful venue, where programming runs from grown-up Christmas pantomimes to the Bridge Project, a series of transatlantic collaborations on serious plays (the likes of Chekhov and, of course, Shakespeare) directed by Sam Mendes.
▶ *From early 2010, the theatre has been operating an informal space in the railway arches beneath Waterloo station. The Old Vic Tunnels has hosted everything from immersive theatre to an 'audio project' by genius graphic novelist Alan Moore.*

Open Air Theatre

Regent's Park, Inner Circle, Marylebone, NW1 4NR (0844 826 4242, www.openairtheatre.org). Baker Street tube. **Tickets** £22-£42.50. Special £20.12 pricing during the Olympics if booked before the end of April. **Credit** AmEx, MC, V. **Map** p396 G3.
The verdant setting of this alfresco theatre lends itself perfectly to summery Shakespeare romps. *A Midsummer Night's Dream* and the Tony-Award winning *Ragtime* will run from 18 May to 8 September in 2012. The standard is a world above village-green dramatics, with the family-friendly Shakespeares joined over the last few years by very popular musicals.
▶ *If you don't want to bring a picnic, good-value, tasty food can be bought at the Garden Café; or plump for traditional tea or Pimm's on the lawn.*

★ Royal Court Theatre

Sloane Square, Chelsea, SW1W 8AS (7565 5000, www.royalcourttheatre.com). Sloane Square tube. **Box office** 10am-6pm Mon-Sat. **Tickets** 10p-£28. **Credit** AmEx, MC, V. **Map** p398 G11.
From John Osborne's *Look Back in Anger*, staged in the theatre's opening year of 1956, to the numerous discoveries of the past decade, among them Sarah Kane, Joe Penhall and Conor McPherson, the emphasis at the Royal Court has always been on new voices in British theatre. Artistic director Dominic Cooke

The World's a Stage

An unprecedented international Bard-fest.

With companies from all over the globe performing plays in London and across the UK, the World Shakespeare Festival, which runs from the Bard's birthday on 23 April through to November 2012, is an extraordinary celebration of a single author.

The RSC is co-ordinating the festival and itself showing a cycle of Shakespeare's shipwreck plays (*The Tempest*, *The Comedy of Errors*, *Twelfth Night* and *Pericles*). Simon Russell Beale will play the title role in *Timon of Athens* at the National. The Iraqi Theatre company brings *Romeo and Juliet in Baghdad* to Lift at the Riverside in June, a music-filled exploration of love across the sectarian Sunni/Shia divide. (Lift also presents a very political Tunisian *Macbeth* in July.)

In May, world-class Japanese director Yukio Ninagawa puts on *Cymbeline* at the Barbican, where Nobel laureate Toni Morrison and Rokia Traore collaborate in *The Desdemona Project*, a new conversation between Othello's murdered wife and her African nurse, Barbary.

It's exciting stuff, but the crown of the festival is to be found at Shakespeare's Globe, where Globe to Globe, a multi-lingual marathon – without the safety net of subtitles – presents all 37 of the Bard's plays, each by a different international company and in a different language.

Most newsworthy is a submission from the world's newest country, South Sudan. *Cymbeline* was included after producers sent in an unsolicited 20-page pitch complete with a personal plea from the new presidential cultural adviser, who wrote about how he used to lie in the bush under the stars, contemplating Shakespeare's plays and trying not to think about the killing in the morning.

Conflict plays a very large part in the bill: the great Wars of the Roses plays, the *Henry VI* trilogy, will be performed in one day by the national theatres of Serbia, Albania and Macedonia. But Shakespeare's comedies have a track record of slipping a serious punch under the nose of the censor: an Afghan company who did a hugely daring *Love's Labour's Lost* in a bombed-out old garden in Kabul, where men and women acted together and held hands, will also perform.

ARTS & ENTERTAINMENT

Shakespeare's Globe. See p346.

Billy Elliot the Musical.

ARTS & ENTERTAINMENT

has injected plenty of politics into the programme, and successfully lowered the age of his audiences in the process. Expect to find rude, lyrical new work by first-time playwrights, as well as better established American and European writers with a message. Look out for quality shorts and more of the usual vividly produced British and international work by young writers.

Royal Shakespeare Company
Information 01789 403444, tickets 0844 800 1110, www.rsc.org.uk. **Box office** *By phone* 10am-6pm Mon-Sat. **Tickets** £5-£48. **Credit** AmEx, MC, V.
Britain's flagship company hasn't had a London base since it quit the Barbican (*see p343*) in 2002, although it is turning its mind towards finding one now of the £100m redevelopment of its home theatres in Stratford-upon-Avon has reached completion. In the meantime, it continues its itinerant existence, now usually appearing for three months from December in the Roundhouse (*see p321*), as well as popping up in smaller venues to stage the new plays that artistic director Michael Boyd has championed.

Shakespeare's Globe
21 New Globe Walk, Bankside, SE1 9DT (7401 9919, www.shakespeares-globe.org). Southwark tube or London Bridge tube/rail. **Box office** *In person* 10am-8pm Mon-Sat; 10am-7pm Sun. *By phone* 10am-5pm Mon-Sat; 10am-4pm Sun. **Tickets** £5-£35. **Credit** AmEx, MC, V. **Map** p402 O7.
Sam Wanamaker's dream to recreate the theatre where Shakespeare first staged many of his plays has become a successful reality, underpinned by

outreach work (you can drop in for regular free Q&As with cast and director). The open-air, standing-room Pit tickets are excellent value, if a little marred by low-flying aircraft. The venue's on great form under current boss Dominic Dromgoole, but comedy is what it usually does best. Expect a range of Shakespeare classics alongside new plays on parallel themes. *Photo p345.*

Long-runners & musicals

★ Billy Elliot the Musical
Victoria Palace Theatre, Victoria Street, Victoria, SW1E 5EA (0844 248 5000, www.billyelliotthemusical.com). Victoria tube/ rail. **Box office** 10am-8.30pm Mon-Sat. **Tickets** £19.50-£95. **Credit** AmEx, MC, V. **Map** p398 H10.
The combination of Elton John's music and a heart-melting yarn about a northern working-class lad with an unlikely talent for ballet has scooped more awards internationally than any other British musical and launched the careers of dozens of young Billies. It remains an uplifting, humane night at the theatre.

Ghost the Musical
Piccadilly Theatre, 4 Denman Street, Piccadilly, W1D 7DY (0844 871 7618, www.ghostthemusical.com). Piccadilly Circus tube. **Box office** *In person* 10am-10pm Mon-Sat. *By phone* 9am-10pm daily. **Tickets** £25-80. **Credit** AmEx, MC, V. **Map** p398 J7.
Packed with special effects and delirious hen weekend parties, *Ghost the Musical* is a gleaming piece of stagecraft whose slick, fabulous staging puts it light years ahead of many of its ageing competitors. It

doesn't have the same romantic appeal as the film: Dave Stewart and Glen Ballad's inserted power ballads are a great workout for the talented leads, but they benchpress your heart instead of caressing it.

Jersey Boys
Prince Edward Theatre, 28 Old Compton Street, Soho, W1D 4HS (0844 482 5151, www.jerseyboyslondon.com). Leicester Square tube. **Box office** *In person* 10am-7.45pm Tue-Sun. *By phone* 24hrs daily. **Tickets** £20-£95. **Credit** AmEx, MC, V. **Map** p416 W2.
This Broadway import had the critics singing the praises of Ryan Molloy, who hits the high notes in Frankie Valli & the Four Seasons' doo-wop standards. The well-trodden storyline of early struggle, success and break-up is elevated by pacy direction.

★ Legally Blonde
Savoy Theatre, the Strand, WC2R 0ET (0844 847 2345, www.legallyblondethemusical.co.uk). Covent Garden tube or Charing Cross tube/rail. **Box office** 10am-7.30pm Mon-Sat. *By phone* 24hrs daily. **Tickets** £29-£66.50. **Credit** AmEx, MC, V. **Map** p416 Z4.
A pepped-up, candy-coloured hymn to sisterhood, in which Malibu Barbie Elle Woods takes on the overprivileged preppies at Harvard and wins. Laurence O'Keefe and Nell Benjamin's music and lyrics give the movie an irresistible makeover: highlights are super-smart rhyming dialogues that actually propel the plot, rhythmic, catchy tunelets and a strong British cast.

Les Misérables
Queen's Theatre, 51 Shaftesbury Avenue, Soho, W1D 6BA (0844 482 5160, www.lesmis.com). Leicester Square or Piccadilly Circus tube. **Box office** *In person* 9am-8pm Mon-Sat. *By phone* 10am-8pm Mon-Sat. **Tickets** £20-£85. **Credit** AmEx, MC, V. **Map** p416 W3.

The RSC's version of Boublil and Schönberg's musical came to the London stage in 1985 – and no fewer than three celebratory versions ran simultaneously on one October night in 2010. The version at the Queen's should manage a few more anniversaries, which has good and bad consequences. When actors have been singing these songs since their first audition, it's easy to take it that half-inch too far. Still, the voices remain lush, the revolutionary sets are film-fabulous, and the lyrics and score (based on Victor Hugo's novel) will be considerably less trivial than whatever's on next door.

★ Matilda the Musical
Cambridge Theatre, 32-34 Earlham Street, Covent Garden, WC2H 9HU (0844 800 1110, www.matildathemusical.com). Covent Garden tube or Charing Cross tube/rail. **Box office** *In person* 10am-8pm daily. *By phone* 10am-6pm Mon-Sat. **Tickets** £20-£59.50. **Credit** AmEx, MC, V. **Map** p397 L6.
Adapted from Roald Dahl's riotous children's novel, with songs by superstar Aussie comedian Tim Minchin, this RSC transfer received rapturous reviews on its first outing in Stratford-upon-Avon and has been hailed already as the new *Billy Elliot*.

Mousetrap
St Martin's Theatre, West Street, Cambridge Circus, Covent Garden, WC2H 9NZ (0844 499 1515, www.the-mousetrap.co.uk). Leicester Square tube. **Box office** 10am-8pm Mon-Sat. **Tickets** £16-£60. **Credit** AmEx, MC, V. **Map** p416 X3.
Running in the West End since 1952, Agatha Christie's drawing-room whodunnit is a murder mystery Methuselah, and will probably still be booking when the last trump sounds.

War Horse
New London Theatre, Drury Lane, Covent Garden, WC2B 5PW (0844 412 4654,

ARTS & ENTERTAINMENT

Matilda the Musical.

Reach For the Sky

Mass participation theatre comes to London.

It's a towering ambition. London's leading independent theatres have announced an unprecedented 2012 collaboration: a three-week festival of theatre, produced with international companies from all over the globe, whose centrepiece will be a huge-scale spectacular show with the working title *Babel*.

Battersea Arts Centre, the Royal Court, Sadler's Wells, Somerset House, the Lyric Hammersmith, Theatre Royal Stratford East and the Young Vic will jointly host World Stages London, to run from 7 May 2012. Headline show *Babel* will be a site-specific promenade for more than 1,000 people per night and is likely to be housed in that underused London icon, Battersea Power Station.

This epic show is inspired by the Old Testament story in which humankind unite to build a tower that would reach heaven. (Their efforts were crushed, so the Bible says, by God, who smote the

tower and created the first language barriers to prevent future international collaborations.)

More than 300 of the world's languages – which were supposedly invented that day – are spoken on the streets of the capital. It is hoped that many of those voices and those experiences will be translated into the multi-layered project. *Babel* will begin locally, with participating theatres curating and building community art towers in east, west, south and central London. The second phase will gather these contributions after the festivals of Diwali and Christmas. The final show will draw on the stories of Londoners, many of whom have roots across the globe. And its creators will recruit a supporting cast of more than 1,000.

The producers are confident that they will be able to sculpt epic theatre out of local experiences.

www.nationaltheatre.org.uk/warhorse). Covent Garden tube. **Box office** *In person* 10am-8pm Mon-Sat. *By phone* 24hrs daily. **Tickets** £15-£55. **Credit** AmEx, MC, V. **Map** p416 Z2.
Transferred from the National Theatre (*see p344*), *War Horse* is an incredibly moving piece of theatre (and a massive critical and popular hit). The play is based on Michael Morpurgo's children's novel about a horse separated from his young master and spirited off to World War I. Bereft Albert duly signs up, to seek Joey in the mud and carnage of Flanders. The real stars are the extraordinary puppet horses. Each visibly manipulated by three actors, who make them gallop, pant and emote as clearly as any human actor, these plywood and leather frames become astonishingly expressive beasts.

OFF-WEST END THEATRES

Almeida
Almeida Street, Islington, N1 1TA (7359 4404, www.almeida.co.uk). Angel tube. **Box office** *In person* 10am-6pm Mon-Sat. *By phone* 10am-7.30pm Mon-Sat. **Tickets** £8-£32. **Credit** AmEx, MC, V. **Map** p400 O1.
Well groomed and with a rather funky bar, the Almeida turns out thoughtfully crafted theatre for grown-ups. Under artistic director Michael Attenborough it has drawn top directors such as Thea Sharrock and Rupert Goold, and premières from Neil LaBute.

★ Battersea Arts Centre (BAC)
Lavender Hill, Battersea, SW11 5TN (7223 2223, www.bac.org.uk). Clapham Common tube, Clapham Junction rail or bus 77, 77A, 345. **Box office** 10am-6pm Mon-Fri; 3-6pm Sat. **Tickets** £3-£10; pay what you can Thur-Sat (phone ahead). **Credit** MC, V.
Housed in the old Battersea Town Hall, the forward-thinking BAC hosts young theatre troupes; expect quirky, fun and physical theatre from the likes of cult companies Kneehigh and 1927. You can drop in Thursday-Saturday for a drink and a glimpse of one of the theatre's pioneering scratch performances – a chance to see a work-in-progress then tell its creators what you thought of it in the bar.

★ Bush
Shepherd's Bush Green, 7 Uxbridge Road, Shepherd's Bush, W12 8LJ (8743 5050, www.bushtheatre.co.uk). Shepherd's Bush Market tube. **Box office** *In person & by phone* noon-7.30pm Mon-Sat (performance days); noon-6pm Mon-Fri (non-performance days). **Tickets** £7-£20. **Credit** AmEx, MC, V.
This diminutive venue punches well above its weight, with well-judged productions and an impressive record of West End transfers. It's famous for its new writers; among the alumni are Stephen Poliakoff and David Edgar.

Festivals Theatre
What not to miss this year.

The **World Shakespeare Festival** is undoubtedly the year's must-see theatre festival (*see p345* **The World's a Stage**). Apart from the Bardic behemoth, the **Greenwich+Docklands International Festival** (www.festival.org) combines acrobatics, dance and theatre, with aerial performances and fireworks over the Queen's House and in Woolwich. Expect equally eye-catching stunts at this year's free street art and outdoor theatre spectacular, held over ten days from late June. At around the same time of year, **LIFT** (the **London International Festival of Theatre**; www.liftfest.org.uk) gathers an extraordinary number of performances (last year, nearly 90 in under a month) under the directorship of Mark Ball.

In July and August, the National Theatre (*see p344*) rolls out a large square of astroturf by the river for **Watch This Space** (www.nationaltheatre.org.uk), a programme of alfresco theatre, dance and circus. Also during the month of August, an eclectic bunch of new, experimental and short shows sprint through the **Camden Fringe** (www.camdenfringe.org). Finally, more outré and challenging work can be seen at January's **London International Mime Festival** (www.mimefest.co.uk), from haunting visual theatre to puppetry for adults.

★ Donmar Warehouse
41 Earlham Street, Covent Garden, WC2H 9LX (0844 871 7624, www.donmarwarehouse.com). Covent Garden or Leicester Square tube. **Box office** *In person* 10am-6pm Mon-Sat. *By phone* 9am-10pm Mon-Sat; 10am-8pm Sun. **Tickets** £12-£30. **Credit** AmEx, MC, V. **Map** p416 Y2.
The Donmar is less a warehouse than a boutique chamber. Multi-award-winning artistic director Michael Grandage kept the venue on the fresh, intelligent path established by Sam Mendes, and his successor, Josie Rourke, promises to do the same. The Donmar's combination of artistic integrity and intimate size, with audience right alongside the stage, has proved hard to resist, with many high-profile film actors appearing: among them Nicole Kidman, Gwyneth Paltrow and Ewan McGregor.

Gate Theatre
Prince Albert, 11 Pembridge Road, Notting Hill, W11 3HQ (7229 0706, www.gatetheatre.co.uk). Notting Hill Gate tube. **Box office** *By phone*

10am-6pm Mon-Fri. **Tickets** £20; £15 reductions. **Credit** MC, V. **Map** p404 Z6.

A doll's house of a theatre, with rickety wooden chairs as seats, the Gate is the only producing theatre in London dedicated to international work.

★ Lyric Hammersmith

Lyric Square, King Street, Hammersmith, W6 0QL (0871 221 1722, www.lyric.co.uk). Hammersmith tube. **Box office** *By phone* 10am-5.30pm Mon-Sat. *In person* 9.30am-7.30pm on performance days. **Tickets** £12.50-£35. **Credit** MC, V.

Artistic director Sean Holmes launched his tenure in 2009 with a pledge to bring writers back into the building, making space for neglected modern classics and new plays alongside the cutting-edge physical and devised work for which the Lyric is known.

Soho Theatre

21 Dean Street, Soho, W1D 3NE (7478 0100, www.sohotheatre.com). Tottenham Court Road tube. **Box office** *In person* 10am-6pm Mon-Sat; 10am-7.30pm performance nights. *By phone* 10am-7pm Mon-Sat. **Tickets** £5-£20. **Credit** MC, V. **Map** p395 K6.

Its cool blue neon lights and front-of-house café help it blend into the Soho landscape, but this theatre has made a name for itself since opening in 2000. It attracts a young, hip crowd and plays very effectively to the theatre/comedy/cabaret crossover scene.
► *For comedy at the Soho, see p298.*

Theatre Royal Stratford East

Gerry Raffles Square, Stratford, E15 1BN (8534 0310, www.stratfordeast.com). Stratford tube/rail/DLR. **Box office** 10am-6pm Mon-Sat. **Tickets** £6-£27. **Credit** MC, V.

The Theatre Royal Stratford East is a community theatre, with many shows written, directed and performed by black or Asian artists. Musicals are big here – *The Harder They Come* went on to West End success – but there is also a Christmas pantomime and harder-hitting fare.

★ Tricycle

269 Kilburn High Road, Kilburn, NW6 7JR (information 7372 6611, tickets 7328 1000, www.tricycle.co.uk). Kilburn tube. **Box office** 10am-9pm Mon-Sat; 2-8pm Sun. **Tickets** £8.50-£29. **Credit** MC, V.

Passionate and political, the Tricycle consistently finds original ways into difficult subjects. It has pioneered its own genre of 'tribunal' docu-dramas.

★ Wilton's Music Hall

Graces Alley, off Ensign Street, E1 8JB (7702 2789, www.wiltons.org.uk). Aldgate East or Tower Hill tube. **Box office** 10am-6pm Mon-Fri. **Tickets** £10-£25. **Credit** MC, V. **Map** p403 S7.

London's last surviving example of the giant pub halls that flourished in the mid 19th century, Wilton's Music Hall once entertained the masses with acts ranging from Chinese performing monkeys to acrobats, contortionists to opera singers. It was here that Victorian music hall star George Leybourne made his name in character as Champagne Charlie, and that the can-can first scandalised London. Roughly 150 years after opening, Wilton's still serves as a theatre, offering an atmospheric stage for everything from situation-specific Bach to Mark Almond – but only just.

★ Young Vic

66 The Cut, Waterloo, SE1 8LZ (7922 2922, www.youngvic.org). Waterloo tube/rail. **Box office** 10am-6pm Mon-Sat. **Tickets** £10-£29.50. **Credit** MC, V. **Map** p402 N8.

As the name suggests, this Vic (actually now in its forties) has more youthful bravura than its older sister up the road, and draws a younger crowd, who pack out the open-air balcony at its popular restaurant and bar on the weekends. They come to see European classics with a modern edge, new writing with an international flavour and collaborations with leading companies.

Escapes & Excursions

Brighton Pier. *See p354.*

Escapes & Excursions

Fast transport links will whisk you to a sampling of Britain's best.

There's so much in London that you could easily spend a lifetime exploring the city. But that isn't at all the same as *wanting* to spend a lifetime exploring the city. Everyone who lives here sometimes feels an irresistible urge to leave, so why would visitors be any different? In this chapter, there are four suggested excursions that should refresh and reinvigorate you, as well as introducing you to the UK's south-east corner. Two are by the sea, but could otherwise hardly be more different: **Brighton** offers traditional seaside kitsch and a full-on nightlife scene, while

Dungeness, **Rye** and **Romney** come with cranky charm and an other-worldly atmosphere. Inland and nestling happily in the lee of the North Downs, **Canterbury** is a lively medieval city, its cathedral and ruined abbey of such historical significance that they're listed as a UNESCO World Heritage Site. And **Cambridge**, as flat as the fenlands it sits upon, is perfect for those who like to peek into cloistered courts and college chapels.

GETTING AROUND

All of the destinations included in this chapter are within easy reach of London, which makes them perfect either for a day trip or a more leisurely overnight stay. **Brighton** and **Cambridge** are the easiest of the four to reach by train; they're both within an hour of London, with rail services running from early in the morning until relatively late at night; **Canterbury** is also a direct rail journey from London, and now with its new high-speed rail link from St Pancras International, it too takes under an hour to get to. It's more of an effort to reach **Dungeness**, **Romney** and **Rye**, but the journey is well worth the effort. If you don't fancy negotiating the train network, and are happy to hire a car, it's a relatively easy journey by road.

For the main attractions, we've included details of opening times, admission prices and transport details, but be aware that these can change without notice: always phone to check. Major sights are open all through the year, but many of the minor ones close out of season, often from November to March.

Before setting out, drop in on the **Britain & London Visitor Centre** (*see p376*) for additional information.

By train

Notwithstanding the occasional strike or weather-related line closure, Britain's rail network is generally reliable. However, ticket prices on some services are insultingly high, and with different rail companies sharing some routes, it's easy to inadvertently pay too much or buy a ticket that limits your options. Factor in varying definitions of peak and off-peak travel and you'll usually be better off discussing your needs at a ticket office window, than buying blind at a machine. If more than two of you are travelling, ask about family and group tickets, which offer excellent value.

The website **www.nationalrail.co.uk** has a good journey planner and gives live advice on engineering works and other delays, which are a

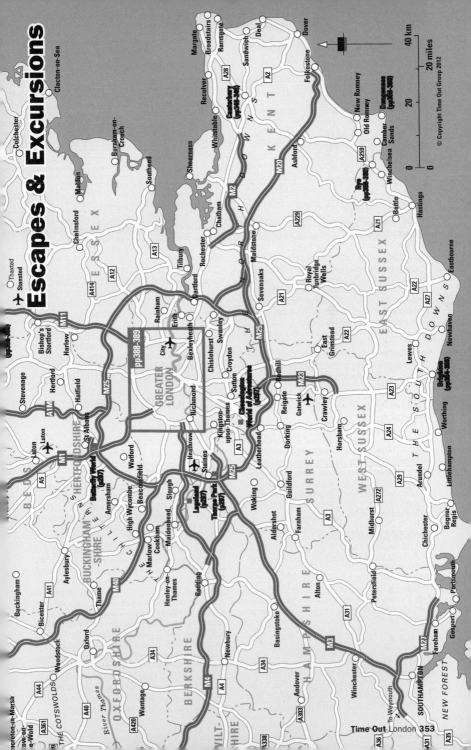

Escapes & Excursions

© Copyright Time Out Group 2012

Brighton

regular occurence, particularly at weekends.
You can buy tickets on the website, too, but
there's generally no advantage, unless your
journey takes you outside the south-eastern
network (in which case, the further ahead you
purchase, the lower the price). National Rail's
phone number is 0845 748 4950.

If you need extra help, there are rail travel
centres in London's mainline stations, as well
as at Heathrow and Gatwick airports. Staff can
give you guidance on timetables and booking.
We specify departure stations in the 'Getting
there' section for each destination; the journey
times cited are the fastest available.

By coach

Coaches operated by **National Express**
(0871 781 8181, www.nationalexpress.com)
are scheduled to run throughout the country.
Services depart from Victoria Coach Station
(*see p364*), which is ten minutes' walk from
Victoria rail and tube stations. **Green Line
Travel** (0844 801 7261, www.greenline.co.uk)
also operates coaches.

Victoria Coach Station
*164 Buckingham Palace Road, Victoria, SW1W
9TP (0843 222 1234, www.tfl.gov.uk). Victoria
tube/rail.* **Map** p400 H11.
Britain's most wide-ranging coach services are run
by National Express (*see p364*). They mostly depart
from Victoria Coach Station, as do the services run
by many other companies to and from Europe; some
depart from Marble Arch.

By car

If you're in a group of three or four, it may be
cheaper to hire a car (*see p367*), especially if
you plan to take in several sights within an area.
The road directions in the listings below should
be used in conjunction with a proper map.

By bicycle

Capital Sport (01296 631671, www.capital-
sport.co.uk) offers gentle cycling tours along
the Thames from London. Leisurely itineraries
include plenty of time to explore royal palaces,
parks and historic attractions; the website
contains full details. Alternatively, try **Country
Lanes** (01590 622627, www.countrylanes.
co.uk), which leads cycling tours all over the
beautiful New Forest in Hampshire.

London-on-Sea

BRIGHTON

Britain's youngest city, England's most popular
tourist destination after London and host to the
nation's biggest annual arts festival outside
Edinburgh, Brighton is thriving. It's also a
bracingly liberal kind of place: the constituency
of Brighton Pavilion elected Britain's first
Green Party MP, Caroline Lucas, in the 2010
General Election. However, novelty is nothing
new to Brighton, which has been evolving
throughout its existence.

Brighton began life as Brighthelmstone, a
small fishing village; it remained so until 1783,
when the future George IV transformed it into a
fashionable retreat. George kept the architect
John Nash busy converting a modest abode into
a bizarre piece of orientalist kitsch; it's now the
Royal Pavilion (*see p355*), and remains an
ostentatious sight. Next door, the **Brighton
Museum & Art Gallery** (Royal Pavilion
Gardens, 03000 290900, www.brighton-hove-
rpml.org.uk) has entertaining displays and
a good permanent art collection.

Lacy, delicate **Brighton Pier**, dating from
the 1890s, is a clutter of hot-dog stands, karaoke
and fairground rides, filled with customers in
the summertime. Still, with seven miles of

coastline, Brighton retains all the traditional seaside resort trappings. Look out for the free **Brighton Fishing Museum** (201 King's Road Arches, on the lower prom between the piers, 01273 723064, www.brightonfishing museum.org.uk) and the **Sea-Life Centre** (*see below*), the world's oldest functioning aquarium.

Brighton's West Pier has fallen victim to a series of fires and the depredations of the elements, its remains are a skeletal monument to its historic past. A spectacular 150m-high viewing tower is planned to open soon at its foot: see www.brightoni360.co.uk for more.

A gay hub, a major student town and a child-friendly spot, Brighton still welcomes weekend gaggles of hen parties, ravers, nudists, discerning vegetarians, surfers, sunseekers and all-round wastrels. Many are satisfied to tumble from station to seafront, calling in at a couple of bars down the hill – and, perhaps, visiting the huge number of independent shops in and around **North Laine**, and in the charming network of narrow cobbled streets known as the **Lanes** – before plunging on to the pier or hobbling over the pebbles.

But to get the best out of Brighton, it's advisable to seek out its unusual little pockets: the busy gay quarter of **Kemp Town**, the savage drinking culture of **Hanover**, the airy terraces of **Montpelier**. Although hilly, the city has an award-winning bus network, with an all-night service on main lines, making all parts easily accessible.

If you're going for something longer than a day trip, Time Out's *Shortlist: Brighton* will prove invaluable.

Royal Pavilion

Brighton, BN1 1EE (03000 290900, www.royalpavilion.org.uk). **Open** *Apr-Sept* 9.30am-5.45pm daily. *Oct-Mar* 10am-5.15pm daily. *Tours* by appointment. Last entry 45mins before closing. **Admission** £9.80; £7.80 reductions; £5.60 under-15s; free under-5s. **Credit** MC, V.

Sea-Life Centre

Marine Parade, BN2 1TB (01273 604234, www.visitsealife.com). **Open** 10am-5pm Mon-Fri; 10am-6pm Sat, Sun. Last entry 1hr before closing. **Admission** £16.20; £11.40-£15 reductions; free under-3s; £48 family. **Credit** MC, V.

Where to eat & drink

Brighton offers a ridiculous amount of dining possibilities for a town of its size, a handful of which would hold their head up in any city in the UK. **Gingerman** (21A Norfolk Square, 01273 326688, www.gingermanrestaurants.com) offers top-quality modern British dishes at accessible prices. At **Bill's** (The Depot, North Road, 01273 692894, www.billsproduce store.co.uk) organic deli and restaurant, diners sit at long communal tables and tuck into buttermilk pancakes, salads and burgers. **Fishy Fishy** (36 East Street, 01273 723 750, www.fishyfishy.co.uk) does laid-back seafood dishes. **Terre à Terre** (71 East Street, 01273 729051, www.terreaterre.co.uk) is an inventive vegetarian restaurant. **Jamie's Italian** (11 Black Lion Street, 01273 915480, www. jamieoliver.com) is an affordable Italian eaterie and is everything you'd expect from brand Jamie. And **Riddle & Finns** (12B Meeting House Lane, 01273 323008, www.riddleand finns.co.uk) is an accomplished champagne and oyster bar.

Of the city's drinking holes, **Brighton Rocks** (6 Rock Place, 01273 600550, www. brightonrockspub.com) is Kemp Town's most talked-up small bar, with a heated terrace, quality cocktails and inspired bar snacks and tapas. Quite possibly the best pub in Brighton is the Basketmakers Arms (12 Gloucester Road, 01273 689006, www.thebasketmakers arms.co.uk), with its comprehensive selection of cask ales and whiskies; another boozer also beloved by ale enthusiasts is the **Hand in Hand** (33 Upper St James Street, 01273 699595). The **Lion & Lobster** (24 Sillwood Street, 01273 327299, www.thelionandlobster.co.uk) is a wonderful little pub with a nice vibe, cool and communal. The **Medicine Chest** (51-55 Brunswick Street East, 01273 770002, www.themedicinechest.co.uk) is a speakeasy-style cocktail bar. Of the gay bars, the most fun

Terre à Terre.

ESCAPES & EXCURSIONS

is to be had at the **Amsterdam Hotel** (11-12 Marine Parade, 01273 688825, www. amsterdam.uk.com). **Doctor Brighton's** (16-17 King's Road, 01273 208113, www. doctorbrightons.co.uk), on the seafront, is also worth a punt, with regular DJs playing house and techno.

Where to stay

Given Brighton's popularity with tourists, it's unsurprising that hotel prices can be on the high side. **Drakes** (43-44 Marine Parade, 01273 696934, www.drakesofbrighton.com, doubles £115-£345) is one of Brighton's high-end designer hotels. The in-house restaurant serves food that is as polished as the surrounds. Another worthwhile option is the typically chic **Myhotel Brighton** (17 Jubilee Street, 01273 900300, www.myhotels.com, doubles £85-£345), which has a penthouse suite containing a 400-year-old carousel horse.

Hotel Pelirocco (10 Regency Square, 01273 327055, www.hotelpelirocco.co.uk, doubles £99-160) describes itself as 'England's most rock 'n' roll hotel'; each of the themed rooms come with a PlayStation 2 to aid recovery from a night in the bar sipping cocktails with Brighton's music types. The pampering **Nineteen** (19 Broad Street, 01273 675529, www.hotelnineteen.co.uk, doubles £70-£120) has just eight rooms in a stylish townhouse.

A good-quality stop on Ship Street is the classy **Hotel du Vin** (nos.2-6, 01273 718588, www.hotelduvin.com, doubles £160-£430). The **Amherst** (2 Lower Rock Gardens, 01273 670131, www.amhersthotel.co.uk, doubles £100-£130) is one of the best bargains among Brighton's contemporary hotels, while the **George IV** (34 Regency Square, 01273 321196, www.georgeivbrighton.co.uk, doubles £72-£155) is surely the best bargain, with many of the rooms offering sea views.

Getting there

By train Trains for Brighton leave from Victoria (50mins; map p400 H10) or King's Cross/St Pancras and London Bridge (1hr 15mins; map p397 L3 & p403 Q8).
By coach National Express coaches for Brighton leave from Victoria Coach Station (1hr 50mins).
By car Take the A23, the M23, then the A23 again to Brighton (approx 1hr 20mins).

Tourist information

Tourist Information Centre *Royal Pavilion, Brighton, BN1 1JS (01273 290337, www.visitbrighton.com).* **Open** 10am-5pm Mon-Sat.

Ancient History

CANTERBURY

The home of the Church of England since St Augustine was based here in 597, the ancient city of Canterbury is rich in atmosphere. Gaze up at its soaring spires, or around you at the enchanting medieval streets, and you'll soon feel blessed, even if you're not an Anglican.

The town's busy tourist trade and large university provide a counterweight to the brooding mass of history present in its old buildings. And, of course, to the glorious **Canterbury Cathedral** (*see p357*); it's at its most inspirational just before dusk, especially if there's music going on within and the coach parties are long gone. Inside, you'll find superb stained glass, stone vaulting and a vast Norman crypt, which since early 2011 has been home to *Transport*, an Anthony Gormley sculpture made from antique Canterbury Cathedral nails. A plaque near the altar marks what is believed to be the spot where Archbishop Thomas Becket was murdered; the Trinity Chapel contains the site of the original shrine, plus the tombs of Henry IV and the Black Prince.

A pilgrimage to Becket's tomb was the focus of one of the earliest and finest long poems in all English literature: Geoffrey Chaucer's *Canterbury Tales*, written in the 14th century. At the exhibition named after the poem (*see p357*), visitors are given a device that they point at tableaux inspired by Chaucer's tales of a knight, a miller, a wife of Bath, and others, enabling them to hear the rollicking stories that Chaucer brought to astonishingly vivid life.

Canterbury Cathedral.

Just down the road from Christ Church Gate lies the **Royal Museum & Art Gallery** (High Street, 01227 452747), a monument to high Victorian values. It's currently closed for refurbishment, expected to reopen in early 2012, when its permanent collections of art by cattle painter Thomas Sidney Cooper, as well as work by Van Dyck and Sickert, will be on display.

Founded to provide shelter for pilgrims, **Eastbridge Hospital** (25 High Street, 01227 471688) retains the smell and feel of ages past. Visitors can tour the hospital and admire the undercroft with its Gothic arches, the Chantry Chapel, the Pilgrims' Chapel and the refectory with an enchanting early 13th-century mural showing Christ in Majesty (there's only one other like this, and it's in France).

The **Roman Museum** (*see below*) has the remains of a townhouse and mosaic floor among its treasures, augmented with computer reconstructions and time tunnels. From here, you get a super view of the cathedral tower. After the Romans comes **St Augustine**, or at least the ruins of the abbey he built (Longport, 01227 767345, www.english-heritage.org.uk). English Heritage has attached a small museum and shop to the site.

Everything you want to see, do or buy in Canterbury is within walking distance. And that includes the seaside – at least, it does if you fancy a long (seven-mile) walk or cycle along the Crab & Winkle Way, a disused railway line to pretty Whitstable.

Canterbury Cathedral
The Precincts, CT1 2EH (01227 762862, www.canterbury-cathedral.org). **Open** *Summer* 9am-5.30pm Mon-Sat; 12.30-2.30pm Sun. *Winter* 9am-5pm Mon-Sat; 12.30-2.30pm Sun. Admission is restricted during services and special events. **Admission** £9; £8 reductions; free under-5s. **Credit** MC, V.

Canterbury Tales
St Margaret's Street, CT1 2TG (01227 479227, www.canterburytales.org.uk). **Open** *Summer* 10am-5pm daily. *Winter* 10am-4.30pm daily. **Admission** £7.95; £5.90-£6.95 reductions; free under-4s. **Credit** MC, V.

Roman Museum
Butchery Lane, CT1 2JR (01227 785575, www.canterbury.co.uk). **Open** 10am-5pm daily. Last entry 45mins before closing. **Admission** £6; £5-£1.50 reductions. **Credit** MC, V.

Where to eat & drink

Chef Michael Caines has added a smart touch to the Canterbury eating scene, with **Michael Caines at Abode** (01227 826684,

www.michaelcaines.com, main courses £22.50-£26.50). The two-Michelin-starred chef's influence is evident in the ambitious, fine dining menu. There's also his **Old Brewery Tavern** (Stour Street, 01227 826682, www.michaelcaines.com, mains £9-£19), where prints of grizzled coopers rolling barrels hang on the walls.

Another notable restaurant is the **Goods Shed** (Station Road West, 01227 459153, www.thegoodsshed.co.uk, mains £10-£18), which occupies a lofty Victorian building, which was formerly a railway freight store. On a raised wooden platform, diners sit at scrubbed tables and choose from the specials chalked on the board. Only ingredients on sale in the farmers' market below are used in the restaurant. For people who care about their food and its provenance, this is heaven. Vegetarians will love **Hutch** (13 Palace Street, 0127 766700, www.thehutchcanterbury.co.uk), which is a dapper little restaurant and a relatively new addition to the Kent foodie scene.

Pub-wise, most of the better ones are owned by Shepherd Neame, the local brewery based up the road in the town of Faversham. The best for real ales is the **Unicorn** (61 St Dunstan's Street, 01227 463187, www.unicorninn.com), which also has a great pub garden for summer drinking. Built in 1370, the **Parrot** (1-9 Church Lane, St Radigands, 01227 762355) is the oldest pub in Canterbury and also one of the oldest buildings. A good choice of ales and cider is served in a charming setting. Recently refurbished, the **White Hart** (Worthgate Place, 01227 765091, www.whitehartcanterbury.co.uk) is gaining a good reputation locally, as is the **Farmhouse**, (11 Dover Street, 01227 456118, www.thefarmhousecanterbury.co.uk), which doubles as a decent restaurant and a lively bar with DJs and bands in the evening.

Where to stay

The third in a small chain of smart hotels created by Andrew Brownsword, **ABode** (30-33 High Street, 01227 766266, www.abodehotels.co.uk, doubles £105-£165) has brought a welcome blend of chic into Canterbury's chintzy accommodation options. The 72 rooms are ordered by price and size ranging from 'comfortable', through 'desirable' and 'enviable' to 'fabulous' (a penthouse with superior views and a tennis court-sized bed). The restaurant (*see left*) is superb.

Canterbury Cathedral Lodge (The Precincts, 01227 865350, www.canterburycathedrallodge.org, doubles £75-£119) is right inside the cathedral precincts. There is bright and comfortable accommodation in a private courtyard and, while the hotel is hardly historic (it's only a decade old), the views certainly are. Nearby, the **Cathedral Gate Hotel** (36 Burgate, 01227 464381, www.cathgate.co.uk, doubles £62-£105) is a splendid old hotel built in 1438. It pre-dates the Christ Church Gate it sits alongside. The 25 rooms, with atmospheric sloping floors and ceilings, are reached via dark narrow corridors and low doorways.

Magnolia House (36 St Dunstan's Terrace, 01227 765121, www.magnoliahousecanter bury.co.uk, doubles £95-£125) is compact but recommended; the breakfast is delicious and well worth lingering over. The walk to and from town takes you through peaceful Westgate Gardens. Opposite St Augustine's Abbey, **Number 7 Longport** is a tiny 15th-century cottage that has been beautifully renovated to become a chic one-bedroom B&B. Further out, the **Ebury Hotel** (65-67 New Dover Road, 01227 768433, www.ebury-hotel.co.uk, doubles £75-£150) is really quite grand-looking, with a sweeping drive and a Gothic exterior. The best bedrooms have views of the garden, but most of them are large, light and comfortable.

Getting there

By train From Victoria to Canterbury East (1hr 20mins; map p398 H10), or from Charing Cross (map p416 Y5) to Canterbury West (1hr 30mins). A new high-speed train service from St Pancras International brings the journey time down to about an hour.
By coach National Express from Victoria Coach Station (1hr 50mins).
By car Take the A2, the M2, then the A2 again (approx 2hrs).

Tourist information

Tourist Information Centre *12-13 Sun Street, Buttermarket, Canterbury, CT1 2HX (01227 378100, www.canterbury.co.uk).* **Open** 9.30am-5pm Mon-Sat; 9.30am-4.30pm Sun.

Wild Horizons

DUNGENESS, ROMNEY & RYE

Perhaps because it's difficult to reach from London (though there are rail links to Rye and Hastings), **Romney Marsh** is other-worldly in a way that conjures up science-fiction scenarios in Tarkovsky movies; you half expect to see Steed and Mrs Peel from *The Avengers* supping ale in the eerily unchanged villages. It's a strange, appealing mix of olde-worlde cobbled streets and ancient inns, sandy beaches, the world's largest expanse of shingle and event-

horizoned marshland, criss-crossed by canals and studded with tiny medieval churches and strange concrete defence constructions dating to the period after World War I. So long as the transport links remain as poor as they are, there probably – hopefully – won't be any real changes here for decades to come. **Hastings** is the ideal starting point for a circular tour (by car) that takes in the towns of Winchelsea and Rye, Romney Marsh and Dungeness.

Winchelsea was built on a never-completed medieval grid pattern, first laid out by King Edward I, when the 'old' settlement was swept into the sea in the storms of 1287. The place is proud of its status as England's smallest town, but really it's a sleepy village of 400 residents. It's almost too quaint to be true – like **Rye**, which is a photogenic jumble of Norman, Tudor and Georgian architecture perched on one of the area's few hills. It's worth taking a look at the medieval Landgate gateway and the **Castle Museum** and 13th-century **Ypres Tower** (*see below*). The **Rye Art Gallery** (107 High Street, 01797 222433, www.ryeartgallery.co.uk) offers a changing series of excellent exhibitions, mostly by local artists.

East from Rye lies **Romney Marsh**, flat as a pancake and laced with cycle paths. Bikes can be hired from **Rye Hire** (1 Cyprus Place, Rye, 01797 223033, www.ryehire.co.uk); it's an ideal way to explore the lonely medieval churches that dot the level marsh. Heading out of Rye along the coast road takes you to **Camber Sands**, a vast sandy beach that's a great spot for kite-flying, riding, sand-yachting and invigorating walking.

Beyond is **Dungeness Point**, a huge beach of flint shingle stretching miles out into the sea. Clustered on this strange promontory are a lighthouse that offers wonderful views and a good café. The light on this remote, gloriously bleak patch of land is odd, reflected from the sea on both sides. The oddness of the landscape is enhanced by the presence of the massive Dungeness nuclear power station that dominates the horizon; such man-made wonders are set against a magnificent natural backdrop.

When the miniature **Romney, Hythe & Dymchurch Railway** train (01797 362353, www.rhdr.org.uk) barrels by, you know you're in an episode of *The Prisoner*. Proudly proclaiming to be the 'world's smallest public railway', it's fully functioning but one-third of the standard size. The diminutive train, built by millionaire racing driver Captain Howey in 1927, even includes a buffet car. Sitting in one of the tiny carriages is a surreal experience, as you meander from the wide-open shingle of the Point behind back gardens and caravan parks, through woodland and fields to arrive at **Hythe** (roughly 13 miles away).

Profile Warner Bros Studio Tour London

Accio! Apprentice wizards summoned to Harry Potter tour.

Wannabe-wizards can stop mourning the end of their favourite film franchise: Warner Bros Studios in Leavesden – where all eight Harry Potter blockbusters were created – is opening its doors to fans for the first time on 31 March 2012.

Studio tours are commonplace in Hollywood, but this will be the first of its kind in Britain, and for followers of the bespectacled child-wizard, the Harry Potter Studio Tour offers a rare opportunity to learn just how JK Rowling's magical world was brought to life in the highest-grossing film series of all time.

The Leavesden Studios, a former aircraft hangar 20 miles from London, are spread over 150,000 square feet. The three-hour walking tour will take in such iconic sets as Hagrid's hut and the Gryffindor common room, plus it offers the chance to check out the special effects, animatronics, props and costumes used in the films.

One of the highlights for many fans will be the set of the Great Hall. It was first seen in *Harry Potter and the Philosopher's Stone* and was designed by

BAFTA-winning production designer Stuart Craig – it's 120 feet long and 40 feet wide with a solid stone floor and has the original tables and benches where Daniel Radcliffe, Emma Watson et al once sat. Another highlight will be Dumbledore's office, which was built for *Harry Potter and the Chamber of Secrets* and is home to the Sorting Hat, the Sword of Gryffindor and Albus Dumbledore's desk.

TICKETS

Tickets must be booked in advance at www.wbstudio tour.co.uk or through approved tour operators; £28 adults, £21 children.

GETTING THERE

The Leavesden Studios are just off the A405, less than 3 miles from Watford town centre. They're easily reached by car via Junction 19 or 20 of the M25, Junction 5 or 6 of the M1 or the A41. Fast trains go direct from London Euston in less than 20 minutes; a shuttle bus to the studios runs from Watford Junction station.

FOUR MORE

Other surefire winners for children in the London area are **Butterfly World**, **Thorpe Park** (home of Europe's fastest rollercoaster), **Legoland**, **Chessington World of Adventures** (with zoo) and **Butterfly World**. For all, *see p297.*

Rye Castle Museum & Ypres Tower

3 East Street, TN31 7JY (01797 226728, www.ryemuseum.co.uk). **Open** *Museum* Apr-Oct 10.30am-5pm Sat, Sun. *Tower* Apr-Oct 10.30am-5pm daily. *Nov-Mar* 10.30am-3.30pm daily. **Admission** *Museum* £2.50; £2 reductions. *Tower* £3; £2.50 reductions. *Both* £5; £4 reductions. **No credit cards**.

Where to eat & drink

You'll find some of the finest food on the south-east coast here. In Rye, the **Landgate Bistro** (5-6 Landgate, Rye, 01797 222829, www.land gatebistro.co.uk, mains £12.80-£18) places its emphasis firmly on local produce such as potted wild rabbit or Romney Marsh lamb with gratin potatoes. One of the best seafood restaurants in the area is **Webbe's at the Fish Café** (17 Tower Street, 01797 222226, www.webbes restaurants.co.uk, mains £11-£18). If you're looking for lovingly prepared food with an emphasis on locally sourced ingredients, there are few better places to eat on the peninsula than the **Romney Bay House Hotel** (*see right*).

If fancy isn't your thing, Rye has plenty of simpler eateries: pasta at **Simply Italian** (The Strand, 01797 226024, www.simplyitalian.co.uk, mains £5.95-£12.50) or sound pub food at any number of lovely boozers in town.

The finest option on the seaside is the **Gallivant** (New Lydd Road, 01797 225057, www.thegallivanthotel.co.uk, mains £15.50-£21) at Camber Sands, which prides itself on its use of locally sourced and eco-friendly produce. Further east, Lydd's **Pilot** (Battery Road, 01797 320314, www.thepilot.uk.com, mains £7.50-£13.50) has a jovial pub atmosphere and the food is decent enough.

Of the many pubs, the **Mermaid Inn** in Rye (Mermaid Street, 01797 223065, www.mermaidinn.co.uk) is one of the best; with cellars dating from 1156 and the main building from 1420, the place oozes history. It's also a hotel and has an accomplished restaurant.

INSIDE TRACK
HANG ON A MINUTE, LADS

The gorgeously modernist De La Warr Pavilion in Bexhill-on-Sea – about five miles west of Hastings – will be conspicuously a part of the Cultural Olympiad from 1 March to 1 September 2012 thanks to a prominent rooftop sculpture by Richard Wilson. A coach will teeter at the edge, in homage to the literally cliff-hanging ending of the classic crime caper *The Italian Job*, featuring British icon Michael Caine.

The tiny, multi-award-winning **Red Lion** (Snargate, 01797 344648) is something of a Romney Marsh institution, famed for the fact that its interior hasn't been touched since World War II. It doesn't offer food, but you're welcome to bring your own.

Where to stay

Luxury guesthouses reign supreme in Rye, and visitors will find plenty of well-run establishments in fascinating buildings. If you want somewhere with character and some individuality, the **Hope Anchor Hotel** (Watchbell Street, 01797 222216, www.thehopeanchor.co.uk, doubles £95-£140) is set in a lovely location at the end of a pretty, cobbled street. The seven guestrooms at the **White Vine House** (24 High Street, 01797 224748, www.whitevinehouse.co.uk, doubles £130-£170) are beautifully appointed and are perfect for romantic weekends away.

Wonderfully located on Rye's quaintest cobbled street, the atmospheric 17th-century **Jeake's House** (Mermaid Street, 01797 222828, www.jeakeshouse.com, doubles £45-£80) has nearly a dozen individually decorated rooms, each taking their name from literary and artistic figures who have visited the area, Radclyffe Hall and Malcolm Lowry among them. The **George** (98 High Street, 01797 222114, www.thegeorge inrye.com) is possibly Rye's premier hotel. It's a handsome coaching inn, dating from 1575, with 24 bedrooms, a Georgian ballroom and an excellent restaurant and bar.

In Winchelsea, **Strand House** (Tanyard's Lane, 01797 226276, www.thestrandhouse. co.uk, doubles £65-£145) dates to the 15th century, and there's a delightful garden. The **Romney Bay House Hotel** (Coast Road, Littlestone-on-Sea, New Romney, 01797 364747, www.romneybayhousehotel.co.uk, doubles £95-£164) is a ten-bedroom mansion designed for Hollywood gossip columnist Hedda Hopper by Sir Clough Williams-Ellis of Portmeirion fame. In Hastings, the **Zanzibar International Hotel** (9 Eversfield Place, 01424 460109, www.zanzibarhotel.co.uk, doubles £89-£220) is a tall, thin seafront house that feels like a private house rather than a boutique hotel.

Getting there

By train From London Bridge or Cannon Street to Rye via Ashford International (approx 1hr 45mins; map p403 Q8 & p402 P7). From Charing Cross, Waterloo East or London Bridge to Hastings (approx 1hr 30mins; map p416 Y5, p399 M8 & p403 Q8).
By car Take the A20, the M20, then the A259 (approx 2hrs 30mins).

Dungeness

Tourist information

Hastings Tourist Information *Queen Square, Hastings, TN34 1TL (01424 451111, www.visit1066country.com).* **Open** 8.30am-6.15pm Mon-Fri; 9am-5pm Sat; 10.30am-4pm Sun.
Rye Tourist Information *4-5 Lion Street, Rye, TN31 7LB (01797 229049, www.visitrye.co.uk).* **Open** *Apr-Sept* 10am-5pm daily. *Oct-Mar* 10am-4pm daily.

Colleges & Culture

CAMBRIDGE

Gorgeous, intimidating Cambridge has the feel of an enclosed city. With the narrow streets and tall old buildings of the town centre, it has a way of conveying disapproval to visitors architecturally – and that's before you even reach the 'Keep off the Grass' signs. But pluck up the courage to pass through those imposing gates with their stern porters: within and behind the colleges are pretty green meadows and the idle River Cam, a place where time seems to have stopped back in the 18th century.

Cambridge first became an academic centre when a fracas at Oxford – involving a dead woman, an arrow and a scholar holding a bow – led to some of the learned monks bidding a hasty farewell to Oxford and a hearty hello to Cambridge. Once the dust settled, the monks needed somewhere to peddle their knowledge: the first college, **Peterhouse** (01223 338200, www.pet.cam.ac.uk), was established in 1284. The original hall survives, though most of the present buildings are from the 19th century. Up the road is **Corpus Christi** (01223 338000, www.corpus.cam.ac.uk), founded in 1352. Its Old Court dates from that time and is linked by a gallery to the 11th-century **St Bene't's Church** (Bene't Street, www.stbenetschurch. org), the oldest surviving building in town.

Past Corpus Christi, grand **King's College** (01223 331100, www.kings.cam.ac.uk) was founded by Henry VI in 1441. Its chapel (01223

331155), built between 1446 and 1515 on a scale that would humble many cathedrals, has breathtaking interior fan vaulting and the original stained glass. Attend a service in term-time to hear its wonderful choirboys.

Continue north to find pretty **Trinity** (01223 338400, www.trin.cam.ac.uk), a college founded in 1336 by Edward III and then refounded by Henry VIII in 1546. A fine crowd of Tudor buildings surrounds the Great Court where, legend has it, Lord Byron would bathe naked in the fountain with his pet bear. Wittgenstein studied and taught here, and the library (a cool and airy design by Wren) is open to visitors at certain times. Within, covered cases contain such treasures as a lock of Newton's hair, a Shakespeare first folio and Otto Robert Frisch's crisp and moving account of the first atomic bomb test. From behind the library, you can see the neo-Gothic Bridge of Sighs that connects the major courts of **St John's** (01223 338600, www.joh.cam.ac.uk) across the Cam.

Each of the 31 Cambridge colleges is an independent entity, so entry times (and, for the more famous ones, prices) vary considerably: www.cam.ac.uk/colleges has the details. But Cambridge isn't only about the colleges. Behind its impressive neoclassical façade, the **Fitzwilliam Museum** (*see p362*) has a superb collection of paintings and sculpture (masterpieces by Titian, Modigliani and Picasso), as well as ancient artefacts from Egypt, Greece and Rome. A short walk south, the 40 relaxing acres of the **Botanic Gardens** (*see p362*) have 8,000 plants; at the entrance, is a descendant of Sir Isaac Newton's apple tree.

Fans of eccentric and ghoulish museums should head to Downing Street. On the south side are both the towering totem poles and toucan-shaped 'lime scoop' of the **Museum of Archaeology & Anthropology** (01223 333516, www.maa-cambridge.org) and the fossils and scintillating gemstones of the **Sedgwick Museum of Earth Sciences** (01223 333456, www.sedgwickmuseum.org). On the north side, you'll find the strange scientific devices and grand orreries of the **Whipple Museum of the History of Science** (01223 330906, www.hps. cam.ac.uk/whipple) and, beneath a suspended whale skeleton, the animal skeletons and stuffed birds of the **Museum of Zoology** (01223 336650, www.museum.zoo.cam.ac.uk).

One of the real treats during a visit to Cambridge is **Kettle's Yard** (*see p362*), once Tate curator Jim Ede's home and now a magnificently atmospheric collection of early 20th-century artists – Miró, Brancusi, Hepworth – arranged just as he left it. Settle in one of Ede's chairs and read a book from his shelves.

Behind the main colleges, the beautiful meadows bordering the willow-shaded Cam are known as the **Backs**. Carpeted with crocuses in spring, the Backs are idyllic for summer strolling and 'punting' (pushing flat boats with long poles). Punts can be hired; **Scudamore's Boatyard** (01223 359750, www.scudamores. com) is the largest operator. If you get handy at the surprisingly difficult skill of punting, you can boat down to the **Orchard Tea Rooms** (45-47 Mill Way, 01223 551 125, www.orchard-grantchester.com), where Ted Hughes and Sylvia Plath courted and Rupert Brooke lodged as a student.

Cambridge University Botanic Gardens

1 Brookside, CB2 1JE (01223 336265, www.botanic.cam.ac.uk). **Open** *Apr-Sept* 10am-6pm daily. *Oct, Feb, Mar* 10am-5pm daily. *Nov-Jan* 10am-4pm daily. **Admission** £4; £3.50 reductions.

Fitzwilliam Museum

Trumpington Street, CB2 1RB (01223 332900, www.fitzmuseum.cam.ac.uk). **Open** 10am-5pm Tue-Sat; noon-5pm Sun. **Admission** free.

Kettle's Yard

Castle Street, CB3 0AQ (01223 748100, www.kettlesyard.co.uk). **Open** *House* 2-4pm Tue-Sun. *Gallery & bookshop* 11.30am-5pm Tue-Sun & bank hol Mon. **Admission** free.

Where to eat & drink

Occupying an enviable riverside spot, **Midsummer House** (Midsummer Common, 01223 369299, www.midsummerhouse.co.uk, £40 3 courses) produces Michelin-starred French food that rises to the occasion. Service is as fussy as you'd expect, but the food is perfectly presented and meticulously prepared in flavour combinations that are never less than intriguing.

The **Cambridge Chop House** (1 King's Parade, 01223 359506, www.chophouses.co.uk, mains £11.50-£25) is a great come-one-come-all bistro opposite King's College, where you can tuck into British comfort food and draught ales. Nearby, the busy subterranean **Rainbow Café** (9A King's Parade, 01223 321551, www.rainbow cafe.co.uk, mains £8-£10) serves cheap, hearty vegetarian food. A branch of **Jamie's Italian** (Old Library, Wheeler Street, 01223 654094, www.jamieoliver.com/italian) opened in 2010 in the historic Guildhall, which is just off the central market square. Reopened and refurbished in 2011, the legendary **Fitzbillies** (52 Trumpington Street, 01223 352500), loved by generations of students, is still the place to go to tuck into a Chelsea bun or teatime treat.

Cambridge has many creaky old inns in which to settle down and enjoy one of the city's decent local ales. The **Eagle** on Bene't Street

(01223 505020) is the most famous – Crick and Watson drank here after fathoming the mysteries of DNA – but there are many others, including the **Pickerel Inn** (30 Magdalene Street, 01223 355068) and, down a back alley a little off the beaten track, the sweet little **Free Press** (Prospect Row, 01223 368337, www.freepresspub.com).

Where to stay

Because of the university's prominence in the city, there are plenty of guesthouses, with a cluster of B&Bs nicely located just across the Cam from the centre of town to the north of Midsummer Common. **Harry's** (39 Milton Road, 01223 503866, www.welcometoharrys. co.uk, doubles £75), **Worth House** (152 Chesterton Road, 01223 316074, www.worth-house.co.uk, doubles £55) and **Victoria Guest House** (57 Arbury Road, 01223 350086, www.victoria-guesthouse.co.uk, doubles £65-£75) are all good value.

The pick of the luxury hotels is the **Hotel du Vin** (15-19 Trumpington Street, 01223 227330, www.hotelduvin.com, doubles £185-£335), a cheerfully but carefully run operation, painstakingly converted from listed terraced houses. A basement bar (with wine cellar) extends the whole length of the hotel, the busy all-day restaurant occupies one end of the ground floor and there's a heated and covered cigar 'room' outside.

DoubleTree by Hilton (Granta Place, Mill Lane, 01223 259988, www.doubletree cambridge.com, doubles £139-£264) is located right on the Cam behind Peterhouse, and has an indoor swimming pool. Finally, the **Hotel Felix** (Whitehouse Lane, Huntingdon Road, 01223 277977, www.hotelfelix.co.uk, doubles £200-£245), a modern hotel centred on a characterful 1852 Victorian mansion, is a little remote for walkers, but it has loads of parking space and a good decked area outside its twinkly bar-restaurant.

Getting there

By train Trains to Cambridge leave from King's Cross (50mins; map p397 L3) or Liverpool Street (map p401 R5; 1hr 15mins).
By coach National Express coaches to Cambridge leave from Victoria Coach Station (1hr 50mins).
By car Take Junction 11 or Junction 12 off the M11.

Tourist information

Cambridge Tourist Information Centre

Peas Hill, CB2 3AD (0871 226 8006, www.visit cambridge.org). **Open** *Apr-Sept* 10am-5pm Mon-Sat; 11am-3pm Sun. *Oct-Mar* 10am-5pm Mon-Sat.

Directory

Getting Around

For information on transport during the London 2012 Games, *see p69*.

ARRIVING & LEAVING

By air

Gatwick Airport *0844 892 0322, www.gatwickairport.com. About 30 miles south of central London, off the M23.*
Of the three rail services that link Gatwick to London, the quickest is the **Gatwick Express** (0845 850 1530, www.gatwickexpress.com) to Victoria; it takes 30mins and runs 3.30am-12.30am daily. Tickets cost £17.90 single or £30.50 for an open return (valid for 30 days). Under-15s pay £8.95 for a single and £11.90 for returns; under-5s go free.
 Southern (0845 127 2920, www.southernrailway.com) also runs a rail service between Gatwick and Victoria, with trains every 5-10mins (every 30mins between 1am and 4am). It takes about 35mins, and costs £12.50 for a single, £13 for a day return (after 9.30am) and £30.80 for an open period return (valid for one month). Under-16s get half-price tickets; under-5s go free.
 If you're staying in King's Cross or Bloomsbury, consider trains run by **Thameslink** (0845 748 4950, www.firstcapitalconnect.co.uk) to St Pancras. Tickets are £9.40 single, £9.50 day return (after 9.32am); £17 for a 30-day open return.
 A **taxi** to the centre costs about £100 and takes a bit over an hour.

Heathrow Airport *0844 335 1801, www.heathrowairport.com. About 15 miles west of central London, off the M4.*
The **Heathrow Express** train (0845 600 1515, www.heathrow express.co.uk) runs to Paddington every 15mins (5.10am-11.25pm daily), and takes 15-20mins. The train can be boarded at the tube station that serves Terminals 1, 2 and 3 (aka Heathrow Central; Terminal 2 is currently closed for rebuilding), or the separate station serving the new Terminal 5; for passengers travelling to or from Terminal 4, a shuttle train connects with Heathrow Central. Tickets cost £18 single (£1 less online, £5 more

if you buy on board) or £32 return (£5 more if you buy on board); under-16s go half-price. Many airlines have check-in desks at Paddington Station.
 The journey by tube into central London is longer but cheaper. The 50-60min **Piccadilly line** ride into central London costs £5 one way (£2.50 under-16s). Trains run every few minutes from about 5am to 11.42pm daily (5.45am-11.30pm Sun).
 The **Heathrow Connect** (0845 678 6975, www.heathrow connect.com) rail service offers direct access to Hayes, Southall, Hanwell, West Ealing, Ealing Broadway and Paddington stations in west and north-west London. The trains run every half-hour, terminating at Heathrow Central (Terminals 1 and 3). From there to Terminal 4 get the free shuttle; between Central and Terminal 5, there's free use of the Heathrow Express. A single from Paddington is £8.50; an open return is £16.50.
 National Express (0871 781 8181, www.nationalexpress.com) runs daily coach services to London Victoria (90mins, 5am-9.35pm daily), leaving Heathrow Central bus terminal every 20-30mins. It's £5.50 for a single (£2.50 under-16s) or £9 (£4.50 under-16s) for a return. A taxi into town will cost £45-£65 and take 30-60mins.

London City Airport *7646 0088, www.londoncityairport.com. About 9 miles east of central London.*
The Docklands Light Railway (DLR) now includes a stop for London City Airport. The journey to Bank station in the City takes around 20mins, and trains run 5.35am-12.17am Mon-Sat or 7.07am-11.17pm Sun. By road, a taxi costs around £30 to central London; less to the City or to Canary Wharf.

Luton Airport *01582 405100, www.london-luton.com. About 30 miles north of central London, J10 off the M1.*
It's about a ten-minute bus ride from the airport to Luton Airport Parkway station. From here, the **Thameslink** rail service (*see left*) calls at many stations (St Pancras International and City among them); journey time is 35-45mins. Trains leave every

15mins or so and cost £12.50 single one-way and £21.50 return, or £13 for a cheap day return (after 9.16am Mon-Fri, all day weekends). Trains between Luton and St Pancras run at least hourly all night.
 By coach, the Luton to Victoria journey takes 60-90mins. **Green Line** (0870 608 7261, www.green line.co.uk) runs a 24hr service. A single is £15 and returns cost £22; under-16s £12 single, £17 return. A taxi to London costs £70-£80.

Stansted Airport *0844 335 1803, www.stanstedairport.com. About 35 miles north-east of central London, J8 off the M11.*
The **Stansted Express** train (0845 748 4950, www.stansted express.com) runs to and from Liverpool Street Station; the journey time is 40-45mins. Trains leave every 15mins, and tickets cost £21 single, £29.80 return; under-16s travel half-price, under-5s free.
 Several companies run coaches to central London. The **Airbus** (0871 781 8181, www.national express.com) coach service from Stansted to Victoria takes at least 80mins. Coaches run roughly every 30mins (24hrs daily), more at peak times. A single is £10.50 (£5.50 for under-16s), return is £17.50 (£9 for under-16s).
 A **taxi** into the centre of London costs around £100.

By coach

Coaches run by **National Express** (0871 781 8181, www.nationalexpress.com), the biggest coach company in the UK, arrive at **Victoria Coach Station** (164 Buckingham Palace Road, SW1W 9TP, 0843 222 1234, www.tfl.gov.uk), a good 10min walk from Victoria tube station. This is where companies such as Eurolines (01582 404511, www.eurolines.com) dock their European services.

By rail

Trains from mainland Europe run by Eurostar (0843 218 6186, www.eurostar.com) arrive at **St Pancras International** (Pancras Road, King's Cross, NW1 2QP, 7843 7688, www.stpancras.com).

DIRECTORY

PUBLIC TRANSPORT

Getting around London on public transport is straightforward but it's certainly not cheap.

Information

Details on timetables and other travel information are provided by **Transport for London** (0843 222 1234, www.tfl.gov.uk/journey planner). Complaints or comments on most forms of public transport can also be taken up with **London TravelWatch** (7505 9000, www. londontravelwatch.org.uk).

Travel Information Centres
TfL's Travel Information Centres provide help with the tube, buses and Docklands Light Railway (DLR; *see p366*). You can find them in **King's Cross tube station**, (7.15am-8.15pm Mon-Sat; 8.15am-7.15pm Sun), and in the stations below. Call 0843 222 1234 for more information.

Euston Station 8.15am-7.15pm Mon-Thur; 8.15am-8.15pm Fri; 8.15am-7.15pm Sat, Sun.
Heathrow Terminals 1, 2 & 3 tube station 7.15am-8.15pm daily.
Liverpool Street tube station 8.15am-7.15pm Mon-Thur; 8.15am-8.15pm Fri; 8.15am-7.15pm Sat, Sun.
Piccadilly Circus tube station 9.15am-7pm daily.
Victoria Station 7.15am-8.15pm Mon-Sat; 8.15am-7.15pm Sun.

Fares & tickets

Tube and DLR fares are based on a system of six zones, stretching 12 miles out from the centre of London. A flat cash fare of £4 per journey applies across zones 1-4 on the tube, and £5 for zones 1-6; customers save up to £2.60 per journey with a pre-pay Oyster card (*see below*). Anyone caught without a ticket or Oyster card is subject to a £50 on-the-spot fine (reduced to £25 if you pay within three weeks).

Oyster cards A pre-paid smart-card, Oyster is the cheapest way of getting around on public transport. You can charge up standard Oyster cards at tube stations, Travel Information Centres (*see above*), some rail stations and newsagents. There is a £3 refundable deposit payable on each card; to collect your deposit, call 0845 330 9876.
 Visitor Oyster cards are available from Gatwick Express

outlets, National Express coaches, Superbreak, visitlondon.com, visit britaindirect.com, Oxford Tube coach service and on Eurostar services. The only difference between Visitor Oysters and 'normal' Oysters is that they come pre-loaded with money.

A tube journey in zone 1 using Oyster pay-as-you-go costs £1.90 (70p for under-16s), compared to the cash fare of £4. A single tube ride within zones 2, 3, 4, 5 or 6 costs £1.40 (70p for under-16s); single journeys from zones 1 through to 6 using Oyster are £4.50 (6.30-9.30am, 4-7pm Mon-Fri) or £2.70 (all other times), or 70p for children. Up to four children pay just £1 each for their fares when accompanied by an adult with a Travelcard.

If you make a number of different journeys using an Oyster pay-as-you-go card on a particular day, the total fare deducted will always be capped at the price of an equivalent Day Travelcard. However, if you only make one journey using Oyster pay-as-you-go, you will only be charged a single Oyster fare.

Day Travelcards If you're only using the tube, DLR, buses and trams, using Oyster to pay as you go will always be capped at the same price as an equivalent Day Travelcard. However, if you're also using National Rail services, Oyster may not be accepted: opt, instead, for a Day Travelcard, a standard ticket with a coded stripe that allows travel across all networks.
 Anytime Day Travelcards can be used all day. They cost from £8 for zones 1-2 (£4 child), up to £15 for zones 1-6 (£7.50 child). Tickets are valid for journeys begun by 4.30am the next day. The cheaper **Off-Peak Day Travelcard** allows travel after 9.30am Mon-Fri and all day at weekends and public holidays. It costs from £6.60 for zones 1-2 up to £8 for zones 1-6.

Children Under-5s travel free on buses and trams without the need to provide any proof of identity. Five- and 10-year-olds can also travel free, but need to obtain a 5-10 Zip Oyster photocard. For details, visit www.tfl.gov.uk/fares or call 0845 330 9876.
 An 11-15 Zip Oyster photocard is needed by 11- to 15-year-olds to pay as they go on the tube/DLR and to buy 7-Day, monthly or longer period Travelcards, and by 11- to 15-year-olds to use the tram to/from Wimbledon for free.

Photocards Photocards are not required for 7-Day Travelcards or Bus Passes, adult-rate Travelcards or Bus Passes charged on an Oyster card. For details of how to obtain 5-10, 11-15 or 16+ Oyster photocards, see www.tfl.gov.uk/fares or call 0845 330 9876.

London Underground

Delays are fairly common, with lines closing at weekends for engineering works. Trains are hot and crowded in rush hour (8-9.30am and 4.30-7pm Mon-Fri). Even so, the 12 colour-coded lines that together comprise the underground rail system – also known as 'the tube' – remain the quickest way to get around London (for a map of the Underground, *see pp414-415*), carrying some 3.5 million passengers every weekday. Comments or complaints are dealt with by **LU Customer Services** on 0845 330 9880 (8am-8pm daily); for lost property, *see p372*.

Using the system You can get Oyster cards from www.tfl.gov. uk/oyster, by calling 0845 330 9876, at tube stations, Travel Information Centres, some rail stations and newsagents. Single or day tickets can be bought from ticket offices or machines. You can buy most tickets and top up Oyster cards at self-service machines. Some ticket offices close early (around 7.30pm); carry a charged-up Oyster card to avoid being stranded.

To enter and exit the tube using an Oyster card, simply touch it to the yellow reader, which will open the gates. Make sure you also touch the card to the reader when you exit the tube, or you'll be charged a higher fare when you next use your card to enter a station. On certain lines, you'll see a pink 'validator' – touch this reader in addition to the yellow entry/exit readers and on some routes it will reduce your fare.

To enter using a paper ticket, place it in the slot with the black magnetic strip facing down, then pull it out of the top to open the gates. Exiting is done in much the same way; however, if you have a single journey ticket, it will be retained by the gate as you leave.

Timetables Tube trains run daily from around 5am (except Sunday, when they start an hour or so later, and Christmas Day, when there's no service). You shouldn't have to wait more than 10mins for a train; during peak times, services should run every 2-3mins. Times of last trains vary; they're usually around 12.30am daily (11.30pm on Sun). The tubes run all night only on New Year's Eve; otherwise, you're limited to night buses (*see right*).

Fares The single fare for adults across the network is £4. Using Oyster pay-as-you-go, the fare varies by zone: zone 1 costs £1.90; zones 1-2 costs £1.90 or £2.50, depending on the time of day; zones 1-6 is £2.70 or £4.50. The single fare for children aged 5-15 is 65p or 75p for any journey depending on the time of day. Under-5s travel for free (*see also p365*).

National Rail & London Overground services

Independently run commuter services co-ordinated by **National Rail** (0845 748 4950, www.national rail.co.uk) leave from the city's main rail stations. Visitors heading to south London, or to more remote destinations such as Hampton Court Palace, will need to use these overground services. Travelcards are valid on these services within the right zones, but not all routes accept Oyster pay-as-you-go; check before you travel.

Operated by Transport for London, meaning it does accept Oyster, the **London Overground** is a fabulously useful new service. Originally the rail line ran through north London from Stratford in the east to Richmond in the south-west, with spurs connecting Willesden Junction in the north-west to Clapham Junction in the south-west, and Gospel Oak in the north to Barking in the east, as well as heading north-west from Euston. Then, in 2010, the reopened East London line was incorporated into the Overground network, connecting trains south of the river to trains to the north: effectively, Crystal Palace, West Croydon and New Cross are now useful, brand-new intermediate stations such as Shoreditch High Street) to Highbury & Islington and the northerly extent of the Overground. Trains run about every 20mins (every half an hour on Sunday).

For lost property, *see p372*.

Docklands Light Railway (DLR)

DLR trains (7363 9700, www.tfl. gov.uk/dlr) run from Bank station (where they connect with the tube

system's Central and Waterloo & City lines) or Tower Gateway, close to Tower Hill tube (Circle and District lines). At Westferry station, the line splits east and south via Island Gardens to Greenwich and Lewisham; a change at Poplar can take you north to Stratford. The easterly branch forks after Canning Town to either Beckton or Woolwich Arsenal. Trains run 5.30am-12.30am daily. For lost property, *see p372*.

Fares Adult single fares on the DLR are the same as for the tube (*see p365*) except for DLR-only journeys in zones 2-3, which cost £4 (£1.40-£2.20 with Oyster pay-as-you-go) or £2 for 11-15s (65p-70p with Oyster pay-as-you-go).

The DLR also offers one-day Rail & River Rover tickets, which add one day's DLR travel to hop-on, hop-off travel on **City Cruises** riverboats (10am-6pm; *see p368*) between Westminster, Waterloo, Tower and Greenwich Piers.

Trains leave Tower Gateway hourly from 10am for a special tour, with a guide adding commentary. It costs £15 for adults or £8 for kids.

Buses

You must have a ticket or valid pass before boarding any bus in zone 1, and before boarding any articulated, single-decker bus ('bendy buses', which are in the process of being phased out) anywhere in the city. You can buy a ticket (or a 1-Day Bus Pass) from machines at bus stops, although they're often not working; better to travel with an Oyster card or some other pass (*see p365*). Inspectors patrol buses at random; if you don't have a ticket or pass, you may be fined £50.

All buses are now low-floor vehicles that are accessible to wheelchair-users and passengers with buggies. The only exceptions are Heritage routes 9 and 15, which are served by the world-famous open-platform Routemaster buses (*see p134* **Get There Greener**).

For lost property, *see p372*.

Fares Using Oyster pay-as-you-go costs £1.30 a trip; your total daily payment, regardless of how many journeys you take, will be capped at £4. Paying with cash at the time of travel costs £2.20 for a single trip. Under-16s travel for free (using an Under-11 or 11-15 Oyster photocard as appropriate; *see p365*). A 1-Day Bus Pass gives unlimited bus and tram travel for £4.

Night buses Many bus routes operate 24hrs a day, seven days a week. There are also some special night buses with an 'N' prefix, which run from about 11pm to 6am. Most night services run every 15-30mins, but busier routes run a service around every 10mins. Fares are the same as for daytime buses; Bus Passes and Travelcards can be used at no extra fare until 4.30am of the morning after they expire.

Green Line buses Green Line buses (0844 801 7261, www.green line.co.uk) serve the suburbs within 40 miles of London. Its office is opposite **Victoria Coach Station** (*see p364*); services run 24hrs.

Tramlink

In south London, trams run between Beckenham, Croydon, Addington and Wimbledon. Travelcards that cover zones 3, 4, 5 or 6 are valid, as are Bus Passes. Cash fares are £2.20 (£1.30 with Oyster pay-as-you-go).

For lost property, *see p372*.

Water transport

Most river services operate every 20-60mins between 10.30am and 5pm, and may run more often and later in summer. For commuters, **Thames Clippers** (0870 781 5049, www.thamesclippers.com) runs a service between Embankment Pier and Royal Arsenal Woolwich Pier; stops include Blackfriars, Bankside, London Bridge, Canary Wharf and Greenwich. A standard day roamer ticket (valid 9am-9pm) costs £12.60, while a single from Embankment to Greenwich is £5.50, or £5 for Oyster cardholders. **Thames Executive Charters** (www. thamesexecutivecharters.com) also offers Travelcard discounts on its River Taxi between Putney and Blackfriars, calling at Wandsworth, Chelsea Harbour, Cadogan Pier and Embankment, meaning a £4.60 standard single becomes £3.10.

Westminster Passenger Service Assocation (7930 2062, www.wpsa.co.uk) runs a daily service from Westminster Pier to Kew, Richmond and Hampton Court from April to October. At around £12 for a single, it's not cheap, but it is a lovely way to see the city, and there are discounts of 33%-50% for Travelcard holders. **Thames River Services** (www.westminsterpier.co.uk) operates from the same pier, offering trips to Greenwich, Tower

Pier and the Thames Barrier. A trip to Greenwich costs £10, though £13.50 buys you a Rivercard, which allows you to hop on and off at will. Travelcard holders get a third off.

For commuter service timetables, plus a full list of leisure operators and services, see www.tfl.gov.uk.

For lost property, *see p372.*

TAXIS

Black cabs

The licensed London taxi, aka 'black cab' (although, since on-car advertising, they've come in many colours), is a much-loved feature of London life. Drivers must pass a test called 'the Knowledge' to prove they know every street in central London, and the shortest route to it.

If a taxi's orange 'For Hire' sign is lit, it can be hailed. If a taxi stops, the cabbie must take you to your destination if it's within seven miles. It can be hard to find an empty cab, especially just after the pubs close. Fares rise after 8pm on weekdays and at weekends.

You can book black cabs from the 24hr **Taxi One-Number** (0871 871 8710, a £2 booking fee applies, plus 12.5% if you pay by credit card), **Radio Taxis** (7272 0272) and **Dial-a-Cab** (7253 5000; credit cards only, with a booking fee of £2 plus a 12.5% handling charge). Comments or complaints about black cabs should be made to the **Public Carriage Office** (0845 602 7000, www.tfl.gov.uk/pco). Note the cab's badge number, which should be displayed in the rear of the cab and on its back bumper.

Minicabs

Minicabs (saloon cars) are generally cheaper than black cabs, but can be less reliable. Only use licensed firms (look for a disc in the front and rear windows), and avoid those that illegally tout for business in the street: drivers may be unlicensed, uninsured and dangerous.

Trustworthy and fully licensed firms include **Addison Lee** (0844 800 6677), which will text you when the car arrives, and **Lady Cabs** (7272 3300), **Ladybirds** (8295 0101) and **Ladycars** (8558 9511), which employ only women drivers. Otherwise, text HOME to 60835 ('60tfl'). Transport for London will then text you the numbers of the two nearest licensed minicab operators and the number for Taxi One-Number, which provides licensed black taxis in London. The

service costs 35p plus standard call rate. Always ask the price when you book and confirm it with the driver.

Motorbike taxis

Passenger Bikes (0844 561 6147, www.passengerbikes.com) and **Taxybikes** (7255 4269, www.addisonlee.com/services/taxybikes) have a minimum £30 charge, and offer fixed airport rates; the bikes are equipped with panniers, and can carry a small to medium suitcase. Central London to Gatwick currently costs £120-£130.

DRIVING

London's roads are often clogged with traffic and roadworks, and parking (*see right*) is a nightmare. Walking or using public transport are better options. If you hire a car, you can use any valid licence from outside the EU for up to a year after arrival. Speed limits in the city are generally 20 or 30mph on most roads. Don't use a mobile phone (unless it's hands-free) while driving or you risk a £1,000 fine.

Car hire

All firms below have branches at the airport; several also have offices in the city centre. Shop around for the best rate; always check the level of insurance included in the price.

Alamo UK: 0870 400 4562, *www.alamo.co.uk.* US: 1-877 222 9075, *www.alamo.com.*
Avis UK: 0844 581 0147, *www.avis.co.uk.* US: 1-800 230 4898, *www.avis.com.*
Budget UK: 0844 544 3439, *www.budget.co.uk.* US: 1-800 472 3325, *www.budget.com.*
Enterprise UK: 0800 800 227, *www.enterprise.co.uk.* US: 1-800 261 7331, *www.enterprise.com.*
Europcar UK: 0871 384 1087, *www.europcar.co.uk.* US: 1-877 940 6900, *www.europcar.com.*
Hertz UK: 0870 844 8844, *www.hertz.co.uk.* US: 1-800 654 3001, *www.hertz.com.*
National UK: 0870 400 4552, *www.nationalcar.co.uk.* US: 1-800 222 9058, *www.nationalcar.com.*
Thrifty UK: 01494 751500, *www.thrifty.co.uk.* US: 1-800 847 4389, *www.thrifty.com.*

Congestion charge

Drivers coming into central London between 7am and 6pm Monday to Friday have to pay £10, a fee known

as the congestion charge. The congestion charge zone is bordered by Marylebone, Euston and King's Cross (N), Old Street roundabout (NE), Aldgate (E), Tower Bridge Road (SE), Elephant & Castle (S), Vauxhall, Victoria (SW), Park Lane and Edgware Road (W); see the map on p390. You'll know when you're about to drive into the charging zone from the red 'C' signs on the road. You can also enter the postcode of your destination at www.tfl.gov.uk/roadusers/congestioncharging to discover if it's within the charging zone.

There are no tollbooths – the scheme is enforced by numberplate recognition from CCTV cameras. Passes can be bought from some newsagents, garages and NCP car parks; you can also pay online at www.tfl.gov.uk/roadusers/congestioncharging, by phone on 0845 900 1234 or by SMS (you'll need to pre-register at the website for the latter option). You can pay any time during the day; payments are also accepted until midnight on the next charging day, although the fee is £12 if you pay then. Expect a fine of £60 if you fail to pay, rising to £120 if you delay payment.

Breakdown services

AA (Automobile Association) *0870 550 0600 information, 0845 788 7766 breakdown, www.theaa.com.*
ETA (Environmental Transport Association) *0845 389 1010, www.eta.co.uk.*
RAC (Royal Automobile Club) *0870 572 2722 information, 0800 828282 breakdown, www.rac.co.uk.*

Parking

Central London is scattered with parking meters, but finding an unoccupied one is usually difficult. Meters cost upwards of £1 for 15mins, and in some areas they are limited to 2hrs. Parking on a single or double yellow line, a red line or in residents' parking areas during the day is illegal, and you may be fined, clamped or towed.

However, in the evening (from 6pm or 7pm in much of central London) and at various times at weekends, parking on single yellow lines is legal and free. If you find a clear spot on a single yellow line during the evening, look for a sign giving the local regulations. Meters also become free at certain times during evenings and weekends.

DIRECTORY

Parking on double yellow lines and red routes is illegal at all times.

NCP 24hr car parks (0845 050 7080, www.ncp.co.uk) are numerous but pricey. Central ones include Carrington Street, Mayfair, W1 (£12/2hrs); Snowsfields, Southwark, SE1 (£8/2hrs); and Brewer Street, Soho, W1 (£13/2hrs).

Clamping & vehicle removal

The immobilising of illegally parked vehicles with a clamp is common in London. There will be a label on the car telling you which payment centre to phone or visit. You'll have to stump up an £80 release fee and show a valid licence. The payment centre will de-clamp your car within four hours. If you don't remove your car at once, it may get clamped again, so wait by your vehicle.

If your car has disappeared, it's either been stolen or, if it was parked illegally, towed to a car pound by the local authorities. A release fee of £200 is levied for removal, plus upwards of £21 per day from the first midnight after removal. You'll also probably get a parking ticket of £60-£100 when you collect the car (reduced by 50% if paid within 14 days). To retrieve your car, call the **Trace Service** hotline (0845 206 8602).

CYCLING

The **Transport for London** (0843 222 1234, www.tfl.gov.uk) cycle hire scheme has been a great success, allowing when-you-want-it access to a string of bicycle stations across central London. The scheme is due to expand westwards to Olympia and eastwards to the Olympic Park.

To hire a bike, go to a docking station, touch the 'Hire a cycle' icon and insert a credit or debit card. The machine will print out a five-digit access code, which you then tap into the docking point of a bike, releasing the cycle, and away you go. £1 buys 24-hour access to the bike and the first 30 minutes are free. Serious cyclists should contact the **London Cycle Network** (www.londoncyclenetwork.org.uk) and **London Cycling Campaign** (7234 9310, www.lcc.org.uk). For details of other London cycle hire companies, *see p339*.

WALKING

The best way to see London is on foot, but the city's street layout is complicated. We've included street maps of central London in the back of this book; the standard Geographers' *London A-Z* and Collins' *London Street Atlas* are useful supplements. There's also route advice at www.tfl.gov.uk/gettingaround.

GUIDED TOURS

By bicycle

The **London Bicycle Tour Company** (*see p339*) runs a range of tours in central London.

By boat

City Cruises: Rail River Rover 7740 0400, www.citycruises.com. **Rates** £15; £7.50 reductions. Combines hop-on, hop-off travel on any regular City Cruise route (pick-ups at Westminster, Waterloo, Tower and Greenwich Piers) with free travel on the DLR.

Jason's Trip Canal Boats www.jasons.co.uk. **Rates** £9 return; £8 reductions. Popular 90min narrowboat tours between Little Venice and Camden.

Thames RIB Experience 7930 5746, www.thamesribexperience. com. **Rates** £32-£45; £19-£27 reductions. Our favourite of the growing number of Thames RIB tours (a RIB is a powerful speedboat) zooms you from the Embankment, either to Canary Wharf (50mins) or the Thames Barrier (80mins), and back. You'll need to book in advance.

Thames River Adventures 0845 453 2002, http://thamesriver adventures.co.uk. **Tours** from £24.99. Want to investigate Tower Bridge, Hampton Court Palace or Regent's Canal under your own steam? Guided kayak tours run from March to October.

By bus

Big Bus Company 7233 9533, www.bigbustours.com. **Rates** £27; £12 reductions; free under-5s. These open-top buses (8.30am-6pm, or 4.30pm in winter) ply over 70 stops covering all the central areas of interest. There's live commentary in English, and a recorded version in eight other languages; you can hop on and off at any stop. Tickets include a river cruise.

Original London Sightseeing Tour 8877 1722, www.theoriginal tour.com. **Rates** £26; £13 reductions; £91 family; free under-5s. OLS's hop-on, hop-off bus tours cover 90 stops in central London, including Marble Arch and Trafalgar Square. Commentary comes in seven languages. Tickets include a river cruise.

London Duck 7928 3132, www. londonducktours.co.uk. **Rates** £21; £14-£17 reductions; £62 family. Tours of Westminster in an amphibious vehicle. The 75min road/river trip starts on Chicheley Street (behind the London Eye) and enters the Thames at Vauxhall.

By air

London Helicopter Tours 7036 1077, www.london helicoptertours.co.uk. **Rates** from £180. Departing from a number of west London locations as well as Battersea Heliport. Tours take in the Thames and the Olympic Park.

Adventure Balloons 01252 844222, www.adventure balloons.co.uk. **Rates** from £185. Flights operate from a number of take-off sites and glide over many of the capital's iconic sights. They run at dawn on weekdays between late April and the middle of August.

By car

Black Taxi Tours of London 7935 9363, www.blacktaxi tours.co.uk. **Rates** £130-£145. Tailored 2hr tours for up to five.

Small Car Big City 7585 0399, www.smallcarbigcity.com. **Rates** £54-£239. Feeling a little retro? Tour town in a classic Mini Cooper.

On foot

Head to **www.walklondon. org.uk** for free walks and events. Good choices for paid group tours include **And Did Those Feet** (8806 4325, www.chr.org.uk), **Performing London** (01234 404774, www.performinglondon. co.uk), **Silver Cane Tours** (07720 715295, www.silver canetours.com) and **Urban Gentry** (8149 6253, www.urban gentry.com). **Original London Walks** (7624 3978, www.walks. com) provides an astonishing 140 different walks on a variety of themes. Idiosyncratic outings follow old London maps (www.londontrails.wordpress.com) or the new London art scene (www.foxandsquirrel.com and streetartlondon.co.uk/tours). **The Guardian** (www.guardian.co.uk/travel/series/london-walks) offers a great set of themed audio walks. And if walking is too slow for you, go for a guided run with **www. londonsightseeingruns.com**.

DIRECTORY

Resources A-Z

TRAVEL ADVICE

For up-to-date information on travel to a specific country – including the latest on safety and security, health issues, local laws and customs – contact your home country government's department of foreign affairs. Most have websites with useful advice for would-be travellers. For information on travelling to the United Kingdom from within the European Union, including details of visa regulations and healthcare provision, see http://europa.eu/travel.

AUSTRALIA
www.smartraveller.gov.au

CANADA
www.voyage.gc.ca

NEW ZEALAND
www.safetravel.govt.nz

REPUBLIC OF IRELAND
http://foreignaffairs.gov.ie

UK
www.fco.gov.uk/travel

USA
www.state.gov/travel

ADDRESSES

London postcodes are rather less helpful than they could be for locating addresses. The first element starts with a compass point – N, E, SE, SW, W and NW, plus the smaller EC (East Central) and WC (West Central). However, the number that follows relates not to geography (unless it's a 1, which indicates central) but to alphabetical order. So N2 is way out in the boondocks (East Finchley), while W2 covers the very central Bayswater.

AGE RESTRICTIONS

Buying/drinking alcohol 18.
Driving 17.
Sex 16.
Smoking 18.

ATTITUDE & ETIQUETTE

Don't mistake reserve for rudeness or indifference: strangers striking up a conversation are likely to be foreign, drunk or mad. The weather is a safe subject on which to broach a conversation. Avoid personal questions or excessive personal contact beyond a handshake.

If you want to really rile a Londoner in the Underground, stand blocking the escalator during rush hour (stand on the right, walk on the left).

BUSINESS

As the financial centre of Europe, London is well equipped to meet the needs of business travellers. The financial action is increasingly centred on Canary Wharf.

Marketing, advertising and entertainment companies have a strong presence in the West End.

Conventions & conferences

Visit London *0870 156 6366, www.visitlondon.com.* Enquiries. **Queen Elizabeth II Conference Centre** *Broad Sanctuary, Westminster, SW1P 3EE (7222 5000, www.qeiicc.co.uk).* *Westminster tube.* **Open** 8am-6pm Mon-Fri. *Conference facilities* 24hrs daily. **Map** p399 K9. Excellent conference facilities.

Couriers & shippers

DHL *0844 248 0999, www.dhl.co.uk.*
UPS *0845 787 7877, www.ups.com.*

Office services

British Monomarks *27 Old Gloucester Street, Holborn, WC1N 3XX (7419 5000, www.britishmono marks.co.uk).* *Holborn tube.* **Open** 9am-5.30pm Mon-Fri. **Credit** AmEx, MC, V. **Map** p397 L5.

CONSUMER

Consumer Direct *0845 404 0506, www.consumerdirect.gov.uk.* Funded by the government's Office of Fair Trading, this is a good place to start for consumer advice on all goods and services.

CUSTOMS

Citizens entering the UK from outside the EU must adhere to duty-free import limits:

● 200 cigarettes or 100 cigarillos or 50 cigars or 250g of tobacco
● 4 litres still table wine plus either 1 litre spirits or strong liqueurs (above 22% abv) or 2 litres fortified wine (under 22% abv), sparkling wine or other liqueurs
● 60cc/ml perfume
● 250cc/ml toilet water
● other goods to the value of no more than £390

The import of meat, poultry, fruit, plants, flowers and protected animals is restricted or forbidden; there are no restrictions on the import or export of currency if travelling from another EU country. If you are travelling from outside the EU, amounts over €10,000 must be declared.

People over the age of 17 arriving from an EU country are able to import unlimited goods for their own personal use, if bought tax-paid (so not duty-free). For more details, see www.hmrc.gov.uk.

DISABLED

As a city that evolved long before the needs of disabled people were considered, London is difficult for wheelchair users, though access and facilities are slowly improving. The capital's bus fleet is now low-floor for easier wheelchair access; there are no steps for any of the city's trams; and all DLR stations have either lifts or ramp access. However, steps and escalators to the tube and overland trains mean they are often of only limited use to wheelchair users. A blue symbol on the tube map (*see pp414-415*) indicates stations with step-free access. The *Step-free Tube Guide*

DIRECTORY

map is free; call 0843 222 1234 for more details. For London Overground, call 0845 601 4867.

Most major attractions and hotels offer good accessibility, though provisions for the hearing- and sight-disabled are patchier. Enquire about facilities in advance. *Access in London* is an invaluable reference book for disabled travellers, with a new edition due in 2012. It's available for a £10 donation (sterling cheque, cash US dollars or via PayPal to gordon.couch@yahoo.com) from **Access Project** (39 Bradley Gardens, W13 8HE, www.accessinlondon.org). Or there's Time Out's *Open London* guide to the capital for disabled people.

Artsline *www.artsline.org.uk*. Information on disabled access to arts and culture.
Can Be Done *Congress House, 14 Lyon Road, Harrow, Middx HA1 2EN (8907 2400, www.canbedone.co.uk). Harrow on the Hill tube/rail.* **Open** 9.30am-5pm Mon-Fri. Disabled-adapted holidays and tours in London, around the UK and worldwide.
Royal Association for Disability & Rehabilitation *250 City Road, EC1V 8AF (7250 3222, 7250 4119 textphone, www.radar.org.uk). Old Street tube/rail.* **Open** 9am-5pm Mon-Fri. **Map** p400 P3.
A national organisation for disabled voluntary groups publishing books and the bimonthly magazine *New Bulletin* (£35/yr).
Tourism for All *0845 124 9971, www.tourismforall.org.uk.* **Open** *Helpline* 9am-5pm Mon-Fri. Information for older people and people with disabilities in relation to accessible accommodation and other tourism services.
Wheelchair Travel & Access Mini Buses *1 Johnston Green, Guildford, Surrey GU2 9XS (01483 233640, www.wheelchairtravel.co.uk).* **Open** 9am-5pm Mon-Fri; 9am-noon Sat. Hires out converted vehicles (driver optional), plus cars with hand controls and wheelchair-adapted vehicles.

DRUGS

Illegal drug use remains higher in London than the UK as a whole, though it's becoming less visible on the streets and in clubs. Despite fierce debate, cannabis has been reclassified from Class C to Class B (where it rejoins amphetamine), but possession of a small amount might attract no more than a

warning for a first offence. More serious Class B and A drugs (ecstasy, LSD, heroin, cocaine and the like) carry stiffer penalties, with a maximum of seven years in prison for possession.

ELECTRICITY

The UK uses the European 220-240V, 50-cycle AC voltage. British plugs use three pins, so travellers with two-pin European appliances should bring an adaptor, as should anyone using US appliances, which run off 110-120V, 60-cycle.

EMBASSIES & CONSULATES

American Embassy *24 Grosvenor Square, Mayfair, W1A 2LQ (7499 9000, http://london.usembassy.gov). Bond Street or Marble Arch tube.* **Open** 8.30am-5.30pm Mon-Fri. **Map** p398 G7.
Australian High Commission *Australia House, Strand, Holborn, WC2B 4LA (7379 4334, www.uk.embassy.gov.au). Holborn or Temple tube.* **Open** 9am-5.20pm Mon-Fri. **Map** p399 M6.
Canadian High Commission *38 Grosvenor Street, Mayfair, W1K 4AA (7258 6600, www.canada.org.uk). Bond Street or Oxford Circus tube.* **Open** 8am-3pm Mon-Thur. **Map** p398 H7.
Embassy of Ireland *17 Grosvenor Place, Belgravia, SW1X 7HR (7235 2171, 7225 7700 passports & visas, www.embassyofireland.co.uk). Hyde Park Corner tube.* **Open** 9.30am-4.30pm Mon-Fri. **Map** p398 G9.
New Zealand High Commission *New Zealand House, 80 Haymarket, St James's, SW1Y 4TQ (7930 8422, www.nzembassy.com). Piccadilly Circus tube.* **Open** 9am-5pm Mon-Fri. **Map** p416 W4.

EMERGENCIES

In the event of a serious accident, fire or other incident, call **999** – free from any phone, including payphones – and ask for an ambulance, the fire service or police. For hospital Accident & Emergency departments, *see p371*; for helplines, *see p371*; for police stations, *see p374*.

GAY & LESBIAN

Time Out Gay & Lesbian London (£12.99) is the ultimate handbook to the capital. The phonelines below offer help and information; for HIV and AIDS, *see p371*.

London Friend *7837 3337, www.londonfriend.org.uk.* **Open** 7.30-9.30pm Mon-Wed, Fri.
London Lesbian & Gay Switchboard *0300 330 0630, www.llgs.org.uk.* **Open** 10am-11pm daily.

HEALTH

British citizens or those working in the UK can go to any general practitioner (GP). People ordinarily resident in the UK, including overseas students, are also permitted to register with a National Health Service (NHS) doctor. If you fall outside these categories, you will have to pay to see a GP. Your hotel concierge should be able to recommend one.

A pharmacist may dispense medicines on receipt of a prescription from a GP. NHS prescriptions cost £7.40; under-16s and over-60s are exempt from charges. Contraception is free for all. If you're not eligible to see an NHS doctor, you'll be charged cost price for any medicines prescribed.

Free emergency medical treatment under the NHS is available to:
● EU nationals and those of Iceland, Norway and Liechtenstein; all may also be entitled to state-provided treatment for non-emergency conditions with an EHIC (European Health Insurance Card)
● nationals of New Zealand, Russia, most former USSR states and the former Yugoslavia
● residents (irrespective of nationality) of Anguilla, Australia, Barbados, the British Virgin Islands, the Falkland Islands, the Isle of Man, Montserrat, Poland, Romania, St Helena and the Turks & Caicos Islands
● anyone who has been in the UK for the previous 12 months, or who has come to the UK to take up permanent residence
● students and trainees whose courses require more than 12 weeks in employment in the first year
● refugees and others who have sought refuge in the UK
● people with HIV/AIDS at a special STD treatment clinic

There are no NHS charges for:
● treatment in A&E wards
● emergency ambulance transport to a hospital
● diagnosis and treatment of certain communicable diseases
● family planning services
● compulsory psychiatric treatment

Accident & emergency

Listed below are most of the central London hospitals that have 24-hour Accident & Emergency (A&E) departments.
Charing Cross Hospital *Fulham Palace Road, Hammersmith, W6 8RF (3311 1234, www.imperial. nhs.uk). Barons Court or Hammersmith tube.*
Chelsea & Westminster Hospital *369 Fulham Road, Chelsea, SW10 9NH (8746 8000, www.chelwest.nhs.uk). South Kensington tube.* **Map** p394 C12.
Royal Free Hospital *Pond Street, Hampstead, NW3 2QG (7794 0500, www.royalfree.nhs.uk). Belsize Park tube or Hampstead Heath rail.*
Royal London Hospital *Whitechapel Road, Whitechapel, E1 1BB (7377 7000, www.bartsandthe london.nhs.uk). Whitechapel tube.*
St Mary's Hospital *Praed Street, Paddington, W2 1NY (3312 6666, www.imperial.nhs.uk). Paddington tube/rail.* **Map** p393 D5.
St Thomas' Hospital *Lambeth Palace Road, Lambeth, SE1 7EH (7188 7188, www.guysandstthomas. nhs.uk). Westminster tube or Waterloo tube/rail.* **Map** p399 L9.
University College Hospital *235 Euston Road, NW1 2BU (0845 155 5000, www.uclh.nhs.uk). Euston Square or Warren Street tube.* **Map** p396 J4.

Complementary medicine

British Homeopathic Association *0870 444 3950, www.trust homeopathy.org.* **Open** *Enquiries* 9am-5pm Mon-Fri. Referrals.

Contraception & abortion

Family planning advice, contraceptive supplies and abortions are free to British citizens on the NHS, and to EU residents and foreign nationals living in Britain. Phone 0845 122 8690 or visit www.fpa.org.uk for your local Family Planning Association. The 'morning after' pill (around £25), effective up to 72 hours after intercourse, is available over the counter at pharmacies.

British Pregnancy Advisory Service *0845 730 4030, www. bpas.org.* **Open** *Helpline* 8am-9pm Mon-Fri; 8.30am-6pm Sat; 9.30am-2.30pm Sun. Callers are referred to their nearest clinic for treatment.
Brook Advisory Centre *7284 6040, 0808 802 1234 helpline, www.brook.org.uk.* **Open** *Helpline*

9am-7pm Mon-Fri. Information on sexual health, contraception and abortion, plus free pregnancy tests for under-25s.
Marie Stopes House *Family Planning Clinic/Well Woman Centre, 108 Whitfield Street, Fitzrovia, W1T 5BE (0845 300 8090, www.mariestopes.org.uk). Warren Street tube.* **Open** *Clinic* 8.30am-5pm Mon, Wed, Fri; 9.30am-6pm Tue, Thur; 9am-4pm Sat. *Helpline* 24hrs daily. **Map** p396 J4.
Contraceptive advice, emergency contraception, pregnancy testing, an abortion service, cervical and health screening or gynaecological services. Fees may apply.

Dentists

Dental care is free for resident students, under-18s and people on benefits. All others must pay. To find an NHS dentist, contact the local Health Authority or a Citizens' Advice Bureau (*see right*).

Dental Emergency Care Service *Guy's Hospital, St Thomas Street, Borough, SE1 9RT (7188 0511). London Bridge tube/rail.* **Open** 9am-5pm Mon-Fri. **Map** p402 Q8.
Queues start forming at 8am; arrive by 10am if you're to be seen at all.

Hospitals

For a list of hospitals with Accident & Emergency departments, *see left*; for other hospitals, consult the *Yellow Pages* directory (also online at www.yell.com).

Opticians

See p276.

Pharmacies

Also called 'chemists' in the UK. Branches of Boots and larger supermarkets have a pharmacy, and there are independents on the high street (*see p276*). Staff can advise on over-the-counter medicines. Most pharmacies keep shop hours (9am-6pm Mon-Sat).

STDs, HIV & AIDS

NHS Genito-Urinary Clinics (such as the Centre for Sexual Health) are affiliated to major hospitals. They provide free, confidential STD testing and treatment, as well as treating other problems such as thrush and cystitis. They also offer

counselling about HIV and other STDs, and can conduct blood tests.
The 24-hour **Sexual Healthline** (0800 567 123, www.nhs.uk/ worthtalkingabout/) is free and confidential. See online for your nearest clinic. For other helplines, *see below*; for abortion and contraception, *see left*.
Mortimer Market Centre for Sexual Health *Mortimer Market, off Capper Street, Bloomsbury, WC1E 6JB (3317 5100). Goodge Street or Warren Street tube.* **Open** 9am-6pm Mon, Thur; 9am-7pm Tue; 1-6pm Wed; 8.30am-3pm Fri. **Map** p396 J4.
Terrence Higgins Trust Lighthouse *314-320 Gray's Inn Road, King Cross,WC1X 8DP (0845 122 1200, www.tht.org.uk). King's Cross tube/rail.* **Open** *Helpline* 10am-10pm Mon-Fri; noon-6pm Sat, Sun. **Map** p397 M5.
Advice for those with HIV/AIDS, their relatives, lovers and friends. It also offers free leaflets about AIDS and safer sex.

HELPLINES

Helplines dealing with sexual health issues are listed under STDs, HIV & AIDS (*see left*).

Alcoholics Anonymous *0845 769 7555, www.alcoholics-anonymous.org.uk.* **Open** 10am-10pm daily.
Citizens' Advice Bureaux *www.citizensadvice.org.uk.* The council-run CABs offer free legal, financial and personal advice. Check the phone book or see the website for your nearest office.
Missing People *0500 700 700, www.missingpeople.org.uk.* **Open** 24hrs daily. Information on anyone reported missing.
NHS Direct *0845 4647, www.nhsdirect.nhs.uk.* **Open** 24hrs daily.
A free, first-stop service for medical advice on all subjects.
Rape & Sexual Abuse Support Centre *0808 802 9999, www.rapecrisis.org.uk.* **Open** noon-2.30pm, 7-9.30pm daily. Information and support.
Samaritans *0845 790 9090, www.samaritans.org.uk.* **Open** 24hrs daily. General helpline for those under emotional stress.
Victim Support *0845 303 0900, www.victimsupport.org.uk.* **Open** 9am-9pm Mon-Fri; 9am-7pm Sat, Sun. **Map** p396 H5.
Emotional and practical support to victims of crime.

DIRECTORY

ID

Passports and photographic driver's licences are acceptable forms of ID.

INSURANCE

Insuring personal belongings can be difficult to arrange once you have arrived, so do so before you leave home. Medical insurance is usually included in travel insurance packages. Unless your country has an arrangement with the UK (see p370), it's important to ensure you have adequate health cover.

INTERNET

Many hotels now have high-speed internet access, whether via a cable or as wireless. Many cafés have wireless access; see below for four central establishments. You'll also find internet terminals in public libraries (see right).

Benugo Bar & Kitchen *BFI Southbank, Belvedere Road, South Bank, SE1 8XT (7401 9000, www.benugo.com). Waterloo tube/rail.* **Open** *11am-11pm Mon-Sat; 11am-10.30pm Sun.*
5th View *Waterstone's, 203-206 Piccadilly, W1J 9HA (7851 2433, www.5thview.co.uk). Piccadilly Circus tube.* **Open** *9am-9pm Mon-Sat; noon-5pm Sun.*
Hummus Brothers *88 Wardour Street, Soho, W1F 0TH (7734 1311, www.hbros.co.uk). Oxford Circus tube.* **Open** *noon-10pm Mon-Wed, Sun; noon-11pm Thur-Sat.*
Peyton & Byrne *Wellcome Collection, 183 Euston Road, Bloomsbury, NW1 2BE (7611 2138, www.peytonandbyrne.com). Euston tube/rail.* **Open** *10am-6pm Mon-Wed, Fri, Sat; 10am-10pm Thur; 11am-6pm Sun.*

LEFT LUGGAGE

Airports

Gatwick Airport *01293 502014 South Terminal, 01293 569900 North Terminal.*
Heathrow Airport *8759 3344.*
London City Airport *7646 0000.*
Stansted Airport *01279 663213.*

Rail & bus stations

Security precautions mean that London stations tend to have left-luggage desks rather than lockers. Call 0845 748 4950 for details.

Charing Cross *7930 5444.* **Open** 7am-11pm daily.
Euston *7387 8699.* **Open** 7am-11pm daily.
King's Cross *7837 4334.* **Open** 7am-11pm daily.
Paddington *7313 1514.* **Open** 7am-11pm daily.
Victoria *7963 0957.* **Open** 7am-midnight daily.

LEGAL HELP

Those in difficulties can visit a Citizens' Advice Bureau (see p371) or contact the groups below. Try the **Legal Services Commission** (0845 345 4345, www.legalservices.gov.uk) for information. If you're arrested, your first call should be to your embassy (see p370).

Law Centres Federation *7839 2998, www.lawcentres.org.uk.* **Open** 10am-5.30pm Mon-Fri. Free legal help for people who can't afford a lawyer and live or work in the immediate area; this office connects you with the nearest centre.

LIBRARIES

Unless you're a resident, you won't be able to join a lending library. At the British Library (see p109), only exhibition areas are open to non-members, but the libraries below can be used for reference by all.

Barbican Library *Barbican Centre, Silk Street, the City, EC2Y 8DS (7638 0569, www.cityof london.gov.uk/barbicanlibrary). Barbican tube.* **Open** 9.30am-5.30pm Mon, Wed; 9.30am-7.30pm Tue, Thur; 9.30am-2pm Fri; 9.30am-4pm Sat. **Map** p400 P5.
Holborn Library *32-38 Theobald's Road, Bloomsbury, WC1X 8PA (7974 6345). Chancery Lane tube.* **Open** 10am-7pm Mon-Fri; 10am-5pm Sat. **Map** p397 M5.
Kensington Central Library *12 Philimore Walk, Kensington, W8 7RX (7361 3010, www.rbkc.gov.uk/libraries). High Street Kensington tube.* **Open** 9.30am-8pm Mon, Tue, Thur; 9.30am-5pm Wed, Fri, Sat.
Marylebone Library *109-117 Marylebone Road, Marylebone, NW1 5PS (7641 1300, www.westminster.gov.uk/libraries). Baker Street tube or Marylebone tube/rail.* **Open** 9.30am-8pm Mon, Tue, Thur, Fri; 9.30am-8pm Wed; 9.30am-5pm Sat; 1.30-5pm Sun. **Map** p393 F4.
Victoria Library *160 Buckingham Palace Road, Belgravia, SW1W*

9UD (7641 1300, www.westminster.gov.uk/libraries). Victoria tube/rail. **Open** 9.30am-8pm Mon; 9.30am-7pm Tue, Thur, Fri; 10am-7pm Wed; 9.30am-5pm Sat. **Map** p398 H10.
Westminster Reference Library *35 St Martin's Street, Westminster, WC2H 7HP (7641 1300, www.westminster.gov.uk/libraries). Leicester Square tube.* **Open** 10am-8pm Mon-Fri; 10am-5pm Sat. **Map** p416 X4.
Women's Library *25 Old Castle Street, Whitechapel, E1 7NT (7320 2222, www.thewomens library.ac.uk). Aldgate tube or Aldgate East tube.* **Open** *Reading room* 9.30am-5pm Tue, Wed, Fri; 9.30am-8pm Thur. **Map** p403 S6.

LOST PROPERTY

Always inform the police if you lose anything, if only to validate insurance claims; see left or the *Yellow Pages* for police station locations. Only dial 999 if violence has occurred; use 0300 123 1212 for non-emergencies. Report lost passports both to the police and to your embassy (see p370).

Airports

For items left on the plane, contact the relevant airline. Otherwise, phone the following:

Gatwick Airport *01253 503162.*
Heathrow Airport *0844 824 3115.*
London City Airport *7646 0000.*
Luton Airport *01582 395219.*
Stansted Airport *01279 663293.*

Public transport

If you've lost property in an overground station or on a train, call 0870 000 5151, and give the operator the details.

Transport for London *Lost Property Office, 200 Baker Street, Marylebone, NW1 5RZ (0845 330 9882, www.tfl.gov.uk). Baker Street tube.* **Open** 8.30am-4pm Mon-Fri. **Map** p396 G4. Allow three working days from the time of loss. If you lose something on a bus, call 0843 222 1234 and ask for the numbers of the depots at either end of the route. For tube losses, pick up a lost property form from any station.

Taxis

The Transport for London office (see above) deals with property found in registered black cabs. Allow seven days from the time of loss. For items lost in a minicab, contact the relevant company.

MEDIA
Magazines

Time Out remains London's only quality listings magazine. Widely available in central London every Tuesday, it gives listings for the week from Thursday. If you want to know what's going on and whether it's any good, this is the place to look.

Nationally, *Loaded, FHM* and *Maxim* are big men's titles, while women often buy *Glamour* and *Grazia* alongside *Vogue, Marie Claire* and *Elle*. The appetite for gossip rags such as *Heat, Closer* and *OK* has abated only slightly.

The *Spectator, Prospect*, the *Economist* and the *New Statesman* are at the serious, political end of the market, with the satirical *Private Eye* bringing some levity to the subject. The *London Review of Books* ponders life and letters in considerable depth. The laudable *Big Issue* is sold across the capital by registered homeless vendors.

Newspapers

London's main daily paper is the sensationalist *Evening Standard*, published Monday to Friday. It became a freesheet in 2009, after a major revamp under a new owner failed to bring in enough sales. In the mornings, in tube station dispensers and discarded in the carriages, you'll still find *Metro*, a free *Standard* spin-off that led a deluge of low-quality free dailies.

Quality national dailies include, from right to left of the political spectrum, the *Daily Telegraph* (best for sport), *The Times*, the *Independent* (which launched a cheap daily digest, *i*, in 2010) and the *Guardian* (best for the arts). All go into overdrive on Saturdays and all have bulging Sunday equivalents bar the *Guardian*, which instead has a sister Sunday paper, the *Observer*. The pink *Financial Times* (daily except Sunday) is the best for business.

In the middle market, the leader is the generally right-leaning *Daily Mail* (and *Mail on Sunday*); the *Daily Express* (and *Sunday Express*) competes.

The tabloid leader is the *Sun*, with the *Daily Star* and the *Mirror* its main lowbrow contenders.

Radio

The stations below are broadcast on standard wavebands as well as digital, where they are joined by some interesting new channels (mostly from the BBC). The format is not yet widespread, but you may be lucky enough to have digital in your hotel room or hire car.

Absolute *105.8 FM*. Laddish rock.
BBC Radio 1 *98.8 FM*. Youth-oriented pop, indie and dance.
BBC Radio 2 *89.1 FM*. Bland during the day; better after dark.
BBC Radio 3 *91.3 FM*. Classical music dominates, but there's also discussion, world music and arts.
BBC Radio 4 *93.5 FM, 198 LW*. The BBC's main speech station is led by news agenda-setter *Today* (6-9am Mon-Fri, 7-9am Sat).
BBC Radio 5 Live *693, 909 AM*. Rolling news and sport. Avoid the morning phone-ins.
BBC London *94.9 FM*. Danny Baker (3-5pm Mon-Fri) is brilliant.
BBC World Service *648 AM*. Some repeats, some new shows, transmitted globally.
Capital FM *95.8 FM*. Pop and chat.
Classic FM *100.9 FM*. Easy-listening classical.
Heart FM *106.2 FM*. Capital for grown-ups.
Kiss *100 FM*. Dance music.
LBC *97.3 FM*. Phone-ins and talk.
Magic *105.4 FM*. Familiar pop.
Smooth *102.2 FM*. Aural wallpaper.
Resonance *104.4 FM*. Arts radio – an inventively oddball mix.
Xfm *104.9 FM*. Alternativish rock.

Television

With a multiplicity of formats, there are plenty of pay-TV options. However, the relative quality of free TV keeps subscriptions from attaining US levels.

The five main free-to-air networks are as follows:

BBC1 The Corporation's mass-market station. Relies too much on soaps, game shows and lifestyle TV, but does have quality offerings. As with all BBC stations, there are no commercials.
BBC2 A reasonably intelligent cultural cross-section, but now upstaged by BBC4 (*see right*).
ITV1 Monotonous weekday mass-appeal shows. ITV2 does much the same on digital.
Channel 4 Extremely successful US imports (the likes of *Ugly Betty* and *ER*), more or less unwatchable

home-grown entertainments and the occasional great documentary.
Five From high culture to lowbrow filth. A strange, unholy mix.

Satellite, digital and cable channels include the following:

BBC3 Often appalling home-grown comedy and dismal documentary.
BBC4 Highbrow stuff, including fine documentaries and dramas.
BBC News Rolling news.
BBC Parliament Live debates.
CBBC, CBeebies Children's programmes, the latter is younger.
Discovery Channel Science and nature documentaries.
E4, More4, Film4 Channel 4's entertainment and movie channels.
Fiver US comedy and drama, plus Australian soaps.
ITV2, ITV3, ITV4 US shows on 2, British reruns on 3 and 4.
Sky News Rolling news.
Sky One Sky's version of ITV.
Sky Sports Four channels.

MONEY

Britain's currency is the pound sterling (£). One pound equals 100 pence (p). Coins are copper (1p, 2p), silver (round: 5p, 10p; seven-sided: 20p, 50p), yellow-gold (£1) or silver in the centre with a yellow-gold edge (£2). Paper notes are blue (£5), orange (£10), purple (£20) or red (£50). You can exchange foreign currency at banks, bureaux de change and post offices; there's no commission charge at the last of these (for addresses of the most central, *see p375*). Many large stores also accept euros (€).

Western Union *0800 833833, www.westernunion.co.uk.* The old standby. Chequepoint (*see p374*) also offers this service.

Banks & ATMs

ATMs can be found inside and outside banks, in some shops and in larger stations. Machines in many commercial premises levy a charge for each withdrawal, usually £1.85. If you're visiting from outside the UK, your card should work via one of the debit networks, but check charges in advance. ATMs also allow you to make withdrawals on your credit card if you know your PIN; you'll be charged interest plus, usually, a currency exchange fee. Generally, getting cash with a card is the cheapest form of currency exchange but there are hidden charges, so do your research.

Credit cards, especially Visa and MasterCard, are accepted in most shops (except small corner shops) and restaurants (except caffs). However, American Express and Diners Club tend to be accepted only at more expensive outlets. You will usually have to have a PIN number to make a purchase. For more, see www.chipandpin.co.uk.

No commission is charged for cashing sterling travellers' cheques if you go to one of the banks affiliated with the issuing company. You do have to pay to cash travellers' cheques in foreign currencies, and to change cash. You will always need to produce ID to cash travellers' cheques.

Bureaux de change

You'll be charged for cashing travellers' cheques or buying and selling foreign currency at bureaux de change. The commission varies. Major stations have bureaux, and there are many in tourist areas and on major shopping streets. Most open 8am-10pm.

Chequepoint *550 Oxford Street, Marylebone, W1C 1LY (7724 6127, www.chequepoint.com). Marble Arch tube.* **Open** 8am-10pm Mon-Sat; 10am-10pm Sun. **Map** p396 G6. **Other locations** throughout the city.

Garden Bureau *30A Jubilee Market Hall, Covent Garden, WC2E 8BE (7240 9921). Covent Garden tube.* **Open** 9am-6pm daily. **Map** p416 Z3.

Thomas Exchange *13 Maddox Street, Mayfair, W1S 2QG (7493 1300, www.thomasexchange.co.uk). Oxford Circus tube.* **Open** 9am-6pm Mon-Fri. **Map** p416 U3.

Lost/stolen credit cards

Report lost or stolen credit cards both to the police and the 24-hour phone lines listed below. Inform your bank by phone and in writing.

American Express *01273 696933, www.americanexpress.com.*
Diners Club *0870 190 0011, www.dinersclub.co.uk.*
MasterCard *0800 964767, www.mastercard.com.*
Visa *0800 891725, www.visa.com.*

Tax

With the exception of food, books, newspapers and a few other items, purchases in the UK are subject to Value Added Tax (VAT), aka sales tax. The rate is currently set at 20%. VAT is included in all prices quoted by mainstream shops, although it may not be included in hotel rates.

Foreign visitors may be able to claim back the VAT paid on most goods that are taken out of the EC (European Community) as part of a scheme generally called 'Tax Free Shopping'. To be able to claim a refund, you must be a non-EC visitor to the UK, or a UK resident emigrating from the EC. When you buy the goods, the retailer will ask to see your passport, and will then ask you to fill in a simple refund form. You need to have one of these forms to make your claim; till receipts alone will not do. If you're leaving the UK direct for outside the EC, you must show your goods and refund form to UK customs at the airport/port from which you're leaving. If you're leaving the EC via another EC country, you must show your goods and refund form to customs staff of that country.

After customs have certified your form, get your refund by posting the form to the retailer from which you bought the goods, posting the form to a commercial refund company or handing your form at a refund booth to get immediate payment. Customs are not responsible for making the refund: when you buy the goods, ask the retailer how the refund is paid.

OPENING HOURS

Government offices close on bank (public) holidays (*see p377*), but big shops often remain open, with only Christmas Day sacrosanct. Most attractions remain open on the other public holidays.

Banks 9am-4.30pm (some close at 3.30pm, some 5.30pm) Mon-Fri; some also Sat mornings.
Businesses 9am-5pm Mon-Fri.
Post offices 9am-5.30pm Mon-Fri; 9am-noon Sat.
Pubs & bars 11am-11pm Mon-Sat; noon-10.30pm Sun.
Shops 10am-6pm Mon-Sat, some to 8pm. Many also open on Sun, usually 11am-5pm or noon-6pm.

POLICE

London's police are used to helping visitors. If you've been robbed, assaulted or involved in a crime, go to your nearest police station. (We've listed a handful in central London; look under 'Police' in Directory Enquiries or call 118 118, 118 500 or 118 888 for more.)

If you have a complaint, ensure that you take the offending officer's identifying number (it should be displayed on his or her epaulette). You can then register a complaint with the **Independent Police Complaints Commission** (90 High Holborn, WC1V 6BH, 0845 300 2002, www.ipcc.gov.uk). In non-emergencies, call 0300 123 1212; for emergencies, *see p370*.

Belgravia Police Station *202-206 Buckingham Palace Road, Pimlico, SW1W 9SX (0300 123 1212). Victoria tube/rail.* **Map** p398 H10.
Camden Police Station *60 Albany Street, Fitzrovia, NW1 4EE (0300 123 1212). Great Portland Street tube.* **Map** p396 H4.
Charing Cross Police Station *Agar Street, Covent Garden, WC2N 4JP (0300 123 1212). Charing Cross tube/rail.* **Map** p416 Y4.
Chelsea Police Station *2 Lucan Place, Chelsea, SW3 3PB (0300 123 1212). South Kensington tube.* **Map** p395 E11.
Islington Police Station *2 Tolpuddle Street, Islington, N1 0YY (0300 123 1212). Angel tube.* **Map** p400 N2.
Kensington Police Station *72 Earl's Court Road, Kensington, W8 6EQ (0300 123 1212). Earl's Court tube.* **Map** p394 B11.
Marylebone Police Station *1-9 Seymour Street, Marylebone, W1H 7BA (0300 123 1212). Marble Arch tube.* **Map** p393 F6.
West End Central Police Station *27 Savile Row, Mayfair, W1S 2EX (0300 123 1212). Piccadilly Circus tube.* **Map** p416 U3.

POSTAL SERVICES

The UK has a fairly reliable postal service. If you have a query, contact Customer Services on 0845 774 0740. For business enquiries, call 0845 795 0950.

Post offices are usually open 9am-5.30pm during the week and 9am-noon on Saturdays, although some post offices shut for lunch and smaller offices may close for one or more afternoons each week. Some central post offices are listed below; for others, call the **Royal Mail** on 0845 722 3344 or check online at www.royalmail.com.

You can buy individual stamps at post offices, and books of four or 12 first- or second-class stamps at newsagents and supermarkets that display the appropriate red sign. A first-class stamp for a regular letter costs 46p; second-class stamps are 36p. It costs 68p to send a postcard abroad. For details of other rates, see www.royalmail.com.

See also p369 **Business: Couriers & shippers**.

Post offices

Post offices are usually open 9am-6pm Mon-Fri and 9am-noon Sat, with the exception of Trafalgar Square Post Office (24-28 William IV Street, WC2N 4DL, 0845 722 3344), which opens 8.30am-6.30pm Mon, Wed-Fri; 9.15am-6.30pm Tue; 9am-5.30pm Sat. Listed below are the other main central London offices. For general enquiries, call 0845 722 3344 or consult www.postoffice.co.uk.

Albemarle Street *nos.43-44, Mayfair, W1S 4DS. Green Park tube.* **Map** p416 U5.
Baker Street *no.111, Marylebone, W1U 6SG. Baker Street tube.* **Map** p396 G5.
Great Portland Street *nos.54-56, Fitzrovia, W1W 7NE. Oxford Circus tube.* **Map** p396 H4.
High Holborn *no.181, Holborn, WC1V 7RL. Holborn tube.* **Map** p416 Y1.

Poste restante

If you want to receive mail while you're away, you can have it sent to Trafalgar Square Post Office (*see above*), where it will be kept for a month. Your name and 'Poste Restante' must be clearly marked on the letter. You'll need ID to collect it.

RELIGION

Times may vary; phone to check.

Anglican & Baptist

Bloomsbury Central Baptist Church *235 Shaftesbury Avenue, Covent Garden, WC2H 8EP (7240 0544, www.bloomsbury.org.uk). Tottenham Court Road tube.* **Services & meetings** 11am, 5.30pm Sun. **Map** p397 Y1.
St Paul's Cathedral *For listings, see p90.* **Services** 7.30am, 8am, 12.30pm, 5pm Mon-Sat; 8am, 10.15am, 11.30am, 3.15pm, 6pm Sun. **Map** p402 O6.
Westminster Abbey *For listings, see p137.* **Services** 7.30am, 8am, 12.30pm, 5pm Mon-Fri; 8am, 9am, 12.30pm, 3pm Sat; 8am, 10am, 11.15am, 3pm, 5.45pm, 6.30pm Sun. **Map** p399 K9.

Buddhist

Buddhapadipa Thai Temple *14 Calonne Road, Wimbledon, SW19 5HJ (8946 1357, www.buddhapadipa.org). Wimbledon tube/rail then bus 93.* **Open** *Temple* 9-6pm Sat, Sun. *Meditation retreat* 7-9pm Tue, Thur; 4-6pm Sat, Sun.
London Buddhist Centre *51 Roman Road, Bethnal Green, E2 0HU (0845 458 4716, www.lbc.org.uk). Bethnal Green tube.* **Open** 10am-5pm Mon-Fri.

Catholic

Brompton Oratory *For listings, see p146.* **Services** 7am, 8am (Latin mass), 10am, 12.30am, 6pm Mon-Fri; 7am, 8am, 10am, 6pm Sat; 7am, 8am, 9am (tridentine), 10am, 11am (sung Latin), 12.30pm, 4.30pm, 7pm Sun. **Map** p395 E10.
Westminster Cathedral *For listings, see p139.* **Services** 7am, 8am, 10.30am, 12.30pm, 1.05pm, 5.30pm Mon-Fri; 8am, 9am, 10.30am, 12.30pm, 6pm Sat; 8am, 9am, 10.30am, noon, 5.30pm, 7pm Sun. **Map** p398 J10.

Islamic

East London Mosque *82-92 Whitechapel Road, Whitechapel, E1 1JQ (7650 3000, www.eastlondonmosque.org.uk). Aldgate East tube.* **Services** *Friday prayer* 1.30pm (1.15pm in winter). **Map** p403 S6.
Islamic Cultural Centre & London Central Mosque *146 Park Road, Marylebone, NW8 7RG (7725 2213, www.iccuk.org). Baker Street tube or bus 13, 113, 274.* **Services** times vary; check website for details.

Jewish

Liberal Jewish Synagogue *28 St John's Wood Road, St John's Wood, NW8 7HA (7286 5181, www.ljs.org). St John's Wood tube.* **Services** 6.45pm Fri; 11am Sat.
West Central Liberal Synagogue *21 Maple Street, Fitzrovia, W1T 4BE (7636 7627, www.wcls.org.uk). Warren Street tube.* **Services** 3pm Sat. **Map** p396 J4.

Methodist & Quaker

Methodist Central Hall *Central Hall, Storey's Gate, Westminster, SW1H 9NH (7222 8010, www.c-h-w.co.uk). St James's Park tube.* **Services** 12.45pm Wed; 11am, 6.30pm Sun. **Map** p399 K9.

Religious Society of Friends (Quakers) *173-177 Euston Road, Bloomsbury, NW1 2BJ (7663 1000, www.quaker.org.uk). Euston tube/rail.* **Meetings** 6.30pm Thur; 11am Sun. **Map** p397 K3.

SAFETY & SECURITY

Despite the riots during 2011, there are no real 'no-go' areas in London, and you're much more likely to get hurt in a car accident than as a result of criminal activity, but thieves haunt busy shopping areas and transport nodes as they do in all cities.

Use common sense and follow some basic rules. Keep wallets and purses out of sight, and handbags securely closed. Never leave bags or coats unattended, beside, under or on the back of a chair – even if they aren't stolen, they're likely to trigger a bomb alert. Don't put bags on the floor near the door of a public toilet. Don't take short cuts through dark alleys and car parks. Keep your passport, cash and credit cards in separate places. Don't carry a wallet in your back pocket. And always be aware of your surroundings.

SMOKING

July 2007 saw the introduction of a ban on smoking in all enclosed public spaces, including pubs, bars, clubs, restaurants, hotel foyers and shops, as well as on public transport. Smokers now face a penalty fee of £50 or a maximum fee of £200 if they are prosecuted for smoking in a smoke-free area. Many bars and clubs offer smoking gardens or terraces.

TELEPHONES

Dialling & codes

London's dialling code is 020; standard landlines have eight digits after that. You don't need to dial the 020 from within the area, so we have not given it in this book.

If you're calling from outside the UK, dial your international access code, then the UK code, 44, then the full London number, omitting the first 0 from the code. For example, to make a call to 020 7813 3000 from the US, dial 011 44 20 7813 3000. To dial abroad from the UK, first dial 00, then the relevant country code from the list below. For more international dialling codes, check the phone book or see www.kropla.com/dialcode.htm.

DIRECTORY

DIRECTORY

Australia 61
Canada 1
New Zealand 64
Republic of Ireland 353
South Africa 27
USA 1

Mobile phones

Mobile phones in the UK operate on the 900 MHz and 1800 MHz GSM frequencies common throughout most of Europe. If you're travelling to the UK from Europe, your phone should be compatible; if you're travelling from the US, you'll need a tri-band handset. Either way, check your phone is set for international roaming, and that your service provider at home has a reciprocal arrangement with a UK provider.

The simplest option may be to buy a 'pay-as-you-go' phone (about £10-£200); there's no monthly fee, you top up talk time using a card. Check before buying whether it can make and receive international calls. **Phones4u** (www.phones4u. co.uk) and **Carphone Warehouse** (www.carphonewarehouse.com), which both have stores throughout the city, offer options.

Operator services

Call 100 for the operator if you have difficulty in dialling; for an alarm call; to make a credit card call; for information about the cost of a call; and for help with international person-to-person calls. Dial 155 for the international operator if you need to reverse the charges (call collect) or if you can't dial direct; this service is very expensive.

Directory enquiries

This service is now provided by various six-digit 118 numbers. They're pretty pricey to call: dial (free) 0800 953 0720 for a rundown of options and prices. The best known is 118 118, which charges 41p per call, then £1.29 per minute thereafter; 118 888 charges 59p per call, then £1.29 per minute; 118 180 charges 70p per call, then 14p per minute. Online, the www.ukphone book.com offers five free credits a day to UK residents; overseas users get the same credits if they keep a positive balance in their account.

Yellow Pages This 24-hour service lists phone numbers of businesses in the UK. Dial 118 247 (£1.33p connection charge plus 40p/min) and identify the type of business you require, and where in London.

Public phones

Public payphones take coins or credit cards (sometimes both). The minimum cost is 60p (including a 40p connection charge), local and national calls are charged at 60p for 30mins then 10p for each subsequent 15mins. Some payphones, such as the counter-top ones found in pubs, require more. International calling cards, offering bargain minutes via a freephone number, are widely available.

Telephone directories

There are several telephone directories for London, divided by area, which contain private and commercial numbers. Available at post offices and libraries, these hefty tomes are also issued free to all residents, as is the invaluable *Yellow Pages* directory (also online at www.yell.com), which lists businesses and services.

TIME

London operates on Greenwich Mean Time (GMT), five hours ahead of the US's Eastern Standard time. In spring (25 March 2012) the UK puts its clocks forward by one hour to British Summer Time. In autumn (28 October 2012), the clocks go back to GMT.

TIPPING

In Britain it's accepted that you tip in taxis, minicabs, restaurants (some waiting staff rely heavily on tips), hotels, hairdressers and some bars (not pubs). Around 10% is normal, but some restaurants add as much as 15%. Always check whether service has been included in your bill: some restaurants include an automatic service charge, but also leave space for a gratuity on your credit card slip.

TOILETS

Pubs and restaurants generally reserve the use of their toilets for customers. However, all mainline rail stations and a few tube stations – Piccadilly Circus, for one – have public toilets (you may be charged a small fee). Department stores usually have loos that you can use free of charge, and museums (most of which no longer charge an entry fee) generally have good facilities. At night, options are worse. The coin-operated toilet booths around the city may be your only option.

TOURIST INFORMATION

In addition to the tourist offices below, there is a brand-new centre by St Paul's (*see p90*).
Britain & London Visitor Centre *1 Regent Street, Piccadilly Circus, SW1Y 4XT (7808 3800, www.visitlondon.com). Piccadilly Circus tube.* **Open** 9.30am-6.30pm Mon; 9am-6.30pm Tue-Fri; 9am-5pm Sat; 10am-4pm Sun. **Map** p416 W4.
Greenwich Tourist Information Centre *Discover Greenwich, Pepys House, 2 Cutty Sark Gardens, SE10 9LW (0870 608 2000, www.greenwichwhs.org.uk). Cutty Sark DLR.* **Open** 10am-5pm daily. **Map** p405 X1.
London Information Centre *Leicester Square, Soho, WC2H 7BP (7292 2333, www.london town.com). Leicester Square tube.* **Open** 10am-6pm daily. *Helpline* 8am-10pm Mon-Fri; 9am-8pm Sat, Sun.
Twickenham Visitor Information Centre *44 York Street, Twickenham, Middx, TW1 3BZ (8734 3363, www.visit richmond.co.uk). Twickenham rail.* **Open** 9am-5.15pm Mon-Thur; 9am-5pm Fri.

VISAS & IMMIGRATION

EU citizens do not require a visa to visit the United Kingdom; citizens of the USA, Canada, Australia, South Africa and New Zealand can also enter with only a passport for tourist visits of up to six months as long as they can show they can support themselves during their visit and plan to return. Go online to www.ukvisas.gov.uk to check your visa status well before you travel, or contact the British embassy, consulate or high commission in your own country. You can arrange visas online at www.fco.gov.uk.

Home Office Immigration & Nationality Bureau *Lunar House, 40 Wellesley Road, Croydon, CR9 1AT (0870 606 7766 enquiries, 0870 241 0645 applications, www.homeoffice.gov.uk).*

WEIGHTS & MEASURES

It has taken a considerable amount of time, and some heavy-handed intervention from the European authorities, but the UK is moving towards full metrication. Distances are still measured in miles but all goods are officially sold in metric quantities, with no legal requirement for the imperial equivalent to be given. We've used the still more common imperial measurements in this guide.

Below are listed some useful conversions, first into the metric equivalents from the imperial measurements, then from the metric units back to imperial:

1 inch (in) = 2.54 centimetres (cm)
1 yard (yd) = 0.91 metres (m)
1 mile = 1.6 kilometres (km)
1 ounce (oz) = 28.35 grams (g)
1 pound (lb) = 0.45 kilograms (kg)
1 UK pint = 0.57 litres (l)
1 US pint = 0.8 UK pints
or 0.46 litres

1 centimetre (cm) = 0.39 inches (in)
1 metre (m) = 1.094 yards (yd)
1 kilometre (km) = 0.62 miles
1 gram (g) = 0.035 ounces (oz)
1 kilogram (kg) = 2.2 pounds (lb)
1 litre (l) = 1.76 UK pints or 2.2 US pints

WHEN TO GO

Climate

The British climate is famously unpredictable, but Weathercall on 0906 850 0401 (60p/min) can offer some guidance. The best websites for weather news and features include www.metoffice. gov.uk, www.weather.com and www.bbc.co.uk/london/weather, which all offer good detailed long-term forecasts and are easily searchable.

Spring extends from March to May, though frosts can last into April. March winds and April showers may be a month early or a month late, but May is often very pleasant.

Summer (June, July and August) can be very unpredictable, with searing heat one day followed by sultry greyness and violent thunderstorms the next. There are usually pleasant sunny days, though they vary greatly in number from year to year. High temperatures, humidity and pollution can create problems for those with hay fever or breathing difficulties, and temperatures down in the tube can be uncomfortably hot in rush hour. Do as the locals do and carry a bottle of water.

Autumn starts in September, although the weather can still have a mild, summery feel. Real autumn comes with October, when the leaves start to fall; on sunny days, the red and gold leaves can be

THE LOCAL CLIMATE

Average temperatures and monthly rainfall in London.

	High (°C/°F)	Low (°C/°F)	Rainfall (mm/in)
Jan	6 / 43	2 / 36	54 / 2.1
Feb	7 / 44	2 / 36	40 / 1.6
Mar	10 / 50	3 / 37	37 / 1.5
Apr	13 / 55	6 / 43	37 / 1.5
May	17 / 63	8 / 46	46 / 1.8
June	20 / 68	12 / 54	45 / 1.8
July	22 / 72	14 / 57	57 / 2.2
Aug	21 / 70	13 / 55	59 / 2.3
Sept	19 / 66	11 / 52	49 / 1.9
Oct	14 / 57	8 / 46	57 / 2.2
Nov	10 / 50	5 / 41	64 / 2.5
Dec	7 / 44	4 / 39	48 / 1.9

breathtaking. When the November cold, grey and wet set in, though, you'll be reminded that London is situated on a northerly latitude.

Winter can have some delightful crisp, cold days, but don't bank on them. The usual scenario is for a disappointingly grey, wet Christmas, followed by a cold snap in January and February, when London may even see a sprinkling of snow, and immediate public transport chaos.

Public holidays

On public holidays (bank holidays), many shops remain open, but public transport services generally run to a Sunday timetable. On Christmas Day, almost everything, including public transport, closes down. All dates below are for 2012.

Good Friday Fri 6 Apr
Easter Monday Mon 9 Apr
May Day Holiday Mon 7 May
Spring Bank Holiday Mon 4 June
Summer Bank Holiday
Mon 27 Aug
Christmas Day Tue 25 Dec
Boxing Day Wed 26 Dec
New Year's Day Tue 1 Jan 2012

WOMEN

London is home to dozens of women's groups and networks; www.wrc.org.uk provides information and many links. It also has Europe's largest women's studies archive, the Women's Library (see p372).

For helplines, see p371; for health issues, see pp371-372.

WORK

Finding short-term work in London can be a full-time job. Temporary

jobs are posted on the Jobs section of Gumtree (www.gumtree.com). It's also worth trying recruitment agencies such as Reed (www.reed. co.uk) or Tate (www.tate.co.uk), or the various London markets for work manning the stalls.

Work permits

With few exceptions, citizens of non-European Economic Area (EEA) countries have to have a work permit before they can legally work in the United Kingdom. Permits are issued only for high-level jobs. A youth mobility scheme is open to young residents of Australia, Canada, Japan and New Zealand, however. The **UK Border Agency** website (www.ukba.home office.gov.uk) has details.

Useful addresses

BUNAC *16 Bowling Green Lane, Clerkenwell, EC1R 0QH (7251 3472, www.bunac.org.uk). Farringdon tube/rail.* **Open** 9.30am-5.30pm Mon-Thur; 9.30am-5pm Fri. **Map** p400 N4.
Council on International Educational Exchange *300 Fore Street, Portland, ME 04101, USA (+1-207 553 4000, www.ciee.org).* **Open** 9am-5pm (EST) Mon-Fri. BUNAC and the CIEE help young people to study, work and travel abroad.
Home Office *Border & Immigration Agency, Lunar House, 40 Wellesley Road, Croydon, Surrey CR9 2BY (0870 606 7766, www.ind.home office.gov.uk).* **Open** *Enquiries by phone* 9am-4.45pm Mon-Thur; 9am-4.30pm Fri.
Advice on whether or not a work permit is required. If it is, application forms can be downloaded from the website.

Content Index

INDEX

INDEX

Venue Index

INDEX

INDEX

Maps

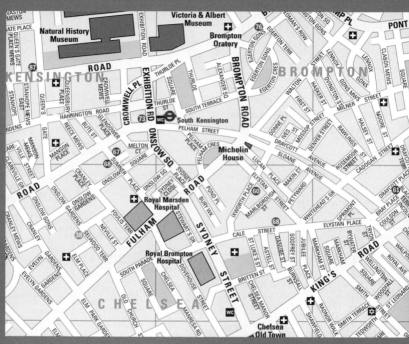

Major sight or landmark	
Railway or coach station	
Underground station	⊖
Park	
Hospital or place of learning	
Casualty unit	✚
Church	✚
Synagogue	✡
Congestion-charge zone	◉
District	MAYFAIR
Theatre	●

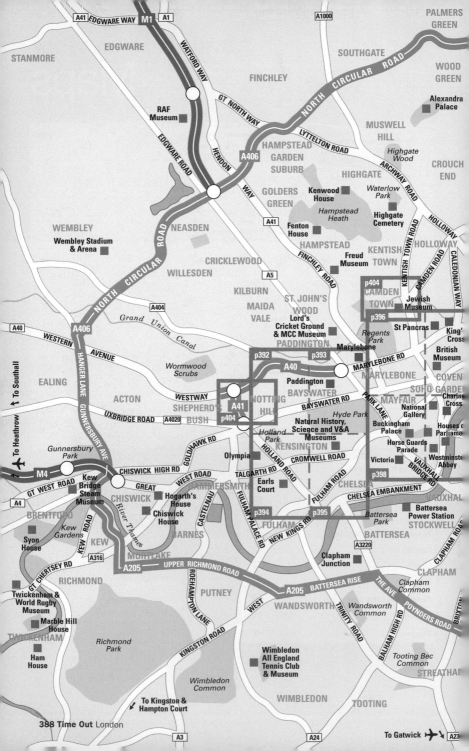

London Overview

Central London
by Area

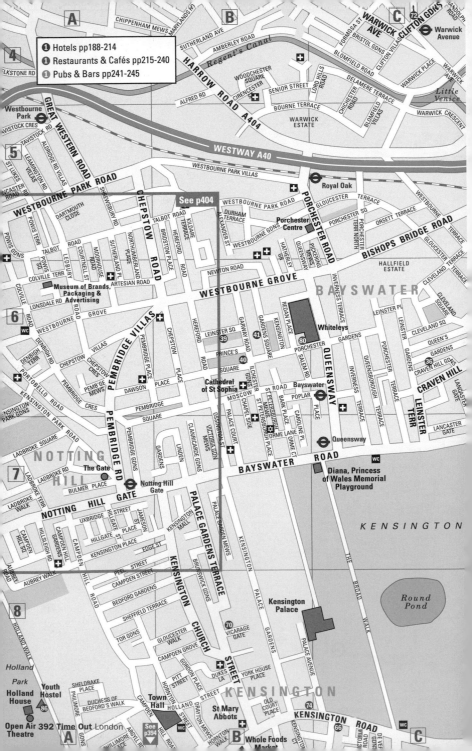

CHIPPENHAM MEWS

4
FOLKSTONE RD

SUTHERLAND AVE

AMBERLEY ROAD

Regent's Canal

WARWICK AVE

CLIFTON GDNS

FORMOSA ST
BRISTOL GDNS

CLIFTON VILLAS
WARWICK AVE

Warwick Avenue

RANDOLPH

WOODCHESTER SQUARE
CIRENCESTER
SENIOR STREET
LORD HILLS ROAD

BLOMFIELD ROAD
DELAMERE TERRACE
WARWICK PLACE

WARWICK AVE

CLIFTON VILLAS

Little Venice

HARROW ROAD A404

ALFRED RD
BOURNE TERRACE

WARWICK ESTATE

CHICHESTER ROAD
BLOMFIELD VILLAS

WARWICK CRESCENT

❶ Hotels pp188-214
❶ Restaurants & Cafés pp215-240
❶ Pubs & Bars pp241-245

Westbourne Park

GREAT WESTERN ROAD
TAVISTOCK CRES
VISTOCK RD

WESTWAY A40

WESTBOURNE PARK VILLAS

Royal Oak

WESTWAY A40

5
ST LUKES RD
LEAMINGTON RD VILLAS
LANCASTER RD

WESTBOURNE PARK ROAD

CHEPSTOW ROAD

See p404

WESTBOURNE PARK ROAD

PORCHESTER ROAD

GLOUCESTER TERRACE

BISHOPS BRIDGE ROAD

WESTBOURNE TERRACE

WESTBOURNE PARK ROAD

WESTBOURNE

TALBOT ROAD
KILDARE TERRACE
HEREFORD

DURHAM TERRACE
ALEXANDER ST

WESTBOURNE GDNS

Porchester Centre

HATHERLEY

PORCHESTER TERRACE NORTH

ORSETT TERRACE

GLOUCESTER TERRACE

WESTBOURNE GROVE

DARTMOUTH CLOSE
SHREWSBURY RD
NORTHUMBERLAND PLACE

BRIDSTOW PLACE

NEWTON ROAD

INVERNESS TERRACE

CLEVELAND TERRACE

B A Y S W A T E R

HALLFIELD ESTATE

CLEVELAND TERRACE

WESTBOURNE PARK ROAD
POWIS TERR
POWIS GDNS
TALBOT
LEDBURY
POWIS SQ
MOORHOUSE ROAD
COURTNELL ST
SUTHERLAND PL
ARTESIAN ROAD
COLVILLE TERR

Museum of Brands,
Packaging &
Advertising

6
WC

COLVILLE ROAD
LONSDALE RD

WESTBOURNE

GROVE

CHEPSTOW

HEREFORD ROAD

LEINSTER SQ
39
PRINCE'S
40

GARWAY ROAD

KENSINGTON GDNS
GARDENS SQUARE

41

REDAN PLACE

80 PORCHESTER

Whiteleys

INVERNESS TERRACE

LEINSTER PL

QUEEN'S GARDENS

LEINSTER

CLEVELAND SQ

CLEVELAND SQ

PORCHESTER

DENBIGH TERR
DENBIGH RD
CHEPSTOW CRES
PEMBRIDGE VILLAS
PEMBRIDGE PLACE

CHEPSTOW PLACE

PRINCE'S SQUARE

ILCHESTER GDNS

MOSCOW ROAD

Bayswater

POPLAR

QUEENSWAY

QUEENSBOROUGH TERRACE

PORCHESTER GARDENS

QUEEN'S GARDENS

CRAVEN HILL GDNS
36
CRAVEN HILL

CRAVEN HILL

LANCASTER GATE

PORTOBELLO ROAD
KENSINGTON PARK GDNS

PEMB GE MEWS
DAWSON PLACE
PEMBRIDGE CRES

PEMBRIDGE
SQUARE

Cathedral
of St Sophia

ST PETERSBURGH MEWS
ST PETERSBURGH PLACE
CHAPEL SIDE
PALACE COURT

BARK PLACE
CAROLINE PL
ORME LANE
ORME CT

CAROLINE PL

LANCASTER TERR

LEINSTER
TERR

PEMBRIDGE GDNS

CLANRICARDE GDNS
VICTORIA GDN MEWS

 OSSINGTON ST

ZORME LANE

Queensway

N O T T I N G
KENSINGTON PARK RD
LADBROKE SQUARE

The Gate

LINDEN GARDENS

PALACE COURT

BAYSWATER ROAD

WC

Diana, Princess
of Wales Memorial
Playground

H I L L
LADBROKE RD
LADBROKE TERR

Notting Hill
Gate

PALACE GARDENS TERRACE

PALACE GDN MEWS

KENSINGTON PALACE GARDENS

K E N S I N G T O N

7
BULMER PLACE

NOTTING HILL GATE

UXBRIDGE STREET
HILLGATE STREET
HILLGATE PLACE

KENSINGTON MALL

THE BROAD WALK

Round Pond

CAMPDEN HILL SQ
AUBREY RD

CAMPDEN HILL GARDENS

KENSINGTON PLACE

EDGE ST

BRUNSWICK GDNS

KENSINGTON

PEEL STREET
CAMPDEN STREET

Kensington Palace

PALACE AVENUE

AUBREY WALK
AUBREY RD

CAMPDEN HILL ROAD

BEDFORD GARDENS

KENSINGTON CHURCH STREET

KENSINGTON GARDENS

8
Holland
Park

HOLLAND WALK

SHEFFIELD TERRACE

TOR GDNS

GLOUCESTER WALK

70 VICARAGE GATE

Holland
House
86

SHELDRAKE PLACE
PHILIMORE

DUCHESS OF BEDFORD'S WALK

CAMPDEN GROVE

PITT STREET
GORDON PLACE

DUKES LA

YORK HOUSE PLACE

OLD COURT PLACE

K E N S I N G T O N

Open Air
Theatre

392 Time Out London

A

ARGYLL RD
PHILIMORE GDNS

See p394

KENSINGTON HIGH

Town
Hall

HORNTON STREET
HOLLAND STREET

St Mary
Abbots

B

Whole Foods
Market

74
KENSINGTON ROAD
66

WC

C

Youth Hostel

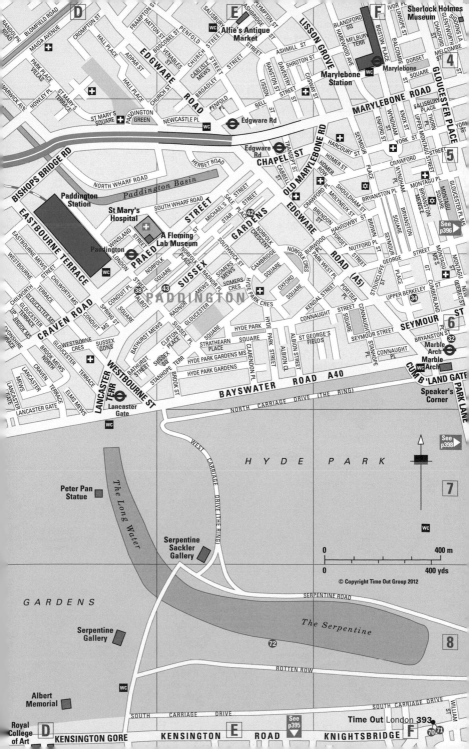

Sherlock Holmes Museum

Alfie's Antique Market

Marylebone Station

Marylebone

Edgware Rd

Edgware Rd

CHAPEL ST

Paddington Station

St Mary's Hospital

A Fleming Lab Museum

Paddington

PADDINGTON

EDGWARE ROAD (A5)

SUSSEX

PRAED STREET

CRAVEN ROAD

See p396

SEYMOUR ST

Marble Arch

Marble Arch

Speaker's Corner

WESTBOURNE ST

LANCASTER TERR

Lancaster Gate

BAYSWATER ROAD A40

NORTH CARRIAGE DRIVE (THE RING)

WEST CARRIAGE DRIVE (THE RING)

HYDE PARK

See p398

Peter Pan Statue

The Long Water

Serpentine Sackler Gallery

GARDENS

SERPENTINE ROAD

The Serpentine

Serpentine Gallery

ROTTEN ROW

Albert Memorial

Royal College of Art

KENSINGTON GORE

KENSINGTON ROAD

KNIGHTSBRIDGE

See p395

0   400 m
0   400 yds

© Copyright Time Out Group 2012

Time Out London **393**

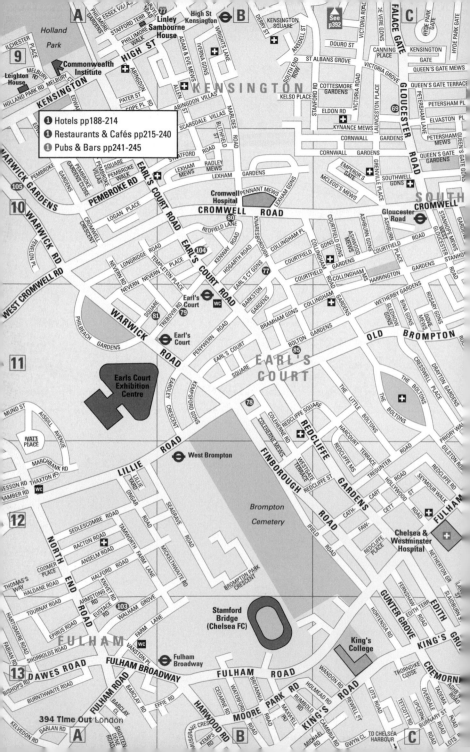

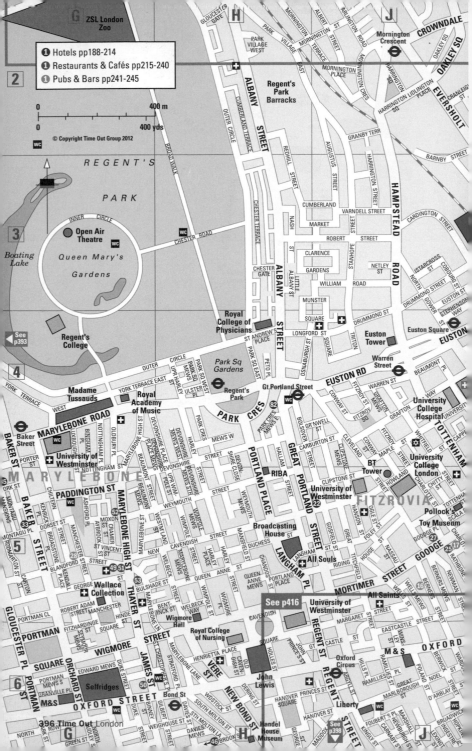

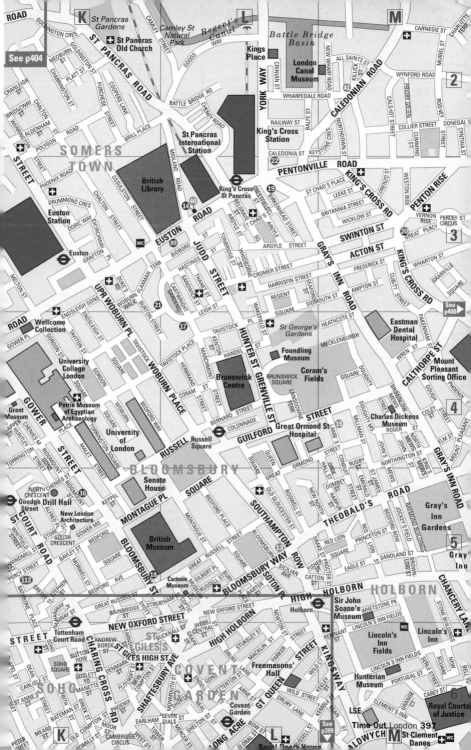

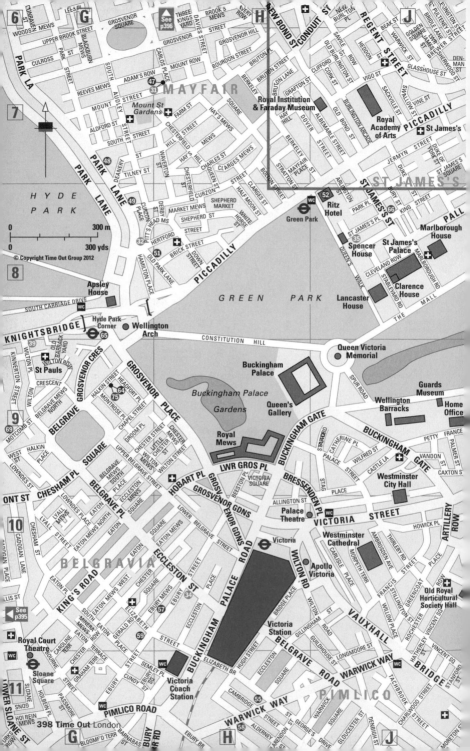

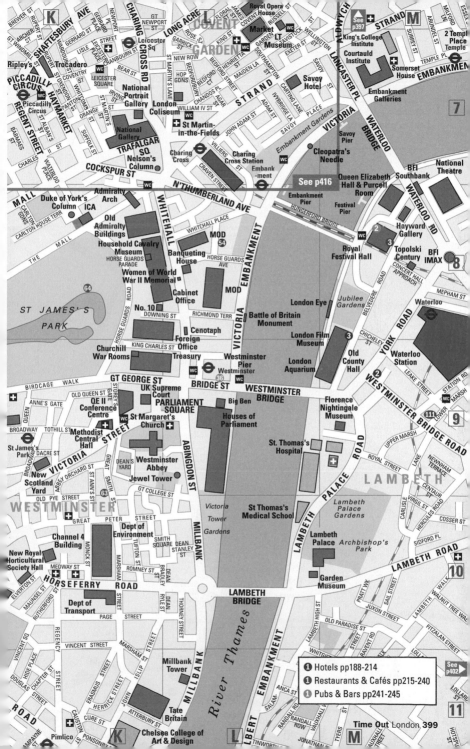

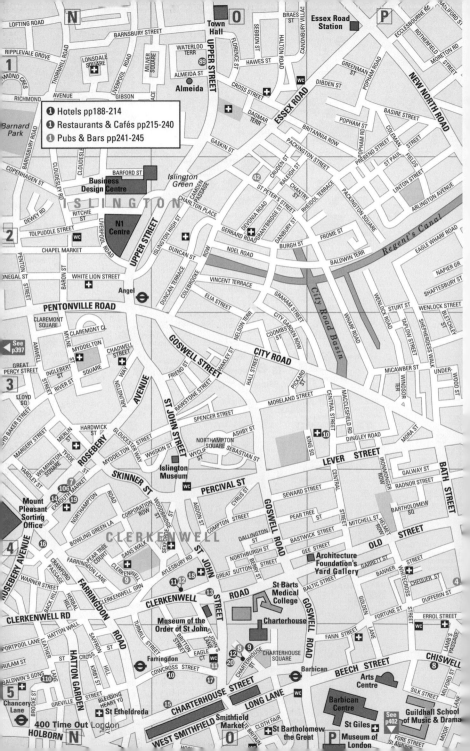

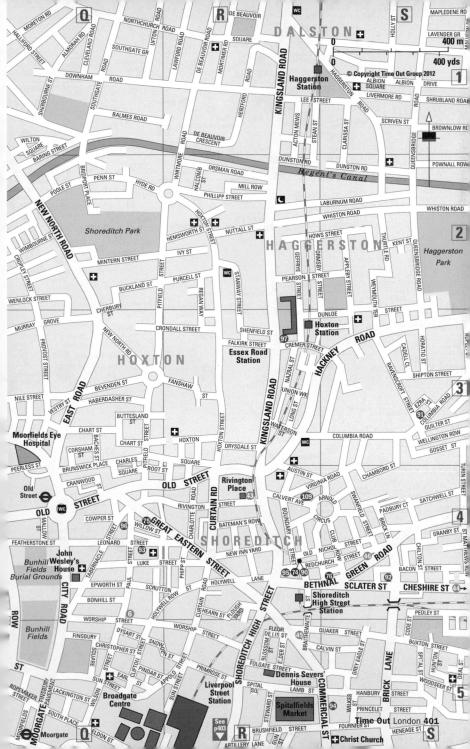

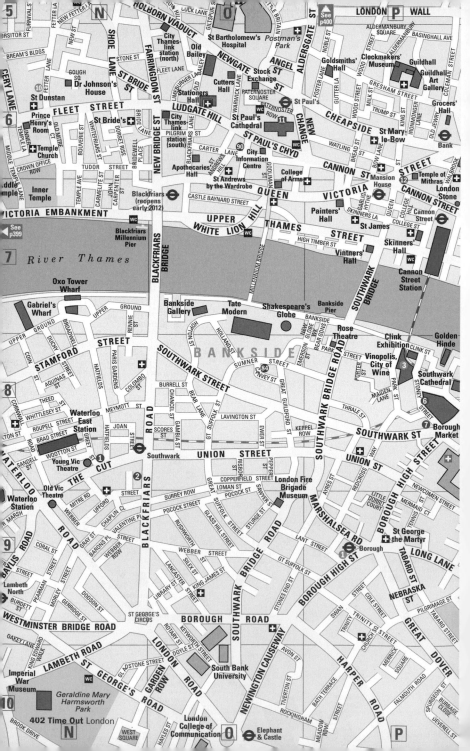

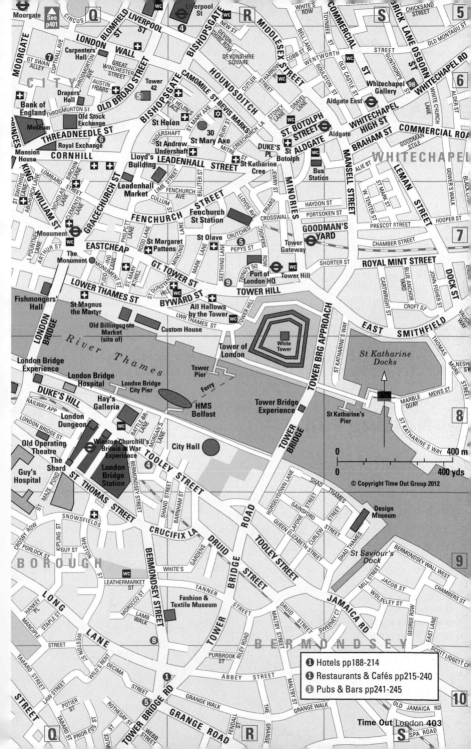

0 Hotels pp188-214
0 Restaurants & Cafés pp215-240
0 Pubs & Bars pp241-245

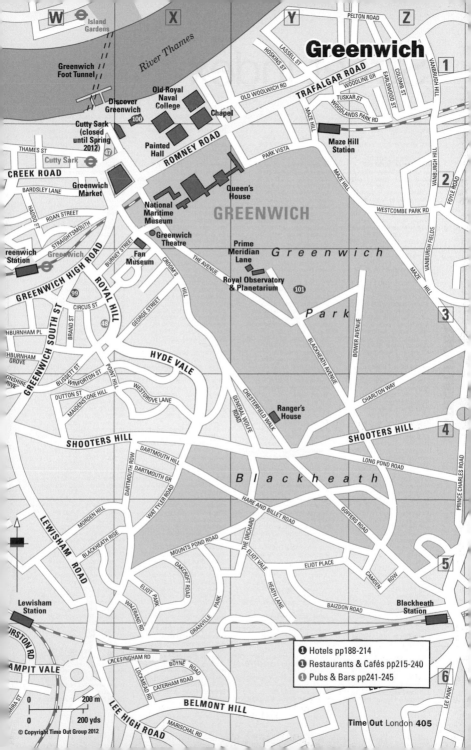

Greenwich

W Island Gardens

River Thames

X

Y PELTON ROAD

Z

1

Greenwich Foot Tunnel

Discover Greenwich

Old Royal Naval College

Chapel

OLD WOOLWICH RD

TRAFALGAR ROAD

HOSKINS ST
LASSELL ST

WOODLINE GR

TUSKAR ST

WOODLANDS PARK RD

EARLSWOOD ST

COLOMB ST

VANBURGH HILL

VANBRUGH HILL

FOYLE ROAD

Cutty Sark (closed until Spring 2012)

100

Painted Hall

ROMNEY ROAD

PARK VISTA

MAZE HILL

Maze Hill Station

THAMES ST

CREEK ROAD

Cutty Sark

Greenwich Market

BARDSLEY LANE

HODD ST

ROAN STREET

STRAIGHTSMOUTH

National Maritime Museum

Queen's House

GREENWICH

WESTCOMBE PARK RD

MAZE HILL

2

Greenwich Station

reenwich Greenwich

GREENWICH HIGH ROAD

ROYAL HILL

BURNEY STREET

Fan Museum

Greenwich Theatre

CROOM'S HILL

THE AVENUE

Prime Meridian Lane

Royal Observatory & Planetarium

101

G r e e n w i c h

VANBURGH FIELDS

MAZE HILL

3

99

CIRCUS ST

GREENWICH SOUTH ST

BRAND ST

48

GEORGE STREET

P a r k

BLACKHEATH AVENUE

BOWER AVENUE

HBURNHAM PL

HBURNHAM GROVE

BLISSETT ST

WYNFORTON ST

POINT HILL

HYDE VALE

WESTGROVE LANE

CHESTERFIELD WALK

GENERAL WOLFE ROAD

CHARLTON WAY

ONSHIRE RIVE

DUTTON ST

MAIDENSTONE HILL

Ranger's House

SHOOTERS HILL

4

PRINCE CHARLES ROAD

LEWISHAM ROAD

SHOOTERS HILL

DARTMOUTH ROW

DARTMOUTH HILL

DARTMOUTH GR

WAT TYLER ROAD

LONG POND ROAD

B l a c k h e a t h

MORDEN HILL

BLACKHEATH RISE

MOUNTS POND ROAD

OAKCROFT ROAD

HARE AND BILLET ROAD

THE ORCHARD

ELIOT VALE

ELIOT PLACE

GOFFERS ROAD

CAMDEN ROW

5

Lewisham Station

ELIOT PARK

WALFRAND RD

GRANVILLE PARK

HEATH LANE

BAIZDON ROAD

Blackheath Station

URSTON RD

MIRA ST

AMPIT VALE

CRICBSINGHAM RD

BOYNE ROAD

LOCKMEAD RD

CATERHAM ROAD

BELMONT HILL

LEE HIGH ROAD

MARISCHAL RD

LEE PARK

6

0 __ 200 m
0 __ 200 yds

❶ Hotels pp188-214
❶ Restaurants & Cafés pp215-240
❶ Pubs & Bars pp241-245

© Copyright Time Out Group 2012

Time Out London **405**

Street Index

STREET INDEX

Street Index

STREET INDEX

STREET INDEX

Street Index

STREET INDEX

London Underground

Transport for London

UNDERGROUND

...ay no more than 5p per minute if calling
...BT landline. There may be a connection charge.
...s from mobiles or other landline providers may vary.

...rney, please check before you travel   Version A TfL 11.2011   Correct at time of going to print

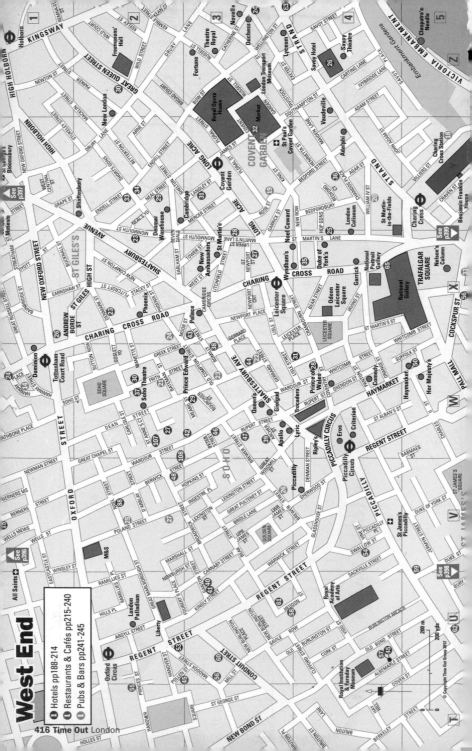

West End

1 Hotels pp188-214
2 Restaurants & Cafés pp215-240
3 Pubs & Bars pp241-245